Ordnance Survey

G000293076

STREET ATLAS
West
Sussex

Contents

III   *Key to map symbols*

IV-V   *Key to map pages*

VI   *Administrative and post code boundaries*

1   *Street maps*

207   *Extra-large-scale map of Brighton town centre*

208   *Town maps of Eastbourne and Hastings*

209   *Town maps of Lewes and Royal Tunbridge Wells*

210   *Index of hospitals, railway stations, schools, shopping centres, street names and universities*

PHILIP'S

First edition published 1988
Fourth edition published 1994
First colour edition published 1997
Reprinted in 1998 by

Ordnance Survey® and George Philip Ltd., a division of
Romsey Road   Octopus Publishing Group Ltd
Maybush   Michelin House
Southampton   81 Fulham Road
SO16 4GU   London SW3 6RB

ISBN 0-540-07319-9 (hardback)
ISBN 0-540-07323-7 (wire-o)

**The mapping between pages 1 and 209 (inclusive) in this atlas is
derived from Ordnance Survey® OSCAR® and Land-Line® data,
and Landranger® mapping.**

Ordnance Survey, OSCAR, Land-Line and Landranger are registered
trade marks of Ordnance Survey, the national mapping agency of
Great Britain.

Printed and bound in Spain by Cayfosa

Digital Data

The exceptionally high-quality mapping
found in this book is available as digital
data in TIFF format, which is easily
convertible to other bit-mapped (raster)
image formats.

The index is also available in digital form
as a standard database table. It contains
all the details found in the printed index
together with the National Grid reference
for the map square in which each entry
is named and feature codes for places
of interest in eight categories such as
education and health.

For further information and to discuss
your requirements, please contact the
Ordnance Survey Solutions Centre on
01703 792929.

Key to map symbols

Symbol	Description
Motorway (with junction number) 22a
Primary route (dual carriageway and single)
A road (dual carriageway and single)
B road (dual carriageway and single)
Minor road (dual carriageway and single)
Other minor road
Road under construction
Railway
Tramway, miniature railway
Rural track, private road or narrow road in urban area
Gate or obstruction to traffic (restrictions may not apply at all times or to all vehicles)
Path, bridleway, byway open to all traffic, road used as a public path
The representation in this atlas of a road, track or path is no evidence of the existence of a right of way

200

156

207

Adjoining page indicators

The map area within the pink band is shown at a larger scale on the page indicated by the red block and arrow

Acad	**Academy**	Mon	**Monument**
Cemy	**Cemetery**	Mus	**Museum**
C Ctr	**Civic Centre**	Obsy	**Observatory**
CH	**Club House**	Pal	**Royal Palace**
Coll	**College**	PH	**Public House**
Ent	**Enterprise**	Recn Gd	**Recreation Ground**
Ex H	**Exhibition Hall**	Resr	**Reservoir**
Ind Est	**Industrial Estate**	Ret Pk	**Retail Park**
Inst	**Institute**	Sch	**School**
Ct	**Law Court**	Sh Ctr	**Shopping Centre**
L Ctr	**Leisure Centre**	Sta	**Station**
LC	**Level Crossing**	TH	**Town Hall/House**
Liby	**Library**	Trad Est	**Trading Estate**
Mkt	**Market**	Univ	**University**
Meml	**Memorial**	YH	**Youth Hostel**

Symbol	Description
British Rail station
Private railway station
Bus, coach station
Ambulance station
Coastguard station
Fire station
Police station
Casualty entrance to hospital
Church, place of worship
H	**Hospital**
i	**Information centre**
P	**Parking**
PO	**Post Office**
Chichester High Sch for Girls	**Important buildings, schools, colleges, universities and hospitals**
County boundaries
River Arun	**Water name**
Stream
River or canal (minor and major)
Water
Tidal water
Woods
Houses
Arundel Castle	**Non-Roman antiquity**
ROMAN VILLA	**Roman antiquity**

■ The dark grey border on the inside edge of some pages indicates that the mapping does not continue onto the adjacent page

■ The small numbers around the edges of the maps identify the 1 kilometre National Grid lines

The scale of the maps is 5.52 cm to 1 km (3½ inches to 1 mile)

0	¼	½	¾	1 mile
0	250m	500m	750m	1 kilometre

The scale of the map on page numbered in red is 11.04 cm to 1 km (7 inches to 1 mile)

0	220 yards	440 yards	660 yards	½ mile
0	125m	250m	375m	½ kilometre

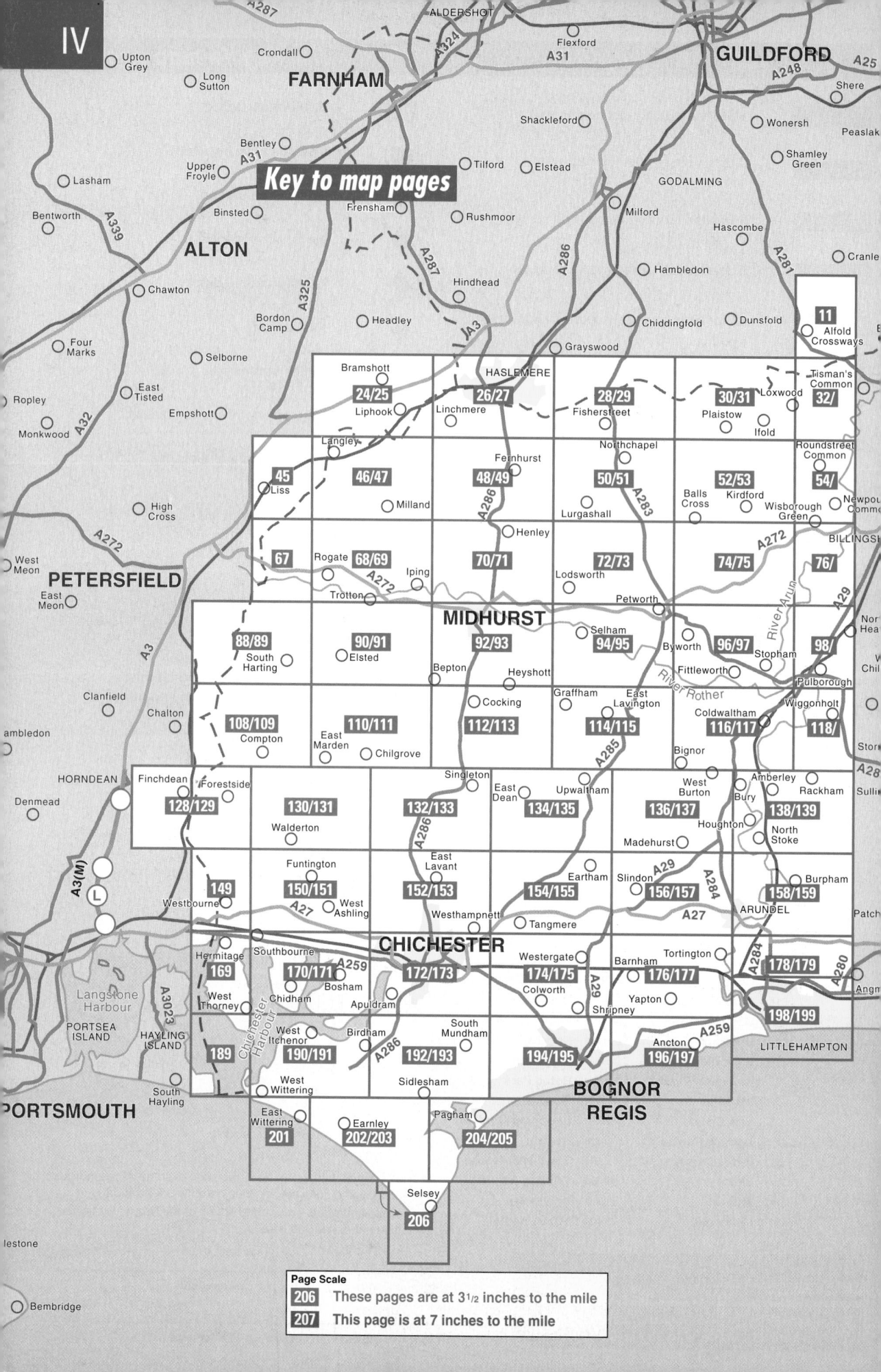

IV

Key to map pages

GUILDFORD

FARNHAM

ALDERSHOT

GODALMING

ALTON

PETERSFIELD

MIDHURST

HASLEMERE

CHICHESTER

BOGNOR
REGIS

PORTSMOUTH

LITTLEHAMPTON

ARUNDEL

24/25	26/27	28/29	30/31	32/
45	46/47	48/49	50/51	52/53	54/
67	68/69	70/71	72/73	74/75	76/
88/89	90/91	92/93	94/95	96/97	98/
108/109	110/111	112/113	114/115	116/117	118/
128/129	130/131	132/133	134/135	136/137	138/139
149	150/151	152/153	154/155	156/157	158/159
169	170/171	172/173	174/175	176/177	178/179
189	190/191	192/193	194/195	196/197	198/199
201	202/203	204/205		
206				

11

Upton Grey
Long Sutton
Crondall
Flexford
Shere
A25
Shackleford
Wonersh
Peaslak
Bentley
Upper Froyle
Tilford
Elstead
Shamley Green
Lasham
Binsted
Frensham
Rushmoor
Milford
Hascombe
Cranle
Bentworth
Headley
Hindhead
Hambledon
Chiddingfold
Dunsfold
Alfold Crossways
Chawton
Four Marks
Bordon Camp
Grayswood
Tisman's Common
Selborne
Loxwood
Ropley
East Tisted
Empshott
Bramshott
Liphook
Linchmere
Fishersreet
Plaistow
Ifold
Roundstreet Common
West Meon
Monkwood
Langley
Fernhurst
Northchapel
Balls Cross
Kirdford
Wisborough Green
Newpou Comme
High Cross
Liss
Milland
Henley
Lurgashall
BILLINGSH
East Meon
Rogate
Iping
Trotton
Lodsworth
Petworth
Clanfield
South Harting
Elsted
Bepton
Heyshott
Selham
Byworth
Stopham
Fittleworth
Pulborough
Chalton
Cocking
Graffham
East Lavington
Coldwaltham
Wiggonholt
Bignor
Stor
HORNDEAN
Finchdean
Forestside
Compton
East Marden
Chilgrove
Singleton
East Dean
Upwaltham
West Burton
Amberley
Rackham
Sulli
Denmead
Walderton
Bury
Houghton
North Stoke
ambledon
East Lavant
Eartham
Slindon
Burpham
Funtington
West Ashling
Westhampnett
Tangmere
Madehurst
Hermitage
Southbourne
Westgate
Barnham
Tortington
West Thorney
Chidham
Bosham
Apuldram
Colworth
Yapton
Shripney
Anton
Langstone Harbour
West Itchenor
Birdham
South Mundham
Ancton
PORTSEA ISLAND
HAYLING ISLAND
West Wittering
Sidlesham
Pagham
South Hayling
East Wittering
Earnley
Selsey

Page Scale

206	These pages are at 3½ inches to the mile
207	This page is at 7 inches to the mile

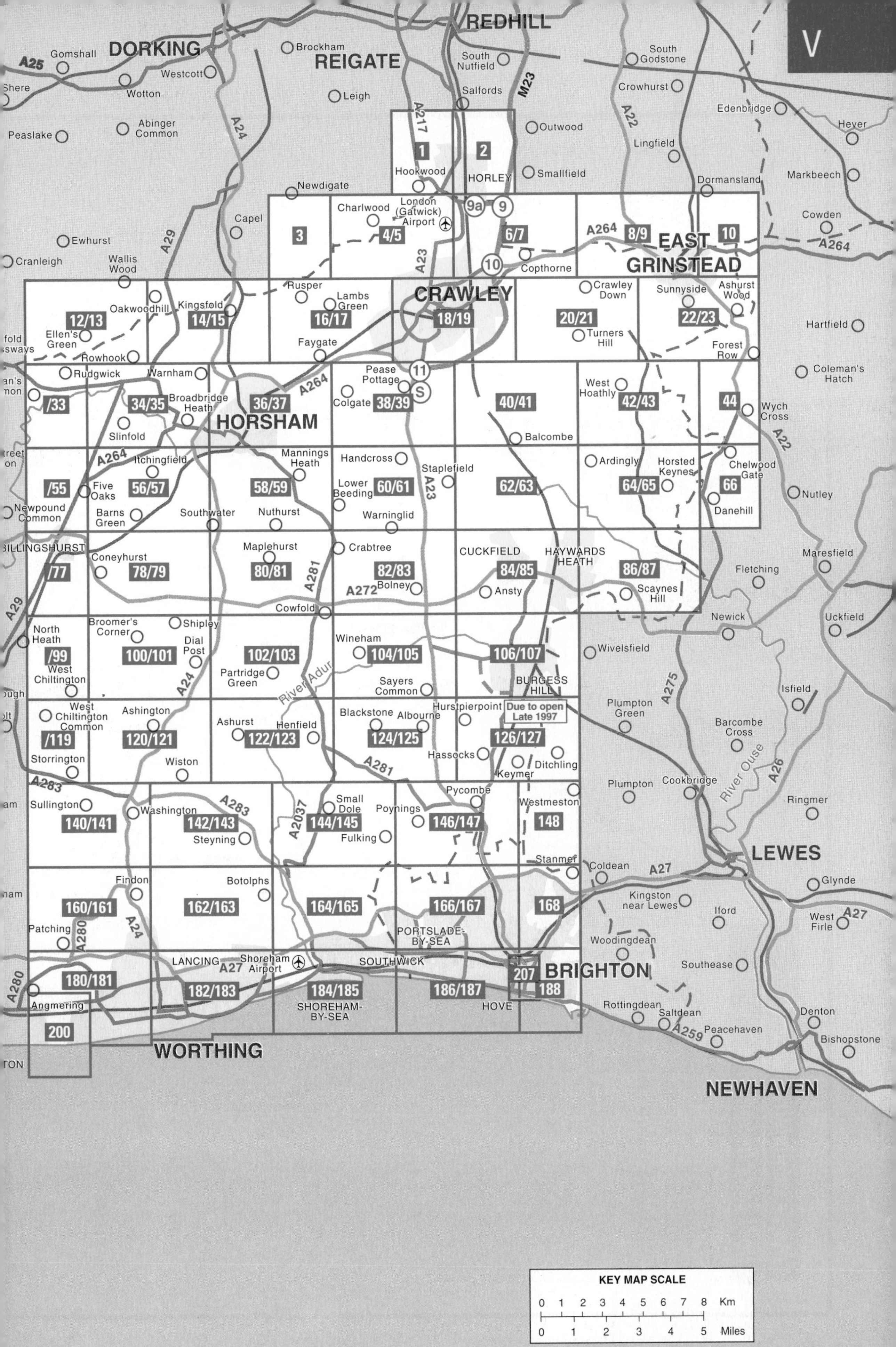

DORKING

REIGATE

REDHILL

A25 Gomshall
Shere
Westcott
Wotton
Peaslake
Abinger Common
Brockham
Leigh
Newdigate
South Nutfield
Salfords
South Godstone
Crowhurst
Edenbridge
Hever
Markbeech
Outwood
Smallfield
Dormansland
Cowden
Ewhurst
Cranleigh
Wallis Wood
Capel
Charlwood
London (Gatwick) Airport
Copthorne
Crawley Down
Sunnyside
Ashurst Wood
Hartfield
Coleman's Hatch
Lingfield

1 Hookwood
2 HORLEY
9a **9**
6/7
10
3
4/5
8/9 **EAST GRINSTEAD**
10
A264

CRAWLEY

Rusper
Lambs Green
Faygate
18/19
Turners Hill
Forest Row
Wych Cross

12/13 Ellen's Green
Oakwoodhill
Kingsfold
14/15
16/17
20/21
22/23
44

Rowhook
Rudgwick
Warnham
Broadbridge Heath
34/35
36/37
Pease Pottage
Colgate
38/39
40/41
Balcombe
West Hoathly
42/43
Chelwood Gate
66

/33
HORSHAM
Slinfold
Itchingfield
Mannings Heath
Handcross
Staplefield
Ardingly
Horsted Keynes
Danehill
Nutley

/55
56/57
58/59
Lower Beeding
60/61
62/63
64/65
Five Oaks
Barns Green
Southwater
Nuthurst
Warninglid
Maresfield
Fletching

Maplehurst
Crabtree
CUCKFIELD HAYWARDS HEATH
Coneyhurst
78/79
80/81
82/83
84/85
86/87
Bolney
A272
Ansty
Scaynes Hill
Newick
Uckfield

77
Wineham
Sayers Common
BURGESS HILL
Wivelsfield

North Heath
Broomer's Corner
Shipley
Dial Post
100/101
102/103
104/105
106/107
Partridge Green
/99
West Chiltington
Due to open Late 1997
Plumpton Green
Isfield
Barcombe Cross

West Chiltington Common
Ashington
Ashurst
Henfield
Blackstone
Albourne
Hurstpierpoint
/119
120/121
122/123
124/125
126/127
Storrington
Wiston
Hassocks
Ditchling
Keymer
Plumpton
Cookbridge
Ringmer

Sullington
Washington
Small Dole
Poynings
Pycombe
Westmeston
140/141
142/143
144/145
146/147
148
Steyning
Fulking
Stanmer
LEWES

Findon
Botolphs
Coldean
Kingston near Lewes
Glynde
160/161
162/163
164/165
166/167
168
Patching
Iford
West Firle
A27
PORTSLADE-BY-SEA
Woodingdean
Southease

LANCING
Shoreham Airport
SOUTHWICK
207
BRIGHTON
180/181
182/183
184/185
186/187
188
HOVE
Rottingdean
Saltdean
Peacehaven
Denton
Bishopstone

Angmering
200
SHOREHAM-BY-SEA
A259

WORTHING

NEWHAVEN

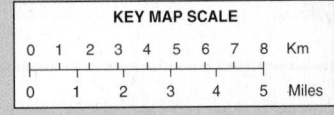

KEY MAP SCALE

0 1 2 3 4 5 6 7 8 Km

0 1 2 3 4 5 Miles

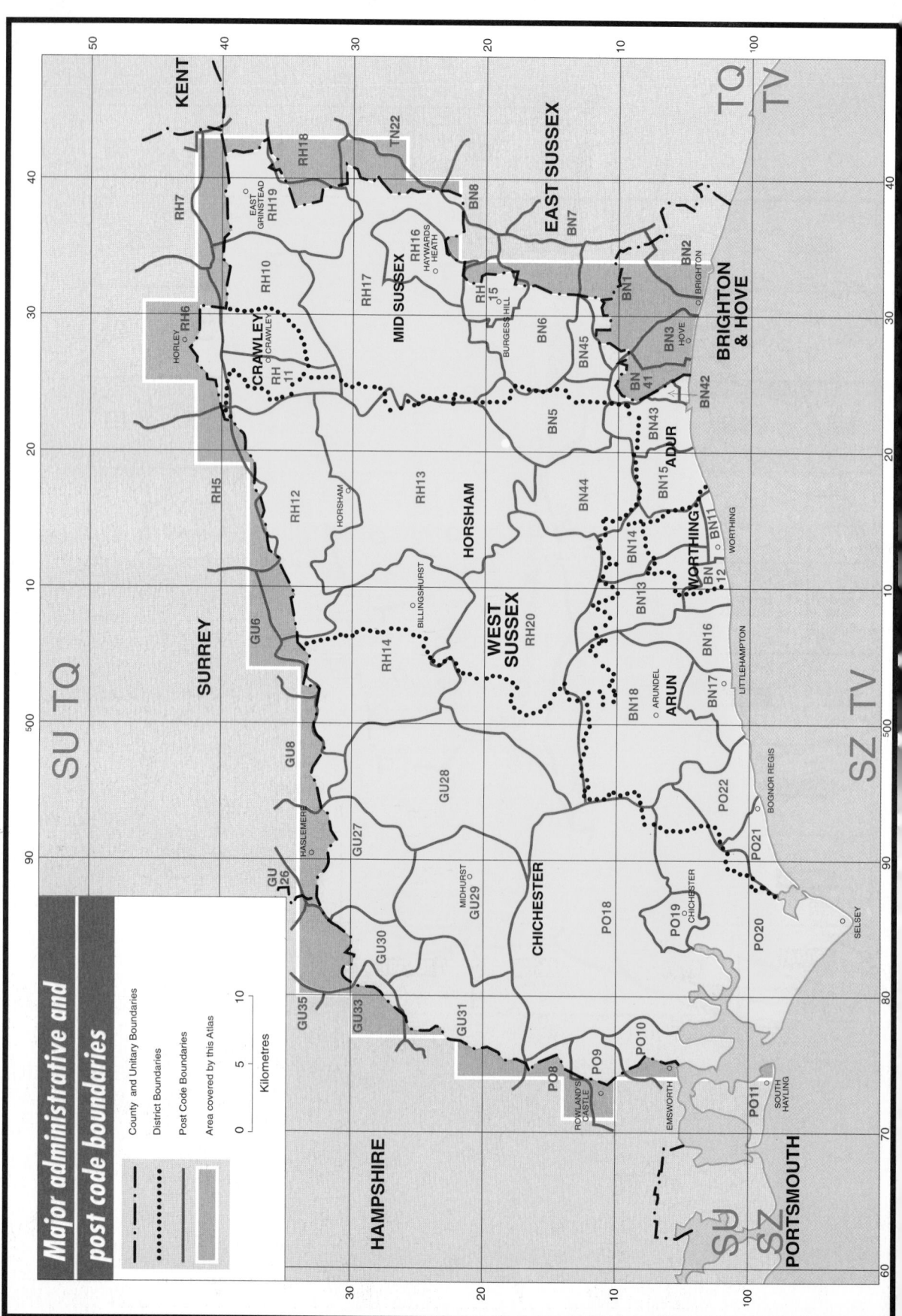

Major administrative and post code boundaries

–·–·–	County and Unitary Boundaries
··········	District Boundaries
———	Post Code Boundaries
	Area covered by this Atlas

Kilometres

0   5   10

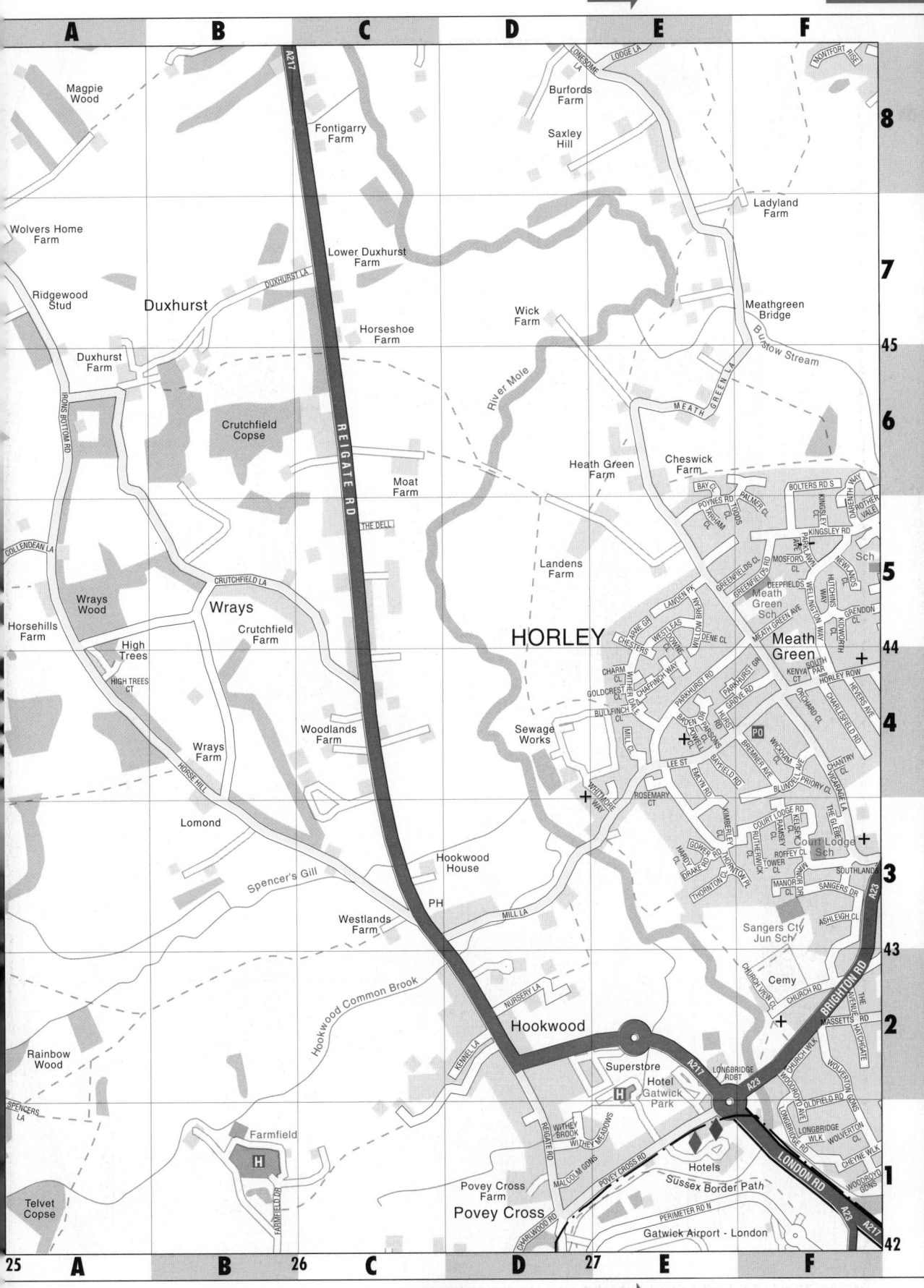
2
A
B
C
D
E
F
Magpie Wood
Fontigarry Farm
Burfords Farm
Saxley Hill
LONESOME LA
LODGE LA
MONTFORT RISE
Ladyland Farm
Wolvers Home Farm
Lower Duxhurst Farm
Ridgewood Stud
Duxhurst
DUXHURST LA
Horseshoe Farm
Wick Farm
Meathgreen Bridge
Burstow Stream
Duxhurst Farm
River Mole
MEATH GREEN LA
IRONS BOTTOM RD
Crutchfield Copse
REIGATE RD
A217
Moat Farm
Heath Green Farm
Cheswick Farm
THE DELL
COLLENDEAN LA
Landens Farm
CRUTCHFIELD LA
Wrays Wood
Wrays
Crutchfield Farm
HORLEY
Meath Green Sch
Meath Green
Horsehills Farm
High Trees
HIGH TREES CT
Sewage Works
Woodlands Farm
Wrays Farm
HORSE HILL
Lomond
Hookwood House
Spencer's Gill
PH
Westlands Farm
MILL LA
Court Lodge Sch
Sangers Cty Jun Sch
Cemy
Hookwood Common Brook
NURSERY LA
Hookwood
KENNEL LA
Rainbow Wood
Superstore
Hotel Gatwick Park
LONGBRIDGE RDBT
BRIGHTON RD
A23
SPENCERS LA
Farmfield
FARMFIELD DR
Telvet Copse
WITHEY BROOK
WITHEY MEADOWS
MALCOLM GDNS
POVEY CROSS RD
Povey Cross Farm
Povey Cross
CHARLWOOD RD
Hotels
Sussex Border Path
PERIMETER RD N
Gatwick Airport - London
LONDON RD
Sch
8
7
45
6
5
44
4
3
43
2
1
42
25
26
27
5

1

A B C D E F

8 Salfords

7

45

6

5

44

4

3

43

2

1

42

28 A B 29 C D 30 E F

HORLEY LODGE LA
WOOD CL
HARWOOD PK
SALBROOK RD
A23
REDHILL DISTRIBUTION CTR
THE ORCHARD BSNS CTR
PEAR TREE HILL
Perry Wood
Picketts
PICKETTS LA
Job's Farm
NEW HOUSE LA
Woolborough Farm
WOOLBOROUGH LA
Orchard Farm
ASTRA BSNS CTR
BEECHWOOD VILLAS
EMPIRE VILLAS
BONEHURST RD
CROSS OAK LA
Lake Cottage
Hunters Moon Farm
Bonehurst Farm
Littlelake Farm
Hathersham Farm
HATHERSHAM LA
Bonehurst Bridge
WILLOW CT
THE GRANGE
BURSTOW HO
BROOKWOOD HO
LONGYARD HO
HAVERSHAM HO
SKIPTON WAY
SAREL WAY
Burstow Stream
LAKE LA
Greatlake Farm
Longyards Shaw
KINGSLEY RD
AVONDALE CL
THE SPINNEY
CARLTON CT
MALLARD CL
BOLTS RD
BENHAMS DR
BENHAMS CL
Sch
GRANARY CL
KILN LA
WAYSIDE
BAKEHOUSE RD
FERN DOWN
YEW TREE CL
LEY CL
CHESTNUT RD
THE CHESTNUTS
LADBROKE RD
CRANBOURNE
HORLEY ROW
1 FALLOWFIELD WAY
2 FAIRSTONE CT
3 HARROWSLEY CT
4 FIELDVIEW
5 WOODHAYES
6 RICKWOOD
7 HAYFIELDS
8 RYELANDS
9 WHITECROFT
10 BROOKWOOD
11 BARLEYMEAD
12 MEADOWSIDE
The Farmhouse (PH)
Tanyard Farm
Brook Wood
LANGSHOTT
THATCHERS CL
SMITHBARN CL
COLLINGWOOD
CARTERSMEAD CL
BIRCHWOOD CL
WOODCOTE
THE FIELDINGS
HERITAGE LAWN
CHEQUERS CL
CHEQUERS DR
B2036
CHATELET CL
THE DELL
HOMEFIELD CL
TANYARD WAY
GREATLAKE CT
HERONS WOOD CT
STOCKFIELD
GRASSMERE
WHEATFIELD WAY
HARVEST CT
HONEYSUCKLE
BRIARS WOOD
MAIZE CROFT
MERIDIAN GR
BROAD MEAD
HEDINGHAM CL
EWELANDS
SAXLEY
LAMBYN CROFT
TWYNER CL
OAKSIDE LA
HAZEL CT
WYSEMEAD
WOODLANDS
COPSE RD
Langshott Wood
Sewage Works
SOUTHLANDS AVE
LE MAY CL
LUMLEY CT
OAKWOOD RD
HEVERS AVE
BRIGHTON RD
Yattendon Sch
BRACKENSIDE
FIRLANDS
GATWICK METRO CTR
HEATHERLANDS
ALEBURY KEEP
OATLANDS
LANGSHOTT LA
THE MEADOWAY
RAYMER WALK
BROADLANDS
RUSSELL CT
ACORN CL
CARLTON TYE
CLARENCE WAY
HILTON CT
CLARENCE CT
Weatherhill Common
WEATHERHILL RD
WEATHERHILL CL
Horley Cty Fst Sch
VICTORIA RD
PARK VIEW
PARKWAY
ALBERT RD
LUMLEY RD
ST HILDA'S CL
YATTENDON RD
WINDMILL CL
BRAMLEY WLK
LONGCHAMP CL
ASHWOOD
WATER VIEW
SMALLFIELD RD
QUEEN'S RD
ELIZABETH CT
KINGS RD
CONSORT WAY
CHURCH RD
MAGNOLIA CT
Liby
PO
STATION RD
ST GEORGES CL
CREWDSON RD
SMALLMEAD
BELGRAVIA CT
Langshott Sch
STONECOURT CL
Oakwood Sch
HORLEY
Harrowsley Green Farm
HIGH ST
CONSORT WAY E
PINE GDNS
RINGLEY AVE
ROSEMARY LA
STATION APP
ROSLAN CT
BALCOMBE RD
Wilgers Farm
PERRYLANDS LA
MASSETTS RD
HAMPTON LODGE
RUSSELLS CRES
THE GROVE
AURUM CL
LOVELANDS
FAIRLAWNS
SILVERLEA GDNS
AVENUE GDNS
Haroldslea Poultry Farm
BURT CL
NORFOLK CL
1 DELTA HO
2 DELTA BGLWS
ATKINSON CT
BALCOMBE GDNS
HAROLDSLEA
Newstead Hall
PEEKS BROOK LA
LINCOLN CL
THE DRIVE
PRIMROSE AVE
Horley Sta
STAFFORD PL
STOCKS CL
CASTLE DR
CHEYNE WLK
UPFIELD
DELTA DR
LIMES AVE
HAROLDSLEA DR
Haroldslea House
FAIRFIELD AVE
HYPERION WLK
MICHAEL CRES
HAROLDSLEA CL
CRESCENT WAY
UPFIELD CL
BAYHORN LA
THE CORONET
BAYHORNE LA
Burstow Stream
The Roughs
Garwick Stream
RIVERSIDE
THE RIDGEWAY
CRESCENT
THE CRESCENT
SPIERS WAY
WALTERSVILLE WAY
THE CLOSE
A217
M23

1
6

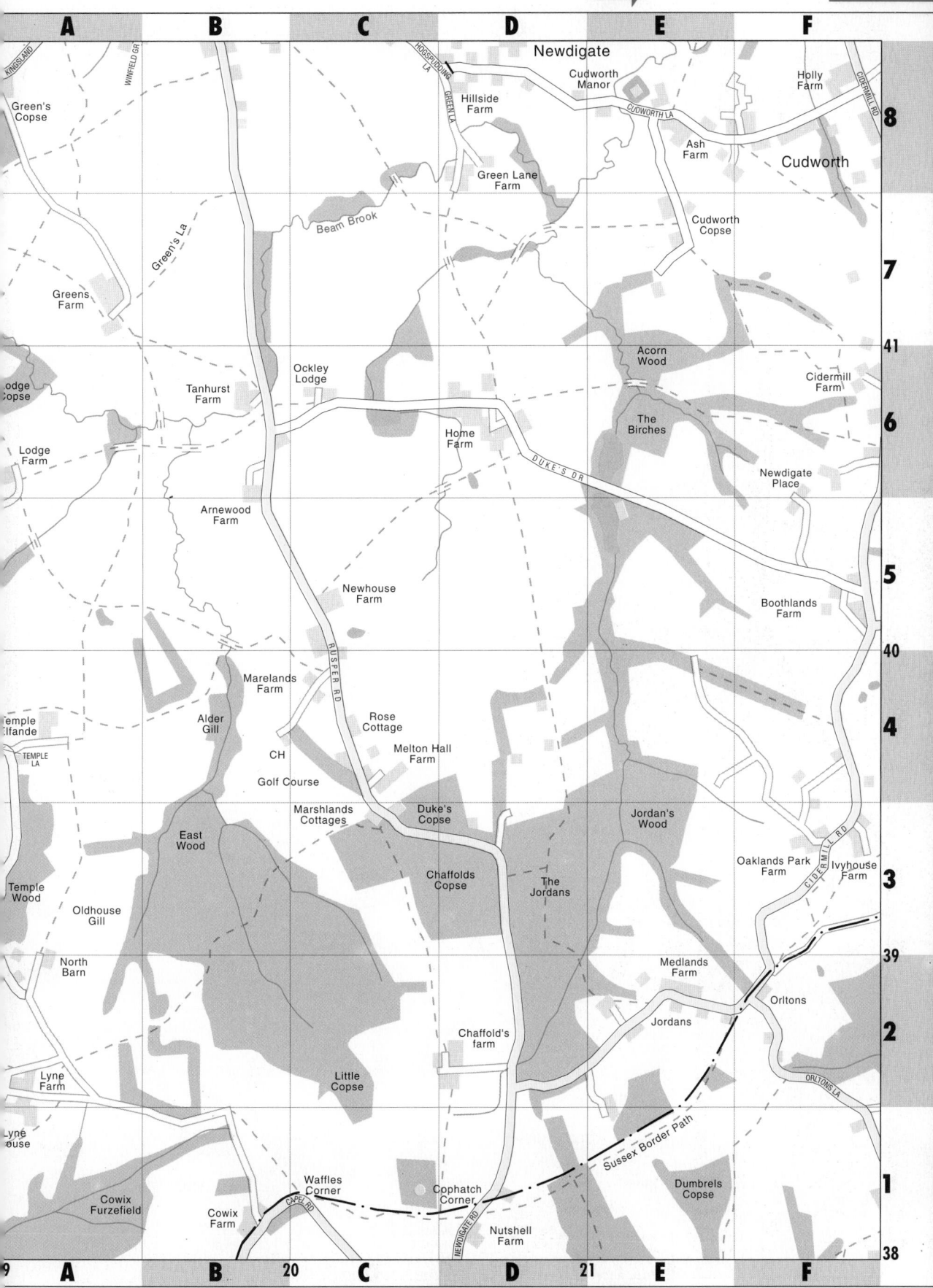

A | B | C | D | E | F

8

Green's Copse

KINGSLAND

WINFIELD GR

HORSSHOEDING LA

Newdigate

Cudworth Manor

Holly Farm

CIDERMILL RD

Hillside Farm

GREEN LA

Ash Farm

CUDWORTH LA

Cudworth

Green's La

Green Lane Farm

Beam Brook

Cudworth Copse

7

Greens Farm

41

Acorn Wood

Cidermill Farm

Lodge Copse

Ockley Lodge

Tanhurst Farm

The Birches

6

Home Farm

DUKE'S DR

Newdigate Place

Lodge Farm

Arnewood Farm

5

Newhouse Farm

Boothlands Farm

RUSPER RD

40

Marelands Farm

4

Temple Ilfande

TEMPLE LA

Alder Gill

Rose Cottage

CH

Melton Hall Farm

Golf Course

Marshlands Cottages

Duke's Copse

Jordan's Wood

Oaklands Park Farm

CIDERMILL RD

Ivyhouse Farm

3

East Wood

Chaffolds Copse

The Jordans

Temple Wood

Oldhouse Gill

39

North Barn

Medlands Farm

Orltons

2

Chaffold's farm

Jordans

Lyne Farm

Little Copse

ORLTONS LA

Lyne ouse

Sussex Border Path

Waffles Corner

CAPEL RD

Cophatch Corner

Dumbrels Copse

1

Cowix Furzefield

Cowix Farm

NEWGATE RD

Nutshell Farm

38

A | B | 20 | C | D | 21 | E | F

A B C D E F

8

7

41

6

5

40

4

3

39

2

1

38

22 A B 23 C D 24 E F

Gildings Farm

Beggarshouse La

Beggarshouse La

Greenings Farm

Greenings

Little Greenings

Furzefield Farm

CIDERMILL RD

Welland Gill

Glover's Plantation

Glover's Wood

STAN HILL

Barfield Farm

Pagewood

RECTORY LA

Glover's Rd

GLENFIELD COTTS

Gatwick Zoo

Welling Barn Farm

Betchworth Works

Sussex Border Path

COUNCIL COTTS

RUSS HILL

Mountnoddy Wood

Russ Hill Farm

CHARLWOOD LA

Gatwick Wena Hotel

Westlands

Waggoners Farm

Westlands Farm

Upper Prestwood Farm

Prestwood Copse

Scrag Copse

ORLTONS LA

Orltons Copse

Gotwick Farm

Tilgate

PRESTWOOD LA

Great Burlands

Man's Brook

Water Hall

Burlands Copse

Lower Prestwood Farm

HILLYBARN RD

Hilly Barn Farmhouse

Ifieldwood

Pockney's Farm

Burlands

Naldretts Farm

Red Gables

Birchfield

IFIELD RD

Little Park Farm

LITTLE PARK ENTERPRISES

CHARLWOOD RD

Ifield Wood

Oak Tree Farm

IFIELD WOOD

Ifield Court Farm

The Druids

Charlwood Place

NORWOODHILL RD

PUDDING LA

Spottles Farm

Charlwood Cty Fst Sch

Charlwood

SWAN LA

ROSEMARY LA

YEW TREE RD

CHAPEL RD

PO

PH

THE STREET

SEWILL CL

PERRYLANDS WY

LOW CNR

ORCHARD COTTS

DOLBY TERR

CHALMERS CT

HORLEY RD

Charlwood Place Farm

Spicer's Bridge

Tifter's Farm

LOWFIELD HEATH RD

Furze Field

Cophall Wood

Ifield Court Hotel

Langhurst Farm

LANGHURST LA

THE MOUNT

The Mount Farm

TWEED LA

1
6

Gatwick Airport-London
North Terminal
LONGBRIDGE RD 1
NORTHWAY 2
CROSSWAY 3
NORTH TERMINAL APP 4
RACECOURSE WAY 5
RACECOURSE RD 6
CHARLWOOD RD
PERIMETER RD N
Sussex Border Path
River Mole
HORLEY RD
Brook Farm
Man's Brook
Brockley Wood
Old Control Tower
Control Tower
1 TIMBERHAM LINK
2 TIMBERHAM WAY
TIMBERHAM FARM RD
CARGO FORECOURT RD
LARKINS RD
OLD CONTROL RD
WINNER WAY
CONTROL TOWER RD
PERIMETER RD S
GATWICK GATE
CHURCH ROAD TRAD EST
CHURCH RD
LOWFIELD WAY
CHURCH ROAD IND EST
Crawter's Bridge
OLD BRIGHTON RD S
A23
Charlwood House
LOWFIELD HEATH RD
Hawthorn Farm
Crawter's Brook
Lowfield Heath
Caravan Park
Ditsworthy
POLES LA
SOUTHWAYS PK
LONDON RD
Gatwick Manor Hotel
Brooklyn Farm
Little Dell
Hydehurst Furze
Rowley Wood
Hyder's Farm
BONNETTS LA
Amberley Farm
Motel
County Oak Ind Est
MERLIN CTR
COUNTY OAK LA
WHITWORTH RD
BETTS WAY
COUNTY OAK WAY
METCALF WAY
FLEMING WAY
Manor Royal
Ind Est
THE SATELLITE BSNS VILLAGE
WALLIS CT
JENNER RD
Ifield Hall
Playing Field
Stafford House
CRAWLEY
Langley Green
Catherington Sch
Langley Green Cty Fst Sch
COUNTY OAK RET PK
KELVIN LA
KELVIN WAY
NEWTON RD
BELL CTR
KELVIN BSNS CTR
STANLEY CTR
BRUNEL CTR
FARADAY RD
1 HAZEL CL
2 BLACKTHORN CL
3 HAWTHORN CL
1 ASHMORE HO
2 LYDDON HO
3 ROWENA HO
4 AUCKLAND CL
CHARLWOOD RD
Stafford Bridge
Ifieldgreen
MULBERRY RD
LANGLEY WALK
MANOR ROYAL
LLOYDS CT
TUSHMORE AVE
CROMPTON WAY
CROMPTON FIELDS
WOOLBOROUGH LA

18
6

5
2
A
B
C
D
E
F
8
7
41
6
5
40
4
3
39
2
1
38
28
29
30
A23
AIRPORT WAY
M23
B2036
B2037
Gatwick Stream
Sussex Border Path
The Coppingham Arms (PH)
Peeks Rough Farm
Bridges Wood
Gatwick Airport-London
Gatwick Airport Sta
South Terminal
LONDON RD
Fern Court Farm
Poplars
Fernhill
Westlands Farm
Burstow Hall
Shipley Bridge Inn
Shipley Bridge
Horleyland Wood
ANTLANDS LA
Shipley Bridge
Courtlands
Sewage Works
Upper Pickett's
Rolls Farm
Black Corner
The Parsons Pig (PH)
BALCOMBE RD
Rowley Farm
Oldlands Farmhouse
Tinsley Bridge
Tinsley Green
Blackcorner Wood
Ind Est
Wellfield Copse
Toovies Farm
Ind Est
Ind Est
Heathy Ground Farm
Crem
The Larches
Forge Wood
Ballast Hole
COPTHORNE WAY
CRAWLEY AVE
Sports Gd
COPTHORNE RD
Grattons Park
Driver's Wood
Wakehams Green Farm
Ind Est
1 LANCASTER CL
2 JAVELIN CT
3 HARRIER CT
4 NIMROD CT
5 BRISTOL CL
6 VICTOR CT
A2011
A2220
19

A B C D E F

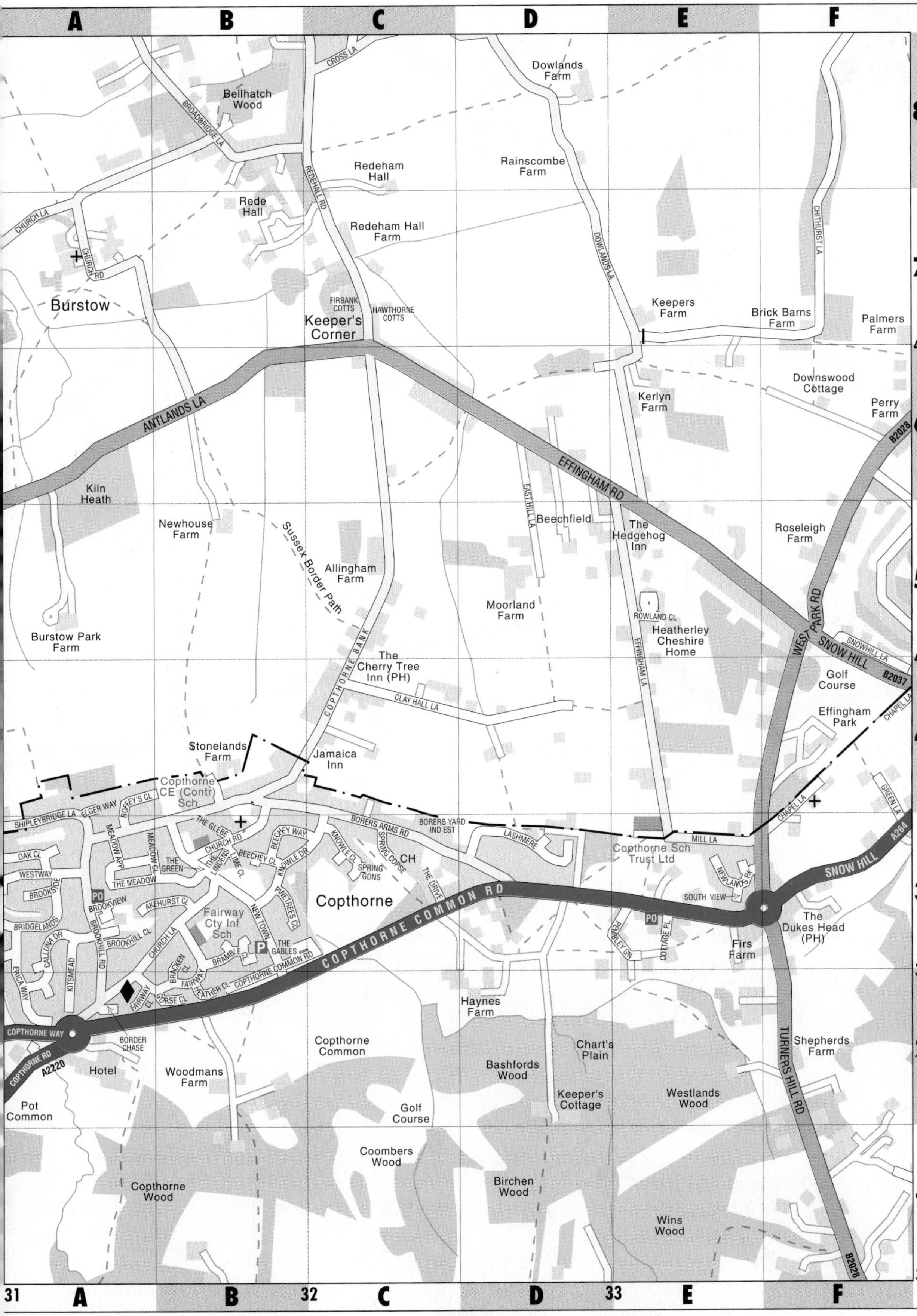

8
7
41
6
5
40
4
39
2
1
38

Bellhatch Wood
Redeham Hall
Rede Hall
Redeham Hall Farm
Dowlands Farm
Rainscombe Farm
Cross La
Broadbridge La
Redhall Rd
Church La
Church Rd
Burstow
Keeper's Corner
Firbank Cotts
Hawthorne Cotts
Keepers Farm
Brick Barns Farm
Palmers Farm
Chithurst La
Downswood Cottage
Perry Farm
Kerlyn Farm
B2028
Antlands La
Kiln Heath
Effingham Rd
Newhouse Farm
Sussex Border Path
Allingham Farm
Beechfield
East Hill La
The Hedgehog Inn
Roseleigh Farm
West Park Rd
Snow Hill
Moorland Farm
Rowland Cl
Heatherley Cheshire Home
Effingham La
Snowhill La
Golf Course
B2037
Copthorne Bank
The Cherry Tree Inn (PH)
Clay Hall La
Effingham Park
Chapel La
Stonelands Farm
Jamaica Inn
Copthorne CE (Contr) Sch
Green La
Shipleybridge La
Ledger Way
Risley's Cl
The Glebe
Borers Arms Rd
Borers Yard Ind Est
Lashmere
Mill La
Copthorne Sch Trust Ltd
A264
Meadow App
Meadow Rd
Church Rd
Beechey Way
Spring La
CH
Oak Cl
Limers
Lime Cl
Beechey Cl
Knowle Cl
Spring Cose
Newlands Pk
Snow Hill
Westway
The Green
Knowle Dr
Spring Gdns
South View
The Dukes Head (PH)
Brookside
Akehurst Cl
Pine Trees Cl
The Drive
PO
Firs Farm
Bridgelands
Callow Dr
PO
Brookview
Brookhill Rd
Fairway Cty Inf Sch
New Town
Cottage Pl
Parley Gn
Erica Way
Kitsmead
Church La
Bracken Cl
Bramble
The Gables
Copthorne
Copthorne Common Rd
Haynes Farm
Chart's Plain
Shepherds Farm
Father Cl
Gorse Cl
Fairway Cl
Copthorne Way
Copthorne Rd
A2220
Border Chase
Hotel
Woodmans Farm
Copthorne Common
Bashfords Wood
Keeper's Cottage
Westlands Wood
Turners Hill Rd
Pot Common
Golf Course
Coombers Wood
Birchen Wood
Copthorne Wood
Wins Wood
B2028
Burstow Park Farm

7

A
B
C
D
E
F
Nevergood Wood
Leighfurze Field
Quarry Farm
EAST PARK LA
Eastpark Farm
B2028
Churchill Stud
A22
WEMBURY PK
WIRE MILL LA
Wire Mill Lake
Homewood
EASTBOURNE RD
HOBBS IND EST
The Plantation
WEST PARK RD
Laylands Farm
Woodcock Bridge
STUBPOND LA
Sewage Works
The Woodcock (PH)
HEATHERWAY
West Park
Cooper's Moors
WOODCOCK HILL
Baker's Wood
Moat Wood
B2028
Perry Farm
A22
Hedgecourt
Domewood
Hedgecourt Lake
Park Farm
Park Wood
HERONS CL
MILL LA
HERONS LEA
COPTHORNE RD
SNOW HILL BSNS CTR
TANGLE OAK
B2037
SNOW HILL
B2037
Felbridge
Felbridge Cty Prim Sch
Snow Hill
Fellcot Farm
LYNDHURST FARM CL
TWITTEN LA
A264
SNOW HILL
CHESTERFIELD CL
ROWPLATT LA
TITHE ORCH
LAKE VIEW RD
Furnace Wood
MCIVER CL
Kenward's Farm
FELCOT RD
WARREN CL
A264
Michaelmas Farm
WHEELERS WAY
CRAWLEY DOWN RD
Gibbshaven Farm
FURNACE RD
FELBRIDGE RD
Furnace Wood
Nurseries
Felbridge Water
The Birches
Furnace Pond
Nurseries.
CUTTINGLYE RD
Stubbits Wood
HOPHURST HILL
Cuttinglye Wood
Greenfield Shaw
Down Park Farm
Parkfields Farm
Gulledge
Sussex Border Path
CUTTINGLYE LA
Hophurst Farm
HAVEN GDNS
FERNHILL CL
FERMANDY LA
HOPHURST LA
TILTWOOD DR
GAGE CL
AVIARY WAY
Worth Way
Railway Shaw
The Larches
8
7
41
6
5
40
4
3
39
2
1
38
34
35
36

7

21

C1
1 THE BROWNINGS
2 BYRON GR
3 CHAUCER AVE
4 TENNYSON RISE
5 THE SAYERS
6 WORDSWORTH RISE

9

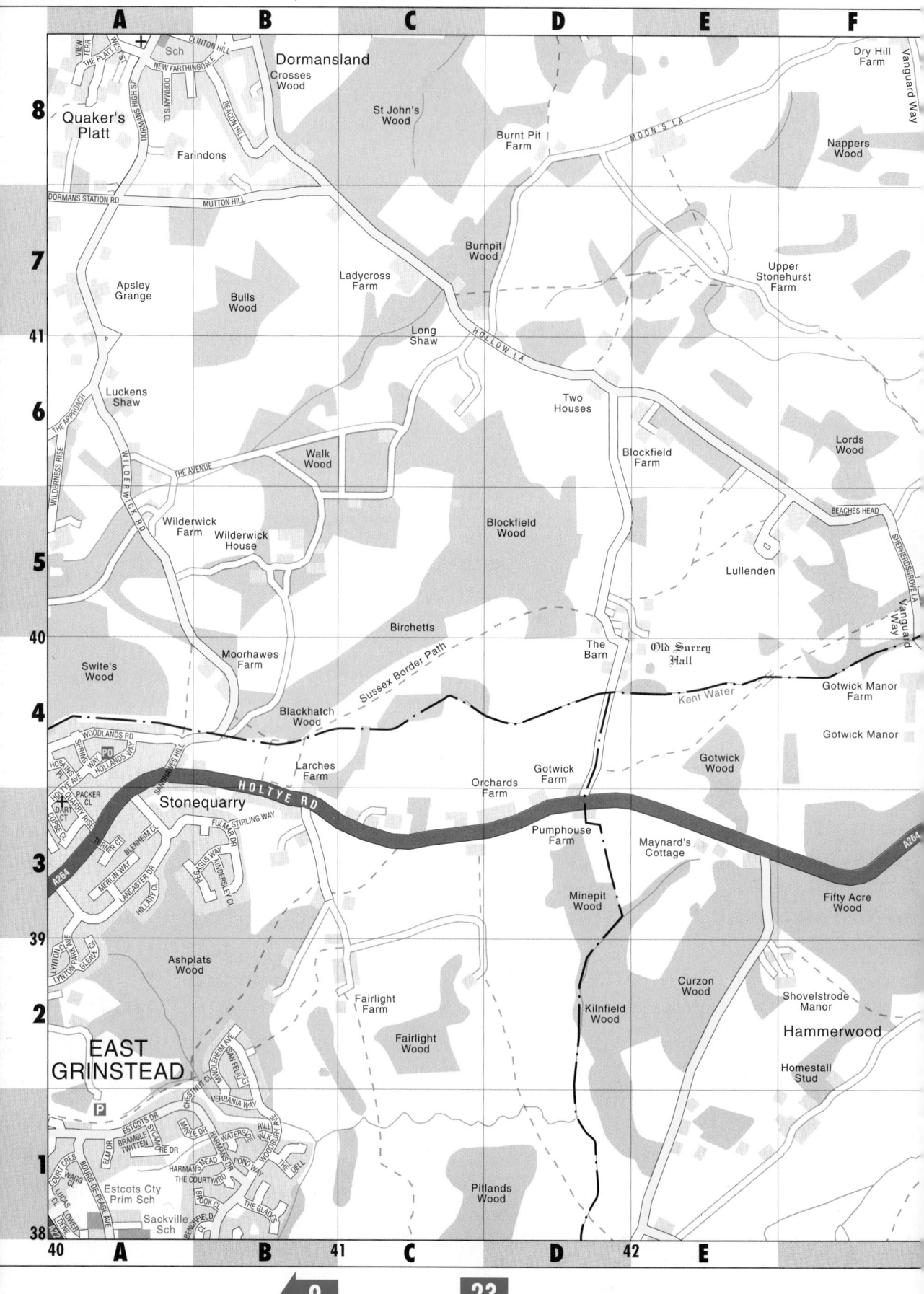
A
B
C
D
E
F
8
7
41
6
5
40
4
3
39
2
1
38
40
41
42
Dormansland
Crosses Wood
Quaker's Platt
Sch
CLINTON HILL
NEW FARTHINGDALE
DORMANS HIGH ST
DORMAN'S CL
BEACON HILL
VIEW TERR
THE PLATT
WEST ST
Farindons
St John's Wood
Burnt Pit Farm
MOON'S LA
Dry Hill Farm
Vanguard Way
Nappers Wood
DORMANS STATION RD
MUTTON HILL
Burnpit Wood
Ladycross Farm
Upper Stonehurst Farm
Apsley Grange
Bulls Wood
Long Shaw
HOLLOW LA
Luckens Shaw
THE APPROACH
Two Houses
Lords Wood
Blockfield Farm
Walk Wood
THE AVENUE
WILDERNESS RISE
WILDERWICK RD
BEACHES HEAD
SHEPHERDSGROVE LA
Wilderwick Farm
Wilderwick House
Blockfield Wood
Lullenden
Birchetts
Vanguard Way
The Barn
Old Surrey Hall
Moorhawes Farm
Swite's Wood
Sussex Border Path
Kent Water
Gotwick Manor Farm
Blackhatch Wood
Gotwick Manor
WOODLANDS RD
SPRINGS WAY
HOLLANDS WAY
PO
SANDHAWES HILL
HOSKINS PL
HOLTYE AVE
Larches Farm
Gotwick Wood
Gotwick Farm
Orchards Farm
PACKER CL
QUARRY RISE
DART CT
COPSE CL
Stonequarry
HOLTYE RD
STIRLING WAY
FULMAR DR
Pumphouse Farm
Maynard's Cottage
A264
TURNER CT
BLENHEIM CL
PEGASUS WAY
KINDERSLEY CL
MERLIN WAY
LANCASTER DR
HILLARY CL
Minepit Wood
Fifty Acre Wood
LYNTON CL
LYNTON PARK AVE
GLEAVE CL
Ashplats Wood
Curzon Wood
Fairlight Farm
Kilnfield Wood
Shovelstrode Manor
Fairlight Wood
Hammerwood
EAST GRINSTEAD
WOODHEIM AVE
SIMON FELIX CT
CHESTNUT CL
VERBANIA WAY
Homestall Stud
P
ESTCOTS DR
BRAMBLE TWITTEN
SYCAMORE DR
MAPLE DR
HARMANS DR
WATERSIDE
HILL WK
WOODBURY AVE
ELM DR
COURT CRES
WAGG CL
BOURG-DE-PEAGE AVE
HARMANS MEAD
THE COURTYARD
POND WAY
THE DELL
Estcots Cty Prim Sch
LUCAS CL
LOWER DENE
BROOK CL
THE GLADES
Sackville Sch
BENCHFIELD CL
Pitlands Wood

9

23

A
B
C
D
E
F
Cranleigh
B2128
Highpark
Sparrow Copse
Bushy Copse
Garson Copse
Little Garson
Holdhurst Farm
White Meads Copse
Great Garson
Boy & Donkey (PH)
Snoxhall Farm
Wey-South Path
ALFOLD RD
VACHERY LA
Thornhurst Brook
Vachery Pond
Lion's La
Wey & Arun Junction Canal (dis)
Water Bridge
Flash Bridge
Hammer Farm
Downs Link
A281
Waterland Farm
Waterbridge Farm
Bridge Farm
Newhouse Farm
Bookers Lee
Little Withybush
Birch Copse
ALFOLD BY-PASS
WILDWOOD LA
KNOWLE LA
HAZELWOOD COTTS
Little Wildwood Farm
Lodge Copse
Butcherhouse Farm
Works
CROSSWAYS COTTS
Pickenswood Copse
Alfold Crossways
LOXWOOD RD
CH
Wildwood Copse
B2133
STONE HATCH
HATCH CL
Wildwood Golf Course
Shrubs Copse
CLAPPERS MEADOW
Ivelle Farm
Furzefield Wood
Aldermoor Copse
Pallinghurst Farm
BAYNARDS RD
HORSHAM RD
Hazel Copse
Highfield Copse
White Lea
Little Birchett
Alfold Farm
HILLHOUSE LA
Hook St
Sussex Border Path
White's Copse
A281
GUILDFORD RD
COOKS HILL
Males Farm
Lower Hill House
8
7
37
6
5
36
4
3
35
2
1
34
04
05
06

A B C D E F

8

7

37

6

5

36

4

3

35

2

1

34

B2128
HORSHAM RD
Whitehall
Norley Farm
Thornhurst Brook
Owlbarn Copse
Longhurst Hill
Windgate Cottage
The Wind Break
SOMMERSBURY LA
Vachery Pond
Vachery House
Home Wood
Brooklands Farm
Baynard's Park
Cobbler's Brook
Vachery Farm
Home Farm
Sharpe's Copse
Collins Farm
Baynard's Park
Tillhouse Farm
Pollingfold Bridge
New Barn
LINACRE DR
Massers Wood
Grub Copse
The Wheatsheaf (PH)
STATION RD
Ruet
FURZEN LA
North Wood
Maybanks Manor
Tolt Garth
Baynards Sta (dis)
LAWNS RD
Starveall Copse
Downs Link
South Wood
BAYNARDS RD
COX GREEN RD
Woodthorpe
HERMONGER LA
Great Inholms
Little Inholms
Hobbs Copse
Sussex Border Path
Little Hawks Hill
CHURCH ST
HAWKRIDGE
Cox Green
Street Copse
The Crickets
Works
LYNWICK ST
PO
The Kings Head (PH)
HIGHCROFT DS
Windacres Farm
Woodsomes Farm
B2128

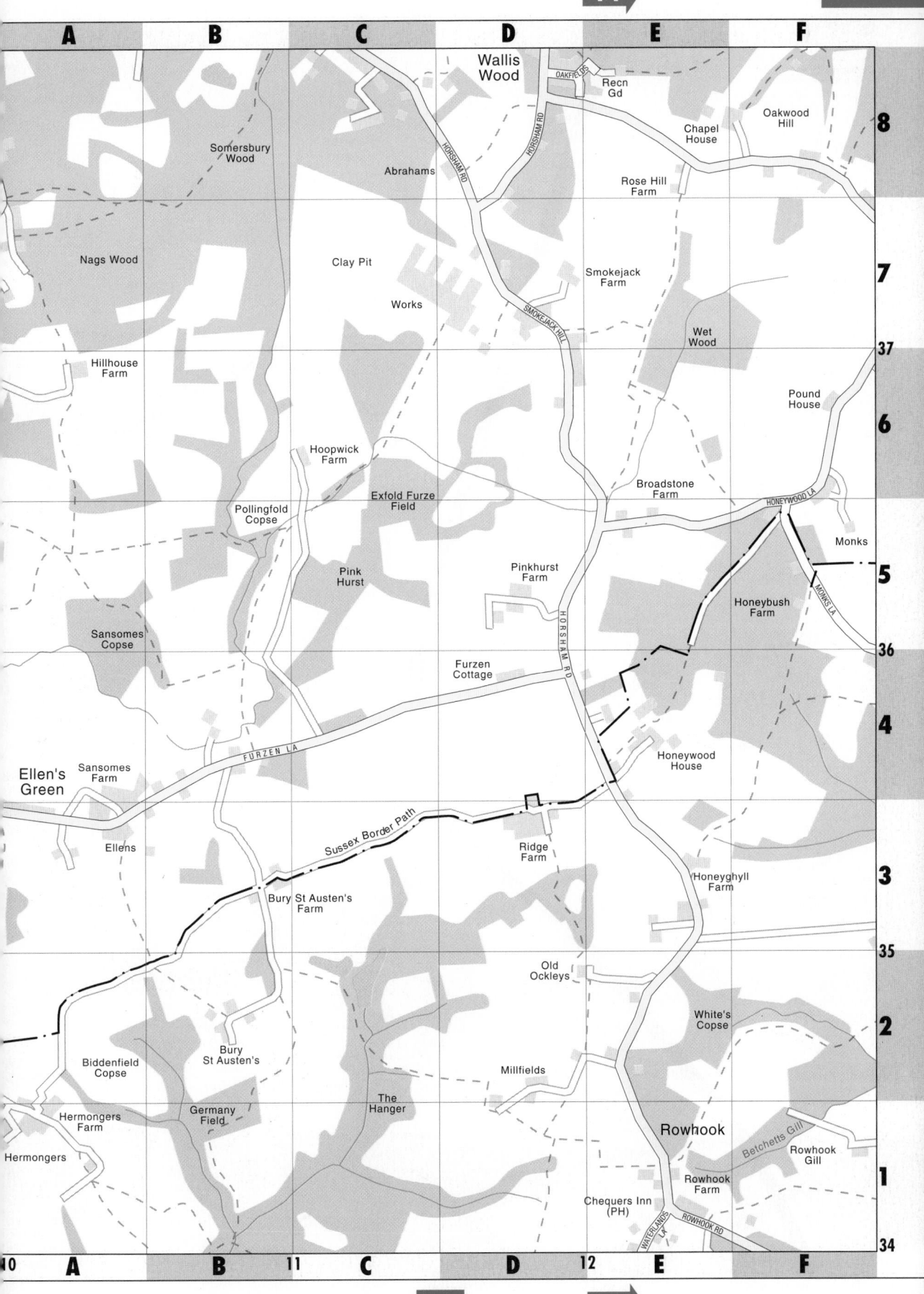

A   B   C   D   E   F

Wallis Wood

Recn Gd

Oakfields

Chapel House

Oakwood Hill

8

Abrahams

Rose Hill Farm

Somersbury Wood

HORSHAM RD

Clay Pit

Smokejack Farm

7

Nags Wood

Works

SMOKEJACK HILL

Wet Wood

37

Hillhouse Farm

Pound House

6

Hoopwick Farm

Exfold Furze Field

Broadstone Farm

HONEYWOOD LA

Pollingfold Copse

Monks

MONKS LA

Pink Hurst

Pinkhurst Farm

Honeybush Farm

5

Sansomes Copse

HORSHAM RD

36

Furzen Cottage

4

Ellen's Green

Sansomes Farm

Honeywood House

FURZEN LA

Sussex Border Path

Ellens

Ridge Farm

Honeyghyll Farm

3

Bury St Austen's Farm

35

Old Ockleys

White's Copse

2

Biddenfield Copse

Bury St Austen's

Millfields

Germany Field

The Hanger

Rowhook

Betchetts Gill

Hermongers Farm

Rowhook Gill

Hermongers

Rowhook Farm

1

Chequers Inn (PH)

WATERLANDS LA

ROWHOOK RD

34

10   A   B   11   C   D   12   E   F

A B C D E F

8
7
37
6
5
36
4
3
35
2
1
34

Chapel Copse
Hale House
Puttocks Bridge
Paynes Green
Timber Gill
The Punchbowl Inn (PH)
Oakdale Farm
North River
Woodhams Farm
Oakwoodhill
Boswells Farm
Place Farm
Rowland Wood
HONEYWOOD LA
RUCKMANS LA
WEARE ST
SMUGGLERS LA
Ruckmans Farm
Potland Hangers
Denne Bridge
Sussex Border Path
Tickfold Gill
Denne Farm
Whitelands Copse
Woodbarn
Whitelands Barn
Monks Farm
Northlands Home Farm
Marches Farm
BOGNOR RD
Stone Farm
MARCHES RD
Joanland Farm
Dawes Farm
Durfold Barn
Chatfolds
Hoopers Barn
Tanners Farm
Charmans Farm
Chatfolds Bridge
Hoopers Copse
Mayes Park House
MAYES LA
Pear Tree Farm
NORTHLANDS RD
Warnham Lodge
Pound Corner
Westbrook House
Benland Wood
Sands Farm
Cider Mill Farm
Threestile Corner
TILLETTS LA
THREESTILE RD
Old Manor
Rowhook Manor
A29

16 →

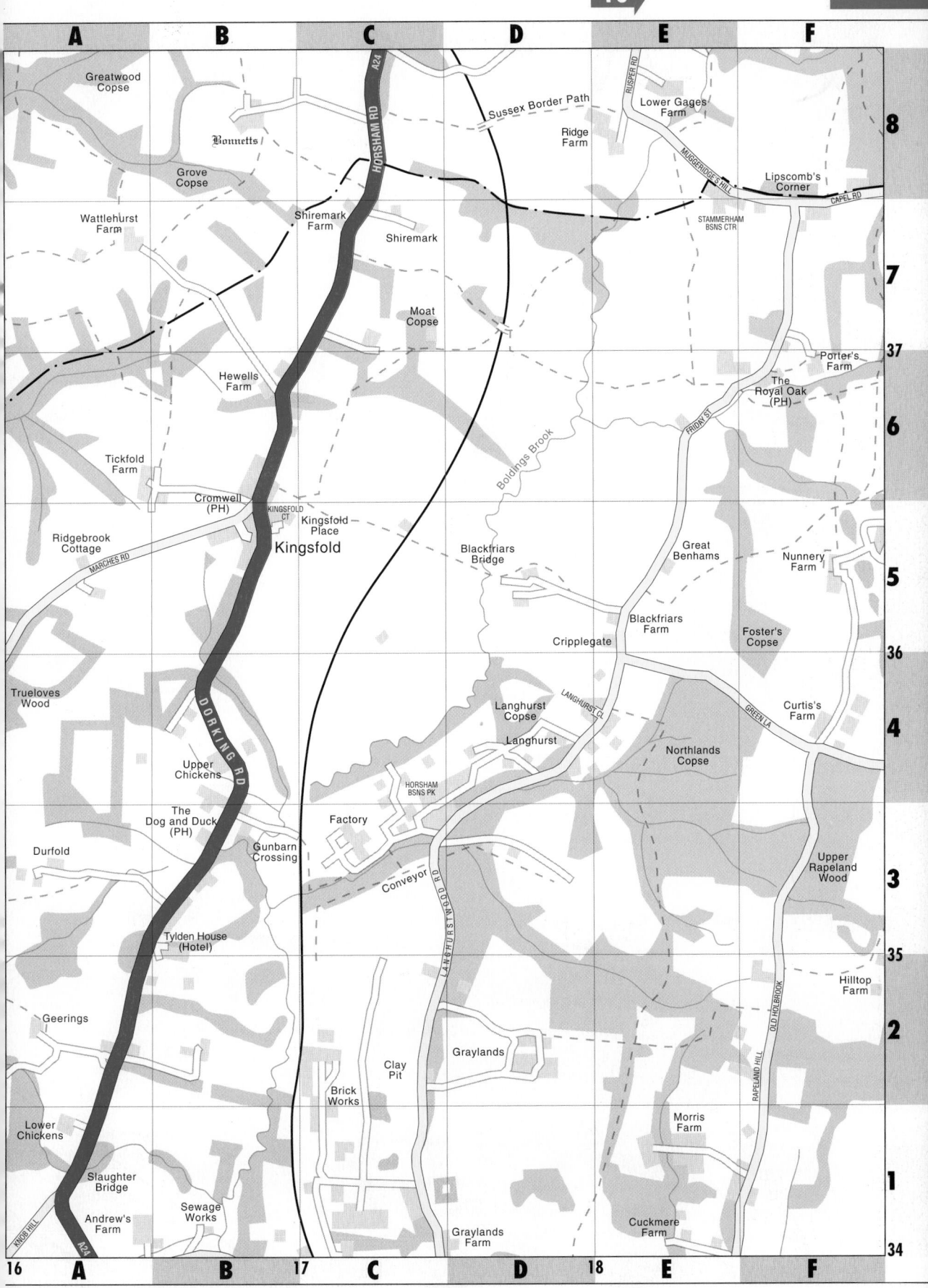

A · B · C · D · E · F

Greatwood Copse

Bonnetts

Grove Copse

Wattlehurst Farm

Shiremark Farm

Shiremark

HORSHAM RD

A24

Sussex Border Path

RUSPER RD

Lower Gages Farm

Ridge Farm

MUGGERIDGE'S HILL

Lipscomb's Corner

CAPEL RD

STAMMERHAM BSNS CTR

8

7

Moat Copse

Porter's Farm

The Royal Oak (PH)

37

6

Hewells Farm

Tickfold Farm

Cromwell (PH)

KINGSFOLD CT

Kingsfold Place

Kingsfold

Ridgebrook Cottage

MARCHES RD

Boldings Brook

Blackfriars Bridge

FRIDAY ST

Great Benhams

Nunnery Farm

Blackfriars Farm

Foster's Copse

5

36

Trueloves Wood

Cripplegate

Langhurst Copse

LANGHURST CL

Langhurst

GREEN LA

Curtis's Farm

Northlands Copse

4

DORKING RD

Upper Chickens

The Dog and Duck (PH)

Durfold

Gunbarn Crossing

Factory

HORSHAM BSNS PK

Conveyor

LANGHURSTWOOD RD

Upper Rapeland Wood

3

35

Tylden House (Hotel)

OLD HOLBROOK

Hilltop Farm

Geerings

Clay Pit

Graylands

RAPELAND HILL

Morris Farm

2

Lower Chickens

Brick Works

Slaughter Bridge

KNOB HILL

A24

Andrew's Farm

Sewage Works

Graylands Farm

Cuckmere Farm

1

34

15
3

8

Rome
Wood

CAPEL RD

New Barn
Farm

Highams

CAPEL RD

NEWGATE RD

Furzefield
Wood

Rusper
House

Venters
Farm

Venters

7

Yew Tree
Cott

Sussex Border Path

HIGH ST

Ghyll Manor
(Hotel)

Chowles

EAST ST

Rusper

37

Horsegills
Wood

Rusper
Cty Prim Sch

PO

PH

COOKS MEAD

COOKS MEADOW

Normans

Millfields
Farm

Cobnor

Lambs Green

6

ASHMORE LA

PETERS HILL

GARDENERS GN

Dialpost
Farm

Pucks
Croft

Baldhorns
Copse

Kiln
Copse

CANONBURY
COTTS

Nurseries

LAMBS GREEN RD

PH

Ashfolds

Sewage
Farm

Cow
Wood

Rusper Court
Farm

Axmas
Farm

Nuns
Wood

Rusper
Nunnery

Manns
Farm

HORSHAM RD

Baldhorns
Park Farm

Baldhorns
Park

Rusper Court
House

River Mole

Saykers

5

36

Old Park

The Lodge

WIMLAND RD

Fay
Cottages

Seers
Croft

FAYGATE LA

4

GREEN LA

Sloughbrook
Gill

Faygate Wood
Farm

Carylls
Farm

Furze
Field

Carylls
Lodge

3

Holming
Wood

Coombers
Farm

Rusper
Copse

North Grange
Farm

KILNWOOD LA

Allingham
Wood

WIMLANDS LA

Culross

35

Caryll's Lea
Farm

2

Hurst
Wood

Hurst
Hill

Breakey
Gill

WIMLAND HILL

Wimland
Farm

Durrants
Copse

Bakehouse
Copse

WIMLAND RD

RUSPER RD

Bush
Copse

FAYGATE
BSNS CTR

OAK WLK

Durrants

Holmbush
Inn
(PH)

Faygate
Sta

PARK RD

1

Hawkesbourne
Farm

Benson's
Cottage

BENSON'S LA

Budd's
Farm

Faygate

CLOVERS
COTTS

CARYLLS
COTTS

CRAWLEY RD

A264

The Castle

34

15
37

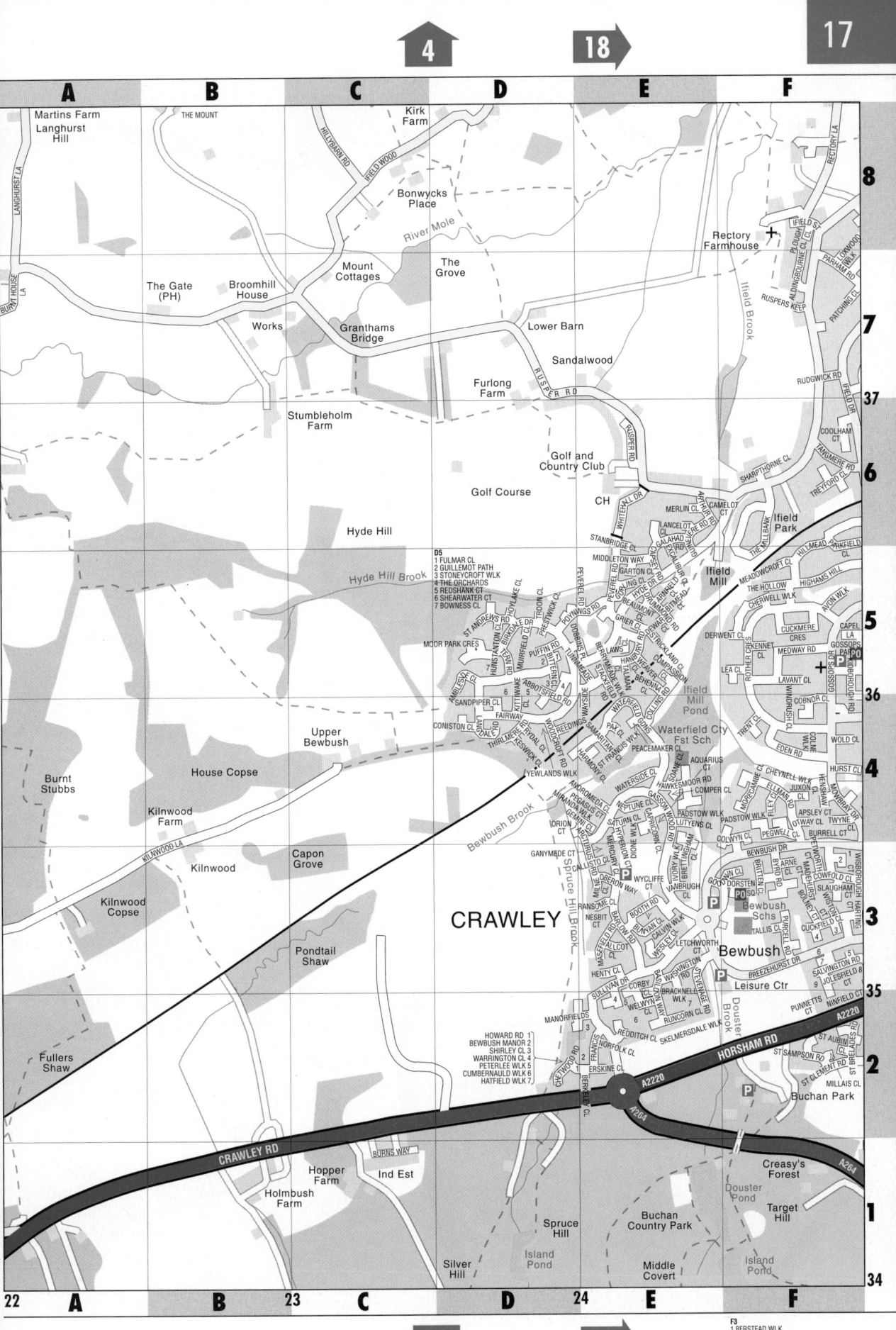

4

18

A B C D E F

8

7

37

6

5

36

4

3

35

2

1

34

22 A B 23 C D 24 E F

38

18

Martins Farm
Langhurst
Hill

THE MOUNT

Kirk
Farm

FIELD WOOD

Bonwycks
Place

HILLBARN RD

LANGHURST LA

BURNT HOUSE LA

River Mole

Ifield Brook

Rectory
Farmhouse

The Gate
(PH)

Broomhill
House

Mount
Cottages

The Grove

Works

Granthams
Bridge

Lower Barn

Sandalwood

RUSPERS KEEP

RECTORY LA

PLOUGH CL

ALDINGBOURNE CL CL

PARHAM RD

IFIELD ST

RUDGWICK RD

IFIELD DR

PATCHING CL

Furlong
Farm

Stumbleholm
Farm

RUSPER RD

Golf and
Country Club

Golf Course

CH

WHITEHALL DR

ARTHUR RD

SHARPTHORNE CL

COOLHAM
CT

TANGMERE RD

TRETFORD CL

Hyde Hill

MERLIN CL

CAMELOT
CT

THE WALL

THE WILLBANK

Ifield
Park

OAKFIELD
CL

HILLMEAD

Hyde Hill Brook

D5
1 FULMAR CL
2 GUILLEMOT PATH
3 STONEYCROFT WLK
4 THE ORCHARDS
5 REDSHANK CT
6 SHEARWATER CT
7 BOWNESS CL

STANBRIDGE CL

GALAHAD

LANCELOT CL

EXCALIBUR RD

MIDDLETON WAY

GARTON CL

HYDE CL

Ifield
Mill

MEADOWCROFT CL

THE HOLLOW

HIGHAMS HILL

CHERWELL WLK

AVON WLK

CAPEL
LA

GOSSOPS
DR PARADE

ST ANDREWS RD

MOOR PARK CRES

PEVEREL RD

PRESTWICK CL

POYNINGS RD

DENMARK RD

BEAUMONT CL

GRIER CL

COMPASSION

DERWENT CL

CUCKMERE
CRES

KENNET CL

ROTHER CRES

MEDWAY RD

LAVANT CL

COBNOR CL

GOSSOPS DR

KIBOROUGH RD

PARK

HURSTANTON CL

BIXLOW CL

HOYLAKE CL

PUFFIN RD

TUNNMERE CL

BERRALL WAY

LAWS

HAND CROSS

RESTRICK RD

COLLINS RD

LEA CL

TRENT CL

COLNE CL

EDEN RD

WOLD CL

ANGLESEA CL

MUIRFIELD RD

KATHWAIKE

ABBOTSFIELD RD

SANDPIPER CL

FAIRWAY

6

2

PAZ

WATERFIELD GDNS

Ifield
Mill
Pond

Waterfield Cty
Fst Sch

PEACEMAKER CL

HURST CL

Upper
Bewbush

CONISTON CL

THIRLMERE RD

RYDAL CL

KESWICK CL

COALE

FREEDINGS

ST FRANCIS RD

HARMONY CL

Burnt
Stubbs

House Copse

Kilnwood
Farm

KILNWOOD LA

Kilnwood

YEWLANDS WLK

Bewbush Brook

ANDROMEDA CL

PEGASUS CL

MIRANDA WLK

ORION

GANNI CL

WATERSIDE CL

HAWKESMOOR RD

COMPER CL

AQUARIUS
CT

NEPTUNE CL

SATURN CL

WOOD RD

PADSTOW WLK

PADSTOW RD

LUTYENS CL

CHEYNELL WLK

JUXON CL

HENSHAW

MORGANA CL

ELLMAN CL

APSLEY CT

TWYNE

BURRELL CT

Kilnwood
Copse

Capon
Grove

Spruce Hill Brook

GANYMEDE CT

DIONE WLK

MILNE CL

OBERON WAY

ASTROLOGER

IVORY CL

BRETT CL

COLWYN CL

PEGWELL CL

BEWBUSH DR

ARNE CL

MAGHULL CL

COWFOLD CL

SLAUGHAM

WISBOROUGH HARTING

AVON CL

BRITTEN CL

BYRD RD

PURCELL

CUCKFIELD CL

Pondtail
Shaw

WYCLIFFE
CT

RANSOME CL

BOOTH RD

BARLOW RD

NESBIT
CT

CALVIN WLK

VANBRUGH
CL

DORSTEN

P

P

Bewbush
Schs

TALLIS CL

6

Bewbush

CRAWLEY

MASFIELD RD

HALLCOT

HENTY CL

SULLIVAN DR

WESLEY CL

LETCHWORTH
CT

STEVENAGE RD

BREEZEHURST DR

SALVINGTON RD

VOLESFIELD CL

Leisure Ctr

P

9

Fullers
Shaw

MANORFIELDS

HOWARD RD 1
BEWBUSH MANOR 2
SHIRLEY CL 3
WARRINGTON CL 4
PETERLEE WLK 5
CUMBERNAULD WLK 6
HATFIELD WLK 7

REDDITCH CL

NORFOLK CL

SKELMERSDALE WLK

RUNCORN CL

CORBY

BRACKNELL CL

WELWYN CL

WASHINGTON RD

PUNNETTS CT

NINFIELD CT

A2220

HORSHAM RD

ST SAMPSON RD

ST AUBIN

ST BRELADES CT

CHETWOOD RD

FRANCIS CL

ERSKINE CL

BERKELEY CL

A2220

ST CLEMENT RD

MILLAIS CL

P

Buchan Park

CRAWLEY RD

BURNS WAY

Hopper
Farm

Ind Est

A264

Douster Brook

Creasy's
Forest

Douster
Pond

Target
Hill

Holmbush
Farm

Spruce
Hill

Buchan
Country Park

Silver
Hill

Island
Pond

Middle
Covert

Island
Pond

F3
1 BERSTEAD WLK
2 DONNINGTON CT
3 HASSOCKS CT
4 PYECOMBE CT
5 TELHAM CT
6 WARBLETON HO
7 CALDBECK HO
8 HALNAKER WLK
9 ICKLESHAM HO

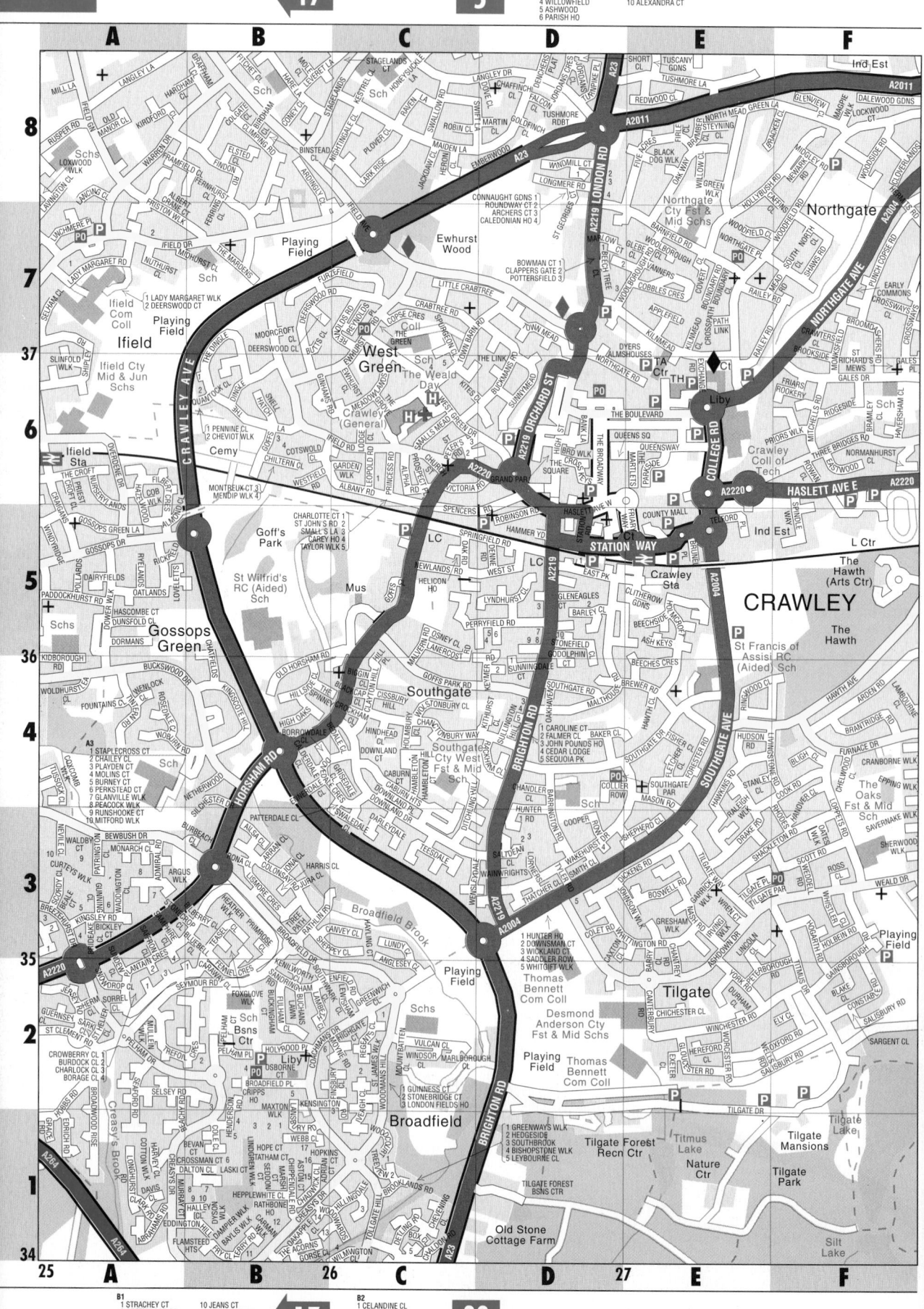

D5
1 THE COURTYARD
2 WALSTEAD HO
3 RAVENDENE CT
4 WILLOWFIELD
5 ASHWOOD
6 PARISH HO
7 PERRYFIELD HO
8 HANDSWORTH HO
9 GLENDON HO
10 ALEXANDRA CT

B1
1 STRACHEY CT
2 GREENWOOD CT
3 SHINWELL WLK
4 WILKINSON CT
5 MORRISON CT
6 ADAMSON CT
7 KEIR HARDIE HO
8 SILKIN WLK
9 HERSCHEL WLK
10 JEANS CT
11 PANKHURST CT
12 SHERATON WLK
13 TIMBERLANDS
14 WOODING GR
15 THOMPSON CT
16 RICHARDSON CT
17 RAMSEY CT

B2
1 CELANDINE CL
2 HENBANE CT
3 SELSEY CT
4 BROADFIELD BARTON
5 ATTLEE HO
6 BALMORAL CT

6
20

A B C D E F

Hazelwick Sch
Milton Mount Fst & Mid Sch
TRINITY CL
HOME CL
FARMLEIGH CL
LEIGHLANDS
Pound Hill
B2036
HEATHFIELD
REIGATE CL
PAYNE CL
HOCKEN MEAD
M23
A2220
COPTHORNE RD
1 HYDE HEATH CT
2 CHERRY TREE CL
Burleys Wood
OLD HOLLOW
A2011
A2004
NORTHGATE AVE
TINSLEY LA S
HAZELWICK MILL LA
WOOLBOROUGH LA
NORTH RD
WOODEND CL
POND WOOD RD
HOLLY CL
ASH RD
GRANGE CL
WEST AVE
Three Bridges
BYCROFT WAY
Gatwick Stream
ST MARY'S DR
DONNE CL
HERRICK CL
MARVELL CL
GRATTONS DR
COBBETT CL
MILTON MOUNT AVE
WOODLANDS
CHAUCER RD
TENNYSON CL
KIPLING CL
SHELLEY CL
BROWNING CL
WORDSWORTH CL
BYRON CL
BURNS RD
PARK WAY
MILTON RD
HARDY CL
1 PENSHURST CL
2 THE PADDOCK
3 SHORT GALLOP
4 GREYHOUND SLIP
5 THE CACKSTONES
BASHFORD WAY
THE COVEY
STACE WAY
THE GROOMS
OAKFIELDS
SHETLAND CL
THE CANTER
HORSESHOE CL
BYERLEY WAY
THE GARRONES
CORONET CL
THE BIRCHES
HAZELWICK AVE
COPPICE WLK
RYE ASH
CROSSWAYS
FORGE LA
FORGE RD
HALLAND CL
CRABBET RD
HENSON RD
RANDALL SCHOFIELD CT
SCALLOWS CL
SCALLOWS RD
KIMBERLEY RD
HAZELWICK RD
MILL RD
WEST WAY
FARM CL
BELVEDERE CT
Sch
NEW ST
WASSAND CL
Coll
GALES DR
THREE BRIDGES RD
JUBILEE WLK
HASLETT AVE E
Three Bridges Sta
Ind Est
Playing Field
STEPHENSON WAY
STEPHENSON PL
STOCKWELL WORKS
RUSSELL WAY
WORTH PARK AVE
STUMBLETTS
MERSWORTH DR
BRIARS WOOD
PINE SHAW
TREVANNE PLAT
OAK DELL
BARNWOOD CL
DENE TYE
WENTWORTH DR
BRIDLE WAY
FELBRIDGE AVE
STIRRUP WAY
OWLETTS
LYTTON DR
SHIRE PARK
THE RIDINGS
KNOLE CL
DEMANS
SEDGEFIELD CL
LINGFIELD DR
Crabbet Park
Pound Hill Cty Fst & Mid Schs
BELLOC CL
MOUNT CL
1 ST IVES
2 ST NICHOLAS CT
3 ST BARNABAS CT
SISSINGHURST CL
BALCOMBE CT
KELSO CL
STATION HILL
SAUNDERS CL
POUND HILL PAR
CLIVE WAY
MOAT WLK
CRAWLEY LA
ALICIA AVE
POUND HILL PL
WORTH RD
THE RISE
HILLCREST CL
Sch
TAUNTON CL
CHEPSTOW CL
HEXHAM CL
MAUNSELL PK
PEARSON RD
ARUNDEL CL
AMBERLEY CL
BODIAM CL
CAMBER CL
SEDGEWICK CL
BURLEYS RD
LONG CL
THE PASTURE
ERIDGE CL
HASTINGS RD
ASHURST DR
MAYFIELD
TURNERS HILL RD
CROWHURST CL
HAZELHURST DR
TICEHURST CL
SALEHURST RD
GREEN LA
OLD ORCHARDS
OSMUND CL
Worth
ATHELSTAN CL
1 GOUDHURST KEEP
2 GOUDHURST CL
3 CROWHURST KEEP
KNEPP CL
LEWES CL
SPRING PLAT
SPRING PLAT CT
BLACKWATER LA
PEVENSEY CL
BANKS RD
COWDRAY CL
TOFTWOOD CL
Worth Way
GEORGIAN CL
CHURCH RD
EDGAR CL
HAROLD RD
SAXON RD
ALFRED CL
Worth Lodge Farm
HAWTH AVE
BURWASH RD
BLACKFOLD RD
BRAMBLETYE
DEDISHAM CL
CHIDDINGLY CL
GREENACRE CL
WILLIAMS WAY
GOSDEN CL
FRESHFIELD CL
COLTASH RD
WALESBEECH
LAMBERHURST WLK
HYLANDS CL
THE CHASE
WATER LEA
BILLINTON DR
WANDLE CL 1
MAYES CL 2
STANIER CL
SEVERN RD
TAMAR CL
JACOBEAN CL
STUART CL
TUDOR CL
ELIZABETHAN WAY
LAUD DR
ST VINCENT CL
COLLINGWOOD CL
BURDETT CL
ALLYINGTON WAY
STREET HILL
WORTH WAY
DOLLIS CL
WESTMINSTER RD
FRANKLIN RD
CLIFTON RD
1 TILLOTSON CL
2 MAYFLOWER CL
3 ALBION CL
4 WELLER CL
5 BETHUNE CL
6 THORNDYKE CL
BALCOMBE RD
CRAVEN RD
STROUDLEY CL
STIRLING CL
GRAVENEY RD
CAMPBELL RD
NELSON CL
TYNE CL
CRANMER WLK
SHELDON CL
BANCROFT RD
TEMPLE CL
REDGRAVE DR
NIVEN CL
OLIVIER RD
Furnace Green
THE GLADE
FURNACE PL
YARMOUTH CL
NORWICH RD
BREYDON WLK
THEYDON CL
Sch
FERONERS CL
BRUNSWICK CL
SHEFFIELD CL
WHEELER RD
ELLISON CL
ELLIOTT CL
CAVELL RD
NEWMAN
EVANS CL
ADELPHI CL
STRAND CL
ALDWYCH CL
SHAFTESBURY RD
DRURY CL
Maidenbower Cty Fst Sch
HARVEST RD
FURNACE DR
FURNACE PAR
WEALD DR
ASHBURNHAM RD
HOLLYE WLK
FOWLER CL
AVELING CL
MARSHALL RD
NORMANDY CL
FENCHURCH RD
SINCLAIR CL
BAXTER CL
MARGARET CL
PARKER CL
LYRIC CL
MAIDENBOWER DR
BENJAMIN RD
PARNELL CL
BRANDON CL
AINTREE RD
EPSOM RD
NEWMARKET RD
FURNACE FARM RD
WARNHAM RD
TUXFORD CL
PROCTOR CL
1 WALKER RD
2 RAWORTH CL
3 STEPNEY CL
4 MAIDENBOWER SQ
5 MAIDENBOWER PL
LUCERNE DR
1 STRUDGATE CL
2 HAWKHURST WLK
3 LOWESTOFT WLK
4 BARTON WLK
5 HEMSBY WLK
6 ORMESBY WLK
7 WAVENEY WLK
8 WROXHAM WLK
9 OULTON WLK
10 HICKLING WLK
ATKINSON RD
WATSON CL
Maidenbower
SYLVAN RD
GOODWOOD CL
FONTWELL CL
LINDEN CL
ST LEONARDS DR
LAUREL CL
CHARLESTON CT
FORESTFIELD
ROSAMUND RD
MARION RD
LONGWOOD VIEW
NYMANS CT
BATEMANS CT
HIGHDOWN CT
LEONARDSLEE CT
WEIRBROOK
WANTAGE CL
BALDWIN CL
STOKES CL
BOSHAM RD
EMSWORTH RD
SHOREHAM RD
CARTER RD
RUSTON CL
TROTTON CL
SALTERNS RD
MOORLAND CL
LANSDOWNE CL
WILSON CL
TANYARD CL
WINTERFOLD
RILLSIDE
FOREST VIEW
Long Wood
1 DONCASTER WLK
2 SHARON CL
3 GRAVETYE CL
4 FERRONERS CT
5 BRUNSWICK CT
HOUGHTON CL
STOPHAM RD
MALHAM CL
CASHER RD
GREATHAM RD
LADYMEAD CL
GODDARD CL
MATTHEWS DR
PALMER RD
HOLDER RD
FLINT CL
PALLINGHAM DR
BOWATER RD
BIRCHWOOD CL
Worthlodge Forest
Furnace Plain
Tilgate Forest Golf Course
BENNETT CL
PENFOLD RD
GATES CL
MERCER CL
BRADBURY RD
GABRIEL RD
BELLAMY CL
DAKIN CL
1 KERDALE CL
2 GIBBONS CL
Flax Field
Brick Field North
CUFFS HILL
JULLETT RD
GREGORY CL
HARPER DR
LYON CL
CH
TILGATE DR
CHAPMAN RD
BARBER CL
MILBORNE CL
DUKE CL
BOLTON RD
Stanford Brook
Brick Field South
Oldhouse Warren
Worth Forest
Whitely Hill
Rugs Corner
WHITELY HILL
B2036
M23

8 7 37 6 5 36 4 3 35 2 1 34

28 A B 29 C D 30 E F

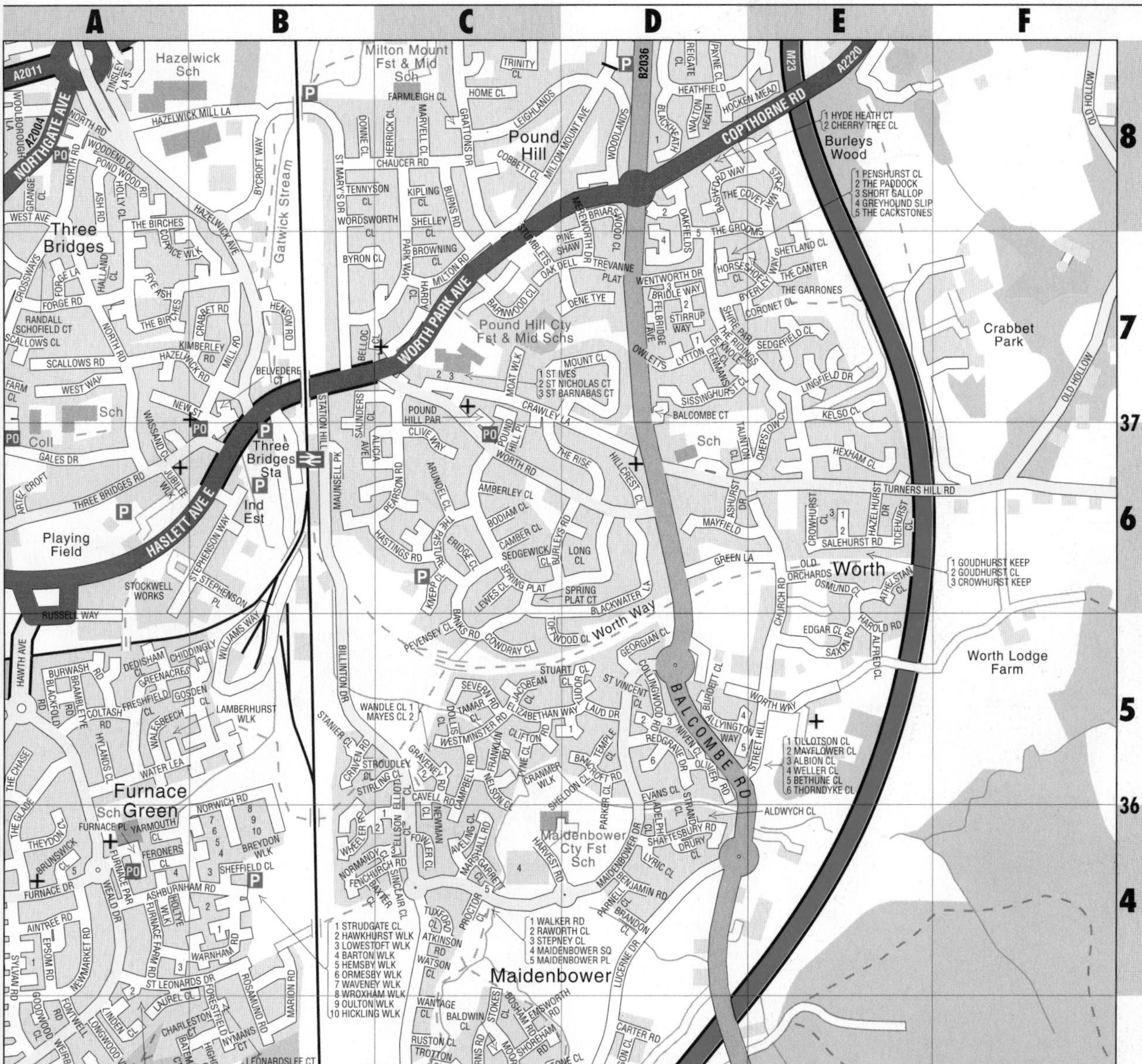

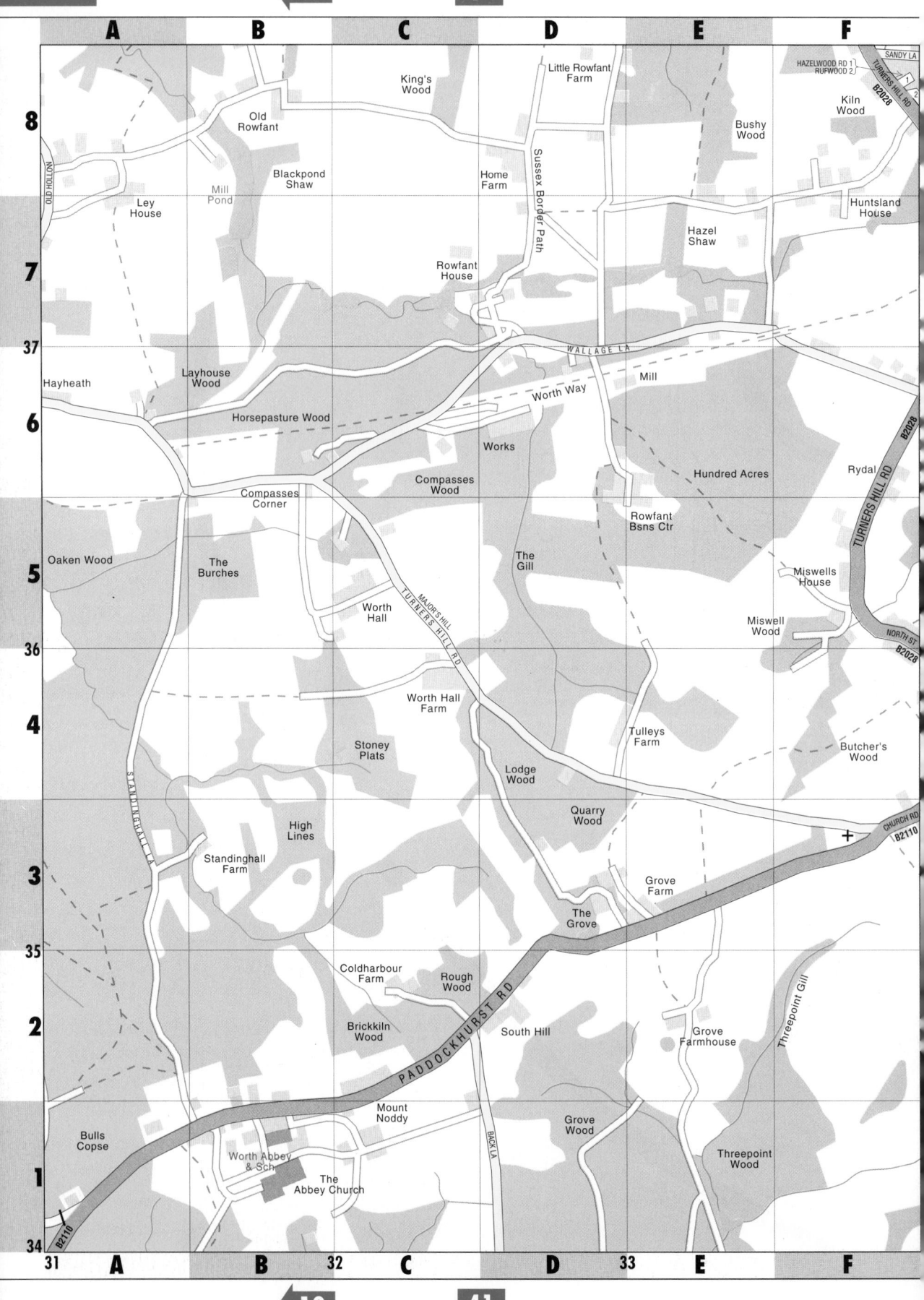

HAZELWOOD RD 1
RUFWOOD 2

SANDY LA

TURNERS HILL RD

B2028

Kiln Wood

Bushy Wood

Huntsland House

Little Rowfant Farm

King's Wood

Old Rowfant

Blackpond Shaw

Home Farm

Sussex Border Path

Hazel Shaw

Ley House

Mill Pond

OLD HOLTYE

Rowfant House

Hayheath

Layhouse Wood

Worth Way

Mill

Horsepasture Wood

Works

Compasses Corner

Compasses Wood

Hundred Acres

Rydal

TURNERS HILL RD

B2028

Oaken Wood

The Burches

The Gill

Rowfant Bsns Ctr

Miswells House

Miswell Wood

NORTH ST

B2028

Worth Hall

MAJOR'S HILL

TURNER'S HILL RD

Worth Hall Farm

Stoney Plats

Lodge Wood

Tulleys Farm

Butcher's Wood

Quarry Wood

High Lines

STANDINGHALL LA

Standinghall Farm

Grove Farm

The Grove

CHURCH RD

B2110

Coldharbour Farm

Rough Wood

PADDOCKHURST RD

Threepoint Gill

Brickkiln Wood

South Hill

Grove Farmhouse

Bulls Copse

Mount Noddy

BACK LA

Grove Wood

Threepoint Wood

Worth Abbey & Sch

The Abbey Church

B2110

A   B   C   D   E   F

8

SANDY LA
SUNNYHILL CL
HOPHURST DR
HOPHURST DR
HILLSIDE
THE COPPICE
HARWARREN
ASH CL
GRANSTON WAY
HARWARD
THE MARTINS
GARDNER LA
LONGS ACRE
BUCKLEY PL
UNDERWOOD WAY
SPINNEY
TILTWOOD DR
HALSLAND
Gulledge Wood
RUFWOOD
VICARAGE RD
BOWERS PL
BIRCH CL
HAZEL WAY
HAZEL CL
COB CL
Worth Way
French Wood
WYN LEY CL
SUNNY AVE
BEECH GDNS
BEECH HOLME
STATION RD
Schs
Brickyard
LA 2
Rushetts Wood
Front Wood
SCHOLARS CT
OLD STATION CL
3
KILN RD
WOODLANDS
Crawley Down

7

Worth Way
GRANGE RD
4
BRICKLANDS
SANDHILL LA
BURLEIGH LA
Sussex Border Path
Tilkhurst Farm
TURNERS HILL RD
SUNNYMEAD 1
RIDGEDALE 2
AUCHINLECK CT 3
ROYAL OAK HO 4
The Grange
Burleigh House Farm

37

Grange Farm
Sandhill
Rainbow Shaw

6

Little Nobs
Fen Place Mill
River Medway
Warren Wood
Peartree Shaw
Moat Shaw
Hurley Farm

5
Burleigh Arches Wood
Home Wood
Mill Wood
MILLWOOD
Ash Leigh Farm
Burleigh Oaks House
Alexander House
Furze Field
TURNER'S HILL RD
B2110

36
MEDWAY
HILL HOUSE CL
EAST ST
Furzewood Farm
Castle Shaw

4
NORTH ST
Turners Hill
Target Shaw
Tickeridge Farm
Kingscote Sta

PO
NOAH'S CT
NEW COTTS
MADEIRA LA
LION LA
Burleigh Farm
Tickeridge Shaw
Bluebell Rly

3
CHURCH RD
B2110
The Crown (PH)
WILLOW RIDGE
WITHYPITTS E
Holstein Wood
South Wood
Sch
Rashes Farm
Spring Wood
Rookery Wood
Stone Wood
WITH WITHYPITTS
Withypitts
Great Wildgoose Wood
Minepit Wood

35
Withy Pitts Farm
Coomberdean Wood
VOWELS LA
Forest Walk
Vowels Gill
Mill Place Wood

2
The Punch Bowl (PH)
Thornhill Cottages
SELSFIELD RD
Selsfield Common
Selsfield Place
Drive Shaw
Bushy Wood
Bramblehill
Selsfield Common
Moatlands
Home Farm

1
Ducknell's Wood
Pine Wood
Warren's Wood
Hastings Wood
Selsfield House
B2028
West Hoathly
Gravetye Manor
Lower Lake

34

34   A   B   35   C   D   36   E   F   34

21
9

F8
1 MIDDLE ROW
2 FOREST LODGE
3 SACKVILLE CT
4 GREAT HOUSE CT
5 PORTLAND HO
6 CORNWALL GDNS

7 NORMANDY CL
8 WILLOW MEAD
9 KINGS COPSE
10 REGAL DR
11 BECKETT WAY

A B C D E F

8
7
37
6
5
36
4
3
35
2
1
34

Great Wood
Coles Wood
CHAUCER AVE
SMOLLETTS
MELTON CRES
CHRISTIES
COPYHOLD RD
THE CLOSE
TENNYSON RISE
GARDEN WOOD RD
BROOKLANDS WAY
B2110
WEST HILL
WEST LA
Liby
PO
HIGH ST
B2110
FAIRFIELD RD

Hill Place Farm
Brook House Farm
Brook House
WEST HILL
HURST FARM RD
QUEEN'S RD
WEST ST
RD
LANGRIDGE
ON WAY
PAIN
DEXTER DR
THE DAKINS
THE JORDANS
ELMSTEAD
SHIP ST
JUDGE'S TERR
BELL HAMMER
PORLAND RD
HERMITAGE LA
KINGFISHER RISE
RICHARD
LOWER MEAD
SAW
YORK AVE
HERONTYE DR

High Grove
Crockshed Wood
IMBERHORNE LA
EAST GRINSTEAD
ASHDOWN VIEW
SOUTHLANDS
NIGHTINGALE CL
ACORN CL
MUSGRAVE AVE
RIDGEWAY
PINE WAY CL
CLAYS CL
WEST LEIGH
GARDEN
HOUSE LA
VICTORIA WAY
STUART WAY
CAVALIER WAY
HAMPTON RD
TUDOR CL
HERONTYE

37
HAZLEDEN CROSS
TURNER'S HILL RD
Coombe Hall Sch
COOMBE HILL RD
Bulrushes Farm
The Meads Cty Prim Sch
Sunnyside
PO
MILL WAY
THE MEADS
MILL COTTS
CORONATION RD
DUNNINGS RD
STEPHENSON DR
CHESTERTON DR
HARWOODS LA
MORTON CL
F7
1 CROMWELL PL
2 CLARENCE DR
3 HARWOODS CL
4 COLLINGWOOD CL

6
Coombe Hall Farm
Dunnings Mill L Complex
Tobias Sch of Art
MEDWAY DR
FOREST VIEW RD
STOCKWELL RD
FARADAY AVE
LISTER AVE
NEWTON RD
MEWS CT

Hazleden Farm
Imberley
Dunning's Wood
Eurythmy Sch
The Beechcroft Towse
Boyles Farm

5
The Plantation
Playing Field
SAINT HILL RD
Rockwood Park
High Wood
Playing Field
Rockingshill Wood
Rushett's Shaw

36
B2110
The Rough
Saint Hill Manor
Saint Hill Green
Jenkin's Wood

4
Ridge Hill Manor
Hen Robin Wood
Saint Hill Farm
WEST HOATHLY RD
Standen Farm
Standen (National Trust)
Busses Farm

Mary Wood
Cock Robin Wood
Jenhurst Wood

3
River Medway
Busses Wood

35
Sussex Border Path

2
Mill Place Farm
Stone Hill House
ADMIRAL'S BRIDGE LA
Weir Wood Resr
Bluebell Rly
Pit Shaw
Admiral's Bridge Wood

1
Birch Farm Nursery
Willet's Bridge
GRINSTEAD LA
Charlwood Farm
Alder Moors

34
Neylands Farm
P
Weir Wood Resr (Nature Reserve)
LEGSHEATH LA

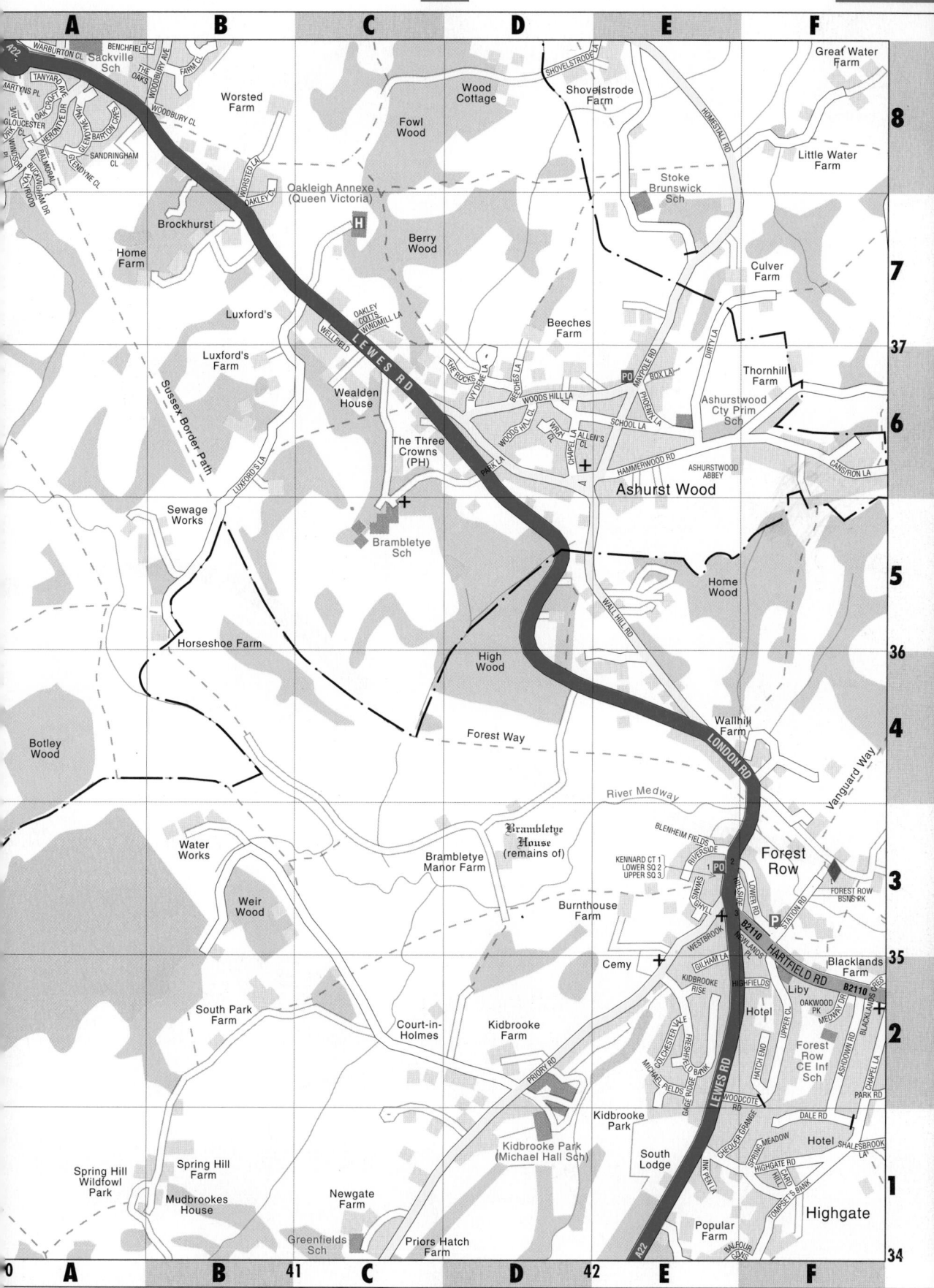
A B C D E F
8
7
37
6
5
36
4
3
35
2
1
34
40 41 42
Sackville Sch
Worsted Farm
Wood Cottage
Shovelstrode Farm
Great Water Farm
Fowl Wood
Little Water Farm
Oakleigh Annexe (Queen Victoria)
Stoke Brunswick Sch
Brockhurst
Berry Wood
Home Farm
Culver Farm
Luxford's
Beeches Farm
Luxford's Farm
Thornhill Farm
Wealden House
Ashurstwood Cty Prim Sch
The Three Crowns (PH)
Ashurst Wood
Ashurstwood Abbey
Sewage Works
Brambletye Sch
Home Wood
Sussex Border Path
Horseshoe Farm
High Wood
Wallhill Farm
Botley Wood
Forest Way
Vanguard Way
River Medway
Brambletye House (remains of)
Water Works
Brambletye Manor Farm
Forest Row
Forest Row Bsns Pk
Weir Wood
Burnthouse Farm
Cemy
Blacklands Farm
Liby
Hotel
South Park Farm
Court-in-Holmes
Kidbrooke Farm
Forest Row CE Inf Sch
Kidbrooke Park
Hotel
Kidbrooke Park (Michael Hall Sch)
South Lodge
Spring Hill Wildfowl Park
Spring Hill Farm
Mudbrookes House
Newgate Farm
Highgate
Popular Farm
Greenfields Sch
Priors Hatch Farm
LEWES RD
LONDON RD
HARTFIELD RD
B2110
A22
WALL HILL RD
HAMMERWOOD RD
SCHOOL LA
WOODS HILL LA
MAYPOLE RD
HOMESTALL RD
DIRTY LA
PRIORY RD
LUXFORD'S LA
KENNARD CT 1
LOWER SQ 2
UPPER SQ 3

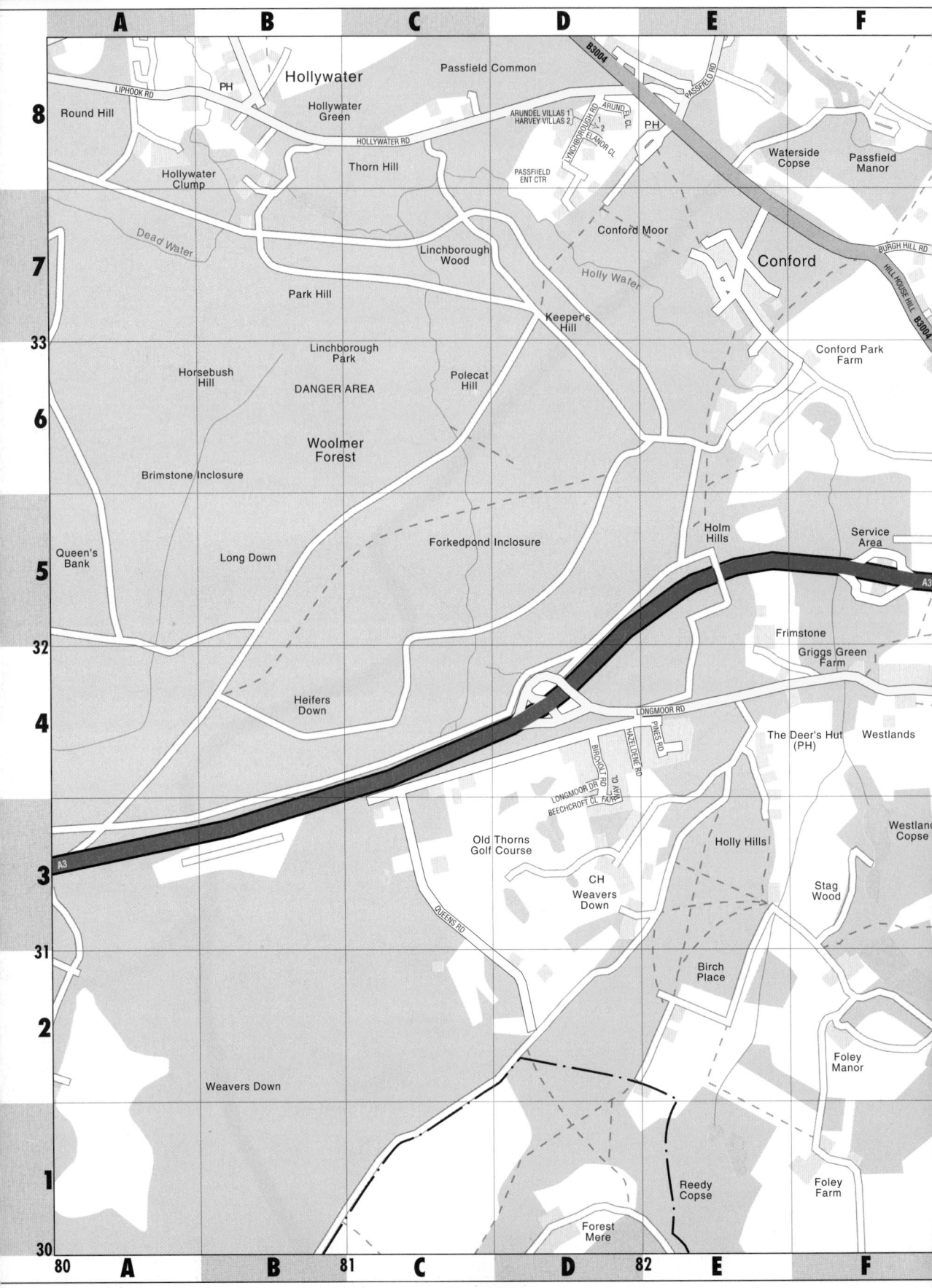
A
B
C
D
E
F
Hollywater
Passfield Common
PH
LIPHOOK RD
Round Hill
Hollywater Green
HOLLYWATER RD
ARUNDEL VILLAS 1
HARVEY VILLAS 2
LYNCHBOROUGH RD
ARUNDEL CL
ELANOR CL
PASSFIELD RD
B3004
PASSFIELD ENT CTR
Thorn Hill
Hollywater Clump
Waterside Copse
Passfield Manor
Dead Water
Linchborough Wood
Conford Moor
Conford
Holly Water
BURGH HILL RD
HILL HOUSE HILL
Park Hill
Keeper's Hill
Linchborough Park
Horsebush Hill
DANGER AREA
Polecat Hill
Conford Park Farm
Woolmer Forest
Brimstone Inclosure
Holm Hills
Service Area
Queen's Bank
Long Down
Forkedpond Inclosure
A3
Frimstone
Griggs Green Farm
Heifers Down
LONGMOOR RD
PINES RD
HAZELDENE RD
BIRCHOLT RD
The Deer's Hut (PH)
Westlands
LONGMOOR DR
BEECHCROFT CL
FAIRWAY CL
Old Thorns Golf Course
Holly Hills
Westland Copse
CH
Weavers Down
Stag Wood
QUEENS RD
Birch Place
Foley Manor
Weavers Down
Reedy Copse
Foley Farm
Forest Mere
8
7
33
6
5
32
4
3
31
2
1
30
80
81
82

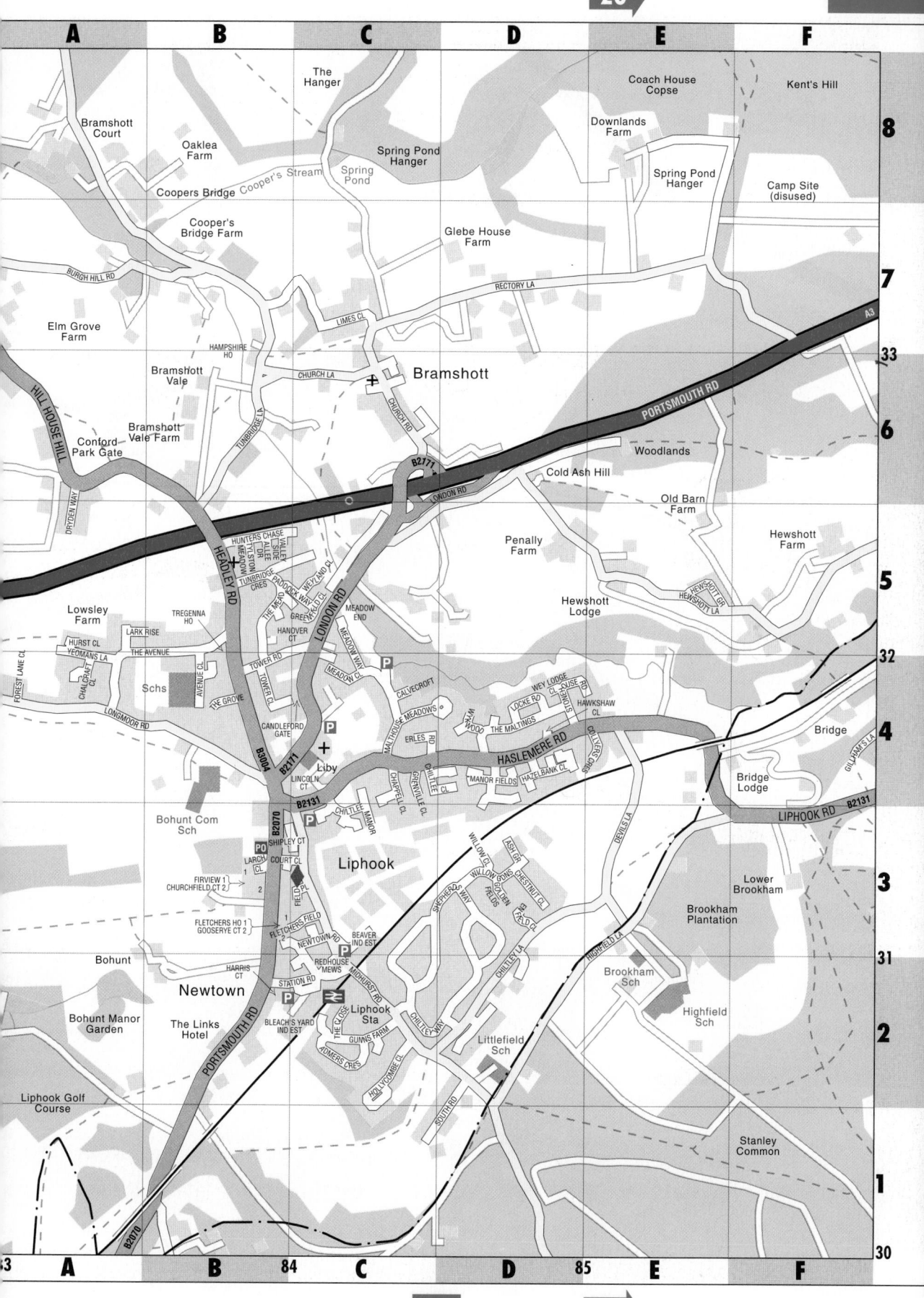

A B C D E F

The Hanger

Coach House Copse

Kent's Hill

Bramshott Court

Oaklea Farm

Spring Pond Hanger

Downlands Farm

Spring Pond Hanger

Camp Site (disused)

Coopers Bridge
Cooper's Stream

Spring Pond

8

Cooper's Bridge Farm

Glebe House Farm

BURGH HILL RD

RECTORY LA

7

Elm Grove Farm

LIMES CL

Bramshott

33

PORTSMOUTH RD

A3

HAMPSHIRE HO

Bramshott Vale

CHURCH LA

CHURCH RD

Woodlands

6

Conford Park Gate

Bramshott Vale Farm

TUNBRIDGE LA

B2171

LONDON RD

Cold Ash Hill

Old Barn Farm

Hewshott Farm

HILL HOUSE HILL

DRYDEN WAY

HUNTERS CHASE
VALLEY SIDE
ALLEE CTR
HYLSTON
TUNBRIDGE CRES
PADDOCK WAY
WEYLAND PL
MEADOW

Penally Farm

HEWSHOTT LA

5

Lowsley Farm

TREGENNA HO
LARK RISE

HEADLEY RD

GREEN LA DO
HANOVER CT

MEADOW END

MEADOW WAY

Hewshott Lodge

HEWSHOTT GR

HURST CL
YEOMANS LA
CHALCRAFT CL
THE AVENUE

THE MEAD
TOWER RD
TOWER CL

MEADOW CL

CALVECROFT

WEY LODGE

LOCKE RD

HAWKSHAW CL

32

FOREST LANE CL

AVENUE CL

THE GROVE

MALTHOUSE MEADOWS

WYKE WOOD

THE MALTINGS

Bridge

Schs

LONGMOOR RD

CANDLEFORD GATE

B3004

B2171

Liby
LINCOLN CT

ERLES RD

CHITTLE CL

HASLEMERE RD

GILLYERD CRES

Bridge Lodge

4

GRENVILLE CL

CHAPPELL CL

MANOR FIELDS

HAZELBANK CL

DEVILS LA

GILLHAM'S LA

LIPHOOK RD

B2131

Bohunt Com Sch

B2070

B2131

CHILTLEE MANOR

Lower Brookham

PO

LARCH CL

SHIPLEY CT

COURT CL

Liphook

WILLOW CL
GUNS
ASH GR
CHESTNUT CL

Brookham Plantation

3

FIRVIEW 1
CHURCHFIELD CT 2

FIELD PL

WILLOW
GDNS

CHILTLEY LA

Brookham Sch

FLETCHERS HO 1
GOOSERYE CT 2

FLETCHERS FIELD

SHEPHERDS WAY

HIGHFIELD LA

31

Bohunt

HARRIS CT

NEWTOWN RD
REDHOUSE MEWS

BEAVER IND EST

MIDHURST RD

Highfield Sch

Newtown

STATION RD

CHILTLEY WAY

PORTSMOUTH RD

P

BLEACH'S YARD IND EST

THE CLOSE

Liphook Sta

GUNNS FARM

Littlefield Sch

2

Bohunt Manor Garden

The Links Hotel

ADMERS CRES

HOLLYCOMBE CL

SOLLARD

Liphook Golf Course

B2070

Stanley Common

1

30

25

A
B
C
D
E
F
8
7
33
6
5
32
4
3
31
2
1
30
86
87
88
GORSE COTTS
Bramshott Chase
Polecat
Playing Field
PORTSMOUTH RD
The Spaniard Inn (Hotel)
Bramshott Common
A3
A287
HINDHEAD RD
NUTCOMBE LA
Woolmer Hill Sch
Frensham Hall Farm
Mast
Holy Cross
Shottermill Cty Jun Sch
Woolmer Hill
Critchmere
SANDY LA
HAMMER LA
WOOLMER HILL RD
HATCHETTS DR
CRITCHMERE HILL
BUFFBEARDS LA
CHERRY TREE AVE
LION LA
AZALEA DR
THE AVENUE
WOODLANDS LA
UNDERWOOD RD
CROFTON
WEYSPRINGS
Sch
STILE GDNS
VICARAGE LA
PRIORS WOOD
1 GLOVERS FIELD
2 ST STEPHEN'S CL
LOWER HANGER
OAK COTTS
DOLPHIN CL
ROEDEER COPSE
CRITCHMERE VALE
MALLARD CL
FIR TREE AVE
SUNVALE CL
SUNVALE AVE
OAK TREE LA
PITFOLD AVE
TROUT RD
MANOR LEA
MANOR CRES
HERON
FOX RD
ELIOT DR
LUCAS FIELD
CHURCH RD
JUNCTION PL
LION GN
B2131
MEADWAY
TIMBERMILL CT
THE MEADS
LIPHOOK RD
Cemy
HAMMER VALE
River Wey
BORDER END
BORDER RD
CHERRIMANS ORCH
PO
Shottermill
HAMMER LA
HEWSHOTT LA
Sewage Works
SHOTTERMILL RD
THE MALLSTREAM
STURT RD
KING'S RD
SICKLE RD
Hammer Moor
MOOR RD
PUTTOCK CL
COPSE RD
HAMMERWOOD COPSE
Springhead
HEATH RD
PEGASUS CL
LINCHMERE RD
NEW RD
SCHOOL RD
DALE VIEW
Sch
STURT AVE
THE ORCHARD
Hammer Bottom
Hammer
MOOR FIELD
CAMELSDALE RD
Gillham's Moor
Hammer Coppice
Cemy
PENNINGTON DR
SPRINGFARM RD
HILLSIDE RD
GILLHAM'S LA
Hammer Hill
HAMMER HILL
Camelsdale
MARLEY COMBE RD
Hill Farm
Gillham's Farm
THE OLD QUARRY
LIPHOOK RD
Ridge Plantations
Marley Combe
Brinksway
MARLEY LA
B2131
Linchmere Common
LINCHMERE RD
Marley Common
The Ridge
DANLEY LA
Sussex Border Path
Marley House
Dale Farm
Linchmere
Church Farm
Cognor Wood
Poison Copse
Ash Copse
Pond Moor
Linchmere Marsh
Golden Valley
Hazel Piece
Hilly Field Copse
Treetop Farm

25
48

28

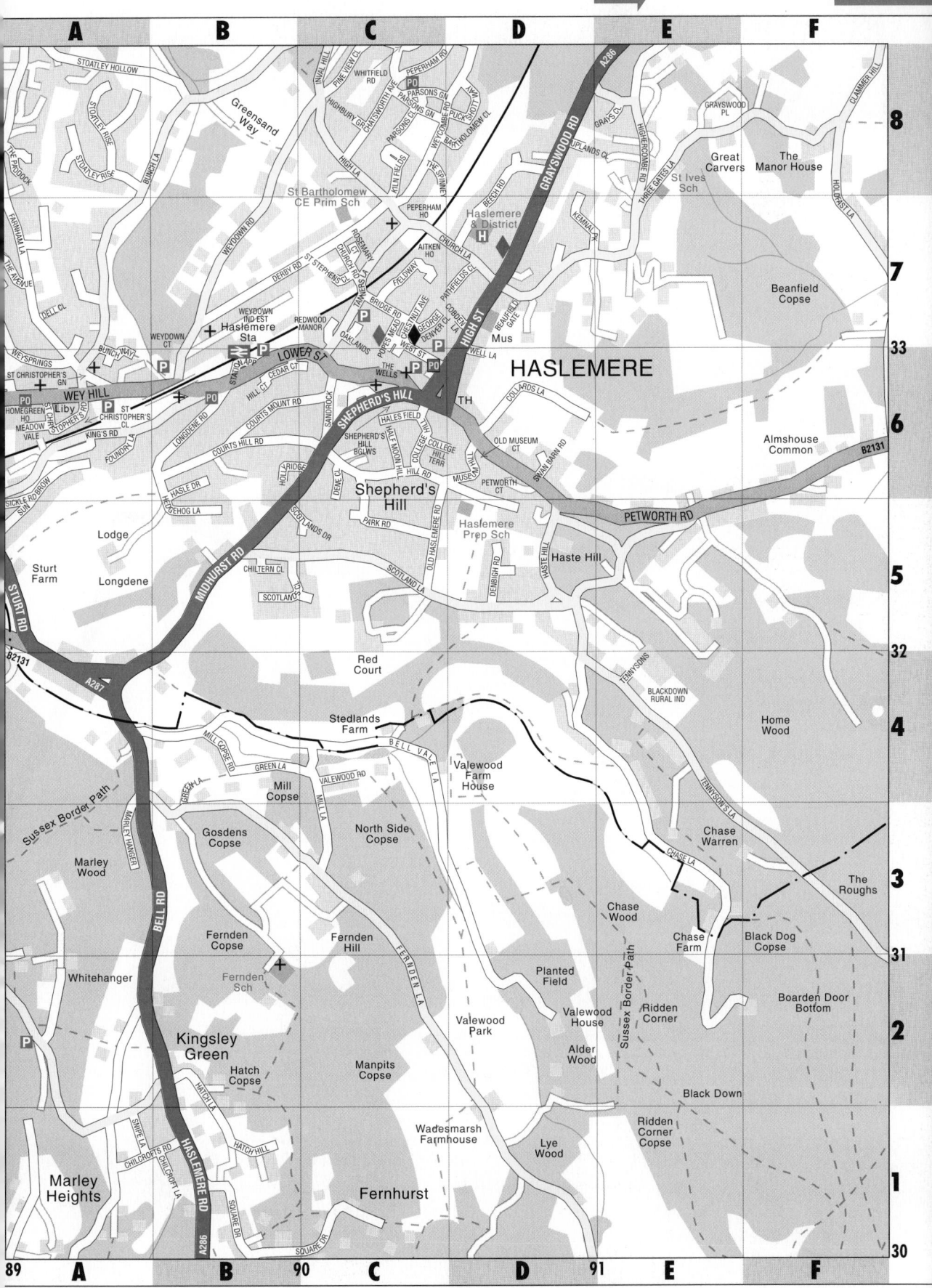

HASLEMERE
Shepherd's Hill
Haste Hill
Greensand Way
St Bartholomew CE Prim Sch
Haslemere & District
Haslemere Sta
Mus
TH
Liby
Great Carvers
The Manor House
St Ives Sch
Beanfield Copse
Almshouse Common
Haslemere Prep Sch
Lodge
Sturt Farm
Longdene
Red Court
Stedlands Farm
Valewood Farm House
Mill Copse
North Side Copse
Gosdens Copse
Marley Wood
Sussex Border Path
Home Wood
Chase Warren
The Roughs
Chase Wood
Chase Farm
Black Dog Copse
Fernden Copse
Fernden Hill
Fernden Sch
Whitehanger
Planted Field
Valewood House
Ridden Corner
Boarden Door Bottom
Valewood Park
Alder Wood
Kingsley Green
Hatch Copse
Manpits Copse
Black Down
Wadesmarsh Farmhouse
Lye Wood
Ridden Corner Copse
Marley Heights
Fernhurst
BLACKDOWN RURAL IND
WEY HILL
LOWER ST
SHEPHERD'S HILL
HIGH ST
GRAYSWOOD RD
MIDHURST RD
STURT RD
BELL RD
HASLEMERE RD
PETWORTH RD
A286
A287
B2131

49
28

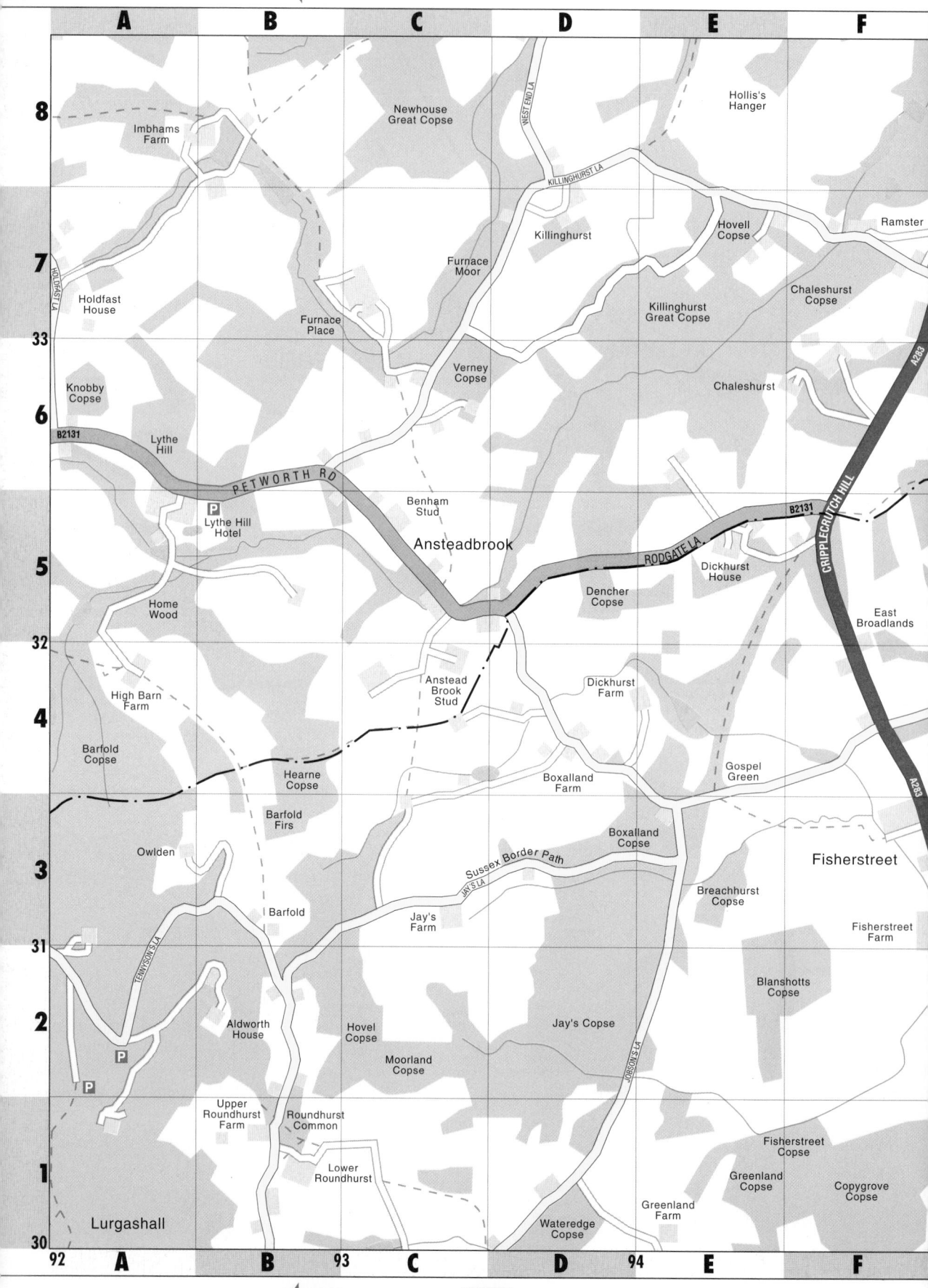

A B C D E F

8 Imbhams Farm · Newhouse Great Copse · WEST END LA · Hollis's Hanger

Holdfast House · KILLINGHURST LA · Hovell Copse · Ramster

7 Holdfast House · Furnace Moor · Killinghurst · Killinghurst Great Copse · Chaleshurst Copse

33 · Furnace Place

Knobby Copse · Verney Copse · Chaleshurst

6 B2131 · Lythe Hill · PETWORTH RD · Benham Stud · B2131

Lythe Hill Hotel · Ansteadbrook · RODGATE LA · Dickhurst House · CRIPPLECRUTCH HILL · A283

5 Home Wood · Dencher Copse · East Broadlands

32 · Anstead Brook Stud · Dickhurst Farm

High Barn Farm · Gospel Green

4 Barfold Copse · Hearne Copse · Boxalland Farm

Barfold Firs · Boxalland Copse · Fisherstreet

Owlden · Sussex Border Path · Breachhurst Copse · Fisherstreet Farm

3 JAY'S LA · Barfold · Jay's Farm · Blanshotts Copse

31 TENNYSON'S LA · Aldworth House · Hovel Copse · Jay's Copse

2 · Moorland Copse · JOBSON'S LA

Upper Roundhurst Farm · Roundhurst Common · Fisherstreet Copse

Greenland Copse · Copygrove Copse

1 Lower Roundhurst · Greenland Farm

Lurgashall · Wateredge Copse

30
92 A B 93 C D 94 E F

8

7

33

6

5

32

4

31

2

1

30

A   **B**   **C**   **D**   **E**   **F**

Windmill Copse

Hungry Corner

Rovehurst Wood

Great Copse

Sparkes Copse

Tugley Farm

Fisherlane Hanger

Gostrode Farm

Griggs Bottom

Fisher Lane Nursery

Little Tugley

FISHER LA

Sussex Border Path

Surrey Copse

Robins Farm

Redlands Farm

GODSTRODE LA

Ramsnest Common

White's Hill

Works

Furze Field

CH

Surrey Belt

Surrey Rough

Big Copse

Pollane Farm

Shillinglee Park Golf Course

Downlands

Downlands Wood

Walk Copse

Shillinglee Park

Upper North Pond

Parkgate

Lower North Pond

Shillinglee Home Farm

Manorhill Copse

Stilland Farm

Gaston's Farm

Newhouse Farm

Turnour's Wood

Deer Tower

New Copse

Nine Acre Rew

Beanfield Copse

Little Hayman's Farm

Eastland Farm

China Bridge

Twenty Four Acres

Haymans Farm

The Lake

Mill Copse

Frith Lodge

The Plantation

Park Mill Farm

Frith Wood

Frith Hill

Dale's Farm Hanger

Dale's Farm

29

A
B
C
D
E
F
8
7
33
6
5
32
4
3
31
2
1
30
98
99
00
Oaken Wood
Canterbury Copse
Ireland
Hurlands Copse
Old Lands
Burntwood Kennels
Peartree Hanger
Oak Wood
PLAISTOW RD
The Hatchetts
Tugley Wood
Inside Copse
Tidy's Copse
Durfold Hall
Durfold Hatch Cottage
Birch Copse
FISHER LA
Dungate Farm
Oakhurst Farm
Upper Ifold Wood
Sussex Border Path
Fisherlane Wood
Durfold Wood
Weald Barkfold Copse
DURFOLD WOOD
Shortland Copse
Downlands Wood
DUNSFOLD RD
East End Farm
Barkfold Hanger
Ashpark Wood
Weald Barkfold
Short's Farm
Works
Oakhurst
Highbridge House
Lyon's Farm
COUNCIL COTTS
Kingspark Wood
Plaistow Cty Inf Sch
PO
WELL BALL
OAKFIELD
THE STREET
BACK LA
LOXWOOD RD
Ifold Copse
Plaistow
Beggars Copse
BUSHFIELD
Birchfold Copse
RICKMAN'S LA
Sparrwood Hangar
Rumbold Wood
Rumbolds Farm
Chilsfold Farm

29
52

32

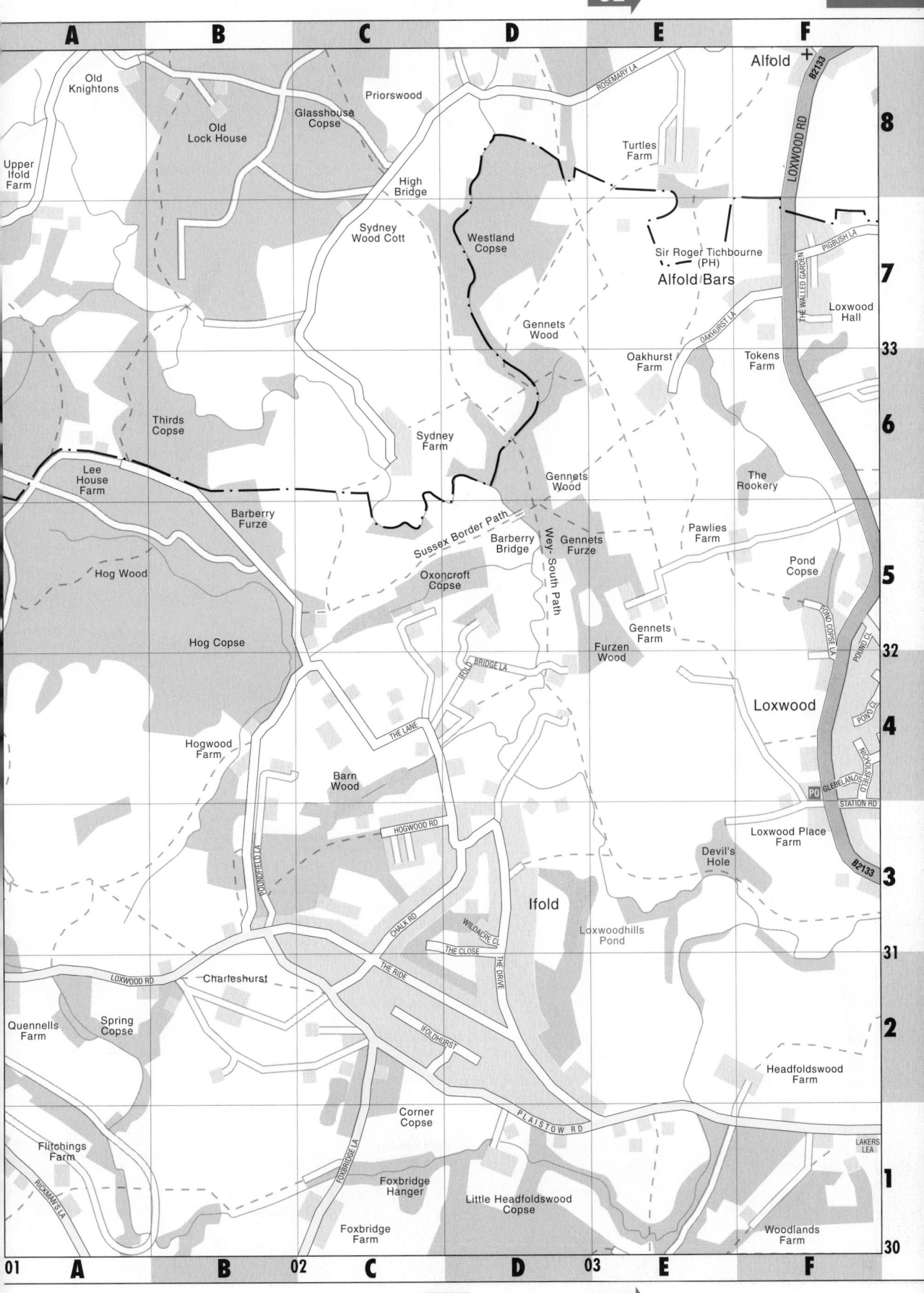

Old Knightons
Upper Ifold Farm
Old Lock House
Glasshouse Copse
Priorswood
High Bridge
Sydney Wood Cott
Westland Copse
Rosemary La
Alfold
B2133
Loxwood Rd
Turtles Farm
Sir Roger Tichbourne (PH)
Alfold Bars
Pigbush La
The Walled Garden
Loxwood Hall
Oakhurst La
Gennets Wood
Oakhurst Farm
Tokens Farm
Thirds Copse
Sydney Farm
Lee House Farm
Gennets Wood
The Rookery
Barberry Furze
Sussex Border Path
Barberry Bridge
Gennets Furze
Pawlies Farm
Wey-South Path
Hog Wood
Oxoncroft Copse
Pond Copse
Pond Copse La
Gennets Farm
Hog Copse
Furzen Wood
Ifold Bridge La
Pound Cl
Loxwood
Pond Cl
The Lane
Hogwood Farm
Barn Wood
Nicholsfield
PO
Glebelands
Station Rd
Hogwood Rd
Loxwood Place Farm
Devil's Hole
B2133
Poundfield La
Chalk Rd
Ifold
Wildacre Cl
Loxwoodhills Pond
The Close
The Ride
The Drive
Loxwood Rd
Charleshurst
Quennells Farm
Spring Copse
Ifoldhurst
Headfoldswood Farm
Corner Copse
Plaistow Rd
Lakers Lea
Flitchings Farm
Foxbridge La
Foxbridge Hanger
Little Headfoldswood Copse
Rickman's La
Foxbridge Farm
Woodlands Farm
A
B
C
D
E
F
8
7
33
6
5
32
4
3
31
2
1
30
01
02
03

53

32

31
11
A
B
C
D
E
F
8
7
33
6
5
32
4
3
31
2
1
30
04
05
06
Lion's Copse
Hook St
Wanbrook Barn
Wanbrook Copse
Basset's Barn
Monckton Hook
Rikkyo Sch in England
The Knob
The Deacons
Hemstocks
Hornshill Wood
Hornshill Farm
A281 GUILDFORD RD
Basset's Copse
Songhurst Farm
Clearmount
PIGBUSH LA
Sussex Border Path
Hope Rough
Primrose Copse
Greenhurst
Old Songhurst Farm
Tisman's
HORNSHILL LA
Mallards Farm
Barnsfold
CROSSWAYS COTTS
Barnsfold Farm House
Tisman's Common
BARNSFOLD LA
Merry Hills
B2133
MERRYHILLS LA
Songhurst New Farm
Woodlands Furze
The Mucky Duck (PH)
Halffurze Field
Great Scrubbs
Hurst Wood
Nursery
Beggars Copse
Pephurst Wood
OAK GR
SPY LA
Spy Farm
Bullhams Wood
Nursery
BADGERS WAY
Loxwood Cty Prim Sch
Pephurst Farm
Corner Copse
LOXWOOD RD
Hale
BURLEY CL
TWO WAYS
STATION RD
FARM CL
Jenkin's Wood
Crabtree Cottage
Crabtree Corner
Round Copse
Baldwin's Knob
The Onslow Arms (PH)
River Arun
Wey - South Path
Brewhurst Mill
BREWHURST LA
Brewhurst Farm
Drungewickhill Farm
BREWHURST LA
COUNCIL COTTS
Newhouse Farm
Birch Copse
Smythies Brow
Drungewick Manor
DRUNGEWICK LA
Sewage Works
Hooklane Copse
River Arun
Flitchfold Farm
Malhamashfold Copse
SKIFF LA
Lakers Lodge
B2133
31
54

12
34

	A	B	C	D	E	F

8

Godley's Copse

Greathouse Farm

Lynwick Hanger

Well Grove

Tip Pond

CHURCH ST

ELSIE RD

KILNFIELD RD

PONDFIELD RD

FOXHOLES

JUBILEE RD

WOODFIELD RD

CHURCH ST

B2128

MARTLET CNR

STATION RD

THE SIDINGS

GASKYNS CL

THURNE WAY

BRIDGE RD

Gravatt's Farm

7

Weyhurst Copse

Rudgwick

Penthorpe Sch

Bowcroft La

Swaynes Farm

Smithers Farm

SMITHERS COTTS

Weyhurst Farm

Bucks Green Sch

PH

THE MARTLETS

PRINCESS MARGARET RD

Rudgwick Cty Prim Sch

A281

33

Woodfalls Manor

PH

Watts Corner

ORCHARD HILL

B2128

QUEEN ELIZABETH RD

PATHFIELD

TATE'S WAY

PATHFIELD RD

PRINCESS ANNE RD

CAK COPSE

Smithers Rough

THE RIDDENS

6

Bucks Green

LOXWOOD RD

Wanford Bridges

River Arun

Downs Link

COOKS HILL

HORSHILL LA

Exfold Farm

MILL COTTS

5

Rolls Farm

ROUNDABOUT COTTS

Warhams

Upper Barn

Pensfold Farm

Chephurst Farm

NALDRETTS LA

Naldretts Farm

PENSFOLD LA

Morelands

Pensfold La

32

Sewage Works

4

Chephurst Copse

Pensfold Furzefield

Rudgwick Grange

Howick Farm

Colin's Cross

Smithwood Copse

Howick Copse

HAVEN RD

3

Tittlesfold Copse

Park Farm

Tittlesfold Farm

31

Mill House

Garlands

Havenhurst Farm

2

Gibbons Mill Farm

River Arun

Gibbons Mill

The Haven

Lower Lodge Farm

PH

Morgan's Green

ORCHURST RD

Marshall's Farm

MARLES LA

Cousins Farm

1

Smerrick's Copse

Heathers Copse

Heathers Farm

30

A   B   C   D   E   F

8

Hyes

Davies
Wood

Roman
Woods

Farthing
Field

Lodge
Farm

Waterland
Farm

Rowhook Hill
House

ROWHOOK HILL
ROWHOOK RD

Townhouse
Copse

A29

7

A281

GUILDFORD RD

Furnacehouse
Farm

A281

A29

River Arun

33

Dedisham

Dedisham
Sch

Townhouse
Farm House

6

Dedisham
Farm

North River

NOWHURST LA

Violets
Farm

Whales
Copse

5

Farm Copse

Hill
House

CLAPGATE LA

Sewage
Works

Rowfold
Farm

Theale
Copse

32

Huntingrove
Farm

STANE ST

Park
STREET

Slinfold
CE (Contr)
Sch

THE STREET

Newbuildings

The
Birches

Theale

4

Kilsyth

Park
House

PARK ST

TANNERY CL

PH

PO

Merle

LYONS RD

3

Slinfold Park
(Golf & Country Park)

CH

SPRING LA

Amber
Field

WEST WAY

COBBLERS

GREENFIELD RD

LYONS CL

MITCHELL GDNS

STREET

THE GRATTONS

LLOYD FIELD RD

PIPERS END

Slinfold

31

Golf
Course

Slinfold
Lodge

MAYDWELL AVE

PARK RD

Downs Link

CLOVER
FIELD

Gaskyns

Meadowhurst

2

Woodstock

Oldhouse
Copse

Works

Hall Land
Rough

HAYES LA

1

Whitebreads

Hayes Grange

A29

Holmbush Manor
Farm

30

10   A   B   11   C   D   12   E   F

14
36

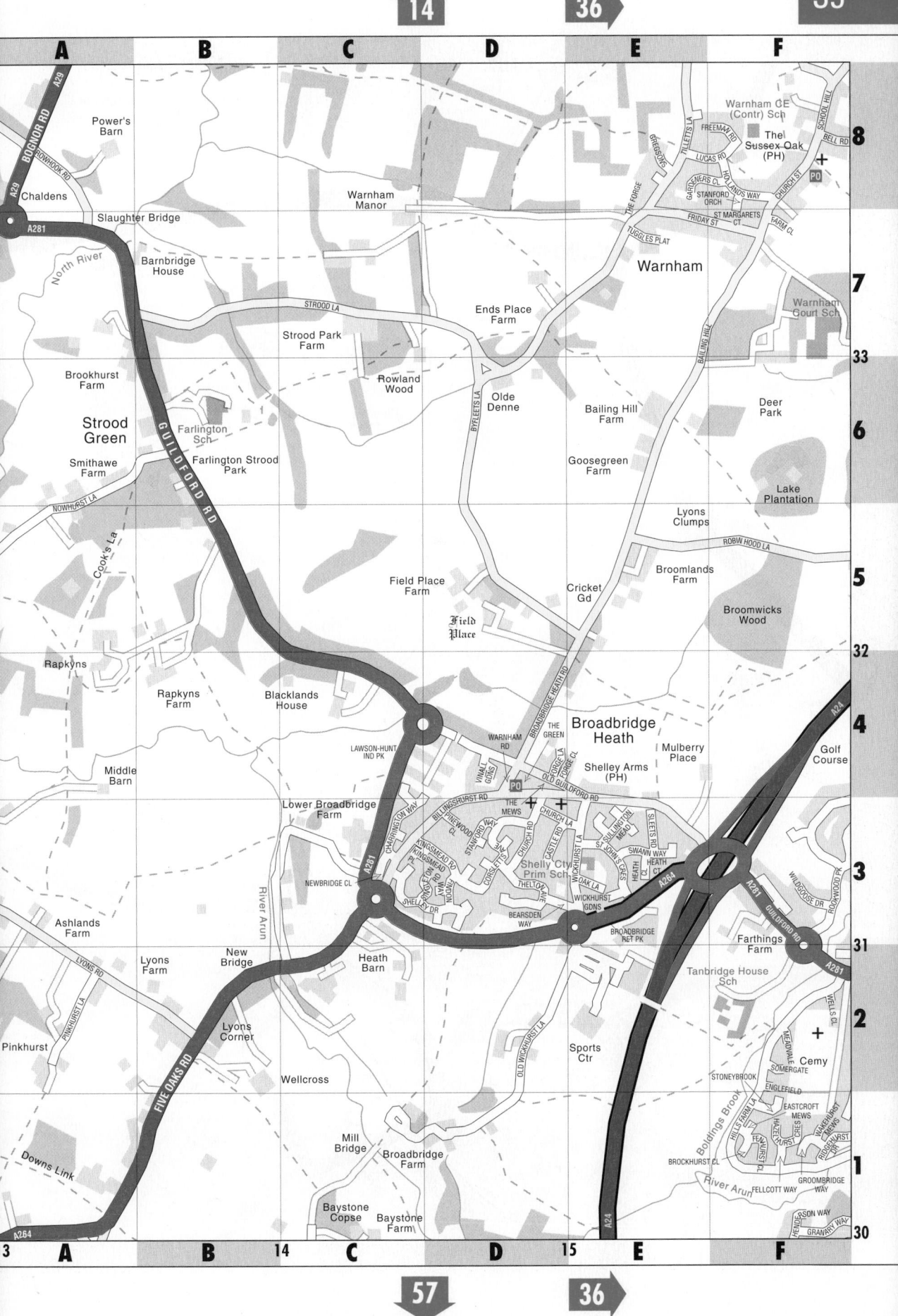
A
B
C
D
E
F
8
7
33
6
5
32
4
3
31
2
1
30
13
14
15
Power's Barn
BOGNOR RD
A29
ROWHOOK RD
Chaldens
Slaughter Bridge
A281
North River
Barnbridge House
Warnham Manor
Warnham CE (Contr) Sch
The Sussex Oak (PH)
PO
Warnham
Ends Place Farm
STROOD LA
Strood Park Farm
Rowland Wood
Olde Denne
BYFLEETS LA
Brookhurst Farm
Strood Green
Farlington Sch
Farlington Strood Park
GUILDFORD RD
Smithawe Farm
NOWHURST LA
Cook's La
Bailing Hill Farm
Goosegreen Farm
Deer Park
Lake Plantation
Warnham Court Sch
BAILING HILL
Lyons Clumps
ROBIN HOOD LA
Broomlands Farm
Broomwicks Wood
Cricket Gd
Field Place Farm
Field Place
Rapkyns
Rapkyns Farm
Blacklands House
BROADBRIDGE HEATH RD
Broadbridge Heath
Mulberry Place
Golf Course
A24
Shelley Arms (PH)
LAWSON-HUNT IND PK
WARNHAM RD
THE GREEN
Middle Barn
Lower Broadbridge Farm
Shelly Cty Prim Sch
NEWBRIDGE CL
A264
BROADBRIDGE RET PK
Ashlands Farm
LYONS RD
Lyons Farm
New Bridge
River Arun
Heath Barn
Farthings Farm
Tanbridge House Sch
PINKHURST LA
Pinkhurst
Lyons Corner
FIVE OAKS RD
Wellcross
OLD WICKHURST LA
Sports Ctr
Cemy
Downs Link
Mill Bridge
Broadbridge Farm
Baystone Copse
Baystone Farm
Boldings Brook
River Arun
BROCKHURST CL
FELLCOTT WAY
GROOMBRIDGE WAY
HENDERSON WAY
GRANARY WAY

57
36

35
15

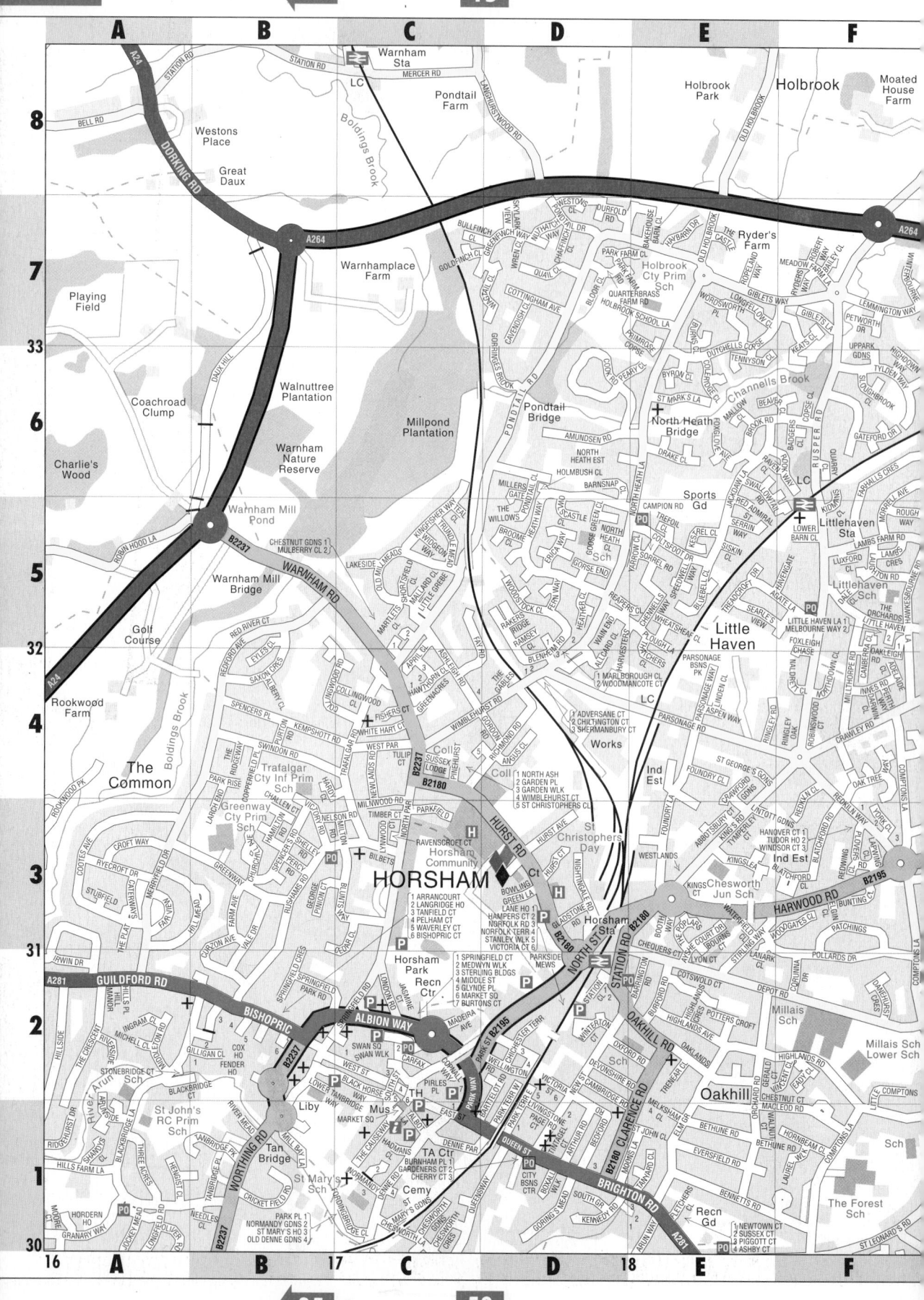
A
B
C
D
E
F
8
7
33
6
5
32
4
3
31
2
1
30
16
17
18
Warnham Sta
LC
STATION RD
MERCER RD
Pondtail Farm
Holbrook Park
Holbrook
Moated House Farm
BELL RD
Westons Place
Great Daux
Boldings Brook
DORKING RD
A24
A264
Ryder's Farm
Warnhamplace Farm
Playing Field
Holbrook Cty Prim Sch
Walnuttree Plantation
Coachroad Clump
Millpond Plantation
Pondtail Bridge
North Heath Bridge
Channells Brook
Charlie's Wood
Warnham Nature Reserve
Sports Gd
Warnham Mill Pond
Littlehaven Sta
Warnham Mill Bridge
WARNHAM RD
B2237
Littlehaven Sch
Golf Course
Little Haven
Rookwood Farm
Works
The Common
Trafalgar Cty Inf Prim Sch
Greenway Cty Prim Sch
Coll
Ind Est
St Christophers Day
HORSHAM
Horsham Community
HURST RD
B2180
B2231
Chesworth Jun Sch
HARWOOD RD
B2195
Horsham Sta
NORTH ST
STATION RD
GUILDFORD RD
A281
BISHOPRIC
ALBION WAY
Horsham Park
Recn Ctr
Millais Sch
Millais Sch Lower Sch
OAKHILL RD
Oakhill
St John's RC Prim Sch
Liby
TH
Mus
Tan Bridge
TA Ctr
CLARENCE RD
BRIGHTON RD
QUEEN ST
WORTHING RD
St Mary's Sch
Cemy
Recn Gd
The Forest Sch
Sch
River Arun

35
58

A B C D E F

8

Castle Copse
Benson's Farm
Cow Barn
Owlscastle Farm
Bush La
Channells Brook
The Cherry Tree (PH)
WIMLAND RD
BROOK LA
BROOK LA
Dobsongill Pond
Rookfield Pond
Beechwood
Middle Hill
TOWER RD
A264
Dobson Gill

7

LC
CRAWLEY RD
CLOVERS WAY
OLD CRAWLEY RD
Newhouse Farm
Roffey Place (Christian Training Ctr)
Roffey Park
Faygate Forest

33

1 BUTTERMERE CL
2 GRASMERE GDNS
Moorhead Farm
CHERRY TREE WLK
The Birches
B2195
CRAWLEY RD
NEW MOORHEAD DR
Roffey Park

6

High Wood
BEEDINGWOOD DR
Beedingwood
Roffey Park Coll

LEMMINGTON WAY
WEYBURN CL
SIMMS PL
BARTHOLOMEW WAY
BIGNOR CL
LANYON MEWS
LANYON CL
EARLES MEADOW
AMBERLEY RD
OAKS
GLENDALE CL
DERWENT CL
LANSDOWN
WHITEFORD RD
LAMBS FARM RD
COMPTON RD
COTTAGE
KINGSMEAD
THE LARCHES
STONYCROFT
BEECH RD
THE OAKS
Roffey Hurst
FOREST RD
Woodside Farm
Stonelodge Plain

5

ROWLANDS
GREENFIELDS WAY
Sch
GREENFIELDS
Sch
LAMBS FARM
GREENFIELDS RD
BROADWOOD
LOCKWOOD
MEADOW
SHEPHERDS
HOLMING
ALLINGHAM
MOORHEAD RD
TURFIELD RD
ROWAN WAY
HOLLY CL
Highbirch Hill
Knights Strength
THE COURTYARD

32

BRIDGES CT
1 WOODBRIDGE CT
2 MANOR CT
LEITH VIEW RD
LIME AVE
Roffey
Sch
KAITHEWOOD HO
NORTH HOLMES CL
CHARMANS CL
ROFFEY CNR
NORFOLK CT
MEDWAY
CEMY
GILLETT HO
Owlbeech Wood
Playing Fields
Whitevane Hill
Race Hill

4

HOWARD RD
CHESTERTON CT
MILLAIS
WINDMILL CL
CRAWLEY RD
LANCING CT
BUTLERS CL
WELLWOOD CL
MURRAY CL
ACORNS
WOODLAND WAY
SOUTH HOLMES CL
FALK MEWS
OWLBEECH WAY
OWLBEECH PL
WOODSIDE
RED DEER CT
FALLOW DEER CT
ROE DEER CT
Sch
Whitevane Pond

3

HAMPTONS BROW
THE GLADE
BELLOC CT
SHELLEY CT
HARWOOD RD
1 OAKHURST MEWS
2 FOREST OAKS
Leechpool & Owlbeech Wood Nature Reserve
Leechpool Wood
Townhouse Copse
St Leonard's Park
Home Farm
Dogkennel Pond
Greenbroom Hill

31

ADWICK CT
ACKTMORN CL
HAMPER'S LA
MILLAIS
HAMPER'S LA
Sandpit Clump
Stew Pond
Dry Pond
Turf Plain
Lily Beds

2

Heron Way Cty Prim Sch
BRAMBLING RD
HAMBLIN
HURST LA
HERON WAY
BENS ACRE
GREB CRES
The Glen
Sunoak Plantation
Sheepwash Wood
Sheepwash Gill
Scragged Oak
Inholme Gill
Scragged Oak Hill
Greenslade Wood
Mick's Cross

1

30

9 A B 20 C D 21 E F

37
17

A
B
C
D
E
F
8
7
33
6
5
32
4
3
31
2
1
30
22
23
24
Holmbush
Hooks Copse
Foxhole Pond
Buchan Hill Forest
Golf Course
Sch
Cottesmore Golf Club
House Pond
Shepherdsfield Farm
TOWER RD
Holmbush Forest
Dobson Gill
Beacon Hill
Black Hill Stud
Water Tower
Sand Plat
FOREST RD
Black Hill
The Dragon Inn (PH)
Road Farm
Rookfield Farm
Colgate Cty Prim Sch
Colgate
Black Hill Wood
Combe Wood
Shelley Cottages
BLACKHOUSE RD
Colgate Lodge
Blackhouse Farm
Colegate Hill
Combe Bottom Wood
Forest Heights Farm
Pearl Cottage
Shelley Farm
SPRINGFIELD LA
New Barn Farm
Combe Bottom
Blindman's Wood
Shelley Middle Gill
St Leonard's Forest
Springfield Farm
Pyefall Gill
Spring Farm
GROUSE RD
Newstead Ghyll
WOODLAND LA
The Larches
Old Springfield Stud
Barnsnap
Stone Edge Nursery
Newstead Gill
Elenge Plat Farm
Barnsnap Wood
Newstead Farm
Old Copse
Lower Grouse Farm
Grouselands
Frenchbridge Gill
Forest Lodge
Hyde Gill
Grouselands Farm
Mount Noddy
The Hyde
Old Copse

37
60

A   B   C   D   E   F

8
7
33
6
5
32
4
3
31
2
1
30

STABLE
COTTS

STABLE
FLATS

Cottesmore
Sch

Water
Tower

South
Lodge

FOREST RD

GROUSE RD

Horsham
Corner

Golf Course

CH

HORSHAM RD

Pease
Pottage

Finches Field
(Sports Gd)

Finches
Shaw

Furze
Field

Shelley Plain
Farm

Hungry
Down

Woodhurst
Plantation

Hydehill
Wood

Nashlands
Farm

Holkham's
Corner

Hoadlands
Farm

Bunnyland

The
Square

Hyde Gill

Darkalley Gill

Creasy's Brook

A264

CREASYS DR

LOWE CL
JARVIS CL

JACKSON RD
CLIMMER

MORTYON RD

Pease Pottage
Forest

Stanford
(Scout Camp Site)

WILLIAM MORRIS
WAY

TILGATE HILL

HOLLINGBOURNE CRES

FARNHAM CL

WYE CL
NC CL

RANMO

1 HOLMAN CL
2 RAMBLERS WAY
3 WILBERFORCE CL

OTFORD
CL

A23

BRIGHTON RD (PEASE POTTAGE HILL)

A264

OLD BRIGHTON RD (NORTH)

BRIGHTON RD

M23

A23

BRIGHTON RD (SOUTH)

11

BANK CL

BLACK SWAN CL

COTSFORD

Woodhurst

TILGATE FOREST
ROW

Crawley Forest
House

Cherry Tree
Farm

The Home
Farm

Tilgate Forest
Lodge

Home
Wood

B2114

Yewtree
Cottages

COOPERS
WOOD

Oak
Cottages

HEADLANDS
COTTS

Handcross
Cty Prim
Sch

GRAVELPIT
CNR

Mast

P

PH

B2110 HIGH ST

A23

B2114

CHADDS
COTTS

1 HILLVIEW GDNS
2 SURRENDEN RISE
3 KINGSWOOD CL
4 WESTCOTT CL

Keepers

Hardriding

Pease Pottage
Service Area

Benson's
Hill

Bensonshill
Wood

High
Wood

High Beeches La

HIGH BEECHES LA

Handcross Park
Sch

Harry's
Wood

Cherrytree
Plantation

New
Pond

PARISH LA

New Buildings
Farm

Highbeeches Forest

Stanford Brook

HIGH BEECHES
COTTS

B2110

Dencombe
Wood

Dencombe
House

Carroty
Wood

Tilgate Forest

Starvemouse
Farm

The
High Beeches
Gardens

Blackfold
Wood

M23

25   A   26   B   C   27   D   E   28   F

A **B** **C** **D** **E** **F**

M23

Oldhouse Warren

Bennetts Rough

B2036 BALCOMBE RD

PADDOCKHURST RD

8

Denches Copse

PH

B2110

Burnt Place

Cowdray Forest

PARISH LA

B2110 LONDON RD

7

Forest House

33

Sherlocks

Monks Forest Cott

B2036

Mount Pleasant Farm

6

Greentrees Farm

Monks Forest

Stanford Brook

HIGH ST

Forest Lodge

Kings Farm

5

Brantridge Forest

Balcombe Forest

Sedgy Gill

32

Highley Manor (Hotel)

Burnt Field

CRAWLEY LA

Scott's Gill

4

Brantridge Forest

Lodgelands

Kelsey House

B2036

Brantridge Forest Farm

Works

Hourglass Wood

BOUNDARY RD

3

HANDCROSS RD

Wellgrove Wood

Balcombe House

B2110

HIGH BEECHES LA

New England Cottages

31

Water Tower

Great Cooper's Corner Farm

Red Bridge

LONDON RD

Half Moon Inn

Knoll Wood

HAYWARDS HEATH RD

2

Brantridge Wood

Casteye Wood

Balcombe

BRAMBLE HILL

PO

Brantridge Park Farm

BRANTRIDGE LA

Pond Wood

Alder Wood

Balcombe CE (Contr) Prim Sch

BRAMBLE MEAD

WESTUP RD

Ashen Wood

Long Shaw

1

Brantridge Park

Banks Wood

Balcombe Sta

JOB'S

NEWLANDS

Westup Farm

Peter's Wood

ROCKS LA

B2036

30

20
42

A B C D E F

8

Cricket
Field

Downside
Wood

Paddockhurst
Park

Great Strudgate
Farm

7

Park
House

Green Wood

Kiln
Wood

33

Monks

Home
Wood

Newhouse
Farm

6

Balcombe Lane

Bushycroft
Wood

The Warren

Little
Strudgate
Farm

Marchants
Banks
Show

Long
Wood

5

STONEY LA

Bloomer's Valley

32

Yewtree
Farm

Fire
Wood

Littlebushy
Wood

Bethlehem
Wood

Upperstaff Wood

BOUNDARY RD

Square
Wood

4

Forest
Farm

The Oaks

Horsebridge
Wood

Ardingly Brook

Wakehurst Place
(Royal Bot Gdn)

Chestnut
Wood

Woodward's
Farm

Tilgate
Wood

PADDOCKHURST LA

Balcombe
Lake

Southfield
Grove

Westwood Valley

3

Walk
Wood

31

Southfield Gill

Tillinghurst
Farm

TILLINGHURST LA

Alder
Wood

Flatfield
Wood

2

Ardingly Resr

WEST
HILL

Great Racks
Wood

Edmond's
Farm

Lullings

Wilton
Villas

Balcombe Mill
(dis)

MILL LA

WEST HILL

Bushy
Wood

STOCKCROFT RD
HAYWARDS HEATH RD
MEADOW CL
DEANLAND RD
TROYMEDE
VICTORIA RD
COOMBERS
FOXWELLS
OLDLANDS AVE
GLEBE VIEW
STUMBLEMEAD

SHELL LA

Great Burrow
Wood

Westhill
Place

30

B2110

LONDON RD

A   B   C   D   E   F

8

Square Wood

Old House Farm

Wayside

Duckyls

Bird's Eye Wood

Giffard's Wood

B2028

Old House

Stonelands

Duckyls Farm

Rocks Wood

Whitestone Wood

7

Longwood Slip

The White Hart (PH)

SELSFIELD RD

33

Chapel Row

THE BEACON

Shagswell Wood

PULLEY'S BROADFIELD

6

Pearcelands

Chiddinglye Farm

Chiddinglye

West Hoathly CE (Contr) Sch

PO

HILLTOP RD

THE HOLLOW

Sheepwash Wood

West Hoathly

NORTH LA

SANDY LA

P

VINOLS CROSS

BATHSFIELD

Lower Barn

Cat Inn (PH)

Priest Ho (Mus)

CHURCH RD

GARDEN HEAD

HOATHLY HILL

TOP RD

BULLDOGS BANK

5

SELSFIELD RD

Chiddinglye Wood

Pearcelands Wood

Philpots Manor Sch

Philpots

Ashurst Wood

32

ASHURST COTTS

Boundary Wood

Philpots Farm

Langridge Farm House

Langridge Wood

4

P

Stonehurst

Coneyburrow Wood

HOOK LA

Courtland Wood

Cob Brook

Grovelands Farm

East Wood

West Wood

South Wood

Barnland Wood

Hook Farm

HAMMINGDEN LA

Newlands Cotts

3

31

Fulling Mill Farm

TILLINGHURST LA

Hoathly Shaw

Ludwell Farm

Whitestone

2

Gardeners Arms (PH)

Scott's Wood

HOOK LA

Whitestone Wood

Furtherhouse Wood

Little London

Horncombe

COB LA

Holly Farm

1

Pickeridge Farm

WATNEY COTTS

Highbrook

Hudds Wood

The Showground

Long Shaw

B2028

Moorlands Wood

30

34   A   B   35   C   D   36   E   F

A **B** **C** **D** **E** **F**

Marl Pit Shaw

Coombe Brook

Blackland Wood

New Coombe Wood

New Coombe Farm

West Hoathly Brickworks

PH

Grinstead Wood

Sharpthorne

HAMSEY RD

STATION RD

MARL PIT RD

HOME PLATE

PO

2

ASHCROFT RD

GLENHAM PL

TOP RD

1 IMAGE CROSS FLATS
2 FOREST RIDGE

Little Cookhams

Cookhams Wood

Courtlands

Bluebell Rly

Sloe Garden Wood

Sussex Border Path

Moon's Wood

Aldern Wood

Deanlands Farm

HORSTED LA

Northwood House

Vaex End

Tanyard

CINDER HILL

Horsted House Farm

Ravenswood Inn

Long Plantation

Blackland Farm

Mayes

Mayes Farm

GRINSTEAD LA

Tits Wood

Miry Copse

Front Wood

Tyes Cross

Courtlands Farm

Wickenden Wood

Wickenden Farm

Round Wood

Piplye Wood

Mayes Wood

Blackdog Cottages

Dodges Farm Cotts

Dodge's Wood

Wickenden Manor

Sandpit Wood

Hang Wood

Restlands

Broadhurst Manor

Meridian Court

Round Wood

Plaw Wood

Plawhatch Hall

Old Plawhatch Farm

PLAW HATCH LA

Horncastle House

Dalingridge Place

Dalingridge Farm

Balcombe Farm

CHILLING ST

BALCOMBE LA

Grinstead Wood

Little Westlands

HURSTWOOD LA

Ass Wood

Hurstwood Farm

Ford

BIRCHGROVE LA

LEGSHEATH LA

Legsheath Farm

BOWERHILL COTTS

Coldharbour Manor

Cripps Manor

Horncastle Wood

Twyford Farm

Twyford Lodge

8

7

33

6

5

32

4

3

31

2

1

30

43
23

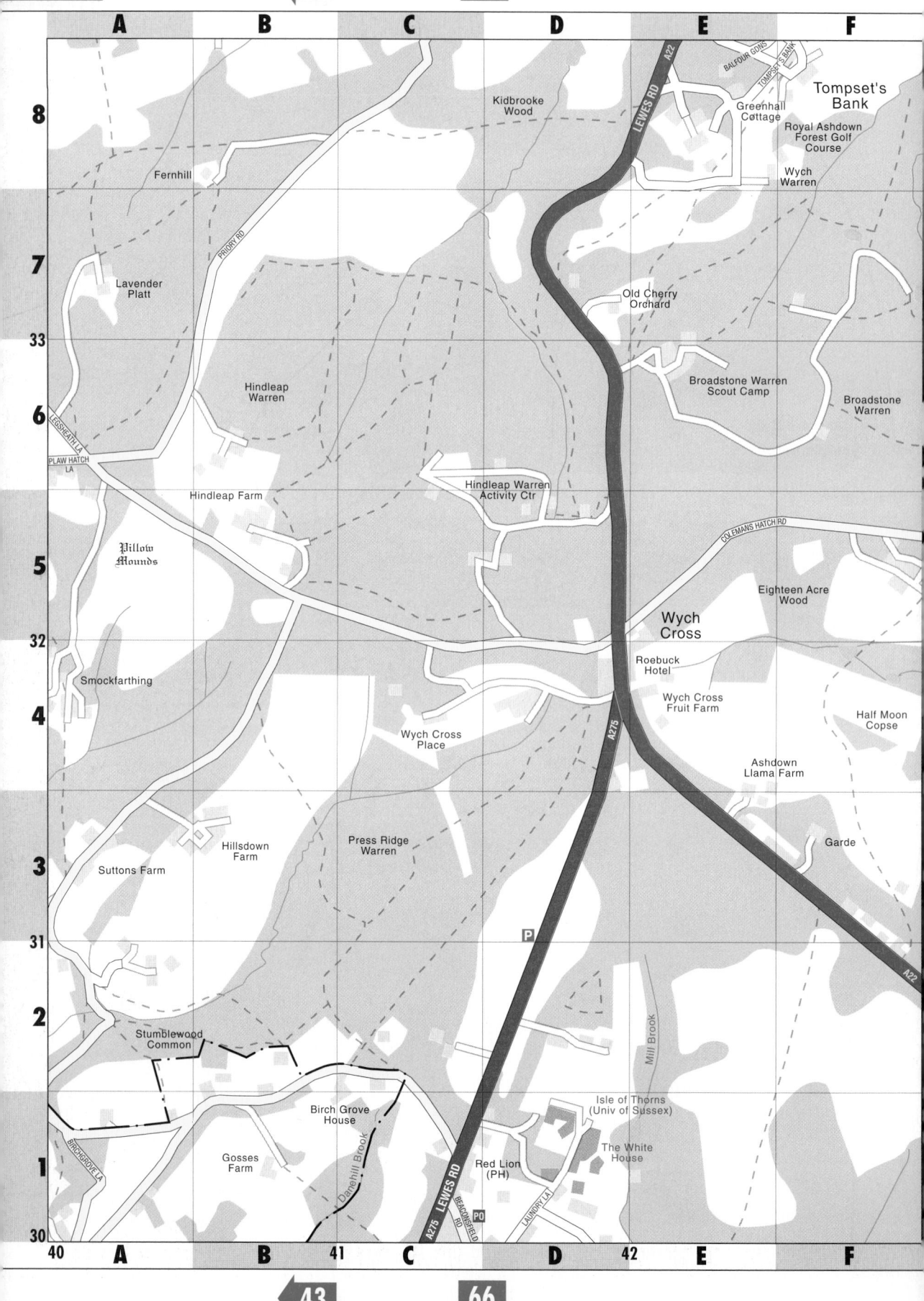
A
B
C
D
E
F
8
7
33
6
5
32
4
3
31
2
1
30
40
41
42
Kidbrooke Wood
Tompset's Bank
Greenhall Cottage
BALFOUR GDNS
TOMPSET'S BANK
A22
LEWES RD
Royal Ashdown Forest Golf Course
Wych Warren
Fernhill
PRIORY RD
Lavender Platt
Old Cherry Orchard
Hindleap Warren
Broadstone Warren Scout Camp
Broadstone Warren
LEGSHEATH LA
PLAW HATCH LA
Hindleap Warren Activity Ctr
Hindleap Farm
COLEMANS HATCH RD
Pillow Mounds
Eighteen Acre Wood
Wych Cross
Roebuck Hotel
Smockfarthing
Wych Cross Fruit Farm
A275
Half Moon Copse
Wych Cross Place
Ashdown Llama Farm
Hillsdown Farm
Press Ridge Warren
Garde
Suttons Farm
P
A22
Stumblewood Common
Mill Brook
Isle of Thorns (Univ of Sussex)
Birch Grove House
The White House
BIRCHGROVE LA
Gosses Farm
Danehill Brook
Red Lion (PH)
A275
LEWES RD
BEACONSFIELD RD
LAUNDRY LA
PO

43
66

A　B　C　D　E　F

Goleigh Farm House

Ham Barn Farm

Works

Moor Park Farm

Westfork

Greatham Bridge

Burgates Farm

CHURCH ST PO

PH

Upper Green
The Blue Bell (PH)

Kippences

HAWLEY RD

HOMEFIELD COTTS

KILN FIELD RD

HAWKS MEAD

West Liss

THE GREEN

ST MARY'S RD

WESTERN RD

BISHBOURNE GDNS

STATION RD

BALFOUR DSP

Brows Farm

Fieldview

Liss

Longmead

LINDEN DR

FARNHAM RD

Sewage Works

NURSERY RD

ANDLERS ASH RD

UPPER MOUNT

Prince's Marsh

LC

STODHAM LA

Andlers Ash Farm

Pruetts

PRUETTS LA

STODHAM LA

Stodham Park

TANKERDALE LA

Longmoor Inclosure

Warren Hill

FOREST RD

FOREST CNR

PINE COTTS

BRIAR WOOD

BERRYLANDS

SHERWOOD CL

PO

NEWFIELD RD

BEECHWOOD

TEMPLE RD

PINE WLK

The Temple Inn (PH)

Liss Forest

The Mint

ROTHERBANK FARM LA

FOREST RISE

River Rother

DUDLEY TERR

KELSEY CL

WOODBOURNE CL

THE ROUNDABOUTS

MILL RD

MILLBROOK CL

SILVER BIRCH

PADDOCK CL

KITCHEN CL

Wyld Green Farm

WYLDE GREEN LA

East Liss

OAK TREE DR

MIDDLE MEADOW

GREENFIELDS

PATRICK'S COPSE RD

LONGACRE

RAKE RD

Little Barn PL

HIGHFIELD GDNS

THE RIDINGS

HATCH LA

Liss Sta

SHOTTERFIELD TERR

SYERS RD

TOPKWOOD

THE OVAL

COPSE CL

MEADOW WLK

TREE CL

LIMES CL

ROMAN MEAD

SPRINGFIELD

LOW RD

COLLARD WAY

MOSS CL

CHASE CL

CHASE CL

INWOOD RD

VINSON RD

PORTLAND SQ

RUSHFIELD RD

PADMORE WAY

BRIDGE MEADOWS

PO

ROTHER House

SUMMERSFIELD

CARDEW RD

LAMBS LEASE

DENNIS WAY

EAST HILL CL

East Hill

Liss Inf & Jun Schs

HILL BROW RD

Hill Side

Hill Brow

Rake Common

Farther Commons

EDGEWOOD CT

WOODLANDS LA

HUNTSBOTTOM LA

MALVERN RD

PLANTATION RD

COMBE RD

B3006

LONDON RD

B2070

PH

Clayton Court

KNOWLES MEADOW

Combe Hill

The Lake

The Wylds

Wylds Farm

WARREN RD

Mangers

REEDS LA

Reeds

Palmers

Whangarei Nursery
Palmers Farm

MINT RD

LC

Home Farm

DUCKMEAD LA

Ciddy Hall

ST PATRICK'S LA

ROCKPIT COTTS

St Patrick's Copse

High Firs House

Highfield Wood

Rake

B2070

PEMBROKE LA

Black Pond

Rake Hanger

Sussex Border Path

Hambledon Piece

Little Dean Bottom

8
7
29
6
5
28
4
27
3
2
27
1
26

A B C D E F

8

7

29

6

5

28

4

3

27

2

1

26

The Broom

Folly Pond

Hilly Fields Copse

Heath Patch

Home Park

Horse Trials Show Gd

Ram's Horn Copse

Sussex Border Path

Langley

The Vineyard

Hutfield Copse

Bishop's Copse

Ripsley Farm

Fox Copse

Ripsley House

PH

B2070

Langley Bridge Farm

Langley Court

Broad Copse

Heath Patch

Brewells Farm

REEDS LA

Little Langley Farm

Langley Wood

BREWELLS LA

Newlands

Rake Firs

Chapel Common

Great Hanger

ST PATRICK'S LA

Rake CE (Contr) Prim Sch

RAKE BSNS PK

Rock Field Firs

Maysleith

The Flying Bull (PH)

◆

Rake

BULL HILL

Coldharbour Park Farm

Coldharbour Wood

Maysleith Hanger

Maysleith Wood

PO

Sun Inn

SANDY LA

B2070

Coldharbour Wood

Hulls Copse

Canhouse Copse

Pot Well

Combeland Farm

CANHOUSE LA

Combe Pond

Canhouse Cottage

Great Trippetts Farm

Goldring

Lower Common Wood

RAKE RD

Combe Lodge Farm

Marsh Wood

Harting Combe

New Barn Farm

80 A B 81 C D 82 E F

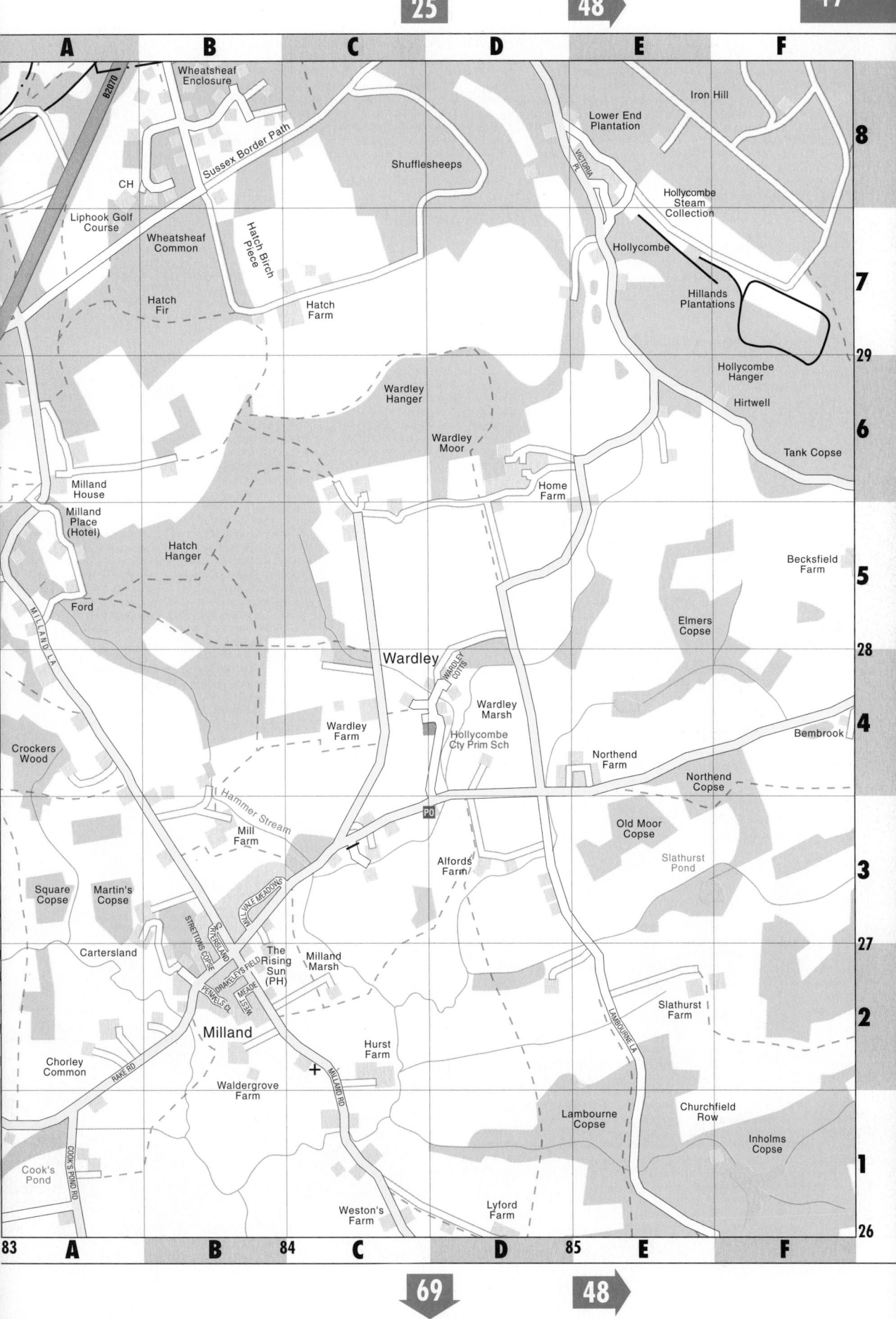

CH

Liphook Golf Course

Wheatsheaf Enclosure

Sussex Border Path

Wheatsheaf Common

Hatch Birch Piece

Shufflesheeps

Lower End Plantation

Iron Hill

VICTORIA PL

Hollycombe Steam Collection

Hollycombe

Hatch Fir

Hatch Farm

Hillands Plantations

Hollycombe Hanger

Hirtwell

Wardley Hanger

Tank Copse

Wardley Moor

Milland House

Home Farm

Milland Place (Hotel)

Hatch Hanger

Becksfield Farm

MILLAND LA

Ford

Elmers Copse

Wardley

Crockers Wood

WARDLEY COTTS

Wardley Marsh

Wardley Farm

Hollycombe Cty Prim Sch

Bembrook

Northend Farm

Northend Copse

Hammer Stream

Mill Farm

PO

Alfords Farm

Old Moor Copse

Slathurst Pond

Square Copse

Martin's Copse

VALE MEADOWS

STRETTONS COPSE

Cartersland

DRAKELEY'S FIELD

RYES RD

PENRELS CL

MEADE

MEAD

The Rising Sun (PH)

Milland Marsh

27

Slathurst Farm

LAMBOURNE LA

Chorley Common

RAKE RD

Milland

Hurst Farm

Waldergrove Farm

MILLAND RD

Lambourne Copse

Churchfield Row

Cook's Pond

COOK'S POND RD

Inholms Copse

Weston's Farm

Lyford Farm

47
26

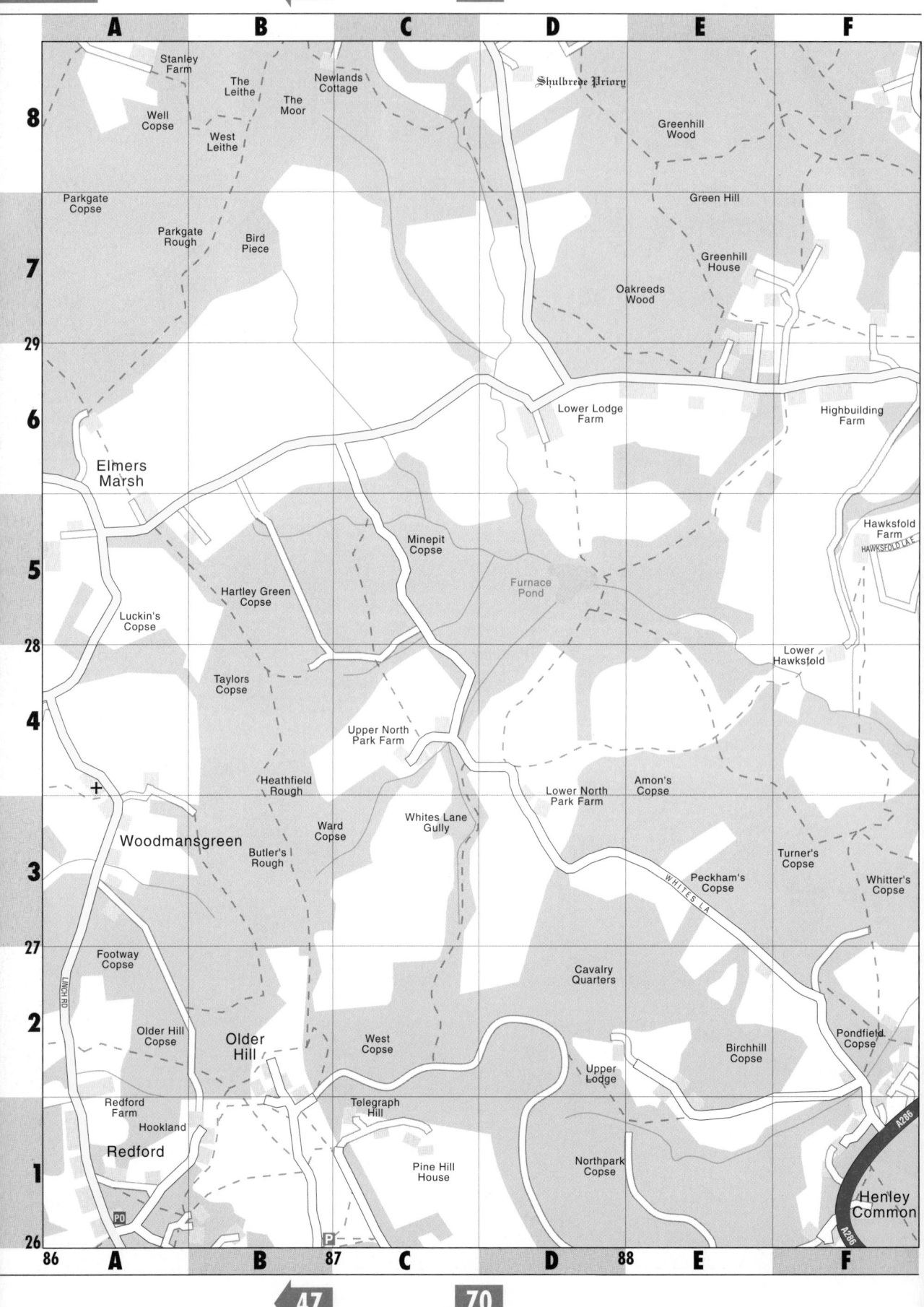
A
B
C
D
E
F
8
7
29
6
5
28
4
3
27
2
1
26
86
87
88
Stanley Farm
The Leithe
Newlands Cottage
The Moor
Shulbrede Priory
Well Copse
West Leithe
Greenhill Wood
Parkgate Copse
Green Hill
Parkgate Rough
Bird Piece
Greenhill House
Oakreeds Wood
Lower Lodge Farm
Highbuilding Farm
Elmers Marsh
Hawksfold Farm
HAWKSFOLD LANE
Minepit Copse
Furnace Pond
Hartley Green Copse
Luckin's Copse
Lower Hawksfold
Taylors Copse
Upper North Park Farm
Heathfield Rough
Amon's Copse
Lower North Park Farm
Woodmansgreen
Ward Copse
Whites Lane Gully
Butler's Rough
Turner's Copse
Peckham's Copse
WHITES LA
Whitter's Copse
Footway Copse
Cavalry Quarters
LINCH RD
Older Hill Copse
Older Hill
West Copse
Pondfield Copse
Birchhill Copse
Upper Lodge
Redford Farm
Telegraph Hill
Hookland
A286
Redford
Pine Hill House
Northpark Copse
Henley Common
PO
P

47
70

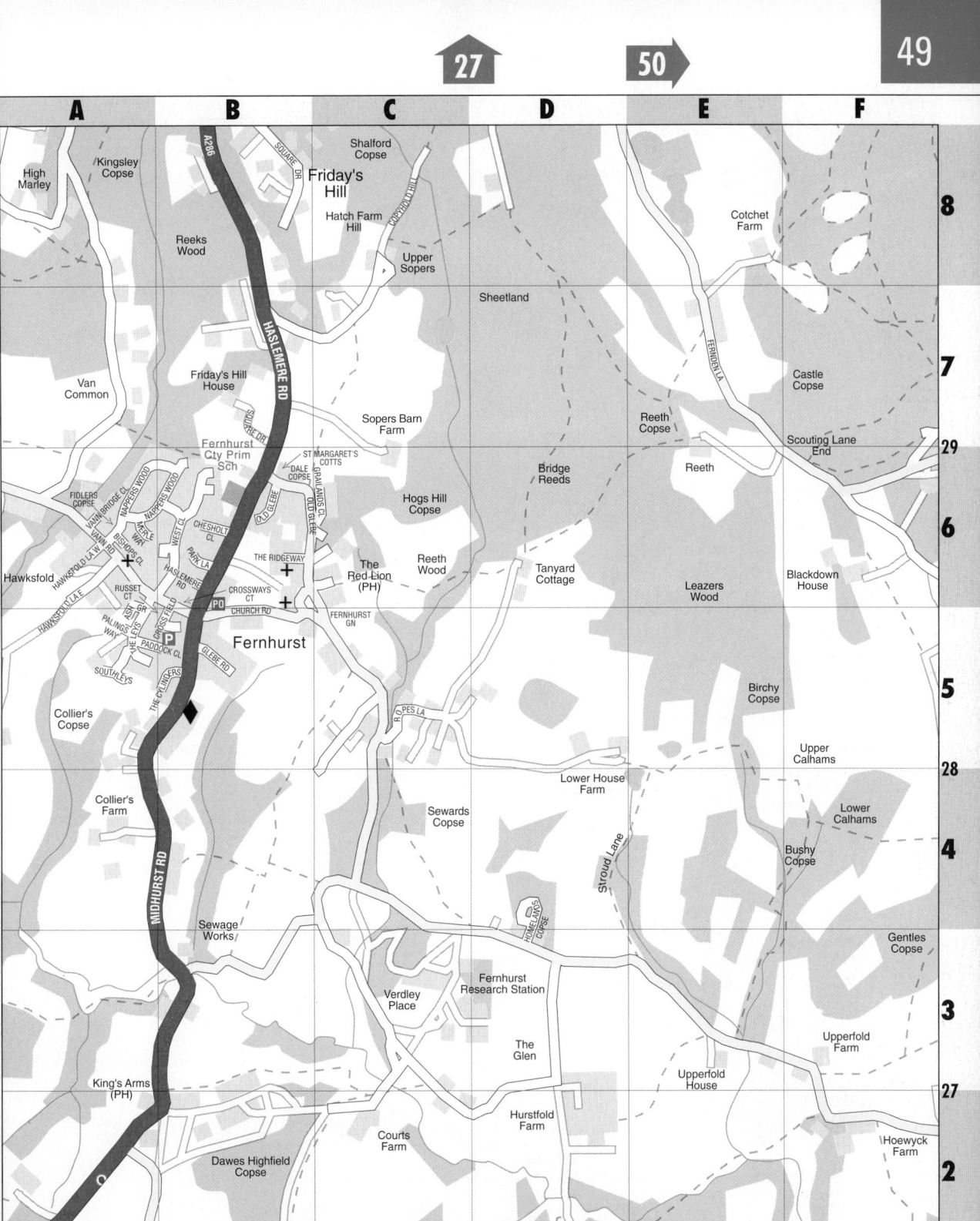

A B C D E F

8

High Marley
Kingsley Copse
Shalford Copse
Friday's Hill
Reeks Wood
Hatch Farm Hill
Cotchet Farm

Upper Sopers

Sheetland

7

Van Common
Friday's Hill House
FERNDEN LA
Castle Copse

Sopers Barn Farm
Reeth Copse
Scouting Lane End

29

Fernhurst Cty Prim Sch
ST MARGARET'S COTTS
Bridge Reeds
Reeth

6

FIDLERS COPSE
DALE COPSE
Hogs Hill Copse
Reeth Wood
Tanyard Cottage
Leazers Wood
Blackdown House

Hawksfold
THE RIDGEWAY
The Red Lion (PH)

PO
CROSSWAYS CT
CHURCH RD
FERNHURST GN

Fernhurst

5

Collier's Copse
RD PES LA
Birchy Copse

Upper Calhams

28

Collier's Farm
Sewards Copse
Lower House Farm
Lower Calhams

Bushy Copse

4

HOMELANDS COPSE
Gentles Copse

Sewage Works
Verdley Place
Fernhurst Research Station
STROUD LANE
Upperfold Farm

3

The Glen
Upperfold House

King's Arms (PH)

27

MIDHURST RD
Courts Farm
Hurstfold Farm
Hoewyck Farm

2

Dawes Highfield Copse

Dawes Farm

Works
Guildford Copse
Surney

1

Henley Copse
Verdley Wood
Overnoons Rough

26

49
28

A
B
C
D
E
F
8
7
6
5
4
3
2
1
29
28
27
26
92
93
94
Rickfield Copse
Abesters Copse
Upper Diddlesford Farm
Fulwick's Copse
Chapel Copse
JOBSON'S LA
Abesters
Bullocks La
New Copse
Diddlesford Manor Farm
Ramsfold Wood
Ramsfold House
Temple of the Winds
FERNDEN LA
Quellwood Common
Shopp Hill Farm
Hookhams Farm
Hillgrove
Blackdown Farm
Tanland Copse
Hobstevens
Upper Barn Hanger
Upper Barn Park Farm
Windfall Wood
Sybs Farm
Navant Hill
Coochway Ground
Mire Hanger
Windfallwood Common
High La
Spring Coppice
Park Farm
Screechhouse Copse
CROSSWAYS
Little Brockhurst
Northurst Farm
Great Brockhurst Farm
The Noah's Ark (PH)
Gatehouse Farm
Dial Green
Goffs Copse
Lurgashall
PO
Gentilshurst Farm
Greengates Farmhouse
GREENGATES
Benefold Copse
Ragham Lodge
Bishop's Hanger
Woodfield Row
HIGHSTEAD LA
Lower Gentilshurst Farm
High Hampstead Farm
Sods Farm
Lickfold Bridge
The Hanger
Chillinghurst Copse
The Lickford Inn (PH)
Mill Pond
Shotter's Farm
Old Mill Farm

49
72

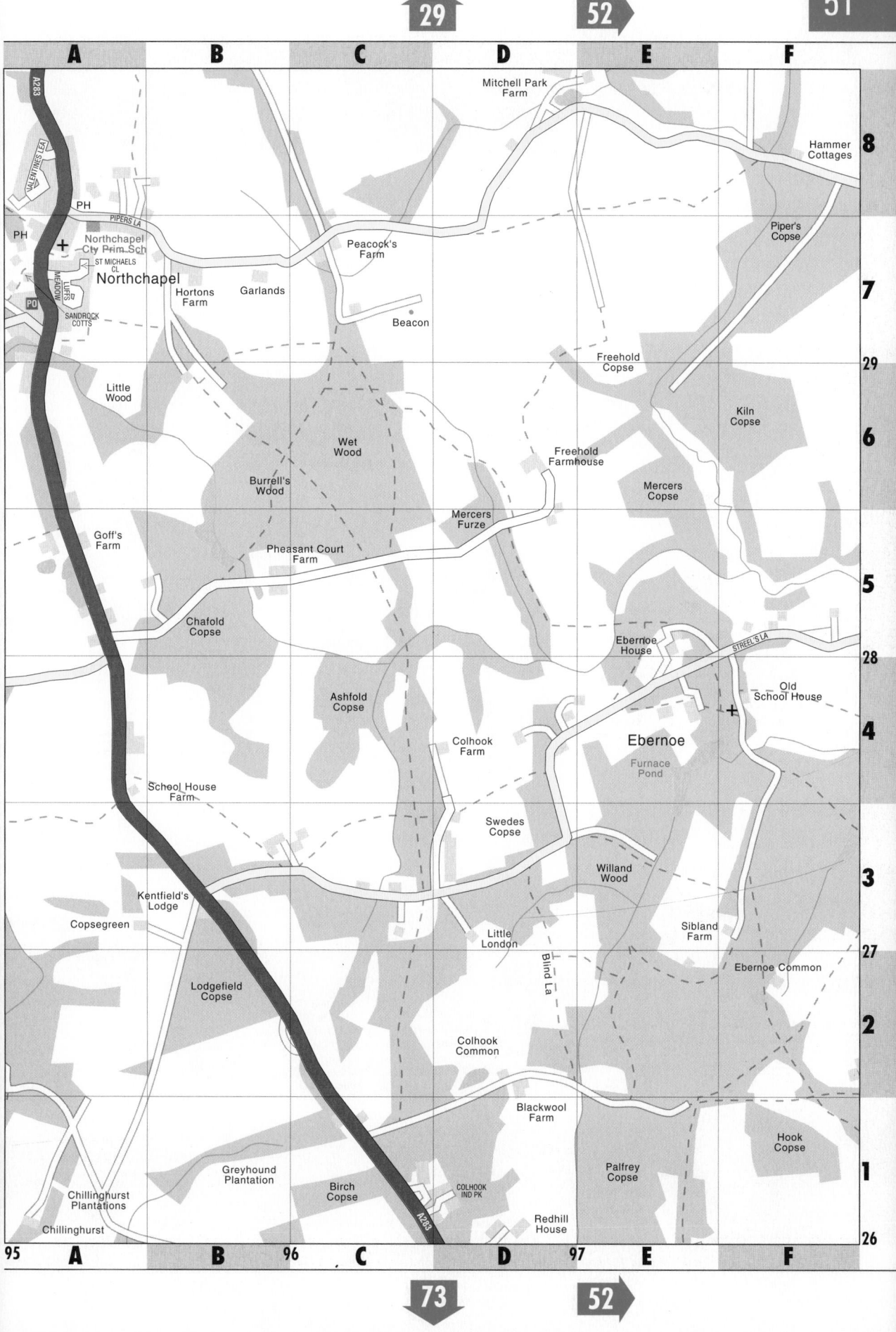

A   B   C   D   E   F

8

7

29

6

5

28

4

3

27

2

1

26

95   A   B   96   C   D   97   E   F

Mitchell Park Farm

Hammer Cottages

Piper's Copse

PH

PIPERS LA

A283

VALENTINE'S LA

Northchapel Cty Prim Sch

PH

ST MICHAELS CL

Northchapel

MEADOW

LUFFS

Peacock's Farm

PO

SANDROCK COTTS

Hortons Farm

Garlands

Beacon

Freehold Copse

Little Wood

Kiln Copse

Wet Wood

Freehold Farmhouse

Burrell's Wood

Mercers Copse

Goff's Farm

Mercers Furze

Pheasant Court Farm

Chafold Copse

Ebernoe House

STREEL'S LA

Old School House

Ashfold Copse

Ebernoe

School House Farm

Colhook Farm

Furnace Pond

Swedes Copse

Willand Wood

Kentfield's Lodge

Little London

Sibland Farm

Copsegreen

Ebernoe Common

Lodgefield Copse

Blind La

Colhook Common

Blackwool Farm

Hook Copse

Greyhound Plantation

Birch Copse

A283

COLHOOK IND PK

Palfrey Copse

Chillinghurst Plantations

Chillinghurst

Redhill House

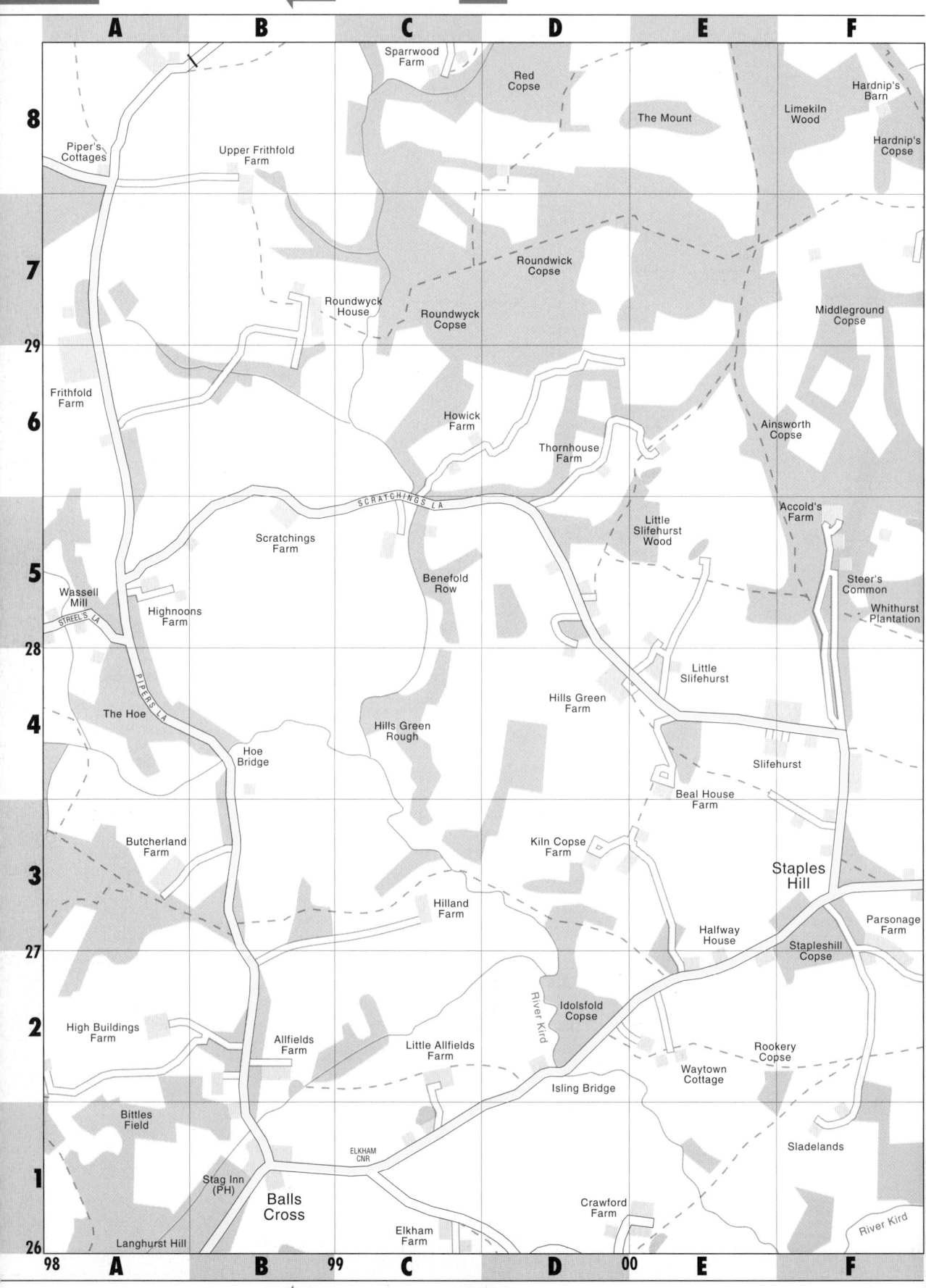

A   B   C   D   E   F

8

7

29

6

5

28

4

3

27

2

1

26

Sparrwood Farm

Red Copse

The Mount

Limekiln Wood

Hardnip's Barn

Hardnip's Copse

Piper's Cottages

Upper Frithfold Farm

Roundwyck House

Roundwyck Copse

Roundwick Copse

Middleground Copse

Frithfold Farm

Howick Farm

Thornhouse Farm

Ainsworth Copse

SCRATCHINGS LA

Scratchings Farm

Benefold Row

Little Slifehurst Wood

Accold's Farm

Wassell Mill

STREEL'S LA

Highnoons Farm

Steer's Common

Whithurst Plantation

PIPERS LA

The Hoe

Hoe Bridge

Hills Green Rough

Hills Green Farm

Little Slifehurst

Little Slifehurst

Slifehurst

Beal House Farm

Butcherland Farm

Kiln Copse Farm

Staples Hill

Hilland Farm

Halfway House

Stapleshill Copse

Parsonage Farm

High Buildings Farm

Allfields Farm

Little Allfields Farm

River Kird

Idolsfold Copse

Rookery Copse

Waytown Cottage

Bittles Field

Isling Bridge

Sladelands

Stag Inn (PH)

ELKHAM CNR

Balls Cross

Crawford Farm

River Kird

Langhurst Hill

Elkham Farm

98   A   B   99   C   D   00   E   F

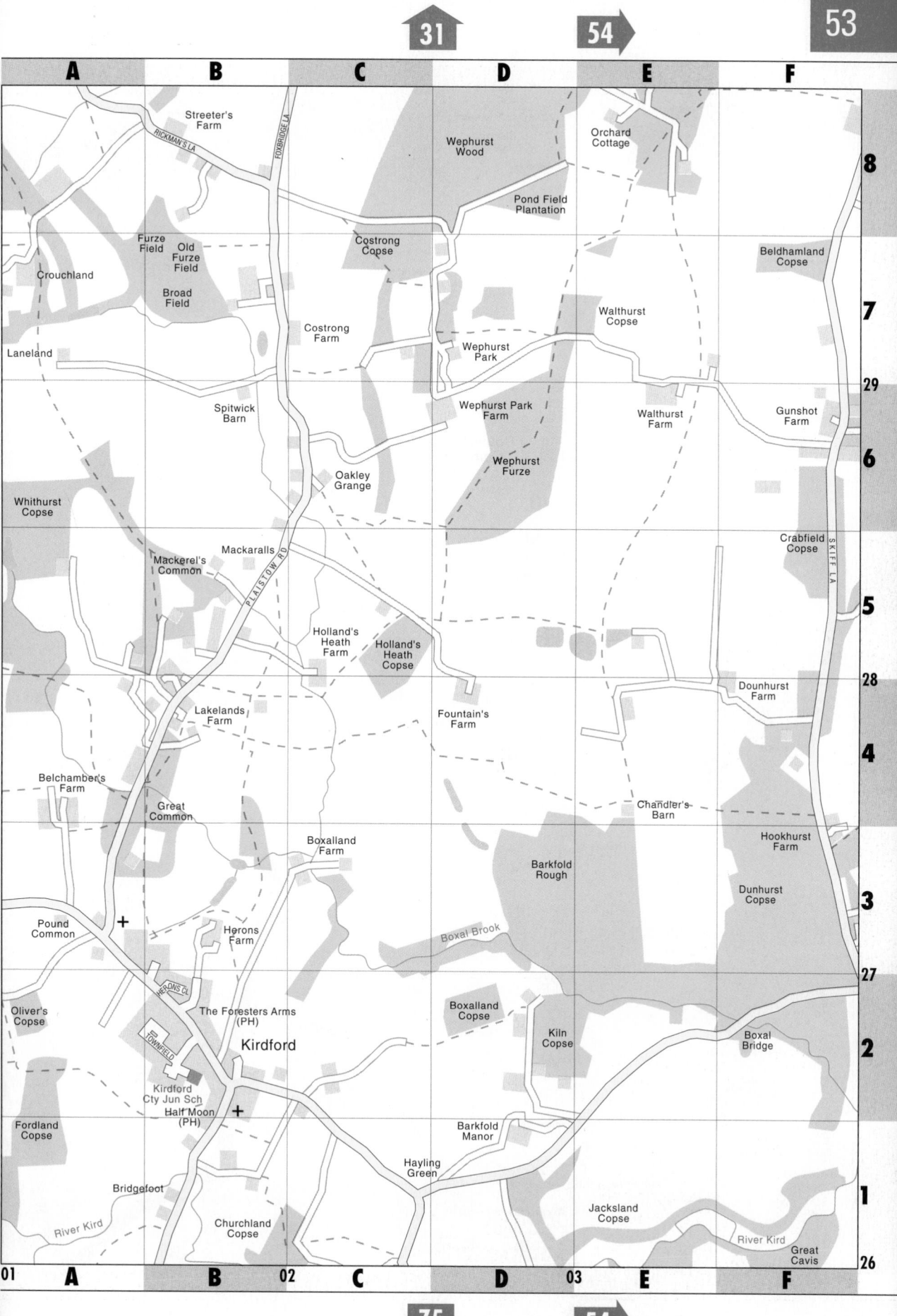

A B C D E F

8

Streeter's Farm

RICKMAN'S LA

Wephurst Wood

Orchard Cottage

Pond Field Plantation

Furze Field

Old Furze Field

FOXBRIDGE LA

Costrong Copse

Beldhamland Copse

7

Broad Field

Crouchland

Costrong Farm

Walthurst Copse

Laneland

Wephurst Park

29

Spitwick Barn

Wephurst Park Farm

Walthurst Farm

Gunshot Farm

6

Whithurst Copse

Oakley Grange

Wephurst Furze

Crabfield Copse

SKIFF LA

Mackaralls

Mackerel's Common

PLAISTOW RD

5

Holland's Heath Farm

Holland's Heath Copse

Dounhurst Farm

28

Lakelands Farm

Fountain's Farm

4

Belchamber's Farm

Great Common

Chandler's Barn

Hookhurst Farm

Boxalland Farm

Barkfold Rough

Dunhurst Copse

3

Pound Common

Herons Farm

Boxal Brook

27

DNS CL

Oliver's Copse

The Foresters Arms (PH)

Boxalland Copse

Kiln Copse

Boxal Bridge

2

TOWNFIELD

Kirdford

Kirdford Cty Jun Sch

Half Moon (PH)

Barkfold Manor

Fordland Copse

Bridgefoot

Hayling Green

Jacksland Copse

1

River Kird

Churchland Copse

River Kird

Great Cavis

26

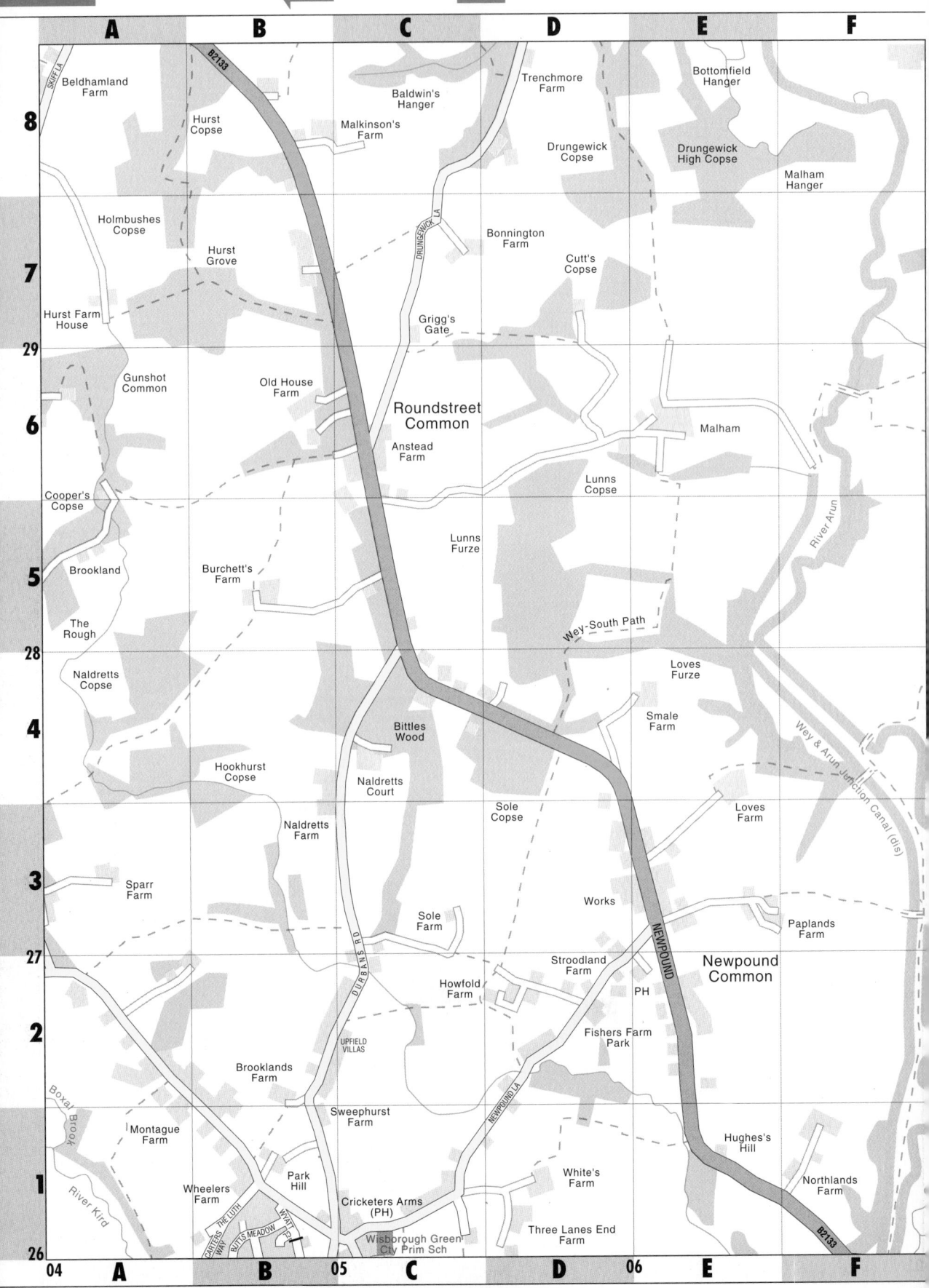

A B C D E F

8

7

29

6

5

28

4

3

27

2

1

26

Skiff La

Beldhamland Farm

Hurst Copse

B2133

Baldwin's Hanger

Malkinson's Farm

Trenchmore Farm

Bottomfield Hanger

Drungewick Copse

Drungewick High Copse

Malham Hanger

Holmbushes Copse

Hurst Grove

Drungewick La

Bonnington Farm

Cutt's Copse

Hurst Farm House

Grigg's Gate

Gunshot Common

Old House Farm

Roundstreet Common

Malham

Cooper's Copse

Anstead Farm

Lunns Copse

River Arun

Brookland

Burchett's Farm

Lunns Furze

Wey-South Path

Loves Furze

The Rough

Naldretts Copse

Bittles Wood

Smale Farm

Wey & Arun Junction Canal (dis)

Hookhurst Copse

Naldretts Court

Loves Farm

Naldretts Farm

Sole Copse

Sparr Farm

Durbans Rd

Sole Farm

Works

Newpound

Newpound Common

Paplands Farm

Stroodland Farm

PH

Howfold Farm

Fishers Farm Park

Upfield Villas

Newpound La

Brooklands Farm

Sweephurst Farm

White's Farm

Hughes's Hill

Montague Farm

Boxal Brook

Wheelers Farm

Park Hill

The Luth

Carters Way

Bytts Meadow

Wrft La

Cricketers Arms (PH)

Three Lanes End Farm

Northlands Farm

River Kird

Wisborough Green Cty Prim Sch

B2133

04 A 05 B C 06 D E F

A B C D E F

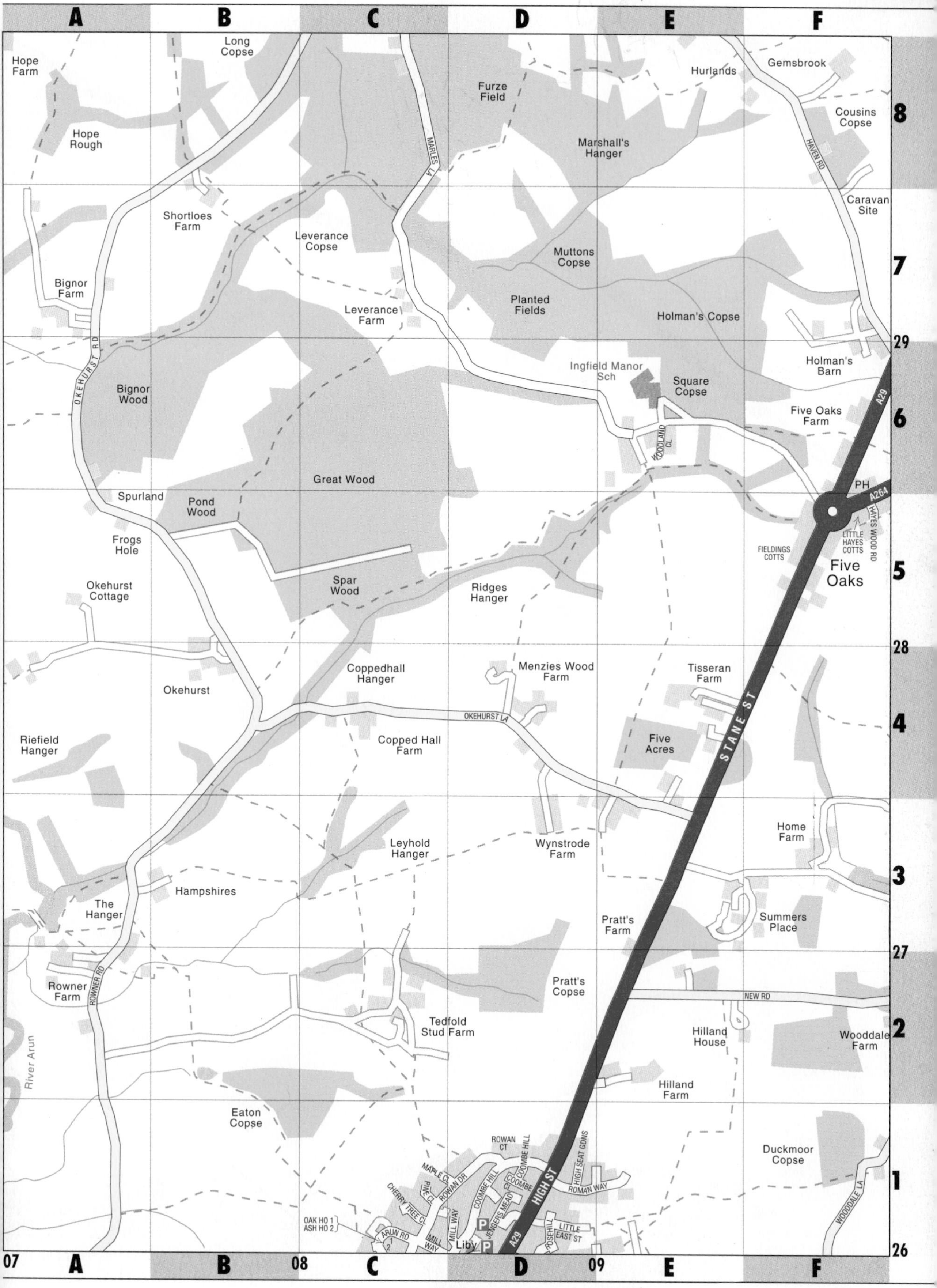

8

Hope Farm
Hope Rough
Long Copse
Furze Field
Hurlands
Gemsbrook
Cousins Copse

Shortloes Farm
Leverance Copse
Marshall's Hanger
Hacker Rd
Caravan Site

Bignor Farm
Leverance Farm
Muttons Copse
Planted Fields
Holman's Copse
7
29
Holman's Barn
A29

Okehurst Rd
Bignor Wood
Ingfield Manor Sch
Square Copse
Woodland Cl
Five Oaks Farm
6

Spurland
Pond Wood
Great Wood
PH
A264
Hayes Wood Rd
Little Hayes Cotts
Fieldings Cotts
Five Oaks
5

Frogs Hole
Okehurst Cottage
Spar Wood
Ridges Hanger
28

Coppedhall Hanger
Menzies Wood Farm
Tisseran Farm
Stane St
4

Okehurst
Okehurst La
Copped Hall Farm
Five Acres

Riefield Hanger
Leyhold Hanger
Wynstrode Farm
Home Farm
3

Hampshires
The Hanger
Pratt's Farm
Summers Place
27

Rowner Rd
Rowner Farm
Tedfold Stud Farm
Pratt's Copse
New Rd
Hilland House
Wooddale Farm
2

River Arun
Eaton Copse
Hilland Farm
Duckmoor Copse
1
26

High St
Rowan Ct
Coombe Hill
High Seat Gdns
Roman Way
Maple Cl
Cherry Tree Cl
Pyke Cl
Rowan Dr
Mill Way
Coombe Hill
Jengers Mead
A29
Rosehill
Little East St
Wooddale La
Oak Ho 1
Ash Ho 2
Arun Rd
Mill Way
Liby
P P

07 A B 08 C D 09 E F

55
34

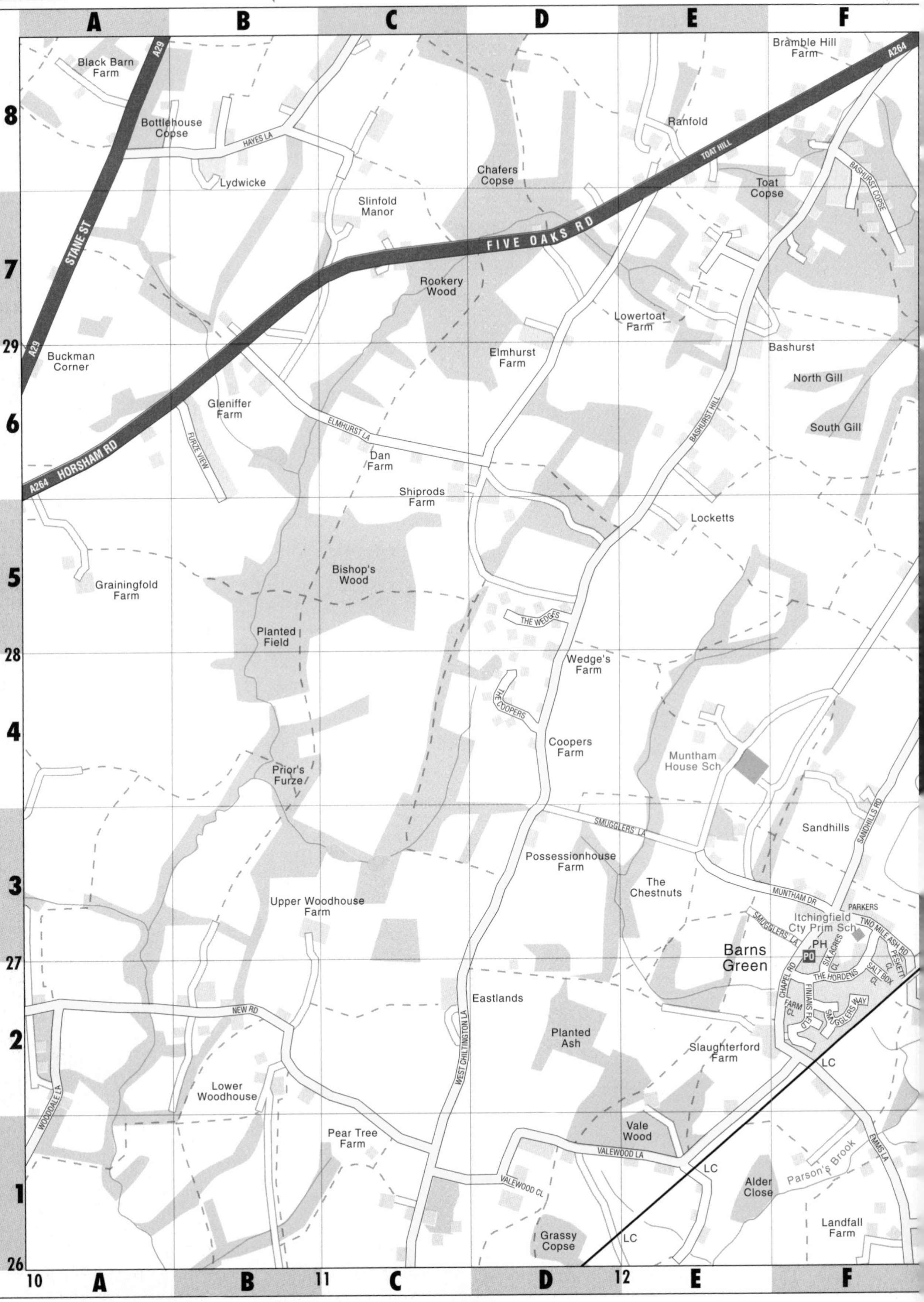

A   B   C   D   E   F

8

Black Barn Farm

Bottlehouse Copse

HAYES LA

Lydwicke

Slinfold Manor

STANE ST

A29

Chafers Copse

Bramble Hill Farm

A264

TOAT HILL

Ranfold

Toat Copse

BASHURST COPSE

FIVE OAKS RD

7

Rookery Wood

Lowertoat Farm

29

Buckman Corner

A29

Elmhurst Farm

Bashurst

North Gill

Gleniffer Farm

6

HORSHAM RD

A264

FURZE VIEW

ELMHURST LA

Dan Farm

Shiprods Farm

BASHURST HILL

South Gill

Locketts

5

Grainingfold Farm

Bishop's Wood

Planted Field

THE WEDGES

Wedge's Farm

28

THE COOPERS

Muntham House Sch

4

Prior's Furze

Coopers Farm

Sandhills

SANDHILLS RD

SMUGGLERS' LA

3

Upper Woodhouse Farm

Possessionhouse Farm

The Chestnuts

MUNTHAM DR

Itchingfield Cty Prim Sch

PARKERS

TWO MILE ASH RD

27

Barns Green

PH

PO

SMUGGLERS LA

ST ADRES

THE HORDENS

PARSONS

PESKETT

SAL BOX

NEW RD

Eastlands

CHAPEL RD

FINNANS CL

FINNANS FM

SMUGGLERS WAY

2

WEST CHILTINGTON LA

Lower Woodhouse

Planted Ash

Slaughterford Farm

LC

WOODDALE LA

Pear Tree Farm

Vale Wood

VALEWOOD LA

LC

Alder Close

Parson's Brook

EBBS LA

Landfall Farm

1

VALEWOOD CL

Grassy Copse

LC

26

10   A   B   11   C   D   12   E   F

55
78

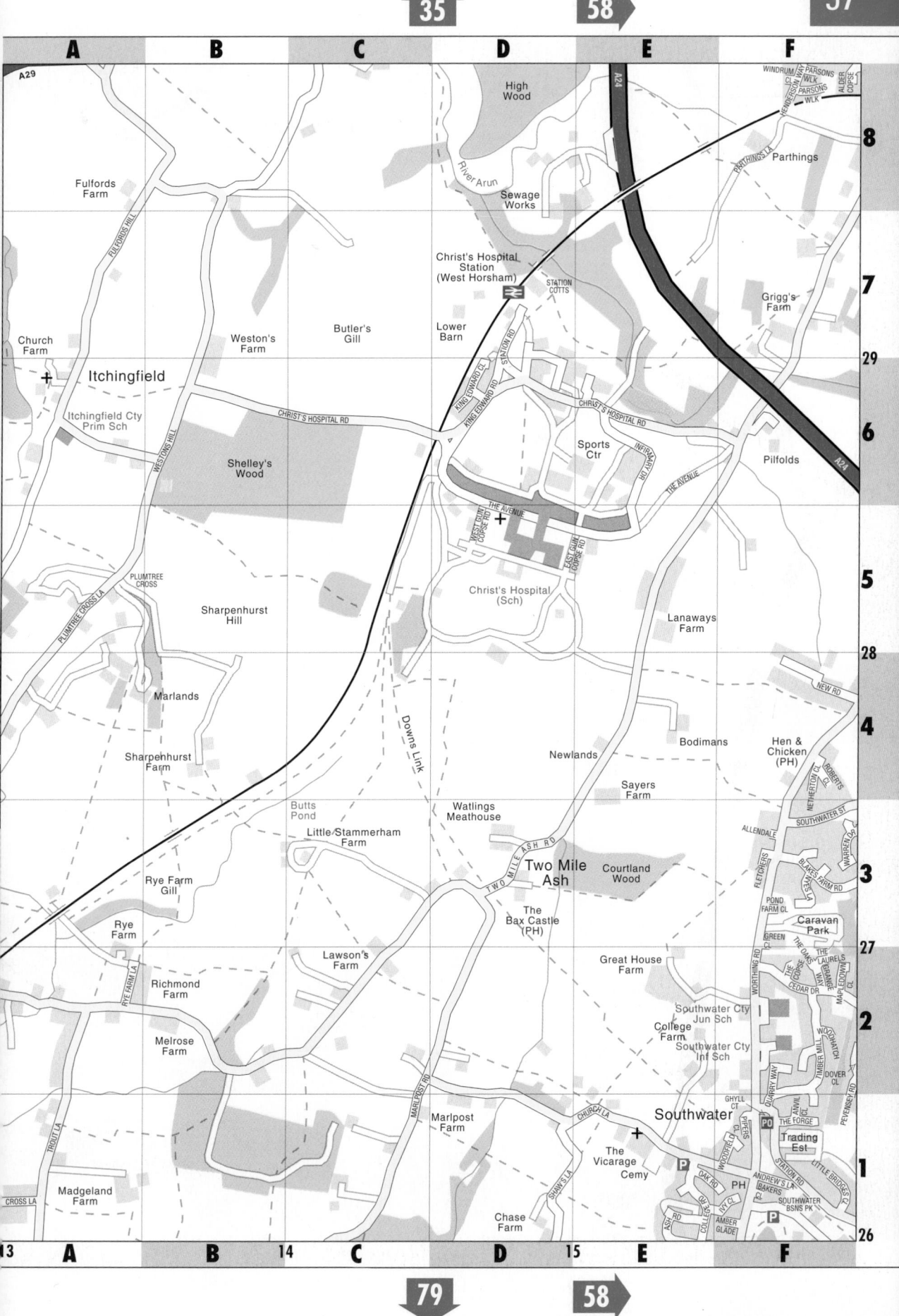

A   B   C   D   E   F

A29

WINDRUM WAY
PARSONS WLK
HENDERSON WAY
PARSONS WLK
ALDER COPSE

8

High Wood

River Arun

Sewage Works

PARTHINGS LA
Parthings

Christ's Hospital Station (West Horsham)

STATION COTTS

A24

7

Grigg's Farm

STATION RD
KING EDWARD CL
KING EDWARD RD

Lower Barn

CHRIST'S HOSPITAL RD

29

Church Farm

+ Itchingfield

Weston's Farm

Butler's Gill

Fulfords Farm

FULFORDS HILL

Itchingfield Cty Prim Sch

CHRIST'S HOSPITAL RD

Sports Ctr

INFIRMARY DR

THE AVENUE

Pilfolds

A24

6

WESTONS HILL

Shelley's Wood

THE AVENUE
WEST GUM COPSE RD
EAST GUM COPSE RD

+

PLUMTREE CROSS

Sharpenhurst Hill

Christ's Hospital (Sch)

Lanaways Farm

5

PLUMTREE CROSS LA

Marlands

28

Sharpenhurst Farm

Downs Link

Newlands

Bodimans

NEW RD

Hen & Chicken (PH)

NETHERTON CL
ROBERTS
SOUTHWATER ST
WARREN DR

4

Sayers Farm

ALLENDALE
FLETCHERS
BLAKES FARM CL
PARK LA
POND FARM CL

Butts Pond

Little Stammerham Farm

Watlings Meathouse

Rye Farm Gill

Two Mile Ash

Courtland Wood

Caravan Park

3

TWO MILE ASH RD

GREEN CL
THE OAKS
THE LAURELS
THE GRANGE
WAY

Rye Farm

The Bax Castle (PH)

27

RYE FARM LA

Lawson's Farm

Great House Farm

WORTHING RD
THE DRIVE
MAPLE DOWN
CEDAR DR

Richmond Farm

Southwater Cty Jun Sch

College Farm

WOODHATCH
TIMBER MILL
MEADOW CL

2

Melrose Farm

MARLPOST RD

Southwater Cty Inf Sch

QUARRY WAY
DOVER CL
PEVENSEY RD

TROUT LA

Marlpost Farm

CHURCH LA

Southwater

GHYLL CT
PO
THE FORGE
ANVIL

1

Madgeland Farm

CROSS LA

The Vicarage

Cemy

+

ANDREW'S LA
LITTLE BRIDGES CT
STATION RD

P

PIPERS
BAKERS
SOUTHWATER BSNS PK
Trading Est

Chase Farm

SHAW'S LA

P

OAK RD
PH
ASH RD
IVY CL
COLLEGE RD
AMBER GLADE

26

HORSHAM

New Town

Tower Hill

Longfield Rd

Boars Head Tavern (PH)

PARTHINGS LANE

TWO MILE ASH RD

TOWER CL

TOWER HILL

SALISBURY RD

OLIVER RD

B2237

WORTHING RD

PICTS HILL

OBME RD

CHESWORTH CL

Denne Meadows Farm

Chesworth Farm

ARUN WAY

HEAD LEY

ATHELSTAN WAY

ST LEONARD'S RD

A281

HERNBROOK DR

BRIGHTON RD

SANDEMAN WAY

KENTWYNS DR

CLOSET

DICKINS WAY

DXLL CRES

Hornbrook Farm

HORNBROOK COPSE

PH

A281

Huxley's Experience Bird of Prey Ctr

Denne Park

Denne Park House

Horsham Golf Course

Amiesmill Farm

White's Bridge

Whitesbridge Farm

Ups and Downs

Alder Copse

Stonepit Wood

KERVES LA

Kerves Brook House

MAGPIE LA

A24

B2237

Hop Oast Farm (Harwood Arabian Stud)

Bourne Hill House

Bulls Farm

King's Farm

Hard's Wood

HARD'S HILL

WORTHING RD

Newfound Out

COLTSTAPLE LA

Hards Farmhouse

Home Farm

SEDGWICK LA

BLAKES FARM RD

KINGS LA

Sunnymeade Farm

Blunts Wood

REEDS LA

Coltstaple Farm

Little Coltstaple Farm

Sedgewick Park

Westlandby Farm

Blake's Farm

SOUTHWATER ST

WILD ORCHID WAY

WARREN DR

LARKSPUR WAY

CHA LOCK WAY

Jackrells Farm

Southwater Street

FAIRVIEW COTTS

Castle Lodge

Sedgwick Castle (remains of)

Home Wood

Castlewood Prim Sch

THE BROOK

THE GLEN

THE DEAN

WINNE WAY

SWAN CL

ROBIN CL

CAMELO CL

CASTLEWOOD RD

JACKRELLS LA

Raylands House

New House Farm

BROADWATER LA

Rushett's Gill

The Wilderness

Sedgwick Park House

Southwater

BODIAM CL

PEVENSEY RD

WALMER CL

YORK CL

BAMBORO CL

CEDAR DR

CROCKHURST

EASTERS CL

PORCHES CL

Easteds Farm

Raylands Park Caravan Site

CORFE CL

WILDSOR CL

ARUNDEL CL

EDINBRO CL

NUTHAM LA

HAZEL CL

CRIPPLEGATE LA

EVERSFIELD

A24

STAKERS LA

Stakers Farm

POLECAT LA

Lockyers Farm

Lower Sedgwick Farm

Nuthurst Farm

37 60

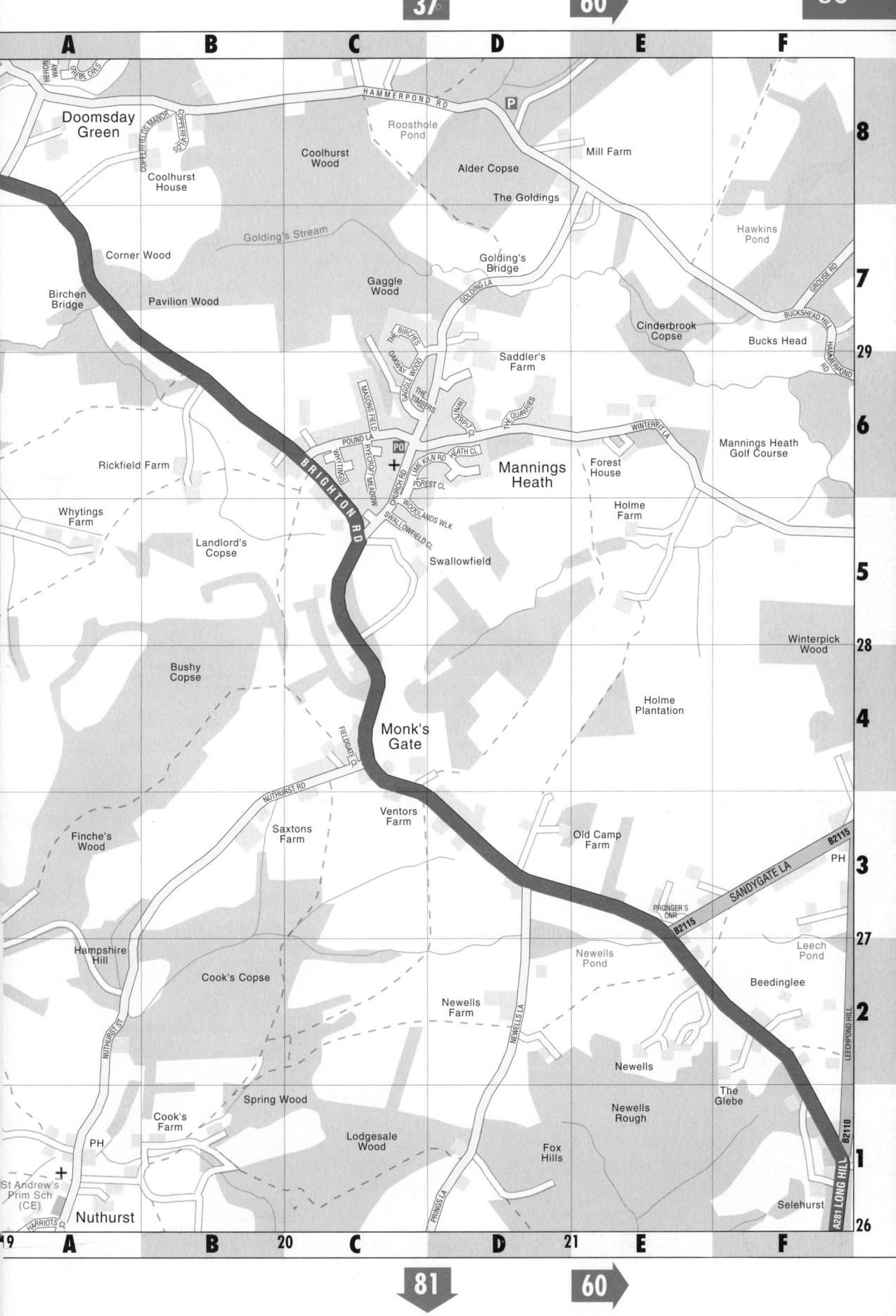
A B C D E F
8 7 29 6 5 28 4 3 27 2 1 26
19 20 21
Doomsday Green
Coolhurst House
Coolhurst Wood
HAMMERPOND RD
Roosthole Pond
Alder Copse
Mill Farm
The Goldings
Golding's Stream
Corner Wood
Golding's Bridge
Hawkins Pond
Birchen Bridge
Pavilion Wood
Gaggle Wood
GOLDING LA
Cinderbrook Copse
Bucks Head
BUCKSHEAD HILL
GROUSE RD
HAMMERPOND RD
Saddler's Farm
THE BIRCHES
OAKWAY
GAGGLE WOOD
THE TIMBERS
MASONS FIELD
WINTERPIT CL
THE QUARRIES
WINTERPIT LA
POUND LA
RYECROFT MEADOW
WHYTINGS
CHURCH RD
LIME KILN RD
HEATH CL
FOREST CL
PO
Mannings Heath
Forest House
Mannings Heath Golf Course
Rickfield Farm
BRIGHTON RD
Whytings Farm
WOODLANDS WLK
SWALLOWFIELD CL
Holme Farm
Landlord's Copse
Swallowfield
Winterpick Wood
Bushy Copse
Holme Plantation
FIELDGATE CL
Monk's Gate
NUTHURST RD
Ventors Farm
Saxtons Farm
Finche's Wood
Old Camp Farm
B2115
SANDYGATE LA
PH
PRONGER'S CNR
Hampshire Hill
Cook's Copse
Newells Pond
Leech Pond
Beedinglee
Newells Farm
NEWELLS LA
NUTHURST ST
Newells
LEECHPOND HILL
The Glebe
Spring Wood
Newells Rough
Cook's Farm
PH
Lodgesale Wood
Fox Hills
B2110
St Andrew's Prim Sch (CE)
PRINGS LA
A281 LONG HILL
Selehurst
Nuthurst
HARRIOTS CL

81 60

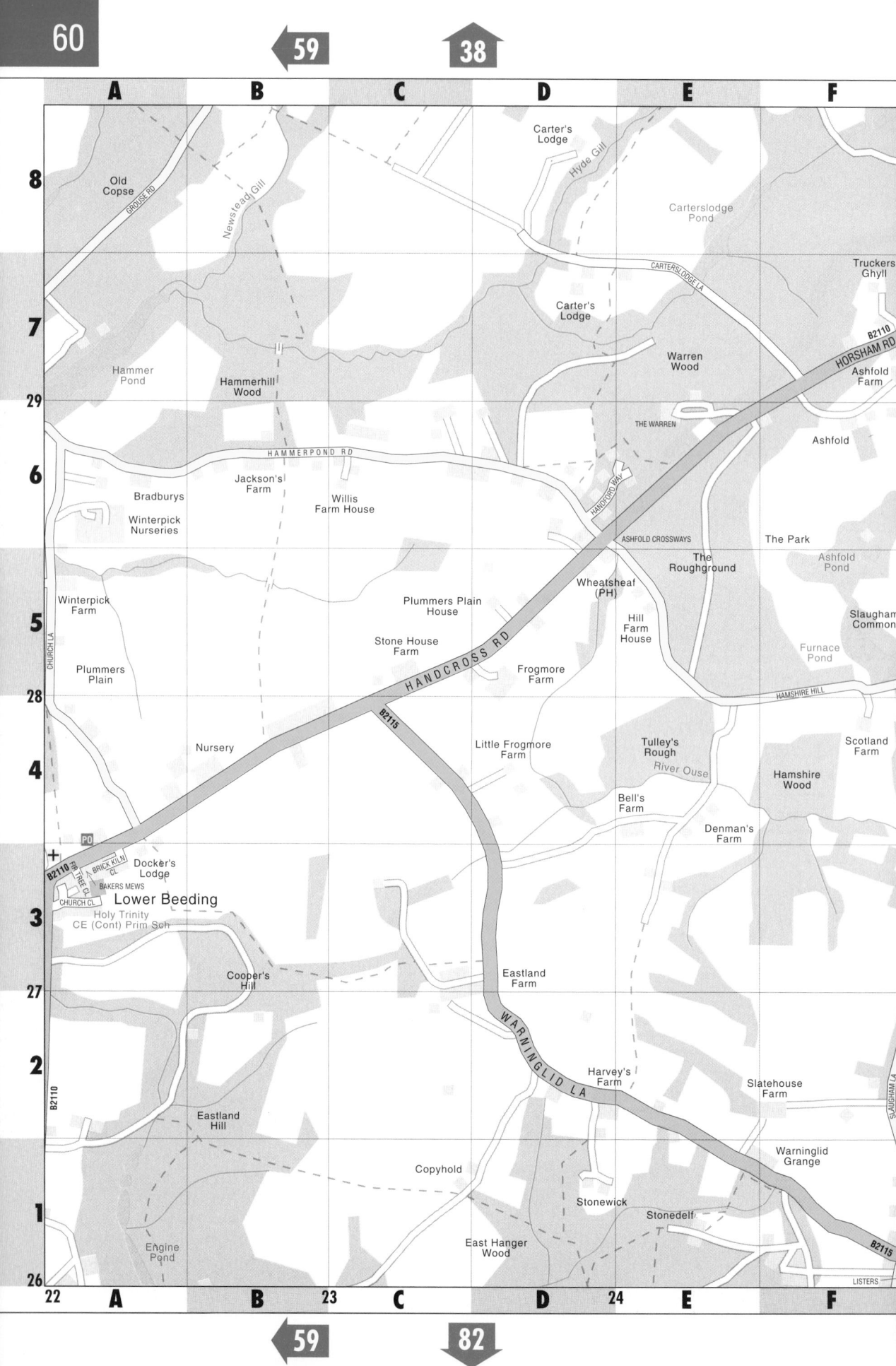

59
38

A B C D E F

8

Old Copse

GROUSE RD

Newstead Gill

Carter's Lodge

Hyde Gill

Carterslodge Pond

7

Hammer Pond

Hammerhill Wood

Carter's Lodge

CARTERSLODGE LA

Warren Wood

Truckers Ghyll

B2110

HORSHAM RD

Ashfold Farm

29

HAMMERPOND RD

THE WARREN

Ashfold

6

Bradburys

Jackson's Farm

Willis Farm House

HANDFORD WAY

ASHFOLD CROSSWAYS

The Roughground

The Park

Ashfold Pond

Winterpick Nurseries

Winterpick Farm

CHURCH LA

Plummers Plain House

Wheatsheaf (PH)

Hill Farm House

Slaugham Common

5

Stone House Farm

HANDCROSS RD

Frogmore Farm

Furnace Pond

Plummers Plain

28

Nursery

B2115

Little Frogmore Farm

River Ouse

Tulley's Rough

Hamshire Hill

Hamshire Wood

Scotland Farm

4

Bell's Farm

Denman's Farm

PO

BRICK KILN CL

Docker's Lodge

+

B2110

FIR TREE CL

BAKERS MEWS

CHURCH CL

Lower Beeding

Holy Trinity CE (Cont) Prim Sch

3

Cooper's Hill

Eastland Farm

27

WARNINGLID LA

2

B2110

Eastland Hill

Harvey's Farm

Slatehouse Farm

SLAUGHAM LA

Copyhold

Warninglid Grange

1

Stonewick

Stonedelf

B2115

Engine Pond

East Hanger Wood

26

LISTERS

22 A B 23 C D 24 E F

59
82

39
62

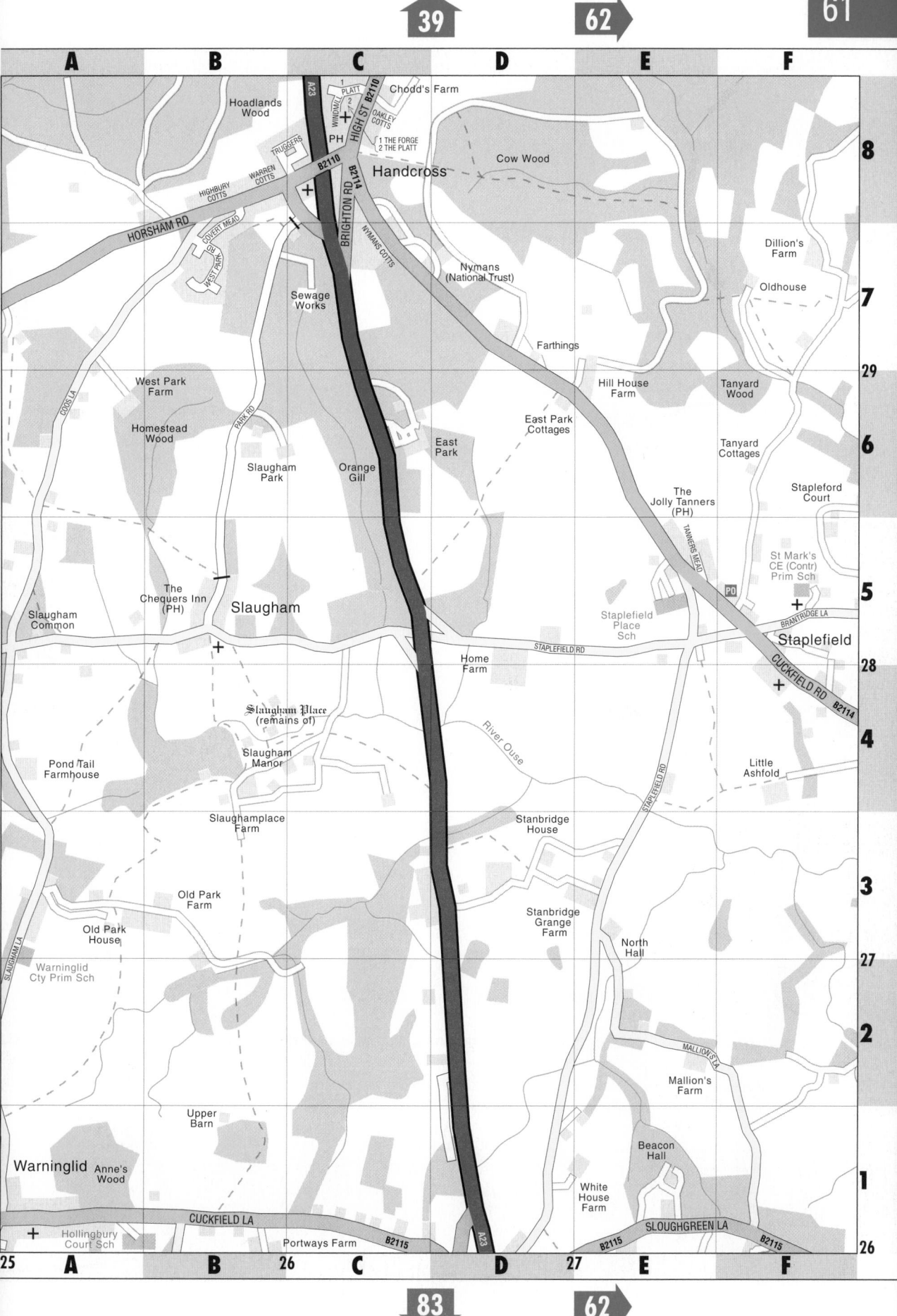
A
B
C
D
E
F
Hoadlands Wood
Chodd's Farm
PLATT
WINDMILL
HIGH ST B2110
OAKLEY COTTS
1 THE FORGE
2 THE PLATT
PH
TRUGGERS
B2110
B2114
Handcross
Cow Wood
HIGHBURY COTTS
WARREN COTTS
HORSHAM RD
COVERT MEAD
WEST PARK RD
BRIGHTON RD
NYMANS COTTS
Nymans (National Trust)
Sewage Works
Dillion's Farm
Oldhouse
Farthings
West Park Farm
Hill House Farm
Tanyard Wood
COOS LA
PARK RD
Homestead Wood
East Park Cottages
East Park
Tanyard Cottages
Slaugham Park
Orange Gill
The Jolly Tanners (PH)
Stapleford Court
TANNERS MEAD
St Mark's CE (Contr) Prim Sch
PO
The Chequers Inn (PH)
Slaugham
Slaugham Common
Staplefield Place Sch
BRANTRIDGE LA
Staplefield
STAPLEFIELD RD
Home Farm
CUCKFIELD RD
B2114
Slaugham Place (remains of)
River Ouse
Slaugham Manor
Pond Tail Farmhouse
Little Ashfold
STAPLEFIELD RD
Slaughamplace Farm
Stanbridge House
Old Park Farm
Stanbridge Grange Farm
Old Park House
North Hall
SLAUGHAM LA
Warninglid Cty Prim Sch
MALLION'S LA
Mallion's Farm
Upper Barn
Beacon Hall
Warninglid
Anne's Wood
White House Farm
CUCKFIELD LA
SLOUGHGREEN LA
Hollingbury Court Sch
Portways Farm
B2115
A23
B2115
B2115
8
7
29
6
5
28
4
3
27
2
1
26
25
26
27

83
62

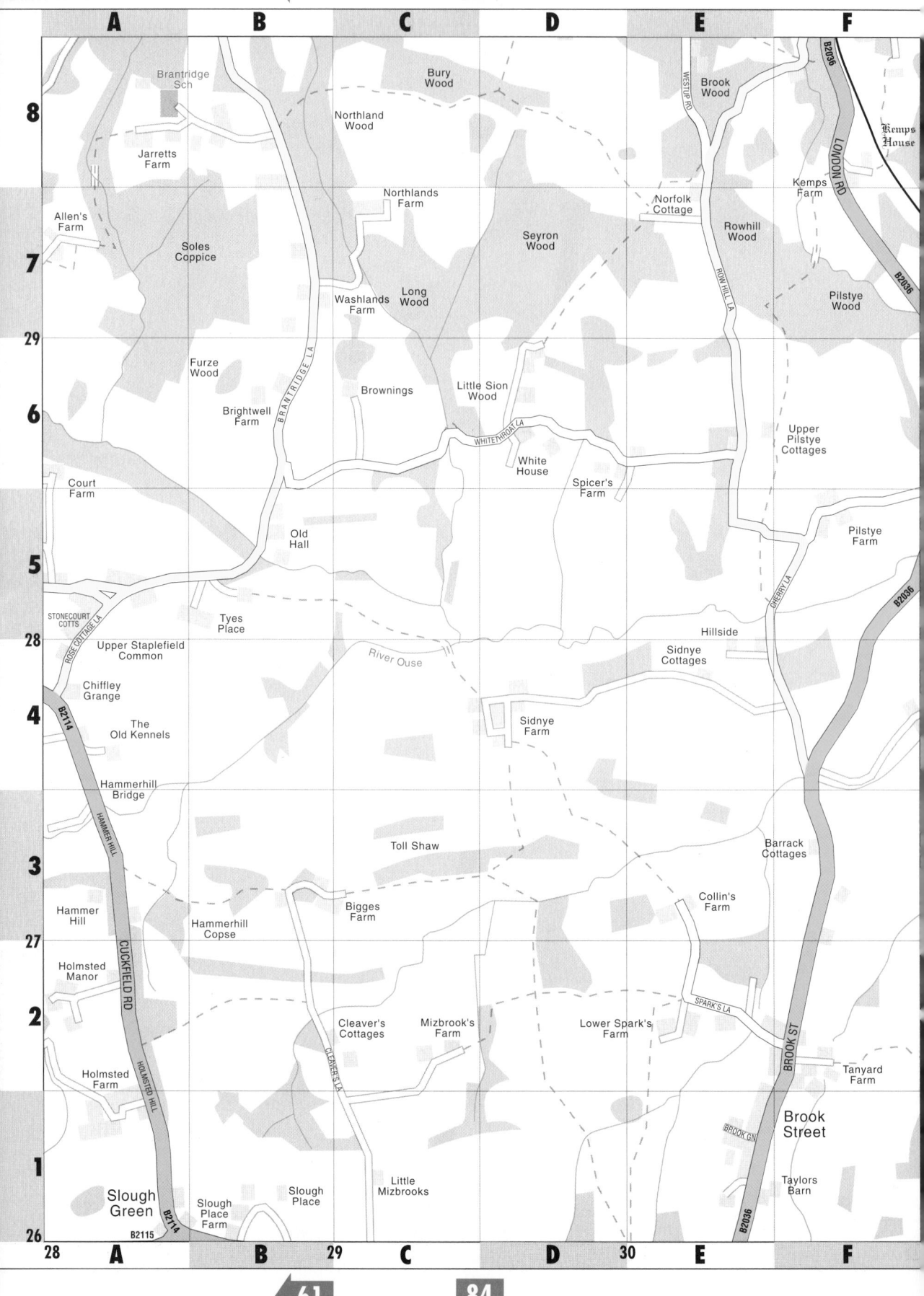

A B C D E F

8

Brantridge Sch

Northland Wood

Bury Wood

Brook Wood

WESTUP RD

Kemps House

Jarretts Farm

Northlands Farm

Norfolk Cottage

Kemps Farm

LONDON RD

Allen's Farm

Seyron Wood

Rowhill Wood

B2036

7

Soles Coppice

ROW HILL LA

Pilstye Wood

29

Furze Wood

Washlands Farm

Long Wood

Little Sion Wood

Brownings

Upper Pilstye Cottages

6

Brightwell Farm

BRANTRIDGE LA

WHITETHROAT LA

White House

Spicer's Farm

Court Farm

Old Hall

Pilstye Farm

5

Stonecourt Cotts

Tyes Place

Hillside

CHERRY LA

B2036

28

ROSE COTTAGE LA

Upper Staplefield Common

River Ouse

Sidnye Cottages

Chiffley Grange

Sidnye Farm

4

B2114

The Old Kennels

Hammerhill Bridge

HAMMER HILL

Barrack Cottages

3

Hammer Hill

Hammerhill Copse

Toll Shaw

Collin's Farm

27

Holmsted Manor

Bigges Farm

SPARK'S LA

2

CUCKFIELD RD

Cleaver's Cottages

Mizbrook's Farm

Lower Spark's Farm

BROOK ST

Tanyard Farm

Holmsted Farm

HOLMSTED HILL

CLEAVER'S LA

BROOK GN

Brook Street

1

Slough Green

Slough Place Farm

Slough Place

Little Mizbrooks

B2036

Taylors Barn

26

B2114

B2115

A B C D E F

41
64
85
64
A
B
C
D
E
F
8
7
29
6
5
28
4
3
27
2
1
26
31
32
33
Glebe Farm
Northlands Wood
Bowder's Farm
Naylands
HAYWARDS HEATH RD
SHELL LA
WEST HILL
BALCOMBE LA
CHURCH LA
Townhouse Farm
Ardingly Resr
Balcombe Place
STONEHALL LA
Stone Hall
Great Saucelands
College Farm
LONDON RD
Furland Wood
CHERRY LA
Sewage Works
Sand's Wood
Alder Wood
Ardingly Coll
Pilstye Ppg Sta
River Ouse
Ryelands Farm
Upper Ryelands Bridge
Ouse Valley Viaduct
River's Wood
Ryelands Wood
COLLEGE RD
Great Bentley Farm
RIVER'S RD
Skew Bridge
River's Farm
Wetlands Wood
Pinetum
BORDEHILL LA
Oak Plantation
Fountain Cottages
Little Bentley Wood
Naldred Farm
COPYHOLD LA
Copyhold Bridge
Borde Hill Gardens
Highgrove Barn
The Tolls
SANDRIDGE LA
HIGH BEECH LA
Haywards Heath Golf Course
Sugworth Wood
Sugworth Farm
CH
Lullings Farm

63
42

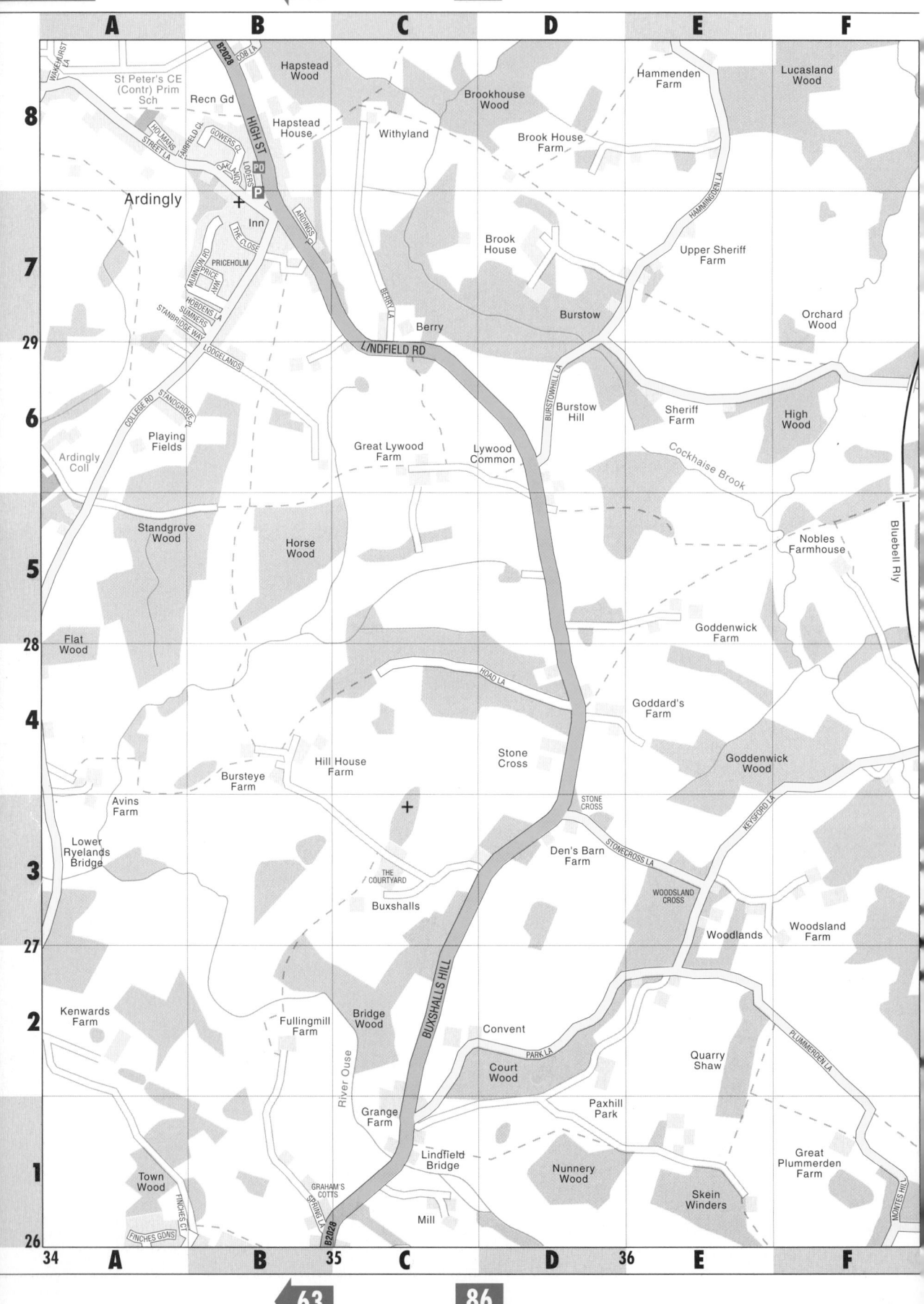
A
B
C
D
E
F
8
7
29
6
5
28
4
3
27
2
1
26
34
35
36
Ardingly
St Peter's CE (Contr) Prim Sch
Recn Gd
Hapstead Wood
Hapstead House
Withyland
Brookhouse Wood
Brook House Farm
Hammenden Farm
Lucasland Wood
HIGH ST
B2028
COB LA
WAKEHURST LA
HOLMANS
STREET LA
FAIRFIELD CL
GOWERS CL
OAKLANDS
LODERS
Inn
THE CLOSE
ARDINGS CL
MUNNION RD
PRICEHOLM
PRICE WAY
HOBDENS LA
SUMNERS
STANBRIDGE WAY
LODGELANDS
COLLEGE RD
STANDGROVE PL
BERRY LA
Berry
LINDFIELD RD
Brook House
Burstow
Upper Sheriff Farm
HAMMINGDEN LA
Orchard Wood
BURSTOWHILL LA
Burstow Hill
Sheriff Farm
High Wood
Playing Fields
Ardingly Coll
Great Lywood Farm
Lywood Common
Cockhaise Brook
Standgrove Wood
Horse Wood
Nobles Farmhouse
Bluebell Rly
Flat Wood
Goddenwick Farm
HOAD LA
Goddard's Farm
Stone Cross
Hill House Farm
Bursteye Farm
Goddenwick Wood
STONE CROSS
Avins Farm
KEYSFORD LA
Lower Ryelands Bridge
Den's Barn Farm
STONECROSS LA
THE COURTYARD
Buxshalls
WOODSLAND CROSS
Woodlands
Woodsland Farm
BUXSHALLS HILL
Kenwards Farm
Fullingmill Farm
Bridge Wood
Convent
PARK LA
Court Wood
Quarry Shaw
PLUMMERDEN LA
River Ouse
Grange Farm
Paxhill Park
Lindfield Bridge
Nunnery Wood
Great Plummerden Farm
Town Wood
GRAHAM'S COTTS
SPRING LA
FINCHES CT
FINCHES GDNS
Mill
Skein Winders
MONTES HILL

63
86

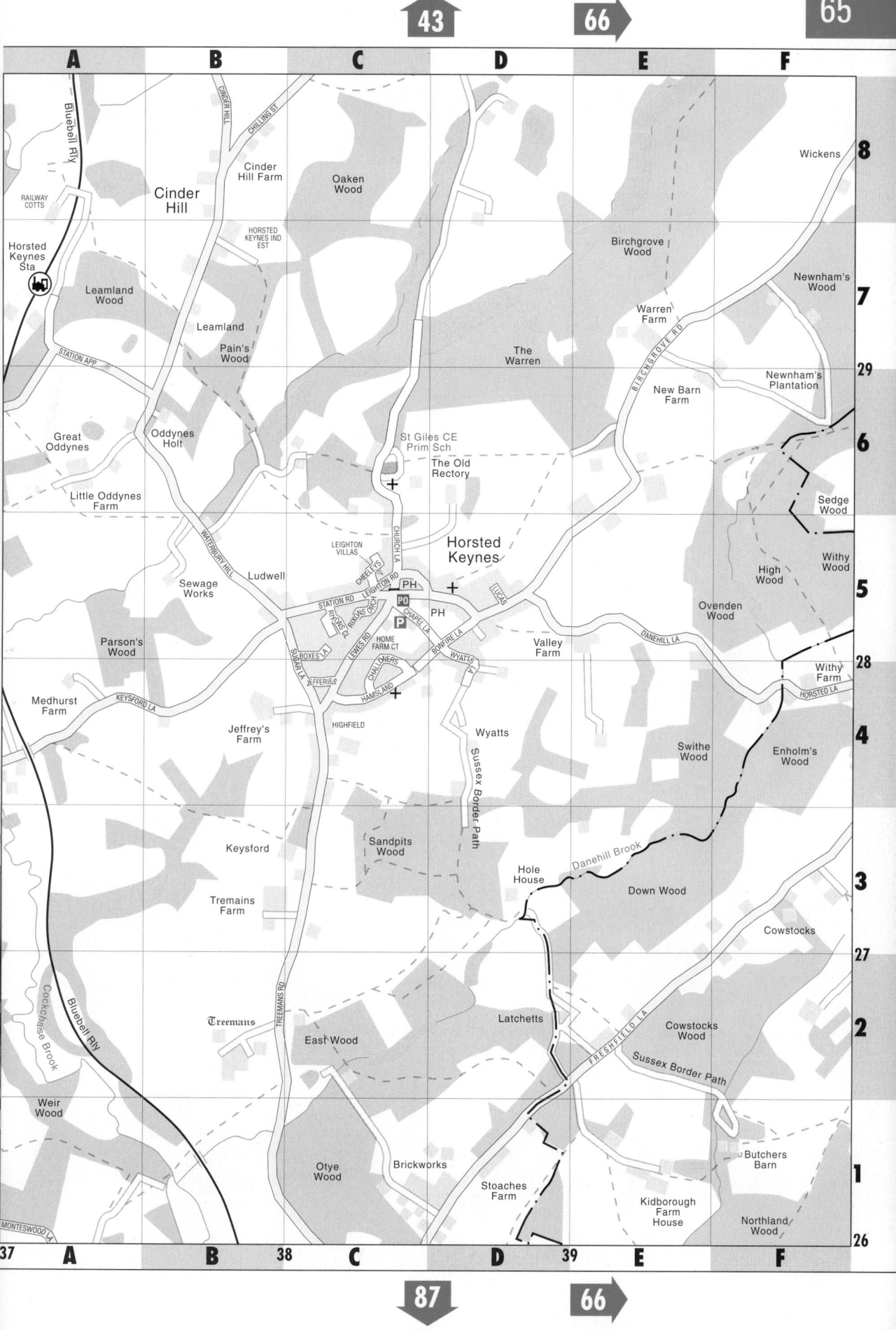

A B C D E F

8
Wickens

Cinder Hill Farm

Cinder Hill

Oaken Wood

Birchgrove Wood

Newnham's Wood
7

RAILWAY COTTS

Horsted Keynes Sta

Leamland Wood

HORSTED KEYNES IND EST

Warren Farm

29

STATION APP

Leamland

Pain's Wood

The Warren

New Barn Farm

Newnham's Plantation

Great Oddynes

Oddynes Holt

6
Sedge Wood

Little Oddynes Farm

St Giles CE Prim Sch

The Old Rectory

BIRCHGROVE RD

High Wood

Withy Wood

WATERBURY HILL

Ludwell

LEIGHTON VILLAS

CHURCH LA

CHEELEYS

Horsted Keynes

LEIGHTON RD

PH

Ovenden Wood

5

Sewage Works

STATION RD

RIMDAS ORCH

PO
P

PH

LUCAS

DANEHILL LA

Parson's Wood

SUGARLA

LEWES RD

CHAPEL LA

BONFIRE LA

WYATTS LA

Valley Farm

28
Withy Farm

HORSTED LA

Medhurst Farm

KEYSFORD LA

JEFFERIES

SUBOXES LA

CHALLONERS

HAMSLAND

HIGHFIELD

Wyatts

Sussex Border Path

Swithe Wood

Enholm's Wood

4

Jeffrey's Farm

Keysford

Sandpits Wood

Hole House

Danehill Brook

Down Wood

3

Cowstocks

Tremains Farm

27

Cockchaise Brook

Bluebell Rly

Treemans

TREEMANS RD

East Wood

Latchetts

FRESHFIELD LA

Sussex Border Path

Cowstocks Wood

2

Weir Wood

Butchers Barn

1

Otye Wood

Brickworks

Stoaches Farm

Kidborough Farm House

Northland Wood

MONTESWOOD LA

26

65
44

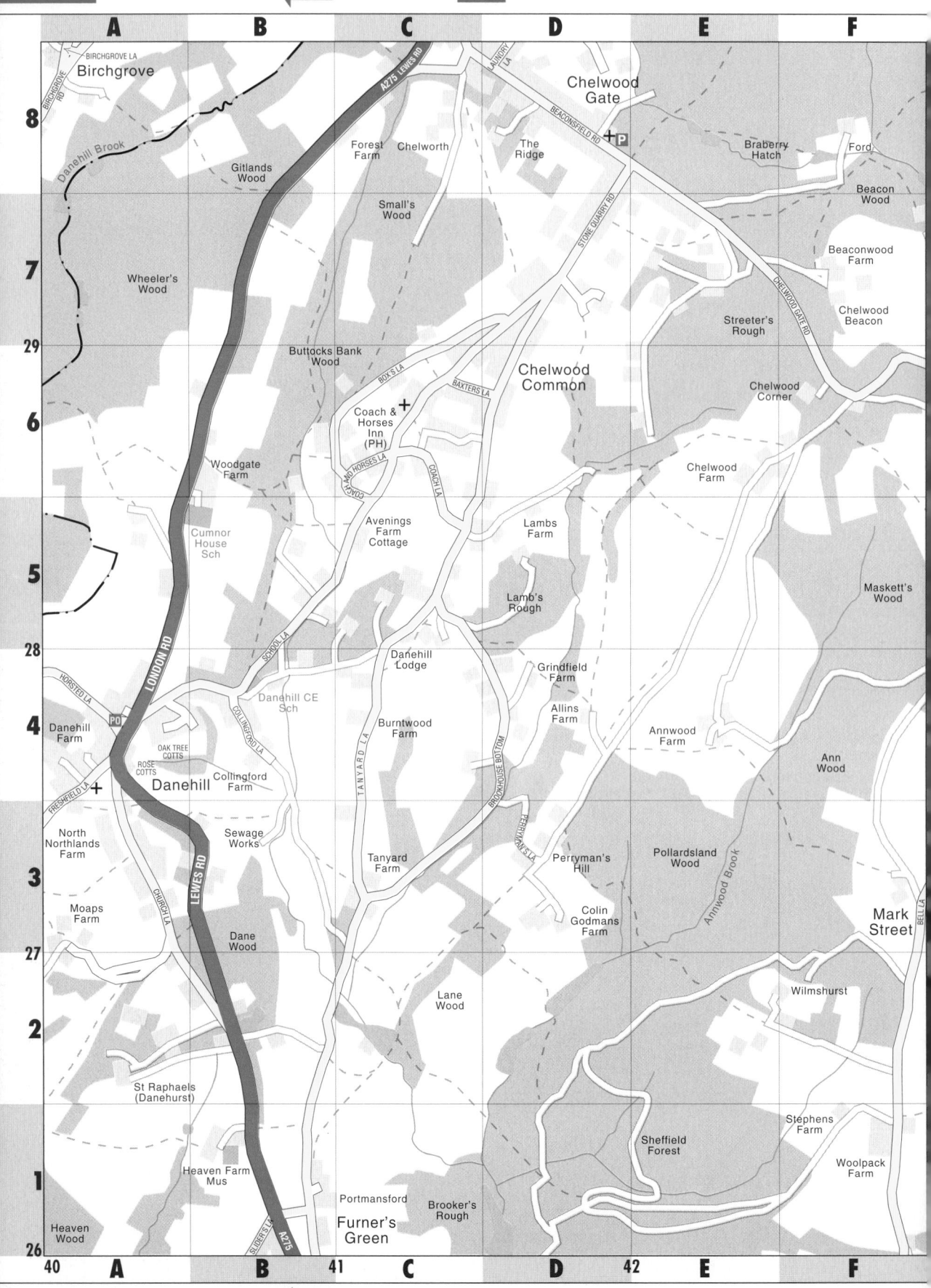
A
B
C
D
E
F
Birchgrove
BIRCHGROVE LA
BIRCHGROVE RD
A275 LEWES RD
LAUNDRY LA
Chelwood Gate
BEACONSFIELD RD
P
Danehill Brook
Gitlands Wood
Forest Farm
Chelworth
The Ridge
Braberry Hatch
Ford
Beacon Wood
Small's Wood
STONE QUARRY RD
Beaconwood Farm
Wheeler's Wood
Streeter's Rough
CHELWOOD GATE RD
Chelwood Beacon
Buttocks Bank Wood
Chelwood Common
BOX'S LA
BAXTERS LA
Chelwood Corner
Coach & Horses Inn (PH)
Woodgate Farm
COACH AND HORSES LA
COACH LA
Chelwood Farm
Avenings Farm Cottage
Lambs Farm
Cumnor House Sch
Maskett's Wood
Lamb's Rough
SCHOOL LA
LONDON RD
Danehill Lodge
Grindfield Farm
HORSTED LA
Danehill CE Sch
PO
Allins Farm
Danehill Farm
Burntwood Farm
Annwood Farm
COLLINGFORD LA
OAK TREE COTTS
ROSE COTTS
Danehill
Collingford Farm
TANYARD LA
BROOKHOUSE BOTTOM
Ann Wood
FRESHFIELD LA
PERRYMAN'S LA
North Northlands Farm
Sewage Works
LEWES RD
Tanyard Farm
Perryman's Hill
Pollardsland Wood
Annwood Brook
CHURCH LA
Colin Godmans Farm
Moaps Farm
Mark Street
BELL LA
Dane Wood
Wilmshurst
Lane Wood
St Raphaels (Danehurst)
Stephens Farm
Sheffield Forest
Heaven Farm Mus
Woolpack Farm
Portmansford
Brooker's Rough
Heaven Wood
SLIDER'S LA
A275
Furner's Green
8
7
29
6
5
28
4
3
27
2
1
26
40
41
42

65

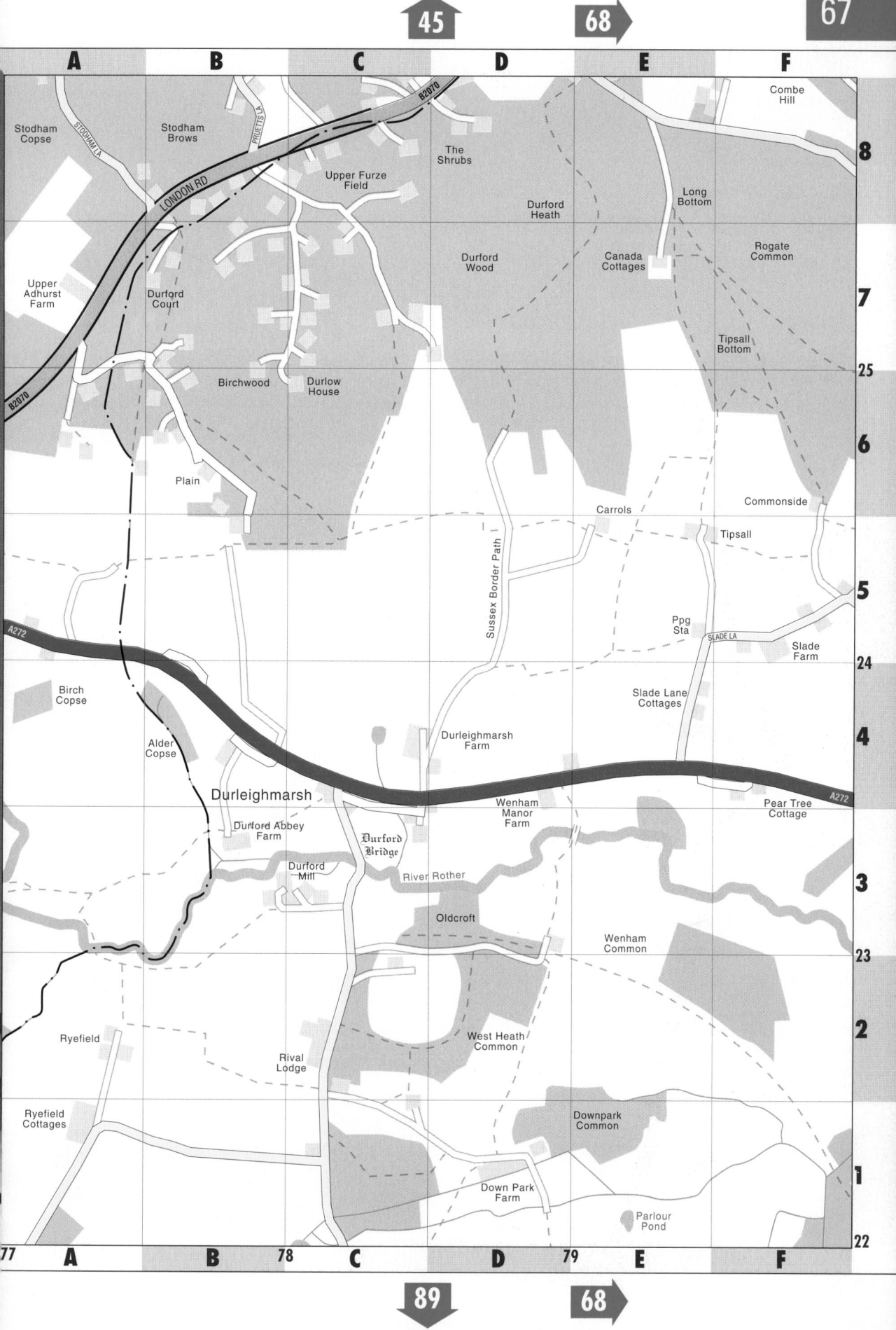

A B C D E F

8

Combe
Hill

Stodham
Copse

Stodham
Brows

The
Shrubs

Upper Furze
Field

Durford
Heath

Long
Bottom

7

Upper
Adhurst
Farm

Durford
Court

Durford
Wood

Canada
Cottages

Rogate
Common

25

Birchwood

Durlow
House

Tipsall
Bottom

6

Plain

Commonside

Carrols

Tipsall

5

Birch
Copse

Sussex Border Path

Ppg
Sta

SLADE LA

Slade
Farm

24

Alder
Copse

Slade Lane
Cottages

4

A272

Durleighmarsh
Farm

Durleighmarsh

Durford Abbey
Farm

Durford
Bridge

Wenham
Manor
Farm

Pear Tree
Cottage

A272

Durford
Mill

River Rother

3

Oldcroft

Wenham
Common

23

Ryefield

Rival
Lodge

West Heath
Common

2

Ryefield
Cottages

Downpark
Common

1

Down Park
Farm

Parlour
Pond

22

77 A B 78 C D 79 E F

67
46

A
B
C
D
E
F
8
7
25
6
5
24
4
3
23
2
1
22
80
81
82
Tullecombe
Tullecombe
(Picnic Place)
Wiseland
Hill
Fyning
Hill
Trotton
Marsh
Cairn
Wood
Rondle
Wood
Redhill
Copse
Fyning
Common
BORDEN LA
Borden
Rogate
Lodge
TERWICK RISE
GATEHOUSE LA
Halecommon
Home
Farm
FYNING LA
Terwick
Common
Dangstein
Ship
Copse
Stonehouse
Home
Farm
Cumber's La
Fyning
PH
Rogate
PO
EAST
LODGE
RED HOUSE CT
PARSONAGE EST
Rogate
CE
(Contr)
Prim Sch
HUGO PLATT
A272
HABIN HILL
GARBITTS LA
Mill's Farm House
Terwick
Land
Fyning
Moor
Sewage
Works
Souter's
Copse
A272
Haben
Farm
Habin
Bridge
Wakeham
Farm
Habin
Mizzards
River Rother
Fair
Oak
Sandhill
Farm
Sandhill
House
The
Mount
New
Barn
Sandilands
Equestrian Ctr

67
90

A B C D E F

8

7

25

6

5

24

4

23

2

22

A B C D E F

Bobbolds Farm

Three Ponds Wood

Borden Wood

Jungle Wood

BORDEN LA

Holm Wood

Cumber's Farm

GATEHOUSE LA

Gatehouse Farm

Cumberspark Wood

MILL LA

ROTHER LA

Trotton

Trotton Bridge

The Keepers Arms (PH)

Terwick Mill

TERWICK LA

Black Pond

Trotton Common

COOK'S POND RD

Hammer Stream

Kingsham Wood

Kingsham Farm

Wick Wood

Pond Copse

CHITHURST LA

New Bridge

Chithurst Manor

Chithurst

Ambletts

Trotton Farm

MILLAND RD

Cemy

MOORHOUSE LA

Robins Farm

ROBIN'S

Stubb Hill

Stubb Hill Farm

Hammer Wood

Hammer Pond

Horn Hill

HAMMER LA

Hammer Stream

Hammer Hanger

River Rother

Crowshole Farm

Iping Marsh

Dunner Hill

LAMBOURNE LA

Queen's Corner

Lyford Copse

Lower Bowley Copse

Titty Hill

Upper Bowley Copse

Bowley Farm

Stubbs Farm House

Coopers Heath

IPING LA

Stedham Marsh

Wispers Copse

Oakham Common

Tentworth

Ash House

STANWATER LA

Hammerwood House

Crouchhouse Farm

Iping

Rotherhill House

Nurseries

HAMILTON CL

COMMON VIEW

PH

SCHOOL LA

ELSTED RD

A272

Stedham Cty Prim Sch

69
48

A   **B**   **C**   **D**   **E**   **F**

A286

8

Woolbeding
Common

Scotland
Farmhouse

Little
Common

West Heath

The
Lair

7

Linch
Old
Rectory

Lord's
Common

Madam's
Farm

KING'S DR

25

Woolhouse
Farm

Pound
Farm

H
King Edward VII

6

St Cuthman's
Sch

Tote
Hill

Great
Common

Pound
Common

Eastshaw
Farm

Hollist
Common

5

Woodgate
Farm

Chapelland
Copse

24

Old
School

Paylins
Copse

Chapelland
Buildings

Cherryorchard
Cottage

4

Lock's
Cottages

Whitters
Farm

Farthings

Old
Buddington

STEDHAM LA

WOOLBEDING LA

EASTSHAW LA

OLD BUDDINGTON LA

BUDDINGTON LA

3

Brambling
Farm

Hurst Hills

Stedham
Mill

BRAMBLING LA

Buddington
Farm

23

MILL LA

Woolbeding

River Rother

HOLLIST LA

Hollist
House

UPPERFIELD

2

Bridgefoot

+
Woolbeding
House

WEAVERS CL

DODSLEY GR

Stedham
Bridge

Stedham
Hall

+

Sewage
Works

Midhurst
Cottage

A286

H

QUEENS

THE ALLEY

1

COMMON VIEW

THE STREET

Stedham

STRATHMOOR
GDNS

Midhurst
Gram Sch
(Contr)

DODSLEY LA

NORTH ST

A272

SCHOOL LA

Great House
Farm

Woolbeding
Bridge

22

69
92

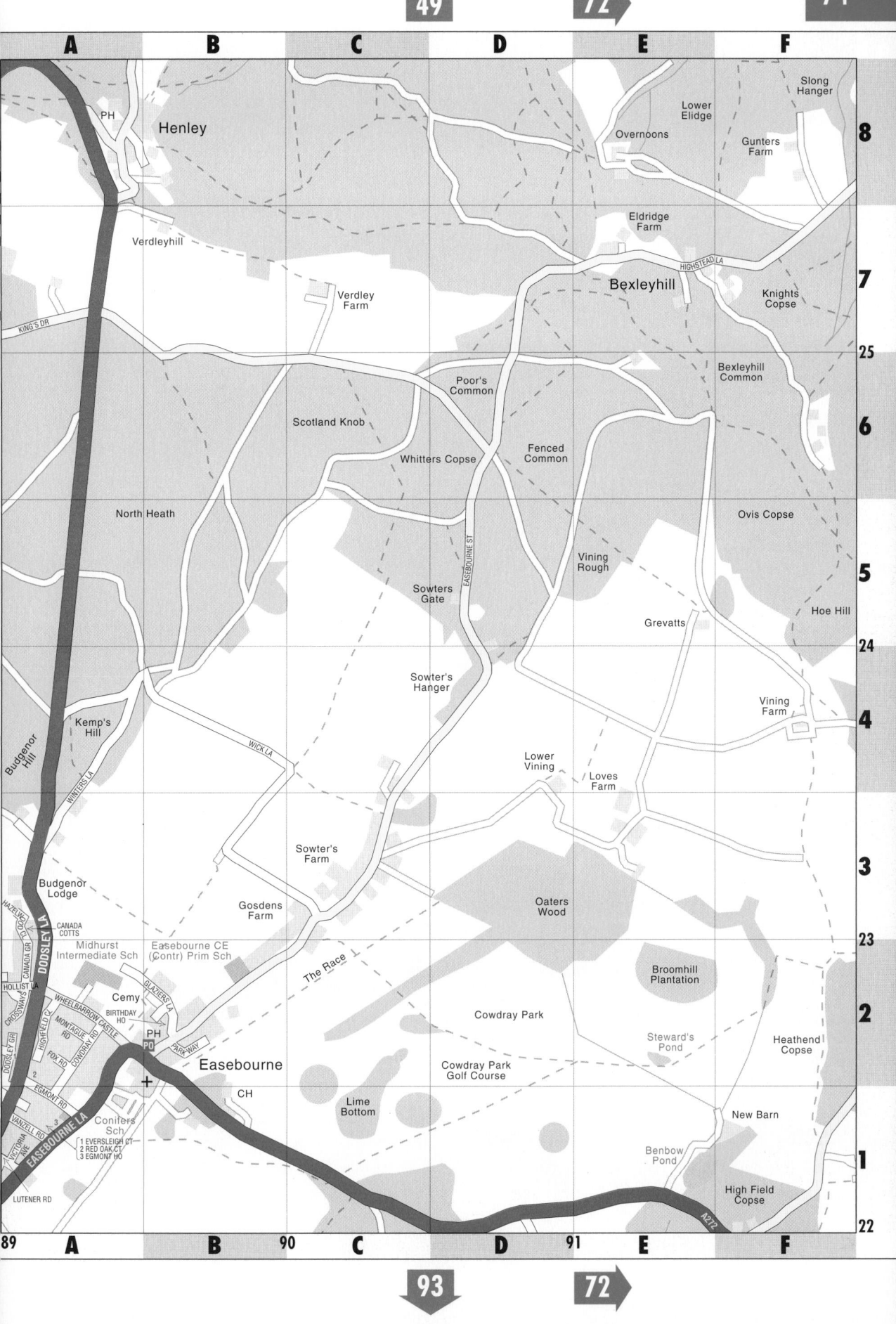

49
72

A   B   C   D   E   F

8

PH

Henley

Slong
Hanger

Lower
Elidge

Overnoons

Gunters
Farm

Verdleyhill

Eldridge
Farm

HIGHSTEAD LA

7

Verdley
Farm

Bexleyhill

Knights
Copse

KING'S DR

25

Poor's
Common

Bexleyhill
Common

Scotland Knob

6

Whitters Copse

Fenced
Common

Ovis Copse

North Heath

EASEBOURNE ST

Vining
Rough

5

Sowters
Gate

Hoe Hill

Grevatts

24

Sowter's
Hanger

Vining
Farm

Budgenor Hill

Kemp's
Hill

WICK LA

4

WINTERS LA

Lower
Vining

Loves
Farm

Sowter's
Farm

3

Budgenor
Lodge

Gosdens
Farm

Oaters
Wood

HAZELINE CT

CANADA GR

DODSLEY LA

CANADA
COTTS

23

Midhurst
Intermediate Sch

Easebourne CE
(Contr) Prim Sch

The Race

Broomhill
Plantation

GLAZIERS LA

HOLLIST CL

Cemy

Cowdray Park

2

WHEELBARROW CASTLE

BIRTHDAY
HO

HIGHFIELD CL

MONTAGUE RD

COWDRAY RD

Steward's
Pond

Heathend
Copse

DODSLEY GR

FOX RD

PH
PO

PARK WAY

Easebourne

Cowdray Park
Golf Course

2

EGMONT RD

CH

Lime
Bottom

New Barn

VANZELL RD

VICTORIA AVE

EASEBOURNE LA

Conifers
Sch

1 EVERSLEIGH CT
2 RED OAK CT
3 EGMONT HO

Benbow
Pond

High Field
Copse

1

LUTENER RD

A272

22

89   A   B   90   C   D   91   E   F

71
50

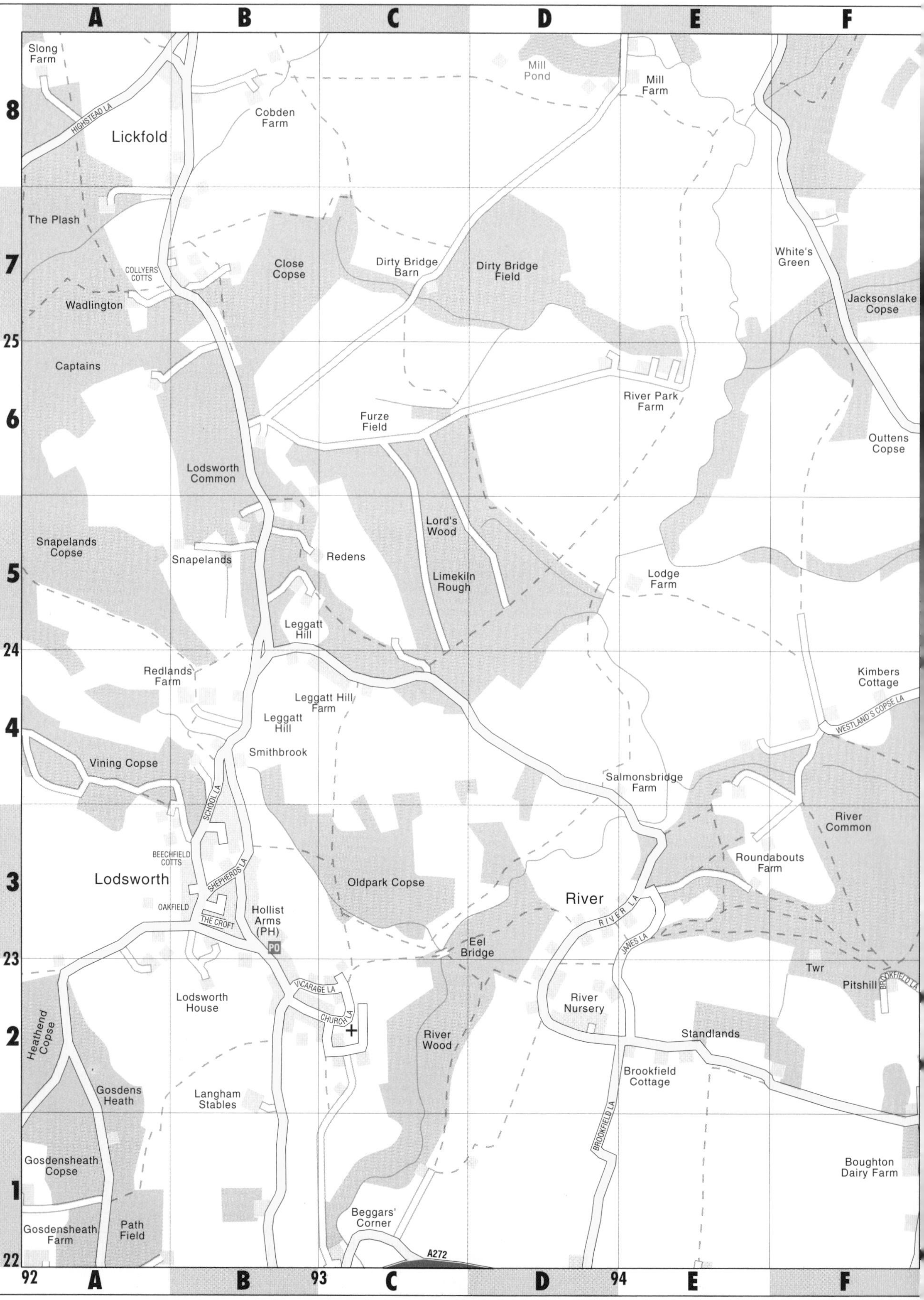

A   **B**   **C**   **D**   **E**   **F**

Slong Farm

HIGHSTEAD LA

Lickfold

Mill Pond

Mill Farm

Cobden Farm

8

The Plash

COLLYERS COTTS

Close Copse

Dirty Bridge Barn

Dirty Bridge Field

White's Green

7

Wadlington

Jacksonslake Copse

25

Captains

River Park Farm

Outtens Copse

6

Furze Field

Lodsworth Common

Lord's Wood

Snapelands Copse

Snapelands

Redens

Limekiln Rough

Lodge Farm

5

Leggatt Hill

Redlands Farm

Kimbers Cottage

24

Leggatt Hill Farm

WESTLANDS COPSE LA

Leggatt Hill

4

Vining Copse

Smithbrook

Salmonsbridge Farm

River Common

SCHOOL LA

Roundabouts Farm

BEECHFIELD COTTS

SHEPHERDS LA

Oldpark Copse

River

RIVER LA

3

Lodsworth

OAKFIELD

THE CROFT

Hollist Arms (PH)

PO

JANES LA

23

Heathend Copse

Lodsworth House

VICARAGE LA

Eel Bridge

River Nursery

Twr

Pitshill

BROOKFIELD LA

CHURCH LA

River Wood

Standlands

2

Gosdens Heath

Langham Stables

Brookfield Cottage

BROOKFIELD LA

Gosdensheath Copse

Boughton Dairy Farm

1

Beggars' Corner

Gosdensheath Farm

Path Field

22

A272

92   **A**   **B**   **93**   **C**   **D**   **94**   **E**   **F**

A   B   C   D   E   F

8

7

25

6

5

24

4

23

3

2

1

22

Glasshouse
Pond
Plantation

Dry
Pond

Stagpark
Farm

Jacksonslake
Plantation

Spring
Pond
Rough

Great
Spring
Pond

Palfrey
Farm

Hoads
Common

Pug's
Bottom
Roughs

Osiers
Farm

Kiln
Copse

Pheasantcopse
Lodge

Little
Spring
Pond

W Twr

W Twr

Burrell's
Cottage

Parkhurst
Farm

Pheasant
Copse

Limbo

Raffling
Wood

Limbo
Farm

Westlands
Copse

Keyfox
Farm

Adelaide
Lodge

WESTLAND'S COPSE LA

Ratford
Farm

Halfmoon
Furze

Shepherds
Cottage

Guntersbridge
Farm

Upper
Copse

Nithurst
Farm

Gunter's
Bridge

Upperton
Common

Mon

Lower
Pond

Upper
Lodge

Upperton

Westbrook
House

Kennels

Cemy

HAMPERS GN

Hampers
Common

Petworth Park
Deer Park

HAMPERS
COMMON
IND EST

NEW RD

Dene
Dip

Upperton
Farm

UPPERTON RD

PARK TERR

LINTON HO

CEMETERY LA

DEAN LA

The Manor
of Dean

Horse
Guards
Inn
(PH)

PO

Upper
Pond

Boat
House

NORTH END CL

NORTHMEAD

Cemy

HORSHAM RD A272

A283

NORTH ST A272

THOMPSON'S
HOSPITAL

GLEBE
VILLAS

A283

95

96

97

A B C D E F

73
52

8

Pug's Bottom
Langhurst Common
Langhurst Farm

Old Elkham Farm

Crawfold Furze

GUNDERSGATE LA

7

Witley Copse

Holland Wood

Old Wood

Medhone Farm

25

Holland Wood Cottage

Petsalls Copses

6

Stedmans Journey

Medhone Copse

5

Blackbrook Farm

No Man's Land

Bennyfold Copse

Wilderness

Bennyfold Farm House

BLACKHOUSE LA

24

Warren Wood

Rushout Wood

4

Moor Farm

Pondtail Copse

3

Westland Farm

Buckfold Farm

GLASSHOUSE LA

A272

23

Lower Roxalls

Oldham Copse

Beechfield

2

Upper Roxalls

Foxhill

Selscome Farm

HORSHAM RD

Hilliers

Oldham Hill

Wickhams Hanger

KINGSPIT LA

Flexham Park

Dairy

A272

Flathurst Stables

1

Flathurst

Brinksole Heath

Brinksole Farm

Montpelier Farm

22

98 A B 99 C D 00 E F

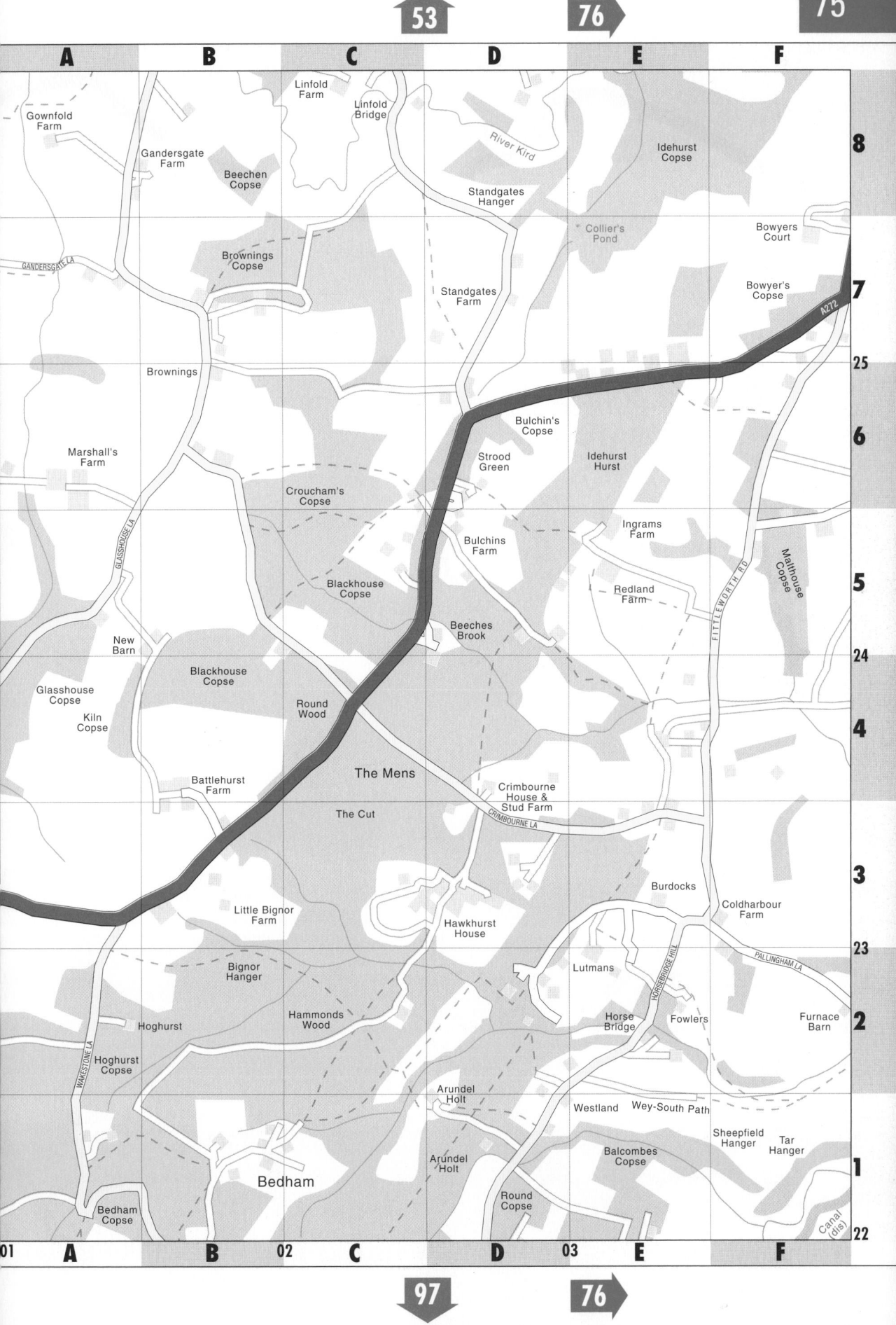

Gownfold
Farm

Linfold
Farm

Linfold
Bridge

River Kird

Idehurst
Copse

Gandersgate
Farm

Beechen
Copse

Standgates
Hanger

Collier's
Pond

Bowyers
Court

GANDERSGATE LA

Brownings
Copse

Standgates
Farm

Bowyer's
Copse

A272

7

25

Brownings

Bulchin's
Copse

Strood
Green

Idehurst
Hurst

6

Marshall's
Farm

Croucham's
Copse

Bulchins
Farm

Ingrams
Farm

Malthouse
Copse

GLASSHOUSE LA

Blackhouse
Copse

Redland
Farm

FITTLEWORTH RD

5

New
Barn

Blackhouse
Copse

Beeches
Brook

24

Glasshouse
Copse

Round
Wood

4

Kiln
Copse

Battlehurst
Farm

The Mens

Crimbourne
House &
Stud Farm

The Cut

CRIMBOURNE LA

Burdocks

Coldharbour
Farm

3

Little Bignor
Farm

Hawkhurst
House

PALLINGHAM LA

23

Bignor
Hanger

Lutmans

HORSEBRIDGE HILL

Hoghurst

Hammonds
Wood

Horse
Bridge

Fowlers

Furnace
Barn

2

WAKESTONE LA

Hoghurst
Copse

Arundel
Holt

Westland

Wey-South Path

Sheepfield
Hanger

Tar
Hanger

Bedham

Arundel
Holt

Balcombes
Copse

1

Bedham
Copse

Round
Copse

Canal
(dis)

22

A   B   C   D   E   F

8

Old Farm

THE LILY

CARTERS WAY

MEADOWBANK

THORNTON MEADOW

PO

BALCHINS CL.

PH   Sch

P

Wisborough Green

GLEBE WAY

WISBOROUGH COMN.

Green Bridge

A272

River Kird

Sewage Works

Wharf Farm

New Bridge

A272

Arun Canal (dis)

Guildenhurst Bridge

7

Tanyard Copse

Harsfold Copse

Orfold Farm

Guildenhurst Manor

25

Streele Farm

6

Harsfold Manor

Harsfold Farm

Harsfold Hanger

River Arun

Lording's Lock

Brockhurst Brook

Lowfold

Tanners Farm

B2133

5

Wey-South Path

Lordings Rough

24

Shipbourne Farm

Frithwood Farm

Woodlands Farm

Knobs Crook

4

Haybarn

Wey & Arun Canal (dis)

Lee Place House

North Wood

Westlands Farm

Wabblegate Farm

3

Northwood Farm

Bramley Field

23

Haybourne

2

Snape Farm

Furnacepond Cottages

PALLINGHAM LA

P   P

Pallingham Manor Farm

Rawstick Copse

1

Toat Wood

Stable Barn Farm

The Thimes

BLACK GATE LA

Brinsbury Coll of Agriculture & Horticulture

STANE ST

A29

22

04   A   B   05   C   D   06   E   F

55
78

A B C D E F
Newbridge Farm
NEWBRIDGE RD
Bridgewaters Farm
The Limeburners (PH)
Parbrook
The Weald Sch
Jun & Inf Schs
Billingshurst
Billingshurst Sta
Ind Est
GILLMANS IND EST
Hammonds
Little Daux Farm
ROSIER COMM CTR
CONEYHURST RD
EAST ST
WEST ST
HIGH ST
ALICKS HILL
STATION RD
LOWER STATION RD
Rosier Gate
Rosier Wood
Beck Copse
Par Brook
Brockhurst Brook
Sewage Works
Great Lordings Wood
LORDINGS RD
Little Gillmans Farm
Kingsfold
Andrew's Hill
Denham's Farm
Lordings Farm
Stonepits Rough
Kingslea Farm
Lordings Cottages
Providence Cottage
STANE ST
MARRINGDEAN RD
Oakdene
Marringdean Farmhouse
Hadfold Farm
Southlands Farm
Marringdean Wood
Hadfold Wood
South House Farm
Adversane
Blacksmiths Arms (PH)
WALNUT TREE COTTS
Coombland Farm
Jackmans Farm
Steepwood Copse
ADVERSANE LA
Highfure
WEST CHILTINGTON LA
Steepwood Farm
Brookdale Farm
Wood Barn Farm
Todhurst Farm (Brinsbury Coll annexe)
8 7 25 6 5 24 4 3 23 2 1 22
07 08 09

99
78

77
56

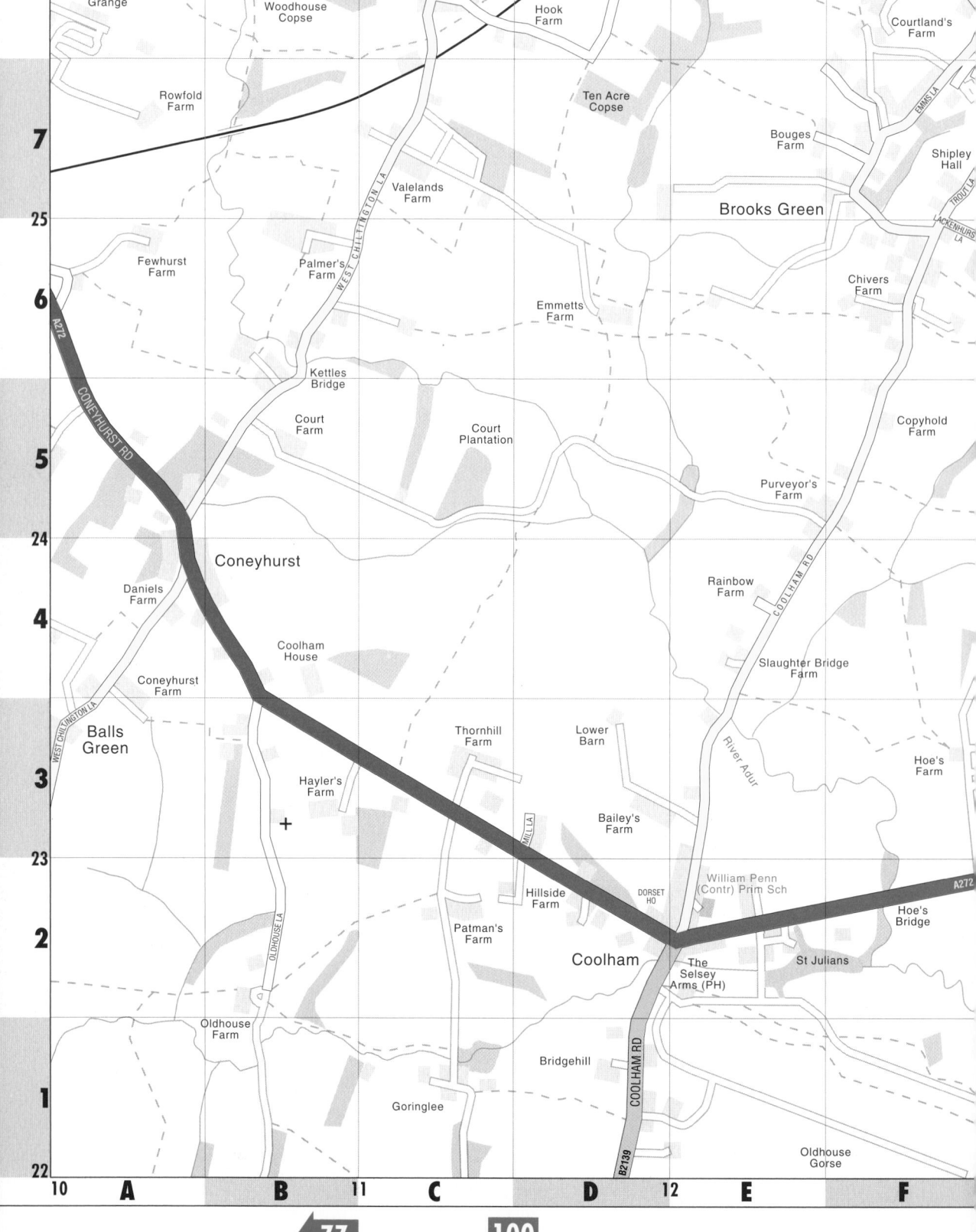
A
B
C
D
E
F
8
7
25
6
5
24
4
3
23
2
1
22
10
11
12
Rowfold
Grange
Woodhouse
Copse
Duncan's
Hook
Farm
Bullbrook House
Farm
Courtland's
Farm
Rowfold
Farm
Ten Acre
Copse
Bouges
Farm
EMMS LA
Shipley
Hall
TROUT LA
Valelands
Farm
WEST CHILTINGTON LA
Brooks Green
Fewhurst
Farm
Palmer's
Farm
Chivers
Farm
A272
Emmetts
Farm
Kettles
Bridge
Court
Farm
Court
Plantation
Copyhold
Farm
CONEYHURST RD
Purveyor's
Farm
Coneyhurst
Daniels
Farm
Rainbow
Farm
COOLHAM RD
Coolham
House
Slaughter Bridge
Farm
Coneyhurst
Farm
WEST CHILTINGTON LA
Balls
Green
Thornhill
Farm
Lower
Barn
River Adur
Hoe's
Farm
Hayler's
Farm
MILL LA
Bailey's
Farm
William Penn
(Contr) Prim Sch
A272
Hillside
Farm
DORSET
HO
Hoe's
Bridge
Patman's
Farm
OLDHOUSE LA
Coolham
The
Selsey
Arms (PH)
St Julians
Oldhouse
Farm
Bridgehill
COOLHAM RD
Goringlee
B2139
Oldhouse
Gorse

77
100

A B C D E F

8

7

25

6

5

24

4

23

3

2

1

22

Madgeland Wood
Crookhorn Farm
Chase Farm
Birch Wood
Birchwood Farm
St Johns Farm
Marlpost Wood
Blinks Wood
Netherwood
The Gill
Middle Wood
Rascals Farm
Lackenhurst Furzefield
Northlands Wood
Woodfords
Trawler's Farm
Woodgetters
The Delph
Newbuildings Plantation
Newbuildings Place
The Plantation
Brick Kiln Farm
Abraham's Plantation
Baker's Farm
Goffsland Farm
Hoe's Wood
Shepherd's Farm
Hartsgravel Bridge
Old Keepers Cott
Hoe's Wood
Renche's Cott
Dragons Green
Hoe's Farm
Oakleigh Farm
The George and Dragon (PH)
Renche's Wood
Cock's Hill
Great Cockshill Wood
Cuckoo Barn
SCOLLIERS CROSSWAYS
DRAGONS GREEN COUNCIL COTTS
Green Street
Shipley Paygate
A272
Butterstocks Farm
Greenstreet Farm
North Lodge
Lodge Farm
Perrets
Jackie's Copse
POUND LA
Spring Wood
Merrik Wood
Ashbrook Bridge
Greenstreet Furzeland
Knepp Park
Knight's Farm
Shipley CE (Contr) Prim Sch
Church Farm North
RED LA

TROUT LA
MARLPOST RD
SHAW'S LA
ASH RD
COLLEGE RD
WORTHING RD
Southwater County Park
WOODLANDS WAY
BEECHWOOD
MILL STRAIGHT
WEALDON CL
THE GABLES
FOXES CL
TREE TOPS
ANDREWS RD
LITTLE C'
FOXFIELD COTTS
OAK CL
CALSC
BASH
THE FIELDINGS
COUNCIL COTTS 1
INGLENOOK 2
ANDREWS COTTS 3
LACKENHURST LA
NETHERWOODS RD
DRAGONS GREEN RD
SHIPLEY RD
BAKER'S LA
DRAGONS LA
SMITHERS HILL LA
SCHOOL LA

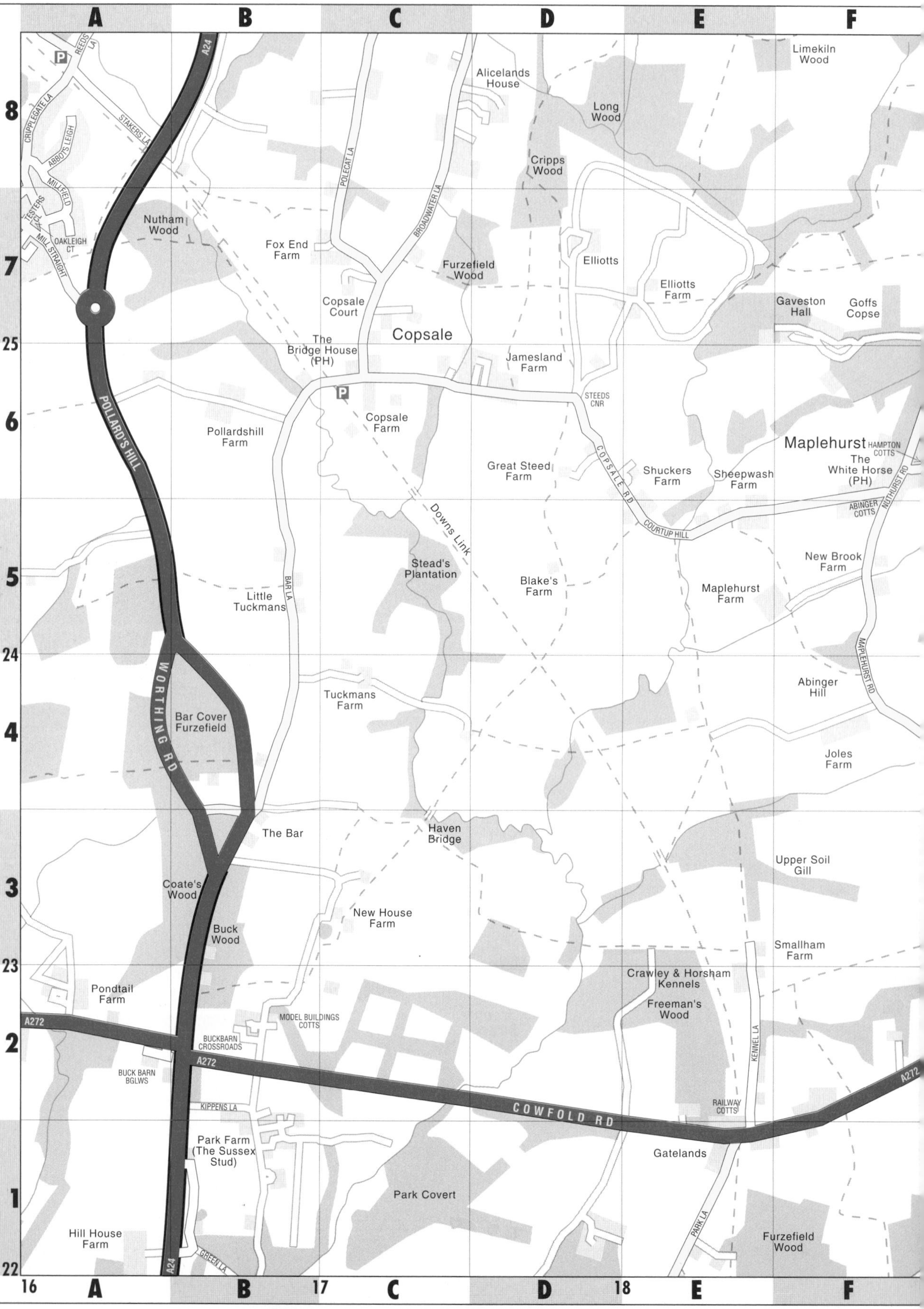

A B C D E F

8

7

25

6

5

24

4

3

23

2

1

22

Limekiln Wood

Alicelands House

Long Wood

Cripps Wood

Fox End Farm

Furzefield Wood

Elliotts

Elliotts Farm

Gaveston Hall

Goffs Copse

Copsale Court

Copsale

The Bridge House (PH)

Jamesland Farm

STEEDS CNR

Maplehurst

HAMPTON COTTS

The White Horse (PH)

ABINGER COTTS

NUTHURST RD

Pollardshill Farm

Copsale Farm

Great Steed Farm

Shuckers Farm

Sheepwash Farm

COURTUP HILL

New Brook Farm

Nutham Wood

POLLARD'S HILL

A24

STAKERS LA

REEDS LA

CRIPPLEGATE LA

ABBOTS LEIGH

MILLFIELD

STERS LA

OAKLEIGH CT

MILL STRAIGHT

POLECAT LA

BROADWATER LA

COPSALE RD

MAPLEHURST RD

Downs Link

BAR LA

Stead's Plantation

Little Tuckmans

Blake's Farm

Maplehurst Farm

Abinger Hill

WORTHING RD

Bar Cover Furzefield

Tuckmans Farm

Joles Farm

Haven Bridge

Upper Soil Gill

The Bar

Coate's Wood

Buck Wood

New House Farm

Smallham Farm

Pondtail Farm

A272

MODEL BUILDINGS COTTS

BUCKBARN CROSSROADS

A272

Crawley & Horsham Kennels

Freeman's Wood

KENNEL LA

BUCK BARN BGLWS

KIPPENS LA

Park Farm (The Sussex Stud)

Cowfold Rd

RAILWAY COTTS

A272

Gatelands

Hill House Farm

A24

GREEN LA

Park Covert

PARK LA

Furzefield Wood

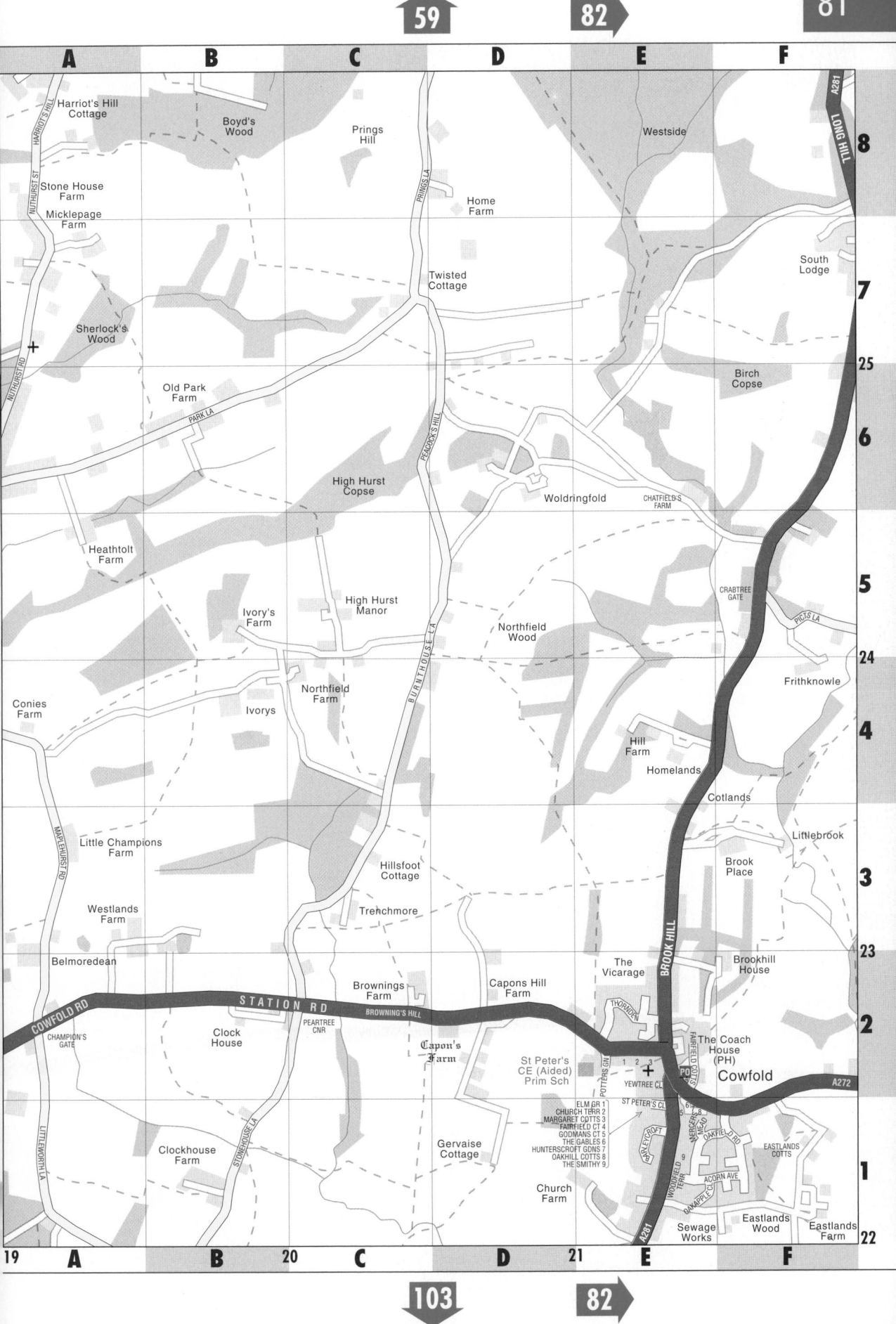

59
82

A   B   C   D   E   F

Harriot's Hill Cottage

Boyd's Wood

Prings Hill

Westside

LONG HILL

A281

8

Stone House Farm

Micklepage Farm

Home Farm

Twisted Cottage

South Lodge

7

Sherlock's Wood

25

Birch Copse

Old Park Farm

PARK LA

PEACOCK'S HILL

PRINGS LA

6

High Hurst Copse

Woldringfold

CHATFIELD'S FARM

CRABTREE GATE

PICTS LA

5

Heathtolt Farm

High Hurst Manor

Northfield Wood

24

Ivory's Farm

Frithknowle

Conies Farm

BURN HOUSE LA

Northfield Farm

Hill Farm

4

Ivorys

Homelands

Cotlands

Little Champions Farm

Littlebrook

MAPLEHURST RD

Brook Place

3

Hillsfoot Cottage

Brookhill House

23

Westlands Farm

Trenchmore

The Vicarage

BROOK HILL

Belmoredean

Brownings Farm

Capons Hill Farm

The Coach House (PH)

Cowfold

2

STATION RD

BROWNING'S HILL

THORNDEN

FAIRFIELD COTTS

A272

COWFOLD RD

CHAMPION'S GATE

Clock House

PEARTREE CNR

POTTERS GN

St Peter's CE (Aided) Prim Sch

YEWTREE CL

ST PETER'S CL

FAIRFIELD

Capon's Farm

ELM GR 1
CHURCH TERR 2
MARGARET COTTS 3
FAIRFIELD CT 4
GODMANS CT 5
THE GABLES 6
HUNTERSCROFT GDNS 7
OAKHILL COTTS 8
THE SMITHY 9

EASTLANDS COTTS

1

STONEHOUSE LA

Clockhouse Farm

Gervaise Cottage

Church Farm

WOODFIELD TERR

ACORN AVE

OAKFIELD RD

Eastlands Wood

LITTLEWORTH LA

A281

Sewage Works

Eastlands Farm

22

19 A   B 20 C   D 21 E   F

103
82

81
60

A
B
C
D
E
F
8
7
25
6
5
24
4
3
23
2
1
22
22
23
24
Hogstolt Hill
Leonardslee Gardens
New Pond
Lydhurst
Rifleman Inn (PH)
THE STREET
Barland's Farm
Freechase Hill
Crabtree
A281
LONG HILL
MILL CL
Minepits Wood
Free Chase Farm
The Lake
The Crabtree Inn (PH)
Furnace Pond
Free Chase
MILL LA
Steep Wood
Peppersgate Farm
Drewitts
PERRYFIELD LA
Round Wood
Den Wood
EARWIG LA
Goodgers
Bushy Platts
Long House
Denwood House
Graffields
Hookland Farm
Bull's Wood
CROSS COLWOOD LA
Chatesgrove
North Farm
Barnfield Wood
Colwood Manor Farm
PICTS LA
Chargrove
Westlands
Pict's Farm
Aglands
Spronkett's
BULL'S LA
Walhurst Manor
SMITH'S CROSS
Homefields
SPRONKETT'S LA
Kings Hill
Upper Barn
Barnfield House
Cooper's Farm
New Barn
Six Acre Shaw
Lyelands
Homewood House
Oakendene Manor
Southlands Farm
Greenacres Farm
A272
A272
OAKDENE IND EST
KENTSTREET LA
Bugshole Copse
WINEHAM LA
Taintfield Wood
Nye's Copse
Red House

81
104

61
84

A
B
C
D
E
F
Paternosters
North
Gravelies
Wood
Great
Thorndean
Farm
North
Gravelies
Farm
Moorfield
Farm
Colwood
Hill
Rout
Farm
Colwood
Court
Wr Twr
Playdells
Farm
Hill House
Farm
Wykehurst
Corner
The Hanger
Broxmead
Broxmead
Farm
Dan Tree
Farm
Wykehurst
Park
Bundys
New Park
Farm
Colwood
Park
Wykehurst
Park
Long
Wood
Horsmanshoad
Black
Forest
Oakview
Farm
Bolney
Wood
Nailard's
Wood
Buncton
Court
Woodland
Farm
Ragget's
Wood
Dalton's
Farm
Bolney
Pickwell
Bookers
Farm
Old
Highlands
Highlands
Bolney
CE (Contr)
Prim Sch
Foxhole
Ormonde
Hall
Hanger
Wood
Eight
Bells
Inn
(PH)
North
Wood
Farney Close Sch
Bolney Court
Foxashes
Purvey's
Cottages
Crosspost
Lovell's
Farm
Little
Gravenhurst
A23
B2115
A272
CUCKFIELD LA
SLOUGHGREEN LA
ORCHARD WAY
BROXMEAD LA
COLWOOD LA
JEREMY'S LA
CROSS COLWOOD LA
PICKWELL LA
PH
SPRINGFIELD COTTS
SPRINGFIELD CL
TOP ST
TYTHE BARN
BOLNEY LODGE LA
CHERRY LA
RYECROFT RD
BUNCTON LA
BOLNEY ST
DROVERS
PAYNESFIELD
BANKSIDE
FOXHOLE LA
P
PO
DIAMOND COTTS
CROSSPOST IND PK
CROSSPOST
COUNCIL COTTS
BOLNEY CHAPEL RD
BOLNEY CROSSWAYS
STAIRBRIDGE LA
8
7
25
6
5
24
4
3
23
2
1
22
25
26
27

105
84

83
62

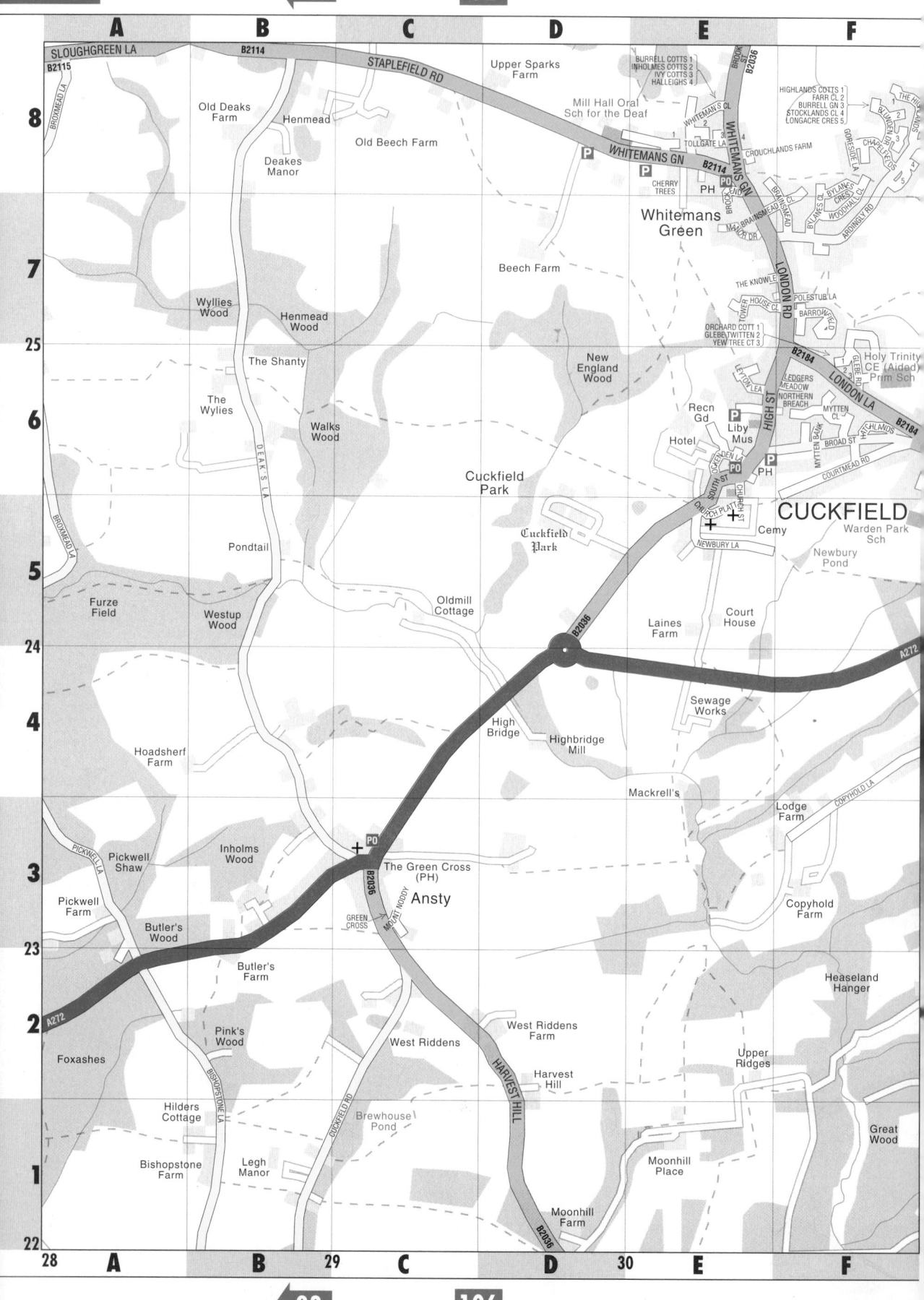
SLOUGHGREEN LA
B2115
B2114
STAPLEFIELD RD
Upper Sparks Farm
Old Deaks Farm
Henmead
Old Beech Farm
Mill Hall Oral Sch for the Deaf
Deakes Manor
WHITEMANS GN
Whitemans Green
Beech Farm
Wyllies Wood
Henmead Wood
The Shanty
New England Wood
The Wylies
Walks Wood
Cuckfield Park
CUCKFIELD
Pondtail
Furze Field
Westup Wood
Oldmill Cottage
Laines Farm
Court House
Sewage Works
High Bridge
Highbridge Mill
Hoadsherf Farm
Mackrell's
Lodge Farm
Inholms Wood
Pickwell Shaw
The Green Cross (PH)
Ansty
Pickwell Farm
Butler's Wood
Copyhold Farm
Butler's Farm
Heaseland Hanger
Pink's Wood
West Riddens Farm
West Riddens
Foxashes
Upper Ridges
Harvest Hill
Hilders Cottage
Brewhouse Pond
Great Wood
Bishopstone Farm
Legh Manor
Moonhill Place
Moonhill Farm
Warden Park Sch
Newbury Pond
Holy Trinity CE (Aided) Prim Sch
LONDON RD
HIGH ST
LONDON LA
A272
B2036
B2184
HARVEST HILL
CUCKFIELD RD
BISHOPSTONE LA
PICKWELL LA
DEAK'S LA
BROXMEAD LA
COPYHOLD LA
A B C D E F
8 7 6 5 4 3 2 1
25 24 23 22
28 29 30

83
106

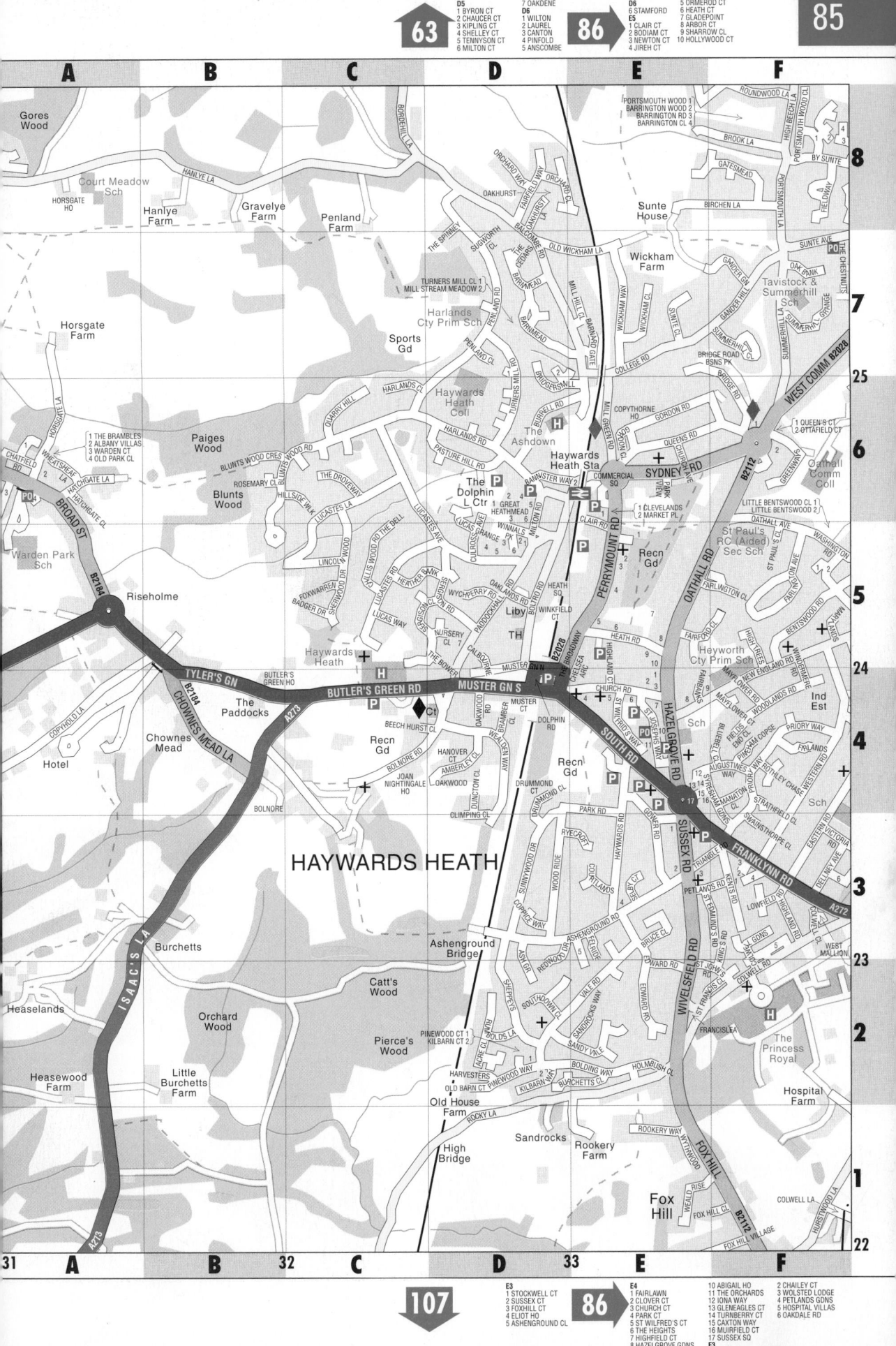

63

D5
1 BYRON CT
2 CHAUCER CT
3 KIPLING CT
4 SHELLEY CT
5 TENNYSON CT
6 MILTON CT

7 OAKDENE
D6
1 WILTON
2 LAUREL
3 CANTON
4 PINFOLD
5 ANSCOMBE

86

D6
6 STAMFORD
E5
1 CLAIR CT
2 BODIAM CT
3 NEWTON CT
4 JIREH CT

5 ORMEROD CT
6 HEATH CT
7 GLADEPOINT
8 ARBOR CT
9 SHARROW CL
10 HOLLYWOOD 1

HAYWARDS HEATH

107

E3
1 STOCKWELL CT
2 SUSSEX CT
3 FOXHILL CT
4 ELIOT HO
5 ASHENGROUND CL

86

E4
1 FAIRLAWN
2 CLOVER CT
3 CHURCH CT
4 PARK CT
5 ST WILFRED'S CT
6 THE HEIGHTS
7 HIGHFIELD CT
8 HAZELGROVE GDNS
9 HEATH CL

10 ABIGAIL HO
11 THE ORCHARDS
12 IONA WAY
13 GLENEAGLES CT
14 TURNBERRY CT
15 CAXTON WAY
16 MUIRFIELD CT
17 SUSSEX SQ
F3
1 HORSTED HO

2 CHAILEY CT
3 WOLSTED LODGE
4 PETLANDS GDNS
5 HOSPITAL VILLAS
6 OAKDALE RD

85
64

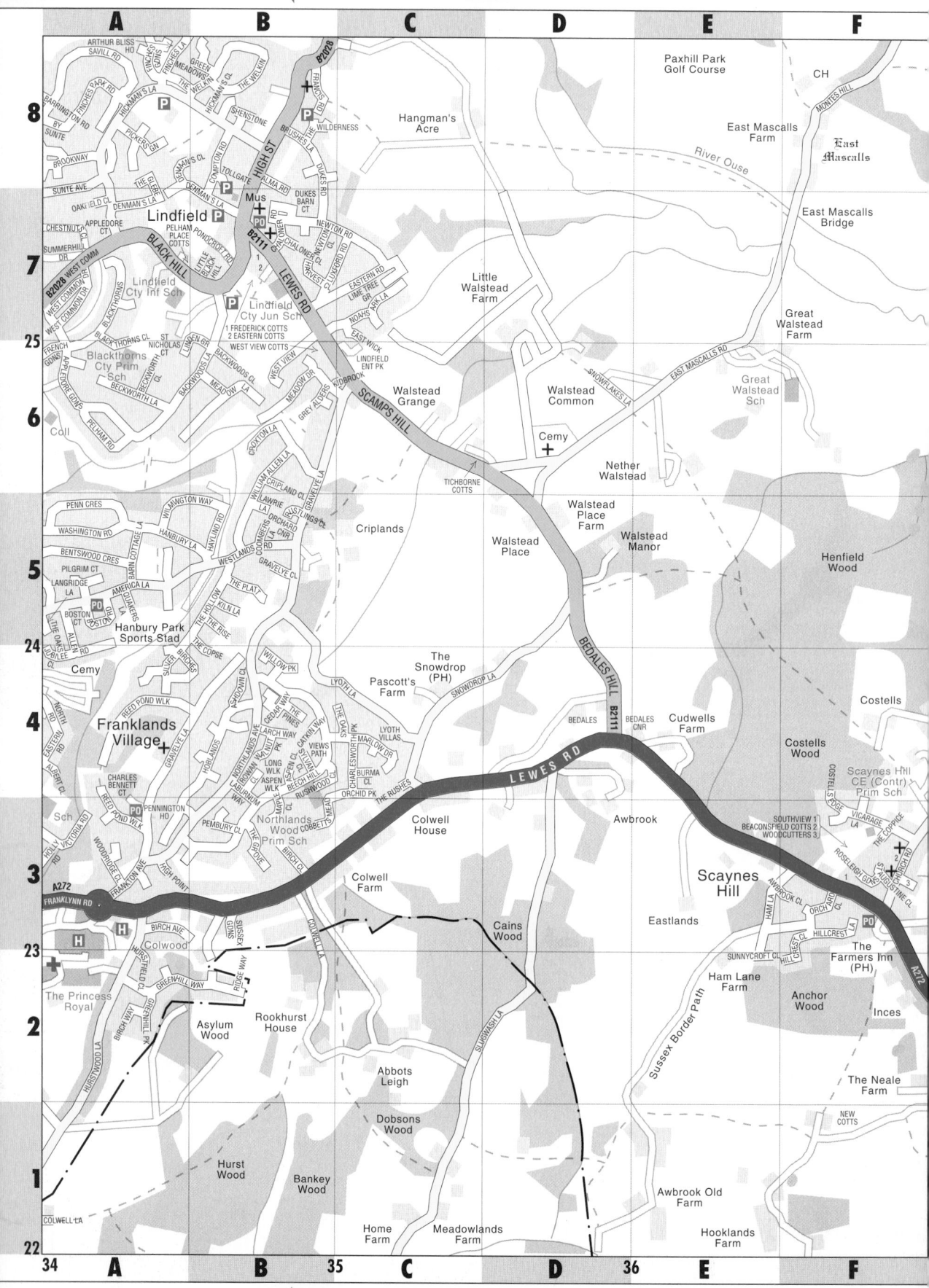
A
B
C
D
E
F
8
7
25
6
5
24
4
3
23
2
1
22
34
35
36
Lindfield
Mus
PO
Lindfield Cty Inf Sch
Lindfield Cty Jun Sch
Blackthorns Cty Prim Sch
Coll
HIGH ST
LEWES RD
BLACK HILL
SCAMPS HILL
BEDALES HILL
B2028
B2111
A272
FRANKLYNN RD
Paxhill Park Golf Course
CH
Hangman's Acre
East Mascalls Farm
East Mascalls
River Ouse
East Mascalls Bridge
Little Walstead Farm
Great Walstead Farm
EAST MASCALLS RD
Great Walstead Sch
Walstead Grange
Walstead Common
Cemy
Nether Walstead
TICHBORNE COTTS
Walstead Place Farm
Cripslands
Walstead Place
Walstead Manor
Henfield Wood
Hanbury Park Sports Stad
Cemy
The Snowdrop (PH)
Pascott's Farm
SNOWDROP LA
Franklands Village
BEDALES
BEDALES CNR
Cudwells Farm
Costells
Costells Wood
Scaynes Hill CE (Contr) Prim Sch
Colwell House
Awbrook
Northlands Wood Prim Sch
Sch
Scaynes Hill
Colwell Farm
Cains Wood
Eastlands
The Farmers Inn (PH)
Colwood
The Princess Royal
Ham Lane Farm
Anchor Wood
Asylum Wood
Rookhurst House
Inces
Sussex Border Path
Abbots Leigh
The Neale Farm
NEW COTTS
Dobsons Wood
Hurst Wood
Bankey Wood
Awbrook Old Farm
Home Farm
Meadowlands Farm
Hooklands Farm
COLWELL LA
SLUGWASH LA
HURSTWOOD LA

85

A
B
C
D
E
F
Cockhaise Mill Farm
COCKHAISE COTTS
Cockhaise Farm
MONTESWOOD LA
Wildboar Bridge
TREEMANS RD
FRESHFIELD LA
Freshfield Crossways
Northland Farm
Freshfield Halt
Freshfields
TOWN PLACE FARM COTTS
Town Place
KETCHE'S LA
King's Wood
Cockhaise Brook
Sussex Border Path
Town Place Farm
Town House Farm
SLIDERS LA
Round Wood
Bluebell Rly
Coneyborough Wood
Freshfield Mill Farm
Freshfield Bridges
Sewage Works
Old Canal
River Ouse
The Sloop Inn (PH)
Home Wood
Hammer Wood
Cole Wood
Nashgill Wood
Pegden House
Freshfield Place
Wapsbourne Wood
Nash Farm
Butterbox Farm
BUTTERBOX LA
Lye Wood
NASH LA
Yew Tree Farm
CHURCH RD
Watlands Farm
Watlands
Massetts
HUNT'S GATE
Wapsbourne Farm
Sennotts
CLEARWATER LA
Hammond's Farm
Sussex Border Path
BLACKBROOK LA
Rock Lodge Vineyard
Blackbrook Bridge
Rock Wood
Lindfield Farm
Warr's Wood
LEWES RD
ANCHOR HILL
Clear Water
Lindfield Wood
Warr's Farm
Great Wood
The Plantation
Chailey Heritage Craft Sch & Hospl (New Heritage)
Broadwater House
WARRS HILL LA
Pellingbridge Farm
BANKS RD
A275
Great Noven Farm
Springfield Farm
A272
8
7
25
6
5
24
4
3
23
2
1
22
37
38
39

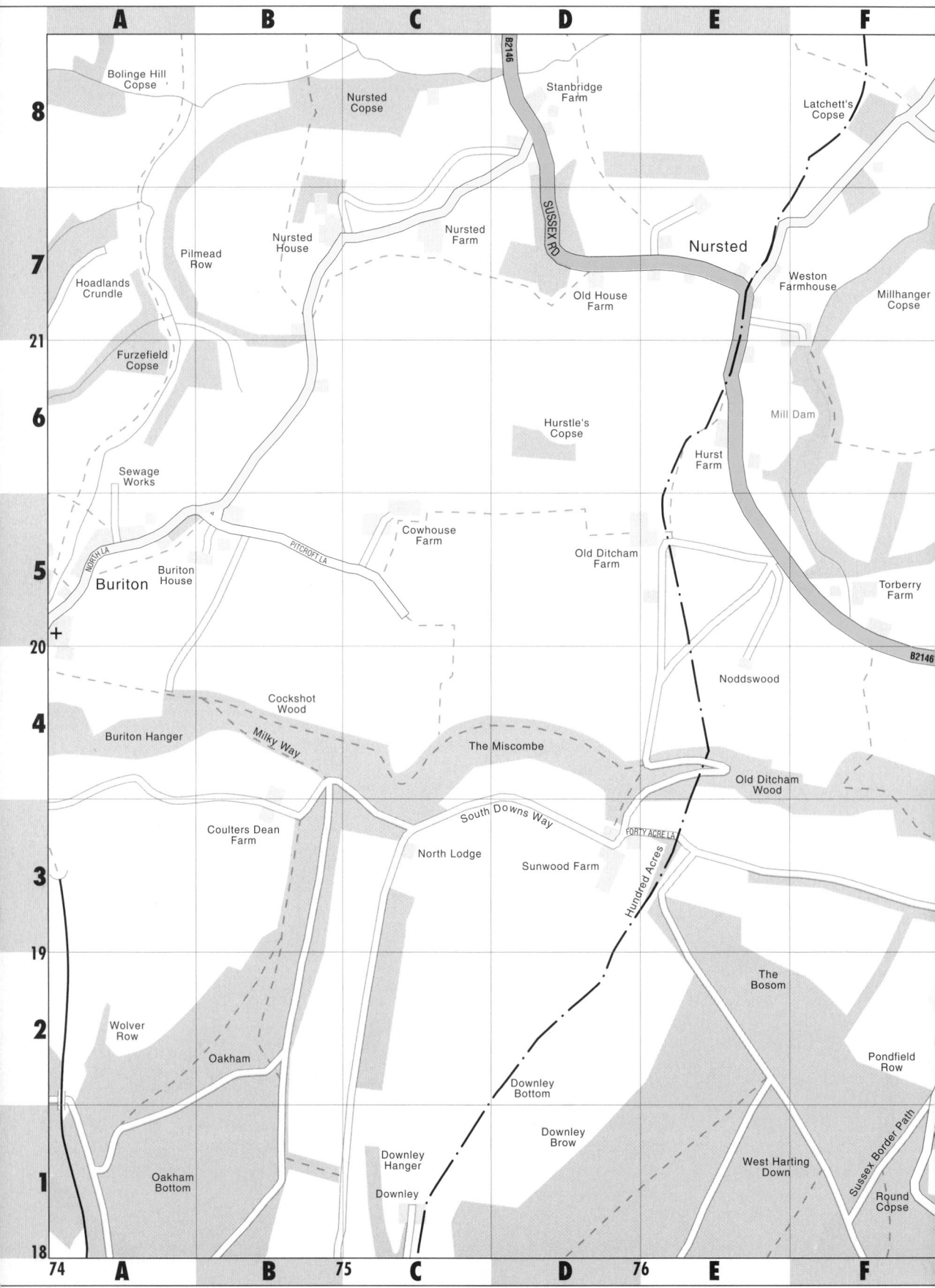

A
B
C
D
E
F
8
7
21
6
5
20
4
3
19
2
1
18
74
75
76
B2146
Bolinge Hill Copse
Nursted Copse
Stanbridge Farm
Latchett's Copse
Nursted House
Nursted Farm
SUSSEX RD
Nursted
Pilmead Row
Hoadlands Crundle
Old House Farm
Weston Farmhouse
Millhanger Copse
Furzefield Copse
Mill Dam
Hurstle's Copse
Hurst Farm
Sewage Works
Cowhouse Farm
Old Ditcham Farm
NORTH LA
PITCROFT LA
Buriton House
Buriton
Torberry Farm
B2146
Noddswood
Cockshot Wood
Buriton Hanger
Milky Way
The Miscombe
Old Ditcham Wood
South Downs Way
FORTY ACRE LA
Coulters Dean Farm
North Lodge
Sunwood Farm
Hundred Acres
The Bosom
Wolver Row
Oakham
Pondfield Row
Downley Bottom
Downley Brow
Sussex Border Path
Downley Hanger
West Harting Down
Oakham Bottom
Round Copse
Downley

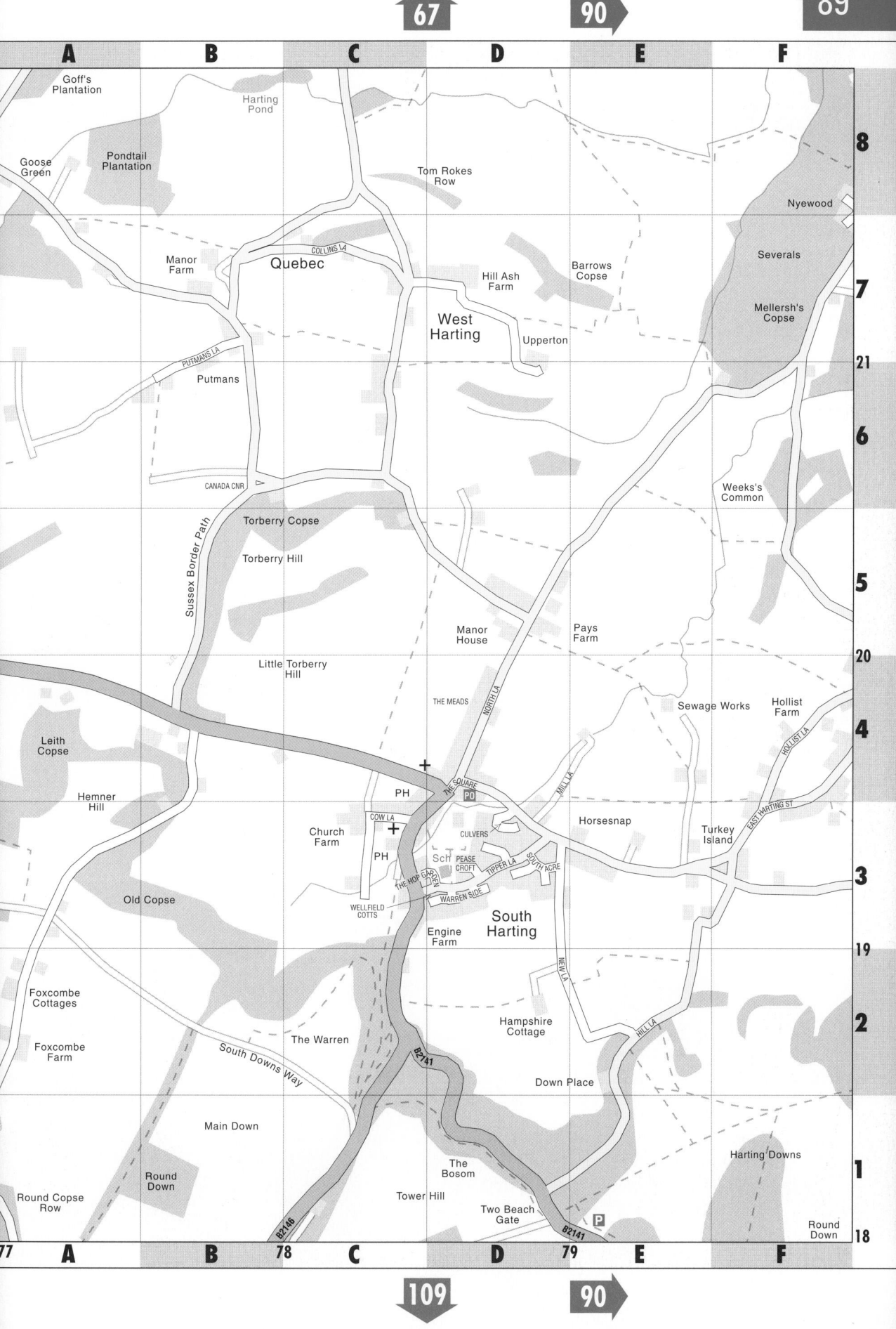
A
B
C
D
E
F
Goff's Plantation
Harting Pond
Goose Green
Pondtail Plantation
Tom Rokes Row
Nyewood
Manor Farm
Quebec
COLLINS LA
Hill Ash Farm
Barrows Copse
Severals
Mellersh's Copse
West Harting
Upperton
PUTMANS LA
Putmans
CANADA CNR
Weeks's Common
Torberry Copse
Torberry Hill
Sussex Border Path
Manor House
Pays Farm
Little Torberry Hill
THE MEADS
NORTH LA
Sewage Works
Hollist Farm
HOLLIST LA
Leith Copse
THE SQUARE
PO
MILL LA
PH
Hemner Hill
COW LA
Horsesnap
Church Farm
CULVERS
Turkey Island
EAST HARTING ST
PH
Sch
PEASE CROFT
TIPPER LA
SOUTH ACRE
THE HOP GARDEN
WARREN SIDE
Old Copse
WELLFIELD COTTS
South Harting
Engine Farm
NEW LA
Foxcombe Cottages
Hampshire Cottage
HILL LA
The Warren
Foxcombe Farm
B2141
South Downs Way
Down Place
Main Down
Harting Downs
The Bosom
Round Down
Round Copse Row
Tower Hill
Two Beach Gate
P
B2146
B2141
Round Down
8
7
21
6
5
20
4
3
19
2
1
18
77
78
79

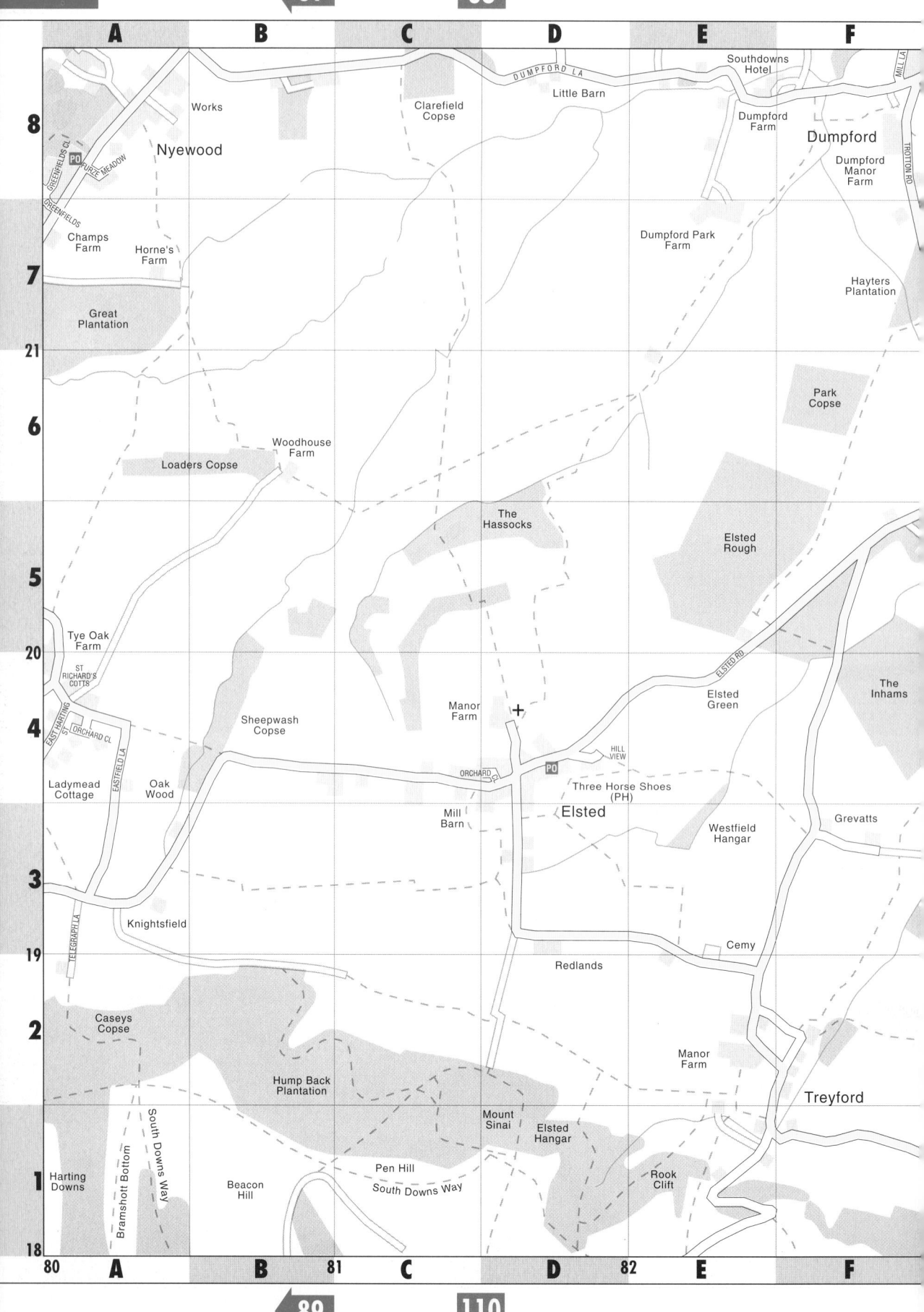

A B C D E F

8

Works

Nyewood

Clarefield
Copse

DUMPFORD LA

Little Barn

Southdowns
Hotel

Dumpford
Farm

Dumpford

MILL LA

TROTTON RD

PO

GREENFIELDS CL

PURLE MEADOW

Dumpford
Manor
Farm

GREENFIELDS

Champs
Farm

Horne's
Farm

7

Great
Plantation

Dumpford Park
Farm

Hayters
Plantation

21

Park
Copse

6

Woodhouse
Farm

Loaders Copse

The
Hassocks

Elsted
Rough

5

Tye Oak
Farm

20

ST
RICHARD'S
COTTS

Sheepwash
Copse

Manor
Farm

+

Elsted
Green

The
Inhams

ELSTED RD

4

EAST HARTING ST

ORCHARD CL

EASTFIELD LA

Oak
Wood

ORCHARD

PO

HILL
VIEW

Three Horse Shoes
(PH)

Elsted

Westfield
Hangar

Grevatts

Ladymead
Cottage

Mill
Barn

3

TELEGRAPH LA

Knightsfield

Redlands

Cemy

19

2

Caseys
Copse

Hump Back
Plantation

Manor
Farm

Treyford

1

Harting
Downs

Bramshott Bottom

South Downs Way

Beacon
Hill

Pen Hill

South Downs Way

Mount
Sinai

Elsted
Hangar

Rook
Clift

18

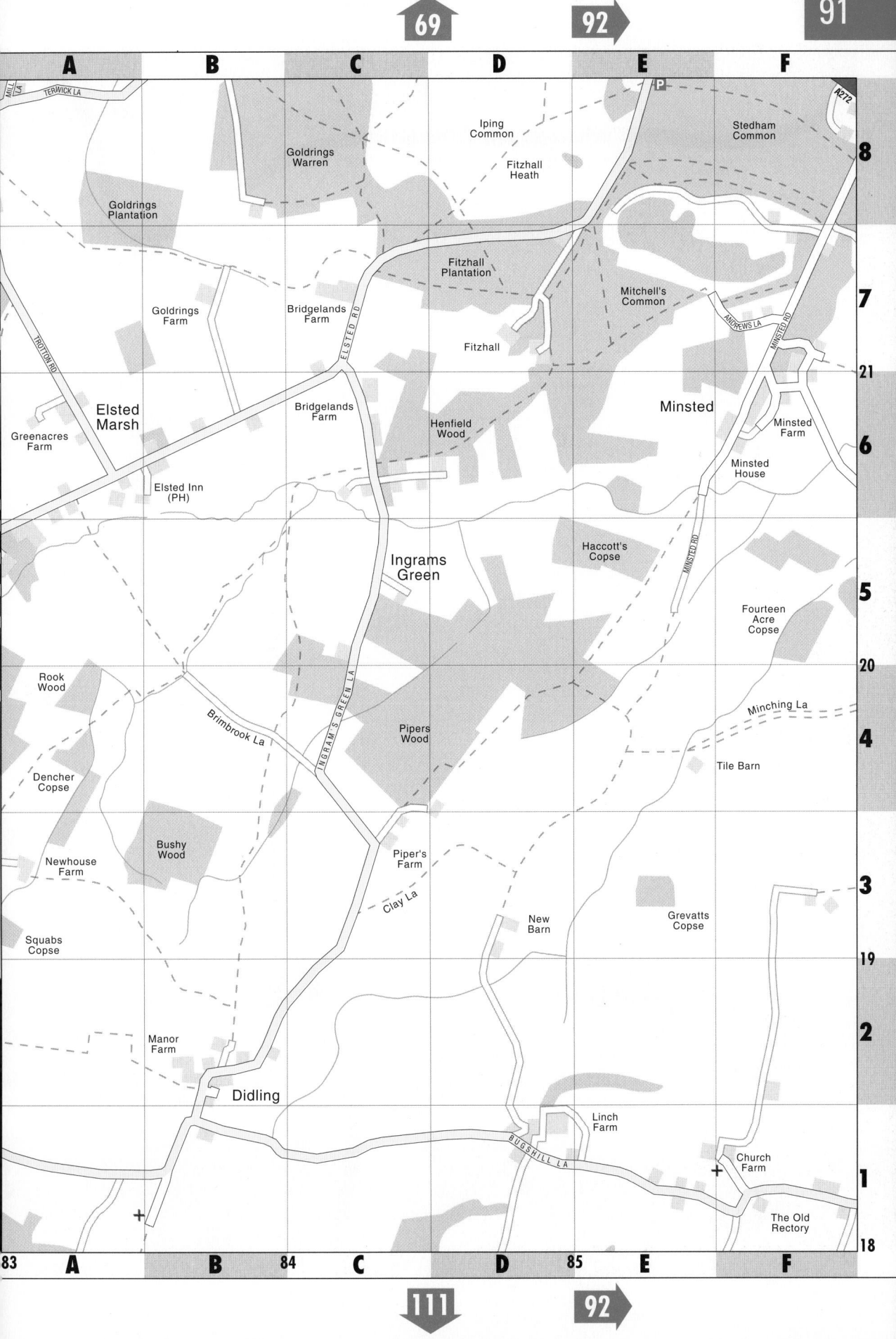

A B C D E F

8

Iping Common

Stedham Common

Goldrings Warren

Fitzhall Heath

Goldrings Plantation

7

Fitzhall Plantation

Mitchell's Common

Goldrings Farm

Bridgelands Farm

ELSTED RD

Fitzhall

ANDREWS LA

MINSTED RD

21

TROTTON RD

Elsted Marsh

Bridgelands Farm

Minsted

Minsted Farm

6

Greenacres Farm

Henfield Wood

Minsted House

Elsted Inn (PH)

MINSTED RD

Ingrams Green

Haccott's Copse

5

Rook Wood

INGRAM'S GREEN LA

Fourteen Acre Copse

20

Brimbrook La

Minching La

4

Pipers Wood

Tile Barn

Dencher Copse

Bushy Wood

3

Newhouse Farm

Piper's Farm

Clay La

New Barn

Grevatts Copse

Squabs Copse

19

Manor Farm

2

Didling

Linch Farm

BUGSHILL LA

Church Farm

1

The Old Rectory

18

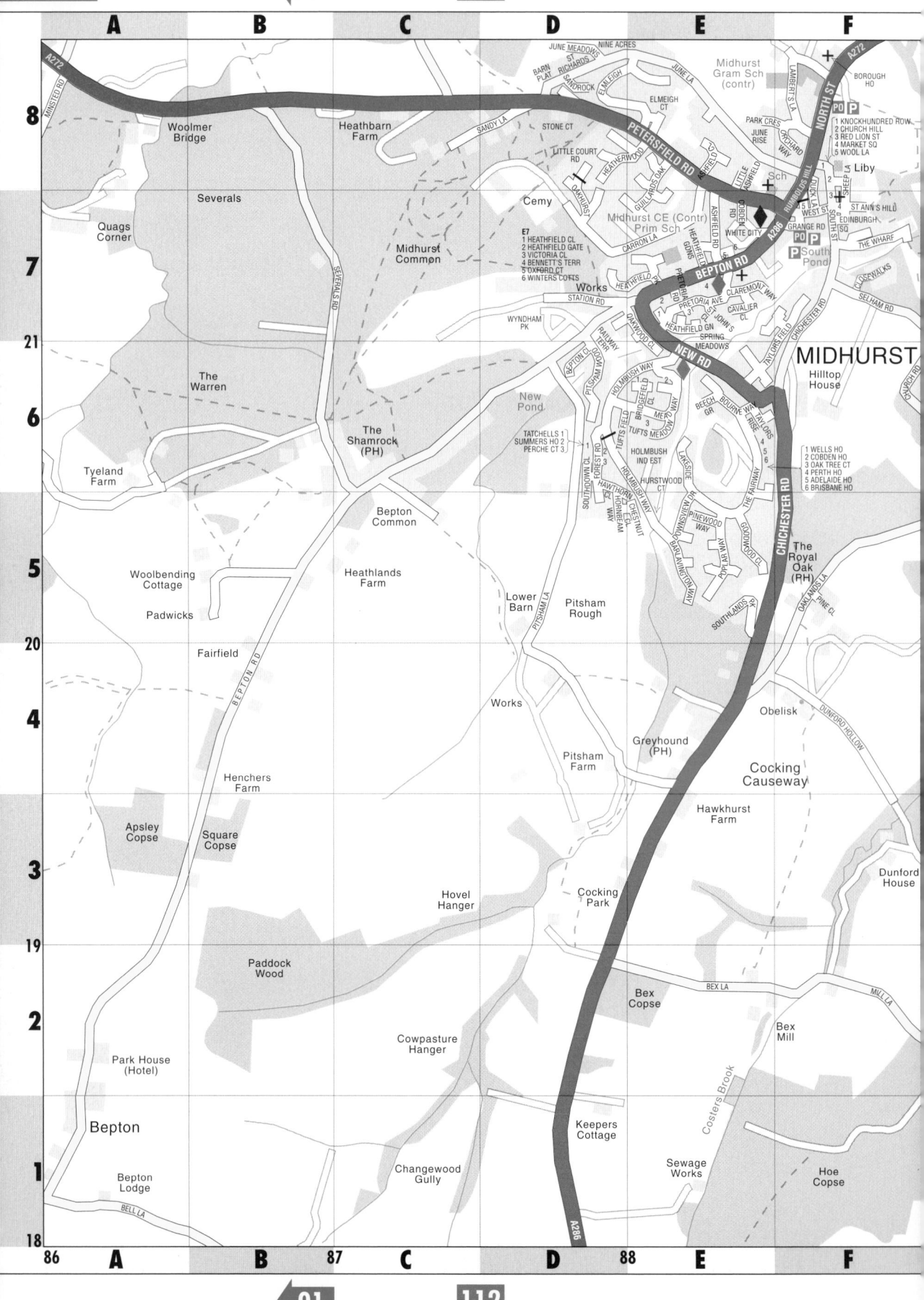
A
B
C
D
E
F
A272
MINSTED RD
Woolmer Bridge
Severals
Quags Corner
Heathbarn Farm
Midhurst Common
Cemy
The Warren
Tyeland Farm
The Shamrock (PH)
Bepton Common
New Pond
Woolbending Cottage
Padwicks
Heathlands Farm
Lower Barn
Pitsham Rough
Fairfield
BEPTON RD
Works
Henchers Farm
Pitsham Farm
Greyhound (PH)
Apsley Copse
Square Copse
Hovel Hanger
Cocking Park
Paddock Wood
Cowpasture Hanger
Park House (Hotel)
Bepton
Bepton Lodge
BELL LA
Changewood Gully
Keepers Cottage
Sewage Works
Bex Copse
BEX LA
Bex Mill
MILL LA
Costers Brook
Hoe Copse
Hawkhurst Farm
Cocking Causeway
Obelisk
DUNFORD HOLLOW
Dunford House
The Royal Oak (PH)
MIDHURST
Hilltop House
CHICHESTER RD
A286
PETERSFIELD RD
BEPTON RD
NEW RD
NORTH ST
Midhurst Gram Sch (contr)
Midhurst CE (Contr) Prim Sch
Liby
South Pond
E7
1 HEATHFIELD CL
2 HEATHFIELD GATE
3 VICTORIA CL
4 BENNETT'S TERR
5 OXFORD CT
6 WINTERS COTTS
1 KNOCKHUNDRED ROW
2 CHURCH HILL
3 RED LION ST
4 MARKET SQ
5 WOOL LA
1 WELLS HO
2 COBDEN HO
3 OAK TREE CT
4 PERTH HO
5 ADELAIDE HO
6 BRISBANE HO
TATCHELLS 1
SUMMERS HO 2
PERCHE CT 3
STATION RD
WYNDHAM PK
SEVERALS RD
PITSHAM LA
SANDY LA
STONE CT
LITTLE COURT RD
JUNE MEADOWS
NINE ACRES
JUNE LA
ELMEIGH CT
BOROUGH HO
ST ANN'S HILL
EDINBURGH SQ
THE WHARF
SELHAM RD
HOLMBUSH IND EST
HURSTWOOD CT
PINEWOOD WAY
SOUTHLANDS PK
OAKLANDS LA
PINE CL
86
87
88
21
20
19
18
8
7
6
5
4
3
2
1

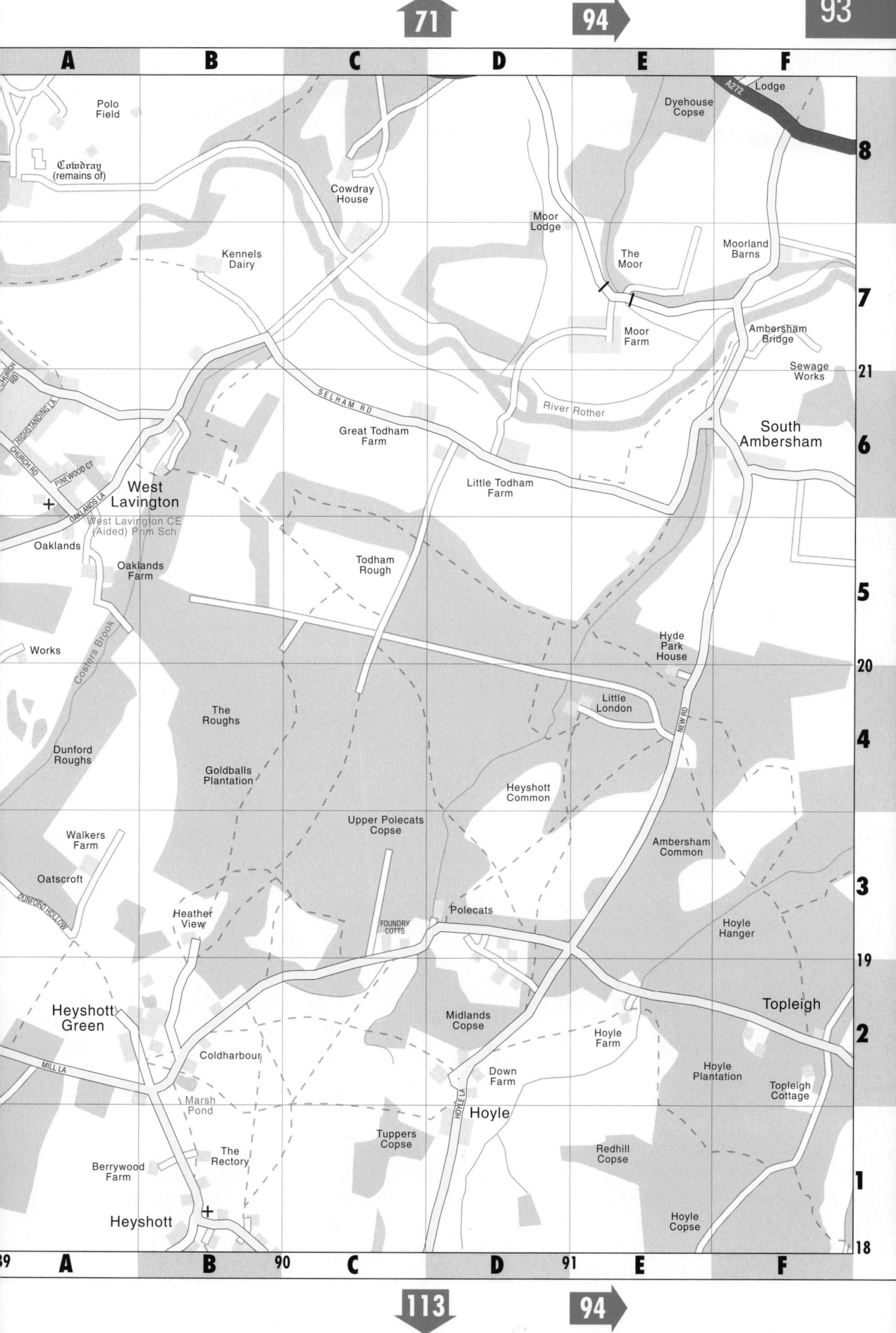

A B C D E F

8

Polo Field

Cowdray (remains of)

Cowdray House

Kennels Dairy

Dyehouse Copse

A272 Lodge

Moor Lodge

The Moor

Moorland Barns

7

Moor Farm

Ambersham Bridge

21

Sewage Works

SELHAM RD

River Rother

South Ambersham

6

Great Todham Farm

Little Todham Farm

West Lavington

HIGHSTANDING LA

CHURCH RD

PINEWOOD CT

OAKLANDS LA

West Lavington CE (Aided) Prim Sch

Oaklands

Oaklands Farm

Todham Rough

5

Costers Brook

Works

Hyde Park House

20

The Roughs

Little London

NEW RD

4

Dunford Roughs

Goldballs Plantation

Heyshott Common

Ambersham Common

Walkers Farm

Oatscroft

DUNFORD HOLLOW

Upper Polecats Copse

Polecats

Hoyle Hanger

3

Heather View

FOUNDRY COTTS

19

Heyshott Green

MILL LA

Midlands Copse

Hoyle Farm

Topleigh

2

Coldharbour

Marsh Pond

HOYLE LA

Down Farm

Hoyle

Hoyle Plantation

Topleigh Cottage

Berrywood Farm

The Rectory

Tuppers Copse

Redhill Copse

1

Heyshott

Hoyle Copse

18

93
72

A   B   C   D   E   F

8
A272

Netherlands
Farm

Halfway
Bridge

Little Common
Cottages

A272

DEAN LA

Noah's Farm Yard
Nature Trail

Moorland
Farm

The
Nore

Lods
Bridge

Grittenham
Farm

SOUTH LA

7

Manor
Farm

River Rother

Sickleham
Cottage

Southdean
Farm

21

Selham

South
Copse

6

The
Priory

+

Hurlands
Farm

The Three
Moles
(PH)

Swath Moor
Barn

Nursery
Wood

Gravel Pit
Wood

SMOKYHOUSE LA

5

Polo
Ground

20

Smoky
House

Selham
House

Fitzlea
Farm

4

High
Wood

Selham
Common

Millborough
House

Fir
Toat

Fitzlea
Wood

Main
Wood

Gallows
Hill

Graffham
Court

Graffham
Common

Barnett's
Bridge

3

Barnett's
Farm

19

Shrublands

The
Potteries

Lavington
Common

2

Wiblings
Farm

Middleheath
Copse

Northwood
Farm

Great
Bury

Homeball
Wood

1

Popple
Hill

Westerland
Stud

Adams
Farm

Lower
Barn

NONNINGTON LA

18
92   A   B   93   C   D   94   E   F

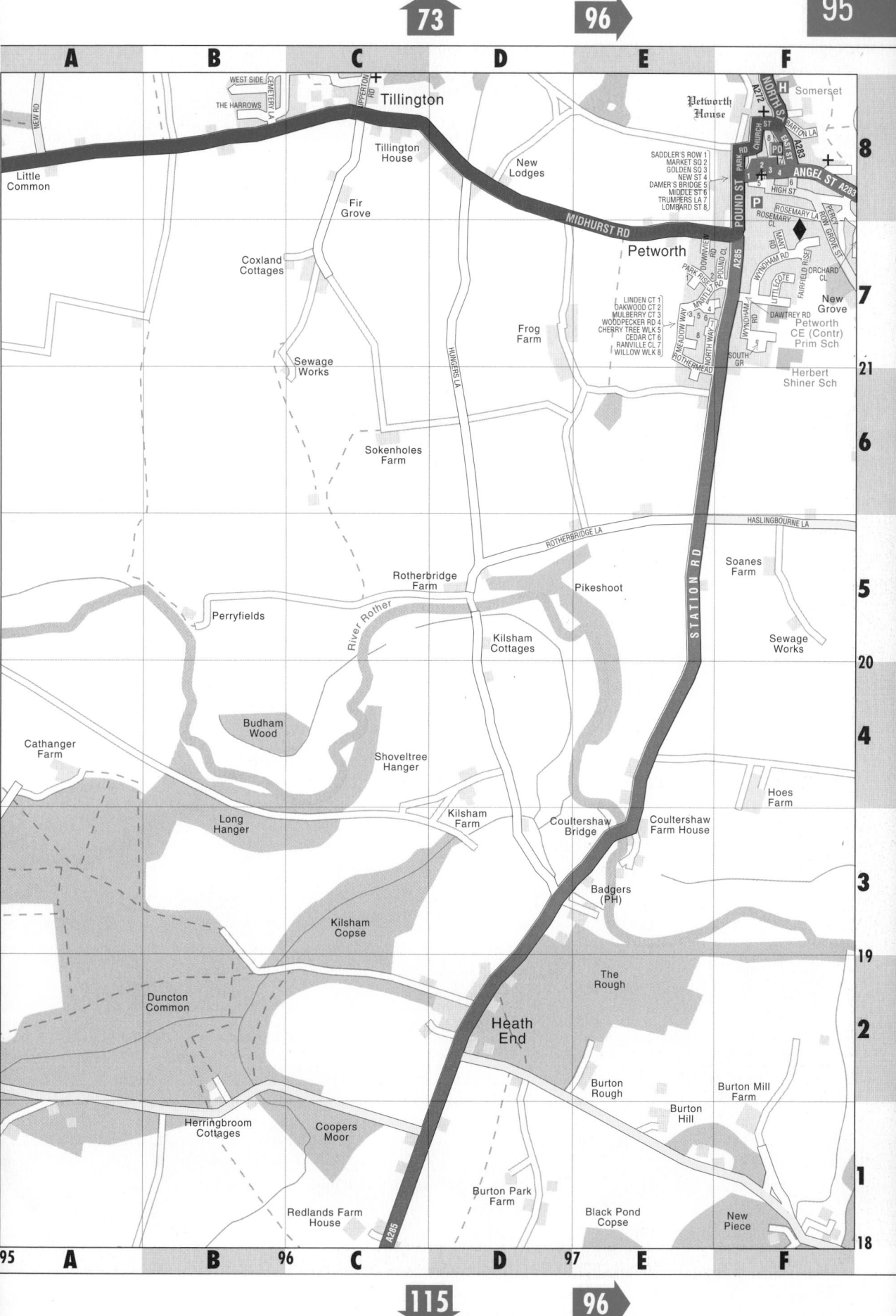

A   B   C   D   E   F

Little
Common

WEST SIDE
THE HARROWS
Tillington
Tillington House
Fir Grove
Coxland Cottages
New Lodges
MIDHURST RD
Petworth House
Somerset
SADDLER'S ROW 1
MARKET SQ 2
GOLDEN SQ 3
NEW ST 4
DAMER'S BRIDGE 5
MIDDLE ST 6
TRUMPERS LA 7
LOMBARD ST 8
ANGEL ST A283
NORTH ST
CHURCH ST
EAST ST
POUND ST
BARTON LA
HIGH ST
A272
PO
H
Petworth
LINDEN CT 1
OAKWOOD CT 2
MULBERRY CT 3
WOODPECKER RD 4
CHERRY TREE WLK 5
CEDAR CT 6
RANVILLE CL 7
WILLOW WLK 8
New Grove
Petworth CE (Contr) Prim Sch
Herbert Shiner Sch
MEADOW WAY
NORTH WAY
ROTHERMEAD
MARTLEY RD
POUND CL
A285
DOWNVIEW RD
PARK RISE
WYNDHAM RD
LITTLECOTE
DAWTREY RD
FAIRFIELD RISE
ORCHARD CL
ROSEMARY LA
SOUTH GR
8
7
21
6

Sewage Works
Sokenholes Farm
Frog Farm
HUNGERS LA

Perryfields
River Rother
Rotherbridge Farm
Kilsham Cottages
Pikeshoot
STATION RD
HASLINGBOURNE LA
Soanes Farm
Sewage Works
ROTHERBRIDGE LA
5
20

Cathanger Farm
Budham Wood
Shoveltree Hanger
Long Hanger
Kilsham Farm
Coultershaw Bridge
Coultershaw Farm House
Hoes Farm
4

Kilsham Copse
Badgers (PH)
3
19

Duncton Common
The Rough
Heath End
Burton Rough
Burton Hill
Burton Mill Farm
2

Herringbroom Cottages
Coopers Moor
Burton Park Farm
Black Pond Copse
New Piece
Redlands Farm House
A285
1
18

95   A   B   96   C   D   97   E   F

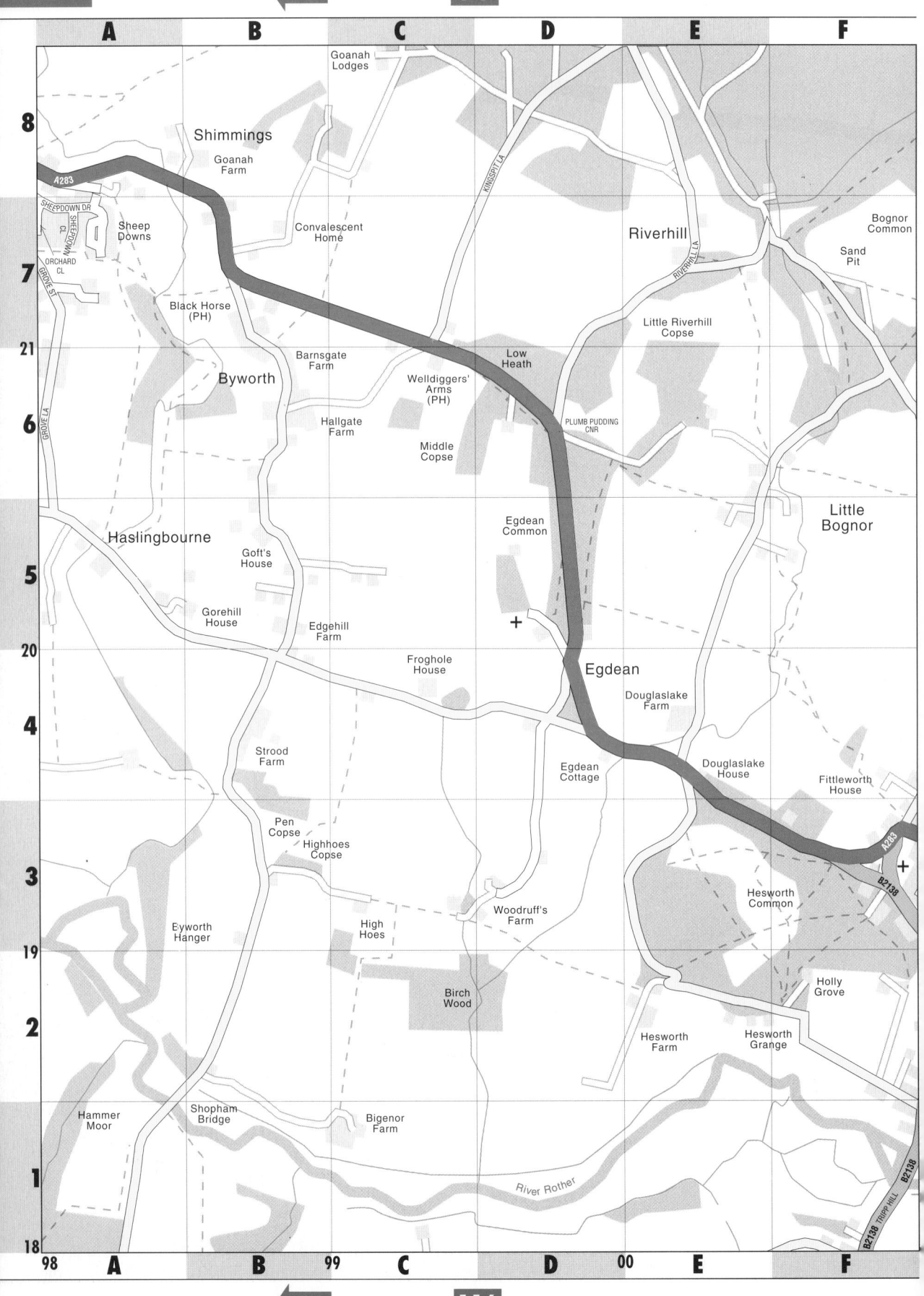

A B C D E F

8

Goanah
Lodges

Shimmings

Goanah
Farm

A283

SHEEPDOWN DR

SHEEPDOWN
CL

Sheep
Downs

Convalescent
Home

Riverhill

Bognor
Common

ORCHARD
CL

7

GROVE ST

Black Horse
(PH)

RIVERHILL LA

Little Riverhill
Copse

Sand
Pit

21

Barnsgate
Farm

Low
Heath

Byworth

Welldiggers'
Arms
(PH)

6

GROVE LA

Hallgate
Farm

Middle
Copse

PLUMB PUDDING
CNR

Little
Bognor

Haslingbourne

Goft's
House

Egdean
Common

5

Gorehill
House

Edgehill
Farm

Froghole
House

Egdean

Douglaslake
Farm

20

Douglaslake
House

Fittleworth
House

4

Strood
Farm

Egdean
Cottage

A283

B2138

Pen
Copse

Highhoes
Copse

Woodruff's
Farm

Hesworth
Common

3

Eyworth
Hanger

High
Hoes

19

Birch
Wood

Holly
Grove

2

Hesworth
Farm

Hesworth
Grange

Hammer
Moor

Shopham
Bridge

Bigenor
Farm

B2138

1

River Rother

B2138 TRIPP HILL

18

98 A B 99 C D 00 E F

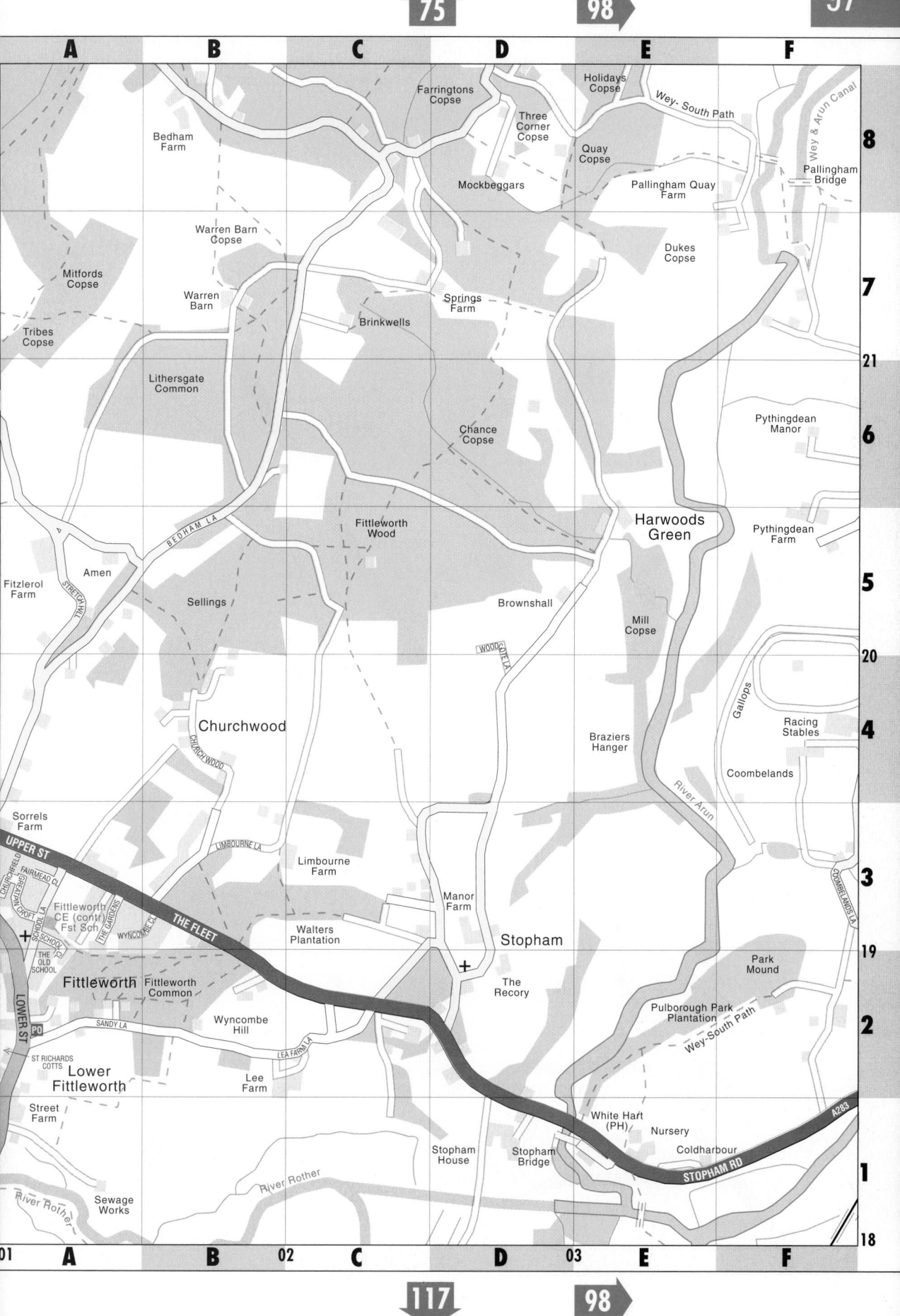

75
98

A **B** **C** **D** **E** **F**

8

Farringtons
Copse

Three
Corner
Copse

Holidays
Copse

Wey- South Path

Wey & Arun Canal

Bedham
Farm

Quay
Copse

Pallingham
Bridge

Mockbeggars

Pallingham Quay
Farm

Warren Barn
Copse

Dukes
Copse

7

Mitfords
Copse

Warren
Barn

Springs
Farm

21

Brinkwells

Tribes
Copse

Lithersgate
Common

Pythingdean
Manor

6

Chance
Copse

Harwoods
Green

Pythingdean
Farm

BEDHAM LA

Fittleworth
Wood

Amen

5

STRETCH HILL

Fitzlerol
Farm

Sellings

Brownshall

Mill
Copse

Gallops

WOOD COT LA

20

Racing
Stables

4

Churchwood

Braziers
Hanger

Coombelands

CHURCHWOOD

River Arun

Sorrels
Farm

UPPER ST

LIMBOURNE LA

Limbourne
Farm

Manor
Farm

Park
Mound

3

FAIRMEAD CL

GRIFFIN'S CROFT

CHURCHFIELD

THE GARDENS

THE FLEET

COOMBELANDS LA

Fittleworth
CE (contr)
Fst Sch

WYNCOMBE CL

Walters
Plantation

Stopham

Pulborough Park
Plantation

Wey-South Path

19

THE OLD
SCHOOL

Fittleworth

Fittleworth
Common

The
Recory

2

LOWER ST

PO

SANDY LA

Wyncombe
Hill

A283

ST RICHARDS
COTTS

LEA FARM LA

Lee
Farm

White Hart
(PH)

Nursery

Lower
Fittleworth

Coldharbour

Street
Farm

Stopham
House

Stopham
Bridge

STOPHAM RD

1

River Rother

Sewage
Works

River Rother

18

117
98

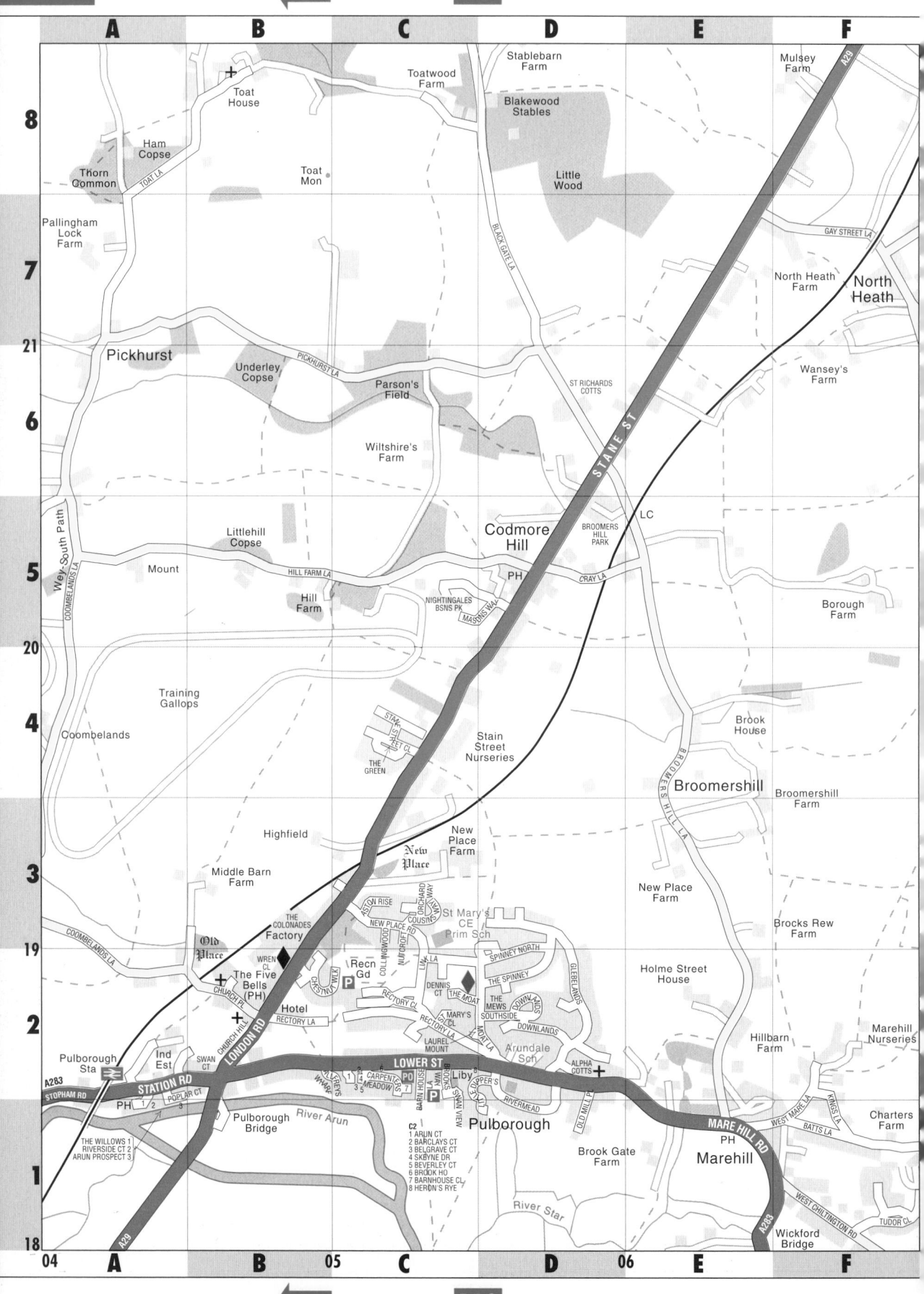

8

7

21

6

5

20

4

3

19

2

1

18

A B C D E F

Mulsey Farm

Stablebarn Farm

Toatwood Farm

Toat House

Blakewood Stables

Ham Copse

Toat Mon

Little Wood

Thorn Common

GAY STREET LA

Pallingham Lock Farm

North Heath Farm

North Heath

Pickhurst

Underley Copse

PICKHURST LA

Parson's Field

ST RICHARDS COTTS

Wansey's Farm

Wiltshire's Farm

Littlehill Copse

Codmore Hill

BROOMERS HILL PARK

LC

Mount

HILL FARM LA

Hill Farm

NIGHTINGALES BSNS PK

PH

CRAY LA

Borough Farm

Training Gallops

MASONS WAY

Coombelands

Brook House

STANE ST CL

Stain Street Nurseries

THE GREEN

Broomershill

Broomershill Farm

Highfield

New Place Farm

New Place

New Place Farm

Brocks Rew Farm

Middle Barn Farm

ORCHARD WAY

NEW PLACE RD

St Mary's CE Prim Sch

COOMBELANDS LA

Old Place

THE COLONADES

Factory

ASH RISE

COUSINS

NUTCROFT RD

COLLINGWOOD

SPINNEY NORTH

Holme Street House

WREN CL

The Five Bells (PH)

CHURCH HILL

CHURCH PL

CHESTNUT RD

Recn Gd
P

LINK LA

DENNIS CT

THE MOAT

THE SPINNEY

GLEBELANDS

DOWN HA'DS

Marehill Nurseries

Hotel

RECTORY LA

RECTORY CL

Mary's Southside

DOWNLANDS

Hillbarn Farm

Pulborough Sta

Ind Est

SWAN CT

LONDON RD

RECTORY LA

LAUREL MOUNT

Arundale Sch

Marehill

A283

STOPHAM RD

STATION RD

PH
1 2
POPLAR CT 3

BAILEYS

LOWER ST

CARPENTERS MEADOW

BARN HOUSE

PO

SWAN VIEW

Liby
P

DIPPER'S

Alpha Cotts

MARE HILL RD

WEST MARE LA

KINGS LA

Charters Farm

Pulborough Bridge

River Arun

C2
1 ARUN CT
2 BARCLAYS CT
3 BELGRAVE CT
4 SKAYNE DR
5 BEVERLEY CT
6 BROOK HO
7 BARNHOUSE CL
8 HERON'S RYE

Pulborough

RIVERMEAD

OLD MILL PL

PH

BATTS LA

WEST CHILTINGTON RD

THE WILLOWS 1
RIVERSIDE CT 2
ARUN PROSPECT 3

Brook Gate Farm

TUDOR CL

A29

River Star

Wickford Bridge

A283

04 A B 05 C D 06 E F

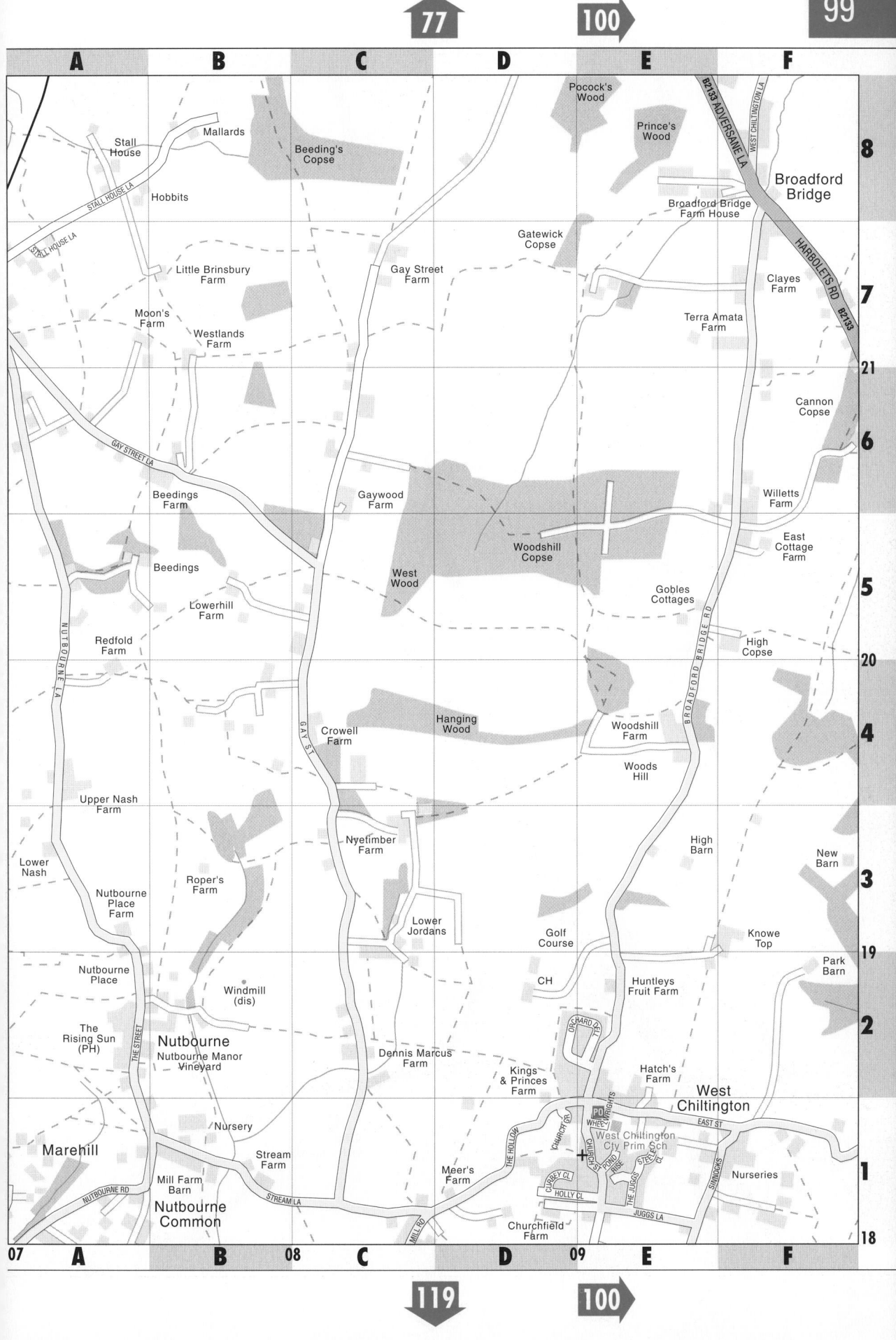

Stall House
Mallards
Beeding's Copse
Pocock's Wood
Prince's Wood
Broadford Bridge
B2133 ADVERSANE LA
WEST CHILTINGTON LA

8

Hobbits
Broadford Bridge Farm House

Little Brinsbury Farm
Gay Street Farm
Gatewick Copse
Clayes Farm
HARBOLETS RD

7

STALL HOUSE LA

Moon's Farm
Terra Amata Farm
B2133

21

Westlands Farm
GAY STREET LA
Cannon Copse

6

Beedings Farm
Gaywood Farm
Willetts Farm

Beedings
Woodshill Copse
East Cottage Farm

NUTBOURNE LA
Lowerhill Farm
West Wood
Gobles Cottages

5

Redfold Farm
High Copse

20

Crowell Farm
Hanging Wood
Woodshill Farm

GAY ST

4

Woods Hill
BROADFORD BRIDGE RD

Upper Nash Farm
Nyetimber Farm
High Barn
New Barn

Lower Nash
Roper's Farm
Lower Jordans
Golf Course
Knowe Top

3

Nutbourne Place Farm
Park Barn

19

Nutbourne Place
Windmill (dis)
CH
Huntleys Fruit Farm

ORCHARD RD

2

The Rising Sun (PH)
Nutbourne
Dennis Marcus Farm
Kings & Princes Farm
Hatch's Farm
West Chiltington

THE STREET
Nutbourne Manor Vineyard
CHURCH RD
WHE...
EAST ST

Nursery
PO
West Chiltington Cfy Prim Sch
Nurseries

Marehill
Stream Farm
THE HOLLOW
CLURBEY CL
HOLLY CL
POND
STEELE CL
THE JUGGS LA
SINNOCKS

1

Mill Farm Barn
Meer's Farm
JUGGS LA

NUTBOURNE RD
STREAM LA
MILL RD
Churchfield Farm

Nutbourne Common

18

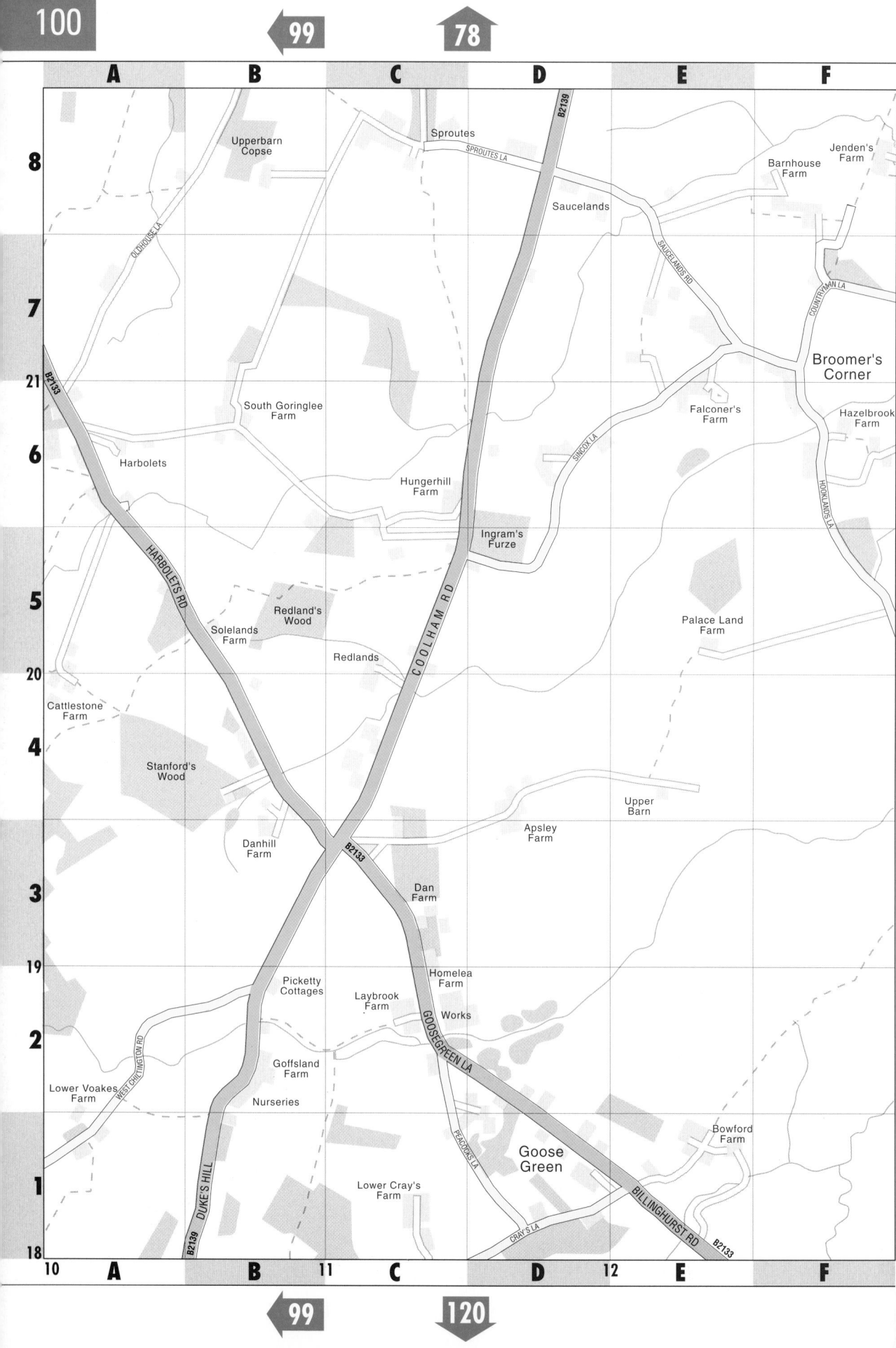
99
78
A
B
C
D
E
F
8
7
21
6
5
20
4
3
19
2
1
18
10
11
12
Sproutes
Sproutes La
Upperbarn Copse
Jenden's Farm
Barnhouse Farm
Saucelands
Oldhouse La
Saucelands Rd
Countryman La
B2139
B2133
Broomer's Corner
South Goringlee Farm
Falconer's Farm
Hazelbrook Farm
Harbolets
Sincox La
Hungerhill Farm
Hooklands La
Ingram's Furze
Harbolets Rd
Coolham Rd
Redland's Wood
Solelands Farm
Palace Land Farm
Redlands
Cattlestone Farm
Stanford's Wood
Upper Barn
Apsley Farm
Danhill Farm
Dan Farm
Homelea Farm
Picketty Cottages
Laybrook Farm
Works
Goosegreen La
West Chiltington Rd
Goffsland Farm
Lower Voakes Farm
Nurseries
Bowford Farm
Peacocks La
Goose Green
Lower Cray's Farm
Duke's Hill
Billinghurst Rd
Cray's La
99
120

A B C D E F

8

7

21

6

5

20

4

3

19

2

1

18

13 A B 14 C D 15 E F

Shipley

School La

Red La Kings Platt

Church Cl

King's Windmill

Capp's Bridge

Church Farm South

Knepp Castle

New Lodge

Kneppmill Pond

Pound Farm

Whitehall

Hampshires Farm

Countryman La

The Countryman (PH)

Pound Cnr

Pound La

Tenchford

Charlwood Barn

Castle La

Smoke House Farm

Hammer Farm

River Adur

Pen Bridge

Lower Barn

Hammer Pond

Swallows La

Honeypools Barn

New Barn Farm

Jackson's Wood

Lancing Brook

Swallows Farm

Brookhouse Farm

Bentons Place Farm

Tory Copse

Dial Post

A24

Worthing Rd

Sewage Works

Bentons La

Worthing Rd

Crown Inn (PH)

Hooklands La

Blonks Farm

Oakwood Farm Cottages

Woodmans Stud

Thistleworth Farm

Bottomhole Copse

Oakwood

Perryland Farm

Furzefield Wood

Hookland Wood

Honeybridge Poultry Farm

Honeybridge La

Grinder's Wood

Basing Hill

Wincaves Park Caravan & Camping Site

Round Wood

Oxcopse Barn

A24

101 80

A B C D E F

8

Hillhouse Lawn

West Grinstead Park

The Coppice

Moon Wood

Griffin's Farm

Well Land Farm

Park Stews

7

Pike Barn

Floodgates Farm

B2135

Steyningroad Lodges

The Rookery

STEYNING RD

21

6

Knepp Castle (remains of)

Bay Bridge

Glebe Farm

West Grinstead

Sandpit Copse

Need's Bridge

Swallows Furzefield

Highlands Buildings

NEED'S HILL

BASSELS LA

Butcher's Row

Need's Farm

5

Rookcross Farm

Clothalls Farm

River Adur

Downs Link

Jolesfield Common

20

Clothalls Farm

Joles Farm

4

Rooklands Farm

Hatterell Bridge

The Green Man (PH)

Jolesfield House

STAPLES HILL

Middlebarn Wood

Hookshile Wood

Sussex Poultry Farm

LITTLE OAK

3

Hobshort's Farm

CHURCH RD

DOWNLANDS

The Partridge (PH)

B2116

19

Convent

Lock Bridge

Lloyts Farm

2

Lock Farm

Moat Farm

1

Flat Dossers

Posbrook's Cottage

Lock Farm

PINLAND RD

Potcommon Furzefield

Pinlands Farm

18

16 A B 17 C D 18 E F

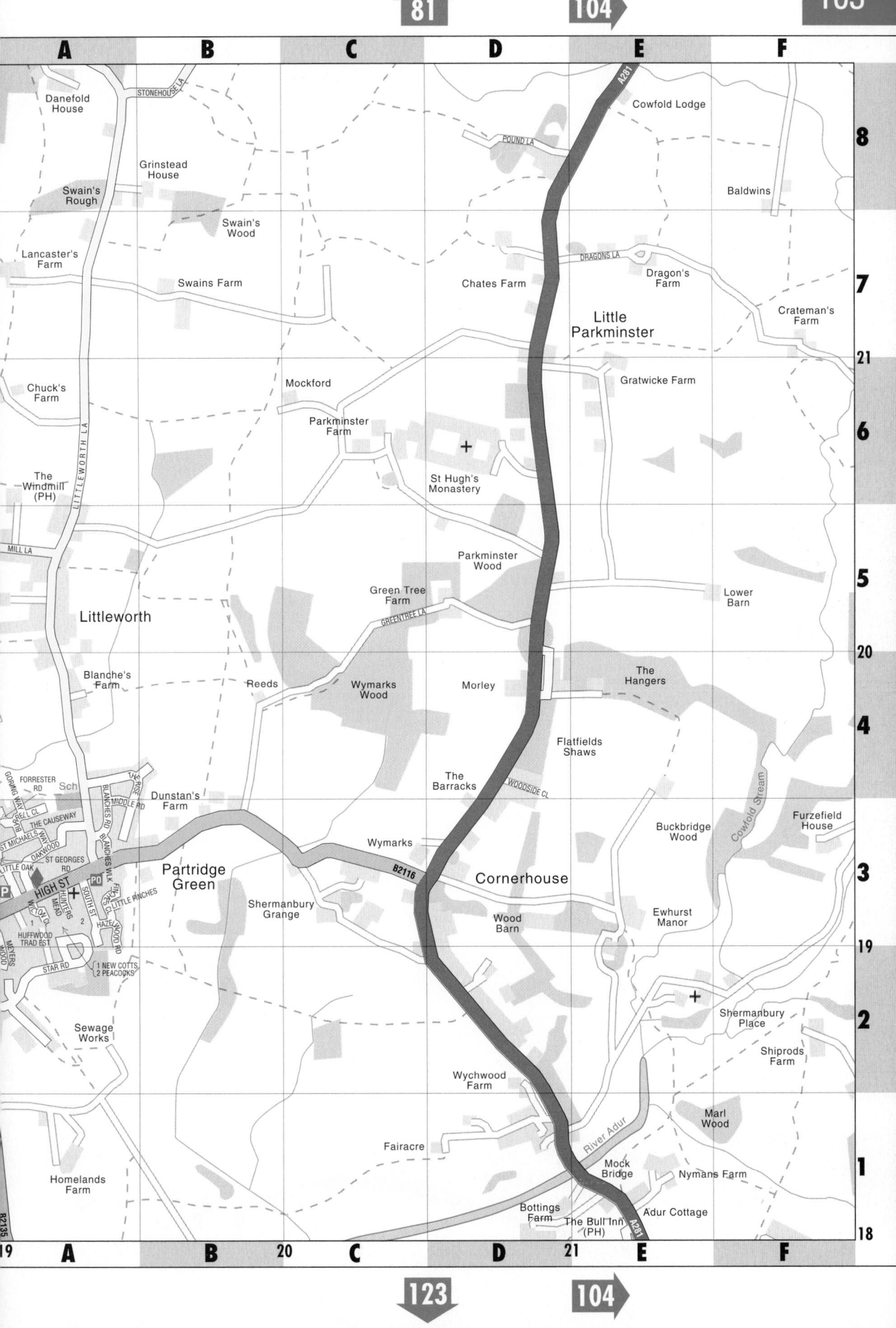

A   B   C   D   E   F

Danefold House

STONEHOUSE LA

Grinstead House

Swain's Rough

Swain's Wood

8

Lancaster's Farm

Swains Farm

POUND LA

Chates Farm

Cowfold Lodge

Baldwins

DRAGONS LA

Dragon's Farm

Crateman's Farm

7

Little Parkminster

21

Chuck's Farm

Mockford

Gratwicke Farm

LITTLEWORTH LA

Parkminster Farm

6

The Windmill (PH)

St Hugh's Monastery

MILL LA

Parkminster Wood

Littleworth

Green Tree Farm

GREENTREE LA

Lower Barn

5

20

Blanche's Farm

Reeds

Wymarks Wood

Morley

The Hangers

4

Flatfields Shaws

The Barracks

WOODSIDE CL

Buckbridge Wood

Cowfold Stream

Furzefield House

FORRESTER RD

Sch

GORING WAY

BELL CL

THE CAUSEWAY

OAKWOOD

ST MICHAELS

St GEORGES RD

BLANCHES RD

MIDDLE RD

BLANCHES WLK

Dunstan's Farm

Wymarks

B2116

Cornerhouse

Ewhurst Manor

3

LITTLE OAK

HIGH ST

PO

HUNTERS MEAD

SOUTH ST

FINCH RD

LITTLE PINCHES

HAZEL WOOD RD

Partridge Green

Shermanbury Grange

Wood Barn

Shermanbury Place

P

WICOL CL

1   2

HUFFWOOD TRAD EST

STAR RD

1 NEW COTTS
2 PEACOCKS

19

2

MEYERS WOOD

Shiprods Farm

Sewage Works

Wychwood Farm

Marl Wood

Homelands Farm

Fairacre

River Adur

Mock Bridge

Nymans Farm

1

R2135

Bottings Farm

The Bull Inn (PH)

Adur Cottage

A281

18

103
82

A B C D E F

8

Cowfold Stream
Bankfield Grange
Westridge Farm
Nyeshill Farm
Dawe's Farm
Purvey's Pit
MOATFIELD LA
KING'S LA
KENT STREET LA
Lower Barn Farm
King's Barn Farm
Coombe House

7

Cowfold Stream
Wilcock's Farm
Kent Street
The Hatch
Old Doctors

21

The Fodges
KENT ST
Twineham Court Farm

6

Buckhatch La
Park Farm
Snakes Harbour Farm
Caravan Park
The Gill
BOB LA
Coombe Farm
The Royal Oak (PH)
WINEHAM LA
Twineham Grange
Twineham Grange Farm

5

Pooks Farm
Oaklands Farm
Grovelands Farm

20

FRYLAND LA
Springlands
Fairoakland
Grovelands
Wineham

4

Furzefield Farm
Waterperry House
FRYLAND LA
FIXCROFT COTTS
Twineham Place Farm
River Adur

+ Cemy

GRATTEN LA

3

Sakeham Farm
Abbeylands Farm
Wyndham Farm
GRATTEN LA
Great Wapses Farm

19

2

Eight Acre Shaw
Fieldland Farm
SAKE EIDE LA
Works
Little Wapses Farm

1

Firtree Wood
Wheatsheaf Inn (PH)
B2116
ALBOURNE RD
Eaton Thorne House
B2116
Firsland Farm

18

22 A B 23 C D 24 E F

83
106

A B C D E F

8

7

21

6

5

20

4

3

19

2

1

18

Brooklands Farm
Garston's Farm
Green Barn
Wantley Wood
Chaites Wood
Tompsetts
Bolney Grange Farm
Whitings
AMBROSE HILL
BOLNEY CHAPEL RD
Chaites Farm
Field Place Farm
Wortleford Wood
Partridge Farm
Sewage Works
Rice Bridge
Stairbridge Farm
STAIRBRIDGE LA
Stair Bridge
BOB LA
Hillmans Farm
COUNCIL COTTS
Twineham Green
Backlands Farm
Tansy Barn
Tansy Wood
Pilgrim Farm
Northlands Farm
BOLNEY GRANGE IND EST
A2300
Hooker's Farm
Hooker's Bridge
PH
JOB'S CNR
JOB'S LA
Dumbrell's Farm
HICKSTEAD LA
A2300
Slipe
War Meml
Little Hickstead Farm
Hickstead
Pook Bourne
Twineham CE Prim (Contr) Sch
Twineham
Hickstead Place
POOKBOURNE LA
Naldretts
Park Farm
Moat Barn
Jumping Course
Naldretts Farm
Barnards
Hickstead International Arena
Hornsdene Farm
Hungerfields
Herrings Bridge
NORTHEND LA
GRATTEN LA
Herrings Farm
New House
New House Farm
TWINEHAM LA
Strood's Farm
COUNCIL COTTS
Pellings
Cobb's Mill
Westhouse Farm
Stuccles Farm
Cobbs Barn
Priory of our Lady
HICKSTEAD PK
B2118
MILL LA
Goldbridge House
Newhouse Farm
THE ACORNS
OAKHURST
JUNCTION LA
Bridger's Farm
Furze Field
Sayers Common
Sports Gd
THE SYCAMORES
KING BSNS CTR
KINGSLAND COTTS
BERRYLANDS
THE CHESTNUTS
HEATH CL
HARVEY CL
Valley Farm
REED'S LA
B2118
PH
A23
Sewage Works
Lanehurst

125
106

105
84
A
B
E
F
8
7
21
6
5
20
4
3
19
2
1
18
28
29
30
C
D
126
19.56.
£ 21.00 + VAT
Hookhouse Wood
Lower Ridges
Hookhouse Farm
Greenacres
Lye's Farm
Streams Farm
Leigh Mill
Woodfield House
A273
BISHOPSTONE LA
Wortleford Bridge
Abbotsford Sch
Bridge Farm House
ISAAC'S LA
Burgess Hill Sewage Works
HAMLIN'S CNR
JOB'S LA
A2300
Dean House Farm
B2036
Bridge Hall
Fairplace Bridge
TATE CRES 1
LILLYWHITE CL 2
SPICERS CL 3
CHILTINGTON CL 4
FAIRBRIDGE WAY
SHEDDINGDEAN BSNS CTR
Sawmill
Goddards Green (Cuckfield Hospl Annexe)
West End Farm
JANE MURRAY WAY
SUSSEX WAY
Goddards' Green
The Sportsman (PH)
CUCKFIELD RD
Gatehouse Farm
Great Wood
GATEHOUSE LA
THE OAKS
CHAFFINCH CL
SHEPHERDS MEAD 1
FAIRFIELD GDNS 2
MAPLE DR
Shalford
PANGDEAN LA
TEMPLE GR
ST MARY'S RD
LEYLANDS RD
Old House
St John's Common
WEST ST
WEST PARK CL
DENHAM RD
SOAMES CT
FAIRFIELD CL
CROMWELL RD
PARK RD
North End Farm
Oaklands Park
MILL LA
POVEYS CL
NEWPORT RD
COLMER CT
SLIMBRIDGE RD
GLOUCESTER RD
Southway Cty Jun Sch
ROYAL GEORGE RD
MARLBOROUGH CT
CONDOR WAY
Eastlands Farm
DANWORTH LA
PARKSIDE
LOWER CHURCH RD
NORMAN RD
STOCKWELL CT
Ind Est
ORCHARD RD
PEARTREE CL
WESTHILL DR
POMPER LA
East Lodge Farm
MALTHOUSE LA
VICTORIA RD
TEKNOL HO
VICTORIA WAY
LONDON RD
QUEEN ELIZABETH AVE
YORK RD
Pickhams Cottage
Old Mill House
AVOCET TRAD EST
VICTORIA CL
GRAVETT CT
STATION RD
CONSORT WAY
VICTORIA IND EST
EDWARD WAY
CHARLES AVE
REGENT BSNS PK
BRAYBON BSNS PK
Road Under Construction
ALBERT DR
Kent's Farm
Hammonds Farm
PAYTON DR
HAMMONDS RIDGE
Superstore
Danworth Farm
Locks Manor
Maltings Farm
MICHELBOURNE CL
HENRY BURT WAY
COLCHINS
WOODCREST RD
Malthouse Theatre
Scotches
CLAYTON DR 1
NIGHTINGALE LA 2
CHANCTONBURY RD
PANGDENE CL

85

A
B
C
D
E
F
8
7
21
6
5
20
4
3
19
2
1
18
31
32
33
A273
ISAAC'S LA
Holmbush Wood
Brooklands Farm
Holmbush Farm
Holmbush Cottages
Folly Farm
ROCKY LA
Kiln Wood
FOX HILL VILLAGE
SCRACE HILL TERR
Fox & Hounds (PH)
Cleavewaters Farm
FOX HILL
B2112
LUNCE'S HILL
Clearwaters Farm
Roger's Farm
CLEARWATERS LA
Lunce's Common
JESTERS
Vale Bridge
Goose Pit
Tilebarn Wood
Brook Lodge
Big Wood
Bedelands Farm Local Nature Reserve
Wivelsfield Cty Prim Sch
CHURCH LA
VALEBRIDGE RD
THEOBALDS RD
Antye Farm
Lunces Hall
Bedelands Farm
VALEBRIDGE CL
DOWNSCROFT
Theobalds
Lowlands Farm
Works
FREEK'S LA
CHICHESTER WAY
CHARLWOOD RD
HAWTHORN CL
COOPERS CL
THE WILLOWS
CHARLWOOD GDNS
VALEBRIDGE DR
LAUREL CL
SPRINGFIELDS FARM IND EST
Works
Great Ote Hall
MARCHANTS WAY
THE HAWTHORNS
MAPLE CL
THE BLACKTHORNS
GRANGE CL
OAKROYD CL
JAMES CL
LADYMEAD
BLACKSTONE WAY
FAULKNERS WAY
BERRY CL
CEDAR CL
CHESTNUT CL
MAPLE DR
LEYLANDS PK
BEDELANDS CL
PO
Recn Gd
FARNLEA
BARKDALE
HUNTINGDON WAY
ROMAINE CL
Great Otehall Wood
Sch
GANDER CL
OAKENFIELD
CHELWOOD CT
AMBERLEY CL
DUMBRILLS CL
LOWLANDS RD
THE SPINNEY
GLADSTONE RD
Manor Field Cty Prim Sch
WELBECK DR
WELBECK CL
BRAMBER WAY
PENWORTH DR
FREEK'S LA
Wivelsfield Sta
GORDON RD
GORDON HO
JANES LA
Ote Hall Farm
SHEDDINGDEAN CL
LEYLANDS RD
MUNNS DR
NOEL GN
JUNCTION CL
STIRLING COURT RD
MANOR RD
World's End
The Royal Oak (PH)
FORGE WAY
MARLE AVE
MILLBANK
RIDGEWAY
THE WITTEN
NOEL RISE
BLACKHOUSE LA
STIRLING CL
WOODLEIGH RD
THE CLOSE
NORTHWAY
MANOR CL
Bankside Farm
HIGHLANDS DR
WINDMILL DR
ST WILFREDS RD
ADUR RD
WOODLAND AVE
EASTDALE RD
WYBERLYE RD
SPANISH CT
DRIVE
THE
MILLERS WAY
MIDFIELDS WLK
ST PETERS RD
WOODLAND CL
THE NURSERY
THE HOLLANDS
ST ANDREWS RD
UPPER
Sch
ST JOHNS RD
MIDFIELDS CL
MIDFIELDS DR
WOODLAND CRES
BROOKWAY
CANTS CL
THE KILN
MANOR RD
THE VINERIES
GOLDEN HILL
JOHNSON DR
PRESCOTT GDNS
MILL PK
LC
NYE RD
CANTS LA
SWANN CL
PARK RD
MILL RD
FIRTOFT CL
1 HUMPHREY LODGE
2 KELSEY CT
3 WARE CT
4 SCRASE LODGE
5 BENJAMIN LODGE
6 PAYTON HO
7 WATTS LODGE
St George's Retreat
1 ST JOHNS CT
2 WARNER CT
JUNCTION RD
ST JOHNS RD
PARK CT
CHURCH CL
CRESCENT RD
CRESCENT
MILL WOOD
Works
Clay Pit
TILERS CL
COPESTAKE DR
QUARRY CL
LOWER CHURCH RD
ST LUKES CT
MIDDLE WAY
KNYVETON CT
RAVENSWOOD RD
MAYFIELD CT
TINDAL CL
EGERTON CL
NORMAN RD
CRESCENT WAY
CHURCH WLK
FOUNDRY CT
TURKEY LA
MANSELL CT
1 YEW TREE COTTS
2 OAK TREE COTTS
3 WRENTHAM HO
MANSION CL
ROLFE DR
Hope Farm
CYPRUS RD
GROVE RD
AVONHURST
INHOLMES PARK RD
CIVIC WAY
THE MARLETS
CHURCH RD
THE BROW
OAKWOOD CL
INHOLMES CL
St Mary's House
Liby
MARKET PL
BARONS CT
CHURCHILL WAY
MARLBOROUGH DR
Mkt
CLEVELAND GDNS
OAKWOOD RD
ROSARY CT
DALEWOOD GDNS
ALEXANDRA RD
BURGESS HILL
B2113 QUEEN ELIZABETH AVE
STATION RD
DOUBLEDAYS
LONGHURST
KINGS WAY
STATION RD
ASHWAY
QUEENS CRES
MEEDS RD
TOWER HO
SILVERDALE RD
Stubs Copse
KEYMER PAR
KEYMER CT
BROAD GREEN
AVE
WOLSTONBURY CT 1
WOLSTONBURY WAY 2
Burgess Hill Sta
WYNNSTAY
GLENDALE RD
BADGERS WLK
Freckborough Manor
Oakmeeds Com Sch
KEYMER RD
FERNDALE RD
WYKEHAM WAY
LURGASHALL
THE HOLT
RUSPERS
Ditchling Common
QUALWALTHAM LA
THE RIDINGS
DROVERS WAY
Burgess Hill Sch
London Meed Cty Prim Sch
Sch
BIRCHWOOD GROVE RD
BURDOCKS DR
SAWYERS CL
KINGS RIDE
BURNERS CL
Pollards Farm
Newick House Sch
WEAVERS CL
OAK HALL PK
THE WARREN
KIRKFORD CL
THATCHERS CL
Ditchling Common Country Park
Ind Est
CHANCTONBURY RD
HOLMESDALE RD
PINEHURST
HAZEL GR
BOUGH BEECHES
BARNSIDE AVE
WINKHURST WAY
WHEELWRIGHT LA
TITCHFIELD CL
SINGLETON WAY
FARM WAY
WOODCREST RD
SADDLERS CL
PRIORY RD
BEECHWOODS
CHILCOMB
PENDEAN
HAMBROOK
ROSEBARN CL
FOLDERS CL
Folders Farm
FOLDERS LA
FRANKLANDS CL
GDNS
KEYMER RD
WOODWARDS CL
B2113
B2112
P

127

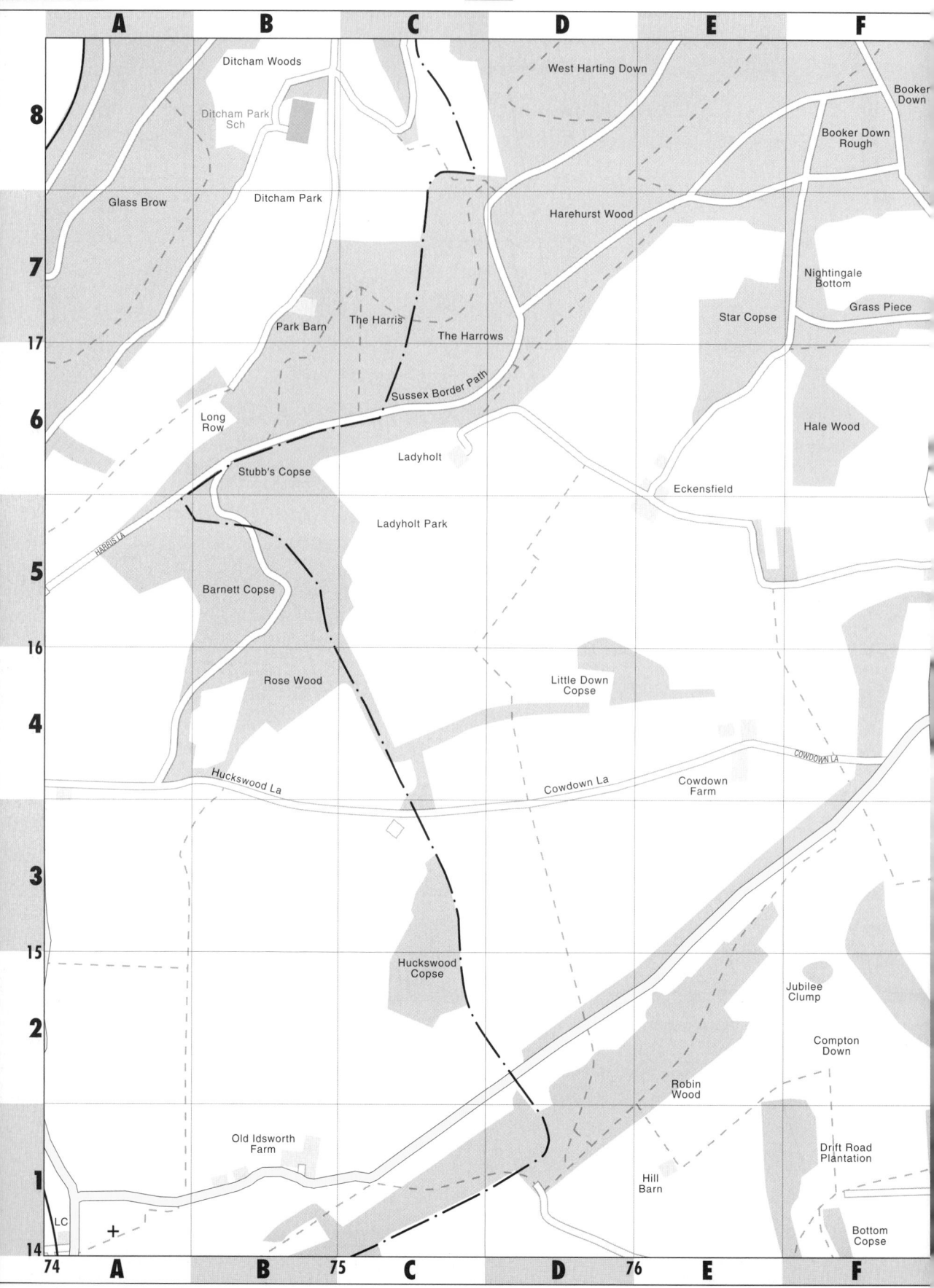

A　　　　B　　　　C　　　　D　　　　E　　　　F

8 Ditcham Woods

West Harting Down

Booker Down

Ditcham Park Sch

Booker Down Rough

Glass Brow

Ditcham Park

Harehurst Wood

7

Nightingale Bottom

Grass Piece

Park Barn

The Harris

17 The Harrows

Star Copse

Sussex Border Path

6 Long Row

Ladyholt

Hale Wood

Stubb's Copse

Eckensfield

HARRIS LA

Ladyholt Park

5 Barnett Copse

16

Rose Wood

Little Down Copse

4

COWDOWN LA

Huckswood La

Cowdown La

Cowdown Farm

3

15 Huckswood Copse

Jubilee Clump

2 Compton Down

Robin Wood

Drift Road Plantation

Old Idsworth Farm

1 Hill Barn

Bottom Copse

LC

14

74　　　A　　　　B　　　　75　　　C　　　　D　　　　76　　　E　　　　F

89 110

A B C D E F

8

Round Down

Garden Wood

B2146

Upper West Wood

Uppark

Stony Wood

Two Beech Bottom

Harting Hill

The Belt

B2141

Whitcombe Bottom

Hudsons Copse

Icehouse Bottom

Bell Vue Hill

Lower West Wood

Deer Barn Bottom

Belt Plain

Kill Devil Copse

7

17

Park Copse

Lawn Bottom

Up Park

Padswood Bottom

B2141

6

Killing Wood

Sixteen Acre Plain

The Forest

Hucksholt Farm

Pads Wood

Bushy Piece

Wills Wood

Edgar Plantation

5

Littlegreen Wood

Compton Corner

Fernbeds Down

16

Littlegreen Sch

Handle Down

4

Compton Park

Hundred Acre Farm

Chalkpit Plantation

Fernbeds Farm

Gold Mine Plantation

Bevis's Thumb

LONG LA

Apple Down

3

15

Telegraph Hill

Compton Farm

East Hanger

PO

Compton

SCHOOL LA

PH

Battines Hill Wood

2

Compton & Up Marden CE (Contr) Prim Sch

West Hanger

B2146

Up Marden Farm

Up Marden

1

14

77 A B 78 C D 79 E F

130 110

109
90
109
131

Bramshott Bottom

South Downs Way

Millpond Bottom

Buriton Farm

Treyford Hill

Little Round Down

Telegraph House

Devil's Jumps

Buriton Hanger

South Downs Way

Philliswood Down

Monkton Copse

North Marden Down

B2141

Germanleith Copse

Bushy Piece

Philliswood Farm

Gutteridge Row

Monkton Farm

North Marden

Royal Oak (PH)

Hooksway

Phillis Wood

Meredon Farm

Hill Lands Farm

Stubbs Copse

Batten Hanger

PHILLISWOOD LA

LONG LA

Long La

Fourways

Newbuildings

Upton Farm

The Glebe House

Manor Place

East Marden

The White Horse (PH)

East Marden Farm

HILLSIDE COTTS

Bow Hill Farm

Chilgrove Hill

Smithy

Faraway

East Marden Down

Chilgrove

B2141

Hill Barn

Whitelands Copse

91
112

A
B
C
D
E
F
8
7
17
6
5
16
4
3
15
2
1
14
Didling Hanger
Didling Hill
Linch Down
Bepton Down
Monkton House
South Downs Way
Linch Ball
Newfarm Plantation
Monkton Wood
Linchball Wood
Winden Wood
Bepton Wood
Winden Field
Several Beeches
Venus Wood
Slippers Row
Westdean Woods
Yewtree Cottage
Keeper's Cottage
Brooms Farm
Stapleash Farm
Rabbit Warren
Colworth Down
Colworth Barn
Stapleash Down
Chilgrove House
HYLTERS'S LA
Colworth Farm
Hylter's Farm
B2141
Ham Wood
83
84
85

132
112

← 111   ↑ 92

A   B   C   D   E   F

8

Horley Farm
Oldhouse Farm
The Richard Cobden (PH)
Mill Hanger
Hampshire Copse

Horley Row
BELL LA
HIGH MEADOW
THE CROFT
A286
Cocking
MILL LA
PO
Sage Barn

7

Stead Combe
Henley La
MALTHOUSE COTTS
CHURCH LA
Sunwool Farm

Harepath Wood
Crypt Farm
CRYPT LA
The Butts
Sun Combe

17

Cocking Down
Middlefield La
Hilltop
Hill Barn Farm
Manorfarm Down

6

South Downs Way
HILLBARN LA

Warren Bottom

HOEFIELD LA
COCKING HILL

5

Stubbs Copse
Highditch Copse
Herringdean Wood
Punters Copse

16

Oak Combe

4

Hacking Copse
The Marlows
Wolverstone Farm

Long Copse
Littlewood Plantation
Singleton Forest

3

Nightingale Wood

Littlewood Farm

15

Middle Barn

2

Wellhanger Copse
Broadham House

A286
Drovers
Collick's Copse
Lady Wood
YORKHURST HILL

1

Downley Cottage

Puttock's Copse
Hill Cottages
A286

14

86   A   B   87   C   D   88   E   F

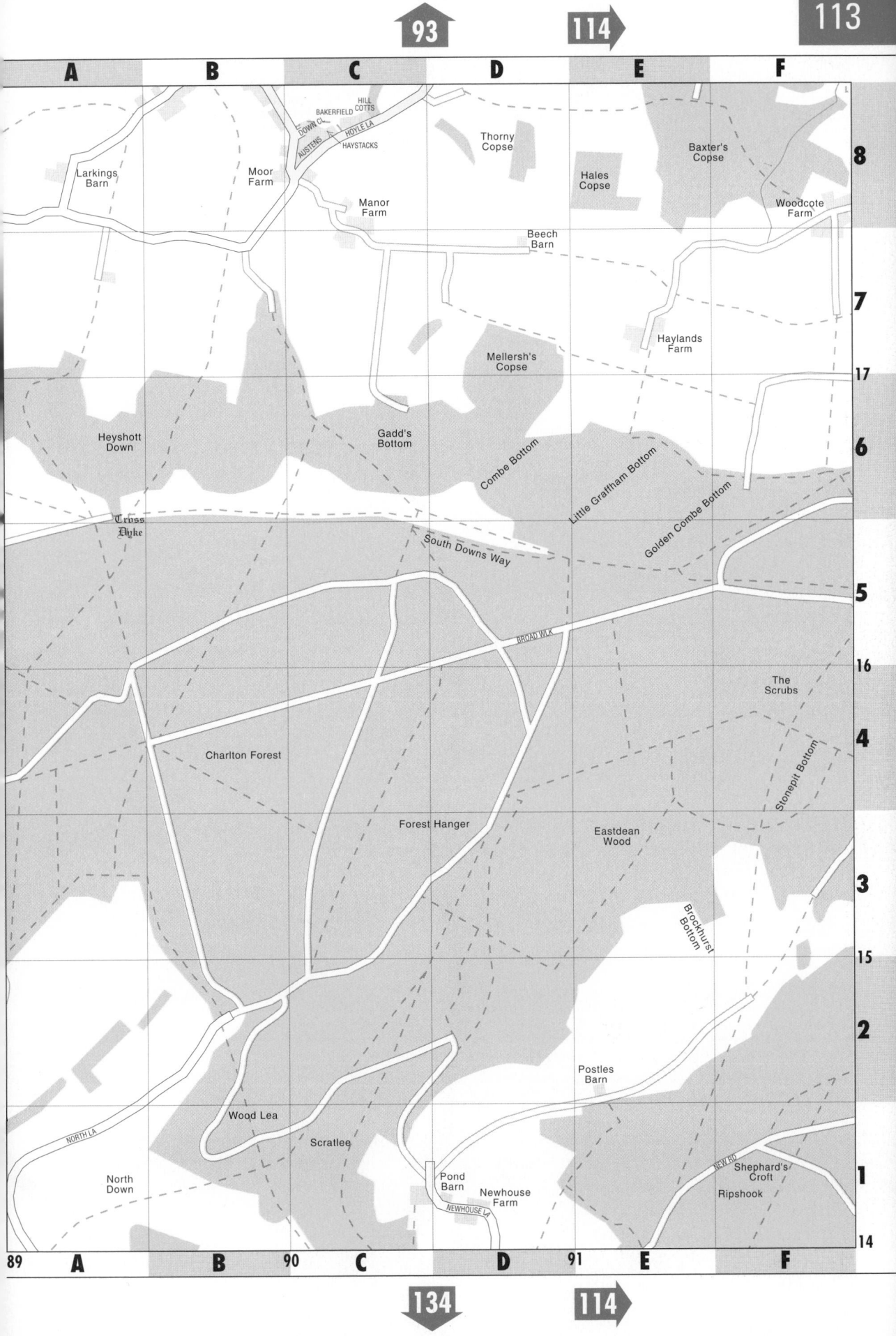

A   B   C   D   E   F

8

7

17

6

5

16

4

3

15

2

1

14

Larkings Barn

Moor Farm

BAKERFIELD
HILL COTTS
DOWN CL
AUSTENS
HOYLE LA
HAYSTACKS

Manor Farm

Thorny Copse

Hales Copse

Baxter's Copse

Woodcote Farm

Beech Barn

Haylands Farm

Mellersh's Copse

Heyshott Down

Gadd's Bottom

Combe Bottom

Little Graffham Bottom

Golden Combe Bottom

Cross Dyke

South Downs Way

BROAD WLK

The Scrubs

Charlton Forest

Stonepit Bottom

Forest Hanger

Eastdean Wood

Brockhurst Bottom

NORTH LA

Wood Lea

Scratlee

Postles Barn

North Down

Pond Barn

Newhouse Farm

NEWHOUSE LA

NEW RD

Shephard's Croft

Ripshook

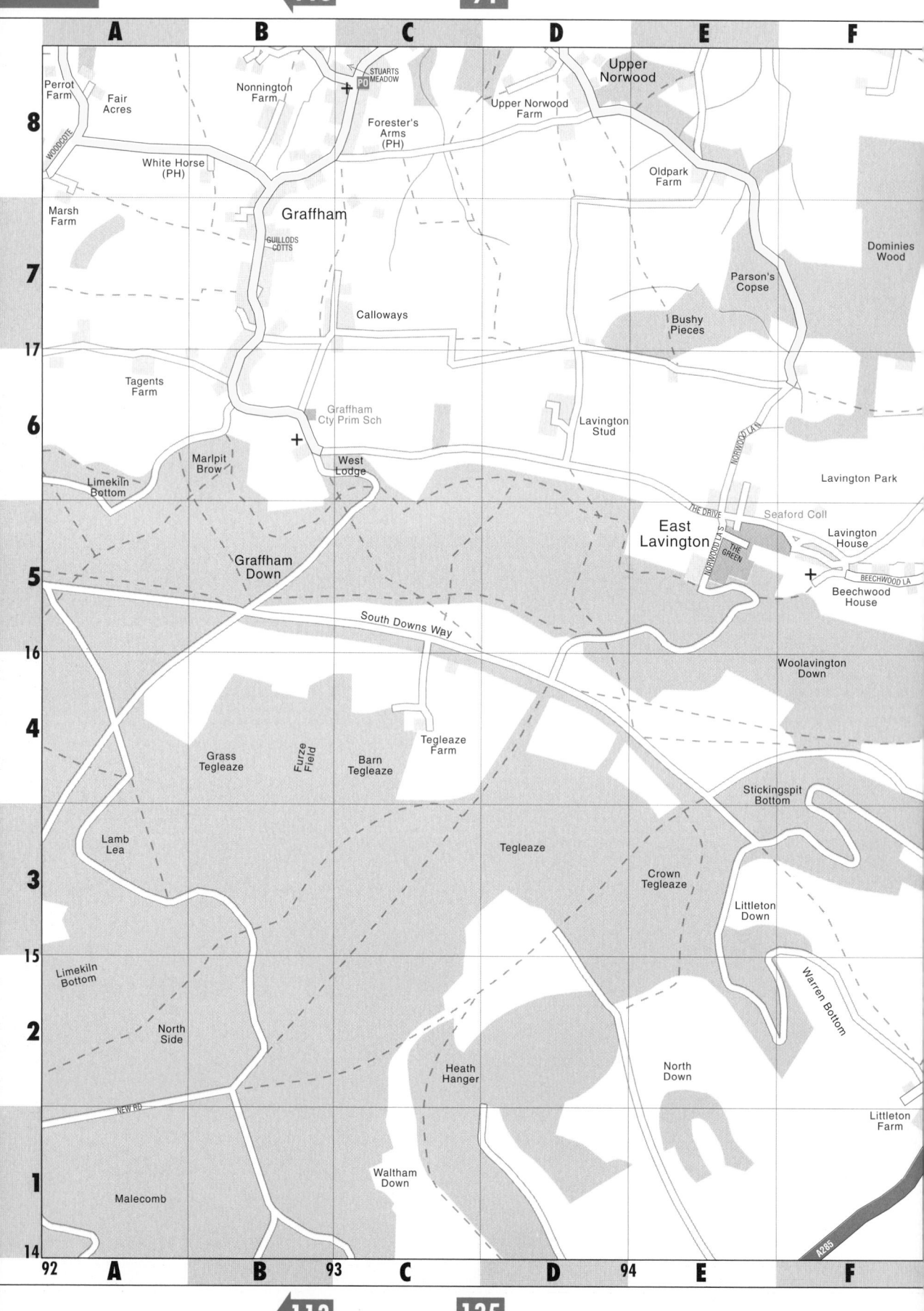

113
94

A   B   C   D   E   F

8

7

17

6

5

16

4

3

15

2

1

14

113
135

92   A   B   93   C   D   94   E   F

Perrot Farm
Fair Acres
Nonnington Farm
STUARTS MEADOW
PO
Upper Norwood
Upper Norwood Farm
WOODCOTE
White Horse (PH)
Forester's Arms (PH)
Graffham
Oldpark Farm
Dominies Wood
Marsh Farm
GUILLODS COTTS
Parson's Copse
Calloways
Bushy Pieces
Tagents Farm
Graffham Cty Prim Sch
Lavington Stud
Lavington Park
Marlpit Brow
West Lodge
NORWOOD LA
Limekiln Bottom
THE DRIVE
Seaford Coll
Lavington House
Graffham Down
East Lavington
NORWOOD LA
THE GREEN
BEECHWOOD LA
Beechwood House
South Downs Way
Woolavington Down
Grass Tegleaze
Furze Field
Barn Tegleaze
Tegleaze Farm
Stickingspit Bottom
Lamb Lea
Tegleaze
Crown Tegleaze
Littleton Down
Limekiln Bottom
Warren Bottom
North Side
Heath Hanger
North Down
Littleton Farm
NEW RD
Waltham Down
Malecomb
A285

A	B	C	D	E	F

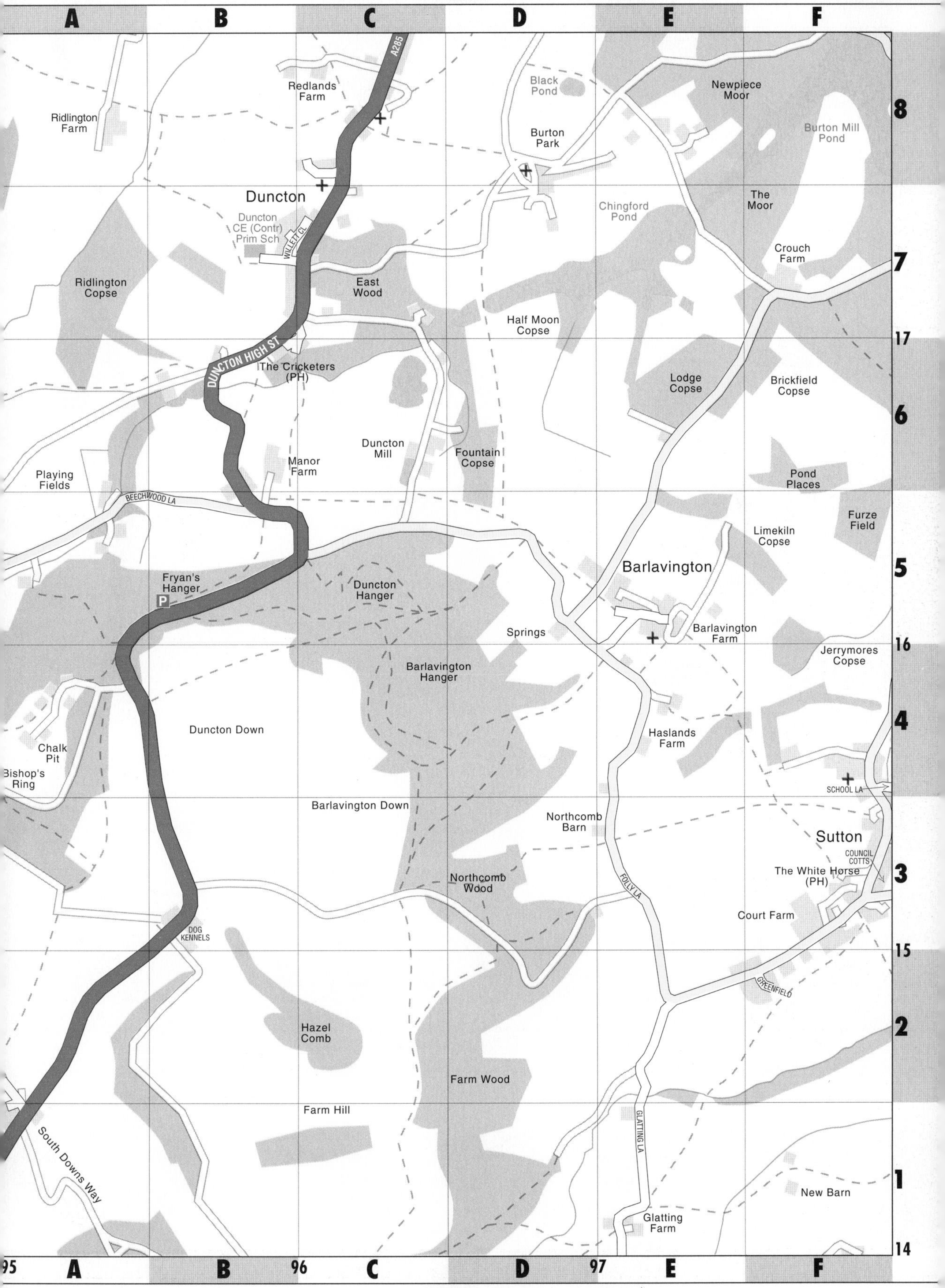

Ridlington Farm

Redlands Farm

Newpiece Moor

Black Pond

Burton Mill Pond

8

Duncton

Burton Park

The Moor

Duncton CE (Contr) Prim Sch

Chingford Pond

Crouch Farm

7

Ridlington Copse

East Wood

Half Moon Copse

17

DUNCTON HIGH ST

The Cricketers (PH)

Lodge Copse

Brickfield Copse

6

Playing Fields

BEECHWOOD LA

Manor Farm

Duncton Mill

Fountain Copse

Pond Places

Furze Field

Fryan's Hanger

Duncton Hanger

Barlavington

Limekiln Copse

5

Springs

Barlavington Farm

Jerrymores Copse

16

Chalk Pit

Bishop's Ring

Barlavington Hanger

Haslands Farm

SCHOOL LA

4

Duncton Down

Barlavington Down

Northcomb Barn

Sutton

FOLLY LA

Council Cotts

The White Horse (PH)

3

DOG KENNELS

Northcomb Wood

Court Farm

GREENFIELD

15

Hazel Comb

2

Farm Wood

GLATTING LA

Farm Hill

New Barn

1

South Downs Way

Glatting Farm

14

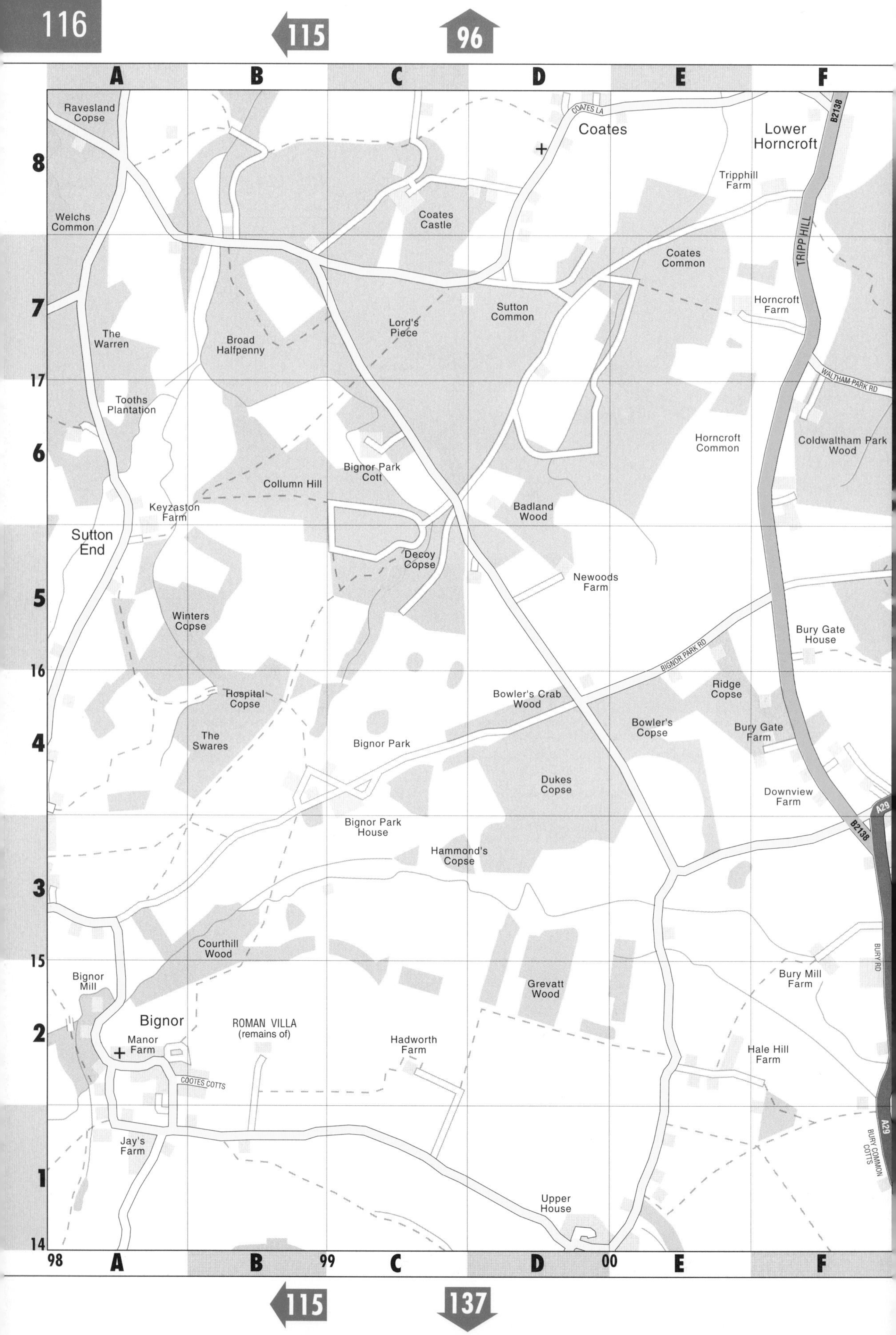

← 115
96 ↑

A **B** **C** **D** **E** **F**

Ravesland Copse

Coates

Lower Horncroft

COATES LA

8

Welchs Common

Coates Castle

Tripphill Farm

B2138

Coates Common

7

The Warren

Broad Halfpenny

Lord's Piece

Sutton Common

Horncroft Farm

TRIPP HILL

17

Tooths Plantation

WALTHAM PARK RD

6

Keyzaston Farm

Collumn Hill

Bignor Park Cott

Badland Wood

Horncroft Common

Coldwaltham Park Wood

Sutton End

Decoy Copse

Newoods Farm

5

Winters Copse

Bury Gate House

16

Hospital Copse

Bowler's Crab Wood

BIGNOR PARK RD

Ridge Copse

4

The Swares

Bignor Park

Bowler's Copse

Bury Gate Farm

Dukes Copse

Downview Farm

B2138

A29

Bignor Park House

Hammond's Copse

3

Courthill Wood

15

Bignor Mill

Grevatt Wood

Bury Mill Farm

BURY RD

2

Bignor

ROMAN VILLA (remains of)

Hadworth Farm

Hale Hill Farm

Manor Farm

COOTES COTTS

A29

BURY COMMON COTTS

Jay's Farm

1

Upper House

14

← 115
137 ↓

97
118

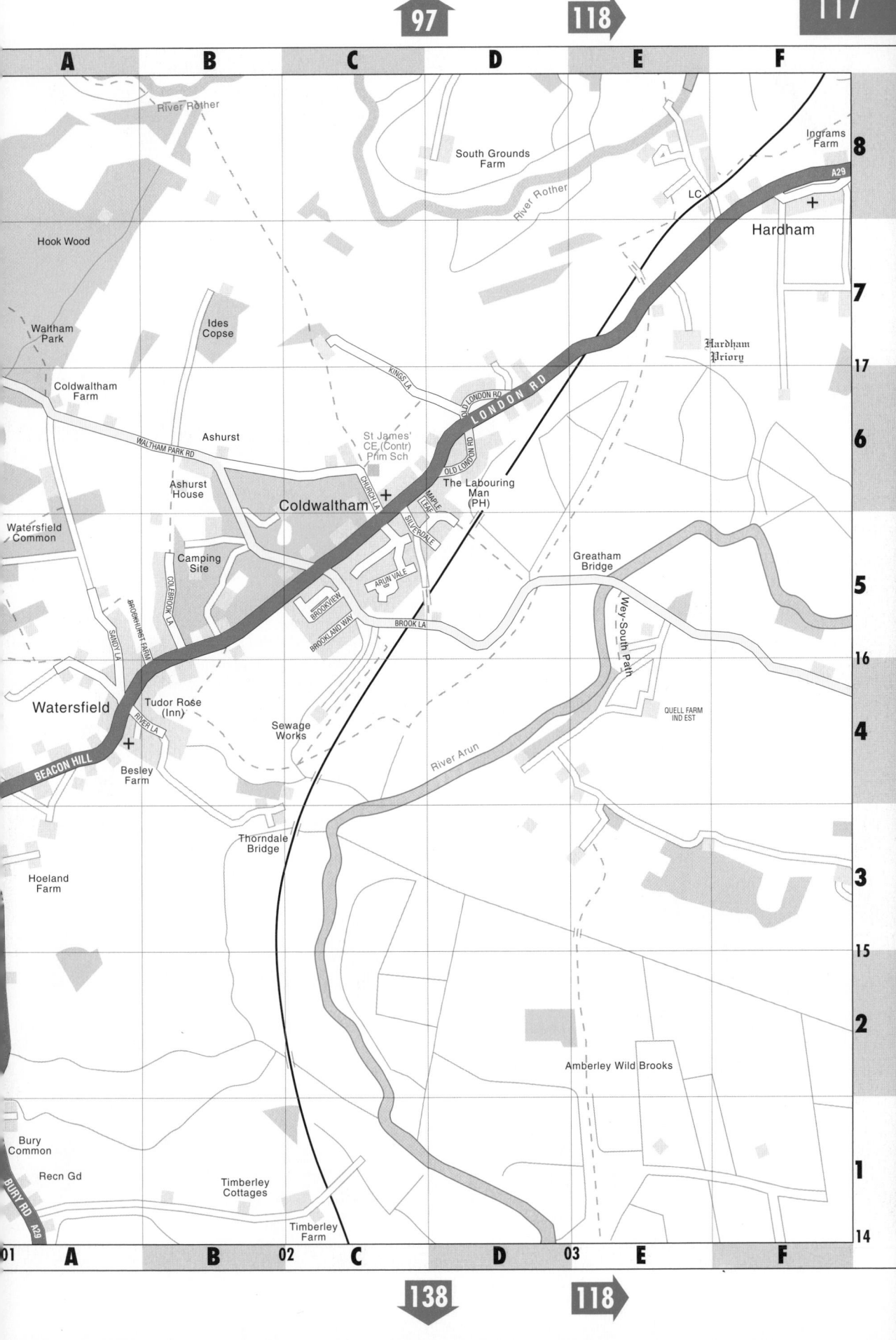
A
B
C
D
E
F
River Rother
South Grounds Farm
Ingrams Farm
A29
LC
Hardham
Hook Wood
Ides Copse
Waltham Park
Hardham Priory
Coldwaltham Farm
KINGS LA
OLD LONDON RD
LONDON RD
Ashurst
WALTHAM PARK RD
St James' CE (Contr) Prim Sch
CHURCH LA
Ashurst House
The Labouring Man (PH)
Coldwaltham
MAPLE LEAF
SILVERDALE
Watersfield Common
Camping Site
Greatham Bridge
ARUN VALE
COLEBROOK LA
BROOKHURST FARM
Wey-South Path
BROOKVIEW
BROOK LA
BROOKLAND WAY
SANDY LA
QUELL FARM IND EST
Watersfield
Tudor Rose (Inn)
RIVER LA
Sewage Works
River Arun
BEACON HILL
Besley Farm
Thorndale Bridge
Hoeland Farm
Amberley Wild Brooks
Bury Common
Recn Gd
BURY RD
Timberley Cottages
Timberley Farm
8
7
17
6
5
16
4
3
15
2
1
14
01
02
03

138
118

117
98

A
B
C
D
E
F
8
7
17
6
5
16
4
3
15
2
1
14
04
05
06
A29
LONDON RD
A283
Sewage Works
River Chilt
Winterfields Farm
Banks Cottage
Lickfold Farm
GOLF CLUB LA
River Arun
Wiggonholt Farm
River Stor
Wiggonholt
Upperton's Barn Visitors Ctr
Rush Brook
Nature Reserve
P
Wiggonholt Common
Redford House
Manor Farm
Greatham
Washingham
Wassel Pond
Northpark Wood
Bog Common
HURSTON LA
Greatham Common
Sparrite Farm
Sparrite Common
Glebe Farm
The Sawyard
Bog Common Cottages
Rackham Common
Parham Farm
Rackham Plantation
Fangrove Hill
Lillywhites Field
Sparrite Farm
West Lodges
Limekiln Plat
Douglas's Lodge
West Plain
Parham Park (Deer Park)
Parham House
Windmill Hill
Rackham Mill (disused)
RACKHAM ST
Rackham House

117
139

A B C D E F

8

Recn Gd

West Chiltington Rd
Nutbourne
Common

Heath
Mill

Nestledown
Nursery

Southlands
Farm

Harborough Gorse
Harborough
Meadow
New Barn La

Finches La

Mill Rd

Whale's Farm

7

Harborough Hill

Foxfields
The Common
The
Birches

Martlets
Birch End
Oak

Southlands La

Sewage
Works

River Chilt

Castlegate

Heathfield
Copse
Kingswood La

Silver Wood

Nyetimber La
Barkworth
Way

Morris Way

Kensington La
Nightingale

Handle Cl
Larch End
Haglands La
Haglands Copse

Smock
Alley

Lordings La

17

Hurston Warren

West Chiltington
Common

Crossways Pk

Common Hill
Garden
Wood Cl

The Hawthorns

Smock Alley

Rushfield
Nurseries

High Bar La

6

Hurston
Warren

Nyetimber Copse

Chiltington Cl
Rambledown La

Crossways

Willow Cl

Highbar
Copse

Linfield Copse
Furze Common Rd

CH

Brook
Chase

Fir Tree La
Fir Tree La

Birch Tree La

Birch Tree Cl
Silver Glade

Threal's La

Champions
Farm

Golf Club La

Golf
Course

Monkmead La

Heather La

Monkmead
Copse

Westward La

Wymidham Lea

Badgers Wood

Bower La
Silver Glade

Grove La

Roundabout
Threals
Copse
High
Spinney

Threal's
Farm

5

Hurston Place
Farm

Sunset La

Spinney La

Perrett's
Copse

Birch Gr

Roundabouts

Roundabout
Farm

16

Hurston Place

West Chiltington Rd

Hareswith
Pond

Greenhurst La

4

Hurston
Street Farm

Poultry
Farm

Northlands La

Northlands

River Stor

Fryern Home
Farm

East
Wantley

Water La

3

Freeland

Sewage
Works

Hurston La

Fryern Rd

Water Lane
Ind Est

Robell Way
Brook
Southdown

Rother Cl
Concorde
Cl

Jubilee Way

Parham
Airfield

Hurston Gr

Melton Dr

Melton Ave

Melton
Cl
Aldermoor La

Birch Gr
Rainbow Way

15

Faithfull
Cres
Dam Way

Rapley
Ave
Kewmare Cres

Longland Ave

Lobs Wood
La

Greenfield Way

Denshire Dr
Kingsland Cl
Downsview Av

Sullington Copse
Banks
Croft
Rowan
Oak Cl

Thakeham Rd

B2139

The
Rydon
Com Sch

2

Southdown
Gliding Club

Cootham

Taisy Mead
Turners Mead
Bramber La

Stavning Cres
Shermanbury
Dr
Spierbridge Rd

Merryfield Rd
Frenches Cl
Frenches

Merryfield
Garden La

Windmill La

Sherston
Cl

Kingsfield
Mead La

Meath La
Woodside Cl

Manley Cl
Heatherlands

Water La

Sullington
Warren

Charity
Farm

Dukes
Row
PH

Cootham Gn

Chanctonbury
L Ctr

Recn
Gd

Reed Cl
Love
La

Holly
Cl

Holly Cl

Riverside
Hawthorn Way

Stor Meadow

Wantley
La

Kingsfield

Sch

Fletcher's
Croft

Liby

Mill La

School Hill

Nightingale La
Nightingale Pk

1

The Crescent

Charella La

Warren Croft
Cassidy Pl
Greenacre Cl
Fox Cft

Brow Cl

The Plantation

Plantation Way

B2139

North St

PO

The Square

Old Mill
Sq

Wisborough

Manley's Hill
Byne

Woodpec

Chantry La

Pulborough Rd

West St
High St

B2139

School Hill

Clay La

New Town Rd
Fox Cft

Amberley Rd

Fern Rd

Monastery La
School La

Rectory Rd

Rectory La
Rectory Cl

Rosemary Cl
Manor Cl

Meadowside

Harwood
Wlk

Meadowside
Meadowside

Lysander
Ho

Washington Rd
A283

14

Amberley Gate

Kithurst La
Kithurst Pk

Link Hill

Monastery

Chanctonbury
Wlk

Brown's La

Storrington

07 A B 08 C D 09 E F

D1
1 WHITE HORSE CT
2 HAMMOND PL
3 MALDEN PL
4 LANGTON PL
5 LINDALE PL

119 100

A
B
C
D
E
F
8
7
17
6
5
16
4
3
15
2
1
14
10
11
12
Nursery
B2139
DUKE'S HILL
Cray's Farm
Woolvens Farm
B2133
BILLINGHURST RD
Town House Farm
Bramblefield
CRAY'S LA
Westlands Farm
Thakeham City Prim Sch
THE STREET
Chesswood Nursery
White Lion Inn (PH)
Thakeham
Thakeham Place
Mill Copse
WOODLAND COTTS
West Wolves Farm
HARDBARROW WOODS
HIGH BAR LA
Warminghurst Farm
Warminghurst
Abingworth
Manor House Buildings
FURZE COMMON RD
GUYHURST SPINNEY
Oast House Farm
Nursery
RECTORY LA
PENN GDNS
STORRINGTON RD
JACKET'S HILL
STRAWBERRY LA
Lancing Brook
Meiros Farm
Nursery
Ashington CE (Contr) Prim Sch
PARK LA
Guyhurst Copse
Park Barn
Green Dene Farm
Church Farm
Pelham House
P
CHURCH LA
Little Thakeham
The Maples
Nursery
MILL LA
Newhouse Farm
MERRYWOOD LA
MERRYWOOD HO
Jinkes Farm
Mitchbourne
MILL LA
A24
Orchardway Farm
WOODLANDS LA
NEWHOUSE LA
TUDOR VILLAGE
SQUIRRELS COPSE
MELROSE PL
MUTTON'S LA
Lower Barn
CRESCENT RISE
Malthouse Farm
B2139
PINE CL
THAKEHAM COPSE
OAK AVE
CHANCTON CL
GORSE BANK CL
BIRCH WAY
CHESTNUT CL
HILLSIDE WLK
ROCK RD
Mutton's Farm
Nursery
HAZELWOOD CL
BUNBURY CL
Longbury Hill
The Rydon Com Sch
HILLSIDE
BRACKEN LA
LONDON RD
HILLSIDE RD
Heath Common
Nurseries
SANDGATE LA
BRACKEN CL
Nursery
HAMPERS LA
SPRING GDNS
GEORGES LA
BLUEBERRY HILL
VERAS WLK
Washington Common
SANCTUARY LA
Sand Pit
BADGERS HOLT
SANDY LA
Rock Place Farm
Rock Farm
ROCK LA
Sandgate Park
P
A24

119 141

101

122

A B C D E F

Wincave Farm
A24
Cow Barn
The Plantation
Bennetts Farm
HOOKLANDS LA
Hooklands Farm
Woodman's Farm
Windsor Common
HONEYBRIDGE LA
Buckells Farm
BILLINGHURST RD
Nursery
SPEAR HILL
Spear Hill
BASING HILL
Capite Wood
Eastlands Farm
Calves Croft
Coombewick
Lion's Wood
Daylands Farm
Holmbush House
Binser's Barn
Martins Farm
Hook Farm
B2133
GREENACRES
RECTORY CL
ALICIA AVE
RECTORY LA
WINDMILL CL
THE CLOSE
WOELFS CL
HILLCREST
THE SANDS
HILLCREST DR
MERLEA CL
TIMS
East Wolves Farm
Baldwin's Wood
America Wood
Frenchland Cottage
Ashington
Jessops Farm
BROADBRIDGE COTTS
Broadbridge Farm
Brownhill
CHURCH LA
FAIRFIELD RD
FAIRFIELD WAY
1 BLACKSMITHS CL
2 MORLEYS
Brownhill Wood
MILL LA
BROOK SIDE
LONDON RD
Sewage Works
LOW WAY
MILL MEAD
LONDON RD
KENSETT'S CNR
Nursery
Common Copse
Fairoak Furzefield Wood
Hawking Sopers
Whitelands Farm
Trickles Wood
Little Wood
Guesses Farm
HOLE ST
NORTH LA
Birch Copse
Hole Street Farm
Lower Holestreet Barn
SPITHANDLE LA
Upper Chancton Farm
Abbott's Farm
Fair Oak Farm
Guessgate Farm
STOCKS FIELD
Wiston
WATER LA
PO
Upper Buncton House

8 7 17 6 5 16 4 3 15 2 1 14

13 A B 14 C D 15 E F

142
122

121
102

A
B
C
D
E
F
8
7
17
6
5
16
4
3
15
2
1
14
Eder Farm
The Capite
Ford Clappers (FB)
River Adur
Bines Bridge
B2135
Martinsland Farm
Hemmicks
Northblows
Bines Green
Honey Bridge
Claylands Farm
FORD LA
Brookwood Farm
Godsmarks Farm
New Barn
HONEYBRIDGE LA
Sopers Farm
GOLDEN LA
Yokenclose Farm
Honeybridge Farm
Hill's Farm
Moor's Head
CHURCH LA
Benfield Farm
Eatons Farm
Ashurst
Peppers Farm
The Fountain Inn (PH)
PEPPER'S LA
SCHOOL LA
Ashurst CE (Aided) Prim Sch
Wellen's Farm
Pepper's
Sweethill Farm
King's Barn Farm
Pepper's Pond
River Adur
Blakes Farm
Furzefield Cottage
Beggars Bush Kennels
SPITHANDLE LA
Bergen-op-Zoom
New Wharf Farm
Horsebridge House
Calcot Wood
Doves Farm
Northover Farm
Upper Northover Farm
Spithandle Rough
Horsebridge Common
Calcot Farm
College Wood Farm
HORSHAM RD
Loves Rough
Huddlestone Wood
B2135
16
17
18

121
143

103
124
Chestham Park
Brightham's Farm
Cibses Cottage
KIDDERS LA
Bines Farm
Betley Bridge
Lidde Hill Farm
ALBOURNE RD
CROUCH HILL
Chess Bridge
Little Betley
Great Betley Farm
Parsonage Wood
Sewage Works
CHESS BROOK GN
River Adur
Parsonage Farm
Chates
St Peter's CE (Aided) Prim Sch
Cemy
L Ctr
Lashmars Hall
Downs Link
Henfield
Blundens Farm
STONEPIT LA
1 CROFT VILLAS
2 WOOLVEN ROW
3 EASTERN TERR
4 HOLMGARTH
West End
UPPER STATION RD
Nursery
Liby
FURNERS LA
WEST END LA
Dear's Farm
LOWER STATION RD
Grays Farm
Nurseries
HOLLANDS LA
Catsfold Farm
Buckwish Farm
Little Barn
Nurseries
Nep Town
Henfield Common
New Inn Farm
Leeches
Spring Hill
BARROW HILL
Harwoods
Barrowhill Farm
Broadmare Farm
The Rye
Rye Farm
Brookside Farm
DAGBROOK LA
Nightingale Hall
New Barn
Dairy
Lipride Farm
NEWBARN LA
Wyckham Wood
144
124

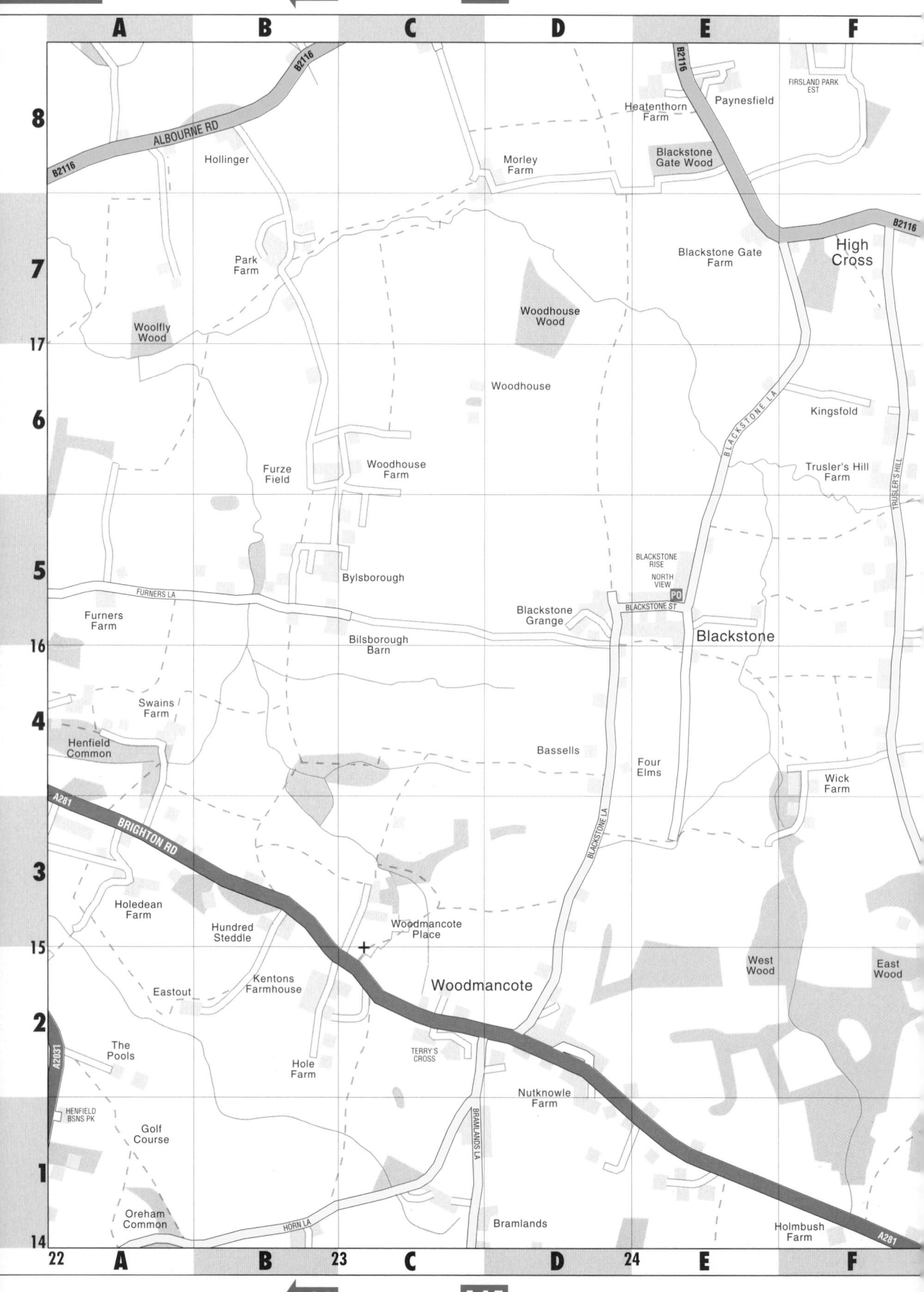

A B C D E F

8

ALBOURNE RD
B2116
B2116

Hollinger

Morley
Farm

Heatenthorn
Farm

Paynesfield

FIRSLAND PARK
EST

Blackstone
Gate Wood

B2116

Park
Farm

Blackstone Gate
Farm

High
Cross

B2116

7

Woolfly
Wood

Woodhouse
Wood

17

BLACKSTONE LA

Kingsfold

Woodhouse

6

Furze
Field

Woodhouse
Farm

Trusler's Hill
Farm

TRUSLER'S HILL

5

Bylsborough

BLACKSTONE
RISE

NORTH
VIEW

PO

BLACKSTONE ST

Blackstone

FURNERS LA

Furners
Farm

Blackstone
Grange

16

Bilsborough
Barn

Swains
Farm

Bassells

Four
Elms

Wick
Farm

4

Henfield
Common

A281

BRIGHTON RD

BLACKSTONE LA

3

Holedean
Farm

Hundred
Steddle

Woodmancote
Place

West
Wood

East
Wood

15

+

Kentons
Farmhouse

Eastout

Woodmancote

2

A2037

The
Pools

Hole
Farm

TERRY'S
CROSS

Nutknowle
Farm

BRAMLANDS LA

HENFIELD
BSNS PK

Golf
Course

1

Oreham
Common

HORN LA

Bramlands

Holmbush
Farm

A281

14

22 A B 23 C D 24 E F

A   B   C   D   E   F

TWINEHAM LA

Whiteoaks Farm

Reed's Farm

REED'S LA

COUNCIL COTTS

8

Coombe Farm

B2118

FURZELAND WAY

Coombe Hill Cottage

Knowles Tooth

Court Bushes Sports Gd

LANGTON LA

BLACKTHORN

WILLOW WAY

HENFIELD RD

High Cross Farm

Potters Field

West Town Farm

Langton Farm

7

NURSERY CL

KEMPS

HURST GDNS

CHESTNUT

Priestfield Farm

Westhouse Farm

Albourne Green

Langton Grange

17

WEALD CL

WESTERN RD

PIERPOINT CL

B2116

Albourne CE (Contr) Prim Sch

THE STREET

BARN CL

2

West Town

ALBOURNE RD

B2116

White Horse (PH)

MANOR

6

ORCHARD WAY

GUNS

MANOR RD

HUNTER'S MEAD 1
BARLEYCROFT 2

THE TWITTEN

Northpark Farm

The Old School

Ladymead

1 2

B2116

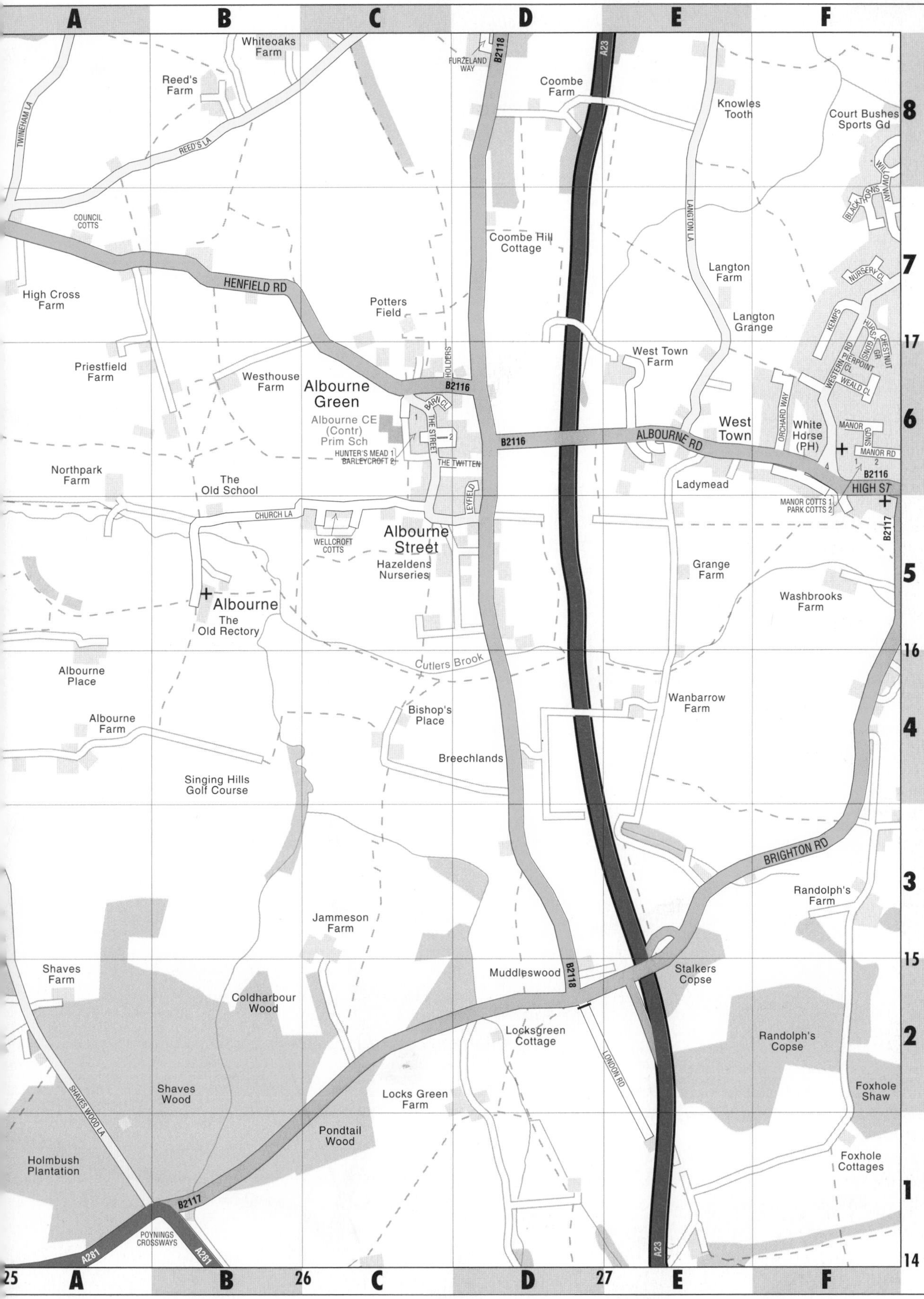

HIGH ST

MANOR COTTS 1
PARK COTTS 2

CHURCH LA

LEYFIELD

Albourne Street

B2117

WELLCROFT COTTS

Hazeldens Nurseries

Grange Farm

5

Washbrooks Farm

+ Albourne

The Old Rectory

Cutlers Brook

16

Albourne Place

Bishop's Place

Wanbarrow Farm

4

Albourne Farm

Breechlands

Singing Hills Golf Course

Randolph's Farm

BRIGHTON RD

3

Jammeson Farm

15

Shaves Farm

Muddleswood

B2118

Stalkers Copse

Coldharbour Wood

Locksgreen Cottage

LONDON RD

Randolph's Copse

2

Shaves Wood

SHAVES WOOD LA

Locks Green Farm

Foxhole Shaw

Pondtail Wood

1

Holmbush Plantation

B2117

A281

POYNINGS CROSSWAYS

A281

A23

Foxhole Cottages

14

25   A   B   26   C   D   27   E   F

A B C D E F

8
Clayton Priory
Ruckford House
Hurstpierpoint Coll
Hammond's Mill Farm
DANWORTH LA
CHALKERS LA
MALTHOUSE LA
WILLOW WAY
MILL RACE
New Close Farm
A273
NIGHTINGALE LA

7
Recn Gd
WHITE'S CL
HANNINGTON PL
BISHOP'S CL
CUCKFIELD RD
WILLOW PINS
IDEN HURST
CE WAY
Highfields Farm
Mill Nursery
New Barn Farm
LONDON RD

17
S LAWRENCE
FAIRFIELD CR
Big Edgerley
St CHRISTOPHER'S RD
WILDERNESS RD
MARCHANTS RD
MERCHANTS CL

6
St Lawrence CE Sch
Liby
Little Park Farm
COLLEGE LA
COLLEGE PL
Hurst Wickham
Clayton Wickham Farm
Friar's Oak Hotel
Woodside Grange
THE BOURNE
BANKSID
THE SPINNEY

5
B2116
HIGH ST
THE GLEBE
TRINITY RD
THE RIBBETTS
RIBBETTS HO
WEST FURLONG CT
CSPT FURLONG LA
PIT RD
WOLFBRG
SOUTH AVE
HASSOCKS RD
St GEORGE'S LA
St GEORGE'S PL
CHERINGTON CL
OFFIELD DR
HIGHFIELD
WICKHAM DR
SPINNY
HURST WICKHAM CL
Hurst Wickham Stables
Belmont
BELMONT LA
Friar's Oak Farm
WILLOW HO 1
GRACE CT 2
PAVILION
BELMONT CL
PRIORY RD
MEADOWS
BRAMBLES
THE CROFT
THE CROWN

16
B2117
Parkview Downsview
HALTON SHAWS
Tott Farm
Tott Hill
LWOL
PINE TREE
CLYNTON CL
RY CL
Cemy
SOUTH AVE
Hassocks
TRIARS OAK RD
LITTLE COPSE RD
LIBSTS
QUEENS DR
KINGS DR

4
RANDIDDLES CL
WICKHAM HILL
THE CROSSWAYS
HURST RD
Ham Farm
STANFORD CL
PINE TREES CT
STONEPOND RD
FARM CL
FRIARS CL
NGR TH CT
RAVENSWOOD
SEMLEY RD
THE WILLOWS
THE GENISTOS
CROWN POINT HO
WOODSLAND CL
WOODSLAND RD
HOLMWOOD
HOLMWOOD CT
CHANCELLORS PK
Hassocks Sch
THE CLOSE
GRAND AVE
ORCHARD LA

Nursery
CHALLOW CL
NORTH BANK
STANFORD AVE
STATION APP
STATION APP
STATION
Hassocks Sta
KEYMER RD
Hassocks Lodge
CLAYTON AVE
WILMINGTON G
B2116
PO

3
Bedlam Street
Danny Lake
NEW WAY LA
STONEPOUND CROSSROADS
POUND GATE
SOUTH BANK
ROSE CT 1
CLAYTON PARK 2
STANFORD TERR 3
STATION COTTS 4
DUNCTON HO 5
THE ORCHARD
OCKENDEN WAY
LAGWOOD CL
DOWNS VIEW RD
BRIGHTON RD
PARKLANDS RD
BROOK AVE
WINDMILL AVE
DALE AVE
SHANDS CL
Downlands Sch

15
Old Wood
Danny
Little Danny
Furzefield
Ockenden's Wood
ANY WOOD RD
HERON'S TYE 1
SANDBROOK 2
ORION PAR 3
FITZJOHN CT 4
Butcher's Wood

2
Hautboyes
Coldharbour Farm
Lag Wood
Halfway

1
The Jack & Jill (PH)
A273
B2112
NEW RD
B2112

14
Ashen Plantation
The Warrene

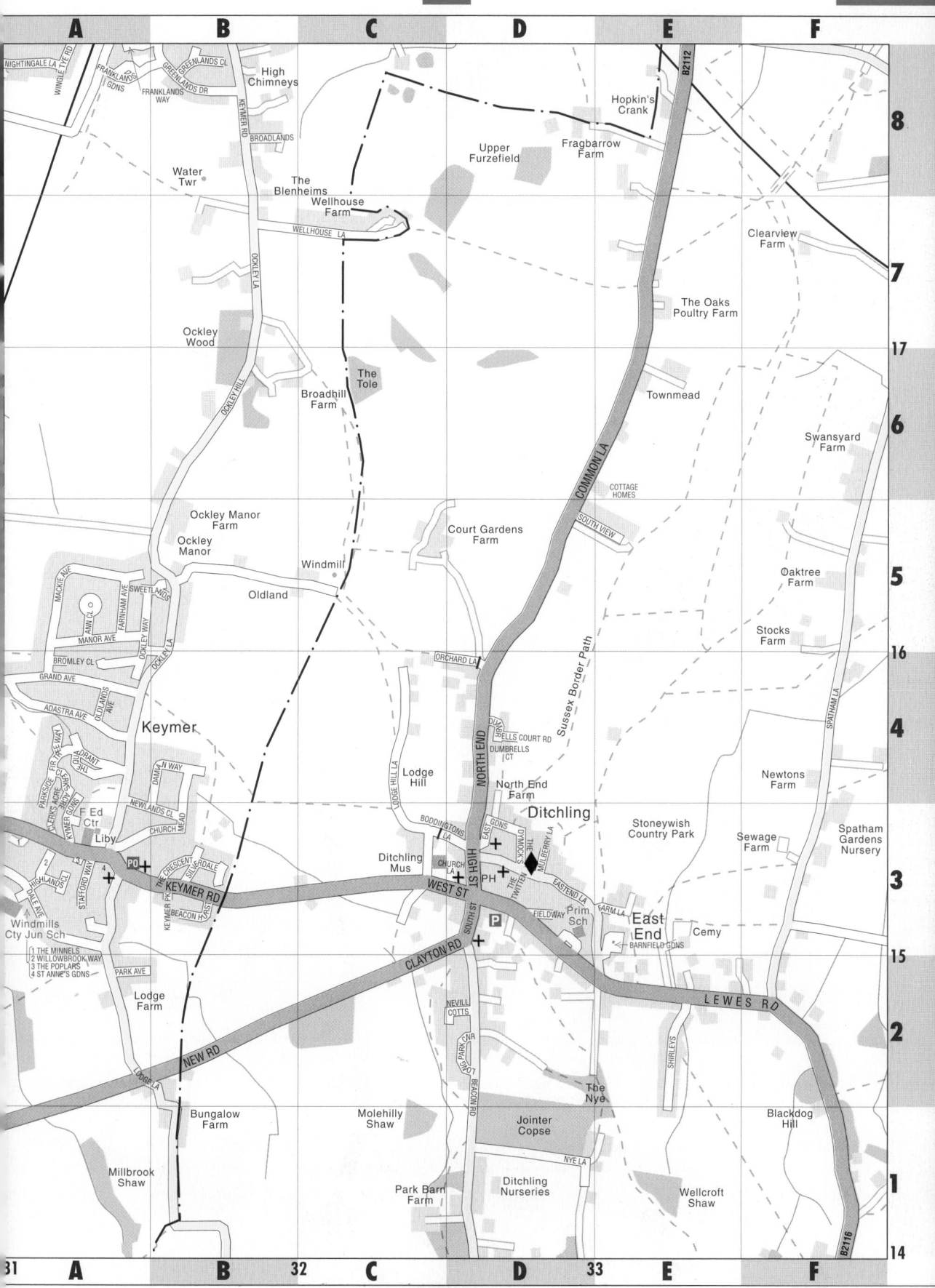
107
A
B
C
D
E
F
High Chimneys
Hopkin's Crank
Upper Furzefield
Fragbarrow Farm
Water Twr
The Blenheims
Wellhouse Farm
WELLHOUSE LA
OCKLEY LA
KEYMER RD
BROADLANDS
Clearview Farm
The Oaks Poultry Farm
Ockley Wood
The Tole
Broadhill Farm
OCKLEY HILL
Townmead
Swansyard Farm
COMMON LA
COTTAGE HOMES
SOUTH VIEW
Ockley Manor Farm
Ockley Manor
Court Gardens Farm
Windmill
Oldland
Oaktree Farm
Stocks Farm
ORCHARD LA
Sussex Border Path
Keymer
Lodge Hill
LODGE HILL LA
NORTH END
DUMBRELLS COURT RD
DUMBRELLS CT
North End Farm
Ditchling
Newtons Farm
Stoneywish Country Park
Sewage Farm
Spatham Gardens Nursery
SPATHAM LA
F Ed Ctr
Liby
PO
KEYMER RD
WEST ST
HIGH ST
Ditchling Mus
PH
P
EASTEND LA
FIELDWAY
Prim Sch
East End
Cemy
BARNFIELD GDNS
FARM LA
Windmills Cty Jun Sch
1 THE MINNELS
2 WILLOWBROOK WAY
3 THE POPLARS
4 ST ANNE'S GDNS
PARK AVE
CLAYTON RD
SOUTH ST
LEWES RD
Lodge Farm
NEVILL COTTS
SHIRLEYS
NEW RD
LODGE LA
BEACON RD
The Nye
Bungalow Farm
Molehilly Shaw
Jointer Copse
Blackdog Hill
NYE LA
Millbrook Shaw
Park Barn Farm
Ditchling Nurseries
Wellcroft Shaw
B2112
B2116
8
7
17
6
5
16
4
3
15
2
1
14
31
32
33
148

A B C D E F

8 Blendworth House
Blendworth Farm
Wick Farm
Oxleys Copse

CRABDEN LA

Wick Hanger

Rectory
Blendworth
CE Inf Sch
Blendworth
St Giles Farm
Murrants Copse

BLENDWORTH LA

7 Cadlington House

Idsworth House

13 Nobles Farm
WOODHOUSE LA
ASHCROFT LA

6 ROWLANDS CASTLE RD
Eastlands
Treadwheel Farm
Idsworth Park
Finchdean
The George (PH)

IDSWORTH CL

Woodhouse
TREADWHEEL RD
Finchdean Farm

DEAN LA

B2149

Pyle Farm

Motleys Copse

MAGPIE RD

5 Calf Dell

12 MAGPIE COTTS
WOODHOUSE LA
Sussex Border Path & Stanton Way

4 The Holt
Woodhouse Ashes Farm
Cherry Row

Monarch's Way

Great Wellsworth

Stein Wood
WELLSWORTH LA

3 HOLT GDNS
WELLSWOOD GDNS
WELLSWOOD MEADOWLANDS
FINCHDEAN RD

BOWES HILL
BROAD CROFT

11 Horsefoot Hill
LINKS LA
GREATFIELD WAY
THE PEAK
UPLANDS RD
Rowlands Castle Sta
The Sling

Golf Course
Recn Gd
THE PEAK
THE FAIRWAY

2 Havant Thicket
P
PO
Rowland's Castle

Long Wood
CH
The Forest

GLEN DALE

Staunton Country Park
LINKS CL
STANSTEAD CL
WOODBERRY LA

KINGS CL
ROYAL GDNS
CASTLE RD
Furzy Plain
MANOR LODGE RD
GATE CL
REDHILL RD
COLLEGE CL

KNIGHT WY
BLACKCAP
KINGFISHER
Red Hill
HILL BROW CL
THE DRIFT
Red Hill Farm

1 P
BRAMBLING RD 1
NUTHATCH CL 2
MALLARD RD
HAZELDEAN DR
Nightingale Bottom

Upper Lake
B2149

10
71 A B 72 C D 73 E F

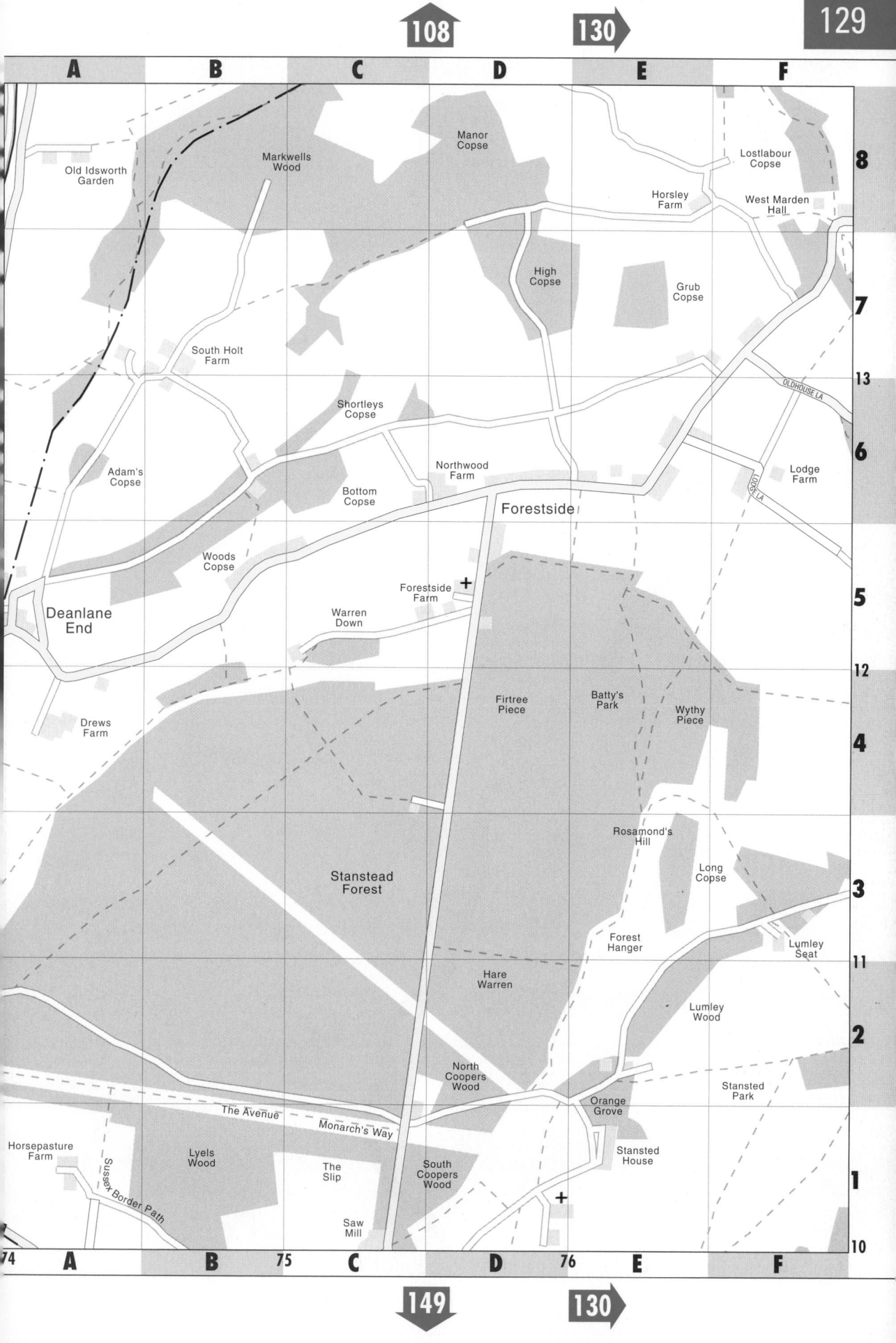

A B C D E F

8

Old Idsworth
Garden

Markwells
Wood

Manor
Copse

Lostlabour
Copse

Horsley
Farm

West Marden
Hall

High
Copse

Grub
Copse

7

South Holt
Farm

OLDHOUSE LA 13

Shortleys
Copse

Northwood
Farm

Lodge
Farm

6

Adam's
Copse

Bottom
Copse

LOCK LA

Forestside

Woods
Copse

Deanlane
End

Forestside
Farm

Warren
Down

Batty's
Park

Firtree
Piece

Wythy
Piece

5

12

Drews
Farm

Rosamond's
Hill

Long
Copse

4

Stanstead
Forest

Forest
Hanger

Lumley
Seat

3

Hare
Warren

Lumley
Wood

11

North
Coopers
Wood

Orange
Grove

Stansted
Park

2

Horsepasture
Farm

The Avenue

Monarch's Way

Sussex Border Path

Lyels
Wood

The
Slip

South
Coopers
Wood

Stansted
House

1

Saw
Mill

74 A B 75 C D 76 E F 10

Hill Farm

Blinkard Copse

Locksash Farm

Grevitts Copse

PH

Down Cotts

B2146

West Marden

Nore Down Wy

Sewage Works

Malthouse Copse

Dolly's Hanger

Lower Farm

Lowerfarm Copse

Wheatcroft

Locksash La

Nore Down

Oldhouse La

Fanny's Row

Lyecommon

Cabragh House

Birchin Copse

Warren Copse

Haslett Copse

Pitlands Farm

Busto Copse

Watergate Farm

Woodbarn

Holmes Row

Watergate Hanger

Inholmes Wood

Watergate Park

Piglegged Row

Broadreed Farm

Dundarroch

Oak Copse

Mitchamer Farm

Mitchamer Cotts

Woodlands La

Monarch's Way

Manor Farm

Cooks La

The Barley Mow (PH)

Brooklands Cotts

Walderton

Woodlands Cottages

Lordington Copse

River Ems

Park Slip

Walderton Down

B2146

Walderton Hill Plantation

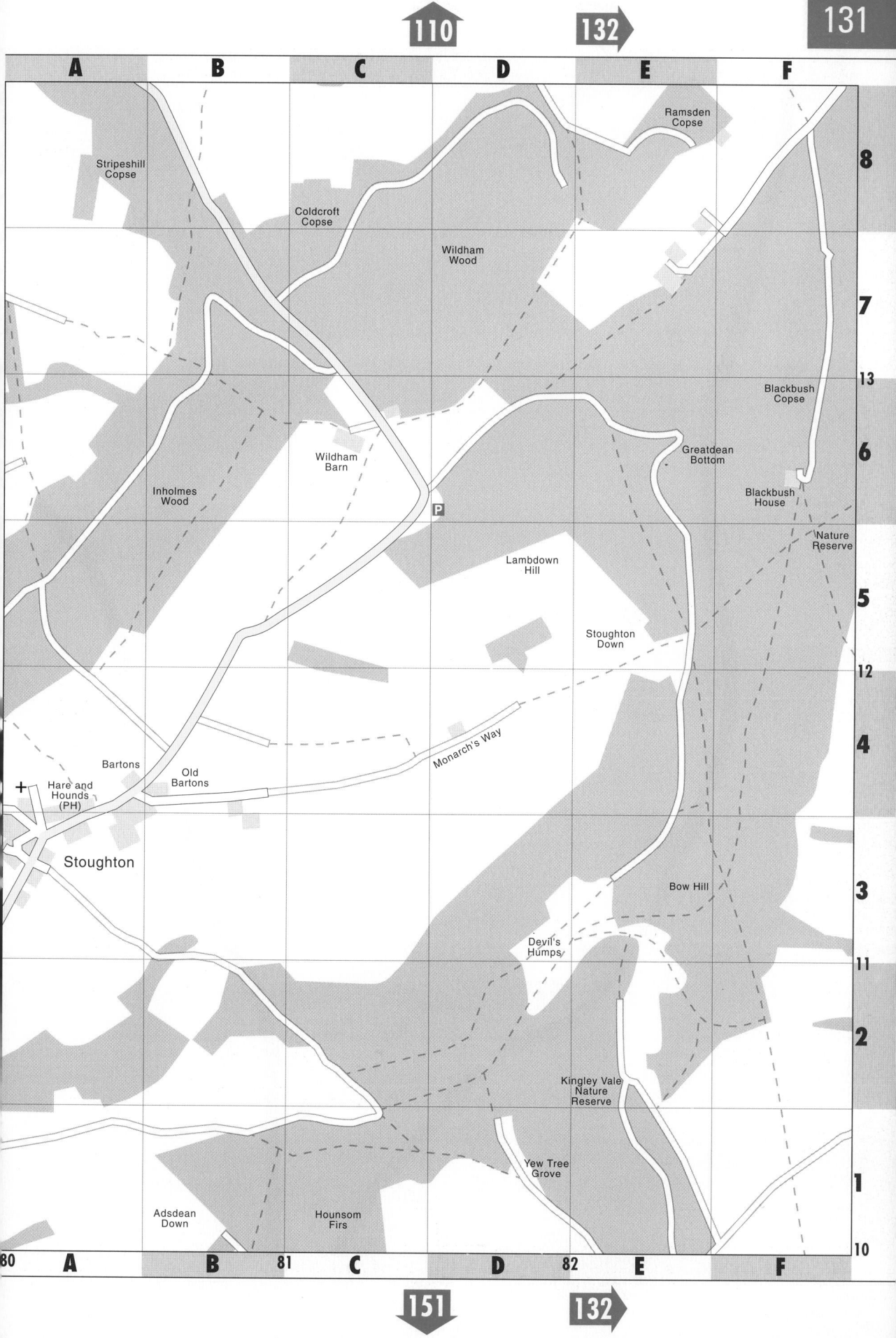

110
132

A B C D E F

8

7

13

Ramsden
Copse

Stripeshill
Copse

Coldcroft
Copse

Wildham
Wood

Blackbush
Copse

6

Wildham
Barn

Inholmes
Wood

P

Greatdean
Bottom

Blackbush
House

Nature
Reserve

5

Lambdown
Hill

Stoughton
Down

12

Bartons

Old
Bartons

Monarch's Way

4

Hare and
Hounds
(PH)

Stoughton

Bow Hill

3

Devil's
Humps

11

2

Kingley Vale
Nature
Reserve

Yew Tree
Grove

1

Adsdean
Down

Hounsom
Firs

10

131
111

A   B   C   D   E   F

8

Hylters

Lodge Hill
Farm

Double
Barn

Withy Bed

Monarch's Way

7

Warren
Barn

Brickkiln
Cottages

HYLTERS LA

Warren
Down

Warren
Hanger

13

Heathbarn
Down

Whitedown
Plantation

Highdown
Plantation

6

Brickkiln
Farm

Goosehill
Camp

Whiteland
Cottages

Whiteland
Copse

WARREN
COTTS

Little
Home
Farm

A286

PHEASANT
COTTS

West Dean
CE (contr)
Prim Sch

PH
PO

5

Hasler's
Steading

HASLER'S LA

Manor
Farm

Bottom
Barn

12

Hensbush
Copse

4

Dean
Cottages

River Lavant

Lawrence
Copse

Rummages
Barn

Preston
Farm

3

Binderton Lane

Crows Hall
Farm

Crows Hall
Copse

11

Welldown
Cottages

BINDERTON LA

2

Welldown

Binderton
House

Ox
Barn

1

Slate
Barn

Langford
Farm

B2141

A286

STAPLE LA

10

83   A   B   84   C   D   85   E   F

131
152

B2141

112
134

A   B   C   D   E   F

8

Levin Down

Honeycomb
Copse

Cucumber
Farm

Levin Down
Clump

Canada
Cottages

Hat
Hill

Ware
Barn

7

Withy
Bed

Singleton CE
(Contr) Prim
Sch

BANKSIDE

NORTH LA

LITTLEDROVE
COTTS

CHARLTON RD

Chills
Down

PO   PH

TH'S LETS

The Fox
Inn
(PH)

Hillside

CHURCH WAY

13

River Lavant

Singleton

Charlton

CHARLTON MILL WAY

Charlton
Farm

Gardens

Home
Farm

Park
Cottage

Manor
Farm

Saw
Mill

6

West Dean Coll

West Dean

Open Air
Museum

Bruton
Gate

West Dean
Park

Bottom
Barn

5

KNIGHT'S HILL

Singletonhill
Plantation

12

Great
Combes

Accident
Corner

Yewtree
Hanger

4

TOWN LA

Westside
Plantation

The
Warren

Arboretum
Cottage

Charlton Down

3

Arboretum

Goodwood
Race Course

P

Calhouns
Plantation

St Roche's
Hill

Masts

Grand Stand

11

Monarch's Way

The
Trundle

P

2

KENNEL HILL

PRINCE'S DR

PARK RD

CHALKPIT LA

Haye's Down

Goodwood Park

Birdless
Grove

1

Lavant Down

Golf
Course

10

86   A   B   87   C   D   88   E   F

153
134

133
113

A **B** **C** **D** **E** **F**

8

Court Hill

Halfmoon
Piece

Green Hill

New Barn

Highdown
Croft

High Down

7

+
PH

13

CHARLTON RD

Manor Farm

PO

MAIN RD

CHAPEL ROW
+

East Dean

DROKE LA

Ide's
Barn

6

Wallerdean
Hill

5

EASTDEAN HILL

Shotter's Ground

Bubholts

Chiseldown

Potcomb

12

Charlton
Park

Park
Hill

Eastdean
Park

Eastdean
Hill

Monarch's Way

4

Goodwood
Country Park

CHALK RD

Pilleygreen
Lodges

SELHURSTPARK RD

3

Picnic
Area

Open
Winkins

11

Appletree
Bottom

The
Plantation

Little
Copse

Red
Copse

2

MOLECOMB BROADWALK

Molecomb
Peak

Halnaker Gallop

1

Hat Hill

Ladys
Winkins

Halnaker
Park

Denge
Bottom

10

89 **A** **B** 90 **C** **D** 91 **E** **F**

A B C D E F

8

Malecomb

Heath Hill

Upwaltham

Upwaltham Farm

Shepherd's Copse

Oxen Down

Lambdown Bottom

Deep Coombe

7

13

DROKE LA

Droke

6

Bonney's Hanger

Upwaltham Hill

Astead Down

Droke Hanger

Benges Wood

Stubbs Wood

5

Selhurstpark Hill

North Wood

Forest Trail

12

SELHURSTPARK RD

St Mary's Farm

Eartham Wood

4

Selhurst Park

Ide's Common

St Mary's Wood

3

Selhurstpark Farm

11

Jackdine Farm

Forest Trail

Monarch's Way

2

Middle Barn

The Rough

Wood Cottage

1

North Barn Farm

Nore Hill Plantation

Bushy Copse

10

135
115

A   B   C   D   E   F

8

Littleton
End

Scotcher's Bottom

Denture

Glatting
Hanger

New
Barn

GLATTING LA

Coldharbour
Farm

Pitchurst
Copse

Lamb
Hanger

Left
Hanger

Westwood Bottom

7

West
Wood

Sutton
Down

Burton Down

Masts

13

P

Bignor
Hill

South Downs Way

6

Gumber
Corner

Dawtrey's
Hooks

Monarch's Way

5

The
Gumber

Great
Bottom

Little Bottom
Wood

12

Gumber
Farm

4

Stammers
Wood

Stammers

3

Oak
Barn

Warren
Barn

11

Ashlee
Wood

2

Great
Down

Home
Farm

Coneygate

The
Plain

1

Northwood
Cottages

Dale Park
House

10

135
156

A B C D E F

8
7
13
6
5
12
4
3
11
2
1
10

West Burton

Bignortail Wood

WEST BURTON RD

Cookes House

Southview Farm

Egg Bottom Coppice

WEST BURTON LA

Hillside Nursery

Nursery

Bury CE (Aided) Prim Sch

Westburton Hill

A29

The White Horse (PH)

Bury Manor Farm

King's Buildings

BURY HILL

Barkhale Wood

South Downs Way

Bury Hill

Coombe Wood

Langham Buildings

The Denture

Wapelgate Corner

Langham Wood

Stammer's Copse

Houghton Forest

Trot Row

Monarch's Way

P

B2139

P

B2139

Picnic Area

Whiteways Lodge

A284

Parletts Farm

LONDON RD

Madehurst

Lower Farm

Newbarn Farm

A29 FAIRMILE BOTTOM

Rewell Hill Wood

Whiteways Plantation

A284

Cemy

98 A B 99 C D 00 E F

← 137   117

| | A | B | C | D | E | F |

A29
BURY RD
THE HOLLOW
Hollow Farm
Prattendens Farm
Timberley Bridge
Amberley Swamp
Wey-South Path
The Sportsman (PH)
RACKHAM RD
RACKHAM ST

8

Bury
NORFOLK COTTS
SQUIRES COTTS
Dorset House Sch
Castle Farm
THE ALLEY
CHURCH ST
HOG LA
ST HIGH
EAST ST
PH PO
HURST CL
ARUN CL
HURST CL

7
PO
CHURCH LA
COOMBE CRES
HANOVER CL
HOUGHTON LA

13
Amberley
SCHOOL RD
Amberley CE (Contr) Sch
TURNPIKE RD
B2139

6
Sewage Works
Recn Gd
END COTTS
MILL LA
Highdown

NEW BARN RD

5
Wysh House
HIGH TITTEN
Downs Farm

River Arun
Amberley Museum

12
South Downs Way
Houghton Bridge

4
Houghton
George & Dragon (PH)
SOUTH LA
Houghton Farm
Bridge Inn
HOUGHTON BRIDGE
Amberley Sta
Stoke Hazel Wood

STOKE RD

3
B2139
Camp Hill
Canada

11
Monarch's Way

2
North Stoke Farm
North Stoke

1
South Wood

10

| 01 | A | B | 02 | C | | D | 03 | E | F |

← 137   158

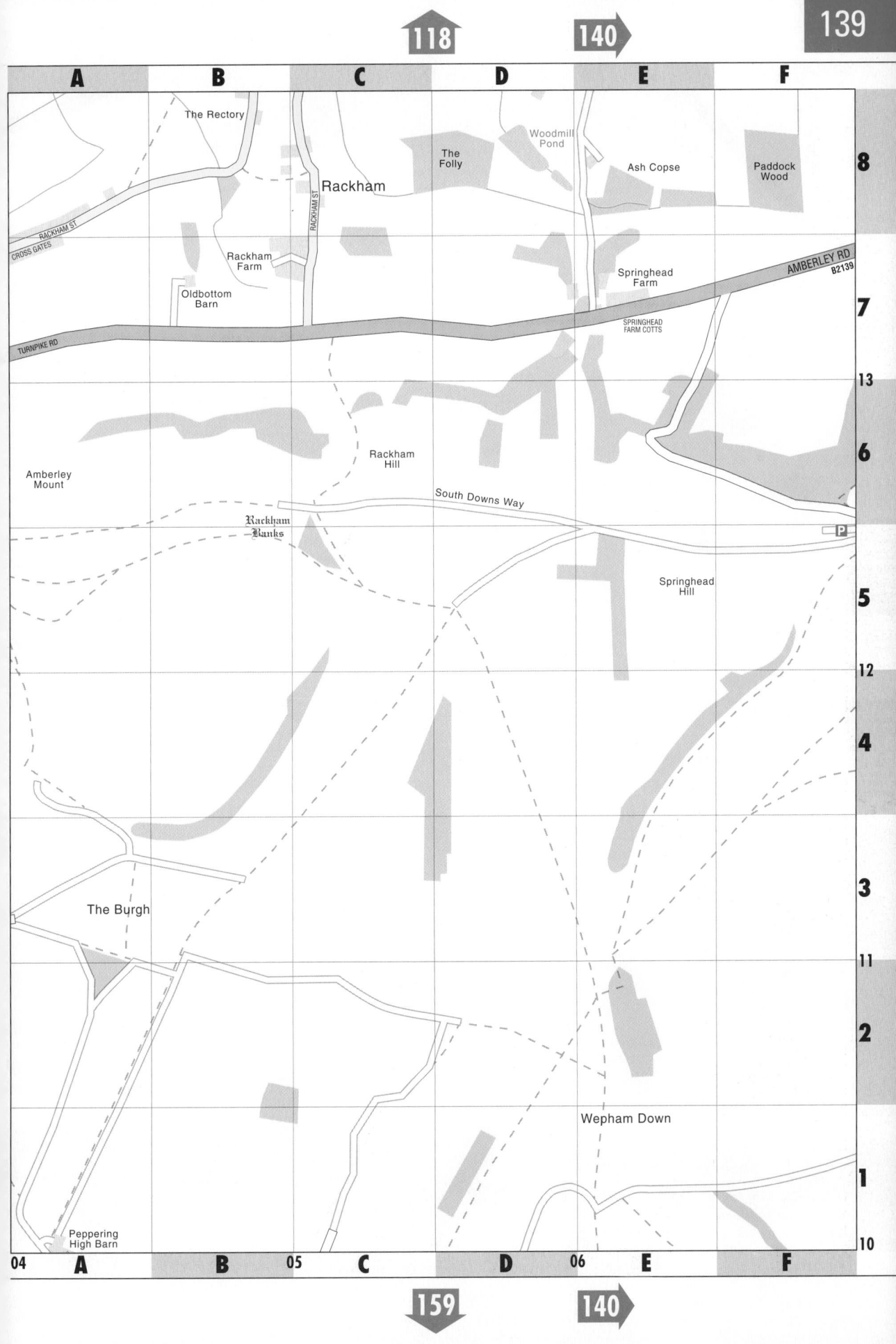

A B C D E F

The Rectory

Woodmill Pond

Ash Copse

Paddock Wood

8

Rackham

The Folly

RACKHAM ST

CROSS GATES

RACKHAM ST

Rackham Farm

Springhead Farm

AMBERLEY RD

B2139

Oldbottom Barn

7

TURNPIKE RD

SPRINGHEAD FARM COTTS

13

Rackham Hill

6

Amberley Mount

South Downs Way

Rackham Banks

P

Springhead Hill

5

12

4

The Burgh

3

11

2

Wepham Down

1

Peppering High Barn

10

04 A B 05 C D 06 E F

◀ **139**
119 ▲

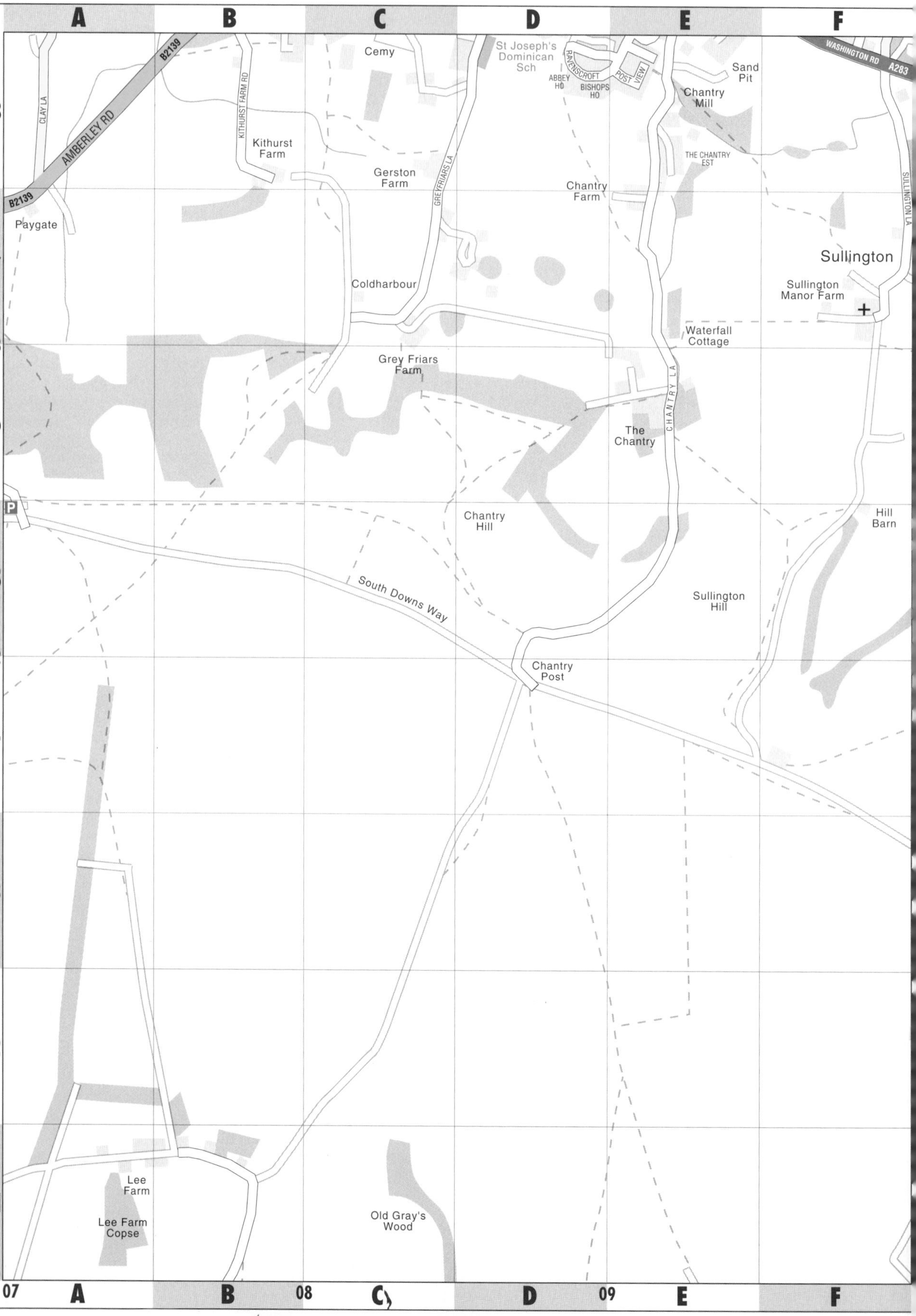

A B C D E F

8

CLAY LA

B2139

AMBERLEY RD

B2139

KITHURST FARM RD

Paygate

Kithurst Farm

Cemy

Gerston Farm

GREYFRIARS LA

St Joseph's Dominican Sch

RAVENSCROFT

ABBEY HO

BISHOPS HO

POST VIEW

WASHINGTON RD A283

Sand Pit

Chantry Mill

THE CHANTRY EST

SULLINGTON LA

7

Coldharbour

Chantry Farm

Sullington

Sullington Manor Farm

+

13

Grey Friars Farm

Waterfall Cottage

6

The Chantry

CHANTRY LA

P

Chantry Hill

Hill Barn

5

South Downs Way

Sullington Hill

12

Chantry Post

4

3

11

2

1

Lee Farm

Lee Farm Copse

Old Gray's Wood

10

07 **A** **B** 08 **C** **D** 09 **E** **F**

◀ **139**
160 ▼

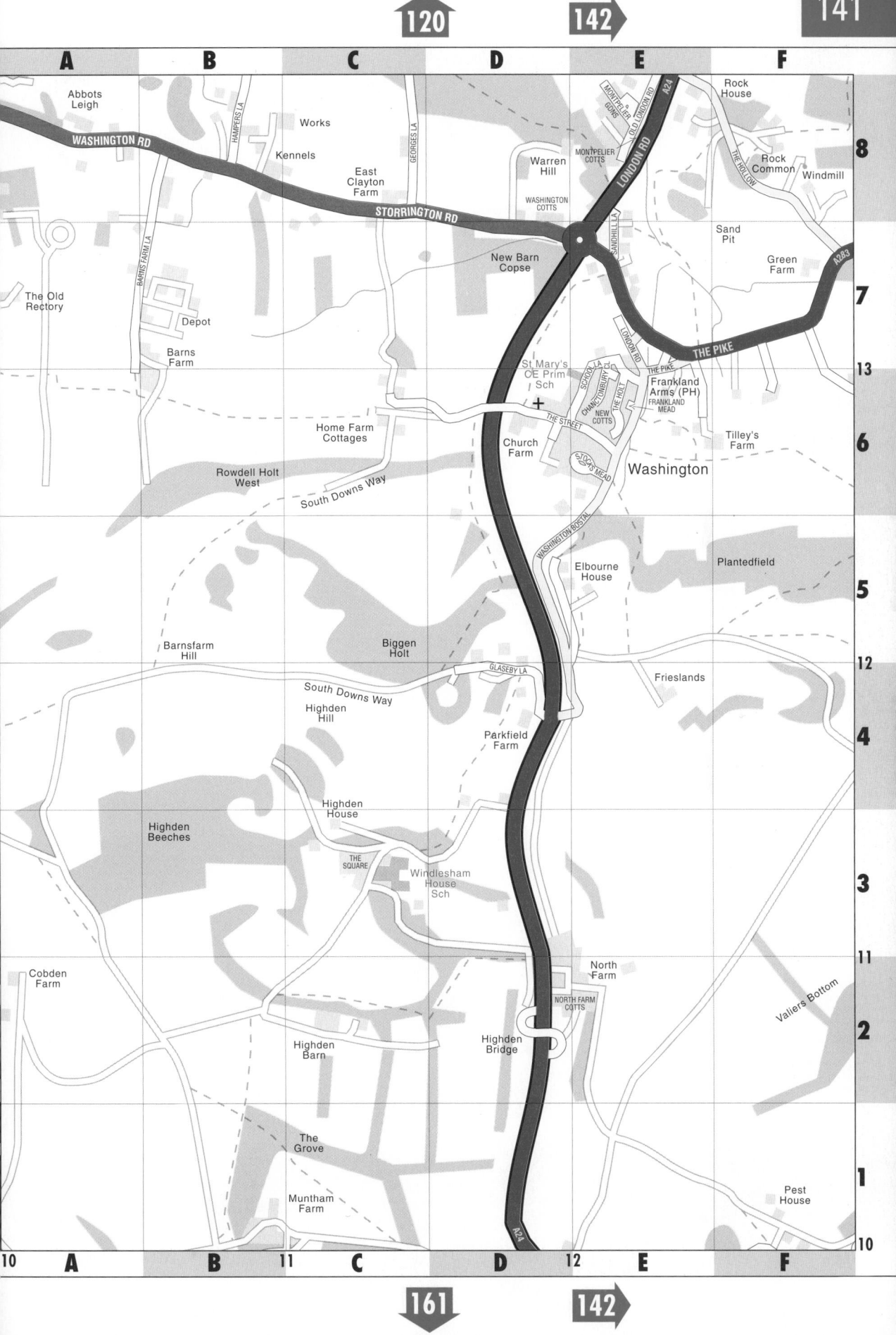

120
142

A B C D E F

Abbots
Leigh

WASHINGTON RD

Works

HAMPERS LA

Kennels

GEORGES LA

East
Clayton
Farm

STORRINGTON RD

Warren
Hill

WASHINGTON
COTTS

MONTPELIER
COTTS

MONTPELIER
GDNS

OLD LONDON RD

A24

LONDON RD

Rock
House

Rock
Common

THE HOLLOW

Windmill

A283

8

The Old
Rectory

BARNS FARM LA

Depot

Barns
Farm

New Barn
Copse

SANDHILL LA

Sand
Pit

Green
Farm

7

LONDON RD

THE PIKE

13

St Mary's
CE Prim
Sch

SCHOOL LA

CHANCTONBURY CL

THE HOLT

THE PIKE

NEW
COTTS

Frankland
Arms (PH)

FRANKLAND
MEAD

Tilley's
Farm

6

Home Farm
Cottages

THE STREET

Church
Farm

STOCKS MEAD

Washington

Rowdell Holt
West

South Downs Way

WASHINGTON BOSTAL

Elbourne
House

Plantedfield

5

Barnsfarm
Hill

Biggen
Holt

Friebslands

12

South Downs Way

GLASEBY LA

Highden
Hill

Parkfield
Farm

4

Highden
Beeches

Highden
House

THE
SQUARE

Windlesham
House
Sch

3

North
Farm

11

Cobden
Farm

Valiers Bottom

NORTH FARM
COTTS

2

Highden
Barn

Highden
Bridge

The
Grove

1

Muntham
Farm

A24

Pest
House

10

10 A B 11 C D 12 E F

A | B | C | D | E | F

8

The Rough

Sevier's Barn

Buncton

Buncton Manor Farm

WATER LA

Refuse Tip

WASHINGTON RD

THE PIKE

A283

Buncton Crossways

The Falconers

7

Lower Chancton Farm

Model Cottages

A283

13

Copyhold Wood

Newcommon Copse

Bushovel Farm

Rokers

MOUSE LA

Weppons

CHANCTONBURY RING RD

Wiston Park

6

Lock's Farm

Owlscroft Barn

Picnic Area

Wiston House

Wiston

Combe Holt

Great Barn Farm

5

Chanctonbury Hill

Chanctonbury Ring

12

4

Chalkpit Wood

Well Bottom

Lion's Bank

Court Plantation

3

South Downs Way

11

Middle Brow

2

Buddington Bottom

Stump Bottom

Steyning Valley

1

Findon Park House

10

13 | A | B | 14 | C | D | 15 | E | F

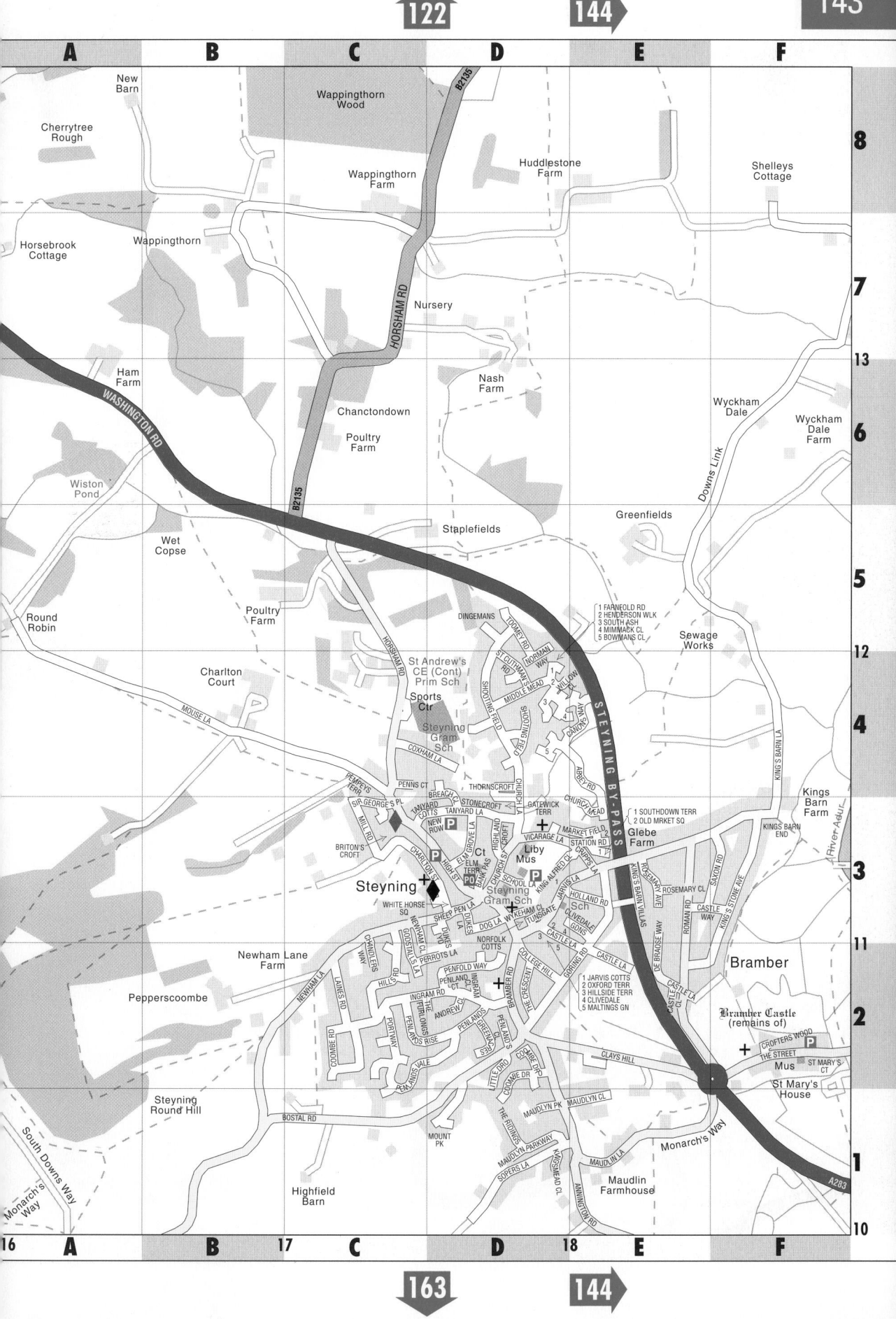

A B C D E F

8

7

13

6

5

12

4

11

3

2

10

New Barn

Cherrytree Rough

Wappingthorn Wood

Wappingthorn Farm

Huddlestone Farm

Shelleys Cottage

Horsebrook Cottage

Wappingthorn

B2135

HORSHAM RD

Nursery

Ham Farm

WASHINGTON RD

Chanctondown

Poultry Farm

Nash Farm

Wyckham Dale

Wyckham Dale Farm

B2135

Wiston Pond

Wet Copse

Staplefields

Downs Link

Greenfields

Round Robin

Poultry Farm

DINGEMANS

1 FARNFOLD RD
2 HENDERSON WLK
3 SOUTH ASH
4 MIMMACK CL
5 BOWMANS CL

Sewage Works

Charlton Court

MOUSE LA

HORSHAM RD

St Andrew's CE (Cont) Prim Sch

Sports Ctr

Steyning Gram Sch

COXHAM LA

MIDDLE MEAD

SHOOTING FIELD

TOOMEY RD

ST CUTHMAN WAY

WILLOW

CANON WAY

STEYNING BY-PASS

ABBEY RD

KING'S BARN LA

Kings Barn Farm

PEMBEYS CT

PENNIS CT

BREACH

SIR GEORGE'S PL

TANYARD COTTS

TANYARD LA

THORNSCROFT

STONECROFT

CHURCH LA

GATEWICK TERR

CHURCH MEAD

1 SOUTHDOWN TERR
2 OLD MRKET SQ

Glebe Farm

KINGS BARN END

River Adur

MILL RD

BRITON'S CROFT

NEW ROW

ELM GROVE LA

HIGH ST

HIGHLAND

VICARAGE LA

MARKET FIELD

STATION RD

CHARLTON ST

Ct

Steyning

CHURCH ST

TANYARD LA

SCHOOL LA

Liby Mus

KING'S ALFRED CT

JARVIS LA

KINGS BARN VILLAS

ROSEMARY AVE

ROSEMARY CL

SAXON RD

ROMAN RD

CASTLE WAY

KING'S STONE AVE

Kings Barn Farm

WHITE HORSE SQ

SHEEP PEN LA

DOG LA

WYKEHAM CL

HOLLAND RD

CLIVEDALE

GDNS

CASTLE LA

Sch

Steyning Gram Sch

DUKES TYE

NEWHAM LA

GOSDENS

VALE

TUNSGATE

Newham Lane Farm

CHANDLERS WAY

HILLS RD

PERROTS LA

INGRAM RD

ANDREW

WYBOURNES

NORFOLK COTTS

BRAMBER RD

THE CRESCENT

COLLEGE HILL

GORSE RD

CASTLE LA

DE BRAOSE WAY

CASTLE CL

CASTLE LA

Bramber

Pepperscoombe

LAINES RD

COOMBE RD

POULTRY

PENLANDS RISE

PENFOLD WAY

HILLS RD

PENLANDS CT

PENLANDS

GREEN CL

LITTLE DRO

COOMBE DR

COOMBE RD

1 JARVIS COTTS
2 OXFORD TERR
3 HILLSIDE TERR
4 CLIVEDALE
5 MALTINGS GN

Bramber Castle (remains of)

CROFTERS WOOD

THE STREET

Mus

ST MARY'S CT

St Mary's House

Steyning Round Hill

BOSTAL RD

PEN LANDS VALE

THE RUINS

MAUDLYN PK

CLAYS HILL

Monarch's Way

South Downs Way

Monarch's Way

MOUNT PK

MAUDLYN PARKWAY

SOPERS LA

KINGSMEAD CL

MAUDLIN LA

ANNINGTON RD

Maudlin Farmhouse

A283

Highfield Barn

A   B   C   D   E   F

8

Stretham
Manor

Westmill
Farm

NEWBARN LA

SHOREHAM RD

HORN LA

A2037

Wood's Mill
Countryside C

Downs Link

Newhall
Farm

NEW HALL LA

SILVER
BIRCHES

HOE WOOD

DOWNS CLO

HOE WS CLO

BEECH

Hoe Wood

7

Wyckham
Farm

New Hall

DOWNSVIEW

WOOD LA

HILL
VIEW

13

TOTTINGTON DR

ORCHARD
CL

Wyckham Dale
Farm

PO

SANDS LA

1

2

3

1 SOUTHVIEW
2 THE OAKS
3 WOODS MILL CL

6

Horton
Wood

Fox & Hounds
(PH)

Small Dole

River Adur

Landfill
Site

MACKLEY'S IND EST

Tottington
Wood

5

Scout
Camp

HILLSIDE LA

Longland
Wood

12

Nightingales

4

Freeland
Cottages

Tottington
Cottages

Horton Hall

Mannings
Farm

Tottington Manor
Farm

Burrells

3

Sele
Priory

Works

Riding
Sch

Upper
Horton

HENFIELD RD

11

CHURCH CL

CHURCH FARM WLK

TUDOR DR

THE
PADDOCKS

THE DRIFTWAY

ST
PETER'S
GN

PEPPERSCOOMBE LA

POUND

BRIDLE CL

Golding Barn
Caravan
Site

PRIORY FIELD

CHURCH LA

DEACONS WAY

DOWNLAND RD

DOWNLAND CL

TRULEIGH

2

SALTINGS WAY

SCHOOL RD

MONKS WAY

WINDMILL
CL

UNDERHILL RD

NEWLAND RD

ADUR
VALLEY
CT

Windmill
Hill

GOLDING BARN FARM
(WORKS)

Room Bottom

RIVERSIDE

Upper Beeding
Cty Prim Sch

HYDE
SQ

HYDE LA

MANOR RD

COLLEGE RD

THE STREET

PO

P

SELE GDNS

HIGH ST

STANDEN
CT

Beeding
Bridge

ADUR
VIEW

DAWN CRES

DAWN CL

NEW RD

THE
FLORETS

HOBS
ACRE

MAUDLIN RD

MAUDLINS FARM RD

1

A283

Upper
Beeding

Castle Town

THE BOSTAL

South Downs Way

STEYNING BY-PASS

A283

SHOREHAM RD

A2037

The Towers
Convent Sch

Monarch's Way

10

Beeding Court
Farm

19   A   20   B   C   20   D   21   E   F

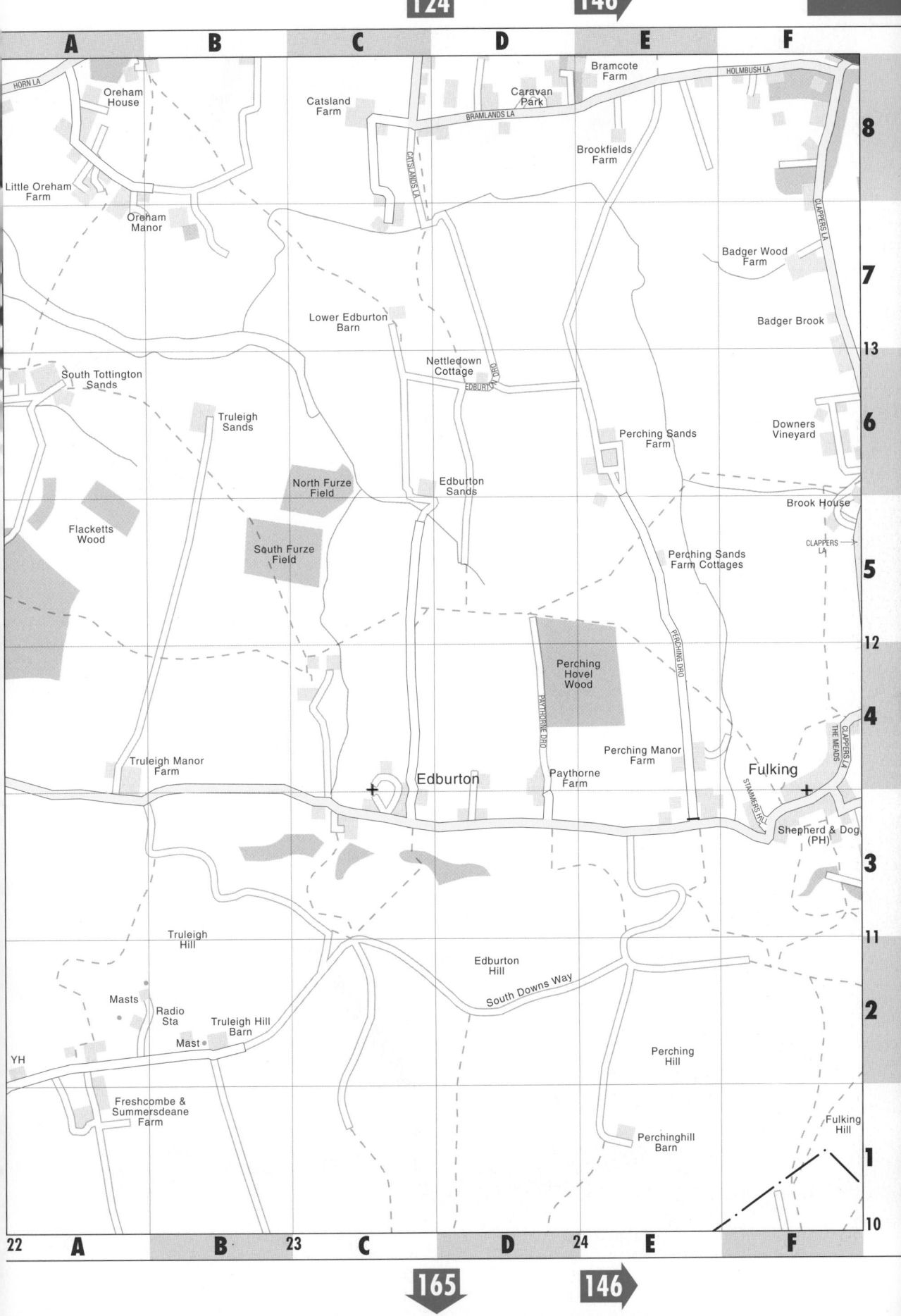

A B C D E F

8
7
13
6
5
12
4
3
11
2
1
10

HORN LA
Oreham House
Little Oreham Farm
Oreham Manor
South Tottington Sands
Truleigh Sands
Flacketts Wood
North Furze Field
South Furze Field
Truleigh Manor Farm
Truleigh Hill
Masts
Radio Sta
Mast
Truleigh Hill Barn
YH
Freshcombe & Summersdeane Farm

Catsland Farm
CATSLANDS LA
BRAMLANDS LA
Bramcote Farm
Caravan Park
HOLMBUSH LA
Brookfields Farm
Lower Edburton Barn
Nettledown Cottage
DRO
EDBURY
Edburton Sands
Edburton
Paythorne Farm
PAYTHORNE DRO
Perching Hovel Wood
Edburton Hill
South Downs Way
Perchinghill Barn

Badger Wood Farm
CLAPPERS LA
Badger Brook
Downers Vineyard
Perching Sands Farm
Brook House
CLAPPERS LA
Perching Sands Farm Cottages
PERCHING DRO
Perching Manor Farm
THE MEADS
CLAPPERS LA
Fulking
STAMMERS HILL
Shepherd & Dog (PH)
Perching Hill
Fulking Hill

145
125

A   B   C   D   E   F

A281

A281

Park Cottages

Park Wood

Newtimber Place

Old Rectory

A23

LONDON RD

Round Hill

8

Stonestaples Wood

Newtimber Wood

CHURCH LA

Redhouse Farm

7

Poynings Grange Farm

WEST RD

A281

A23

13

Cobsham Rough

Newtimber Holt

CLAPPERS LA

Grange Lodge Cottages

CROSSWAYS COTTS

Newtimber Hill

6

High Beeches

BEGGAR'S LA

MILL CT
MILL CL

MILL LA

Poynings

North Hill

5

ROYAL OAK COTTS

West Hill

DYKE CL

12

PH

PO

Cemy

4

Wickhurst Barn

East Hill

Saddlescombe

3

Devil's Dyke

P

Devil's Dyke Hotel

Devil's Dyke

P

Sussex Border Path
South Downs Way

Summer Down

11

Ewe Bottom

2

CH

Pond Brow

DEVIL'S DYKE RD

Dyke Golf Course

P

1

Devil's Dyke Farm

10

25 A   B 26 C   D 27 E   F

145
166

Wolstonbury

Wolstonbury Hill

Wellcombe Bottom

Clayton

+

UNDERHILL LA

Clayton Holt

Rockrose

Clayton Windmills

P   Jill   Jack

MILL LA

Chantry

CLAYTON HILL

Clayton Tunnel

New Barn Farm

13

South Downs Way

WEST RD

DALE HILL   PYECOMBE

Pyecombe

CH

Pyecombe Golf Course

6

Wayfield Farm

CHURCH HILL

THE WISHE-

SCHOOL LA

Rag Bottom

Cow Down

Riding School

PH

CHURCH LA

A273

Haresdean

Middle Brow

5

12

LONDON RD

South Hill

Sussex Border Path

Holt Bottom

Pangdean Farm

Pangdean Holt

War Meml

South Hill

Poor Brow

South Hill Cottages

11

South Hill Farm

Deep Bottom

The Pylons

Hogtrough Bottom

Scare Hill

Varncombe Hill

Sussex Border Path

Ewebottom Hill

Ewe Bottom

10

A23

Waterhall Golf Course

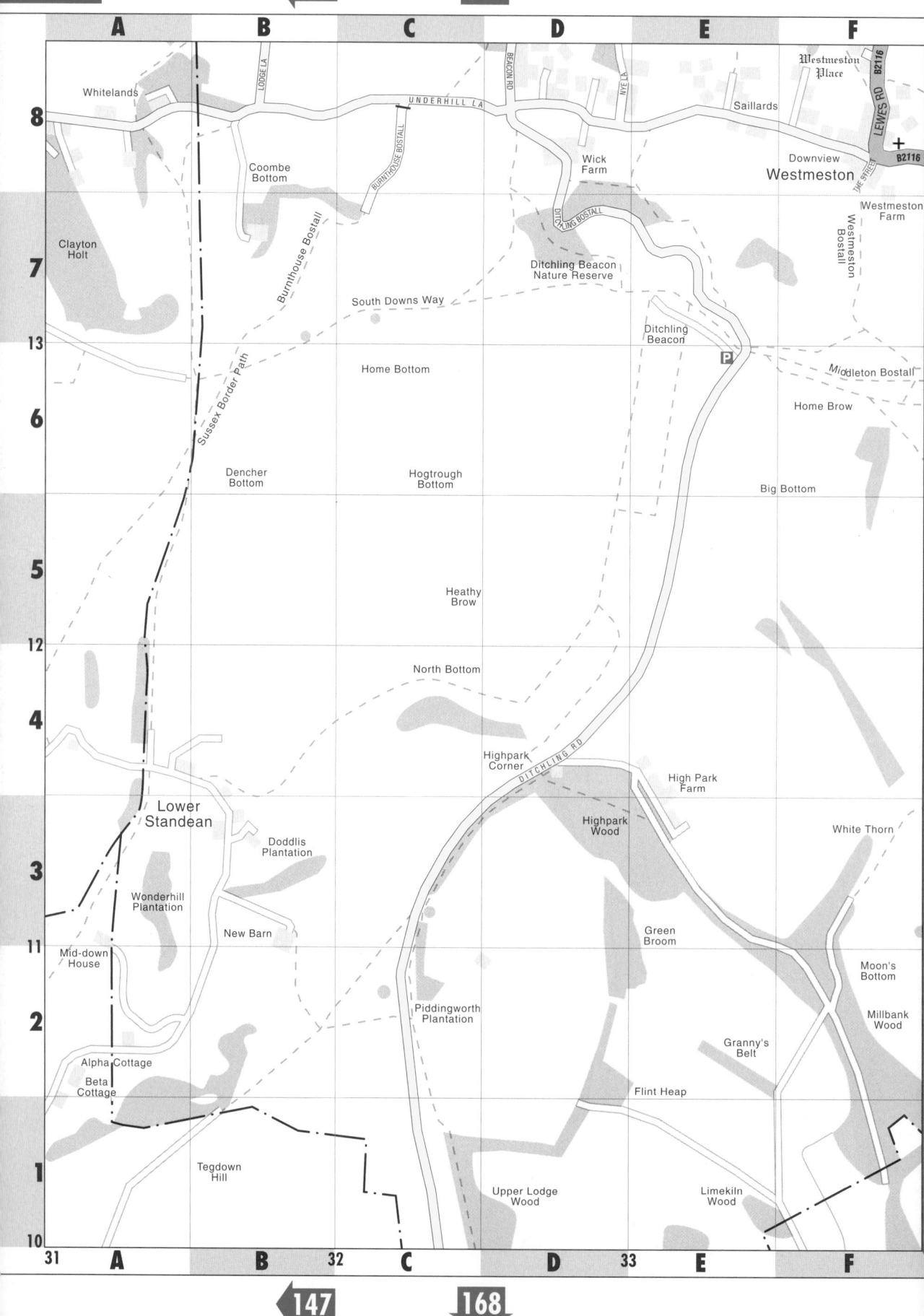

A   B   C   D   E   F

8   Whitelands   Coombe Bottom   UNDERHILL LA   Wick Farm   Saillards   Westmeston Place   LEWES RD   B2116   Downview   Westmeston   B2116

7   Clayton Holt   Burnthouse Bostall   South Downs Way   Ditchling Beacon Nature Reserve   Westmeston Farm   Westmeston Bostall

13   Ditchling Beacon   Middleton Bostall

6   Home Bottom   Home Brow

    Dencher Bottom   Hogtrough Bottom   Big Bottom

5   Heathy Brow

12   North Bottom

4   Highpark Corner   DITCHLING RD   High Park Farm

    Lower Standean   Doddlis Plantation   Highpark Wood   White Thorn

3   Wonderhill Plantation   Green Broom   Moon's Bottom

11   New Barn   Millbank Wood

    Mid-down House   Piddingworth Plantation   Granny's Belt

2   Alpha Cottage   Beta Cottage   Flint Heap

1   Tegdown Hill   Upper Lodge Wood   Limekiln Wood

10

31   A   B   32   C   D   33   E   F

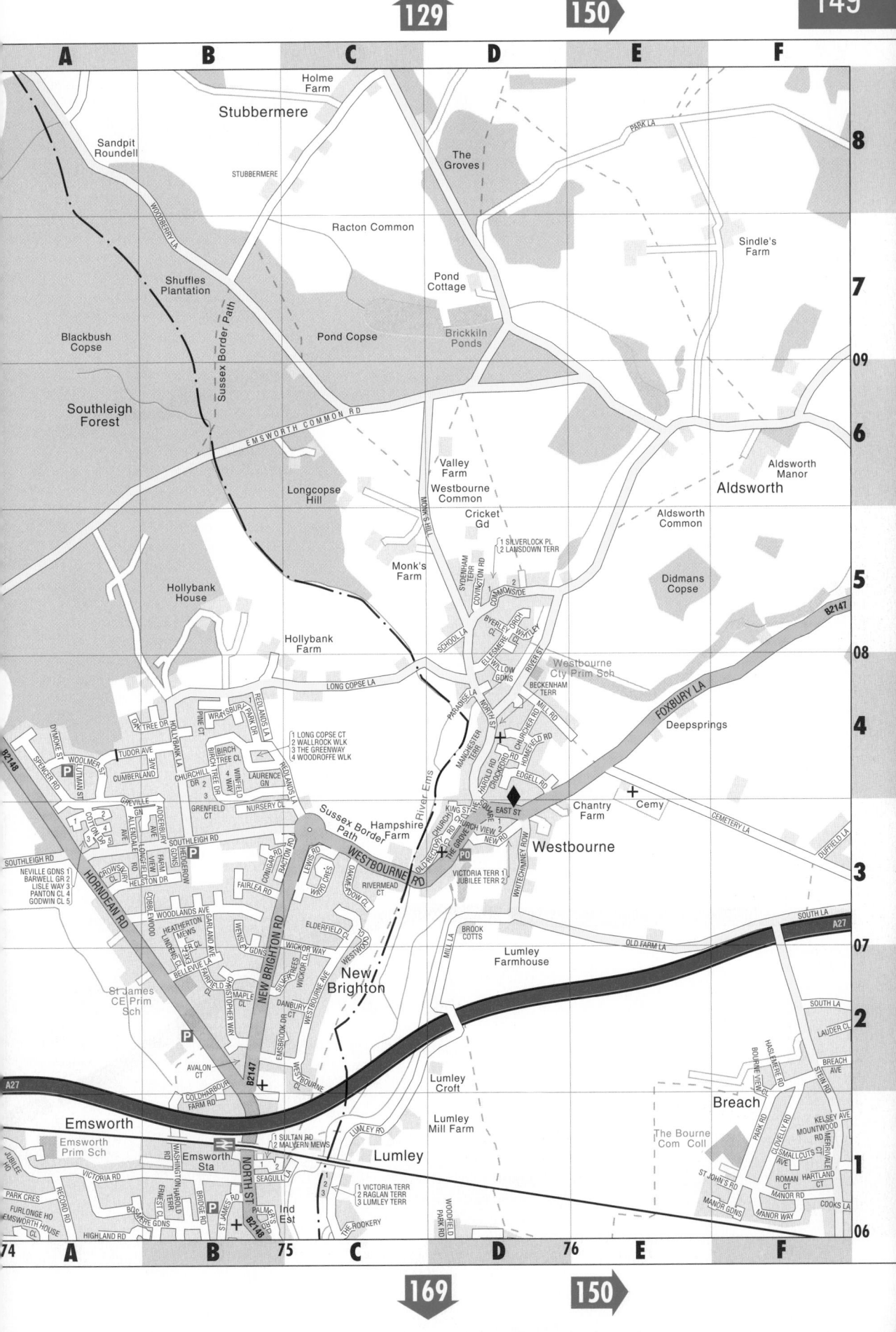

A B C D E F

8

7

09

6

5

08

4

07

3

2

1

06

Holme Farm

Stubbermere

Sandpit Roundell

Stubbermere

The Groves

Park La

Sindle's Farm

Racton Common

Shuffles Plantation

Pond Cottage

Blackbush Copse

WOODBERRY LA

Pond Copse

Brickkiln Ponds

Sussex Border Path

Southleigh Forest

EMSWORTH COMMON RD

Longcopse Hill

Valley Farm

Westbourne Common

Aldsworth Manor

Aldsworth

Cricket Gd

Aldsworth Common

MONK'S HILL

Monk's Farm

1 SILVERLOCK PL
2 LANSDOWN TERR

Didmans Copse

B2147

Hollybank House

SYDENHAM TERR

COVINGTON RD

COMMONSIDE

Hollybank Farm

SCHOOL LA

BYERLEY CL

WHITLEY ORCH

Westbourne Cty Prim Sch

08

LONG COPSE LA

ELLESMERE ORCH

WILLOW GDNS

River St

BECKENHAM TERR

FOXBURY LA

4

1 LONG COPSE CT
2 WALLROCK WLK
3 THE GREENWAY
4 WOODROFFE WLK

OAK TREE DR

REDLANDS LA

PARK DR

BIRCH TREE CL

REDLANDS LA

WRA'SBURY

PINE CT

PARADISE LA

MANCHESTER TERR

NORTH ST

MILL RD

HONEYFIELD RD

CHURCHER RD

Deepsprings

WOLMER ST

SPENCER RD

TUDOR AVE

HOLLYBANK LA

CUMBERLAND CT

CHURCHILL DR

WINFIELD

LAURENCE GN

3 4 WAY

CROCKFORD RD

HAROLD RD

EDGELL RD

Cemy

B2148

DYMOKE ST

PUTMAN ST

GREVILLE GN

NURSERY CL

Sussex Border Path

EAST ST

CEMETERY LA

DUFFIELD LA

Chantry Farm

ADDERBURY AVE

ALLENDALE AVE

LONGFIELD

COTTON LA

Hampshire Farm

KING ST

THE SQUARE

Westbourne

NEVILLE GDNS 1
BARWELL GR 2
LISLE WAY 3
PANTON CL 4
GODWIN CL 5

Southleigh RD

HEDGEROW

FARM

GRENFIELD CT

COMIGAR RD

LEWIS RD

BACTON RD

WESTBOURNE RD

OLD RECTORY

CHURCH RD

CHURCH VIEW

NEW RD

PO

Victoria Terr 1
Jubilee Terr 2

HORNDEAN RD

CROWSBURY CL

FAIRLEA RD

NEW BRIGHTON RD

GARLAND RD

FAIRFIELD

WENSLEY GDNS

River Ems

GAME MEADOW CL

Rivermead CT

WHITCHIMNEY ROW

SOUTH LA

A27

COBBLEWOOD

Woodlands Ave

HEATHERTON MEWS

LINDENS CL

FIR CL

ELDERFIELD CL

WICKOR WAY

WICKOR CL

Brook Cotts

Lumley Farmhouse

OLD FARM LA

SOUTH LA

St James CE Prim Sch

BELLEVUE LA

CHRISTOPHER WAY

MAPLE CL

DANBURY CL

SILVERLEES

WESTBOURNE AVE

New Brighton

WESTBROOK

MILL LA

HASLEMERE RD

BOURNE VIEW

LAUDER CL

BREACH AVE

AVALON CT

EMSBROOK DR

WESTBOURNE WAY

B2147

COLDHARBOUR FARM RD

Lumley Croft

Lumley Mill Farm

PARK LA

CLOVELLY RD

STEIN RD

Breach

MOUNTWOOD RD

MERIVALE AVE

KELSEY AVE

SMALLCUTS AVE

ROMAN CT

HARTLAND CT

A27

Emsworth

Emsworth Prim Sch

Emsworth Sta

WASHINGTON HAROLD TERR

ERNEST RD

NORTH ST

SEAGULL LA

1 SULTAN RD
2 MALVERN MEWS

Lumley

LUMLEY RD

WOODFIELD PARK RD

The Bourne Com Coll

St John's Rd

MANOR GDNS

MANOR RD

COOKS LA

MANOR WAY

JUBILEE RD

PARK CRES

RECORD RD

VICTORIA RD

BRIDGE RD

ST JAMES RD

BOSMERE GDNS

B2148

PALM

Ind Est

1 VICTORIA TERR
2 RAGLAN TERR
3 LUMLEY TERR

THE ROOKERY

FURLONGE HO
EMSWORTH HOUSE CL

HIGHLAND RD

74 75 76

A B C D E F

149 130

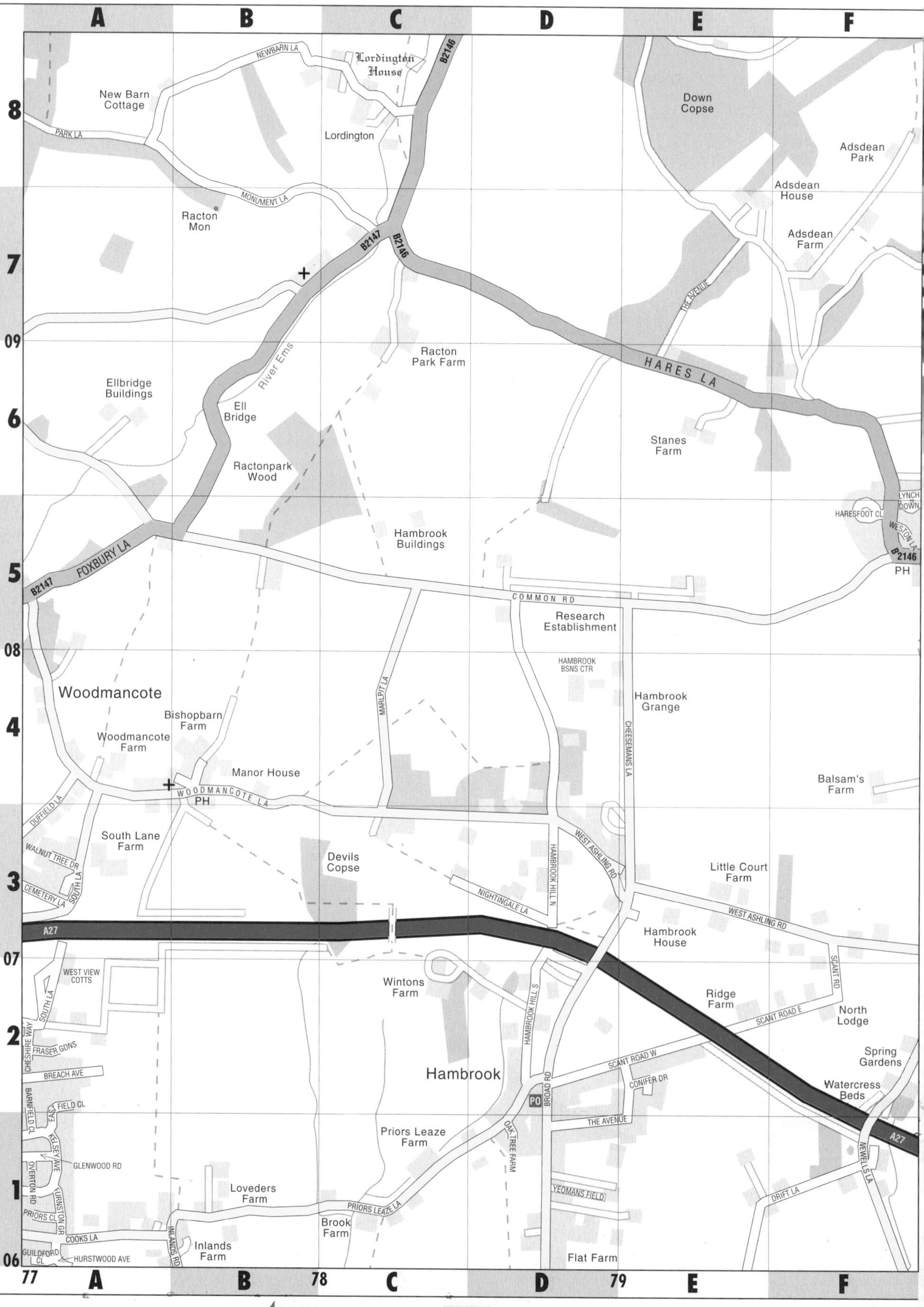

A   B   C   D   E   F

8

New Barn
Cottage

NEWBARN LA

Lordington
House

B2146

Down
Copse

Adsdean
Park

Adsdean
House

PARK LA

Lordington

MONUMENT LA

Adsdean
Farm

Racton
Mon

7

B2147

B2146

+

09

River Ems

Racton
Park Farm

HARES LA

Ellbridge
Buildings

Ell
Bridge

6

Stanes
Farm

LYNCH
DOWN

Ractonpark
Wood

HARESFOOT CL

WESTON LA

B2146

PH

Hambrook
Buildings

5

FOXBURY LA

B2147

COMMON RD

Research
Establishment

08

HAMBROOK
BSNS CTR

Woodmancote

MARLPIT LA

Hambrook
Grange

CHEESSMANS LA

4

Bishopbarn
Farm

Woodmancote
Farm

Manor House

WOODMANCOTE LA

PH

+

Balsam's
Farm

DUFFIELD LA

WALNUT TREE DR

South Lane
Farm

Devils
Copse

WEST ASHLING RD

Little Court
Farm

3

CEMETERY LA

SOUTH LA

NIGHTINGALE LA

HAMBROOK HILL S

WEST ASHLING RD

A27

07

Hambrook
House

SCANT RD

WEST VIEW
COTTS

Wintons
Farm

Ridge
Farm

North
Lodge

2

CHESHIRE WAY

SOUTH LA

FRASER GDNS

BREACH AVE

Hambrook

HAMBROOK HILL S

SCANT ROAD E

Spring
Gardens

BARNFIELD CL

EAST FIELD CL

BROAD RD

SCANT ROAD W

THE AVENUE

CONIFER DR

Watercress
Beds

A27

Priors Leaze
Farm

PO

OAK TREE FARM

PEWELL LA

KELSEY AVE

KURNSTON GR

GLENWOOD RD

Loveders
Farm

PRIORS LEAZE LA

YEOMANS FIELD

DRIFT LA

1

OVERTON RD

PRIORS CL

Brook
Farm

GUILDFORD
L CL

HURSTWOOD AVE

COOKS LA

INLANDS RD

Inlands
Farm

Flat Farm

06

77   A   B   78   C   D   79   E   F

149 170

131
152

A
B
C
D
E
F
8
7
09
6
5
08
4
3
07
2
1
06
80
81
82
Funtington Plantation
East Plantation
Funtington Down
Stoke Down
Downs Farm
West Copse
Lodge
Upper Wood Lynch
Bowhill House
BOWHILL LA
Lodge
Blackhill's Row
Funtington Down House
DOWNS RD
Hollandsfield
Woodend
Poultry Farm
West Stoke House
THE BROAD WLK
The Old Rectory
Broadley Copse
West Stoke
LYNCH DOWN
Dellfield
FIVE ACRES
DAVYS CT
Ashling Wood
WOODEND
Stoke Wood
CHURCH LA
ADMIRALS WLK
Lye Wood
PO
Funtington
Coopersfield
Southwood Farm
LYE LA
Moor Barn
B2178
B2146
WATERY LA
Horse and Groom (PH)
Ashling Park
Northbrook Farm
LYE LA
East Ashling
Nurseries
SANDY LA
West Ashling
PH
DOWN ST
Densworth
East Ashling Farm
Dickers Farm
MILLPOND LA
KNIGHTS COTTS
HEATHER CL
Dickers Copse
B2178
SCHOOL DELL
MALT HOUSE LA
Funtington Cty Prim Sch
Ryelands Farm
MILL RD
MALTHOUSE COTTS
SOUTHBROOK RD
Mount Pleasant
EDITH COTTS
Mouthey's Copse
Southbrook Farm
NEWELLS LA
Greenland's Copse
MOUTHEY'S LA
Waterloo Farm
SOUTHBROOK RD
Tryways Farm
Oak Wood
Oakwood Sch
Merryfields Plantation
Scuttle Gate
The Osiers
Breadbare Copse
Mouthey's Common
RATHAM LA
Breeches Copse
Oakwood Farm
Ratham House
Knapp Copse
CLAY LA
Robin Hill Farm
Doublebarn
Ratham Mill
RATHAM LA
B2146
Chalcroft Copse
New Barn
BROOKS LA
A27

171
152

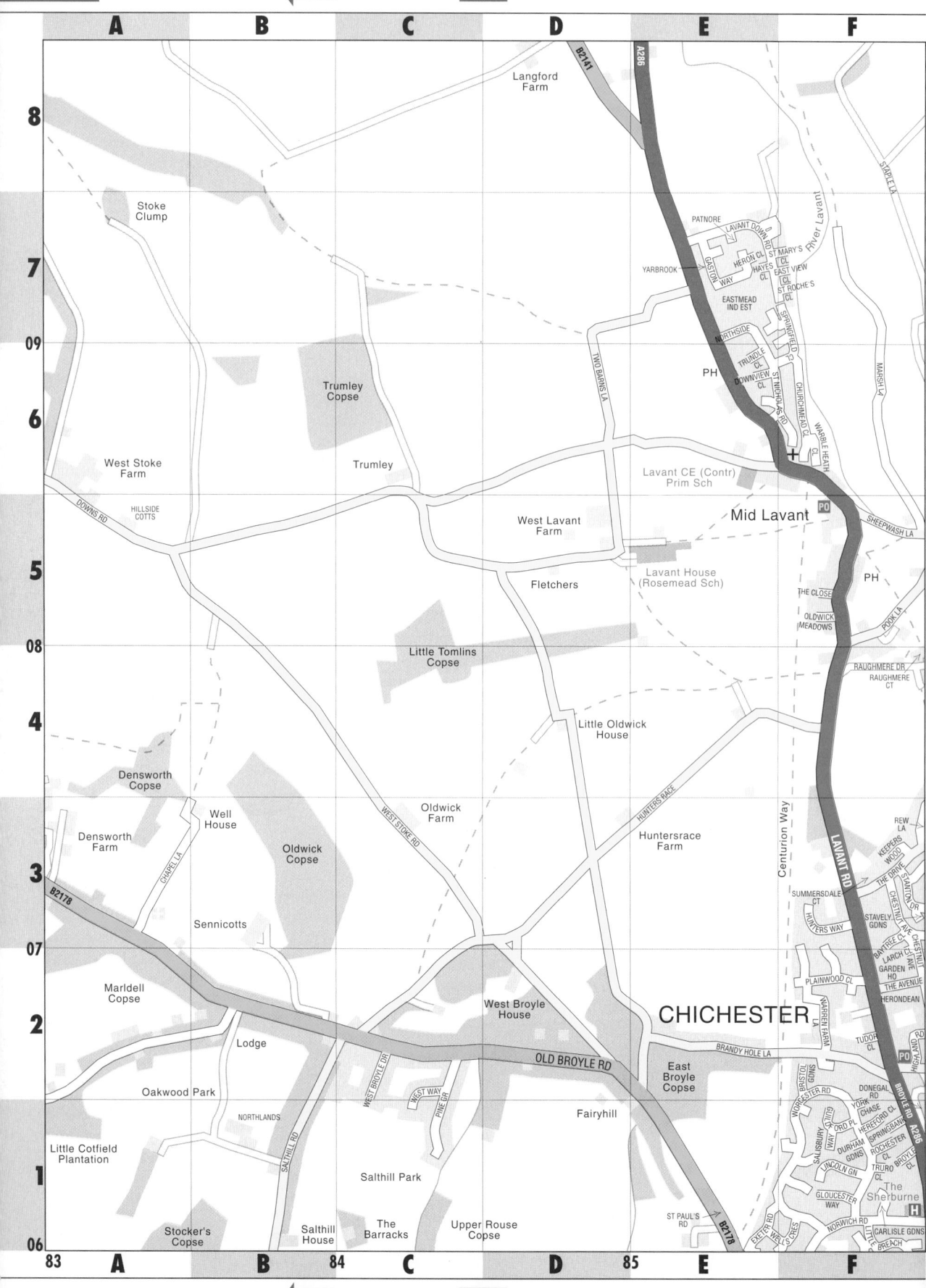

A B C D E F

8

7

09

6

5

08

4

08

3

07

2

07

1

06

83 A 84 B C 85 D E F

Langford Farm

B2141

A286

Stoke Clump

Patnore

LAVANT DOWN RD

GASTON WAY

HERON CL

ST MARY'S CL

HAYES CL

EAST VIEW

ST ROCHE'S CL

Yarbrook

EASTMEAD IND EST

NORTHSIDE

SPRINGFIELD

TRUNDLE CL

DOWNVIEW CL

ST NICHOLAS RD

CHURCHMEAD CL

River Lavant

STARTLE LA

MARSH LA

Trumley Copse

TWO BARNS LA

PH

WARBLE HEATH

West Stoke Farm

Trumley

DOWNS RD

HILLSIDE COTTS

Lavant CE (Contr) Prim Sch

Mid Lavant

PO

SHEEPWASH LA

West Lavant Farm

Fletchers

Lavant House (Rosemead Sch)

THE CLOSE

OLDWICK MEADOWS

PH

POOK LA

Little Tomlins Copse

RAUGHMERE DR

RAUGHMERE CT

Densworth Copse

Little Oldwick House

WEST STOKE RD

Oldwick Farm

HUNTERS RACE

Centurion Way

REW LA

Well House

CHAPEL LA

Densworth Farm

Oldwick Copse

Huntersrace Farm

LAVANT RD

KEEPERS WOOD

THE DRIVE

STANTON CL

CHESTNUT DR

STAVELEY GDNS

HUNTERS WAY

SUMMERSDALE CT

BAYTREE CL

CHESTNUT AVE

LARCH CL

GARDEN HO

THE AVENUE

HERONDEAN

B2178

Sennicotts

Marldell Copse

Lodge

WEST BROYLE DR

West Broyle House

CHICHESTER

BRANDY HOLE LA

PLAINWOOD CL

WARREN FARM LA

TUDOR CL

PO

A286

Oakwood Park

NORTHLANDS

WEST WAY

PINE GR

East Broyle Copse

OLD BROYLE RD

Fairyhill

WORCESTER RD

DONEGAL RD

YORK CHASE

HEREFORD CL

SPRINGBANK

ROCHESTER CL

TRURO CL

BROYLE RD

Little Cotfield Plantation

SALTHILL RD

Salthill Park

St PAUL'S RD

B2178

GUILDFORD PL

SALISBURY GDNS

DURHAM CL

LINCOLN GN

EXETER RD

WELLS CRES

The Sherburne

GLOUCESTER WAY

NORWICH RD

CARLISLE GDNS

BREACH

Stocker's Copse

Salthill House

The Barracks

Upper Rouse Copse

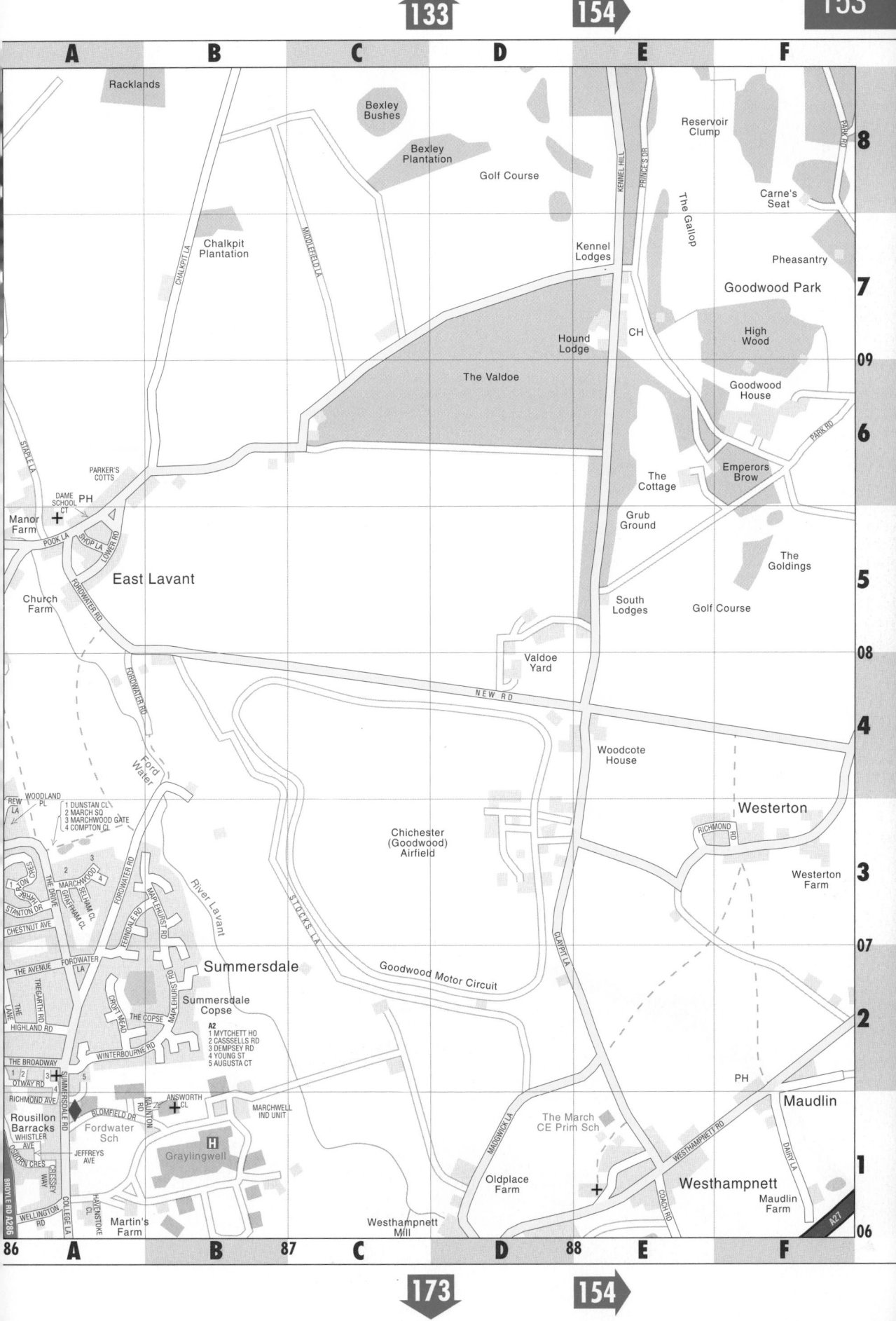
A
B
C
D
E
F
Racklands
Bexley Bushes
Bexley Plantation
Golf Course
Reservoir Clump
Carne's Seat
The Gallop
Pheasantry
Goodwood Park
High Wood
Goodwood House
Emperors Brow
The Cottage
Grub Ground
The Goldings
Golf Course
South Lodges
Chalkpit Plantation
Kennel Lodges
Hound Lodge
CH
The Valdoe
KENNEL HILL
PRINCE'S DR
PARK RD
CHALKPIT LA
MIDDLEFIELD LA
STAPLE LA
PARKER'S COTTS
DAME SCHOOL CT
PH
Manor Farm
POOK LA
SHOP LA
LOWER RD
East Lavant
Church Farm
FORDWATER RD
Valdoe Yard
NEW RD
Woodcote House
Westerton
RICHMOND RD
Westerton Farm
Ford Water
WOODLAND PL
REW LA
1 DUNSTAN CL
2 MARCH SQ
3 MARCHWOOD GATE
4 COMPTON CL
Chichester (Goodwood) Airfield
River Lavant
STOCKS LA
CLAYPIT LA
Goodwood Motor Circuit
Summersdale
Summersdale Copse
A2
1 MYTCHETT HO
2 CASSSELLS RD
3 DEMPSEY RD
4 YOUNG ST
5 AUGUSTA CT
MARCHWOOD
SELHAM CL
GRAFFHAM CL
THE DRIVE
STANTON DR
CHESTNUT AVE
THE AVENUE
FORDWATER LA
TREGARTH RD
THE LANE
HIGHLAND RD
THE BROADWAY
OTWAY RD
RICHMOND AVE
FERNDALE RD
MAPLEHURST RD
CROFT MEAD
THE COPSE
WINTERBOURNE RD
SUMMERSDALE RD
BLOMFIELD DR
NAUNTON RD
ANSWORTH CL
MARCHWELL IND UNIT
Rousillon Barracks
WHISTLER AVE
OSBORN CRES
JEFFREYS AVE
CRESSEY WAY
WELLINGTON RD
COLLEGE LA
HAVENSTOKE CL
BROYLE RD A286
Fordwater Sch
Graylingwell
H
Martin's Farm
Westhampnett Mill
MADGWICK LA
Oldplace Farm
The March CE Prim Sch
COACH RD
WESTHAMPNETT RD
Westhampnett
PH
Maudlin
DAIRY LA
Maudlin Farm
A27
8
7
09
6
5
08
4
3
07
2
1
06
86
87
88

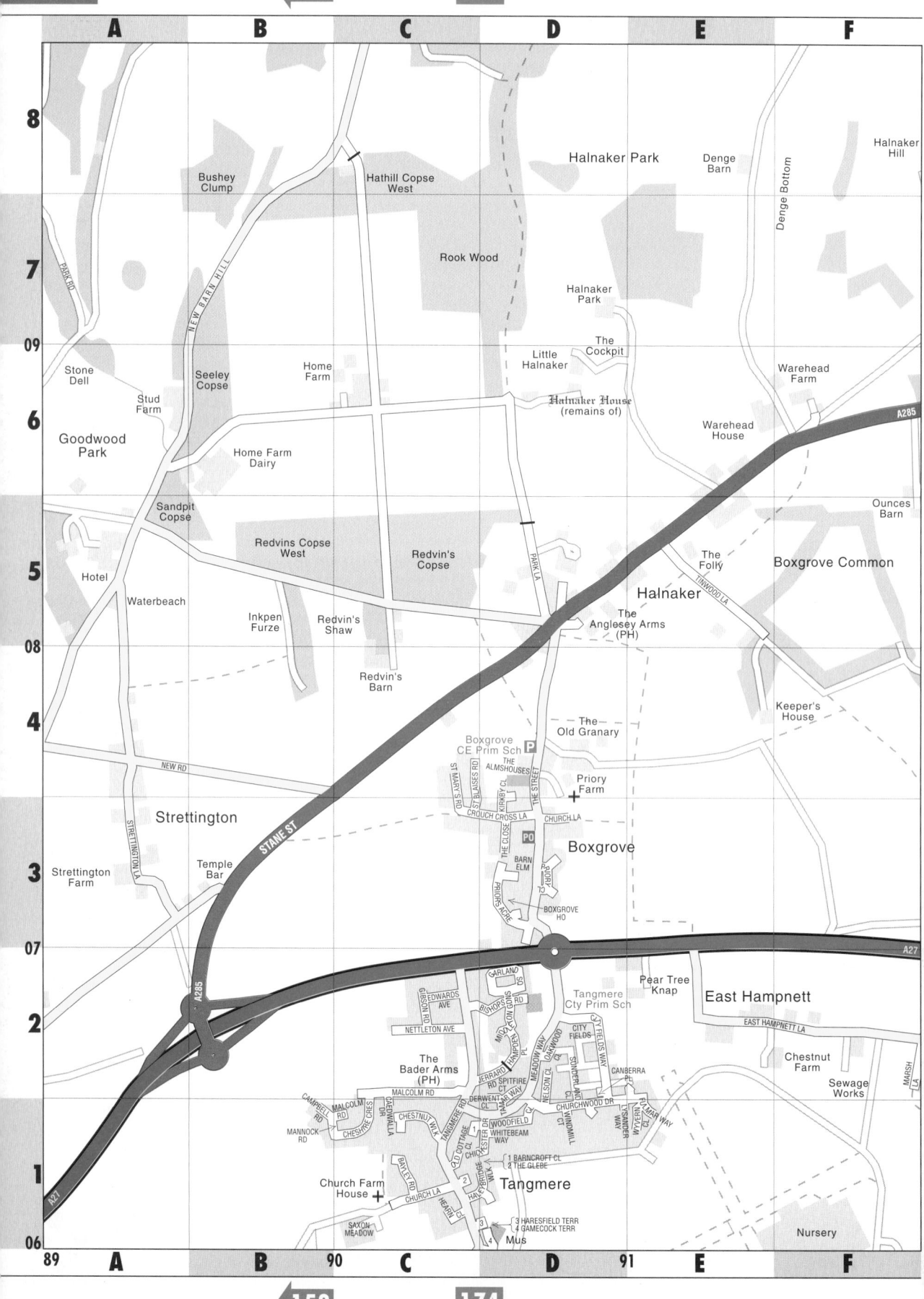

153
134

A B C D E F

8

Bushey
Clump

Hathill Copse
West

Halnaker Park

Denge
Barn

Denge Bottom

Halnaker
Hill

7

Rook Wood

NEW BARN HILL

Halnaker
Park

09

Stone
Dell

Seeley
Copse

Home
Farm

Little
Halnaker

The
Cockpit

Warehead
Farm

A285

Stud
Farm

6

Goodwood
Park

Home Farm
Dairy

Halnaker House
(remains of)

Warehead
House

Ounces
Barn

Sandpit
Copse

Redvins Copse
West

Redvin's
Copse

PARK LA

The
Folly

Boxgrove Common

5

Hotel

Halnaker

Waterbeach

Inkpen
Furze

Redvin's
Shaw

TINWOOD LA

Keeper's
House

08

Redvin's
Barn

The
Anglesey Arms
(PH)

The
Old Granary

4

NEW RD

Boxgrove
CE Prim Sch P

THE
ALMSHOUSES

Priory
Farm

STANE ST

STRETTINGTON LA

Strettington

ST MARY'S RD

ST BLAISES RD

KIRBY CL

THE STREET

CROUCH CROSS LA

CHURCH LA

Boxgrove

3

Strettington
Farm

Temple
Bar

THE CLOSE

BARN
ELM

PO

A285

PRIORS ACRE

BOXGROVE
HO

07

A27

A27

A27

GARLAND

Pear Tree
Knap

East Hampnett

2

GIBSON RD

BISHOPS RD

ST EDWARDS
AVE

TANGMERE GDNS

Tangmere
Cty Prim Sch

CITY
FIELDS

EAST HAMPNETT LA

NETTLETON AVE

MEADOW CL

OAKWOOD

CITY FIELDS WAY

CANBERRA
PL

Chestnut
Farm

The
Bader Arms
(PH)

GERRARD
RD SPITFIRE

NELSON CL

SAUNDERS
CL

CHURCHWOOD DR

WINDMILL
CT

LYSANDER
WAY

TANGMERE RD

MALCOLM RD

TANE WAY

LAMAR WAY

MARSH LA

Sewage
Works

CAMPBELL RD

MALCOLM
RD

CADEWALLA
DR

CHESTNUT WLK

DERWENT CL

WOODFIELD

WHITEBEAM
WAY

1 BARNCROFT CL
2 THE GLEBE

MANNOCK
RD

CHESHIRE CRES

CHESTER DR

OLD COTTAGE

CHICHESTER

HAY BRIDGE WLK

1

Church Farm
House

BAYLEY RD

CHURCH LA

HEARN

Tangmere

SAXON
MEADOW

3 HARESFIELD TERR
4 GAMECOCK TERR

Mus

06

Nursery

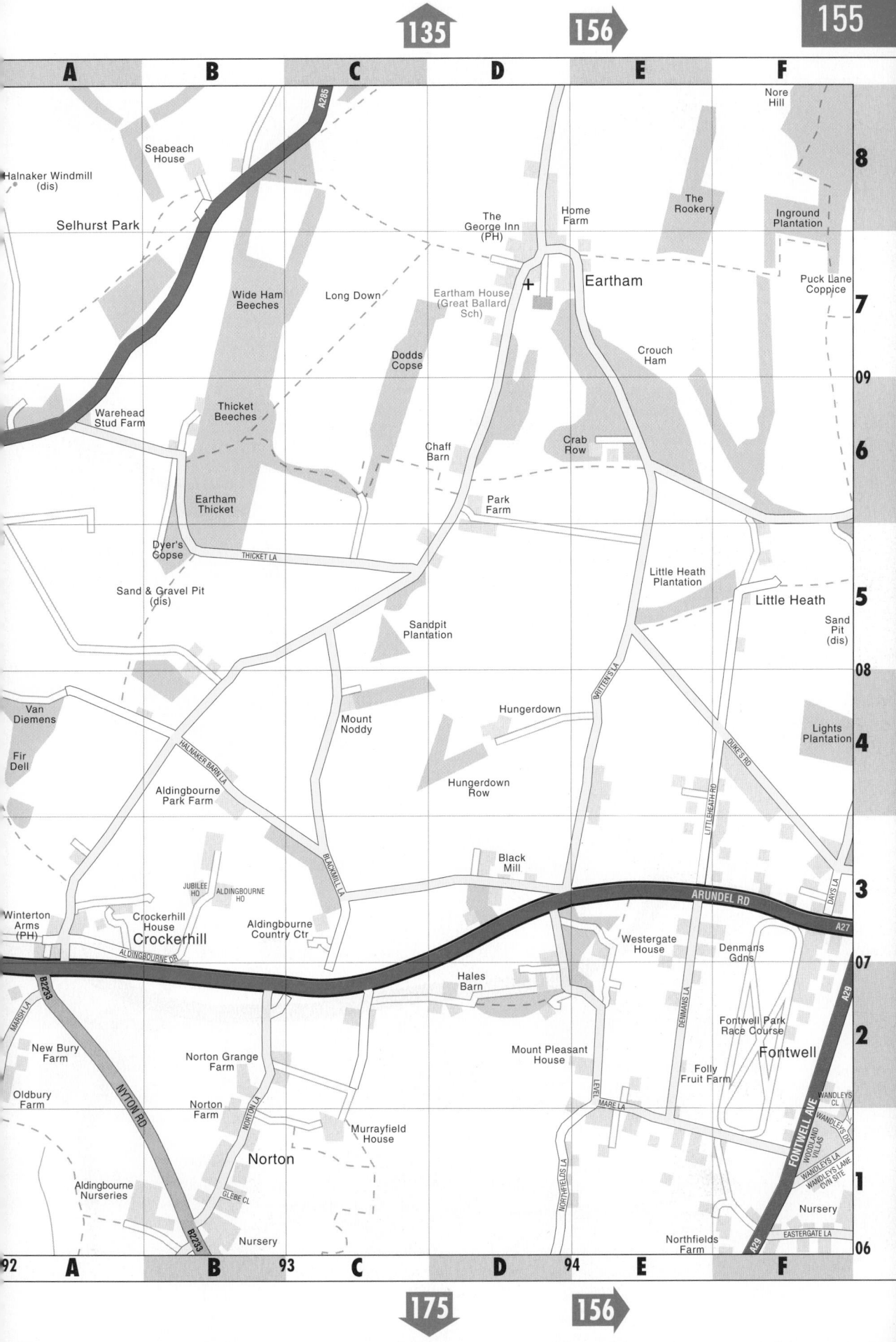

135
156
A
B
C
D
E
F
Nore Hill
Seabeach House
Halnaker Windmill (dis)
Selhurst Park
A285
The Rookery
Home Farm
The George Inn (PH)
Inground Plantation
Eartham
Puck Lane Coppice
Wide Ham Beeches
Long Down
Eartham House (Great Ballard Sch)
Crouch Ham
Dodds Copse
Warehead Stud Farm
Thicket Beeches
Chaff Barn
Crab Row
Park Farm
Eartham Thicket
Dyer's Copse
THICKET LA
Little Heath Plantation
Little Heath
Sand & Gravel Pit (dis)
Sandpit Plantation
Sand Pit (dis)
Van Diemens
Hungerdown
BRITTEN'S LA
Mount Noddy
Lights Plantation
Fir Dell
HALNAKER BARN LA
DUKE'S RD
Aldingbourne Park Farm
Hungerdown Row
LITTLEHEATH RD
Black Mill
BLACKMILL LA
JUBILEE HO
ALDINGBOURNE HO
ARUNDEL RD
DAYS LA
Winterton Arms (PH)
Crockerhill House
Crockerhill
Aldingbourne Country Ctr
Westergate House
Denmans Gdns
A27
ALDINGBOURNE DR
Hales Barn
B2233
MARSH LA
A29
DENMANS LA
Fontwell Park Race Course
New Bury Farm
Norton Grange Farm
Mount Pleasant House
Fontwell
Folly Fruit Farm
Oldbury Farm
NYTON RD
Norton Farm
NORTON LA
LEVEL
MARE LA
WANDLEYS CL
WANDLEYS DR
FONTWELL AVE
WOODLAND VILLAS
Murrayfield House
Norton
WANDLEYS LA
WANDLEYS LANE CVN SITE
Aldingbourne Nurseries
GLEBE CL
NORTHFIELDS LA
Nursery
Nursery
Northfields Farm
EASTERGATE LA
8
7
09
6
5
08
4
3
07
2
1
06
92
93
94
175
156

◀ 155   136 ▲

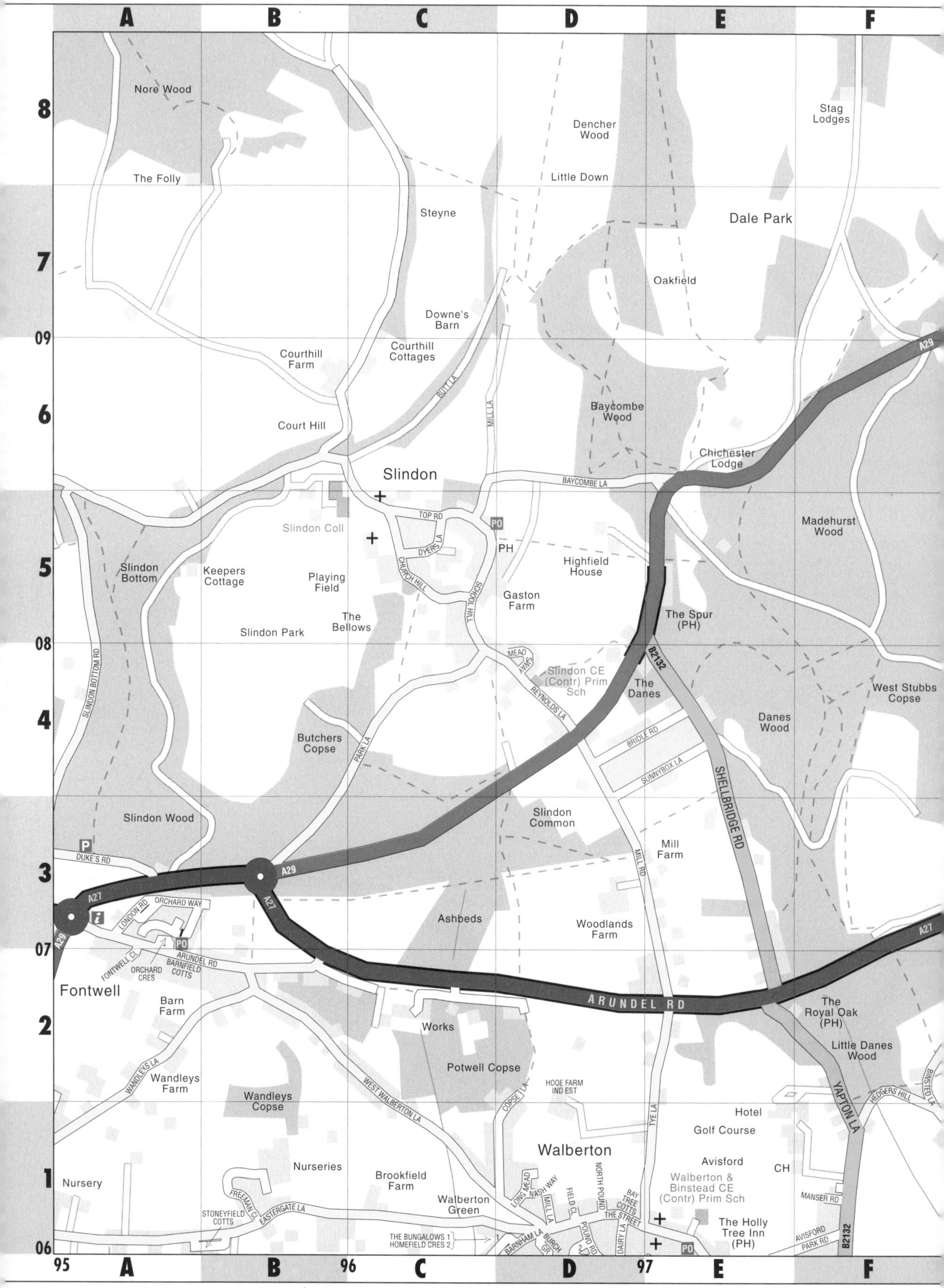

A   B   C   D   E   F

8

Nore Wood

Stag Lodges

Dencher Wood

The Folly

Steyne

Little Down

Dale Park

7

Downe's Barn

Oakfield

09

Courthill Farm

Courthill Cottages

BUTT LA

A29

6

Court Hill

MILL LA

Baycombe Wood

Chichester Lodge

Slindon

BAYCOMBE LA

TOP RD

Madehurst Wood

Slindon Coll

DYERS LA

PO

PH

Highfield House

The Spur (PH)

5

Slindon Bottom

Keepers Cottage

Playing Field

CHURCH HILL

SCHOOL HILL

Gaston Farm

B2132

West Stubbs Copse

The Bellows

MEAD WAY

The Danes

08

Slindon Park

Slindon CE (Contr) Prim Sch

REYNOLDS LA

Danes Wood

4

Butchers Copse

PARK LA

BRIDLE RD

SUNNYBOX LA

SHELLBRIDGE RD

Slindon Wood

Slindon Common

MILL RD

Mill Farm

P
DUKE'S RD

3

A29

A27

Ashbeds

Woodlands Farm

A27

A27
A29

i
LONDON RD

ORCHARD WAY

07

PO

ARUNDEL RD

FONTWELL CL

ORCHARD CRES

BARNFIELD COTTS

ARUNDEL RD

The Royal Oak (PH)

Fontwell

Barn Farm

Works

Little Danes Wood

YAPTON LA

HEDGERS HILL

BINSTED LA

2

WANDLEYS LA

Wandleys Farm

Wandleys Copse

WEST WALBERTON LA

Potwell Copse

HOOE FARM IND EST

COPSE LA

TYE LA

Hotel

Golf Course

CH

MANSER RD

1

Nursery

Nurseries

Brookfield Farm

Walberton Green

Walberton

LONG MEAD

NASH WAY

MILL LA

FIELD CL

NORTH POUND

POUND RD

BAY TREE COTTS

THE STREET

DAIRY LA

Avisford

Walberton & Binstead CE (Contr) Prim Sch

The Holly Tree Inn (PH)

PO

AVISFORD PARK RD

B2132

FREEMANS CL

STONEYFIELD COTTS

EASTERGATE LA

THE BUNGALOWS 1
HOMEFIELD CRES 2

BARNHAM LA

BURGH

06

95   A   B   96   C   D   97   E   F

137
158

A
B
C
D
E
F
Madehurst Cottage
Black Barn Farm
Fairmile Bottom Nature Trail
Dalesdown Wood
Lonebeech Plantation
Duchess Lodge
Horse Shoe Plantation
Yewtree Gate
Rewell Hill
Punchbowl
FAIRMILE BOTTOM
A29
A284
Park Rough
Arundel Park
Sherwood Rough
LONDON RD
Training Gallops
The Rough
Rewell Wood
Screens Wood
Green Doors Lodge
Rewell House
LONG LA
Rough Copse
Cricket Hill Farm
Goblestubb's Copse
ARUNDEL RD
HAVENWOOD CVN PK
Arundel Resort Hotel
The Waterwoods
Scotland Barn
CHICHESTER RD
A27
Paine's Wood
Brickkiln Copse
Winchers Copse
Barn's Copse
Singer's Piece
Scotland
CANADA RD
ELLIS CL
JARVIS RD
HILL TERR
DUKES CL
PEARSON RD
LANE CL
GREEN
HERINGTON RD
BINSTED LA
Arundel CE (Aided) Prim Sch
Stewards Copse
Pedler's Croft
Binsted Wood
HAZEL GR
OAK END
TORTON HILL RD
BERNARD RD
PRIORY RD
Tortington Common
Ash Piece
BIRCH CL
DALLOWAY RD
STEWARDS RISE
HIGH RIDGE CL
MAXWELL RD
The Black Horse (PH)
Church Farm
Binsted
FORD RD
8
7
09
6
5
08
4
3
07
2
1
06
98
99
00

177
158

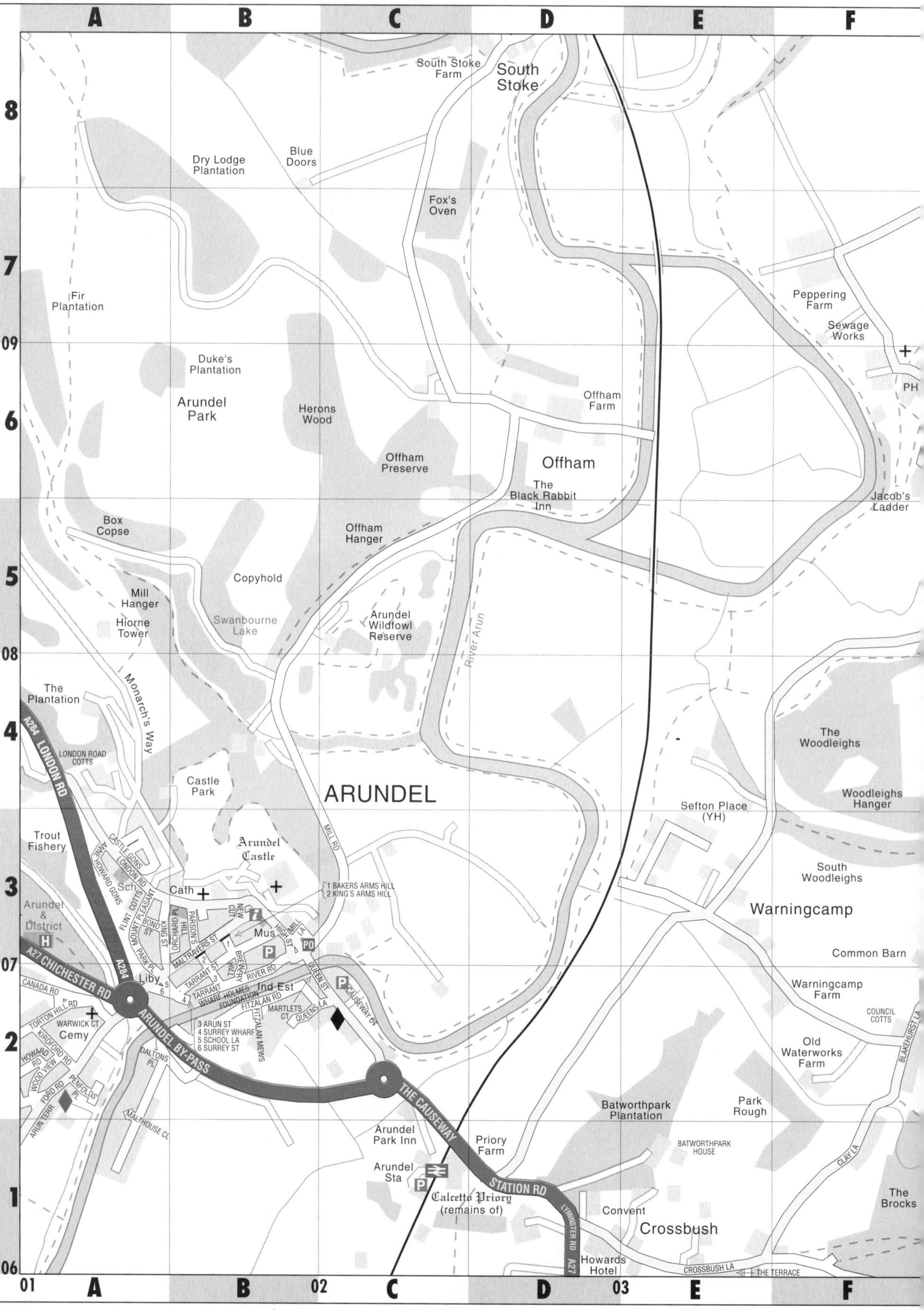

A B C D E F

8

7

09

6

5

08

4

3

07

2

1

06

South Stoke Farm
South Stoke

Dry Lodge Plantation
Blue Doors

Fox's Oven

Fir Plantation

Peppering Farm

Sewage Works

PH

Duke's Plantation

Arundel Park

Herons Wood

Offham Farm

Offham

Jacob's Ladder

Box Copse

Offham Preserve

The Black Rabbit Inn

Copyhold

Offham Hanger

Mill Hanger

Swanbourne Lake

Arundel Wildfowl Reserve

River Arun

Hiorne Tower

The Woodleighs

The Plantation

Woodleighs Hanger

London Road Cotts

A284 LONDON RD

Monarch's Way

Castle Park

ARUNDEL

Sefton Place (YH)

South Woodleighs

Trout Fishery

Arundel Castle

Warningcamp

Arundel & District

H

Cath

1 Bakers Arms Hill
2 King's Arms Hill

MILL RD

Common Barn

A27 CHICHESTER RD

Cemy

Warwick Ct

Liby

Mus

Ind Est

Wharf Holmes Foundation

3 Arun St
4 Surrey Wharf
5 School La
6 Surrey St

Martlets Ct

Queens La

Warningcamp Farm

Council Cotts

Old Waterworks Farm

ARUNDEL BY-PASS

Fitzalan Mews

THE CAUSEWAY

Park Rough

Canada Rd

Daltons Pl

Malthouse Cl

Arundel Park Inn

Priory Farm

Batworthpark Plantation

BATWORTHPARK HOUSE

Howard Rd
Wood View
Penfolds Pl
Ford Rd
Arun Terr

Arundel Sta

STATION RD

Calcetto Priory (remains of)

Convent

Crossbush

LYMINSTER RD A27

The Brocks

Howards Hotel

CROSSBUSH LA

THE TERRACE

A | B | C | D | E | F

Peppering High Barn

Burpham High Barn

8

PEPPERING LA

COOMBE LA

Norfolk Clump

Perry Hill

Barpham Hill

7

09

Burpham

Upper Barpham

6

Wepham

COUNCIL COTTS

Drillsfield Copse

The Conyers

New Down

Tenantry Copse

Upper Oldfield Copse

Oaken Copse

5

08

The Knell

Monarch's Way

Upper Wepham Wood

Lower Oldfield Copse

4

Warningcamp Hill

Angmering Park

Angmering Park Stud Farm

BLAKEHURST LA

Hill Barn

Gibbet Piece

Lower Wepham Wood

The Beeches

3

07

Wepham Ball

Bushy Field

2

Blakehurst Farm

Blakehurst Copse

Coots Dale

Braxby Copse

The Dover

Kitpease Copse

South Fields

Reed's Copse

Quakerscorner Copse

Butler's Copse

Hammerpot Copse

P

1

The Isles

Sailor's Copse

Priorslease Copse

Priorslease Farm

The Lions

Poling Copse

06

04 | A | 05 | B | C | 06 | D | E | F

A B C D E F

8
7
09
6
5
08
4
07
3
2
07
1
06

07 A B 08 C D 09 E F

Harrow Hill
Blackpatch Hill
Lower Barpham
Beech Copse
Michelgrove House
MICHELGROVE COTTS
Myrtle Grove Farm
Monarch's Way
Michelgrove Park
Michelgrove Park Lodges
Stables
Longfurlong Barn
LONGFURLONG LA
A280
Barnstake Copse
Patching Rough
Patching Hill
The Buckmans
Stonyland Copse
LONG FURLONG
Church Copse
Selden Fields
Surgeon's Fields
Patching Copse
Clapham Farm
Olivers Copse
Parham Fields
THE STREET
Patching
HILLSIDE COTTS
COUNCIL COTTS
CHURCH CL
OAKLANDS CL
Norfolk House
SWILLAGE LA
SELDEN LA
Selden Farm
Jewshead Wood
Patching Farm
COLDHARBOUR LA
Clapham & Patching CE (Contr) Prim Sch
COUNCIL COTTS
THE STREET
PO
CLAPHAM CL
Clapham
FRANCE LA
A280
Wyatt's Copse
The Harehams

141
162

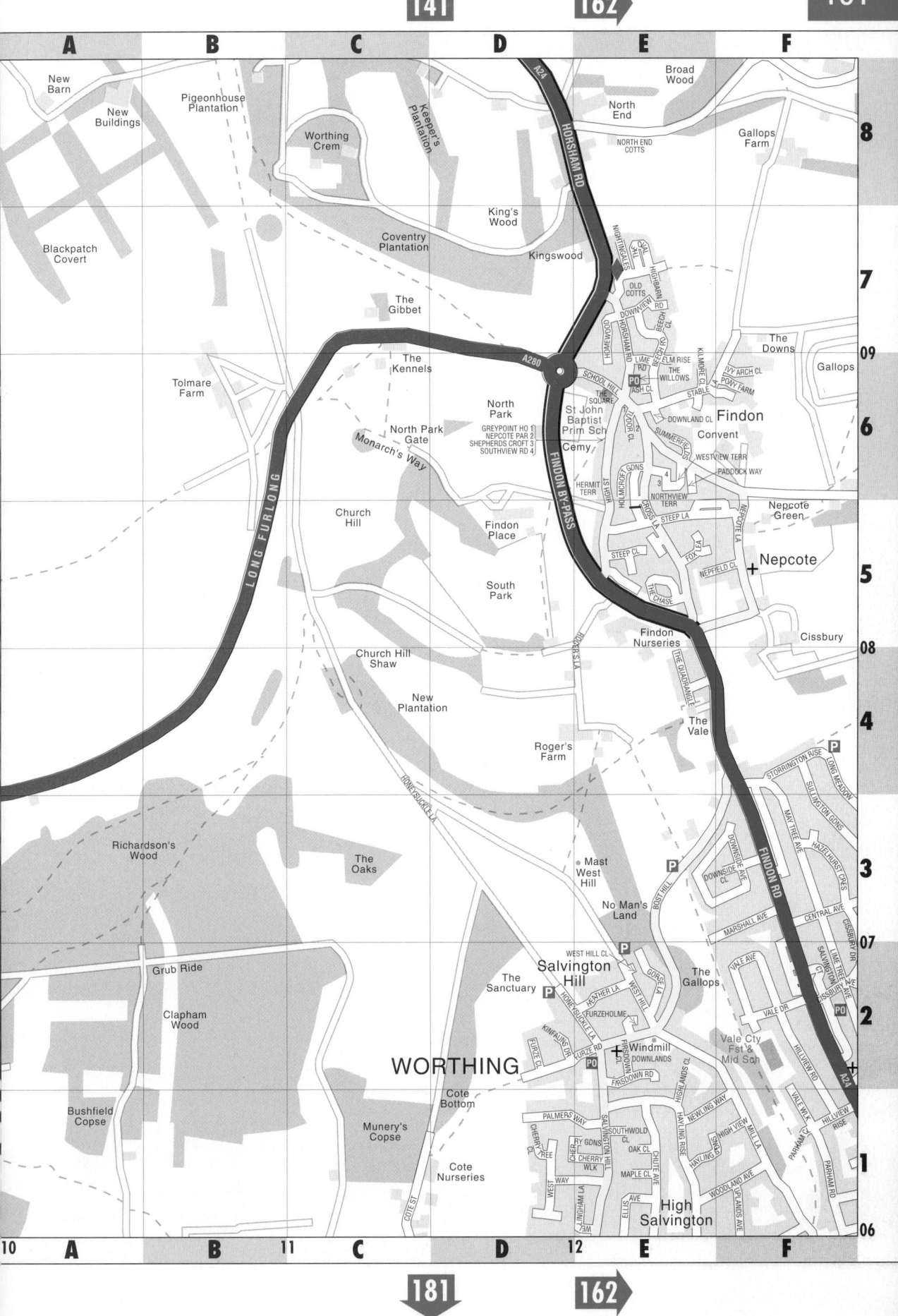
A
B
C
D
E
F
New Barn
New Buildings
Pigeonhouse Plantation
Worthing Crem
Keeper's Plantation
Broad Wood
North End
NORTH END COTTS
Gallops Farm
HORSHAM RD
A24
Blackpatch Covert
Coventry Plantation
King's Wood
Kingswood
The Gibbet
The Kennels
A280
Tolmare Farm
The Downs
Gallops
North Park
North Park Gate
Monarch's Way
St John Baptist Prim Sch
Cemy
Findon
Convent
Nepcote Green
Nepcote
Church Hill
Findon Place
South Park
LONG FURLONG
FINDON BY-PASS
Findon Nurseries
Cissbury
Church Hill Shaw
New Plantation
Roger's Farm
The Vale
Richardson's Wood
The Oaks
Mast
West Hill
No Man's Land
Grub Ride
Clapham Wood
The Sanctuary
Salvington Hill
The Gallops
Windmill
WORTHING
Vale Cty Fst & Mid Sch
Bushfield Copse
Cote Bottom
Munery's Copse
Cote Nurseries
High Salvington
FINDON RD
HONEYSUCKLE LA
COTE ST
ROGERS LA
BOST HILL
GREYPOINT HO 1
NEPCOTE PAR 2
SHEPHERDS CROFT 3
SOUTHVIEW RD 4
NIGHTINGALES
OLD COTTS
DOWNVIEW RD
HIGHBARN
BEECH CL
HOMEWOOD
HORSHAM RD
LIME RD
ELM RISE
THE WILLOWS
KILMORE CL
IVY ARCH CL
PONY FARM
SCHOOL HILL
THE SQUARE
ASH CL
STABLE
DOWNLAND CL
TUDOR CL
SUMMERFIELDS
WESTVIEW TERR
PADDOCK WAY
HOLMCROFT GDNS
HERMIT TERR
HIGH ST
NORTHVIEW TERR
CROSS LA
STEEP LA
NEPCOTE LA
STEEP CL
FOX LEA
NEPFIELD CL
THE CHASE
THE QUADRANGLE
STORRINGTON RISE
LONG MEADOW
SULLINGTON GDNS
MAY TREE AVE
HAZELHURST CRES
DOWNSIDE AVE
DOWNSIDE CL
CENTRAL AVE
MARSHALL AVE
CISSBURY DR
SALVINGTON CT
LIME TREE AVE
CISSBURY AVE
VALE AVE
VALE DR
HILLVIEW RD
WEST HILL CL
GORSE LA
WEST HILL
HEATHER LA
FURZEHOLME
KINFAUNS DR
FURZE CL
FURZE RD
FIRSDOWN CL
DOWNLANDS
FIRSDOWN RD
HIGHLANDS CL
NEWLING WAY
HAYLING RISE
HIGH VIEW
SHIPS
MILL LA
HAYLING RISE
VALE WLK
PARHAM CL
HILLVIEW RISE
PARHAM RD
PALMERS WAY
CHERRY TREE CL
CHERRY GDNS
CHERRY WLK
SALVINGTON HILL
SOUTHWOLD CL
OAK CL
CHUTE AVE
MAPLE CL
WEST WAY
WELLINGHAM LA
ELLIS AVE
WOODLAND AVE
UPLANDS AVE
8
7
09
6
5
08
4
3
07
2
1
06
10
11
12

181
162

161
142

	A	B	C	D	E	F

8

New Barn

Church Wood

Findon Park Farm

No Man's Land

New Hill Barn

7

Monarch's Way

Park Brow

09

Gallops

Lychpole Bottom

6

P

Canada Bottom

5

Cissbury Ring

08

Cissbury Farm

Hill Barn Covert

4

Cissbury Plantation

Lychpole Farm

Shipdens Holt

Deep Bottom

Vineyard Hill

3

Long Meadow Gdns

Sutlington Gdns

Central Ave

Sheepcombe Hanger

Lychpole Hill

07

Cissbury Gdns

Hollingbury Gdns

Shepherds Mead

Mount Carvey

Tenants Hill

2

Cissbury Ave

Findon Valley

Coombe Rise

P

1

Lime Tree Ave

Liby

Aldwick Cres

Ashfold Ave

Kearsley Dr

The Heights

Franklands Cl

Allendale Ave

Worthing Golf Course

Lambleys Barn

Greatham Rd

Wantley Rd

A24

Findon Rd

Floral Dean Ct

Mayfield Cl

CH

Lamberts La

06

13	A		B	14	C		D	15	E		F

161
182

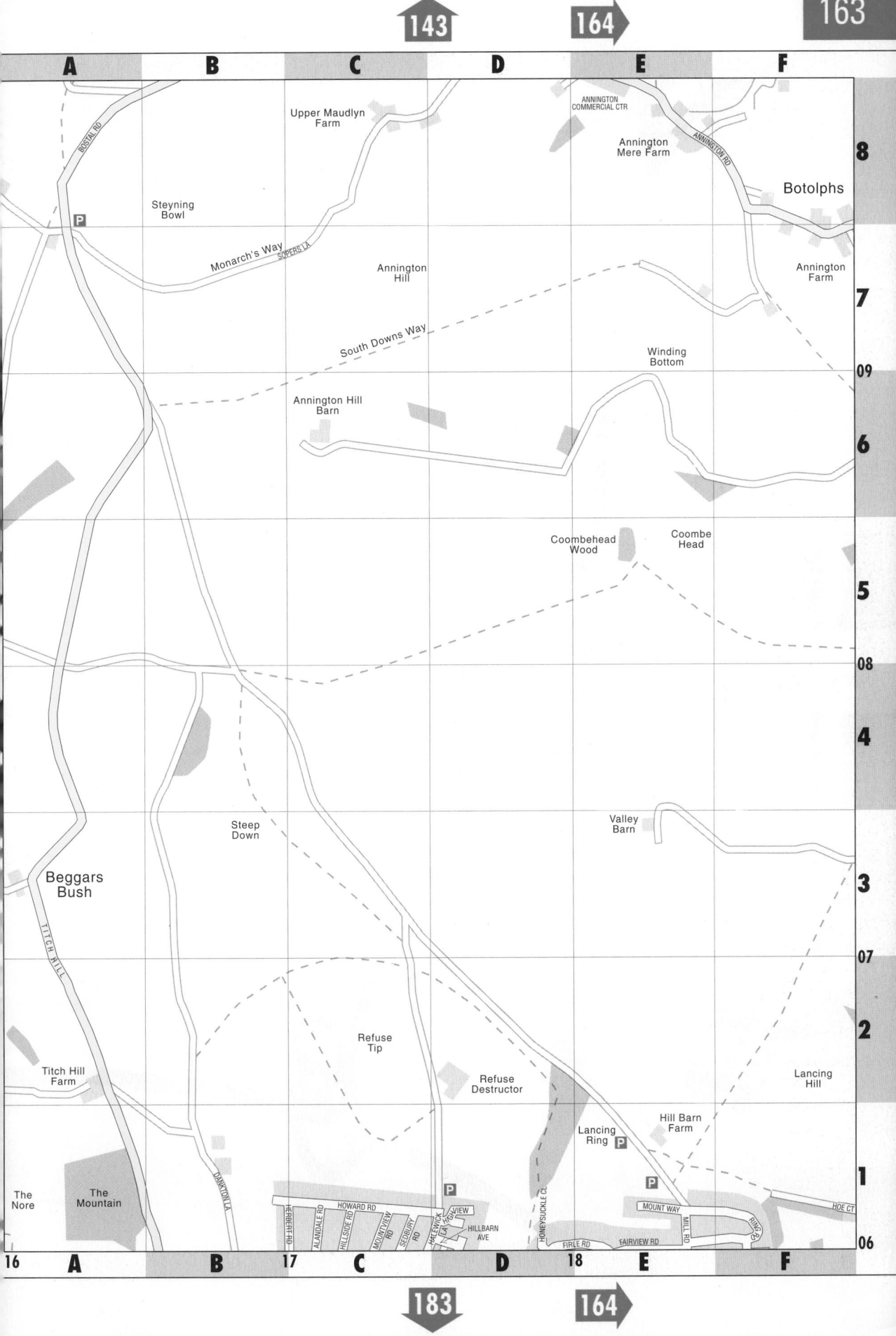

A B C D E F

8

ROSTAL RD

Upper Maudlyn Farm

ANNINGTON COMMERCIAL CTR

Annington Mere Farm

ANNINGTON RD

Botolphs

Steyning Bowl

P

Monarch's Way

SOPERS LA

Annington Hill

Annington Farm

7

09

South Downs Way

Winding Bottom

Annington Hill Barn

6

Coombehead Wood

Coombe Head

5

08

4

Valley Barn

Steep Down

Beggars Bush

3

07

TITCH HILL

Refuse Tip

2

Titch Hill Farm

Refuse Destructor

Lancing Hill

DANKTON LA

Lancing Ring

P

Hill Barn Farm

1

The Nore

The Mountain

HERBERT RD

ALANDALE RD

HOWARD RD

HILLSIDE RD

MOUNTVIEW RD

SEDBURY RD

LA

HILLVIEW

HILLBARN AVE

HONEYSUCKLE CL

P

P

Mount Way

MILL RD

RING RD

HOE CT

FIRLE RD

FAIRVIEW RD

06

16 A B 17 C D 18 E F

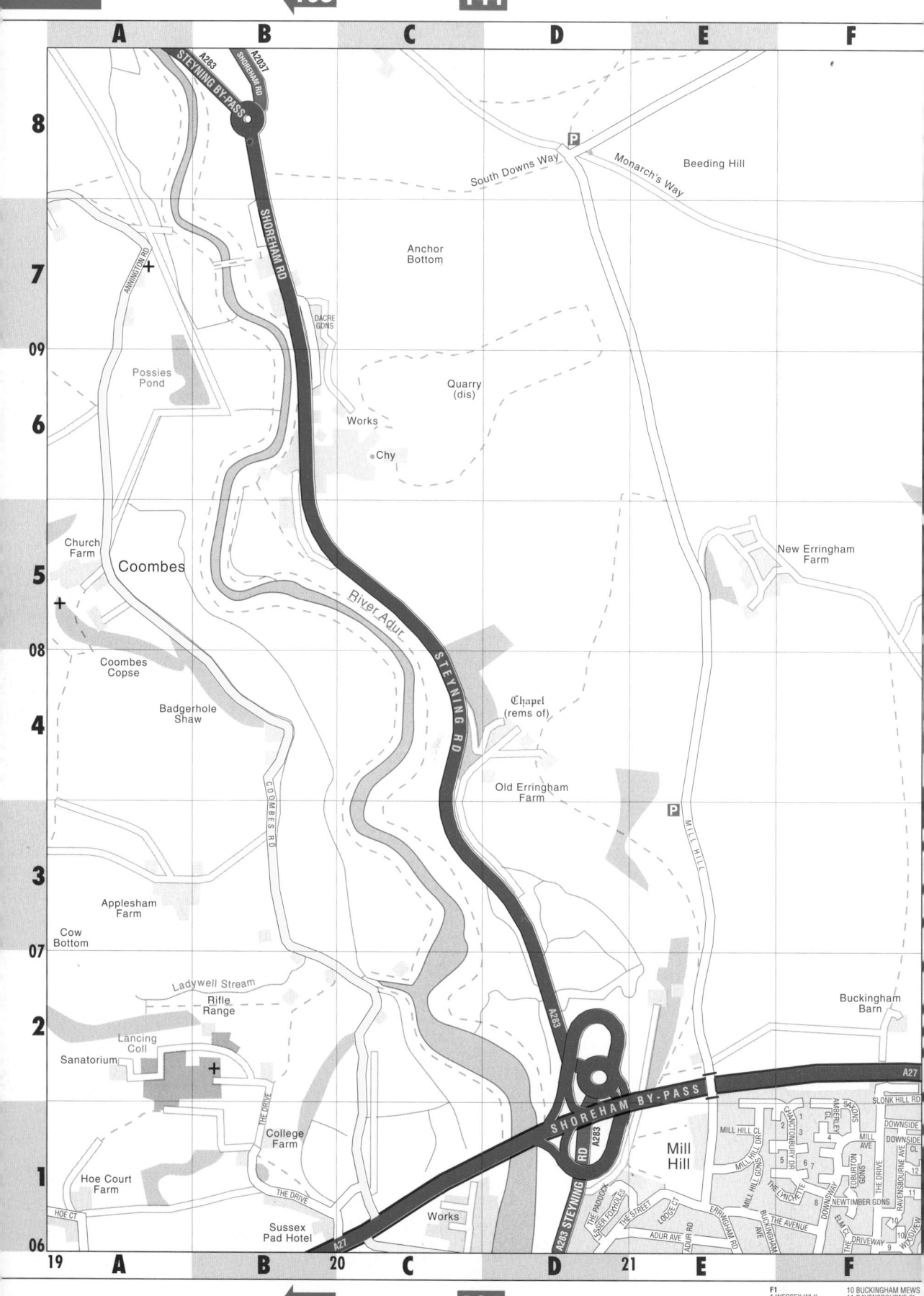

163
144

A   B   C   D   E   F

8

7

09

6

5

08

4

3

07

2

1

06

19   A   B   20   C   D   21   E   F

163
184

STEYNING BY-PASS
A283
A2037
SHOREHAM RD

South Downs Way
Monarch's Way
Beeding Hill

P

Anchor
Bottom

DACRE
GDNS

Possies
Pond

Quarry
(dis)

Works

Chy

Church
Farm

Coombes

New Erringham
Farm

River Adur

Coombes
Copse

Badgerhole
Shaw

Chapel
(rems of)

Old Erringham
Farm

P

COOMBES RD

STEYNING RD

Applesham
Farm

Cow
Bottom

Ladywell Stream

Rifle
Range

Lancing
Coll

Sanatorium

Buckingham
Barn

A283

A27

SHOREHAM BY-PASS

SLONK HILL RD

DOWNSIDE

DOWNSIDE CL

MILL HILL

THE DRIVE

Mill
Hill

THE DRIVE

College
Farm

Hoe Court
Farm

HOE CT

Sussex
Pad Hotel

A27

A283 STEYNING RD

Works

THE PADDOCK
LESSER FOXHOLES
THE STREET
LOOSE CT
ADUR AVE
ADUR RD
ERRINGHAM RD

NEWTIMBER GDNS

THE AVENUE

THE DRIVEWAY

F1
1 WESSEX WLK
2 WESTMORLAND WLK
3 WARWICK WLK
4 ANNINGTON GDNS
5 CISSBURY WAY
6 BLACKPATCH GR
7 WOLSTONBURY WLK
8 NORMANSCOURT
9 NORMAN CRES
10 BUCKINGHAM MEWS
11 RAVENSBOURNE CL
12 CYPRESS CL

145
166
A
B
C
D
E
F
8
7
09
6
5
08
4
3
07
2
1
06
22
23
24
The Warren
Bushy Bottom
Summers Deane
Tenant Hill
Hazelhalt Bottom
Thundersbarrow Hill
Cockroast Hill
Sussex Border Path
Mossy Bottom
Monarch's Way
Whitelot Bottom
Cockroast Bottom
Mileoak Barn
Mile Oak Farm
A27
Mossy Bottom Barn
Mile Oak
Crooked Moon
Southwick Hill
Mile Oak Cty Prim Sch
Coll
SHOREHAM BY-PASS
Slonk Hill
NEW BARN CL 1
MARJORAM PL 2
FENNEL WLK 3
BERBERIS CT 4
5 JUNIPER WLK
6 SAFFRON CL
7 BERGAMOT CRES
8 THYME CL
HAZELHOLT 1
PADDOCK CT 2
BEECH CL 3
HILLBANK CL 4
COMPASS CT
1 LOWER DR
2 WINDMILL PAR
Superstore
Herons Dale Sch
Holmbush Cty Fst Sch
Cemy
Buckingham Park Recn Gd
Southlands General
SLONK HILL RD
UPPER SHOREHAM RD
A270 UPPER SHOREHAM RD
OLD SHOREHAM RD
A270
B2167
KINGSTON BROADWAY
KINGSTON WAY
ROYAL GEORGE PAR
FAIRFIELD CL
BUCI CRES
FRANKLIN RD
SOUTHVIEW CL
HOLMBUSH WAY
UPTON AVE
CHURCH HOUSE CL
185
166

A B C D E F

8

Scabes Castle

Golf Course

DEVIL'S DYKE RD

P

7

CH

Golf Farm

Skeleton Hovel

09

Benfield Valley

6

Brighton & Hove Golf Course

Round Hill

P

Mount Zion

5

Benfield Hill

West Hove Golf Course

Monarch's Way

08

CH

A27

SHOREHAM BY-PASS

FOREDOWN RD

New Barn

Foredown Hill

A27

West Blatchington Inf Sch

West Blatchington Jun Sch

Monarch's Way

1 NUTLEY CL
2 MIDHURST CL

PORTSLADE -BY-SEA

Foredown Tower

BUSH TERR

Benfield Valley Golf Course

CH

SYLVESTER WAY

THE MEADOWS

ST HELEN'S DR

Hangleton Park

Hangleton Cty Inf & Jun Sch

3

Sports Ctr

Portslade Com Coll (Lower)

NORTH LA

St Helen's Park

07

HANGLETON LA

Recn Gd

CHURCHILL

Windmill (dis)

Windmill CL

ST PETER

2

Hillside Sch

Hangleton

Hove Park Sch (Lower)

GREENLEAS

WESTWAY

Liby

HANGLETON RD

Blatchington Mill Sch

Sch

Superstore

SHANKLIN CT 1
SANDOWN CT 2
RYDE CT 3

PO

Knoll Cty Inf Sch

1 THE PARADE
2 QUEEN'S PAR

CHURCH

1

Portslade Com Coll

PO

LINDFIELD

ROBINS ROW

Portslade Village

Easthill Park

Allot Gdns

ST RICHARD'S CT

A2038

Goldstone Cty Jun Sch

West Blatchington Allot Gdns

06

TO B2195

1 BIRCH CT
2 ILEX CT

Schs

BENFIELD CRES

Cemy

25

A

26

B

C

26

D

27

E

F

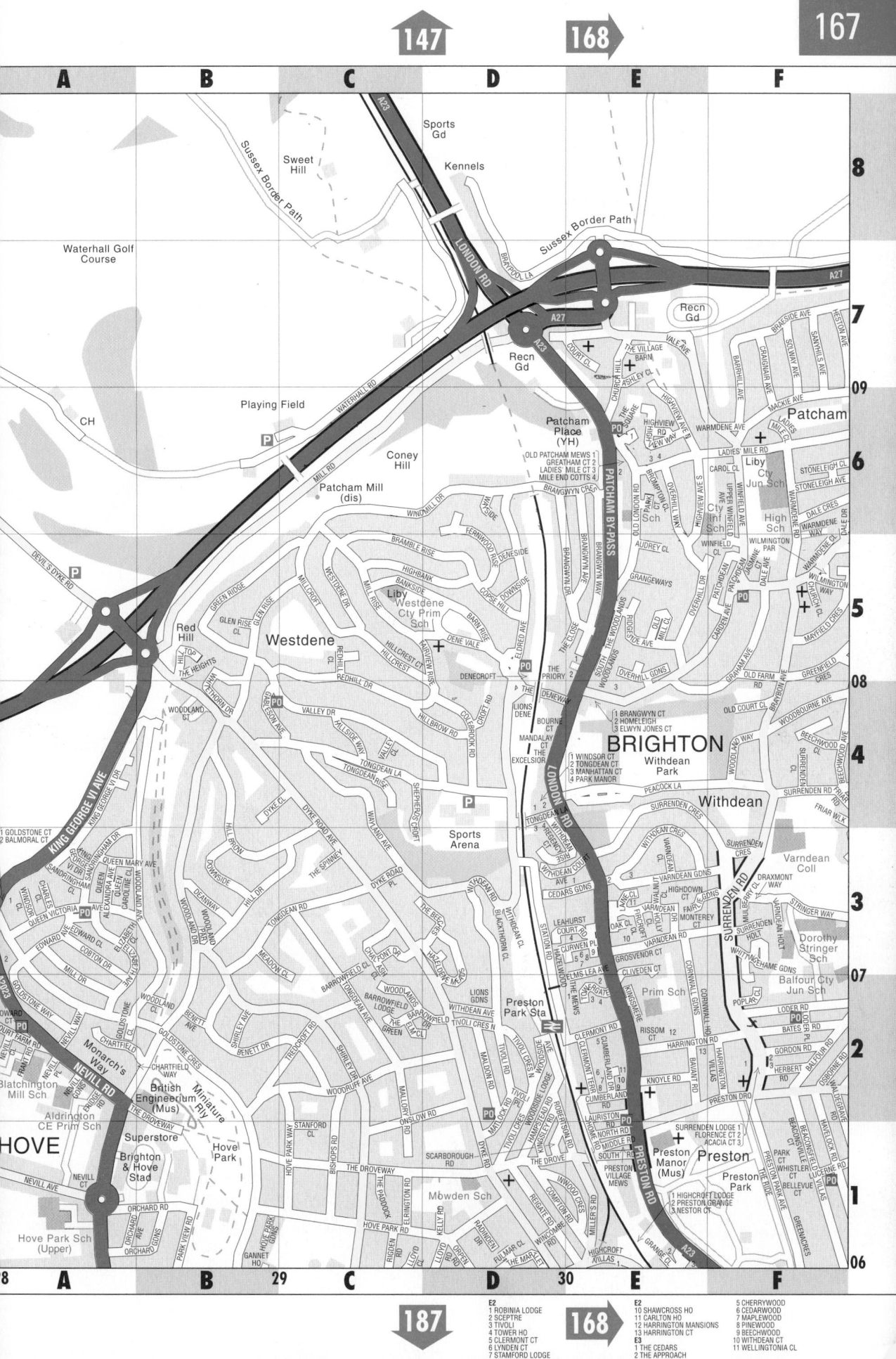

E2
1 ROBINIA LODGE
2 SCEPTRE
3 TIVOLI
4 TOWER HO
5 CLERMONT CT
6 LYNDEN CT
7 STAMFORD LODGE
8 CUMBERLAND LODGE
9 CENTENARY HO

E2
10 SHAWCROSS HO
11 CARLTON HO
12 HARRINGTON MANSIONS
13 HARRINGTON CT

E3
1 THE CEDARS
2 THE APPROACH
3 WITHDEAN HALL
4 LEAHURST CT

5 CHERRYWOOD
6 CEDARWOOD
7 MAPLEWOOD
8 PINEWOOD
9 BEECHWOOD
10 WITHDEAN CT
11 WELLINGTONIA CL

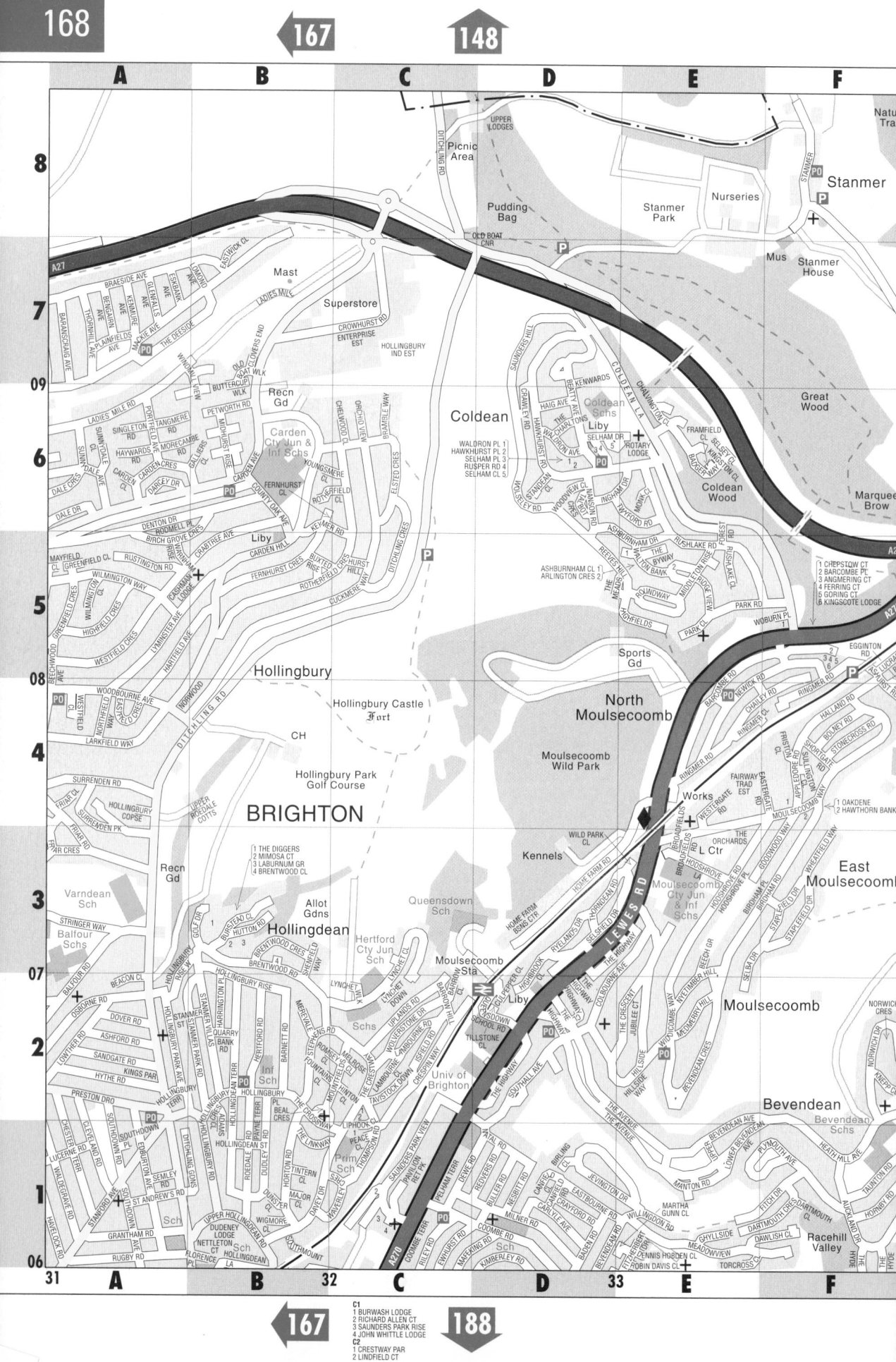

167
148
167
188

C1
1 BURWASH LODGE
2 RICHARD ALLEN CT
3 SAUNDERS PARK RISE
4 JOHN WHITTLE LODGE
C2
1 CRESTWAY PAR
2 LINDFIELD CT

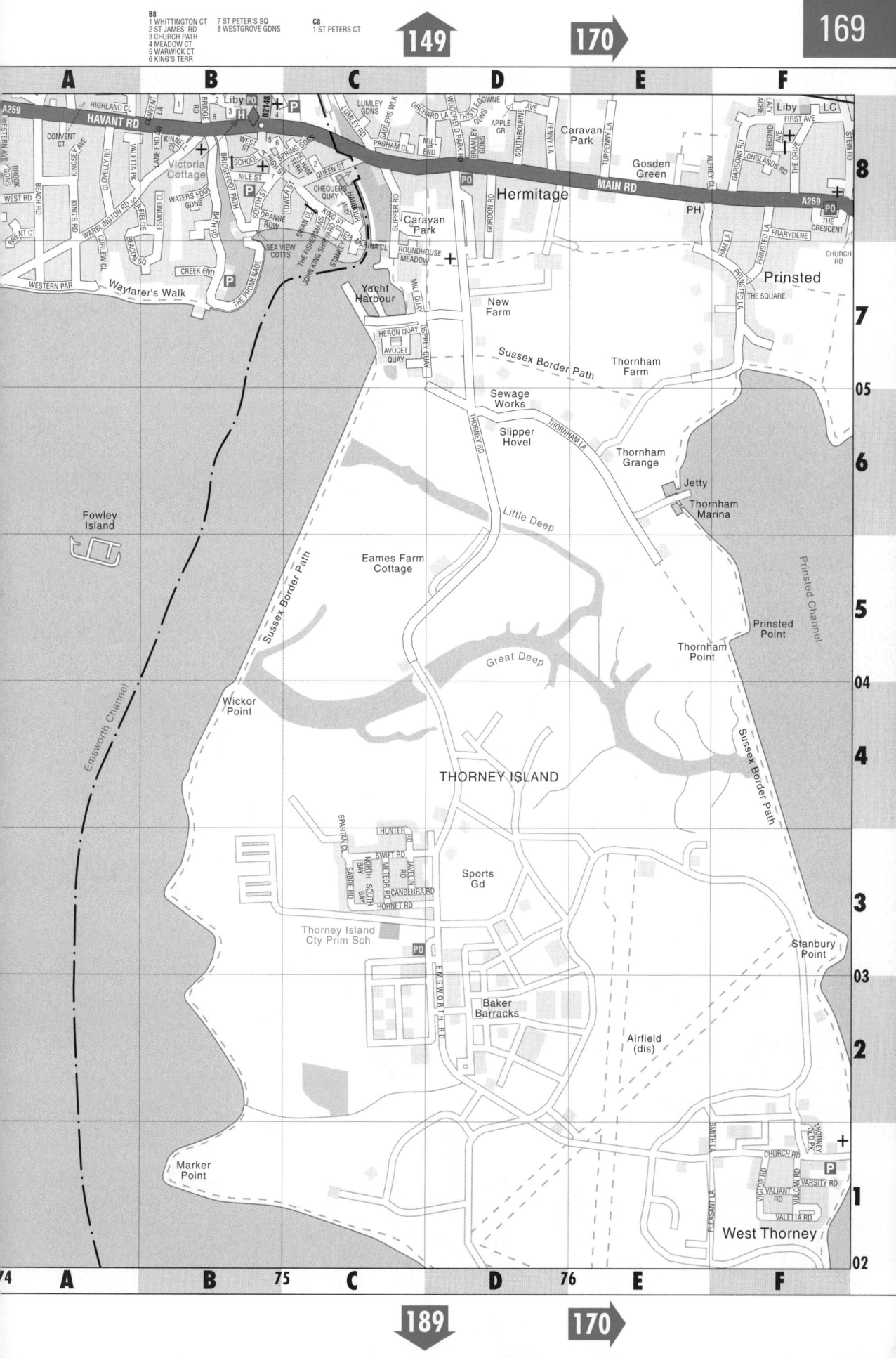

B8
1 WHITTINGTON CT
2 ST JAMES' RD
3 CHURCH PATH
4 MEADOW CT
5 WARWICK CT
6 KING'S TERR

7 ST PETER'S SQ
8 WESTGROVE GDNS

C8
1 ST PETERS CT

HAVANT RD

A259

Highland Cl
Convent La
Kinnel Dr
Bridge Rd
Liby PO
B2148
P

Western Ave
Brook Gdns
West Rd
Kings Rd
Valetta Rd
Sea Fields
Esmond Cl
Beacon Sq
Warblington Rd
Curlew Cl
Convent Ct
Regent Ct
Western Par
Lane End Dr
Coldavy Cl
Clayton Rd

Victoria
Cottage

Waters Edge Gdns
School La
Bath Rd
Bridgefoot Path
South St
Nile St
Spring Gdns
West St
Tower La

Sea View
Cotts

Creek End
P
The Promenade

Wayfarer's Walk

John King Ship Yard
The Fisherman's
Marina Cl
Swan Cl
Orange Row
King St
Old Yard

Chequers
Quay
Harbour
Way
Queen St
Reeds Pl

Lumley Gdns
Lumley Rd
Pagham Cl
Sea St

Orchard La
Woodfield Park Rd
Mill End
Brawley Gdns
Gordon Rd
Thistle Downe
Apple Gr
Southbourne Ave
Penny La

Caravan
Park

Gosden
Green

Liby LC
First Ave
Lazy Acre
Garsons Rd
Longlands Rd
The Drive
Stein Rd
PO
The Crescent
A259
Prinsted
Alfrey Cl
Ham La
Cross St La
Prinsted La
Frarydene
Church Rd
The Square

PH

MAIN RD

Hermitage

Caravan
Park
Roundhouse
Meadow

Yacht
Harbour

Heron Quay
Avocet Quay
Osprey Quay
Mill Quay

New
Farm

Sussex Border Path

Thornham
Farm

Sewage
Works

Slipper
Hovel

Thornham La
Thorney Rd

Thornham
Grange

Jetty
Thornham
Marina

Little Deep

Fowley
Island

Sussex Border Path

Emsworth Channel

Eames Farm
Cottage

Great Deep

Thornham
Point

Prinsted
Point

Prinsted Channel

Wickor
Point

Sussex Border Path

THORNEY ISLAND

Spartan Cl
Hunter Rd
Swift Rd
Meteor Rd
Javelin Rd
Canberra Rd
Sabre Rd
Hornet Rd
North Bay
South Bay

Sports
Gd

Stanbury
Point

Thorney Island
Cty Prim Sch

PO
Emsworth Rd

Baker
Barracks

Airfield
(dis)

Marker
Point

Smiths La
Pleasant La
Victor Rd
Valiant Rd
Valetta Rd
Vulcan Rd
Church Rd
Varsity Rd
Thorney
Old Pk
P

West Thorney

169
150

A   B   C   D   E   F

Southbourne Halt
LODGEBURY CL
Southbourne
Cty Jun & Inf Schs
Southbourne
Caravan Site
NEW RD
MOSDELL RD
GOODW... CT
INLANDS RD
LC
Ham Brook

Works
Longacres
DRIFT LA
GREEN LA
LC
Nutbourne Halt
LC
FLAT RD
BROAD RD
Flat Farm
8

A259
PO
MAIN RD
SCHOOL LA
BELL HO
FARM LA
Nursery
POTTERY LA
BROAD MEADOW
MANSFIELD COTTS
MAYBUSH DR
PH
IVYDENE CRES
The Bosham Inn
HAMSTEAD MEADOW

Nutbourne
A259
7

05
Marsh Farm
COT LA
Chidholm Parochial (Contr) Prim Sch

6

CHIDHAM LA
Eastfield Farm

5
Chidham Point
STEELS LA
Middleton Farm
Landing Stages
HARBOUR WAY

04
Old House at Home (PH)
MARSH LA
Easton Farm

4
Hovel Barn
Chidmere Pond
Chidham
Hard

Thorney Channel

3

New Barn
Cobner Farm
Bosham Channel

03

2
Cullimer's Pond

Cobner Hard

1
Hard
Cobner House

02
77   A   B   78   C   D   79   E   F

169
190

151
172

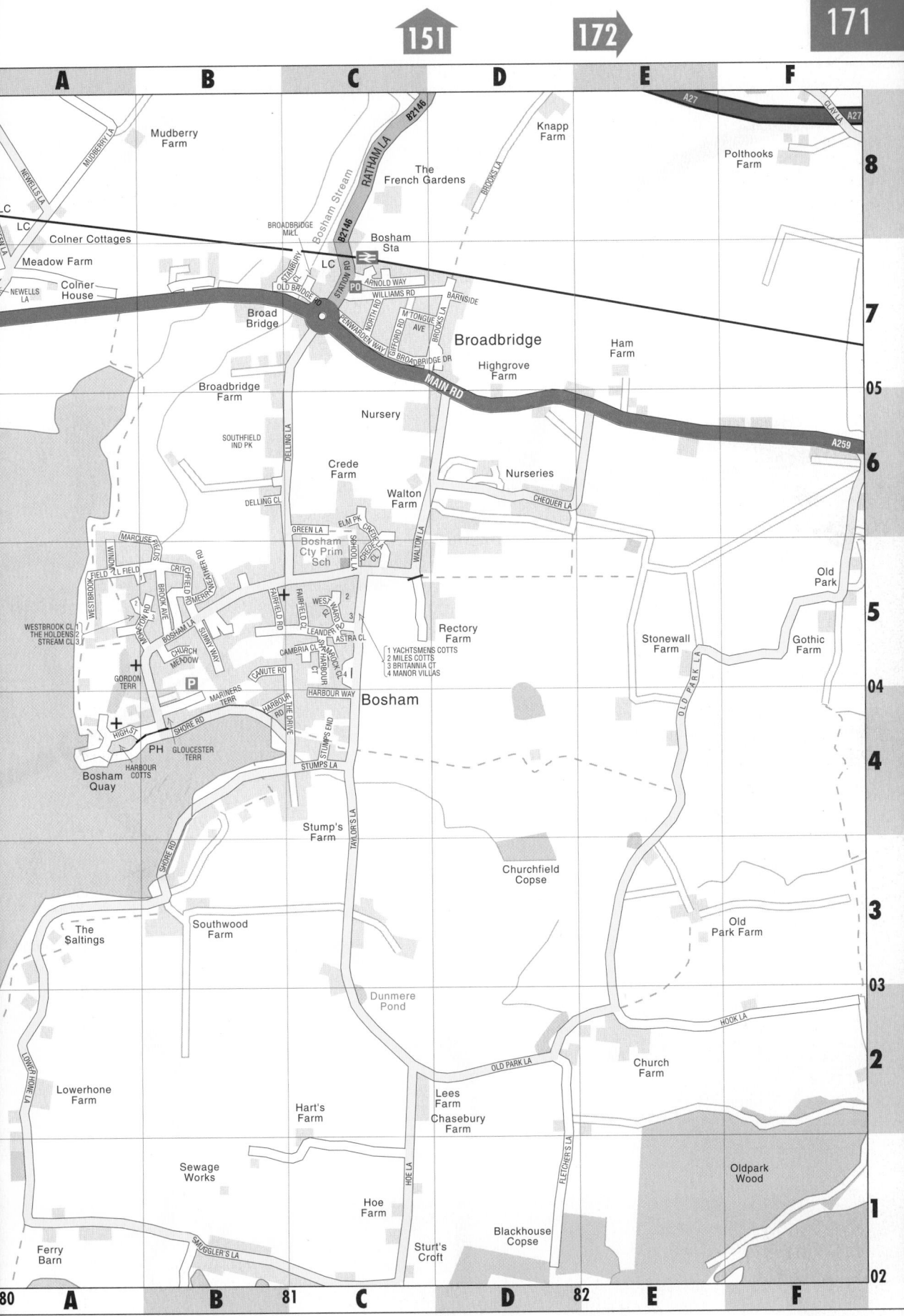
A
B
C
D
E
F
Mudberry Farm
Knapp Farm
Polthooks Farm
The French Gardens
RATHAM LA
B2146
A27
CLAY LA
MUDBERRY LA
NEWELLS LA
BROOKS LA
Bosham Stream
LC
Colner Cottages
BROADBRIDGE MILL
Bosham Sta
Meadow Farm
Colner House
NEWELLS LA
STANBURY CL
OLD BRIDGE RD
STATION RD
ARNOLD WAY
WILLIAMS RD
BARNSIDE
NORTH RD
M'TONGUE AVE
GIFFORD RD
Broad Bridge
PENWARDEN WAY
BROADBRIDGE DR
Broadbridge
Ham Farm
Highgrove Farm
MAIN RD
Broadbridge Farm
Nursery
A259
SOUTHFIELD IND PK
DELLING LA
Crede Farm
Nurseries
Walton Farm
CHEQUER LA
DELLING CL
GREEN LA
ELM PK
CREDE CL
Bosham Cty Prim Sch
SCHOOL LA
WALTON LA
MARCUSE FIELDS
WINDMILL FIELD
WESTBROOK FIELD
CRITCHFIELD RD
MERRYWEATHER RD
FAIRFIELD RD
FAIRFIELD CL
WEST WARD CL
Old Park
WESTBROOK CL 1
THE HOLDENS 2
STREAM CL 3
MORETON RD
BROOK AVE
BOSHAM LA
SUNNY WAY
LEANDER
ASTRA CL
Rectory Farm
Stonewall Farm
Gothic Farm
CHURCH MEADOW
CAMBRIA CL
SHAMROCK CL
HARBOUR CT
1 YACHTSMENS COTTS
2 MILES COTTS
3 BRITANNIA CT
4 MANOR VILLAS
GORDON TERR
CANUTE RD
MARINERS TERR
HARBOUR WAY
Bosham
HARBOUR RD
THE DRIVE
HIGH ST
SHORE RD
STUMPS END
PH
GLOUCESTER TERR
HARBOUR COTTS
Bosham Quay
STUMPS LA
OLD PARK LA
Stump's Farm
TAYLOR'S LA
SHORE RD
Churchfield Copse
Southwood Farm
The Saltings
Old Park Farm
Dunmere Pond
HOOK LA
OLD PARK LA
Church Farm
LOWER HONE LA
Lowerhone Farm
Lees Farm
Hart's Farm
Chasebury Farm
Sewage Works
HOE LA
FLETCHER'S LA
Oldpark Wood
Hoe Farm
Blackhouse Copse
Sturt's Croft
Ferry Barn
SMUGGLER'S LA
8
7
05
6
5
04
4
3
03
2
1
02
80
81
82

191
172

171 152

F7
1 PAULUS CT
2 PASCOE CT
3 DENISON CT
4 LANCASTRIAN GRANGE
5 THE PROVIDENCE
6 PROVIDENCE PL

A B C D E F

8

7

05

6

5

04

4

3

03

2

1

02

83 84 85

171 192

CHICHESTER
NOVIOMAGVS

Hardham's Farm
Orchard Cotts
Bethwines Farm
The Barn House
Salthill Lodge
New Cottages
Centurian Way
Jessie Younghusband Cty Prim Sch
St Anthony's Sch
Royal West Sussex
Mead House
Bishop Luffa CE Sch (Aided)
Fishbourne Sta
Fishbourne
FISHBOURNE ROMAN PALACE (remains of)
Fishbourne CE (Contr) Sch
Parklands Cty Prim Sch
The Maltings
Cty H
Liby
Mkt
Woolstaplers
Fishbourne Road E
Watersmeet
Superstore
Westgate
Chichester Coll of Arts, Science & Tech
The Close
Leggatt's Farm
Mill Pond
Main Rd
Fishbourne Rd W
The Manor
Lower Turnpike Nursery
Cathedral Way
Westgate L Ctr
Southgate City Bsns Ctr
Chichester Sta
Terminus Mill
Lawrence Farm
Manor Farm
Chichester By-Pass
Chichester High Sch for Girls
The Courtyard
South Bank
King's Ave
Heather Cl
Lacey Ho
Sewage Works
River Lavant
Church Farm
Common Farm
Stock Bridge Rd
Rymans
Apuldram Manor Farm
Apuldram
Mile Pond Farm
Mile Pond
Turnpike Cl 1
Forge Cl 2
Cutfield Cl 3
Poyntz Cl 4
Manor Cl
Stockbridge
St George's Dr
Boat Yard
Dell Quay
Crown & Anchor Inn (PH)
Dell Quay Rd
Birdham Rd
Donnington Pk
Donnington Manor
Selsey Rd
Crouchers
Windmill Farm
Black Horse (PH)
Donnington
Pelleys La
Chichester Canal
Fishbourne Channel

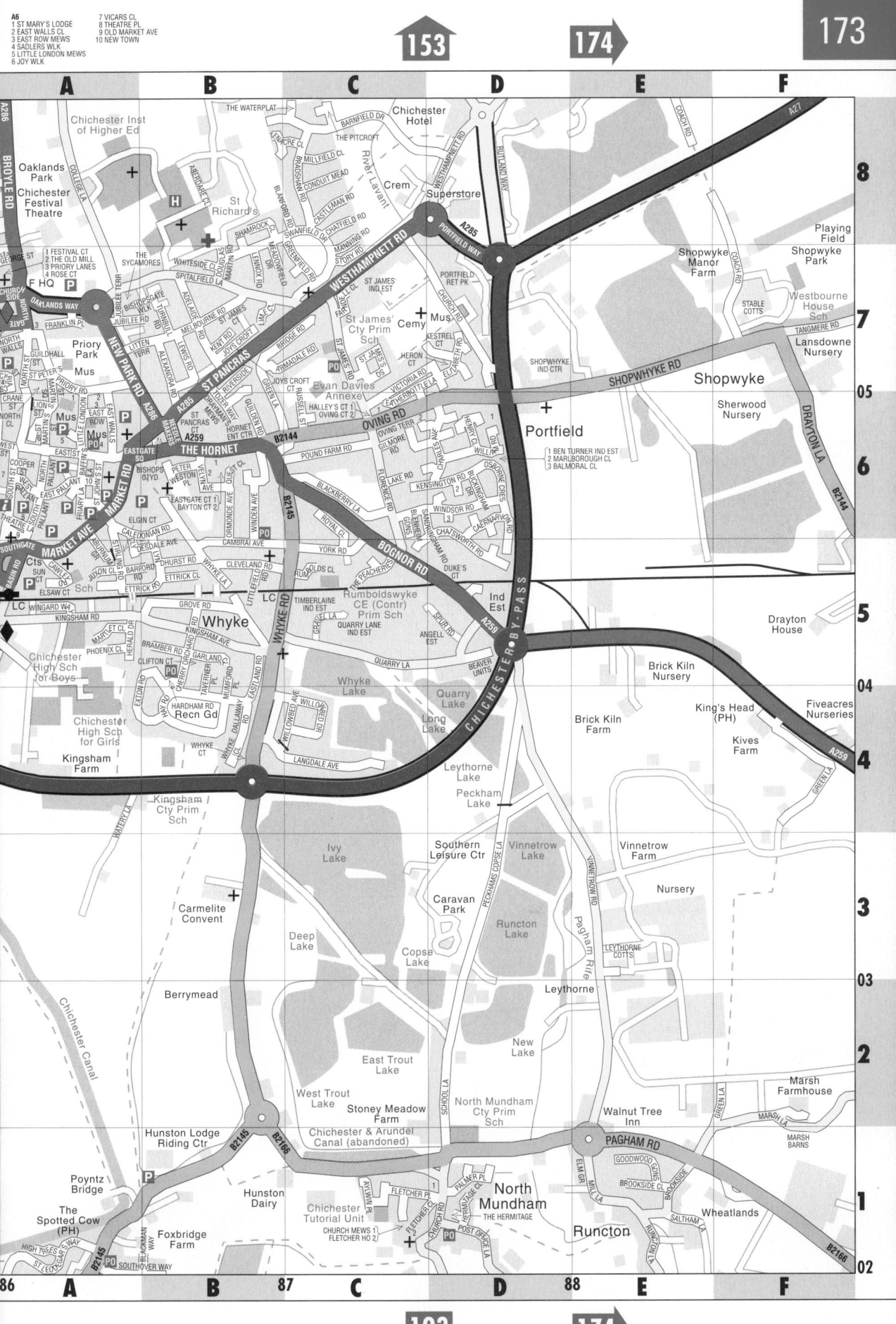

A6
1 ST MARY'S LODGE   7 VICARS CL
2 EAST WALLS CL   8 THEATRE PL
3 EAST ROW MEWS   9 OLD MARKET AVE
4 SADLERS WLK   10 NEW TOWN
5 LITTLE LONDON MEWS
6 JOY WLK

173
154

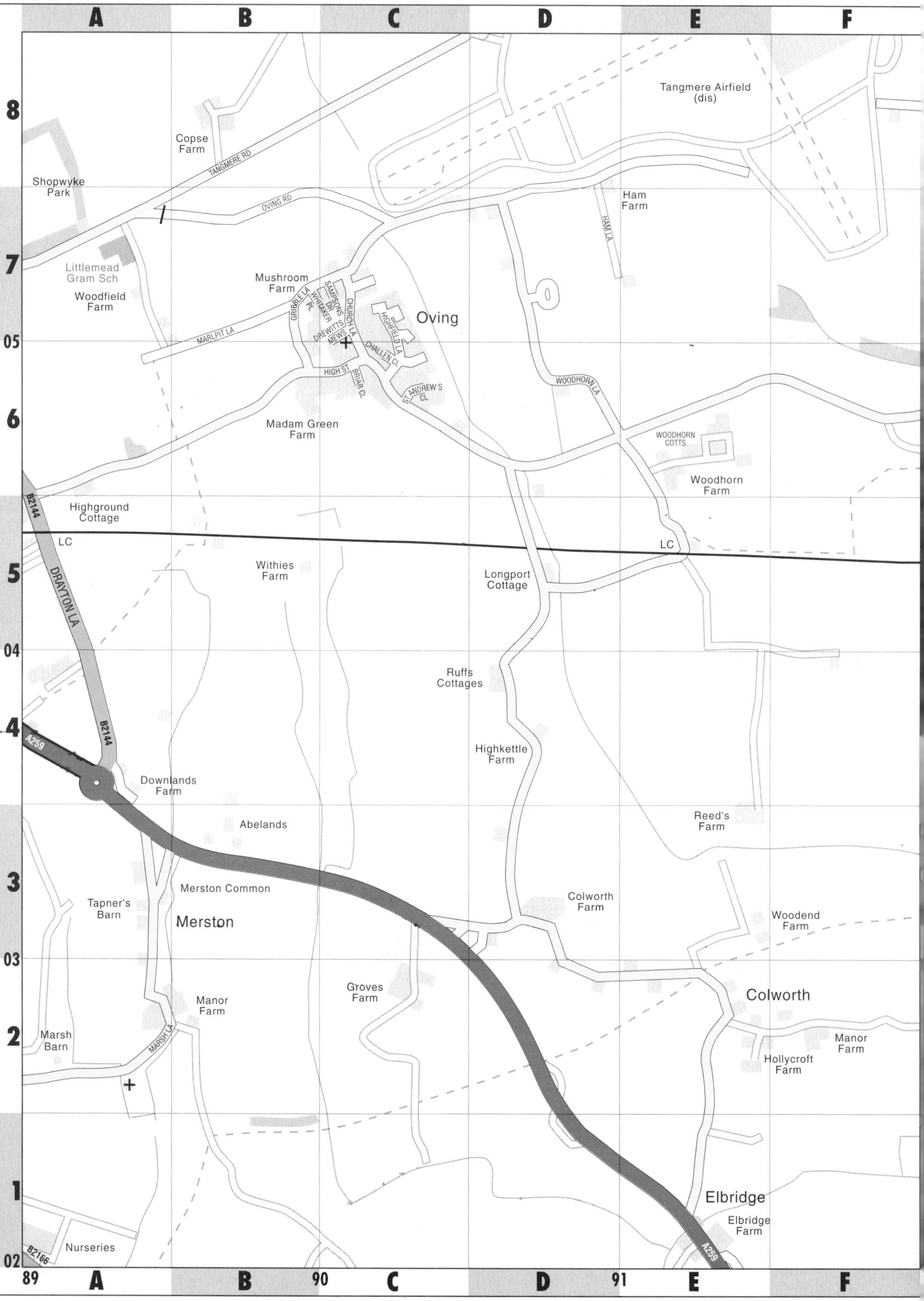

A · B · C · D · E · F

8

Tangmere Airfield
(dis)

Copse
Farm

TANGMERE RD

Shopwyke
Park

OVING RD

Ham
Farm

FRM LA

7

Littlemead
Gram Sch

Woodfield
Farm

Mushroom
Farm

GRIBBLE LA
SAMPSONS
DR
WHITAKER
PL
DREWITTS
MEWS

CHURCH LA

HIGHFIELD LA

Oving

MARLPIT LA

CHALLEN CL

05

HIGH ST

BRIAR CL

ST ANDREW'S
CL

WOODHORN LA

WOODHORN
COTTS

6

Madam Green
Farm

Woodhorn
Farm

B2144

Highground
Cottage

LC

LC

DRAYTON LA

Withies
Farm

Longport
Cottage

5

04

Ruffs
Cottages

4

B2144

A259

Highkettle
Farm

Reed's
Farm

Downlands
Farm

Abelands

Colworth
Farm

Woodend
Farm

3

Tapner's
Barn

Merston Common

Merston

03

MARSH LA

Manor
Farm

Groves
Farm

Colworth

Manor
Farm

2

Marsh
Barn

Hollycroft
Farm

1

Elbridge

Elbridge
Farm

B2166

Nurseries

A259

02

89 · A · B · 90 · C · D · 91 · E · F

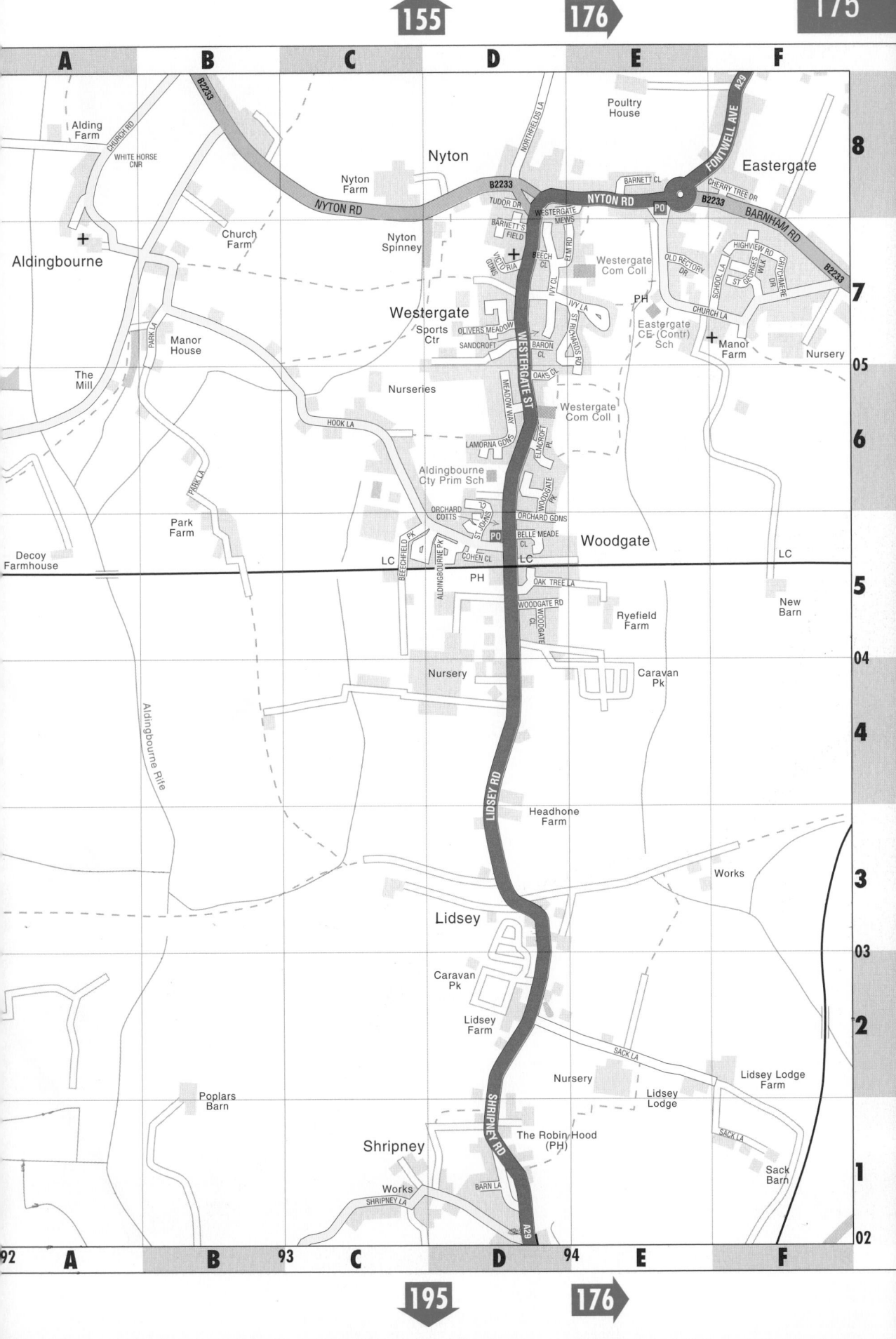

155
176

A　B　C　D　E　F

8

B2233

Alding
Farm

WHITE HORSE
CNR

CHURCH RD

Nyton
Farm

Nyton

NYTON RD

B2233

Poultry
House

FONTWELL AVE

A29

Eastergate

8

BARNETT CL

PO

Cherry Tree Dr

B2233

BARNHAM RD

B2233

Aldingbourne

Church Farm

Nyton
Spinney

TUDOR DR

BARNETT'S
FIELD

WESTERGATE
MEWS

VICTORIA GDNS

BEECH CL

IVY CL

ELM RD

Westergate
Com Coll

PH

Old Rectory Dr

HIGHVIEW RD

ST GEORGES

SCHOOL LA

CRITCHMERE WLK

7

Manor
House

PARK LA

Westergate

Sports
Ctr

OLIVERS MEADOW

SANDCROFT

IVY LA

ST HILDA'S RD

BARON CL

Eastergate
CE (Contr)
Sch

CHURCH LA

Manor
Farm

Nursery

05

The
Mill

Nurseries

WESTERGATE ST

MEADOW WAY

OAKS CL

Westergate
Com Coll

7

HOOK LA

6

6

PARK LA

LAMORNA GDNS

ELMCROFT PL

WOODGATE PK

Aldingbourne
Cty Prim Sch

Park
Farm

ORCHARD
COTTS

ST JOHNS

PO

ORCHARD GDNS

BELLE MEADE

Woodgate

Decoy
Farmhouse

LC

BEECHFIELD PK

ALDINGBOURNE PK

COHEN CL

PH

LC

OAK TREE LA

WOODGATE RD

WOODGATE CL

Ryefield
Farm

New
Barn

LC

5

5

04

Nursery

Caravan
Pk

04

Aldingbourne Rife

LIDSEY RD

Headhone
Farm

4

4

Works

3

3

Lidsey

03

03

Caravan
Pk

Lidsey
Farm

SACK LA

Nursery

Lidsey Lodge
Farm

2

2

Poplars
Barn

SHRIPNEY RD

Lidsey
Lodge

SACK LA

Shripney

The Robin Hood
(PH)

Sack
Barn

1

Works

BARN LA

1

SHRIPNEY LA

A29

02

92　A　B　93　C　D　94　E　F　02

195
176

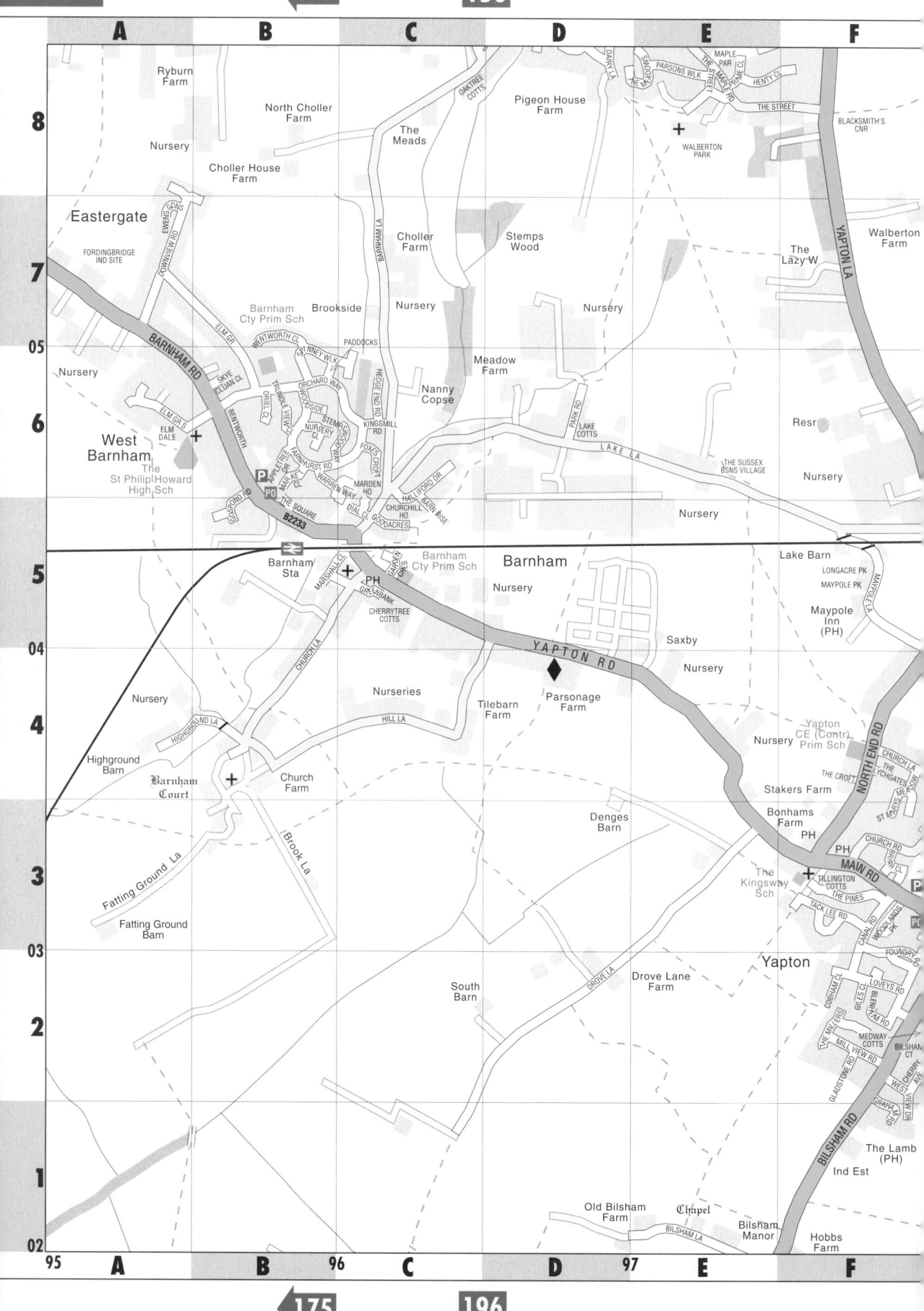
175
156
A
B
C
D
E
F
Ryburn Farm
North Choller Farm
Pigeon House Farm
Nursery
Choller House Farm
The Meads
Walberton Park
Blacksmith's Cnr
Eastergate
Fordingbridge Ind Site
Choller Farm
Stemps Wood
Walberton Farm
The Lazy W
Yapton La
Barnham Cty Prim Sch
Brookside
Nursery
Barnham Rd
Meadow Farm
Nanny Copse
West Barnham
The St Philip Howard High Sch
Lake La
The Sussex Bsns Village
Resr
Nursery
B2233
Barnham Sta
Barnham Cty Prim Sch
Barnham
Lake Barn
Longacre Pk
Maypole Pk
Maypole Inn (PH)
Nursery
Saxby
Yapton Rd
Nurseries
Tilebarn Farm
Parsonage Farm
Hill La
Highground Barn
Barnham Court
Church Farm
Yapton CE (Contr) Prim Sch
Stakers Farm
Bonhams Farm
North End Rd
Denges Barn
Brook La
Fatting Ground La
Fatting Ground Barn
The Kingsway Sch
Main Rd
Yapton
Drove Lane Farm
Drove La
South Barn
Bilsham Rd
The Lamb (PH)
Ind Est
Old Bilsham Farm
Chapel
Bilsham Manor
Hobbs Farm
Bilsham La
8
7
05
6
5
04
4
3
03
2
1
02
95
96
97
175
196

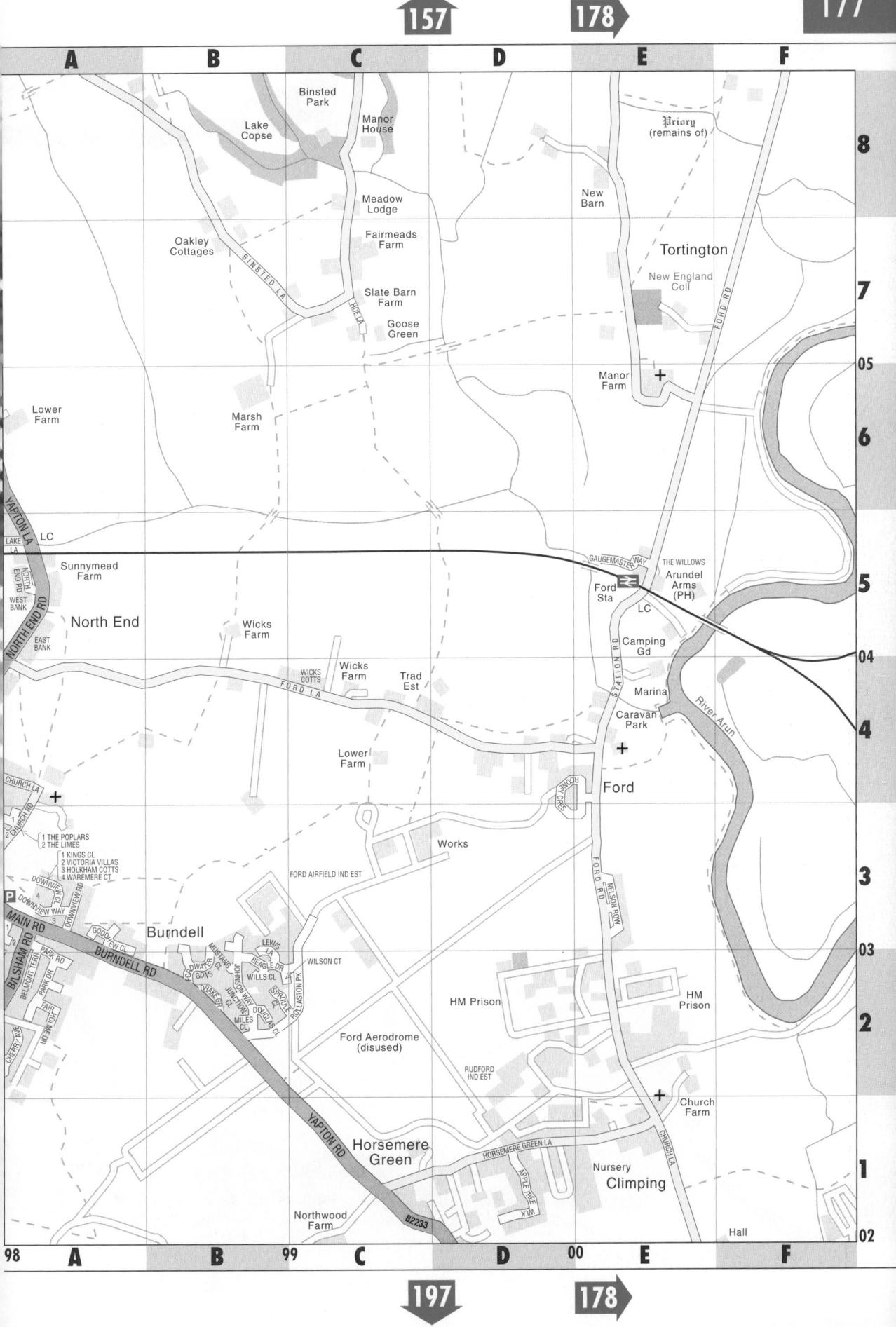
157
178
A
B
C
D
E
F
8
7
05
6
5
04
4
3
03
2
1
02
98
99
00
Binsted Park
Lake Copse
Manor House
Meadow Lodge
Fairmeads Farm
Oakley Cottages
BINSTED LA
Slate Barn Farm
HOE LA
Goose Green
Marsh Farm
Lower Farm
Priory (remains of)
New Barn
Tortington
New England Coll
FORD RD
Manor Farm
YAPTON LA
LC
LAKE LA
Sunnymead Farm
NORTH END RD
WEST BANK
North End
EAST BANK
Wicks Farm
GAUGEMASTER WAY
THE WILLOWS
Arundel Arms (PH)
Ford Sta
Camping Gd
STATION RD
WICKS COTTS
Wicks Farm
Trad Est
FORD LA
Marina
Caravan Park
River Arun
Lower Farm
Ford
RODNEY CRES
CHURCH LA
CHURCH RD
1 THE POPLARS
2 THE LIMES
1 KINGS CL
2 VICTORIA VILLAS
3 HOLKHAM COTTS
4 WAREMERE CT
Works
FORD AIRFIELD IND EST
DOWNVIEW CL
DOWNVIEW WAY
DOWNVIEW RD
P
MAIN RD
Burndell
GOODVIEW CL
BURNDELL RD
BILSHAM RD
BELMONT TERR
PARK RD
PARK DR
MUSTANG CL
FORDWATER GDNS
LEWIS LA
BEAGLE DR
WILLS CL
JOHNSON WAY
JUNCTION CL
DRAKE GR
SPROULE CL
ROLLASTON PK
WILSON CT
MILES CL
DOUGLAS CL
FAIRHOLME DR
CHERRY AVE
NELSON ROW
HM Prison
HM Prison
Ford Aerodrome (disused)
RUDFORD IND EST
Church Farm
YAPTON RD
Horsemere Green
HORSEMERE GREEN LA
CHURCH LA
APPLE TREE WLK
Nursery
Climping
Northwood Farm
B2233
Hall
197
178

A   B   C   D   E   F

8   7   05   6   5   04   4   03   3   2   1   02

River Arun

LC

Broomhurst Farm

Knucker Hole

LC

Arundel Junction

Brook Barn Farm

Court Wick Park

Littlehampton Junction

Nursery

Sewage Works

Caravan Park

River Arun

A259

Littlehampton Marina

Ret Pk

BRIDGE RD

B2187

Broad Piece

Riverside Ind Est

Forsters Yd

Quayside

Stubbs Copse

A27

A284

A27

CROSSBUSH LA

Calceto Farm

Brookfield

Brooklawns

LYMINSTER RD

CHURCH RD

Church Farm

THE PADDOCK

Lyminster

Brookside Caravan Park

Black Ditch

Thornlea Caravan Park

KINGSMEAD

PENARTH GDNS

ARUNDEL DR

OLD MEAD RD

WOODCOTE LA

PH
Caravan Park

Nurseries

Nurseries

Nurseries

Nurseries

GRANARY WAY

MILL FULLERS WLK

HEARNFIELD RD

TODDINGTON LA

LC

Hollyacre

Toddington

LITTLEHAMPTON

A259

B2187

A284

EAGLES CHASE

SWIFT WAY

EDWARDS WAY

REDWING

FALCON

ROBIN CL

FINCHES CL

KESTREL WAY

NEW COURTWICK LA

L MINSTER LA

COURTWICK LA

SANDFIELD AVE

COOMES WAY

SEATON CL

SEATON RD

SEATON LA

GRIFFIN CRES

OSPREY DR

1 OSPREY CL
2 SEATON PARK COTTS
3 LYMINSTER GATE

BARN CL

HOLLY DR

ON PK

Nurseries

A259

WORTHING RD

LA

HAWTHORN RD

Wick

MARTELLO ENT CTR

NORTHWAY RD

WINDLESHAM CT

GLEBE RD

Sch

WICK ST

BEACONSFIELD RD

GLADONN

Sch

CORNFIELD CL

Cornfield Sch

Caravan Park

OAKCROFT GDNS

Cemy

B2187

A259

WILLOW BRO

GREENFIELDS

JOYCE CL

ELSPRING MEAD

WHEATCROFT

STEAN FURLONG

BROOK RD

COLE RD

CHERRY

WICK PAR

CLARENCE

HEIG GN

HIGHFIELD

WHITE ACRE

MEAD

POTTERS

COURTWICK LA

THE CROSSWAYS

GRAND AVE

SELWYN

DEAL

LANDSDOWNE RD

STANLEY RD

HARTING RD

NORTH ST

1 NURSERY GDNS
2 TRUE BLUE PREC
3 GLADSTONE TERR

THORNCROFT RD

SELWAY LA

TOWNSEND CRES

THRGATE RD

LEDSHAM WAY

ARUNDEL RD

GREENSIDE

CLUN RD

BELLOC RD

MANNING RD

LINESIDE Ind Est

LINESIDE WAY

198

WHITELEA RD

WEST WAY

Sch

Prim Sch

CLUB

The Littlehampton Com Sch

HORSHAM RD

PEREGRINE CT

BELLSCROFT

OSMONDE CL

DALE DAVIES CL

GOSDEN CRES

Flora McDonald Cty Jun Sch

WICKBOURNE HO

WICK FARM CL

PEEL CL

FORT RD

CHAPEL CL

ROMAN BELVNGHAM CRES

WATER LA

JAYS CL

WHITEWAYS

BLAKEHURST WAY

HIGHDOWN DR

PARH

AMBERLEY CL

GROVE CRES

GROVE RD

HILL RD

FALKLAND AVE

Harwood Ind Est

ARUNSIDE Ind Est

HARWOOD ROAD ENT UNITS

HARWOOD RD

LINDEN PK

CHAPEL CL

LOUDOUN RD

EAST HAM RD

MANTLING RD

CORNWALL RD

CORNWALL GDNS

YORK GDNS

YORK RD

FIELD CL

Inf Sch

Jun Sch

Elm Grove Cty Inf Sch

PATERSON WILSON RD

ELMGROVE RD

DORSET CL

STANHOPE RD

PO

NORMAN CL

SOUTHFIELDS RD

PARKSIDE GDNS

MEADOW WAY

ESHER DR

SYDE AVE

P

LINDEN RD

TALBOT RD

MAXWELL RD

GLOUCESTER RD

GLOUCESTER PL

GLOUCESTER LA

HOWARD RD

B2140

A284

CONNAUGHT RD

FRANCISCAN WAY

ST MARTINS

DUKE ST

AVON RD

WINTERTON LODGE

MERTON LODGE

EAST ST

FITZROY CT

ST MARY'S CL

ST MARY'S RD

RAYDEN CL

ST FLORA'S RD

Sports Field

1 HEATHCOURT
2 REDWOOD CT

SHORT FURLONG

THE ESTUARY

WINTER

CARAVAN PARK

P

1 PHAROS QUAY
2 ALPHA CT
3 SMALLCROFT CL
4 PEPPER CT

TERMINUS RD

WHARF RD

RIVER RD

ALBERT

HIGH ST

SPARKS

SUREY CL

TERMINUS PL

PURBECK PL

Mkt

PO

BAT RD

ARCADE

FITZALAN RD

CHURCH ST

GODA RD

Littlehampton

FERRY RD

ROPE WLK

ALDWICK HO 1
FELPHAM HO 2
MARDEN HO 3
ALDINGBOURNE HO 4
PAGHAM HO 5
SINGLETON HO 6
FUNTINGTON HO 7
BOXGROVE HO 8
HOUGHTON HO 9
CHILGROVE HO 10

D1
1 ANCHOR SPRINGS
2 DUKE'S CT
3 ST MARTIN'S LA
4 WYCHCROFT
5 HOWARD PL
6 MADEHURST CT
7 ROSE CT
8 HAMPTON CT
9 ANTONIA CT
10 THE ARCADE
11 EVANS GDNS

D2
1 MERTON DR
2 QUANTOCKS
3 MALTHOUSE PAS
4 HAMPTON FIELDS

E1
1 ST MARY'S GDNS
2 TEMPLE CT
3 AMENIC CT
4 WHITE LODGE
5 SUMMERLEA GDNS

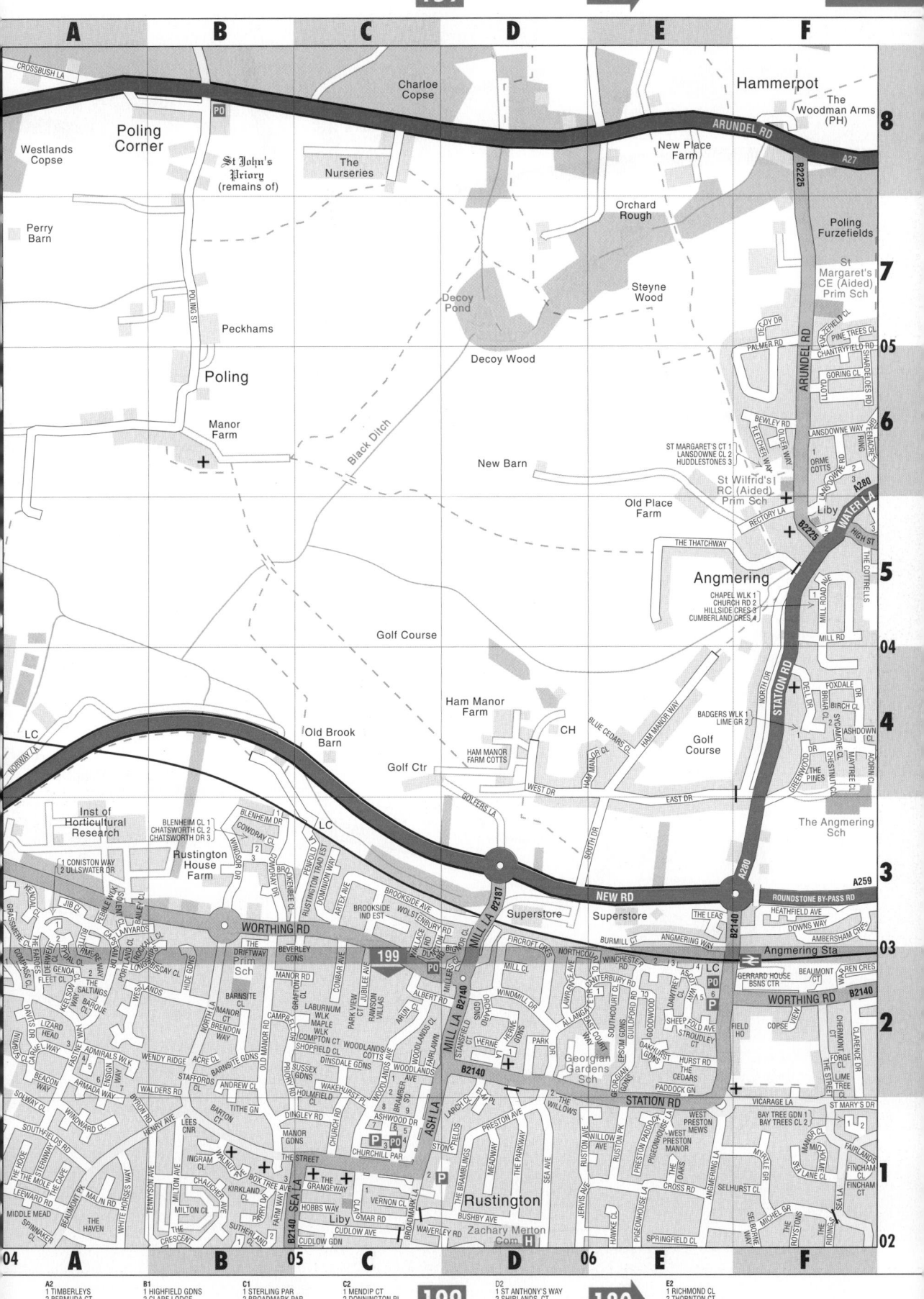

159
180
199
180

Crossbush La

Poling Corner

Westlands Copse

St John's Priory (remains of)

The Nurseries

Charloe Copse

Hammerpot

The Woodman Arms (PH)

ARUNDEL RD

A27

New Place Farm

Poling Furzefields

St Margaret's CE (Aided) Prim Sch

Perry Barn

Orchard Rough

Peckhams

Decoy Pond

Steyne Wood

Poling

Decoy Wood

Manor Farm

Black Ditch

New Barn

New Place Farm

Old Place Farm

St Wilfrid's RC (Aided) Prim Sch

ST MARGARET'S CT 1
LANSDOWNE CL 2
HUDDLESTONES 3

Angmering

CHAPEL WLK 1
CHURCH RD 2
HILLSIDE CRES 3
CUMBERLAND CRES 4

THE THATCHWAY

RECTORY LA

Liby

WATER LA

HIGH ST

THE COTTRELLS

MILL RD

Golf Course

Ham Manor Farm

CH

Old Brook Barn

BLUE CEDARS CL

HAM MANOR WAY

Golf Course

The Angmering Sch

BADGERS WLK 1
LIME GR 2

FOXDALE

The Pines

Golf Ctr

HAM MANOR FARM COTTS

WEST DR

EAST DR

Inst of Horticultural Research

BLENHEIM CL 1
CHATSWORTH CL 2
CHATSWORTH DR 3

BLENHEIM DR

Rustington House Farm

1 CONISTON WAY
2 ULLSWATER DR

WORTHING RD

Superstore

NEW RD

Superstore

THE LEAS

ROUNDSTONE BY-PASS RD

A259

Heathfield Ave
Downs Way
Ambersham Cres

Angmering Way

Angmering Sta

Angmering Way

WORTHING RD

B2140

The Driftway Prim Sch

BROOKSIDE IND EST

Superstore

Mill Cl

Windmill Dr

Georgian Gardens Sch

Gerrard House Bsns Ctr

FIELD HO

Rustington

Zachary Merton Com H

STATION RD

West Preston Manor

179
160

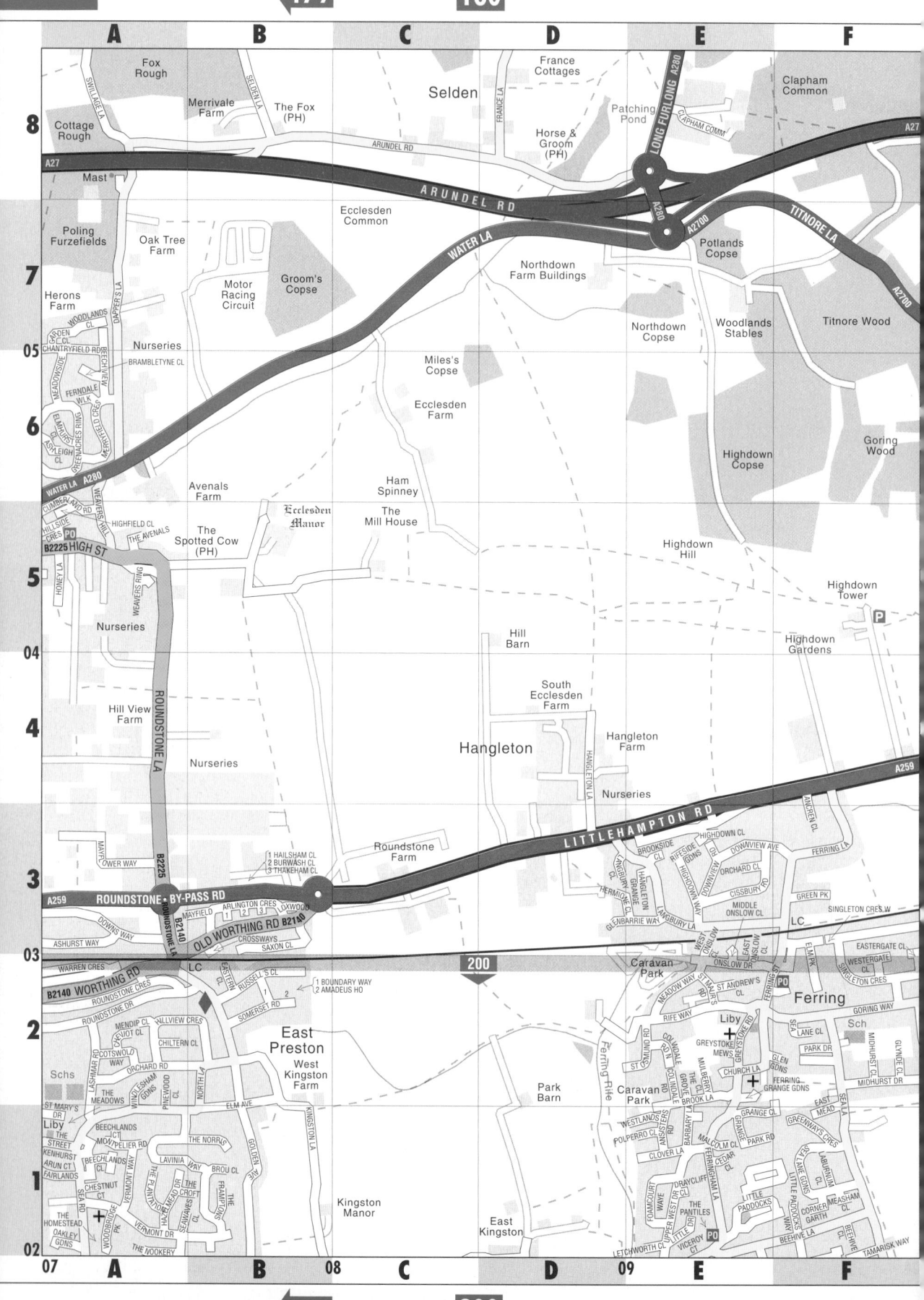
A
B
C
D
E
F
8
7
05
6
5
04
4
3
03
2
1
02
07
08
09
Fox Rough
Cottage Rough
Merrivale Farm
The Fox (PH)
Selden
France Cottages
Patching Pond
Clapham Common
Horse & Groom (PH)
SWILLAGE LA
SELDEN LA
FRANCE LA
LONG FURLONG
A280
CLAPHAM COMM
ARUNDEL RD
A27
Mast
ARUNDEL RD
Ecclesden Common
Poling Furzefields
Oak Tree Farm
WATER LA
A2700
TITNORE LA
Potlands Copse
Northdown Farm Buildings
Motor Racing Circuit
Groom's Copse
Herons Farm
DAPPER'S LA
WOODLANDS CL
GARDEN CL
CHANTRYFIELD RD
BEECHVIEW
Nurseries
BRAMBLETYNE CL
MEADOWSIDE
FERNDALE WLK
ELMHURST CL
GREENACRES RING
MERRYFIELD CRES
ASHLEIGH CL
Northdown Copse
Woodlands Stables
Titnore Wood
Miles's Copse
Ecclesden Farm
Goring Wood
Highdown Copse
WATER LA
A280
WEAVERS HILL
Avenals Farm
Ham Spinney
CUMBERLAND RD
HILLSIDE CRES
PO
HIGHFIELD CL
THE AVENALS
Ecclesden Manor
The Mill House
The Spotted Cow (PH)
B2225 HIGH ST
Highdown Hill
HONEY LA
WEAVERS RING
Highdown Tower
P
Nurseries
Hill Barn
Highdown Gardens
Hill View Farm
ROUNDSTONE LA
South Ecclesden Farm
Hangleton
Hangleton Farm
HANGLETON LA
Nurseries
A259
ANGREN CL
LITTLEHAMPTON RD
Roundstone Farm
MAYFLOWER WAY
B2225
1 HAILSHAM CL
2 BURWASH CL
3 THAKEHAM CL
BROOKSIDE CL
RIFESIDE GDNS
HIGHDOWN CL
DOWNVIEW AVE
FERRING LA
LANGBURY CL
HANGLETON GRANGE
HIGHDOWN WAY
DOWNVIEW RD
ORCHARD CL
CISSBURY RD
HERMIONE CL
GREEN PK
MIDDLE ONSLOW CL
SINGLETON CRES W
A259
ROUNDSTONE BY-PASS RD
ARLINGTON CRES
LOXWOOD
MAYFIELD
ROUNDSTONE LA
B2140
OLD WORTHING RD B2140
DOWNS WAY
CROSSWAYS
SAXON CL
ASHURST WAY
GLENBARRIE WAY
LANGBURY LA
WEST ONSLOW CL
EAST ONSLOW CL
LC
ELM PK
EASTERGATE CL
WESTERGATE CL
SINGLETON CRES
WARREN CRES
LC
200
Caravan Park
ONSLOW DR
B2140 WORTHING RD
ROUNDSTONE CRES
EASTERN CL
RUSSELL'S CL
1 BOUNDARY WAY
2 AMADEUS HO
MEADOW WAY
ST MAUR'S RD
ST ANDREW'S CL
FERRING ST
PO
Ferring
ROUNDSTONE DR
SOMERSET RD
RIFE WAY
GORING WAY
MENDIP CL
HILLVIEW CRES
CHEVIOT CL
East Preston
Liby
Sch
CHILTERN CL
ST OSMUND RD
COLWADE
GREYSTOKE RD
SEA LANE CL
MIDHURST CL
GLYNDE CL
COTSWOLD WAY
GREYSTOKE MEWS
PARK DR
Ferring Rife
ORCHARD RD
West Kingston Farm
CHURCH LA
GLEN GDNS
Schs
LASHMAR RD
WINDLESHAM GDNS
PINEWOOD CL
NORTH LA
FERRING GRANGE GDNS
MIDHURST DR
THE MEADOWS
Park Barn
Caravan Park
COLWADE RD
THE CL
MULBERRY
BROOK LA
ST MARY'S DR
ELM AVE
KINGSTON LA
EAST MEAD
SEA LA
Liby
THE STREET
BEECHLANDS CT
WESTLANDS
GRANGE CL
GREENWAYS CRES
MONTPELIER RD
THE NORRIS
POLPERRO CL
ANSISTERS RD
BARBARY LA
GRANGE
PARK RD
KENHURST
BEECHLANDS CL
LAVINIA WAY
GOLDEN AVE
MALCOLM CL
SEA LANE GDNS
LABURNUM CL
ARUN CT
FAIRLANDS
BROU CL
CLOVER LA
FERRINGHAM LA
CEDAR CL
SEA RD
CHESTNUT CT
VERMONT WAY
THE PLANTATION
HAZELMEAD DR
THE CROFT
FRAMPTONS
THE
FOAMCOURT WAYE
DRAYCLIFF CL
LITTLE PADDOCKS
LITTLE PADDOCKS WAY
MEASHAM CL
THE HOMESTEAD
WOODBRIDGE PK
SEAWAVES CL
Kingston Manor
UPPER WEST DR
THE PANTILES
CORNER GARTH
East Kingston
LITTLE DR
PO
BEEHIVE LA
BEEHIVE CL
OAKLEY GDNS
VERMONT DR
LETCHWORTH CL
VICEROY CT
TAMARISK WAY
THE NOOKERY

179
200

161
182

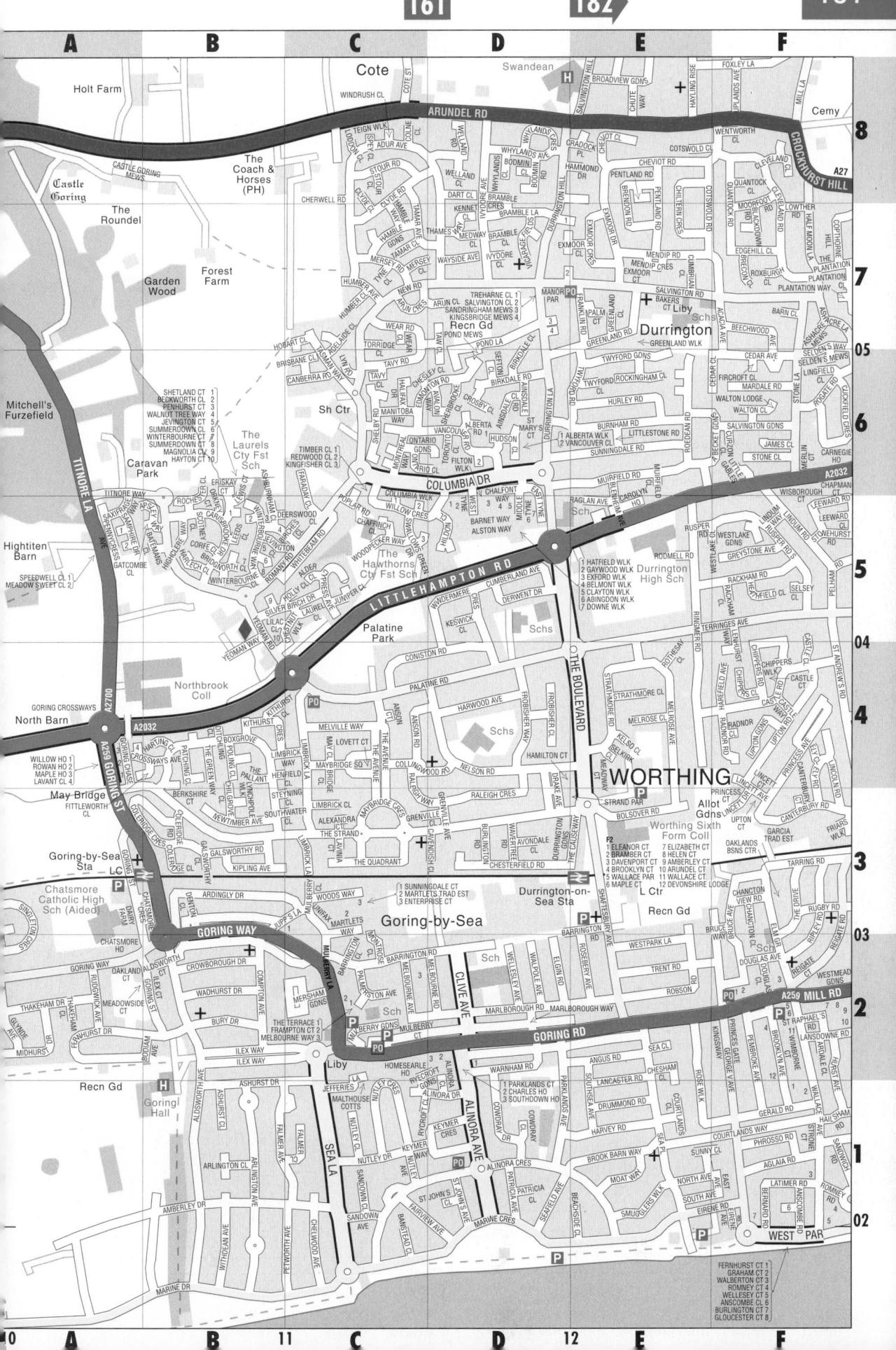
A
B
C
D
E
F
Cote
Swandean
Holt Farm
WINDRUSH CL
COTE ST
ARUNDEL RD
BROADVIEW GDNS
SALVINGTON HILL
CHUTE WAY
HAYLING RISE
UPLANDS AVE
FOXLEY LA
MILL LA
Cemy
CROCKHURST HILL
A27
WENTWORTH CL
COTSWOLD CL
CHEVIOT RD
CLEVELAND CL
QUANTOCK CL
LOWTHER RD
HALF MOON LA
COPTHORNE HILL
The Coach & Horses (PH)
CASTLE GORING MEWS
Castle Goring
The Roundel
Forest Farm
Garden Wood
CHERWELL RD
TEIGN WLK
ADUR AVE
STOUR RD
WELLAND CL
DART CL
KENNET CL
THAMES WAY
MEDWAY
WAYSIDE AVE
IVYDORE AVE
BRAMBLE LA
BRAMBLE CRES
WHYLANDS AVE
WHYLANDS CRES
BODMIN CL
CRADOCK PL
CHEVIOT CL
HAMMOND DR
DURRINGTON HILL
PENTLAND RD
BRENDON RD
CHILTERN CRES
COTSWOLD RD
EXMOOR DR
EXMOOR CRES
MENDIP RD
MENDIP CRES
CUMBRIAN CL
EDGEHILL CL
ROXBURGH CL
PLANTATION WAY
THE PLANTATION
HUMBER AVE
HUMBER CL
MERSEY RD
NEW RD
ARUN CRES
ARUN CL
TREHARNE CL 1
SALVINGTON CL 2
SANDRINGHAM MEWS 3
KINGSBRIDGE MEWS 4
Recn Gd
POND MEWS
POND LA
MANOR PAR
FRANKLIN RD
PALM CT
GREENLAND RD
GREENLAND WLK
SALVINGTON RD
BAKERS CT
Liby
Schs
Durrington
ACACIA AVE
BARN CL
BEECHWOOD AVE
ASHACRE LA
ASHACRE MEWS
SELDEN'S WAY
SELDEN'S MEWS
LINGFIELD CL
ROGATE RD
CUCKFIELD CRES
HOBART CL
BRISBANE CL
CANBERRA RD
ADELAIDE CL
TASMAN WAY
WEAR RD
TORRIDGE CL
TAVY RD
TAVY CL
HALIFAX DR
EDMONTON RD
CHESLEY CL
AVALON WAY
SHERBROOKE WAY
SEFTON CL
BIRKDALE RD
CROSBY CL
AINSDALE CL
TWYFORD GDNS
TWYFORD RD
ROCKINGHAM CL
HURLEY RD
BURNHAM RD
LITTLESTONE RD
SUNNINGDALE RD
CEDAR AVE
CEDAR CL
FIRCROFT CL
MARDALE RD
WALTON LODGE
WALTON CL
SALVINGTON GDNS
JAMES CL
STONE CL
STONE LA
MERLIN CT
CARNEGIE HO
Mitchell's Furzefield
SHETLAND CT 1
BECKWORTH CL 2
PENHURST CT 3
WALNUT TREE WAY 4
JEVINGTON CT 5
SUMMERDOWN CL 6
WINTERBOURNE CT 7
SUMMERDOWN CT 8
MAGNOLIA CL 9
HAYTON CT 10
The Laurels Cty Fst Sch
Sh Ctr
MANITOBA WAY
SHELBY RD
ALBERTA RD
VANCOUVER RD
ST MARY'S CT
HUDSON CL
1 ALBERTA WLK
2 VANCOUVER CL
ONTARIO GDNS
ONTARIO CL
FILTON WLK
TIMBER CL 1
REDWOOD CL 2
KINGFISHER CL 3
Caravan Park
TITNORE LA
TITNORE WAY
ERISKAY CT
ROCHESTER CL
ORKNEY CL
LEWIS CT
ASHBURNHAM CL
FARADAY CL
COLUMBIA DR
COLUMBIA WLK
WILLOW CRES
CHALFONT WAY
WEST TYNE
MIDDLE TYNE
EAST TYNE
BARNET WAY
ALSTON WAY
HILTON CL
RAGLAN AVE
CAROLYN HO
BLENHEIM AVE
MUIRFIELD RD
MUIRFIELD CT
A2032
WISBOROUGH CT
CHAPMAN CT
LEWARD RD
LEEWARD CL
LINDUM WAY
LINDUM RD
STONEHURST RD
RUSPER RD
RUSPER RD S
WESTLAKE GDNS
WESTLAKE CL
GREYSTONE AVE
RODMELL RD
Durrington High Sch
PELHAM RD
SAXIFRAGE WAY
SAMPHIRE DR
APSLEY WAY
BATEMANS CT
GATCOMBE CL
SPEEDWELL CL 1
MEADOW SWEET CL 2
Hightiten Barn
HIGHCLERE WAY
HARLECH CL
CORFE CL
CARISBROOKE DR
LEEDS CL
BRIDGNORTH CL
WINTERBOURNE WAY
DEERSWOOD CL
JEVINGTON
BIRCHES CL
ROMANY RD
WHITEBEAM RD
POPLAR RD
CHAFFINCH CL
WOODPECKER WAY
SWALLOWS GREEN
The Hawthorns Cty Fst Sch
ALDER CL
CYPRESS AVE
HOLLY CL
SILVER BIRCH DR
JUNIPER CL
LAUREL CL
LILAC CL
CHESTNUT WLK
YEOMAN WAY
YEOMAN RD
LITTLEHAMPTON RD
1 HATFIELD WLK
2 GAYWOOD WLK
3 EXFORD WLK
4 BELMONT WLK
5 CLAYTON WLK
6 ABINGDON WLK
7 DOWNE WLK
RACKHAM RD
RACKHAM CL
HEATHFIELD CL
SELSEY CL
WINDERMERE CRES
CUMBERLAND AVE
DERWENT DR
KESWICK CL
Palatine Park
Schs
CONISTON RD
THE BOULEVARD
ROTHESAY CL
RINGMER RD
TERRINGES AVE
LENHURST WAY
HAREFIELD AVE
CHIPPERS RD
CHIPPERS WLK
CHIPPERS CL
CASTLE RD
CASTLE CL
CASTLE WAY
ST ANDREW'S RD
Northbrook Coll
GORING CROSSWAYS
North Barn
A2700
PALATINE RD
HARWOOD AVE
FROBISHER WAY
FROBISHER CL
STRATHMORE RD
STRATHMORE CL
MELROSE CL
MELROSE AVE
RADNOR CL
RADNOR RD
UPTON GDNS
UPTON RD
KITHURST CL
KITHURST CRES
BOXGROVE
DITCHLING
POLING CL
PATCHING CL
THE GREEN WAY
HARTING CL
CROSSWAYS AVE
GORING CHASE
A259 GORING ST
WILLOW HO 1
ROWAN HO 2
MAPLE HO 3
LAVANT CL 4
MELVILLE WAY
LOVETT CT
MAY CL
ANSON CT
ANSON RD
THE AVENUE
Schs
KELSO CL
SELKIRK CL
HAMILTON CT
PRINCESS AVE
ELY CL
ELY RD
LINCOLN RD
LIMBRICK WAY
HENFIELD CL
STEYNING CL
SOUTHWATER CL
MAYBRIDGE SQ
COLLINGWOOD RD
NELSON RD
RALEIGH CRES
RALEIGH WAY
DRAKE AVE
MEADWAY
WORTHING
STRAND PAR
PRINCESS CT
LINCETT AVE
LINCETT DR
CANTERBURY RD
CANTERBURY CL
May Bridge
FITTLEWORTH CL
BERKSHIRE CT
THE PALLANT
LYNCHPOLE WLK
NEWTIMBER AVE
CHILGROVE CL
LIMBRICK CL
ALEXANDRA CT
THE STRAND
MAYBRIDGE CRES
GRENVILLE CT
GRENVILLE AVE
CAVENDISH CL
BURLINGTON RD
WAVERTREE RD
AVONDALE CL
DURRINGTON GDNS
THE CAUSEWAY
BOLSOVER RD
Allot Gdns
Worthing Sixth Form Coll
UPTON CT
GARCIA TRAD EST
FRIARS WLK
OAKLANDS BSNS CTR
COLERIDGE CRES
COLERIDGE CL
GALSWORTHY RD
GALSWORTHY
KIPLING AVE
THE QUADRANT
LAVINIA CT
CHESTERFIELD RD
F2
1 ELEANOR CT
2 BRAMBER CT
3 DAVENPORT CT
4 BROOKLYN CT
5 WALLACE PAR
6 MAPLE CT
7 ELIZABETH CT
8 HELEN CT
9 AMBERLEY CT
10 ARUNDEL CT
11 WALLACE CT
12 DEVONSHIRE LODGE
Goring-by-Sea Sta
LC
TARRING RD
Chatsmore Catholic High Sch (Aided)
SINGLETON CRES
DAIRY FARM
CHATSMORE CRES
ARDINGLY DR
DENTON CL
MULBERRY CL
WOODS WAY
UNIFAX
1 SUNNINGDALE CT
2 MARTLETS TRAD EST
3 ENTERPRISE CT
Durrington-on-Sea Sta
SHAFTESBURY AVE
L Ctr
Recn Gd
CHANCTON VIEW RD
CHANCTON CL
THE DRIVE
RUGBY RD
RIPLEY RD
REIGATE RD
JUPP'S LA
MARTLETS WAY
Goring-by-Sea
GORING WAY
CHATSMORE HO
MONTROSE CL
BARRINGTON CL
BARRINGTON RD
BARRINGTON RD
WESTPARK LA
BRUCE WAY
BRUCE AVE
ELM GR
Sch
DOUGLAS AVE
DOUGLAS CL
REIGATE CL
WESTMEAD GDNS
GORING WAY
OAKLAND CT
ALDSWORTH CT
CROWBOROUGH DR
COMPTON AVE
MULBERRY LA
MELBOURNE AVE
MELBOURNE RD
CLIVE AVE
WELLESLEY AVE
WALPOLE AVE
ELGIN RD
ROSEBERY AVE
TRENT RD
ROBSON RD
A259 MILL RD
THAKEHAM DR
THAKEHAM CL
RUDGWICK AVE
MEADOWSIDE CT
ILEX CT
GORING ST
WADHURST DR
MERSHAM GDNS
PALMERSTON AVE
Sch
MARLBOROUGH RD
MARLBOROUGH WAY
ST RAPHAEL'S RD
LANSDOWNE RD
GLYNDE AVE
FERNHURST DR
MIDHURST DR
BURY DR
THE TERRACE 1
FRAMPTON CT 2
MELBOURNE WAY 3
MULBERRY GDNS
MULBERRY CT
GORING RD
SEA CL
BODIAM AVE
ILEX WAY
Liby
HOMESEARLE HO
ALINORA CL
WARNHAM RD
ANGUS RD
CHESHAM CL
KINGSWAY
PRINCES GATE
GEORGE V AVE
PEMBROKE AVE
BROOKLYN AVE
WIMBORNE CL
WALLACE AVE
ARDALE CL
HURST AVE
Recn Gd
Goring Hall
ALDSWORTH AVE
ASHURST DR
ASHURST CL
JEFFERIES LA
MALTHOUSE COTTS
NUTLEY CRES
RYECROFT GDNS
RYECROFT DR
ALINORA DR
1 PARKLANDS CT
2 CHARLES HO
3 SOUTHDOWN HO
SOUTHSEA AVE
LANCASTER RD
DRUMMOND RD
COURTLANDS
ROSE WLK
GERALD RD
HAILSHAM RD
FALMER AVE
FALMER CL
SEA LA
NUTLEY CL
KEYMER CRES
ALINORA AVE
COWDRAY DR
COWDRAY CL
PARKLANDS AVE
HARVEY RD
COURTLANDS WAY
PHROSSO RD
STRONE AVE
SANDWICH RD
ARLINGTON CL
ARLINGTON AVE
NUTLEY DR
KEYMER WAY
NUTLEY AVE
ALINORA CRES
SEA PL
BROOK BARN WAY
SUNNY CL
AGLAIA RD
ROMNEY RD
SANDOWN CL
ST JOHN'S CL
ST JOHN'S AVE
PATRICIA AVE
PATRICIA CL
SEAFIELD AVE
MOAT WAY
NORTH AVE
EAST AVE
SOUTH AVE
LATIMER RD
ANSCOMBE RD
BERNARD RD
AMBERLEY DR
SANDOWN AVE
BANSTEAD CL
FAIRVIEW AVE
MARINE CRES
BEACHSIDE CL
SMUGGLERS WLK
EIRENE RD
EIRENE AVE
WEST PAR
WITHDEAN AVE
PETWORTH AVE
CHELWOOD AVE
MARINE DR
FERNHURST CT 1
GRAHAM CT 2
WALBERTON CT 3
ROMNEY CT 4
WELLESEY CT 5
ANSCOMBE CL 6
BURLINGTON CT 7
GLOUCESTER CT 8
8
7
05
6
5
04
4
3
03
2
1
02
10
11
12

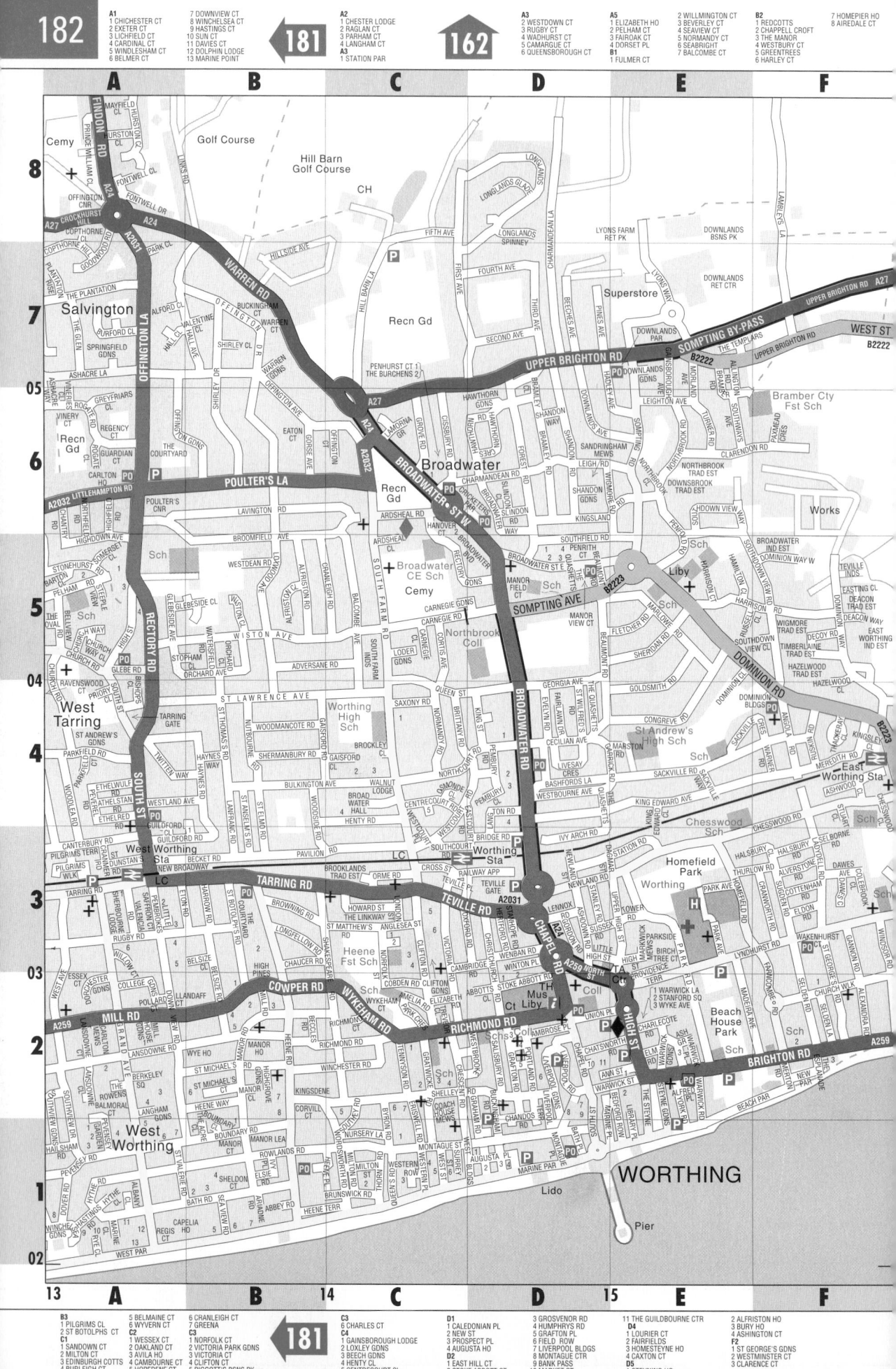
182
A1
1 CHICHESTER CT
2 EXETER CT
3 LICHFIELD CT
4 CARDINAL CT
5 WINDLESHAM CT
6 BELMER CT
7 DOWNVIEW CT
8 WINCHELSEA CT
9 HASTINGS CT
10 SUN CT
11 DAVIES CT
12 DOLPHIN LODGE
13 MARINE POINT
181
A2
1 CHESTER LODGE
2 RAGLAN CT
3 PARHAM CT
4 LANGHAM CT
A3
1 STATION PAR
162
A3
2 WESTDOWN CT
3 RUGBY CT
4 WADHURST CT
5 CAMARGUE CT
6 QUEENSBOROUGH CT
A5
1 ELIZABETH HO
2 PELHAM CT
3 FAIROAK CT
4 DORSET PL
B1
1 FULMER CT
2 WILLMINGTON CT
3 BEVERLEY CT
4 SEAVIEW CT
5 NORMANDY CT
6 SEABRIGHT
7 BALCOMBE CT
B2
1 REDCOTTS
2 CHAPPELL CROFT
3 THE MANOR
4 WESTBURY CT
5 GREENTREES
6 HARLEY CT
7 HOMEPIER HO
8 AIREDALE CT
A B C D E F
8 7 6 5 4 3 2 1
05 04 03 02
Cemy
Golf Course
Hill Barn Golf Course
CH
FINDON RD
A24
A27
CROCKHURST HILL
OFFINGTON CNR
COPTHORNE HILL
FONTWELL DR
WARREN RD
LINKS RD
FIFTH AVE
FOURTH AVE
SECOND AVE
FIRST AVE
THIRD AVE
CHARMANDEAN LA
LONGLANDS
LONGLANDS SPINNEY
LYONS FARM RET PK
DOWNLANDS BSNS PK
DOWNLANDS RET CTR
LAMBLEYS LA
Superstore
UPPER BRIGHTON RD
SOMPTING BY-PASS
WEST ST
B2222
Salvington
OFFINGTON LA
Recn Gd
Bramber Cty Fst Sch
Broadwater
BROADWATER ST W
POULTER'S LA
A2032
LITTLEHAMPTON RD
POULTER'S CNR
NORTHBROOK TRAD EST
DOWNSBROOK TRAD EST
Works
Broadwater CE Sch
Cemy
Sch
Liby
SOMPTING AVE
B2223
Northbrook Coll
DOMINION RD
BROADWATER IND EST
EASTING CL
DEACON TRAD EST
WIGMORE TRAD EST
TIMBERLAINE TRAD EST
HAZELWOOD TRAD EST
EAST WORTHING IND EST
West Tarring
RECTORY RD
SOUTH ST
Worthing High Sch
BROADWATER RD
St Andrew's High Sch
East Worthing Sta
Chesswood Sch
West Worthing Sta
TARRING RD
TEVILLE RD
Worthing Sta
Homefield Park
Worthing
H
A2031
CHAPEL RD
COWPER RD
WYKEHAM RD
MILL RD
A259
Heene Fst Sch
RICHMOND RD
TH
Mus
Liby
Coll
HIGH ST
TA Ctr
Beach House Park
BRIGHTON RD
West Worthing
WEST PAR
MARINE PAR
Lido
WORTHING
Pier
13 A B 14 C D 15 E F
B3
1 PILGRIMS CL
2 ST BOTOLPHS CT
C1
1 SANDOWN CT
2 MILTON CT
3 EDINBURGH COTTS
4 BURLEIGH CT
5 BELMAINE CT
6 WYVERN CT
C2
1 WESSEX CT
2 OAKLAND CT
3 AVILA HO
4 CAMBOURNE CT
5 HOPEDENE CT
6 CRANLEIGH CT
7 GREENA
C3
1 NORFOLK CT
2 VICTORIA PARK GDNS
3 VICTORIA CT
4 CLIFTON CT
5 PIGGOTT'S BSNS PK
181
C3
6 CHARLES CT
C4
1 GAINSBOROUGH LODGE
2 LOXLEY GDNS
3 BEECH GDNS
4 HENTY CL
5 CENTRECOURT CL
D1
1 CALEDONIAN PL
2 NEW ST
3 PROSPECT PL
4 AUGUSTA HO
D2
1 EAST HILL CT
2 STOKE ABBOTT CT
3 GROSVENOR RD
4 HUMPHRYS RD
5 GRAFTON PL
6 FIELD ROW
7 LIVERPOOL BLDGS
8 MONTAGUE CTR
9 BANK PASS
10 MARKET ST
11 THE GUILDBOURNE CTR
D4
1 LOURIER CT
2 FAIRFIELDS
3 HOMESTEYNE HO
4 CAXTON CT
D5
1 STEYNING HO
2 ALFRISTON HO
3 BURY HO
4 ASHINGTON CT
F2
1 ST GEORGE'S GDNS
2 WESTMINSTER CT
3 CLARENCE CT

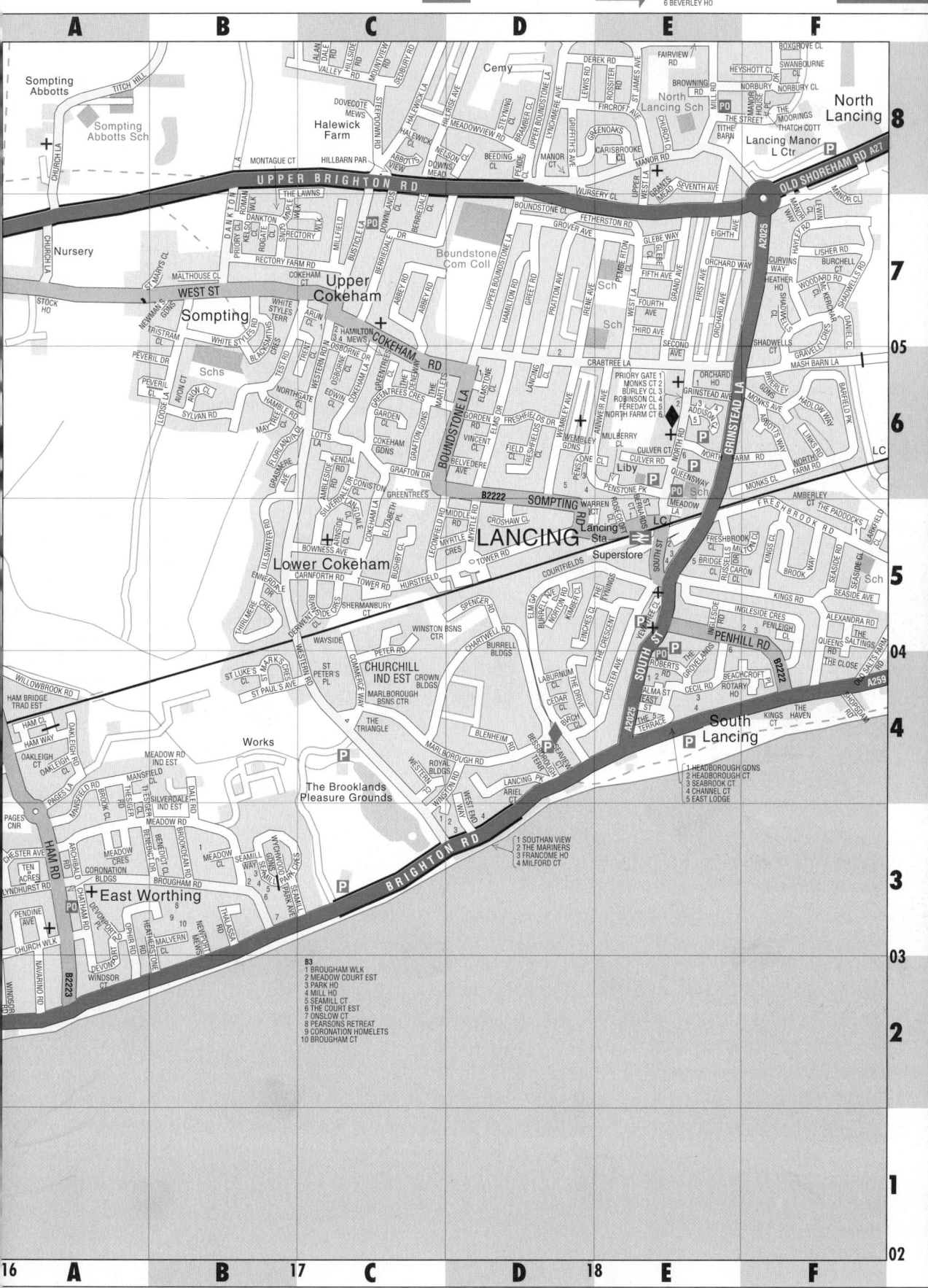

C7
1 BALL TREE CROFT
2 WESTERN LODGE
3 SOUTH LODGE
4 INGLECROFT CT

163

D6
1 CHERRY TREE LODGE
2 CRABTREE LODGE
3 ST NICHOLAS' CT
4 ST DAVID'S GATE
5 ST JOHN'S CT

184

E5
1 ST ROBERT'S LODGE
2 STATION PAR
3 FRESHBROOK CT
4 THE WILLOWS
5 RUSSELL CT
6 BEVERLEY HO

F5
1 COWLEY DR
2 OAKLANDS
3 HAZELWOOD LODGE

B3
1 BROUGHAM WLK
2 MEADOW COURT EST
3 PARK HO
4 MILL HO
5 SEAMILL CT
6 THE COURT EST
7 ONSLOW CT
8 PEARSONS RETREAT
9 CORONATION HOMELETS
10 BROUGHAM CT

1 SOUTHAN VIEW
2 THE MARINERS
3 FRANCOME HO
4 MILFORD CT

1 HEADBOROUGH GDNS
2 HEADBOROUGH CT
3 SEABROOK CT
4 CHANNEL CT
5 EAST LODGE

F7
1 CLEMENT'S CT
2 WEPPONS
3 CECIL NORRIS HO
4 NORMANHURST
5 OAKLAND CT
6 TINTAGEL CT

7 SWANBOROUGH CT
8 MANNINGS
9 GLYNDEBOURNE CT
10 PASHLEY CT
11 RIVERSIDE BSNS CTR

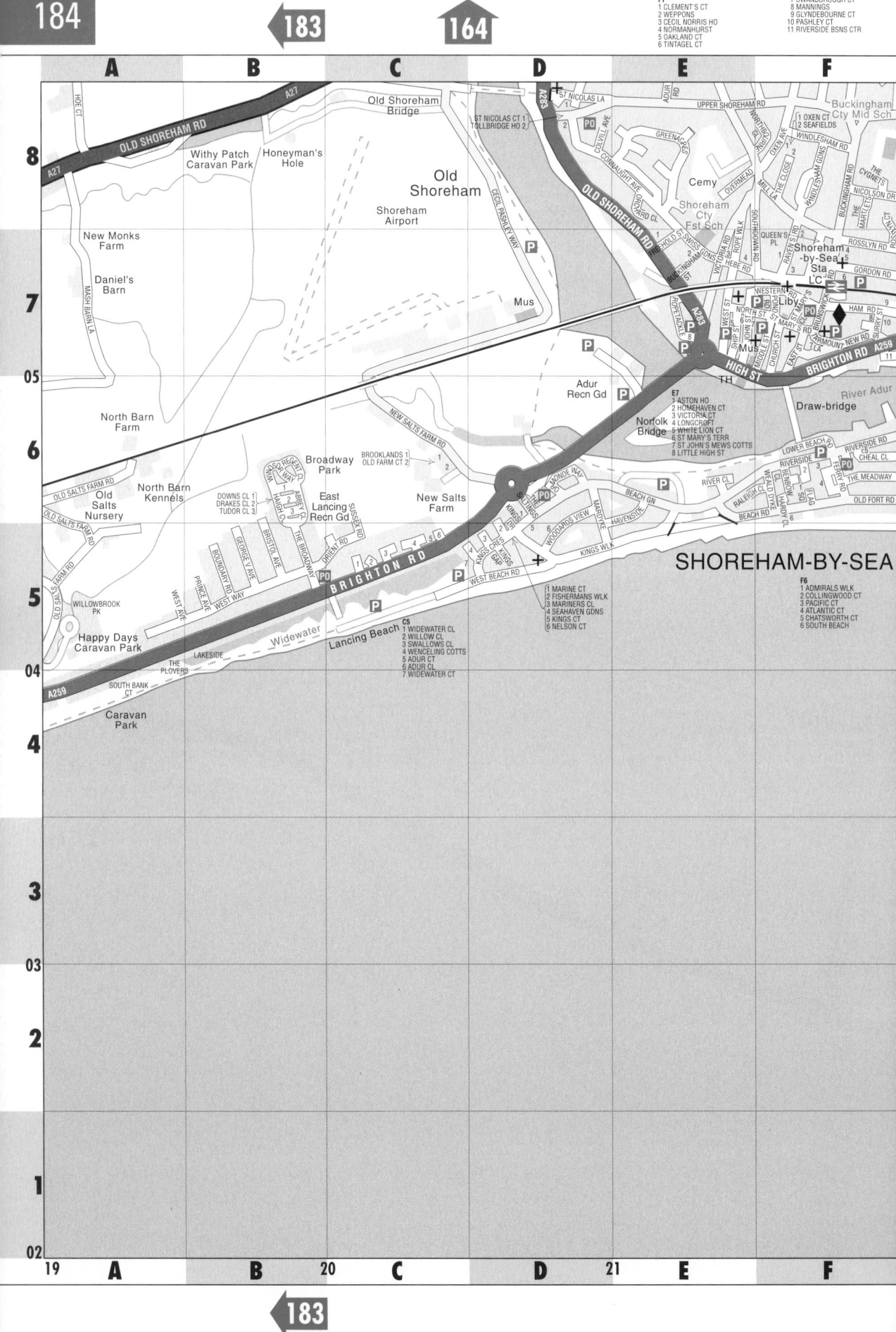

SHOREHAM-BY-SEA

C5
1 WIDEWATER CL
2 WILLOW CL
3 SWALLOWS CL
4 WENCELING COTTS
5 ADUR CT
6 ADUR CL
7 WIDEWATER CT

1 MARINE CT
2 FISHERMANS WLK
3 MARINERS CL
4 SEAHAVEN GDNS
5 KINGS CT
6 NELSON CT

E7
1 ASTON HO
2 HOMEHAVEN CT
3 VICTORIA CT
4 LONGCROFT
5 WHITE LION CT
6 ST MARY'S TERR
7 ST JOHN S MEWS COTTS
8 LITTLE HIGH ST

F6
1 ADMIRALS WLK
2 COLLINGWOOD CT
3 PACIFIC CT
4 ATLANTIC CT
5 CHATSWORTH CT
6 SOUTH BEACH

C8
1 LONEY CT
2 FRASER CT
3 MILWARD CT
4 PENSTONE CT
5 JULIAN CT
6 WILMOT CT

7 OSBORNE CT
8 HOLMBUSH CT
9 DOWNES CT
10 ADUR CT
11 BROADWAY CT
12 WISTON CT
13 ARUN CT

C8
14 ARUNDEL CT
15 RECTORY CT
16 CAIUS CT
17 KINGSTON CT

E7
1 SCHOOL CL
2 TWITTEN CL
3 GREEN CT
4 GREEN CL
5 WATLING CL
6 SPRING GDNS

7 STATION RD
8 WATLING CT
9 GRANGE CT
10 LOCKS CT
11 COATES CT
12 ROCK CL
13 CHANNEL VIEW

14 SEA HO

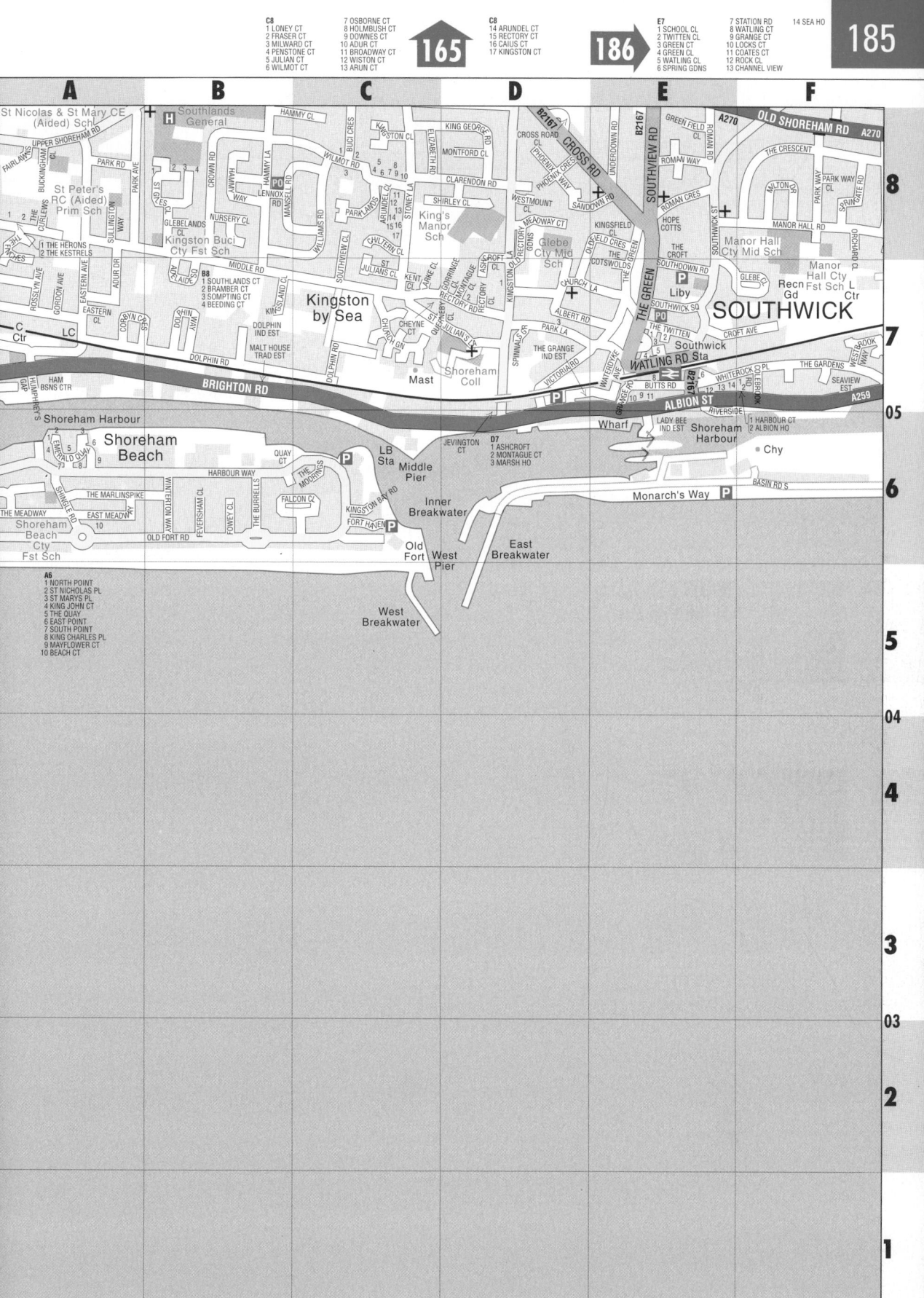

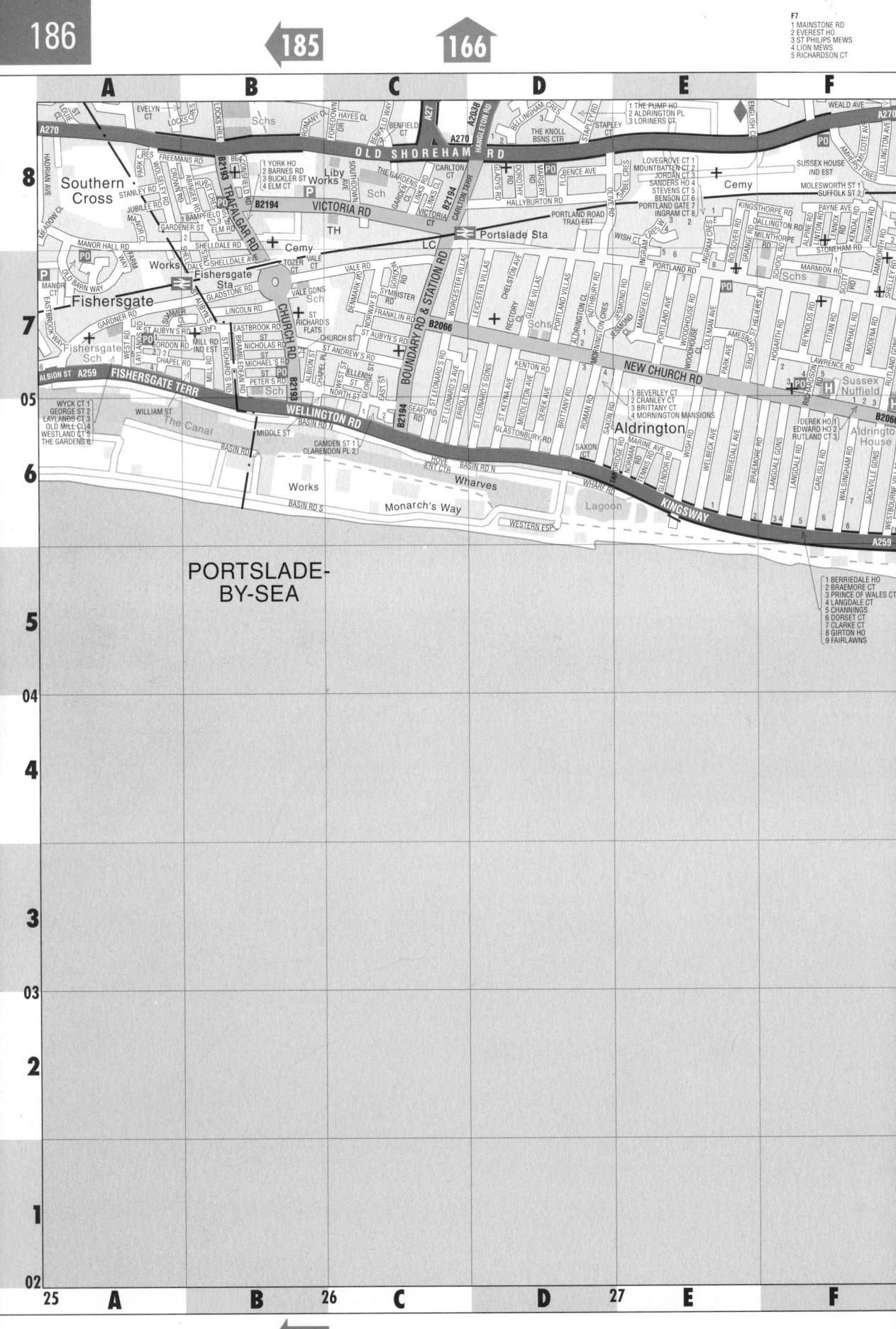

185

166

F7
1 MAINSTONE RD
2 EVEREST HO
3 ST PHILIPS MEWS
4 LION MEWS
5 RICHARDSON CT

185

B7
1 CONWAY CT
2 CLARENDON HO
3 ELLEN HO
4 GOLDSTONE HO
5 LIVINGSTONE HO
6 CLIFTONVILLE CT
7 STEYNING CT
8 BRAMBER CT
9 EATON CT
10 GRANVILLE CT
11 HADDINGTON ST
12 MALVERN ST
13 MONMOUTH ST
C7
1 DEVONSHIRE CT
2 CORNWALL CT
3 SOMERSET CT
4 JANESTON CT
5 STIRLING CT
6 BRECON CT
7 ELIZABETH CT
8 PHILIP CT
9 BALTIMORE CT
10 DRIVE LODGE
11 EATON MANOR
12 VERIC
13 VALVERDE HO
14 VALENTINE CT
15 HEREFORD CT
16 GAINSBOROUGH HO
17 EATON GATE
18 CHARIS CT
19 EATON HALL
20 EATON GARDENS MANSIONS
167
C7
21 VANBRUGH CT
D7
1 COWDRAY CT
2 GOODWOOD CT
3 CROMWELL CT
4 WILLOW CT
188
D7
5 KINSALE CT
6 PALMEIRA HO
7 BELL MEAD
8 AMBER CT
9 CONISTON CT
10 SOMERHILL CT
11 BERESFORD CT
12 ST ANN'S CT
A
B
C
D
E
F
OLD SHOREHAM RD
CROMWELL RD
DAVIGDOR RD
CHURCH RD
NEW CHURCH RD
WESTERN RD
KINGSWAY
KING'S RD
SACKVILLE RD
HOVE ST
THE DRIVE
GRAND AVE
DYKE RD
MONTPELIER RD
PRESTON RD
QUEEN'S RD
Aldrington Sta
Hove Sta
Sussex Cty Cricket Gd
Recn Gd
Newman Sch
Playing Field
King Alfred (Swimming Pool & Sports Ctr)
1 BATH CT
2 BENHAM CT
3 SPA CT
1 KINGS MEWS
2 WINDSOR LODGE
3 DURHAM CT
4 WARNHAM CT
5 ASHLEY CT
6 OLIVER HO
7 HAMILTON MANSIONS
8 THE PRIORY
Monarch's Way
1 LANSDOWNE SQ
2 BRUNSWICK MEWS
3 DONKEY MEWS
4 UPPER MARKET ST
5 LOWER MARKET ST
6 KERRISON MEWS
7 CHAPEL MEWS
8 EMBASSY CT
HOVE
BRIGHTON
The Brighton Ctr
West Pier (dis)
207
8
7
05
6
5
04
4
3
03
2
1
02
For full street detail of the highlighted area see page 207.
28
29
30
A6
1 BLENHEIM CT
2 PEMBROKE CT
3 WENDOVER GRANGE
4 AYMER HO
5 DOLPHIN CT
6 PRINCES CT
7 HOVE MANOR
8 FAIRLAWNS
9 VICEROY LODGE
10 BLUEBIRD CT
11 LANCASTER CT
C6
1 MARLBOROUGH CT
2 COPTHORNE CT
3 NORMANDY HO
4 BOWEN CT
5 GROVE CT
6 THE AMBASSADORS
7 WILBURY GRANGE
8 HAREWODD CT
9 VICTORIA GR
10 ST JOHN'S PL
11 WILBURY LODGE
12 ASHDOWN
13 SUSSEX CT
14 THE ATHENAEUM
15 SANDRINGHAM LODGE
16 HATFIELD CT
17 AMBER CT
18 PALMEIRA MANSIONS
19 AVENUE CT
20 PALMEIRA CT
21 VICTORIA CT
22 COOMBE LEA
23 GRAND AVENUE MANSIONS
24 ALBERT MEWS
D6
1 ABERGAVENNY HO
2 ROCHESTER CL
3 ROCHESTER CT
4 GWYDYR MANSIONS
5 KITILEAR CT
6 SOMERHILL LODGE
7 ST ANNES WELL HO
8 FARM MEWS
9 LANSDOWNE MEWS
E5
1 LITTLE WESTERN ST
2 NORFOLK BLDGS
3 NORFOLK MEWS
4 NORFOLK ST
5 WESTERN TERR
6 SILLWOOD HALL
7 SILLWOOD CT
8 OSPREY HO
9 SILLWOOD PL
10 FRED EMERY CT
11 KINGSLEY CT
12 CAVENDISH HO
13 BEDFORD TOWERS
14 HAMPTON ST
15 MITRE HO
16 REGENCY MEWS
188
17 RUSSELL MEWS
18 SUSSEX HEIGHTS
19 METROPOLE CT
20 ABBOTTS
21 ASTRA HO
E6
1 THE VINERIES
2 WORCESTER CT
3 KENYA CT
4 VERNON CT
5 BRAEMAR HO
6 MONTPELIER PL
7 MONTPELIER LODGE
8 HEATHER CT
9 MONTPELIER TERR
10 VICTORIA PL
E7
1 WESTCOMBE
2 BERKELEY CT
3 DERBY CT
4 WARWICK CT
5 RICHMOND CT
6 MARSTON CT
7 LORRAINE CT
8 CHESTER CT
9 YORK CT
10 WINDLESHAM CT
11 PAVILION CT
12 WESTMORLAND CT

B8
1 ST SAVIOURS CT
2 ROUND HILL RD
3 ROUND HILL ST
4 DITCHLING CT
5 MAYO CT
6 CENTENARY IND EST
7 ASHDOWN RD

C5
1 LAKE VIEW
2 HILARY LODGE
3 THE GRAPERIES
4 SLOANE CT
5 PATCHING LODGE

187

C5
6 JACQUELINE DU PRE CT
7 EVELYN GLENNIE CT
8 COURTNEY KING CT

C6
1 FINSBURY LODGE
2 HIGHDEN

168

C6
3 WESTMOUNT
4 CROWN HILL
5 SYDNEY TIDY HO
6 ATTREE CT
7 CORN CT
8 BARN FIELD GDNS
9 WINDERMERE CT

C8
1 FREEHOLD TERR
2 LEWIS CT
3 PEVENSEY RD
4 FAIRLIGHT PL
5 ST LEONARD'S RD
6 OLD VIADUCT CT
7 SHANKLIN CT
8 NEWMARKET TERR

F5
1 SANDERSTEAD
2 KINGSFOLD
3 BYLANDS
4 GRINSTEAD MOUNT
5 LANCING CT
6 HURSTWOOD
7 COTSWOLD PL
8 WELLSBOURNE
9 SOUTH LODGE
10 LICHFIELD CT
11 FRAMFIELD
12 RYECROFT
13 WALTER MAY HO

A B C D E F

C7
1 AINSWORTH HO
2 BARCLAY HO
3 NAPIER HO
4 JOHNSON BANK
5 UPPER WELLINGTON RD
6 ST MARTIN'S FLATS
7 CORONATION ST
8 NORMANTON ST

HAYBOURNE CL 1
NINFIELD PL 2
HORSHAM CL 3
WISTON WAY 4
PULBOROUGH CL 5
SEVELANDS CL 6

7 SWANBOROUGH PL
8 TILLINGTON
9 BROCKHURST
10 LINCHMERE

Whitehawk Camp

EXCEAT CL 1
ASHINGTON CT 2
AMBERLEY LODGE 3
COLGATE CL 4
UCKFIELD CL 5
ALFRISTON CL 6
PENHURST PL 7
FAYGATE CT 8

LOWER CHALVINGTON PL 1
BURLOW CL 2
WARBLETON CL 3
LIONS CT 4

1 HENLEY CT
2 ROEDEAN CT

ARUNDEL TERR 1
DE COURCEL RD 2
COURCELS 3

1 PORTSIDE
2 THE OCTAGON
3 STARBOARD CT
4 MARINERS QUAY
5 TRAFALGAR GATE

London Road Sta
Round Hill
Cemy
Crem
Race Hill
Brighton Sta
Brighton General
Brighton Race Course
Stands
Queen's Park
Whitehawk
Royal Pavilion
Mus & Art Gall
Royal Sussex
Kemp Town
East Brighton Park
Stanley Deason L Ctr
Black Rock
Sea Life Ctr
Palace Pier
BRIGHTON
Volks Electric Rly
Brighton Marina Village
IRB Sta
Brighton Marina

207

31 A B 32 C D 33 E F

For full street detail of the highlighted area see page 207.

187

C4
1 SOMERSET POINT
2 WARWICK MOUNT
3 ESSEX PL
4 MONTAGUE ST
5 ST GEORGE'S TERR
6 MONTAGUE CT
7 MARINE TERRACE MEWS
8 ROYAL CRESCENT MEWS
9 ST ANNE'S CT
10 ROYAL CRESCENT MANSIONS
11 COLLEGE ST
12 TELEGRAPH ST
13 GARNET HO
14 DANNY SHELDON HO
15 CLARENDON PL
16 BLOOMSBURY ST
17 BLOOMSBURY PL
18 PORTLAND PL

D4
1 COURTNEY KING HO
2 CHAPEL TERR
3 SEYMOUR SQ
4 SEYMOUR ST
5 SEYMOUR HO
6 SUDELEY TERR
7 UPPER SUDELEY ST
8 MILLFIELD COTTS
9 EASTERN TERR MEWS
10 EASTERN TERR
11 BELGRAVE PL
12 SURREY HO
13 SWEDA CT
14 PERCIVAL TERR
15 CHICHESTER CL
16 CLARENDON TERR
17 ST MARY'S SQ
18 KEMP TOWN PL
19 CHICHESTER TERR

E4
1 PLAYDEN CL
2 PRINCE REGENT'S CT
3 BRISTOL MEWS
4 SUSSEX MEWS
5 RUGBY CT
6 ARUNDEL CT
7 BELL TOWER IND EST
8 HOLLINGBOURNE CT
9 LONGHURST

169
190

A B C D E F

8

7

01

Longmere
Point

6

Pilsey Sand

Pilsey Island

5

Chichester Harbour

00

4

Stocker's Lake

East
Head

3

99

Black
Point

HAYLING ISLAND

The
Spit

Lifeboat
Station

2

FISHERMAN'S WLK

EASTOKE AVE

WITTERING RD

SELSEY CL

EARNLEY RD

HASLEMERE GDNS

SIDLESHAM CL

TICHENOR RD

PAGHAM GDNS

BRACKLESHAM RD

SEAFARERS WLK

BIRDHAM RD

HAVEN RD

BOSMERE RD

NUTBOURNE RD

SANDY POINT RD

CORONATION RD

TRELOAR RD

WHEATLANDS CRES

P

South Hayling

1

HAVEN RD

WHEATLANDS AVE

PO

SOUTHWOOD RD

SANDY BEACH
EST

P

98

A B C D E F

8

7

01

6

00

5

00

4

99

3

2

99

1

98

Thorney Channel

Cobnor
Point

Chichester
Harbour

Chichester Channel

Ferry P

Chalkdock
Point

Ship
Inn

THE STREET

Itchenor
Park

P

West
Itchenor

Pilsey
Island

FARM
COTTS

Itchenor
House

ITCHENOR RD

Redlands

REDLANDS LA

Ella
Nore

Rookwood
House

ROOKWOOD LA

ROOKWO

Rookwood Lane
House

SHEEPWASH LA

Wicks Farm
Caravan Park

Lane End
House

Tara

B2179

Gate
Lodge

ELLANORE LA

Walnut Tree
House

MALTHOUSE
COTTS

CHAPEL LA

ACRE ST

Holmes
Farm

Nunnington Farm
Caravan Park

Speedscroft

Roman Landing

SUMMERFIELD RD

West Wittering
Parochial (Contr)
Prim Sch

P
O

ELMSTEAD
GDNS

ELMSTEAD PARK RD

MEADOW LA

ELMS LA

PIGGERY HALL LA

Snow
Hill

COASTGUARDS
COTTS

COASTGUARD LA

LOCKSASH CL

CUNLIFFE CL

POUND RD

PH

MIDDLEFIELD

ROYCE CL

ROYCE WAY

MIDWOOD
CL

ELMS RIDE

ELMS WAY

Home
Farm

BRIAR
AVE

FURZEFIELD

THE WAD

West
Wittering

THE BYEWAY

SEAWARD DR

WELLSFLD

CAKEHAM RD

B2179

171   192

A   **B**   **C**   **D**   **E**   **F**

Trew's Copse

Upper Wolve's Copse

Copperas Point

Ferry P

Fletcher's Copse

Bosham Hoe

8

CHANDLERS REACH

Lower Wolves Copse

Salterns Copse

ORCHARD RD

Longmore

TUFF'S HARD

Salterns Lock

Ship Yard

7

Chichester Canal

Longmore Point

ALFSTONE CL

SPINNEY LA

Birdham Pool

THE CAUSEWAY

01

LOCK LA

Westlands Copse

Westlands Pier

Westlands

6

Westlands Farm

COURT BARN LA

Oldhouse Farm

GREENACRES

WESTLANDS LA

Birdham

Birdham Fruit Farm

CHALKDOCK LA

Ham Lodge

Hammonds Farm

OAK MEADOW

Broomer Farm

GLEBE FIELD RD

ST JAMES'S

KEWELL'S CNR

MARTINS LA

A286

5

CLAYTONS CNR

SPRINGFIELD CL

Lippering Farm

PESCOTT'S CL

CHERRY LA

Birdham CE (Contr) Prim Sch

TICHENOR RD

CHURCH

Redmoor

00

THE SALTINGS

CROOKED LA

LONGMEADOW GDNS

MAIN RD

ALANDALE RD

FLORENCE CL

CHAFFER LA

Nurseries

Shipton Green

FARNE LA

Whitestone Farm

4

BURLOW CL

PO

SHIPTON GREEN LA

1 OLD SCHOOL CL
2 FARNE CL

Roman Way Country Club

Holt Place

B2179

A286

3

Lamb Inn (PH)

Nurseries

PINKS LA

B2198

Guy's Farm

Northleigh Farm

99

The Bell Inn

Cherry Cottage

HUNDREDSTEDDLE LA

BELL LA

FIRST AVE

2

Hundredsteddle Farm

Carthagena Farm

Batchmere's Farm

Hale Farm

Nurseries

BATCHMERE RD

Somerley

SOMERLEY LA

Thatched Cottage

BATCHMERE EST

TILE BARN EST

ALMODINGTON LA

Windmill (dis)

SECOND AVE

1

TILE BARN LA

BRACKLESHAM LA

Glen Nurseries

Mill House

STUBCROFT LA

B2198

BROOKERS LA

A   81   **C**   **D**   82   **E**   **F**

202   192

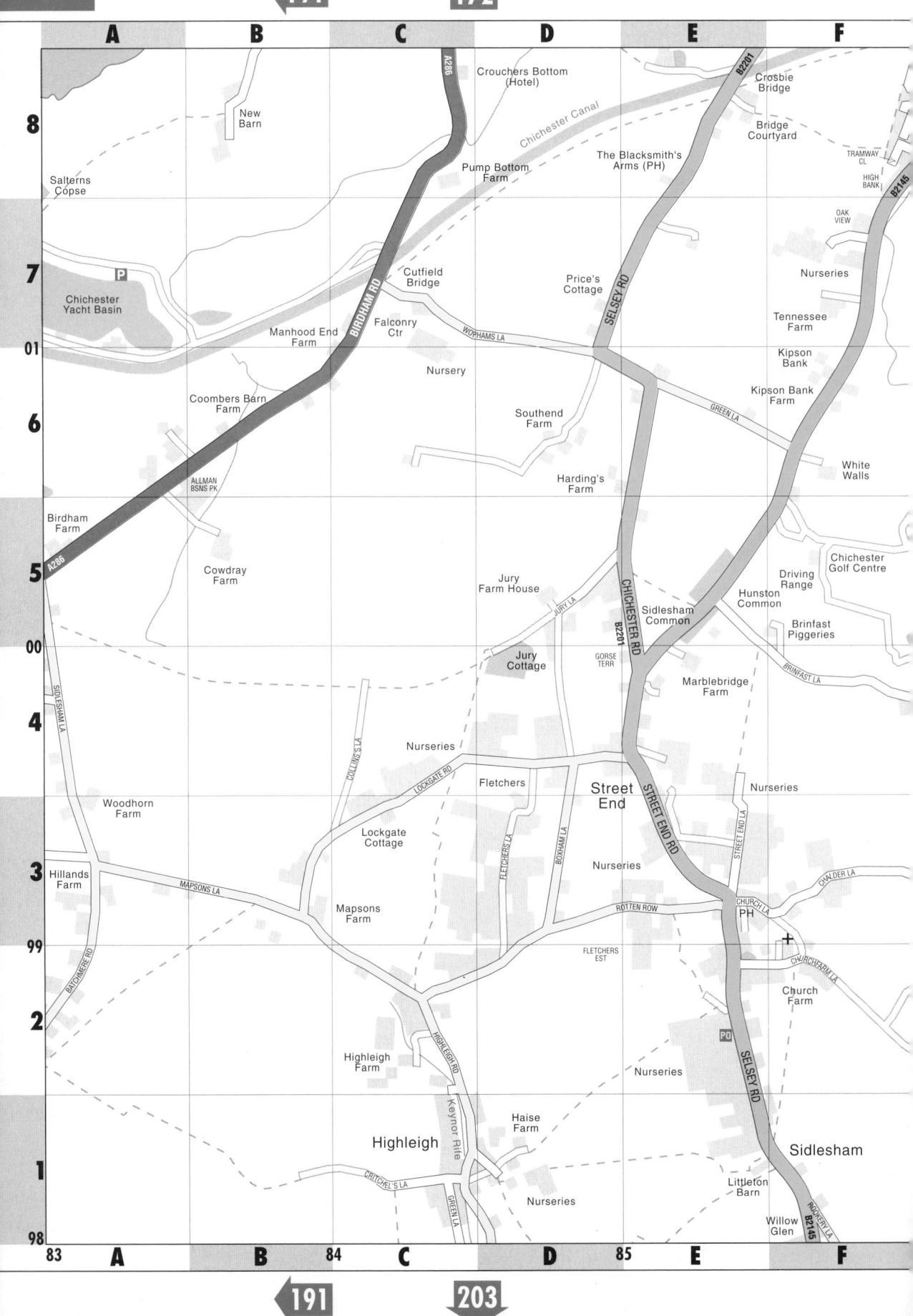

191
172

A B C D E F

8

Salterns
Copse

New
Barn

Crouchers Bottom
(Hotel)

Chichester Canal

The Blacksmith's
Arms (PH)

Crosbie
Bridge

Bridge
Courtyard

TRAMWAY
CL

HIGH
BANK

B2201

B2145

OAK
VIEW

7

Chichester
Yacht Basin

P

Cutfield
Bridge

Manhood End
Farm

Falconry
Ctr

WOPHAMS LA

Pump Bottom
Farm

Price's
Cottage

SELSEY RD

Nurseries

Tennessee
Farm

BIRDHAM RD

A286

01

Coombers Barn
Farm

Nursery

Kipson
Bank

Kipson Bank
Farm

GREEN LA

6

Southend
Farm

Harding's
Farm

White
Walls

ALLMAN
BSNS PK

5

Birdham
Farm

A286

Cowdray
Farm

Jury
Farm House

JURY LA

CHICHESTER RD

B2201

Sidlesham
Common

Driving
Range

Chichester
Golf Centre

Hunston
Common

Brinfast
Piggeries

00

Jury
Cottage

GORSE
TERR

Marblebridge
Farm

BRINFAST LA

4

SIDLESHAM LA

COLLINS S LA

Nurseries

LOCKGATE RD

Fletchers

Street
End

STREET END LA

Nurseries

Woodhorn
Farm

Lockgate
Cottage

FLETCHERS LA

BOXHAM LA

STREET END RD

Nurseries

3

Hillands
Farm

MAPSONS LA

Mapsons
Farm

ROTTEN ROW

CHALDER LA

CHURCH LA

PH

99

BATCHMERE RD

FLETCHERS
EST

CHURCHFARM LA

Church
Farm

2

HIGHLEIGH RD

Highleigh
Farm

Haise
Farm

Nurseries

PO

SELSEY RD

1

KEYNOR RIFE

Highleigh

GREEN LA

Nurseries

Sidlesham

Littleton
Barn

B2145

ROOKERY LA

98

Willow
Glen

CRITCHEL S LA

83 A 84 B C 84 D 85 E F

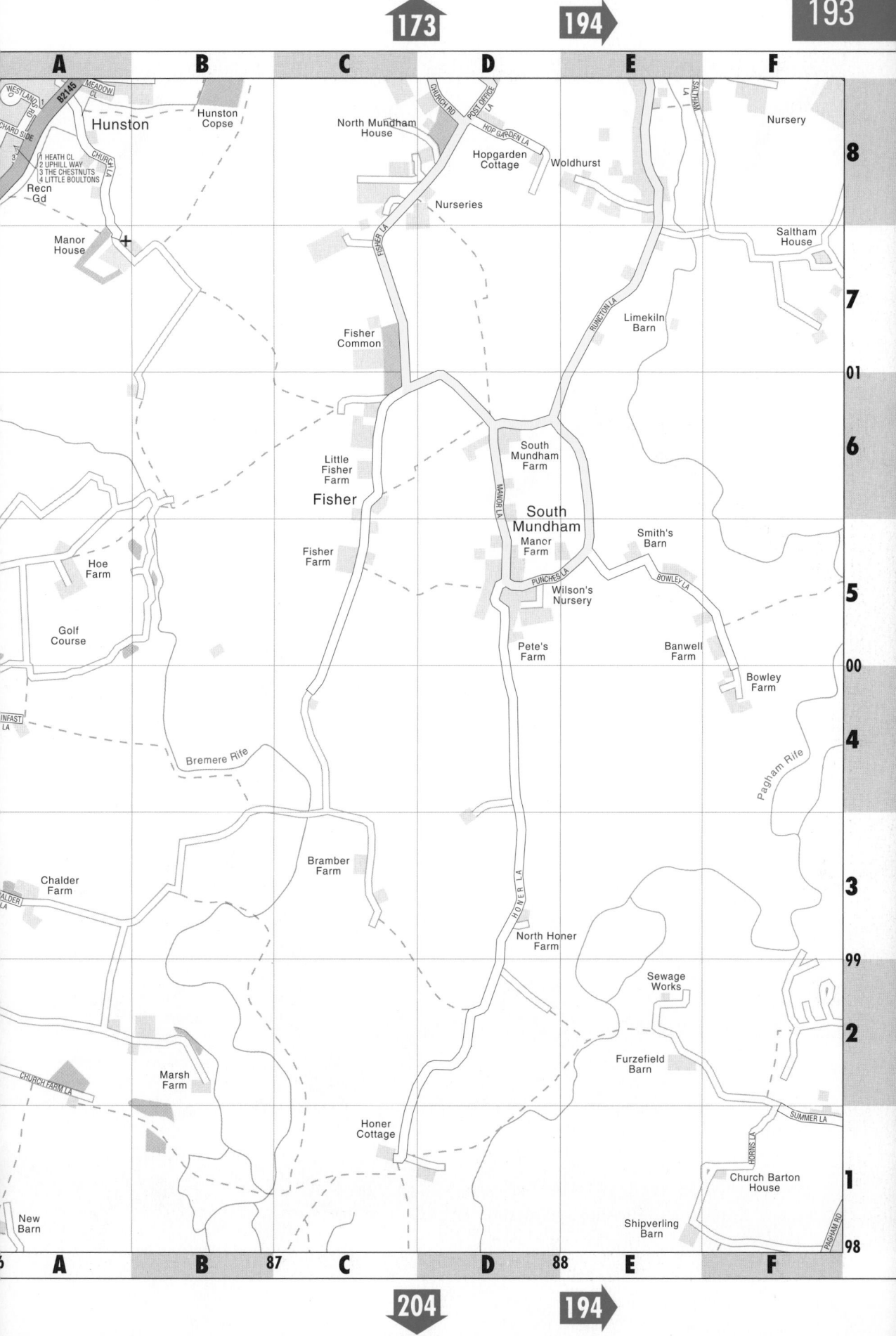

A B C D E F

WESTLANDS MEADOW CL B2145
ORCHARD SIDE
Hunston Hunston Copse North Mundham House CHURCH RD POST OFFICE LA HOP GARDEN LA Nursery
1 HEATH CL Hopgarden Cottage Woldhurst SALTHAM LA
2 UPHILL WAY CHURCH LA Nurseries Saltham House
3 THE CHESTNUTS
4 LITTLE BOULTONS
Recn Gd
8

Manor House FISHER LA RUNCTON LA Limekiln Barn
7
01

Fisher Common
6

Little Fisher Farm South Mundham Farm
Fisher MANOR LA Smith's Barn
Hoe Farm Fisher Farm South Mundham BOWLEY LA
Manor Farm 5
Golf Course PUNCHES LA Wilson's Nursery Banwell Farm 00
Pete's Farm Bowley Farm 4

INFAST LA Bremere Rife Pagham Rife

Chalder Farm Bramber Farm 3
ALDER LA HONER LA 99
North Honer Farm 2
Sewage Works
CHURCH FARM LA Marsh Farm Furzefield Barn SUMMER LA
Honer Cottage HORRIS LA Church Barton House 1
New Barn Shipverling Barn PAGHAM RD 98

A 87 B C D 88 E F

193 174

A B C D E F

8
7
01
6
5
00
4
3
99
2
1
98

B2166

Manor Nursery

New Barn

PAGHAM RD

Newlands Nursery

Butterlees Farm

Park Farm

A259

CHICHESTER RD

Babsham Farm

BARSHAM LA

LOATS LA
GREYSTOKE AVE
BRADWICK AVE
BRASMAS WAY
NEWBARN LA
HIGHFI...
WINSTON CRES

Orchard Caravan Park

Newbarn La

GLENELG CT

Crimsham Manor Farm

Royal Oak Inn (PH)

Lagness

Trafalgar Cottage

Park Farmhouse

Chalcroft Nurseries
CENTRAL...
Cemy
DAVIDS CL
CHALCRAFT LA
THE HOLLIES

Pennicott's Farm

LOWER BOGNOR RD

Neale's Farm

Morells Farm

Pagham Rife

Copyhold Farm

MALDOUGH...
DOWNING
LIDL CL
CHURCHILL AVE
WINDSOR
REGENTS WAY
SELWYN
HUGHES
CAMBRIDGE
ST JOHN'S
AMBERLE...

Bogno Regis Com Coll
BROOK
RUNNYMEDE CT
HAMPTON CT

Sefter Farm

SEFTER RD

ETON CL
ST PETER'S CL
BLENHEIM CT
FIELDS WAY
CAMBRIDGE WLK THE PRESIDENT
KEBLE
QUEENS
SELSEY
FITZWILLIAM
PETERHOUSE
LAVIN...
PO
HASTIN...

Sefter Bottom

PAGHAM RD

PINEHURST PK
RUSBRIDGE
COPTHORNE WAY
LINCOLN AVE
ELIZABETH
ELIZABETH TERR

PINE WLK
STEWART'S LA
COVENTRY WAY
WELLS WAY
WAKEFIELDS WAY
PEMBROKE WAY
SOUTHWARK
NUFFIELD CL
KINGSTON
OXFORD DR
EXETER CL
QUEENS
PUTNEY
WESTMINSTER DR
RIPON
TRINITY WAY
GREYFRIARS...
NEWHAYES...

CHRISTCHURCH CRES

ALDWICK RD B2166

HOOK LA
ROSE GREEN RD
ROSSALYN
LODSWORTH
MANTS FARM CT
CRES
MAYTEL
MEADOW
RODNEY CL
ROSE GREEN RD
GROSVENOR GDNS
AVISFORD TERR
PO
HAZEL GR
ROBINS DR
ST RICHARD'S DR
PARKFIELD AVE
BIRCH CL
CEDAR
SEFTON AVE
ST RICHARD'S WAY
ROCHESTER WAY
SINNEY GDNS
MARGARET...
MALMAYNE CT
STANBROK
SALISBURY CL
LICHFIELD GDNS
THE HOPGARTON
ALDWICK GDNS
SOUTH AVE
WEST AVE
THRUSLOES
BN

Rose Green Cty Jun Sch

HOOK LA
RALEIGH RD
GREYVILLE
CARLTON AVE
Rose Green
P
ST ANTHONY'S WLK
STAPLETON CL
BLONDEL DR
GOSSAMER LA
GOODMAN
CEDAR CL
GOODWOOD...
OLD PL
ALDWICK FIELD LA
LITTLE BABSHAM
LECROFT
WEST WOOD
ALDWICK
BLACKSMITHS...
GILWYN...
CURLESCROFT
GI...

BRIDORLEY CL
FLETCHER CL
FROBISHER RD
HAWKINS
Rose Green Cty Inf Sch
Liby P
VALENTS
WALLSEND
GUNWIN
WILLOWHALE AVE
WILMAN
Aldwick
THE POUND
WYDE...
OLD PL
BARRACK LA
CURLESCROFT
CHAWKMARE COPPICE
MAUJ...
...

DOWNLANDS
MILL PARK RD
ROSS CL
LENNOX RD
ESHER
NYETIMBER CL
BUCKNOR CL
COTTAGE CL
ELDRIDGE CRES
BELL
WILLOWHALE GN
BOXGROVE GDNS
LANGMERE GDNS
FERNHURST GDNS
HAMILTON GDNS
ALBOROUGH WAY
STIRLING
EDINBURGH
ALDWICK ST
CORAL
REDWOOD CT
PO 4
ALDWICK PL
WOODSTOCK GDNS
ALDWICK AVE
HORNBEAM CL
SHORECROFT

Caravan Site

PAGHAM WAY
SPRINGFIELD
PRIORS WAY
WARWICK
LEDBURY CT
GLOSTER DR
THE CRES
NYETIMBERS
FERN CT
MALVERN WAY
GREENLEA AVE
MICKLAM CL
RUISLIP GDNS
STONEY STILE LA
PRYORS GN
CYPRESS GDNS
BARRACK LA
SEAGOURT
ALDWICK BAY...
CHEVELEY GDNS
WYCHWOOD
LARCH...
CRAIGWELL LA
GRANGE
FISH LA
...

SYLVIA CL
SUMMER LA
PO
OAKLAND CT
CANTERBURY CL
Nyetimber
WINDMILL LA
A BECKET'S LA
NYETIMBER
PILGRIMS WAY
TARGET GATE
GARRY
WOLSEY
INGLEWOOD CL
LANGLEY GR
HAYDON
HESTON GR
COLT'S BAY
KINGSWAY
WATERS EDGE
CRAIGWELL...
THE DRIVE

FLEMING WAY
HARBOUR VIEW RD
CHURCH LANE
ELM LA
SUSSEX DR
BARTON CL
MANOR PK
MILLARS CL
APPLE GR
WILLOW
WEST DR
SINGLETON
BOWLING GREEN LA
THE CLEVETS
THE ORCHARD
HUNTERS
MANOR WAY
THE CLOSE
THE FAIRWAY
BECK...
CARON'S CL
CRAIGWELL MANOR
QUEENSWAY
CLOCK HO
PO

THE COURT
PRINCES CROFT
THE ABBOTS
CARDINAL'S DR
GREENWAYS
KINGS DR
MEADOW WAY
TITHE BARN CL
REGIS AVE
LITTLE BARN CL

1 GILWYNES CT
2 THE COURTYARD
3 WALLFIELD
4 RAVENWOOD CT
5 ALDWICK GRANGE

1 COASTGUARD PAR
2 FISHERMAN'S WLK

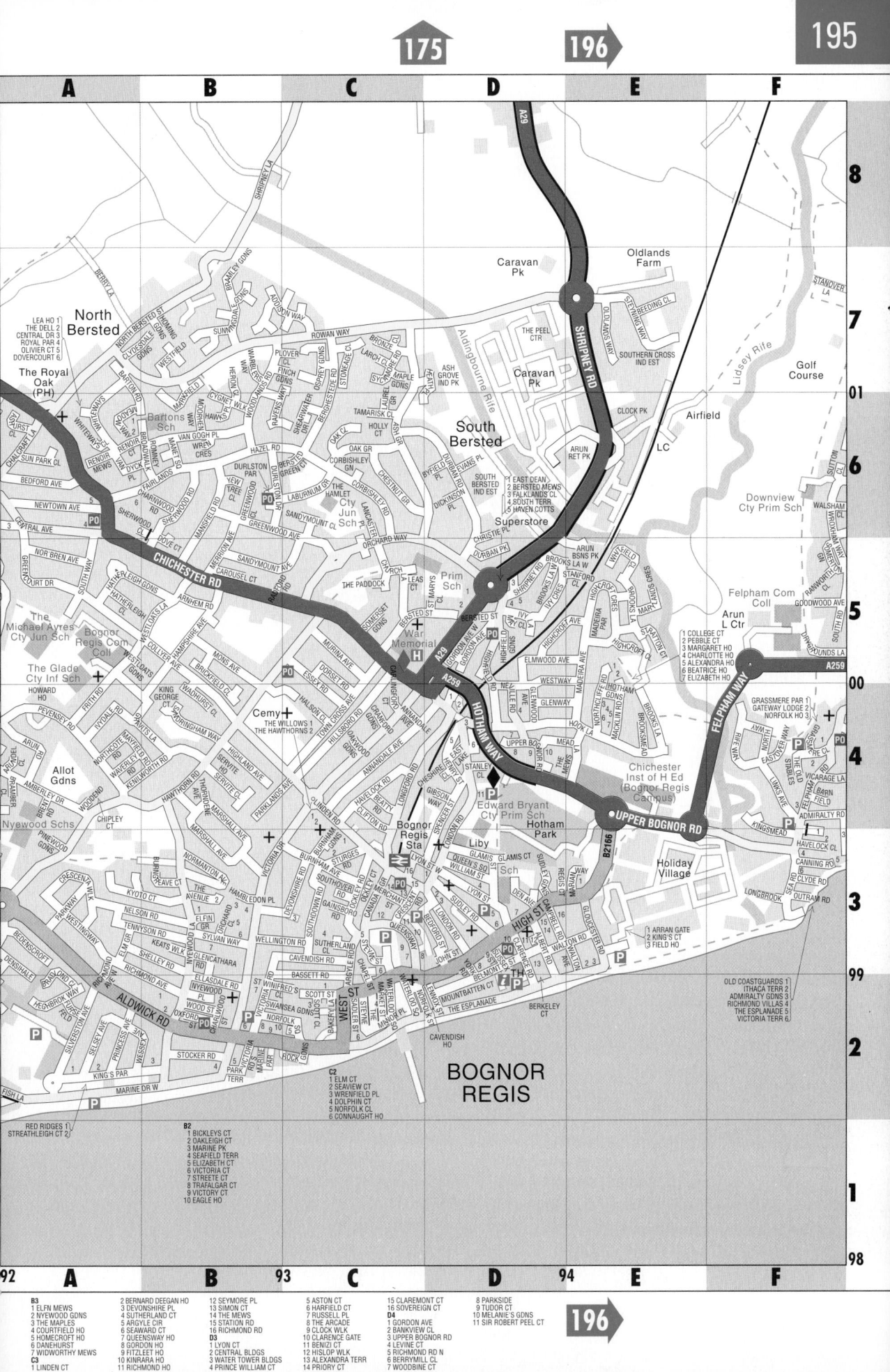

175
196
A
B
C
D
E
F
8
7
01
6
5
00
4
3
99
2
1
98
92
93
94
North Bersted
LEA HO 1
THE DELL 2
CENTRAL DR 3
ROYAL PAR 4
OLIVIER CT 5
DOVERCOURT 6
The Royal Oak (PH)
Bartons Sch
South Bersted
Caravan Pk
Oldlands Farm
THE PEEL CTR
Caravan Pk
SOUTHERN CROSS IND EST
ASH GROVE IND PK
Aldingbourne Rife
Lidsey Rife
Golf Course
Airfield
CLOCK PK
ARUN RET PK
LC
SHRIPNEY RD
SHRIPNEY LA
BERRY LA
A29
ROWAN WAY
STANOVER LA
1 EAST DEAN
2 BERSTED MEWS
3 FALKLANDS CL
4 SOUTH TERR
5 HAVEN COTTS
SOUTH BERSTED IND EST
Superstore
Downview Cty Prim Sch
City Jun Sch
THE HAMLET
ARUN BSNS PK
CHICHESTER RD
Prim Sch
THE PADDOCK
Felpham Com Coll
Arun L Ctr
1 COLLEGE CT
2 PEBBLE CT
3 MARGARET HO
4 CHARLOTTE HO
5 ALEXANDRA HO
6 BEATRICE HO
7 ELIZABETH HO
A259
FELPHAM WAY
The Michael Ayres Cty Jun Sch
Bognor Regis Com Coll
The Glade Cty Inf Sch
HOWARD HO
KING GEORGE CT
War Memorial
Cemy
THE WILLOWS 1
THE HAWTHORNS 2
HOTHAM WAY
GRASSMERE PAR 1
GATEWAY LODGE 2
NORFOLK HO 3
Allot Gdns
Nyewood Schs
CHIPLEY CT
Chichester Inst of H Ed (Bognor Regis Campus)
Edward Bryant Cty Prim Sch
Hotham Park
UPPER BOGNOR RD
Bognor Regis Sta
Liby
Sch
Holiday Village
B2166
HIGH ST
1 ARRAN GATE
2 KING'S CT
3 FIELD HO
OLD COASTGUARDS 1
ITHACA TERR 2
ADMIRALTY GDNS 3
RICHMOND VILLAS 4
THE ESPLANADE 5
VICTORIA TERR 6
ALDWICK RD
WEST ST
THE ESPLANADE
BERKELEY CT
CAVENDISH HO
TH
BOGNOR REGIS
MARINE DR W
RED RIDGES 1
STREATHLEIGH CT 2
C2
1 ELM CT
2 SEAVIEW CT
3 WRENFIELD PL
4 DOLPHIN CT
5 NORFOLK CL
6 CONNAUGHT HO
B2
1 BICKLEYS CT
2 OAKLEIGH CT
3 MARINE PK
4 SEAFIELD TERR
5 ELIZABETH CT
6 VICTORIA CT
7 STREETE CT
8 TRAFALGAR CT
9 VICTORY CT
10 EAGLE HO
B3
1 ELFN MEWS
2 NYEWOOD GDNS
3 THE MAPLES
4 COURTFIELD HO
5 HOMECROFT HO
6 DANEHURST
7 WIDWORTHY MEWS
C3
1 LINDEN CT
2 BERNARD DEEGAN HO
3 DEVONSHIRE PL
4 SUTHERLAND CT
5 ARGYLE CIR
6 SEAWARD CT
7 QUEENSWAY HO
8 GORDON HO
9 FITZLEET HO
10 KINRARA HO
11 RICHMOND HO
12 SEYMORE PL
13 SIMON CT
14 THE MEWS
15 STATION RD
16 RICHMOND RD
D3
1 LYON CT
2 CENTRAL BLDGS
3 WATER TOWER BLDGS
4 PRINCE WILLIAM CT
5 ASTON CT
6 HARFIELD CT
7 RUSSELL PL
8 THE ARCADE
9 CLOCK WLK
10 CLARENCE GATE
11 BENIZI CT
12 HISLOP WLK
13 ALEXANDRA TERR
14 PRIORY CT
15 CLAREMONT CT
16 SOVEREIGN CT
D4
1 GORDON AVE
2 BANKVIEW CL
3 UPPER BOGNOR RD
4 LEVINE CT
5 RICHMOND RD N
6 BERRYMILL CL
7 WOODBINE CT
8 PARKSIDE
9 TUDOR CT
10 MELANIE'S GDNS
11 SIR ROBERT PEEL CT
196

195
176

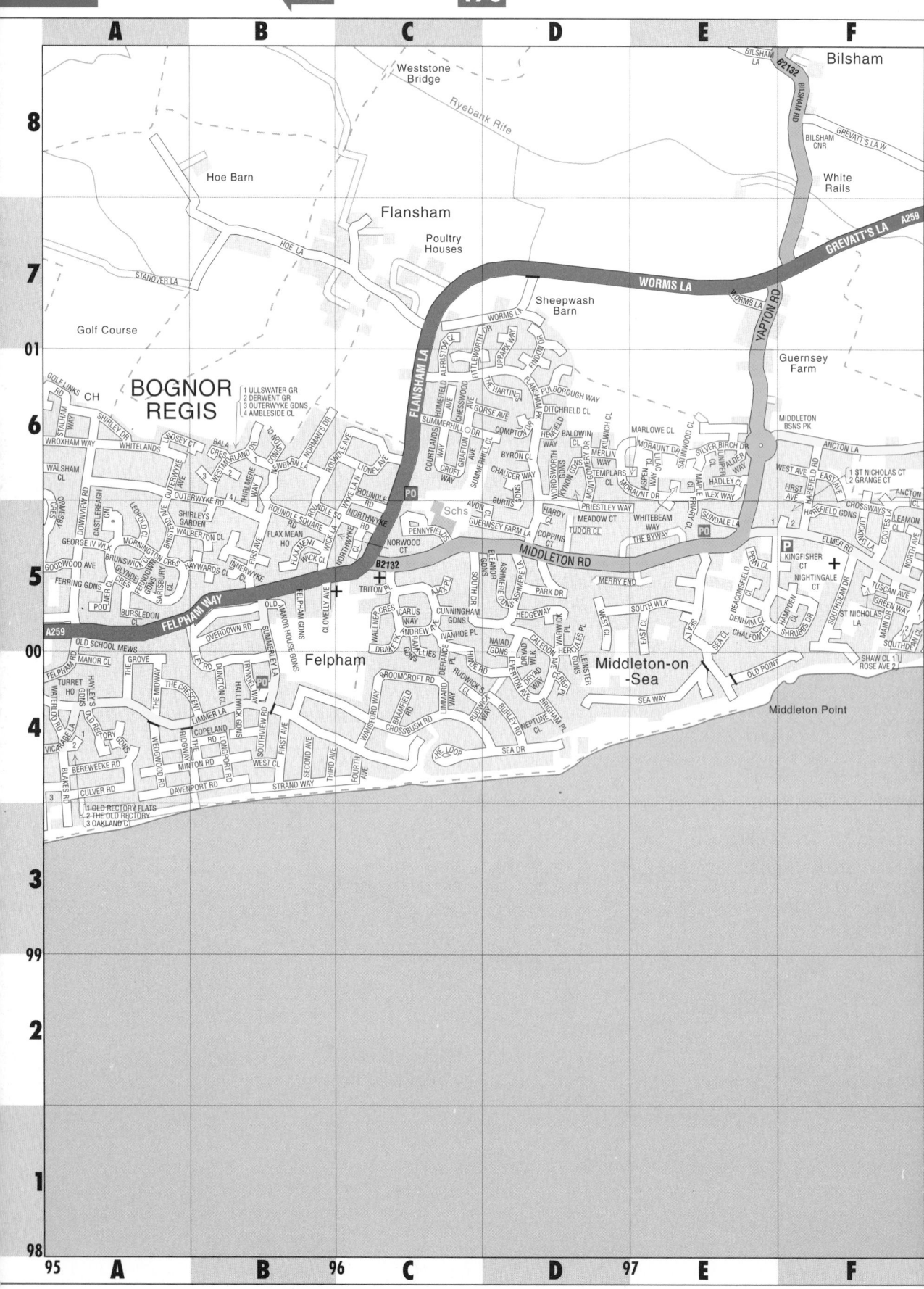
Bilsham
Weststone Bridge
Ryebank Rife
Hoe Barn
Flansham
Poultry Houses
White Rails
Golf Course
Sheepwash Barn
Guernsey Farm
BOGNOR REGIS
Felpham
Middleton-on -Sea
Middleton Point
WORMS LA
GREVATT'S LA
FLANSHAM LA
YAPTON RD
MIDDLETON RD
FELPHAM WAY
BILSHAM RD
HOE LA
STANOVER LA
1 ULLSWATER GR
2 DERWENT GR
3 OUTERWYKE GDNS
4 AMBLESIDE CL
1 OLD RECTORY FLATS
2 THE OLD RECTORY
3 OAKLAND CT
1 ST NICHOLAS CT
2 GRANGE CT
MIDDLETON BSNS PK

195

A259

CROOKTHORN LA

B2233

YAPTON RD

GREVATT'S LA

GREVATT'S LA W

St Mary's CE
(Aided)
Prim Sch

CROOKTHORN LA

Hobb's Farm

Kent's
Farm

LANGMEAD CL

Sewage
Works

Ryebank Rife

Grevatt's
Bridge

Hobbs' New
Barn

Ryebank
House

Climping
Camp Site

The Black Horse
(PH)

CLIMPING ST

New
Barn

Atherington

BREADLA

Ancton

ANCTON LA

KINGSMEAD GDNS

Elmer

Bailiffscourt
Hotel

P

Cudlow
Barn

KINGSMEAD RD

SUNNYMEAD

ANCTON WAY

NORTH AVE E

ANCTON DR

ANCTON LODGE LA

LODGE CL

MEADOW WLK

FARM CNR

LANE END

THE CLOSE

LAYNE

ARUNDEL WAY

FARM CL

NORFOLK WAY

ELM DR

STABLE
FIELD

ALLEYNE WAY

ELMER CL

SEA WAY

THE HARD

ELMER CT

Poole
Place

NORTH AVE S

WEST DR

ELMER RD

CENTRAL DR

EAST DR

DEEPDENE CL

TEMPLESHEEN RD

VILLA PLAGE

MANOR WAY

PO

THE JETTY

1 SUSSEX CT
2 SUSSEX VILLAGE
3 MANOR CT

197
178

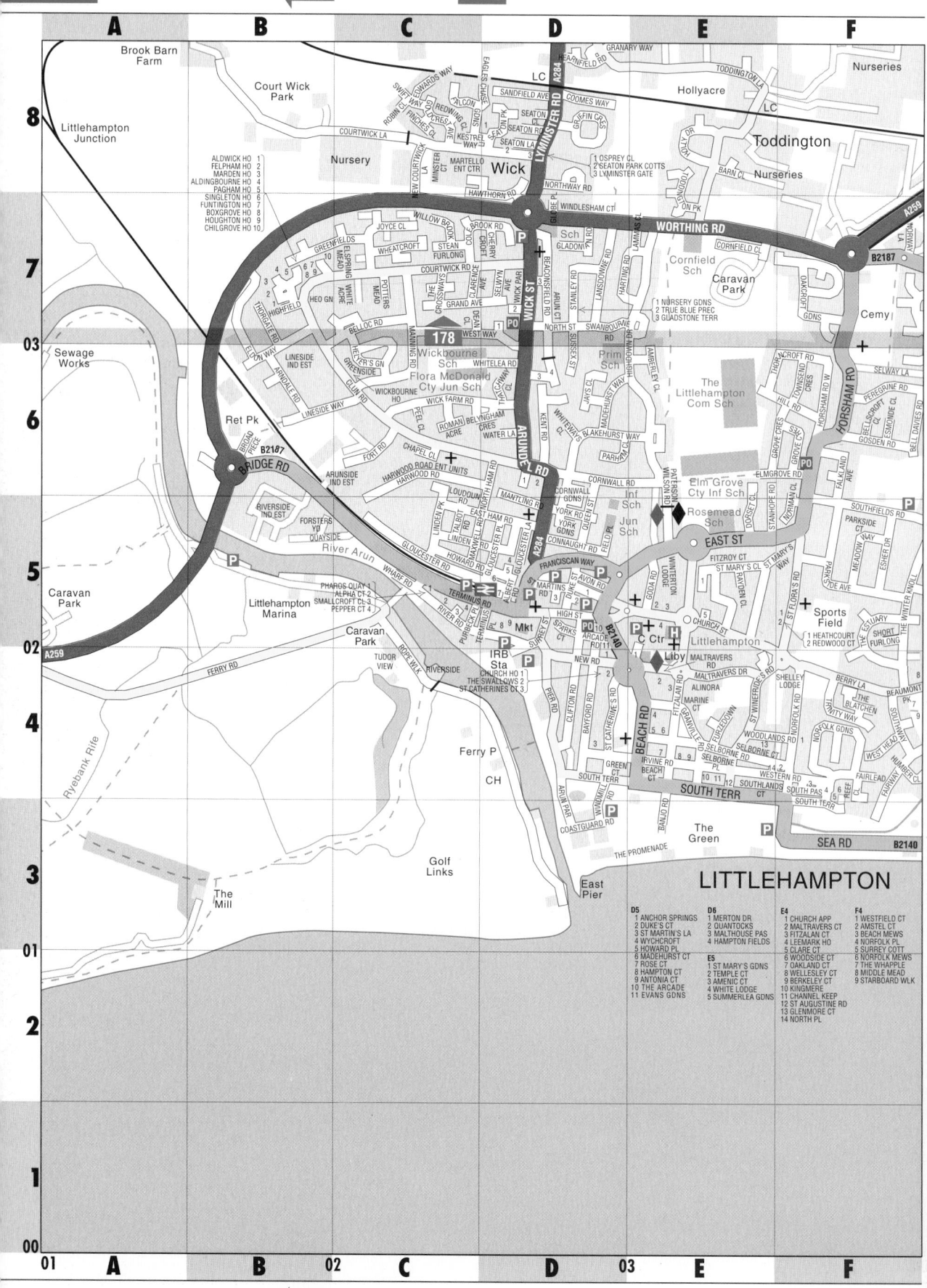
A
B
C
D
E
F
8
7
03
6
5
02
4
3
01
2
1
00
01
02
03
Brook Barn Farm
Court Wick Park
Littlehampton Junction
Nursery
Wick
Hollyacre
Toddington
Nurseries
LC
GRANARY WAY
TODDINGTON LA
SANDFIELD AVE
COOMES WAY
COURTWICK LA
LYMINSTER RD
A284
ALDWICK HO 1
FELPHAM HO 2
MARDEN HO 3
ALDINGBOURNE HO 4
PAGHAM HO 5
SINGLETON HO 6
FUNTINGTON HO 7
BOXGROVE HO 8
HOUGHTON HO 9
CHILGROVE HO 10
1 OSPREY CL
2 SEATON PARK COTTS
3 LYMINSTER GATE
NORTHWAY RD
HAWTHORN RD
WINDLESHAM CT
WORTHING RD
A259
B2187
CORNFIELD CL
Cornfield Sch
Caravan Park
Cemy
Sch
WILLOW BROOK
JOYCE CL
GREENFIELDS
WHEATCROFT
STEAN FURLONG
COURTWICK RD
GRAND AVE
HIGHFIELD
BELLOC RD
WEST WAY
WICK ST
1 NURSERY GDNS
2 TRUE BLUE PREC
3 GLADSTONE TERR
NORTH ST
SWANBOURNE RD
Sewage Works
LINESIDE IND EST
Wickbourne Sch
Flora McDonald Cty Jun Sch
WHITELEA RD
Prim Sch
The Littlehampton Com Sch
HORSHAM RD
LINESIDE WAY
WICK FARM RD
Ret Pk
BRIDGE RD
ARUNDEL RD
BLAKEHURST WAY
CHAPEL CL
HARWOOD ROAD ENT UNITS
HARWOOD RD
ARUNSIDE IND EST
CORNWALL RD
ELMGROVE RD
Elm Grove Cty Inf Sch
Inf Sch
Jun Sch
Rosemead Sch
SOUTHFIELDS RD
RIVERSIDE IND EST
FORSTERS YD
QUAYSIDE
River Arun
CONNAUGHT RD
EAST ST
FITZROY CT
FRANCISCAN WAY
Caravan Park
Littlehampton Marina
PHAROS QUAY 1
ALPHA CT 2
SMALLCROFT CL 3
PEPPER CT 4
TERMINUS RD
HIGH ST
Mkt
C Ctr
Liby
Littlehampton
CHURCH ST
Sports Field
1 HEATHCOURT
2 REDWOOD CT
A259
FERRY RD
Caravan Park
TUDOR VIEW
ROPE WLK
RIVERSIDE
IRB Sta
CHURCH HO 1
THE SWALLOWS 2
ST CATHERINES CT 3
NEW RD
MALTRAVERS RD
MALTRAVERS DR
ALINORA
MARINE CT
SHELLEY LODGE
BEACH RD
B2140
Ryebank Rife
Ferry P
CH
IRVINE RD
SOUTH TERR
WESTERN RD
SOUTHLANDS
SOUTH PAS
COASTGUARD RD
The Green
SEA RD
B2140
THE PROMENADE
Golf Links
East Pier
The Mill
LITTLEHAMPTON
D5
1 ANCHOR SPRINGS
2 DUKE'S CT
3 ST MARTIN'S LA
4 WYCHCROFT
5 HOWARD PL
6 MADEHURST CT
7 ROSE CT
8 HAMPTON CT
9 ANTONIA CT
10 THE ARCADE
11 EVANS GDNS
D6
1 MERTON DR
2 QUANTOCKS
3 MALTHOUSE PAS
4 HAMPTON FIELDS
E5
1 ST MARY'S GDNS
2 TEMPLE CT
3 AMENIC CT
4 WHITE LODGE
5 SUMMERLEA GDNS
E4
1 CHURCH APP
2 MALTRAVERS CT
3 FITZALAN CT
4 LEEMARK HO
5 CLARE CT
6 WOODSIDE CT
7 OAKLAND CT
8 WELLESLEY CT
9 BERKELEY CT
10 KINGMERE
11 CHANNEL KEEP
12 ST AUGUSTINE RD
13 GLENMORE CT
14 NORTH PL
F4
1 WESTFIELD CT
2 AMSTEL CT
3 BEACH MEWS
4 NORFOLK PL
5 SURREY COTT
6 NORFOLK MEWS
7 THE WHAPPLE
8 MIDDLE MEAD
9 STARBOARD WLK

197

179
200
A
B
C
D
E
F
8
7
03
6
5
02
4
3
01
2
1
00
04
05
06
Ham Manor Farm
Old Brook Barn
Golf Ctr
CH
Golf Course
Inst of Horticultural Research
Rustington House Farm
The Angmering Sch
NEW RD
ROUNDSTONE BY-PASS RD
WORTHING RD
STATION RD
MILL LA
ASH LA
SEA LA
SEA RD
THE STREET
Superstore
Angmering Sta
Prim Sch
Georgian Gardens Sch
Rustington
Zachary Merton Com
Liby
Sports Ctr
BROADMARK BEACH
A6
1 TIMBERLEYS
2 BERMUDA CT
3 SCHOONER CT
4 BEAUFORT CT
5 THE MOORINGS
6 SEXTANT CT
7 MOUNTBATTEN CT
B3
1 ALDWICK C
2 CLIMPING CT
3 RACKHAM RD
4 FITZALAN CT
5 PETWORTH CT
6 DOWNSIDE CT
7 HOWARDS WAY
B4
1 NORDSETER LODGE
2 MARIGOLDS LODGE
3 KIRDFORD CL
4 KNIGHTSCROFT CL
5 BEACH CT
6 SELSEY CT
7 COPPETS WOOD
8 NORFOLK CT
9 RAWSON CT
B5
1 HIGHFIELD GDNS
2 CLARE LODGE
3 RICHMOND CT
C4
1 ILEX HO
2 FLINT HO
3 HERON'S COURT CL
4 SHAFTESBURY CT
5 SEAVIEW GDNS
6 HAWTHORN CL
7 RAVENS CROFT
C5
1 STERLING PAR
2 BROADMARK PAR
3 CHURCHILL CT
4 BROADMARK HO
5 WHITECROFT
6 EASTERGATE GN
7 FITTLEWORTH GDN
8 CHICHESTER CT
9 ARUNDEL GDN
C6
1 MENDIP CT
2 DONNINGTON PL
D6
1 ST ANTHONY'S WAY
2 SHIRLANDS CT
E6
1 RICHMOND CL
2 THORNTON CT
3 MUNMERE WAY
4 COPPER HALL CL
5 CRUNDENS CNR
6 STATION PAR

199
180

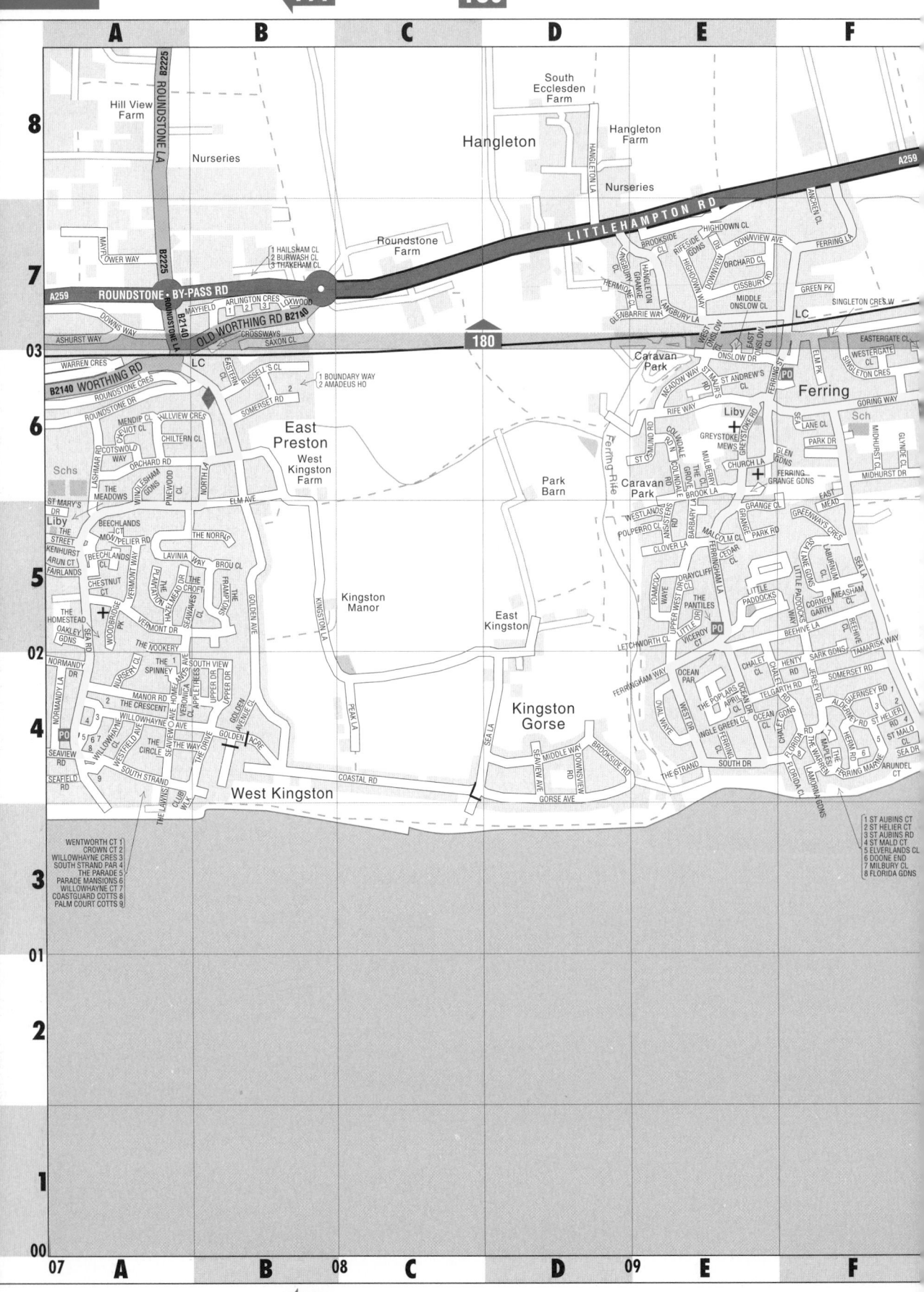
A
B
C
D
E
F
8
7
03
6
5
02
4
3
01
2
1
00
07
08
09
Hill View Farm
Nurseries
ROUNDSTONE LA
B2225
South Ecclesden Farm
Hangleton
Hangleton Farm
HANGLETON LA
Nurseries
A259
LITTLEHAMPTON RD
Roundstone Farm
1 HAILSHAM CL
2 BURWASH CL
3 THAKEHAM CL
ROUNDSTONE BY-PASS RD
MAYFIELD
ARLINGTON CRES
LOXWOOD
OLD WORTHING RD
B2140
CROSSWAYS
SAXON CL
DOWNS WAY
ASHURST WAY
180
WARREN CRES
LC
B2140 WORTHING RD
ROUNDSTONE CRES
ROUNDSTONE DR
EASTERN CL
RUSSELL'S CL
1 BOUNDARY WAY
2 AMADEUS HO
SOMERSET RD
East Preston
West Kingston Farm
MENDIP CL
HILLVIEW CRES
CHEVIOT CL
CHILTERN CL
COTSWOLD WAY
ORCHARD RD
Schs
LASHMAR RD
THE MEADOWS
WINDLESHAM GDNS
PINEWOOD CL
NORTH LA
ELM AVE
ST MARY'S DR
Liby
THE STREET
KENHURST
ARUN CT
FAIRLANDS
BEECHLANDS CT
MONTPELIER RD
BEECHLANDS CL
THE NORRIS
LAVINIA WAY
BROU CL
CHESTNUT CT
VERMONT WAY
THE PLANTATION
HAZELMEAD DR
THE CROFT
THE FRAMPTONS
SEAWAVES CL
THE HOMESTEAD
OAKLEY GDNS
SEA RD
WOODBRIDGE PK
VERMONT DR
THE NOOKERY
GOLDEN AVE
KINGSTON LA
Kingston Manor
NORMANDY DR
NORMANDY LA
NURSERY CL
THE SPINNEY
HOMELANDS AVE
SOUTH VIEW
UPPER DR
MANOR RD
THE CRESCENT
WILLOWHAYNE AVE
APPLETREES
VERONICA CL
GOLDEN AVENUE CL
GOLDEN ACRE
WILLOWHAYNE CL
WESTFIELD AVE
THE CIRCLE
SEAVIEW AVE
THE WAY
THE DRIVE
PO
SEAVIEW RD
SEAFIELD RD
SOUTH STRAND
THE LAWNS
CLUB WLK
West Kingston
COASTAL RD
PEAK LA
SEA LA
East Kingston
Park Barn
Kingston Gorse
SEAVIEW AVE
MIDDLE WAY
DOWNSVIEW RD
BROOKSIDE RD
GORSE AVE
WENTWORTH CT 1
CROWN CT 2
WILLOWHAYNE CRES 3
SOUTH STRAND PAR 4
THE PARADE 5
PARADE MANSIONS 6
WILLOWHAYNE CT 7
COASTGUARD COTTS 8
PALM COURT COTTS 9
BROOKSIDE CL
LANGBURY CL
HANGLETON GRANGE
HERMIONE CL
GLENBARRIE WAY
LANGBURY LA
RIFESIDE GDNS
HIGHDOWN CL
HIGHDOWN WAY
DOWNVIEW RD
DOWNVIEW AVE
ORCHARD CL
CISSBURY RD
MIDDLE ONSLOW CL
WEST ONSLOW CL
EAST ONSLOW CL
ANGREN CL
FERRING LA
GREEN PK
SINGLETON CRES W
EASTERGATE CL
WESTERGATE CL
SINGLETON CRES
ELM PK
Caravan Park
ONSLOW DR
MEADOW WAY
ST MAURS RD
ST ANDREW'S CL
FERRING ST
Ferring
GORING WAY
RIFE WAY
Liby
GREYSTOKE MEWS
GREYSTOKE RD
SEA LANE CL
PARK DR
Sch
MIDHURST CL
GLYNDE CL
MIDHURST DR
ST OSMUND RD
COLINDALE RD N
COLINDALE RD
MULBERRY GROVE
THE CL
CHURCH LA
GLEN GDNS
FERRING GRANGE GDNS
Ferring Rife
Caravan Park
BROOK LA
EAST MEAD
WESTLANDS
POLPERRO CL
ANNSTERS RD
BARBARY LA
GRANGE CL
GRANGE PARK RD
GREENWAYS CRES
CLOVER LA
MALCOLM CL
CEDAR CL
FERRINGHAM LA
SEA LANE GDNS
LABURNUM GR
SEA LA
FOAMCOURT WAYE
DRAYCLIFF CL
UPPER WEST DR
THE PANTILES
LITTLE PADDOCKS
LITTLE PADDOCKS WAY
CORNER GARTH
MEASHAM CL
LITTLE DR
VICEROY CT
BEEHIVE LA
BEEHIVE CL
TAMARISK WAY
LETCHWORTH CL
FERRINGHAM WAY
OCEAN PAR
CHALET CL
HENTY RD
SARK GDNS
SOMERSET RD
JERSEY RD
THE POPLARS
APRIL CL
OCEAN DR
TELGARTH RD
GUERNSEY RD
ALDERNEY RD
ST HELIER RD
OVAL WAYE
WEST DR
INGLE GREEN CL
FERRING CL
OCEAN CL
CHALET GDNS
FLORIDA RD
THE WARREN
MAPLES
HERM RD
ST MALO CL
SEA DR
THE STRAND
SOUTH DR
FLORIDA CL
LAMORNA GDNS
FERRING MARINE
ARUNDEL CT
1 ST AUBINS CT
2 ST HELIER CT
3 ST AUBINS RD
4 ST MALO CT
5 ELVERLANDS CL
6 DOONE END
7 MILBURY CL
8 FLORIDA GDNS

199

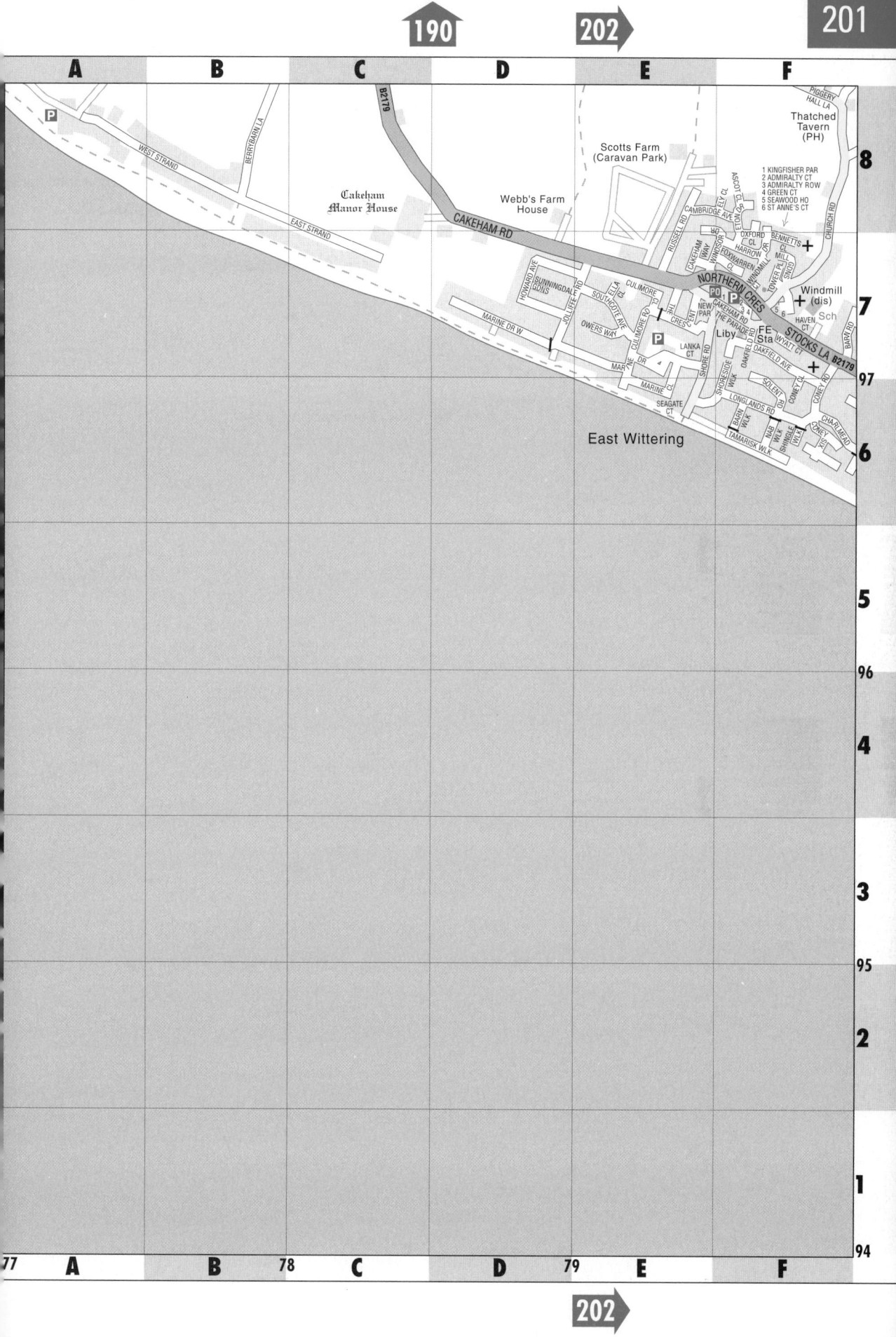

190
202

A B C D E F

8
7
97
6

5
96
4
3
95
2
1
94

B2179

WEST STRAND

BERRYBARN LA

Cakeham
Manor House

EAST STRAND

CAKEHAM RD

Webb's Farm
House

Scotts Farm
(Caravan Park)

Thatched
Tavern
(PH)

PIGGERY
HALL LA

1 KINGFISHER PAR
2 ADMIRALTY CT
3 ADMIRALTY ROW
4 GREEN CT
5 SEAWOOD HO
6 ST ANNE'S CT

CAMBRIDGE AVE
RUSSELL RD
ELY CL
COSSY RD
CHURCH RD

CAKEHAM WAY
WINDSOR CL
OXFORD CL
HARROW CL
BENNETTS CL
MILL RD
FOXWARREN CL
WINDMILL RD
TOWER PL

NORTHERN CRES

Windmill
(dis)

Sch

HAVEN CT

STOCKS LA B2179

BARN RD

CULIMORE
SOUTHCOTE AVE
LELA CL
CRESCENT
NEW/PAR
THE PARADE

FE
Sta

WYATT CT

Liby

HOWARD AVE
SUNNINGDALE GDNS

JOLLIFFE RD
CULIMORE RD

MARINE DR W

OWERS WAY

MARINE DR

MAR

MARINE CL

SEAGATE CT

LANKA CT

SHORE RD

SHORESIDE WLK

OAKFIELD RD
OAKFIELD AVE

CAKEHAM RD

SOLENT RD
LONGLANDS RD

CONEY DR
CORNEY RD
CONEY RD

East Wittering

BARN WLK
TAMARISK WLK
IVY WLK
SHINGLE WLK
CHARLMEAD
XXX
ONE

77 A B 78 C D 79 E F

201
191

A
B
C
D
E
F
8
7
97
6
5
96
4
3
95
2
1
94
80
81
82
Mus
CHURCH FARM LA
CHURCH FARM CT
HILTON PK
EAST WITTERING BSNS CTR
Stubcroft Farm
B2198
Cherry Tree Farm
SOMERLEY LA
THIRD AVE
Batchmere Estate
Almodington
ALMODINGTON LA
BOOKERS LA
Somerley Farm
EARNLEY RD
MANHOOD COTTS
EASTON LA
CLAYTON LA
STUBCROFT LA
BRACKLESHAM LA
FIELD RD
MEADOWS RD
WESSEX AVE
Holiday Centre
EARNLEY MANOR CL
Earnley Grange
Grange Farm
SOUTHDOWN CT
B2179
DOWNVIEW CL
BARTON WAY
CLAPPERS LA
CHURCH COTTS
Manor Farm
Earnley
STOCKS LA
Camping Site
BRACKLESHAM CT
SEAFIELD CL
SEAFIELD WAY
NAGELS CL
KIMBRIDGE PK
MIDDLETON CL
GRAYSWOOD AVE
ELM CL
PEERLEY RD
KIMBRIDGE RD
PEERLEY CL
LEGION WAY
KESTREL CL
PLOVER CL
BEECH AVE
GARDEN AVE
Bracklesham
Grange Rife
CORMORANT WAY
WEST BRACKLESHAM DR
SANDPIPER CT
BRACKLESHAM CL
ROSTOCK CT
POND RD
SANDRINGHAM CL
DROVE LA
BOURNE CT
PO
HARMONY DR
WESTERLEY GDNS
AZARA PAR
ELMDENE CT
ARMADA CT
WILTON CL
SHALBOURNE CRES
P
FIRST AVE
FARM RD
AVEBURY CL
Marsh Barn
THIRD AVE
EAST BRACKLESHAM DR
MARINES DE
WALMSLEYS WAY
Marsh Farm
SEAFIELDS
SILVER WAY
Sussex Beach Holiday Village
LEIGH CT
STONEY LA
BYWAVES
Bracklesham Bay

201

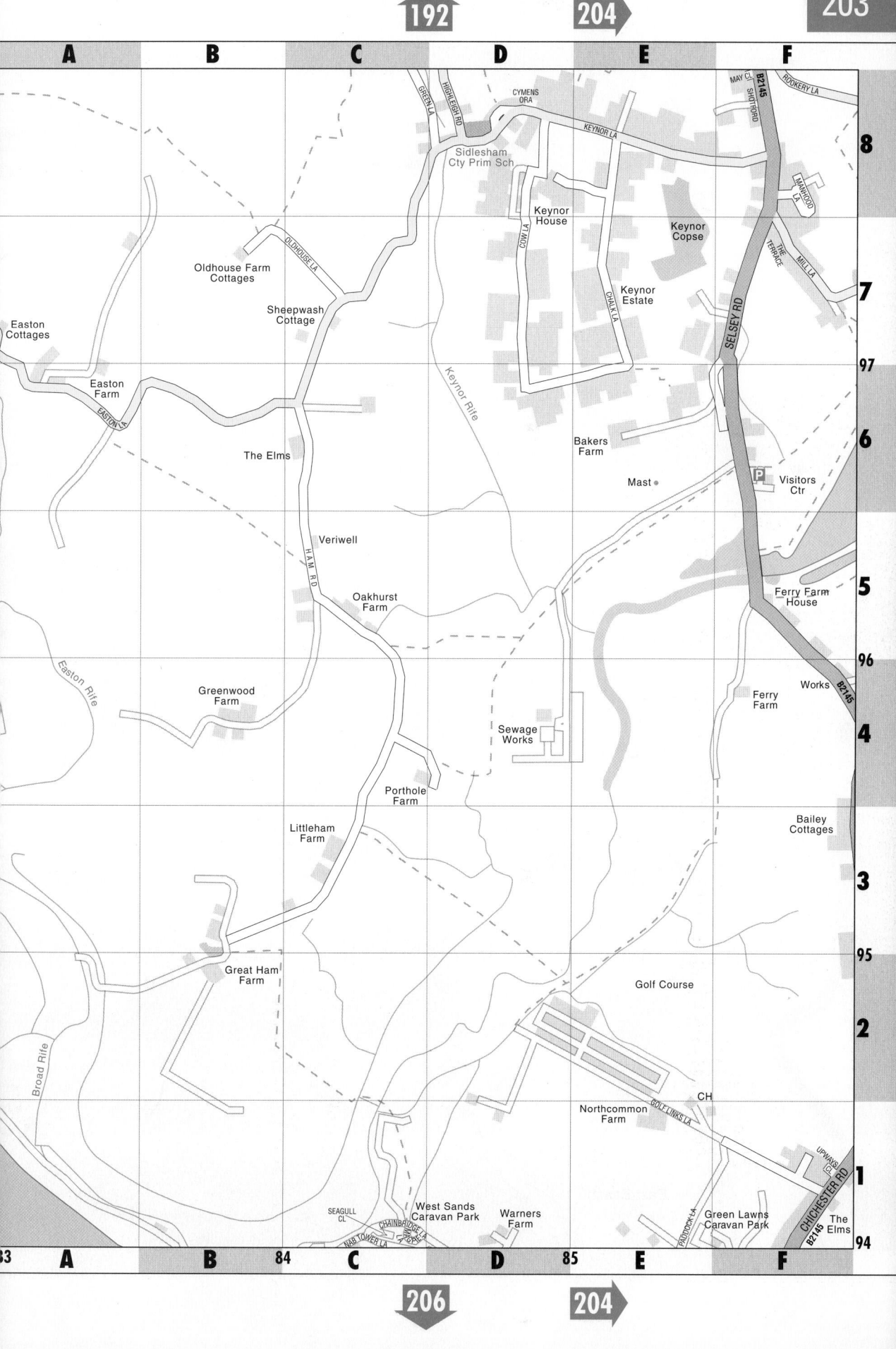

A B C D E F

8
7
97
6
5
96
4
3
95
2
1
94

Easton Cottages

Easton Farm

EASTON LA

The Elms

Oldhouse Farm Cottages

OLDHOUSE LA

Sheepwash Cottage

GREEN LA

HIGHLEIGH RD

CYMENS ORA

Sidlesham Cty Prim Sch

KEYNOR LA

Keynor House

COW LA

Keynor Estate

CHALK LA

Keynor Copse

MAY CL

SHOTFORD

B2145

ROOKERY LA

MANWOOD LA

THE TERRACE

MILL LA

SELSEY RD

Bakers Farm

Mast •

P Visitors Ctr

Keynor Rife

HAM RD

Veriwell

Oakhurst Farm

Greenwood Farm

Porthole Farm

Littleham Farm

Easton Rife

Broad Rife

Sewage Works

B2145

Ferry Farm House

Works

Ferry Farm

Bailey Cottages

Great Ham Farm

Golf Course

Northcommon Farm

GOLF LINKS LA

CH

UPWAYS CL

CHICHESTER RD

B2145

The Elms

SEAGULL CL

CHAINBRIDGE LA

NAB TOWER LA

West Sands Caravan Park

Warners Farm

PADDOCK LA

Green Lawns Caravan Park

83

203
193

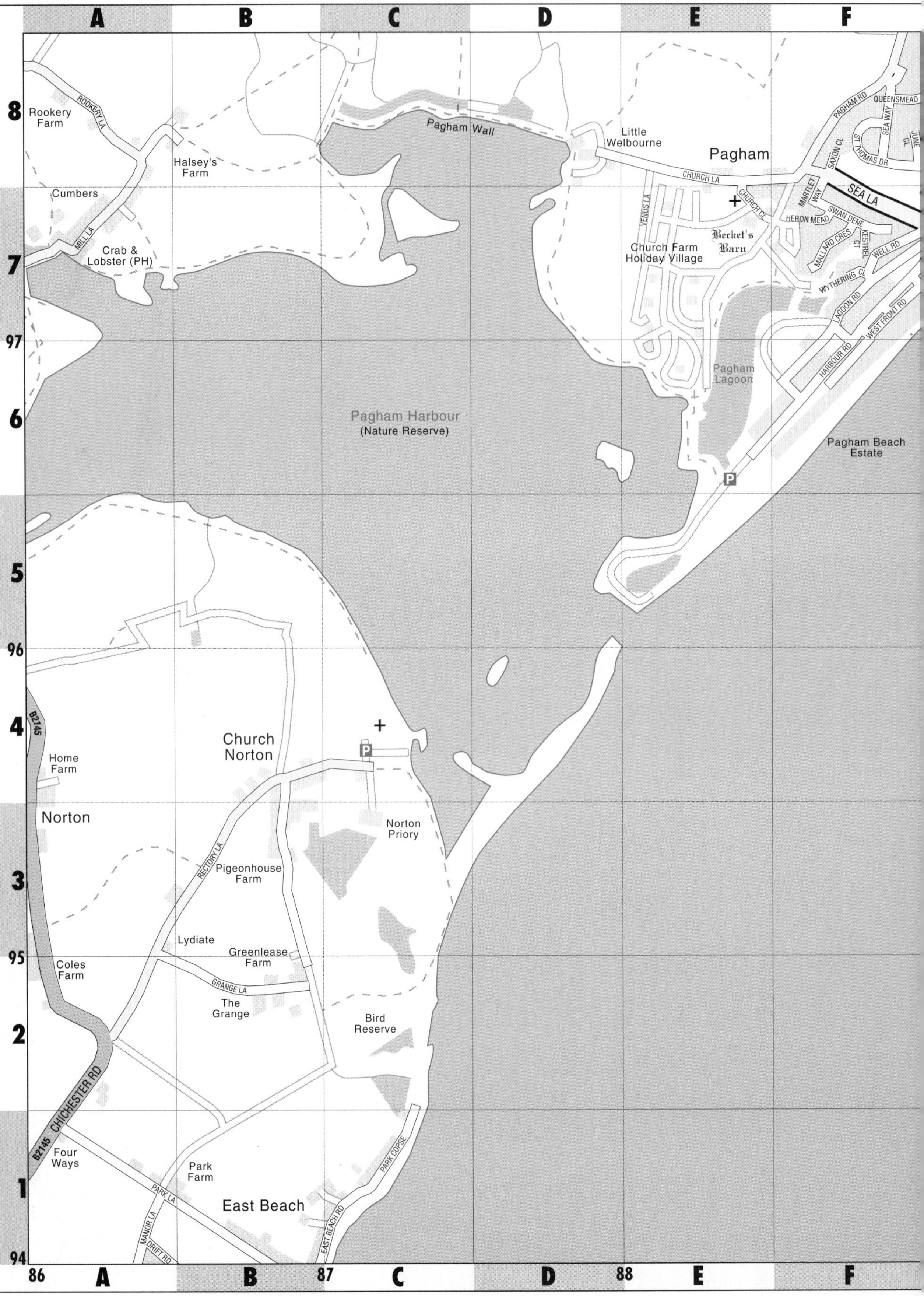

| | A | B | C | D | E | F |

8 Rookery Farm

ROOKERY LA

Halsey's Farm

Pagham Wall

Little Welbourne

Pagham

PAGHAM RD
QUEENSMEAD
SEA WAY
ST THOMAS DR
JUNE
SAXON CL

Cumbers

CHURCH LA

SEA LA

MILL LA

7 Crab & Lobster (PH)

VENUS LA
CHURCH CL

Church Farm Holiday Village

Becket's Barn

MARTLET WAY
HERON MEAD
SWAN DENE
KESTREL CT
NELL RD
MALLARD CRES

WYTHERING CL

97

HARBOUR RD
LAGOON RD
WEST FRONT RD

Pagham Lagoon

6 Pagham Harbour (Nature Reserve)

Pagham Beach Estate

P

5

96

B2145

4 Home Farm

Church Norton

+

P

Norton Priory

Norton

RECTORY LA

3 Pigeonhouse Farm

Lydiate

Greenlease Farm

95 Coles Farm

GRANGE LA

The Grange

Bird Reserve

2

CHICHESTER RD

B2145

1 Four Ways

Park Farm

PARK LA

PARK CORSE

East Beach

MANOR LA
DRIFT RD
EAST BEACH RD

94

86 | A | B | 87 | C | D | 88 | E | F

203
206

	A	B	C	D	E	F

THE CRESCENT
BISHOPS CL
ABBOTTSBURY
BARONS MEAD
GOLDEN ACRE
PAYNE CL
VIEW RD
THE VIEW
CHURCH WAY
EAST MEAD
KINGS DR
PRIORY CL
REGIS AVE
THE GREEN
SHIRLEY CL
THE GLADE
THE FAIRWAY
ARUN WAY
BAY WLK
THE BYE WAY
THE CAUSEWAY
LEDRA DR
VISCOUNT DR
THE DUNE
Aldwick Bay
Estate
BURNHAM
CONWAY DR
DURHAM WAY
ASHCROFT
WEBB CL
SILVERDALE CL
CHANNEL VIEW
TITHE BARN CT 1
BAY CT 2

BOGNOR REGIS

THE ARCADE
THE WOODS
SANDY RD
EAST FRONT RD
BLACK RD

1 ST THOMAS CT
2 CHURCHILL WLK
3 MULBERRY CT

8

7

97

6

5

96

4

3

95

2

1

94

9   A   B   90   C   D   91   E   F

203
204

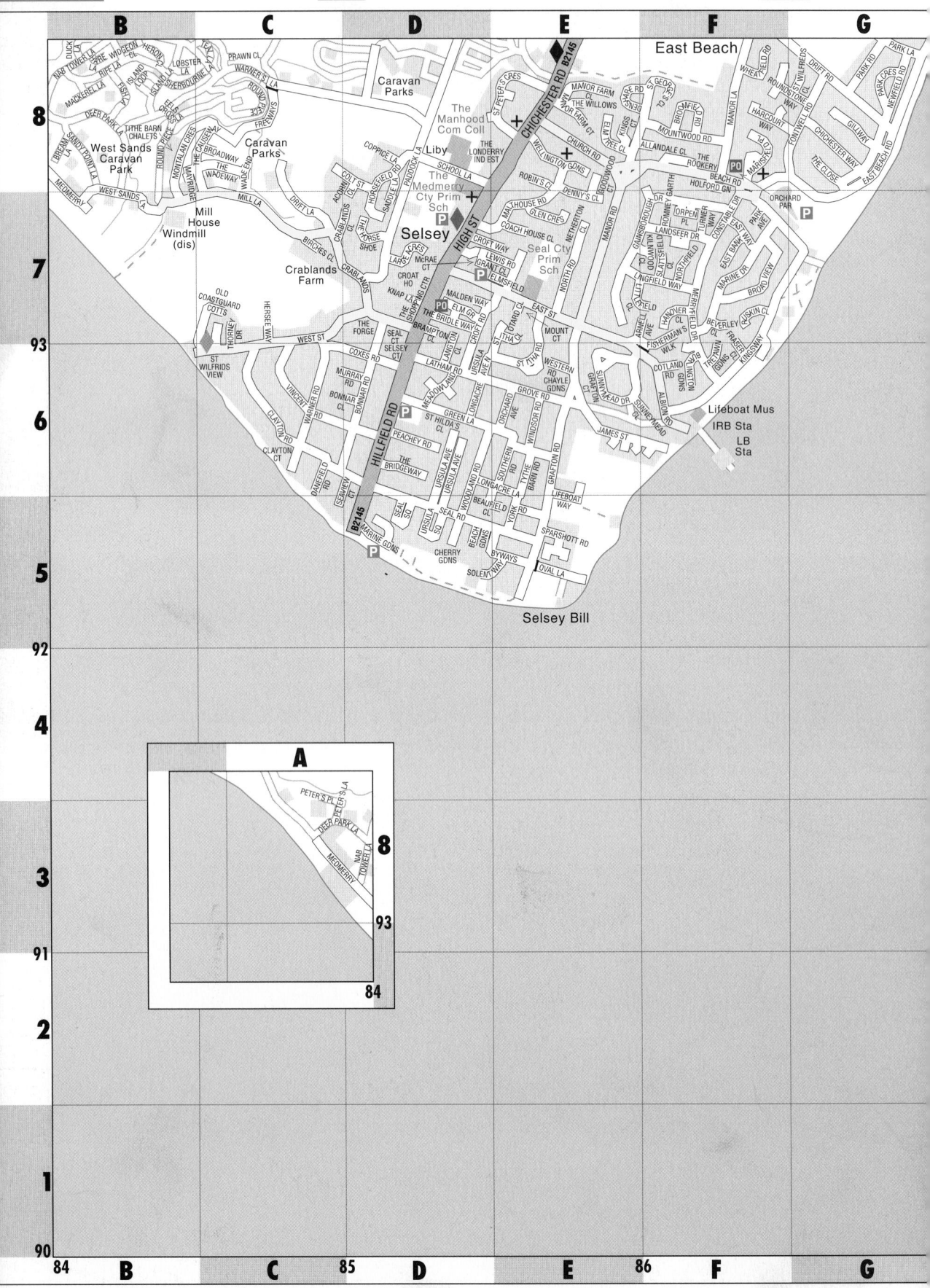
B
C
D
E
F
G
East Beach
Caravan Parks
The Manhood Com Coll
Liby
The Medmerry Cty Prim Sch
Selsey
Seal Cty Prim Sch
West Sands Caravan Park
Caravan Parks
Mill House Windmill (dis)
Crablands Farm
CHICHESTER RD
B2145
HIGH ST
HILLFIELD RD
WEST ST
EAST ST
MILL LA
SCHOOL LA
MANOR RD
MANOR LA
BEACH RD
HOLFORD GN
MOUNTWOOD RD
ALLANDALE CL
THE ROOKERY
CHURCH RD
WELLINGTON GDNS
GOODWOOD CT
ROBIN'S CL
DENNY'S CL
MALTHOUSE RD
GLEN CRES
COACH HOUSE CL
CROFT WAY
LEWIS RD
GRANT CL
ELMSFIELD
NORTH RD
NETHERTON CL
MANOR FARM CL
THE WILLOWS
ELM TREE CL
KINGS CT
ST PETER'S CRES
THE LONDERRY IND EST
PADDOCK LA
COPPICE LA
COLT ST
HORSEFIELD RD
SADDLE LA
ACORN CL
CRABLANDS CL
CRABLANDS
THE HORSE SHOE
LARK ACRES
McRAE CT
CROAT HO
KNAP LA
THE SHOPPING CTR
MALDEN WAY
ELM GR
THE BRIDLE WAY
BRAMPTON CL
THE FORGE
SEAL CT
SELSEY CT
COXES RD
LATHAM RD
LANGTON CL
CROFT RD
URSULA AVE N
ST ITHA CL
ST ITHA RD
OTARD CL
MOUNT CT
WESTERN RD
CHAYLE GDNS
GROVE RD
MEADOWLAND
LONGACRE
ORCHARD AVE
WINDSOR RD
GREEN LA
ST HILDA'S CL
PEACHEY RD
THE BRIDGEWAY
MURRAY RD
BONNAR CL
BONNAR RD
VINCENT RD
WARNER RD
CLAYTON RD
CLAYTON CT
DANEFIELD RD
SEAVIEW CT
SEAL SQ
URSULA SQ
URSULA AVE
SEAL RD
WOODLAND RD
SOUTHERN RD
TYTHE BARN RD
LONGACRE LA
BEAUFIELD CL
YORK RD
GRAFTON RD
LIFEBOAT WAY
SPARSHOTT RD
BEACH GDNS
CHERRY GDNS
MARINE GDNS
BYWAYS
SOLENT WAY
OVAL LA
Selsey Bill
JAMES ST
SUNNYMEAD DR
SUNNYMEAD CL
GRAFTON CT
ALBION RD
COTLAND RD
BURLINGTON GDNS
TREWIN GDNS
FRASER CL
KINGSWAY
BEVERLEY CL
FISHERMAN'S WLK
MERRYFIELD DR
HANOVER CL
ARNELL AVE
LITTLEFIELD CL
LINGFIELD WAY
NORTHFIELD CL
SLATTSFIELD CL
KILNWOOD CL
GAINSBOROUGH DR
ROMNEY GARTH
ORPEN PL
TURNER WAY
LANDSEER DR
CONSTABLE DR
EAST WAY
EAST BANK WAY
MARINE DR
BROAD VIEW
RUSKIN CL
PARK AVE
ORCHARD PAR
Lifeboat Mus
IRB Sta
LB Sta
BROOMFIELD RD
WHEATFIELD RD
ROUNDSTONE WAY
ST WILFREDS CL
HARCOURT WAY
MARISFIELD PL
FONTWELL RD
DRIFT RD
PARK RD
PARK CRES
NEWFIELD RD
PARK LA
GILLWAY
CHICHESTER WAY
THE CLOSE
EAST BEACH RD
PRAWN CL
WARNER'S LA
ROUND PIECE
FREEWAYS
LOBSTER LA
SHERBOURNE LA
HERON CL
WIDGEON
ISLAND LA
ISLAND LOOP
FISH LA
RIFE LA
MACKEREL LA
NAB TOWER LA
DUCK LA
DEER PARK LA
TITHE BARN CHALETS
BREAM LA
SANDY POINT LA
MONTALAN CRES
THE CAUSEWAY
BROADWAY
THE WADEWAY
WADE END
MAYRIDGE
WEST SANDS LA
MEDMERRY
DRIFT LA
BIRCHES CL
OLD COASTGUARD COTTS
THORNEY DR
HERSEE WAY
ST WILFRIDS VIEW
8
7
93
6
5
92
4
3
91
2
1
90
84
85
86
A
PETER'S PL
ST PETER'S LA
DEER PARK LA
NAB TOWER LA
MEDMERRY

Scale: 7 inches to 1 mile
110 yards
1/8 mile
125 m
250 m
187
187
188
188
207
F7
1 PRESTONVILLE CT
2 RUSSELL CRES
3 GROVE VILLA
4 BUCKINGHAM CL
5 NEWSTEAD
6 ST ANNE'S CT
7 ST ANNE'S HO
8 CASPIAN CT
9 TERMINUS PL
B8
1 THE CEDARS
2 THE WILLOWS
3 HOLLY BANK
4 THE LAURELS
F
A
B
8
055
7
050
6
045
5
040
4
036
305
310
315
UPPER HAMILTON RD
PARKMORE TERR
PRESTON RD
BEACONSFIELD RD
PRESTON CIR
VIADUCT RD
OLD SHOREHAM RD
NEW ENGLAND RD
STANFORD RD
HAMILTON RD
BRIGDEN ST
YORK VILLAS
HOWARD TERR
PRESTONVILLE RD
SEVEN DIALS
BUCKINGHAM PL
BATH ST
TERMINUS RD
DYKE RD
LONDON RD
UPPER LEWES RD
LEWES RD
UNION RD
DITCHLING RD
STANLEY RD
ROSE HILL TERR
CIRCUS PAR
St Bartholomew's CE Prim Sch
Brighton Sta
Mus
PRINCE'S CRES
CRESCENT MANSIONS
BROMLEY RD
EDINBURGH RD
CALEDONIAN RD
THE OPEN MKT
PHOENIX BREWERY HALLS
BRUNSWICK ROW
Brighton Coll of Tech
Univ
TRAFALGAR ST
CHEAPSIDE
YORK PL
RICHMOND PL
ST PETER'S PL
SURREY ST
QUEEN'S RD
GLOUCESTER PL
GRAND PAR
Victoria Gardens
MARLBOROUGH PL
North Laine
Mus & Art Gall
Liby
Royal Pavilion
The Lanes
WESTERN RD
NORTH ST
WEST ST
The Brighton Ctr
KING'S RD
Esplanade
GRAND JUNCTION RD
OLD STEINE
PAVILION PAR
EDWARD ST
ST JAMES'S ST
MARINE PAR
MADEIRA DR
Sea Life Ctr
Palace Pier
BRIGHTON
Volks Electric Rly
LAVENDER HO 1
HAMPSHIRE CT 2
MARINE GDNS 3
A6
1 THEOBALD HO
2 GLOUCESTER PAS
3 BLENHEIM PL
4 MARLBOROUGH PL
5 BELBOURNE CT
B5
1 PILOT HO
2 MANTELL HO
3 MARINE VIEW
4 PARK ROAD TERR
5 CARLTON PL
6 DERBY PL
7 UPPER PARK PL
8 ST JOHN'S MOUNT
9 TYSON PL
B5
10 ARDINGLY CT
11 CAVENDISH ST
12 KEBBELL LODGE
13 ST JAMES' HO
14 MALTHOUSE CT
15 HEREFORD CT
16 WILTSHIRE HO
B6
1 WATERLOO PL
2 BLAKE CT
3 ALBION HO
4 THORNSDALE
5 CHURCH WAY
6 ECCLESDEN
7 HIGHLEIGH
8 GROVE BANK
9 NORMANHURST
10 DINAPORE HO
11 RICHMOND HTS
12 COURTLANDS
13 CRANBROOK
14 ASHTON LODGE
15 SAXONBURY
B6
16 NELSON PL
17 GLYNLEIGH
18 COASTAL COUNTIES HO
19 WINDMILL TERR
B7
1 HOLT LODGE
2 THE PINES
3 HAZEL BANK
4 THE LINDENS

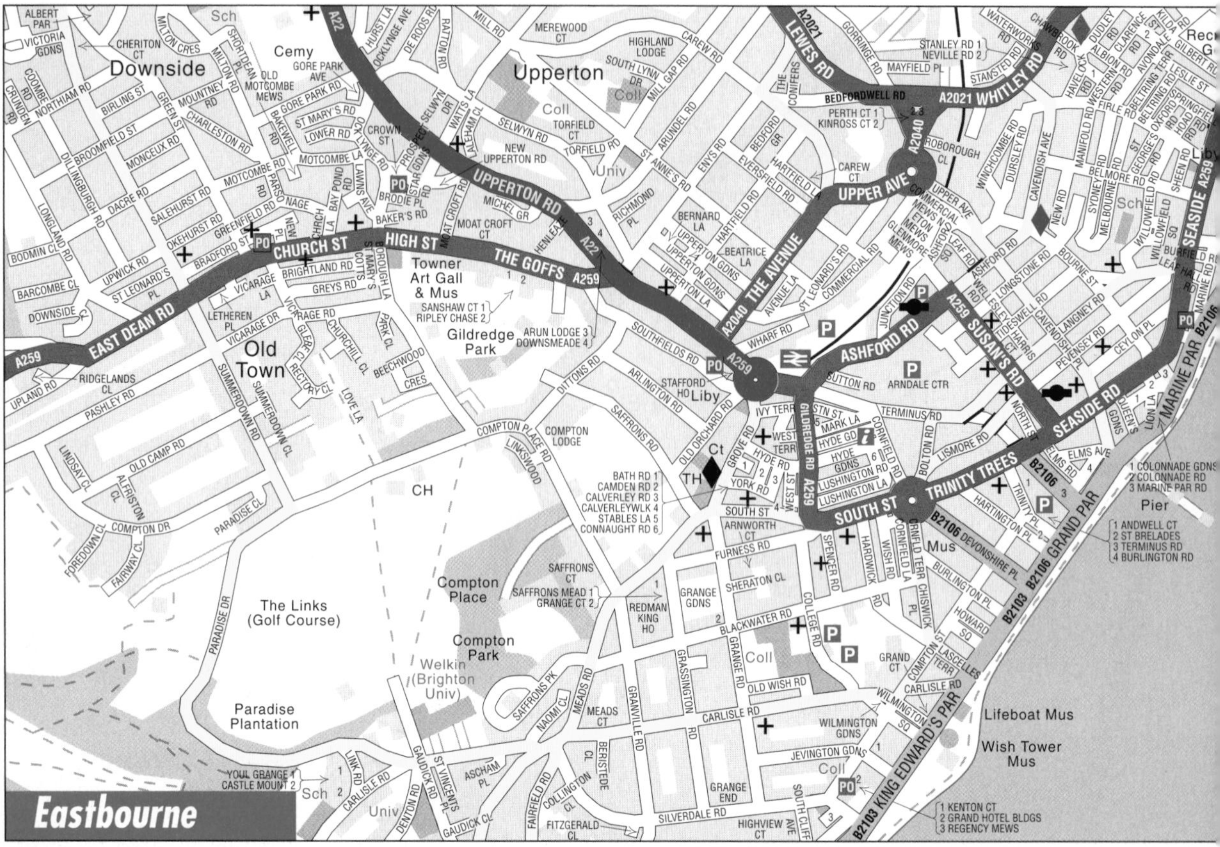

Eastbourne

Downside · Upperton · Old Town · Gildredge Park · Compton Place · The Links (Golf Course) · Compton Park · Paradise Plantation · Welkin (Brighton Univ) · Pier · Lifeboat Mus · Wish Tower Mus

Towner Art Gall & Mus · Saffrons Park · Coll · Univ

Streets: ALBERT PAR · VICTORIA GDNS · CHERITON RD · GORE PARK RD · OLD MOTCOMBE MEWS · NORTHIAM RD · BIRLING ST · MOUNTNEY RD · MOTCOMBE RD · CHARLESTON RD · BROOMFIELD ST · MONCEUX RD · SALEHURST RD · DACRE RD · BODMIN RD · OKEHURST CL · GREENFIELD RD · UPWICK RD · BRADFORD ST · ST LEONARDS RD · BARCOMBE RD · DOWNSIDE · RIDGELANDS · PASHLEY RD · UPLAND RD · LINDSAY CL · OLD CAMP RD · ALFRISTON RD · FRIDAY ST · FAIRWAY CL · PARADISE DR · CHURCH ST · HIGH ST · THE GOFFS · A259 · EAST DEAN RD · A259 · VICARAGE LA · VICARAGE DR · RECTORY CL · LOVE LA · SUMMERDOWN RD · COMPTON PLACE RD · COMPTON LODGE · SAFFRONS RD · ARLINGTON RD · DITTONS RD · UPPERTON RD · THE AVENUE · A2040 · UPPER AVE · A2040 · CAREW RD · LEWES RD · A2021 · WHITLEY RD · A2021 · SEASIDE · A259 · MARINE PAR · B2106 · SUSANS RD · ASHFORD RD · SEASIDE RD · TRINITY TREES · B2106 · SOUTH ST · GRAND PAR · B2103 · KING EDWARD'S PAR · B2103 · BATH RD · CAMDEN RD · CALVERLEY RD · STABLES LA · CONNAUGHT RD · ANWORTH RD · FURNESS RD · GRANGE RD · BLACKWATER RD · OLD WISH RD · CARLISLE RD · MEADS RD · GRANVILLE RD · JEVINGTON GDNS · WILMINGTON GDNS · GRANGE END · HIGHVIEW AVE · SILVERDALE RD · SOUTH CLIFF

1 COLONNADE GDNS · 2 COLONNADE RD · 3 MARINE PAR RD
1 ANDWELL CT · 2 ST BRELADES · 3 TERMINUS RD · 4 BURLINGTON RD
1 KENTON CT · 2 GRAND HOTEL BLDGS · 3 REGENCY MEWS
1 YOUL GRANGE · 2 CASTLE MOUNT

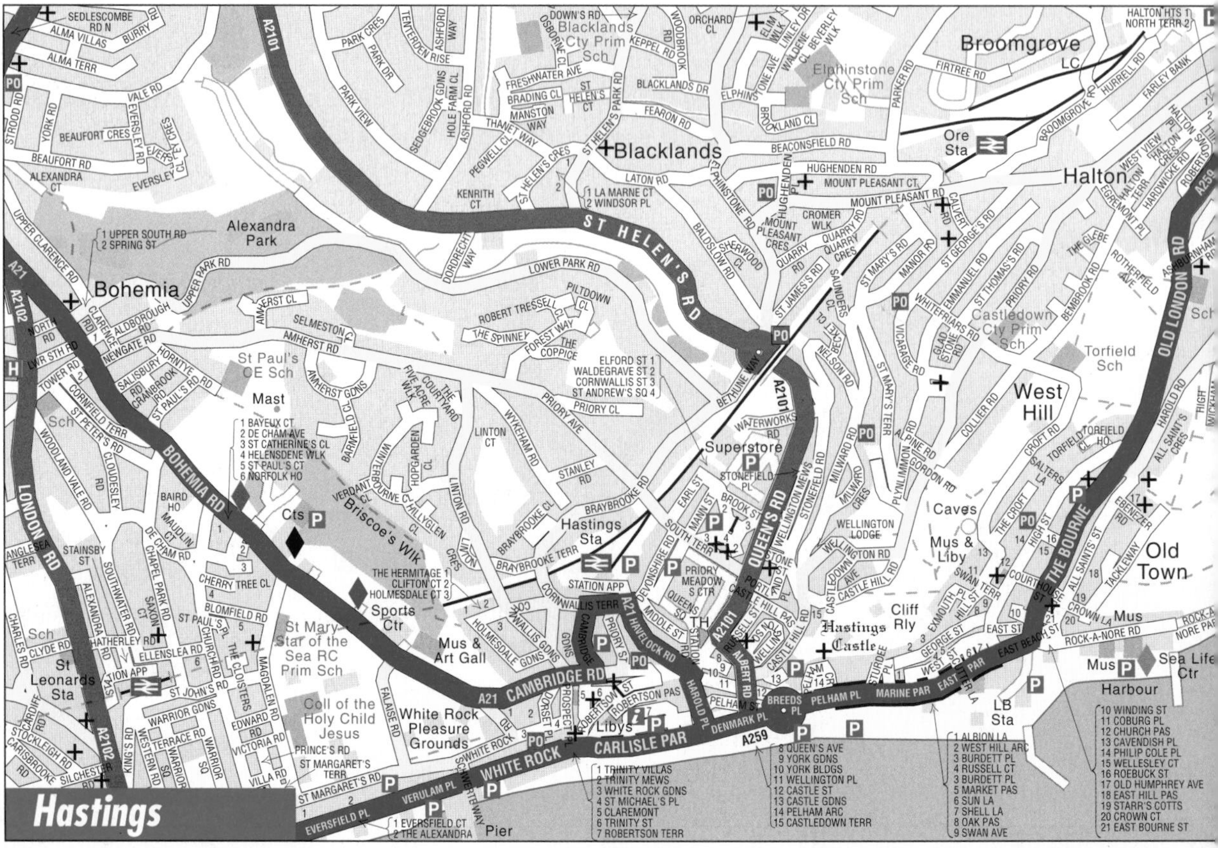

Hastings

Broomgrove · Blacklands · Halton · West Hill · Bohemia · Alexandra Park · Old Town · White Rock Pleasure Grounds · Harbour

Blacklands Cty Prim Sch · Elphinstone Cty Prim Sch · Castledown Cty Prim Sch · Torfield Sch · St Paul's CE Sch · St Mary-Star of the Sea RC Prim Sch · Coll of the Holy Child Jesus · Hastings Sta · Ore Sta · St Leonards Sta

Mus & Art Gall · Mus & Liby · Hastings Castle · Cliff Rly · Sea Life Ctr · Caves · Superstore · Sports Ctr

Streets: SEDLESCOMBE RD N · ALMA VILLAS · ALMA TERR · BURRY · STRODD RD · BEAUFORT CRES · BEAUFORT RD · ALEXANDRA CT · VALE RD · PARK CRES · PARK DR · PARK VIEW · TENTERDEN RISE · ASHFORD WAY · FRESHWATER AVE · BRADING CL · MANSTON WAY · THANET WAY · DOWN'S RD · ORCHARD · WOODBROOK · KEPPEL RD · BLACKLANDS DR · ST HELEN'S RD · FEARON RD · BEACONSFIELD RD · HUGHENDEN RD · MOUNT PLEASANT RD · CROMER WLK · LATON RD · QUARRY CRES · UPPER CLARENCE RD · UPPER PARK RD · LOWER PARK RD · ST HELEN'S RD · BOHEMIA RD · AMHERST RD · ROBERT TRESSELL CL · PILTDOWN · THE SPINNEY · FOREST WAY · THE COPPICE · ELFORD ST · WALDEGRAVE ST · CORNWALLIS ST · ST ANDREW'S SQ · PRIORY AVE · PRIORY CL · LINTON RD · WYKEHAM RD · STANLEY RD · LONDON RD · A21 · A2102 · CAMBRIDGE RD · A21 · WHITE ROCK · CARLISLE PAR · A259 · QUEEN'S RD · A2101 · OLD LONDON RD · A259 · THE BOURNE · MARINE PAR · EAST PAR · ROCK-A-NORE RD

1 UPPER SOUTH RD · 2 SPRING ST
1 BAYEUX CT · 2 DE CHAM AVE · 3 ST CATHERINE'S CL · 4 HELENSDENE WLK · 5 ST PAUL'S CT · 6 NORFOLK HO
1 TRINITY VILLAS · 2 TRINITY MEWS · 3 WHITE ROCK GDNS · 4 ST MICHAEL'S PL · 5 CLAREMONT · 6 TRINITY ST · 7 ROBERTSON TERR
1 EVERSFIELD CT · 2 THE ALEXANDRA
1 ALBION LA · 2 WEST HILL ARC · 3 BURDETT PL · 4 RUSSELL CT · 5 BURDETT PL · 6 SUN LA · 7 SHELL LA · 8 OAK PAS · 9 SWAN AVE
8 QUEEN'S AVE · 9 YORK GDNS · 10 YORK BLDGS · 11 WELLINGTON PL · 12 CASTLE ST · 13 CASTLE GDNS · 14 PELHAM ARC · 15 CASTLEDOWN TERR
10 WINDING ST · 11 COBURG PL · 12 CHURCH PAS · 13 CAVENDISH PL · 14 PHILIP COLE PL · 15 WELLESLEY CT · 16 ROEBUCK ST · 17 OLD HUMPHREY AVE · 18 EAST HILL PAS · 19 STARR'S COTTS · 20 CROWN CT · 21 EAST BOURNE ST

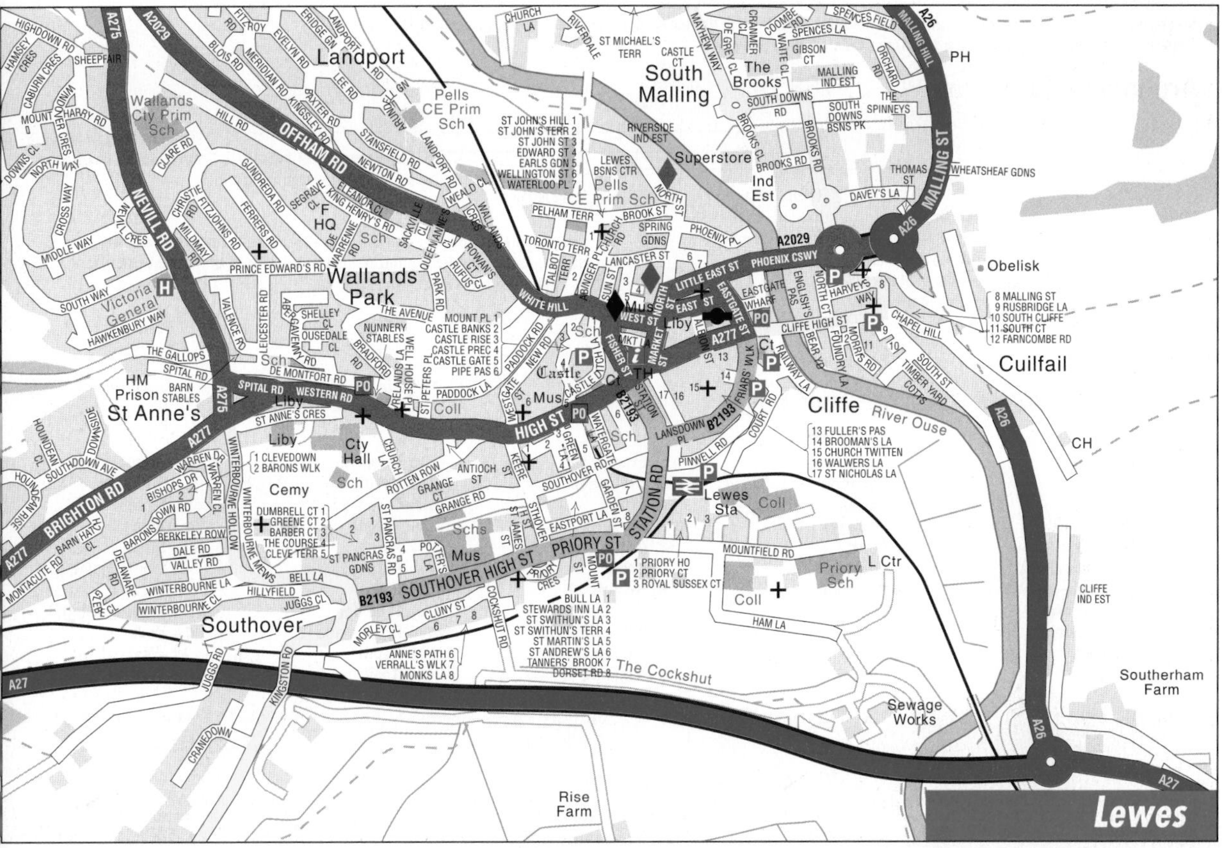

Lewes

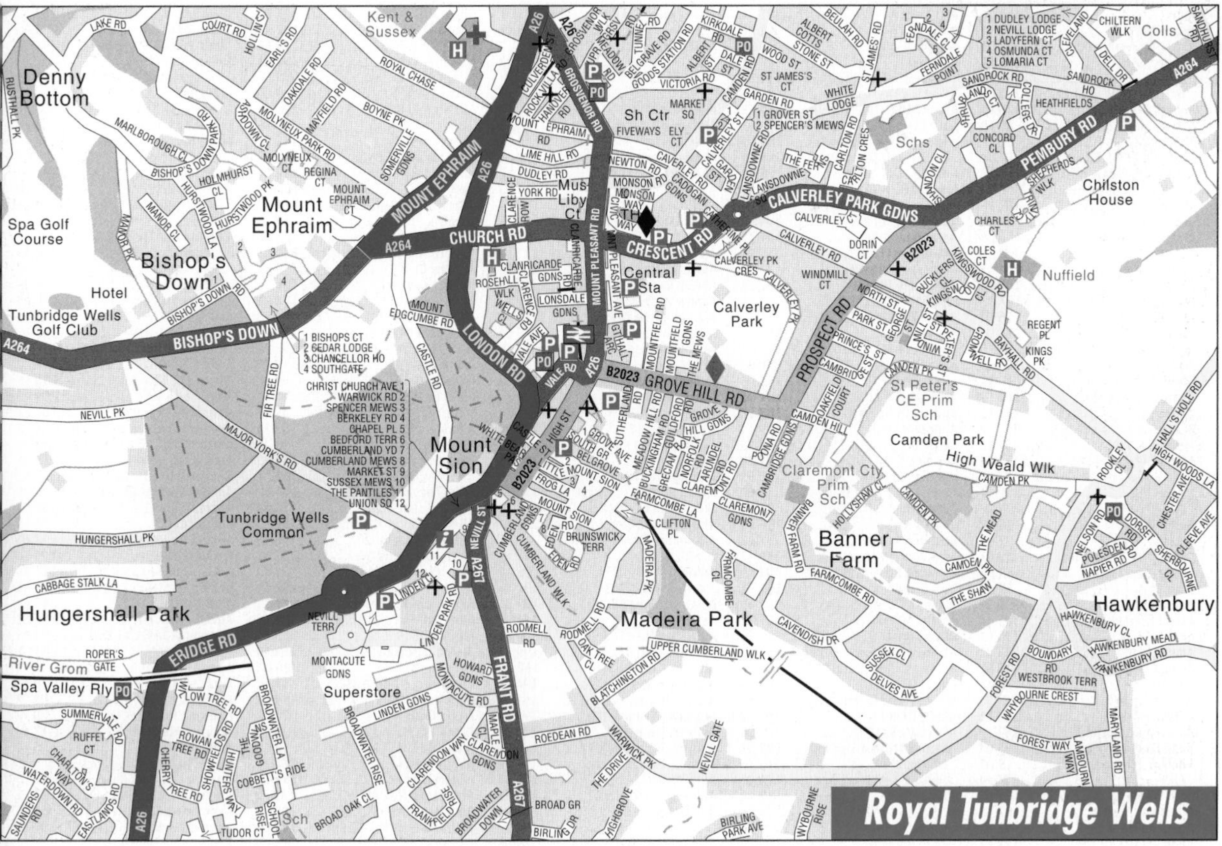

Landport · South Malling · The Brooks · South Downs · Ind Est · Obelisk · Cuilfail · Wallands Park · Victoria General H · St Anne's · HM Prison · Castle · Cliffe · River Ouse · City Hall · Cemy · Southover · Southover High St · Priory St · Lewes Sta · Priory L Ctr · Priory Sch · The Cockshut · Rise Farm · Sewage Works · Southerham Farm · Cliffe Ind Est

Roads: A275, A2029, OFFHAM RD, NEVILL RD, A277, BRIGHTON RD, HIGH ST, STATION RD, B2193, A26, A27, SPITAL RD, WESTERN RD, WHITE HILL

8 MALLING ST
9 RUSBRIDGE LA
10 SOUTH CLIFFE
11 SOUTH CT
12 FARNCOMBE RD

13 FULLER'S PAS
14 BROOMAN'S LA
15 CHURCH TWITTEN
16 WALWERS LA
17 ST NICHOLAS LA

1 PRIORY HO
2 PRIORY CT
3 ROYAL SUSSEX CT

1 CLEVEDOWN
2 BARONS WLK

Royal Tunbridge Wells

Denny Bottom · Mount Ephraim · Bishop's Down · Spa Golf Course · Hotel · Tunbridge Wells Golf Club · Tunbridge Wells Common · Hungershall Park · Calverley Park Gdns · Chilston House · Nuffield · Calverley Park · Central Sta · Mount Sion · The Pantiles · Madeira Park · Banner Farm · Hawkenbury · Camden Park · High Weald Wlk · St Peter's CE Prim Sch · Claremont City Prim Sch · Superstore · Spa Valley Rly · River Grom

Roads: A26, A264, A267, A26, MOUNT EPHRAIM, CHURCH RD, LONDON RD, BISHOP'S DOWN, GROVE HILL RD, CRESCENT RD, PEMBURY RD, PROSPECT RD, B2023, FRANT RD, ERIDGE RD

Index

Street names are listed alphabetically and show the locality, the Postcode District, the page number and a reference to the square in which the name falls on the map page

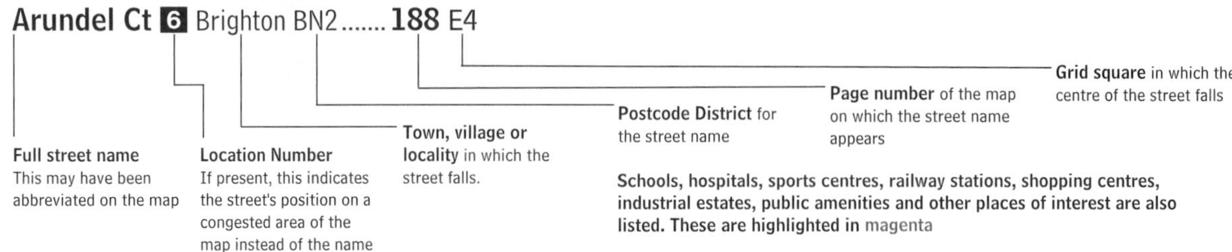

Arundel Ct 6 Brighton BN2 .... 188 E4
Grid square in which the centre of the street falls
Page number of the map on which the street name appears
Postcode District for the street name
Town, village or locality in which the street falls.
Full street name
This may have been abbreviated on the map
Location Number
If present, this indicates the street's position on a congested area of the map instead of the name
Schools, hospitals, sports centres, railway stations, shopping centres, industrial estates, public amenities and other places of interest are also listed. These are highlighted in magenta

Abbreviations used in the index

App	Approach	Cl	Close	Ent	Enterprise	La	Lane	Rdbt	Roundabout
Arc	Arcade	Comm	Common	Espl	Esplanade	N	North	S	South
Ave	Avenue	Cnr	Corner	Est	Estate	Orch	Orchard	Sq	Square
Bvd	Boulevard	Cotts	Cottages	Gdns	Gardens	Par	Parade	Strs	Stairs
Bldgs	Buildings	Ct	Court	Gn	Green	Pk	Park	Stps	Steps
Bsns Pk	Business Park	Ctyd	Courtyard	Gr	Grove	Pas	Passage	St	Street, Saint
Bsns Ctr	Business Centre	Cres	Crescent	Hts	Heights	Pl	Place	Terr	Terrace
Bglws	Bungalows	Dr	Drive	Ho	House	Prec	Precinct	Trad Est	Trading Estate
Cswy	Causeway	Dro	Drove	Ind Est	Industrial Estate	Prom	Promenade	Wlk	Walk
Ctr	Centre	E	East	Intc	Interchange	Ret Pk	Retail Park	W	West
Cir	Circus	Emb	Embankment	Junc	Junction	Rd	Road	Yd	Yard

A'becket Gdns BN13 181 F6
A'becket's Ave PO21 194 B1
Abberton Field BN6 126 B5
Abbey Church The
Brighton RH10 20 B1
Abbey Cl BN15 184 B6
Abbey Ho RH20 140 D8
Abbey Rd Brighton BN2 188 D4
Lancing BN15 183 C7
Steyning BN44 143 E4
Worthing BN11 182 B1
Abbots Cl BN6 126 E4
Abbots Leigh RH13 80 A8
Abbotsbury Ct RH13 36 E3
Abbotsfield Rd RH11 17 D4
Abbotsford Sch RH15 106 E6
Abbotswood Wlk BN16 199 C4
Abbotts [20] BN1 187 E5
Abbotts Cl BN11 182 D2
Abbotts View BN15 183 C8
Abbotts Way BN15 183 F6
Abbottsbury PO21 205 A8
Aberdeen Rd BN2 188 C8
Abergavenny Ho [1] BN3 187 D6
Abigail Ho [10] RH16 85 E4
Abingdon Wlk BN13 181 D5
Abinger Cotts RH13 80 F5
Abinger Rd BN41 186 B8
Abrahams Rd RH11 18 A1
Acacia Ave Hove BN3 166 F1
Worthing BN13 181 F7
Acacia Ct BN1 167 F2
Acorn Ave RH13 81 F1
Acorn Cl Angmering BN16 179 F4
East Grinstead RH19 22 E8
Horley RH6 2 C4
Selsey PO20 206 D8
Acorn End PO21 194 D2
Acorns RH13 37 A4
Acorns The Crawley RH11 18 B1
Sayers Common BN6 105 D2
Acre Cl Haywards Heath RH16 85 D2
Rustington BN16 199 B6
Acre Cl The BN11 182 B1
Acre St PO20 190 F2
Adams Cl BN1 168 B2
Adamson Ct [6] RH11 18 B1
Adastra Ave BN6 127 A4
Adderbury Ave PO10 149 B3
Addison Cl BN15 183 E6
Addison Rd BN1, BN3 187 E7
Addison Way PO22 195 C7
Adelaide Cl Crawley RH11 5 D1
Horsham RH12 36 F4
Worthing BN13 181 C7
Adelaide Cres BN3 187 C5
Adelaide Ho GU29 92 E6
Adelaide Rd PO19 173 B7
Adelaide Sq BN43 185 B7
Adelphi Cl RH10 19 D4
Admers Cres GU30 25 C2
Admiral Rd RH11 18 A3
Admiral's Bridge La RH19 22 C2
Admirals Wlk Funtington PO18 151 A5
Littlehampton BN16 199 A6
[1] Shoreham-by-Sea BN43 184 F6
Admiralty Ct PO20 201 F7
Admiralty Gdns PO22 195 F3
Admiralty Rd PO22 195 F4
Admiralty Row PO20 201 F7
Adrian Ct RH11 18 B1
Adur Ave
Shoreham-by-Sea BN43 164 E1
Worthing BN13 181 C8
Adur Cl [6] BN15 184 C5
Adur Ct
[5] Shoreham-by-Sea BN15 184 C5
[10] Shoreham-by-Sea BN43 185 C8
Adur Dr BN43 185 A7
Adur Rd Burgess Hill RH15 107 C4
Shoreham-by-Sea BN43 184 E8
Adur Valley Ct BN44 144 B2
Adur View BN44 144 A2
Adversane Ct RH12 36 D4
Adversane La RH14 77 D2
Adversane Rd BN14 182 B5
Agate La RH12 36 F5
Aglaia Rd BN11 181 F1
Agnes St BN2 188 C7
Aigburth Ave PO21 194 D3
Ailsa Cl RH11 18 B3
Ainsdale Cl BN13 181 D6
Ainsdale Rd BN13 181 D6
Ainsworth Ho [1] BN2 188 C7
Aintree Rd RH10 19 A4
Air St BN1 207 F5
Airedale Ct [8] BN11 182 B2
Airport Way RH6 6 B8
Airport Way Rdbt W RH6 5 F8
Aitken Ho GU27 27 C7
Ajax Pl PO22 196 C5
Akehurst Cl RH10 7 B3
Alan Way BN2 188 F5
Alandale Rd Birdham PO20 191 F4
Sompting BN15 163 C1
Albany Cl BN11 182 A1
Albany Mews BN3 187 B6
Albany Rd RH11 18 C6
Albany Villas Cuckfield RH17 85 A6
Hove BN3 187 B6
Albert Cl RH16 86 A4
Albert Crane Ct RH11 18 A8
Albert Dr RH15 106 E2
Albert Mews [24] BN3 187 C6
Albert Rd Bognor Regis PO21 195 D3
Brighton BN1 207 F6
Fishbourne PO19 172 C6
Horley RH6 2 A3
Littlehampton BN17 198 D5
Rustington BN16 199 C6
Southwick BN42 185 D7
Alberta Rd BN13 181 D6
Alberta Wlk BN13 181 D6
Albery Cl RH12 36 B4
Albion Cl RH10 19 D5
Albion Ct RH15 106 F2
Albion Hill BN2 207 B6
Albion Ho [3] Brighton BN2 207 B6
Southwick BN42 185 F7
Albion Rd PO20 206 F6
Albion St Brighton BN2 207 B6
Portslade-by-Sea BN41 186 B7
Southwick BN42 185 E7
Albion Way RH12 36 C2
Alborough Way PO21 194 D2
Albourne CE (C) Prim Sch
BN6 125 C6
Albourne Cl BN2 188 F7
Albourne Rd Henfield BN5 124 A8
Hurstpierpoint BN6 125 E6
Albury Keep RH6 2 B4
Aldbourne Dr PO21 194 D2
Alder Cl Crawley Down RH10 21 B8
Worthing BN13 181 C5
Alder Copse RH12 57 F8
Alder Way PO22 196 E6
Aldermoor Ave RH20 119 E3
Alderney Rd BN12 200 F4
Alders Ave RH19 9 E3
Alders View Dr RH19 9 E3
Aldingbourne Cl RH11 17 F7
Aldingbourne Ctry Ctr PO18 155 C3
Aldingbourne Cty Prim Sch
PO20 175 D6
Aldingbourne Dr PO18, PO20 155 B3
Aldingbourne Ho
Crockerhill PO18 155 B3
Littlehampton BN17 178 B3
Aldingbourne Pk PO20 175 D5
Aldrich Cl BN2 188 F6
Aldrington Ave BN3 187 A8
Aldrington CE Fst Sch BN3 186 F7
Aldrington CE Prim Sch BN3 167 A2
Aldrington Cl BN3 186 D7
Aldrington House (Hospl)
BN3 186 F6
Aldrington Pl BN3 186 D8
Aldrington Sta BN3 187 A8
Aldsworth Ave BN12 181 B1
Aldsworth Ct BN12 181 B2
Aldwick Ave PO21 194 F2
Aldwick Cl [1] BN16 199 B3
Aldwick Cres BN14 162 A1
Aldwick Felds PO21 194 F2
Aldwick Gdns PO21 194 F3
Aldwick Grange PO21 194 E2
Aldwick Ho BN17 178 B3
Aldwick Hundred PO21 194 E1
Aldwick Pl PO21 194 F2
Aldwick Rd PO21 195 B2
Aldwick St PO21 194 E2
Aldwych Cl RH10 19 D4
Alexander Cl PO21 194 E2
Alexandra Ct [10] Crawley RH11 18 D5
Worthing BN12 181 C3
Alexandra Ho PO22 195 E4
Alexandra Rd Burgess Hill RH15 107 C2
Chichester PO19 173 B7
Lancing BN15 183 F5
Alexandra Rd Worthing BN11 182 F2
Alexandra Terr [13] PO21 195 D3
Alexandra Villas BN1 207 F6
Alfold By-Pass GU6 11 A5
Alfold La GU6 11 A7
Alfold Rd GU6 11 B7
Alford Cl BN14 182 A7
Alfred Cl RH10 19 E5
Alfred Pl BN11 182 E2
Alfred Rd BN1 207 F6
Alfrey Cl PO10 169 E8
Alfriston Cl Bognor Regis PO22 196 C6
Brighton BN2 188 F6
Worthing BN14 182 B5
Alfriston Ho [2] BN14 182 D5
Alfriston Rd BN14 182 B5
Alice St BN3 187 D5
Alicia Ave Ashington RH20 121 A5
Crawley RH10 19 C6
Alicks Hill RH14 77 D8
Alinora Ave BN12 181 D1
Alinora Cl BN12 181 D1
Alinora Cres BN12 181 D1
Alinora Dr BN12 181 D1
Allandale Cl PO20 206 F8
Allangate Dr BN16 199 D6
Allcard Cl RH12 36 D4
Allcot Cl RH11 17 E3
Allee Dr GU30 25 B5
Allen Rd RH16 86 A4
Allen's Cl RH19 23 D6
Allendale RH13 57 F3
Allendale Ave
New Brighton PO10 149 A3
Worthing BN14 162 A1
Alley The Amberley BN18 138 D7
Stedham GU29 70 A1
Alleyne Way PO22 197 B5
Allfreys Wharf RH20 98 B2
Allingham Gdns RH12 37 B5
Allington Rd BN14 182 E7
Allman Bsns Pk PO20 192 B6
Allyington Way RH10 19 D5
Alma Rd RH16 86 B8
Alma St BN15 183 E4
Almodington La PO20 202 F8
Almond Cl RH11 18 A5
Almshouses The PO18 154 D4
Alperton Cl PO21 194 C1
Alpha Cotts RH20 98 D2
Alpha Ct BN17 198 C5
Alpha Rd RH11 18 C6
Alpine Rd BN3 186 F8
Alston Way BN13 181 D5
Alverstone Rd BN11 182 F3
Amadeus Ho BN16 200 B6
Ambassadors The [6] BN3 187 C6
Amber Ct [17] Hove BN3 187 C6
[8] Hove BN3 187 D7
Amber Glade RH13 57 F1
Amberley CE (C) Sch BN18 138 E7
Amberley Cl Burgess Hill RH15 107 A5
Crawley RH10 19 C6
Amberley Cl
Haywards Heath RH16 85 D4
Horsham RH12 37 A6
Hove BN3 166 E3
Littlehampton BN17 198 E6
Shoreham-by-Sea BN43 164 F1
Amberley Ct Lancing BN15 183 F6
[9] Worthing BN11 181 F2
Amberley Dr
Bognor Regis PO21 195 A4
Hove BN3 166 E3
Worthing BN12 181 B1
Amberley Gate RH20 119 B1
Amberley Lodge BN2 207 A7
Amberley Mus BN18 138 D5
Amberley Rd RH20 140 A8
Horsham RH12 37 A6
Littlehampton BN16 199 C4
Amberley Sta BN18 138 D4
Ambermarle The BN2 207 A4
Ambersham Cres BN16 179 F3
Ambleside Cl
Bognor Regis PO22 196 B6
Crawley RH11 17 D5
Ambleside Rd BN15 183 C6
Ambrose Hill RH17 105 B7
Ambrose Pl BN11 182 D2
Amelia Rd BN11 182 C2
Amenic Ct [3] BN17 198 E5
America La RH16 86 A5
Amesbury Cres BN3 186 E7
Amherst Cres BN3 186 F8
Amstel Ct [2] BN17 198 F4
Amundsen Rd RH12 36 D6
Anchor Hill RH17 87 A2
Anchor Springs [1] BN17 198 D5
Ancren Cl BN12 180 F3
Ancton Cl PO22 196 F5
Ancton Dr PO22 197 A6
Ancton La PO22 196 F6
Ancton Lodge La PO22 197 A5
Ancton Way PO22 197 B5
Andlers Ash Rd GU33 45 A3
Andrew Ave PO22 196 C5
Andrew Cl Rustington BN16 199 B6
Steyning BN44 143 D2
Andrew's La RH13 57 F1
Andrews Cotts RH13 79 F7
Andrews La GU29 91 F7
Andrews Rd RH13 79 F7
Andromeda Cl RH11 17 E4
Angel St GU28 95 F8
Angell Est PO19 173 D5
Anglesea St BN11 182 C3
Anglesey Cl RH11 18 C2
Angmering Ct BN1 168 F5
Angmering La BN16 199 E5
Angmering Sch The BN16 179 F3
Angmering Sta BN16 199 F6
Angmering Way BN16 179 E3
Angola Rd BN14 182 F4
Angus Cl RH12 36 D4
Angus Rd BN12 181 E2

Ann Cl BN6 127 A5
Ann St Brighton BN1 207 A7
Worthing BN11 182 E2
Annandale Ave PO21 195 C4
Anne Howard Gdns BN18 158 A3
Annington Commercial Ctr BN44 163 E8
Annington Gdns 4 BN43 164 F1
Annington Rd BN44, BN15 163 F8
Annweir Ave BN15 183 E6
Anscombe 5 RH16 85 D6
Anscombe Cl BN11 181 F1
Anscombe Rd BN11 181 F1
Ansisters Rd BN12 200 E5
Anson Ct BN12 181 C4
Anson Rd Bognor Regis PO21 194 B2
Worthing BN12 181 C4
Ansty Cl BN2 188 E5
Answorth Cl PO19 153 B1
Antlands La RH6 7 B6
Antlands La E RH6 6 F5
Antlands La W RH6 6 E6
Antonia Ct 9 BN17 198 D5
Anvil Cl Billingshurst RH14 77 C8
Portslade-by-Sea BN41 166 B2
Southwater RH13 57 F1
Apple Gr Bognor Regis PO21 194 B1
Hermitage PO10 169 D8
Apple Tree Wlk BN17 177 D1
Appledore Ct RH16 86 A7
Appledore Gdns RH16 86 A6
Appledore Rd BN2 168 F4
Appledram La N PO19, PO20 172 C6
Appledram La S PO20 172 C4
Applefield RH10 18 E7
Applesham Ave BN3 166 E2
Applesham Way BN41 166 A1
Appletree Dr PO22 176 B6
Appletrees BN16 200 B4
Approach The 2 Brighton BN1 167 E3
Dormansland RH19 9 F6
April Cl Horsham RH12 36 C4
Kingston Gorse BN12 200 E4
Apsley Ct RH11 17 F4
Apsley Way BN13 181 B5
Aquarius Ct RH11 17 E4
Arbor Ct 8 RH16 85 E5
Arcade Rd BN17 198 D5
Arcade The
8 Bognor Regis PO21 195 D3
10 Littlehampton BN17 198 D5
Archers Ct RH11 18 D8
Archibald Rd BN11 183 A3
Arcturus Rd RH11 17 E3
Ardale Cl BN11 181 F2
Arden Rd RH10 18 F4
Ardingly Cl RH11 18 B8
Ardingly Coll RH17 64 A6
Ardingly Ct 10 BN2 207 B5
Ardingly Dr BN12 181 B3
Ardingly Rd RH17 84 F7
Ardingly St BN2 207 B5
Ardings Cl RH17 64 B7
Ardmore Sch BN11 182 D2
Ardsheal Cl BN14 182 C5
Ardsheal Rd BN14 182 C6
Argus Wlk RH11 18 A3
Argyle Cir 5 PO21 195 C3
Argyle Rd Bognor Regis PO21 195 C3
Brighton BN1 207 F8
Ariadne Rd BN11 182 B1
Ariel Ct BN15 183 D4
Arkendale RH19 9 A4
Arlington Ave BN12 181 B1
Arlington Cl BN12 181 B1
Arlington Cres Brighton BN1 168 E5
East Preston BN16 180 B3
Armada Ct PO20 202 B5
Armada Way BN16 199 A6
Armadale Rd PO19 173 C7
Armdale Rd BN17 198 B6
Arne Cl RH11 17 F3
Arne Gr RH6 1 E5
Arnell Ave PO20 206 E7
Arnfield Cl RH11 17 E5
Arnhem Rd PO21 195 B5
Arnold St BN2 188 C7
Arnold Way PO18 171 C7
Arnside Cl BN15 183 C5
Arran Cl RH11 18 B3
Arran Gate PO21 195 E3
Arrancourt RH12 36 B2
Arrivals Rd RH6 5 F8
Artel Croft RH10 19 A6
Artex Ave BN16 179 C3
Arthur Bliss Ho RH16 86 A8
Arthur Rd Crawley RH11 17 E6
Horsham RH13 36 D1
Arthur St BN3 187 A8
Arun Bsns Pk PO22 195 E5
Arun Cl Amberley BN18 138 E7
Lancing BN15 183 C7
Rustington BN16 199 C6
Worthing BN13 181 D7
Arun Cres BN13 181 C7
Arun Ct East Preston BN16 200 A5
Littlehampton BN17 178 D3
1 Pulborough RH20 98 C2
13 Shoreham-by-Sea BN43 185 C8
Arun L Ctr PO22 195 F5
Arun Par BN17 198 D3
Arun Prospect RH20 98 A1
Arun Rd Billingshurst RH14 55 C1
Bognor Regis PO21 195 A4
Arun Ret Pk PO22 195 E6
Arun St BN18 158 B2
Arun Terr BN18 158 A2
Arun Vale RH20 117 C5
Arun Vale Cty Inf Sch BN17 198 D5
Arun Way Bognor Regis PO21 205 B8
Horsham RH13 36 E1
Arundale Sch RH20 98 D2
Arundel By-Pass BN18 158 B2
Arundel Castle BN18 158 B3
Arundel CE (A) Prim Sch BN18 157 F2
Arundel Cl Bognor Regis PO21 195 A4
Conford GU30 24 D8
Crawley RH10 19 C6
Shoreham-by-Sea BN43 185 C8
Southwater RH13 58 A1
Arundel Ct 6 Brighton BN2 188 E4
Burgess Hill RH15 106 F4
Ferring BN12 200 F4
14 Shoreham-by-Sea BN43 185 C8
10 Worthing BN11 181 F2
Arundel & District Hospl BN18 158 A3
Arundel Dr BN17 178 C5
Arundel Gdn 9 BN16 199 C5
Arundel Mews 10 BN2 188 E4
Arundel Pl BN2 188 E3
Arundel Rd Angmering BN16 179 F6
Brighton BN2 188 E4
Fontwell BN18, PO20 155 F3
Littlehampton BN17 198 D6
Selden BN13, BN16 180 C8
Walberton BN18 156 D2
Walberton BN18 156 D2
Worthing BN13 181 D8
Arundel St BN2 188 E3
Arundel Sta BN18 158 C1
Arundel Terr BN2 188 E3
Arundel Villas GU30 24 D8
Arundel Way PO22 197 B5
Arundel Wildfowl Reserve BN18 158 C5
Arunside RH12 36 A1
Arunside Cty Prim Sch RH12 36 A2
Arunside Ind Est BN17 198 C6
Ascot Cl PO20 201 F8
Ascot Way BN16 199 E6
Ash Cl Crawley Down RH10 21 C8
Findon BN14 161 E6
Hove BN3 167 C3
Ash Ct BN42 165 F1
Ash Gr Bognor Regis PO22 195 C6
Fernhurst GU27 49 A6
Haywards Heath RH16 85 D2
Liphook GU30 25 D3
Worthing BN11 182 E2
Ash Grove Ind Pk PO22 195 D7
Ash Ho RH14 55 C1
Ash Keys RH10 18 E5
Ash La BN16 199 C5
Ash Rd Crawley RH10 19 A8
Southwater RH13 57 E1
Ashacre La BN13 182 A7
Ashacre Mews BN13 181 F7
Ashacre Way BN13 182 A6
Ashburnham Cl Brighton BN1 168 E5
Chichester PO19 172 D7
Worthing BN13 181 B5
Ashburnham Dr BN1 168 E5
Ashburnham Rd RH10 19 A4
Ashby Ct RH13 36 E1
Ashcroft 1 BN43 185 D7
Ashcroft Cl BN43 185 D8
Ashcroft La PO8 128 F6
Ashcroft Way PO21 205 A8
Ashdown 12 BN3 187 C6
Ashdown Cl Angmering BN16 179 F4
Haywards Heath RH16 86 B4
Ashdown Dr RH10 18 E3
Ashdown Gate RH19 9 D2
Ashdown Hospl The RH16 85 D6
Ashdown Llama Farm RH18 44 E4
Ashdown Rd 7 Brighton BN2 188 B8
Forest Row RH18 23 F2
Worthing BN11 182 D3
Ashdown View RH19 22 E7
Ashenground Cl 5 RH16 85 E3
Ashenground Rd RH16 85 E3
Ashfield Cl GU29 92 E8
Ashfield Rd GU29 92 E7
Ashfold Ave BN14 162 A1
Ashfold Crossways RH17 60 D6
Ashford Rd BN1 168 A2
Ashington CE (C) Prim Sch RH20 120 F5
Ashington Ct Brighton BN2 188 F6
4 Worthing BN14 182 D5
Ashleigh Cl Angmering BN16 180 A6
Horley RH6 1 F3
Ashleigh Rd RH12 36 C4
Ashley Cl BN1 167 E7
Ashley Ct BN3 187 C5
Ashlings Way Hove BN3 166 E2
Shoreham-by-Sea BN43 165 B1
Ashmere Gdns PO22 196 D5
Ashmere La PO22 196 D5
Ashmore Ho RH11 5 D1
Ashmore La RH12 16 C6
Ashton Gdns BN16 199 C4
Ashton Lodge 14 BN2 207 B6
Ashton Rise BN2 207 B6
Ashurst CE (A) Prim Sch BN44 122 D5
Ashurst Cl Bognor Regis PO21 195 A6
Horsham RH12 37 A5
Worthing BN12 181 B1
Ashurst Cotts RH19 42 F4
Ashurst Dr Crawley RH10 19 D6
Ashurst Dr Worthing BN12 181 B1
Ashurst Rd BN1, BN2 168 F5
Ashurst Way BN16 180 A3
Ashurstwood Abbey RH19 23 E6
Ashurstwood Cty Prim Sch RH19 23 E6
Ashway RH15 107 A2
Ashwood 5 RH11 18 D5
Ashwood Cl BN11 182 F4
Ashwood Dr BN16 199 C5
Ashwyn Bsns Ctr RH15 106 F5
Aspen Cl RH16 86 B4
Aspen Way Horsham RH12 36 E4
Middleton-on-Sea PO22 196 E6
Aspen Wlk RH16 86 B4
Aston Ct 5 Bognor Regis PO21 195 D3
Crawley RH11 18 B1
Aston Ho 1 BN43 184 E7
Aston Rise RH20 98 C3
Astra Bsns Ctr RH1 2 A7
Astra Cl PO18 171 C5
Astra Ho 21 BN1 187 E5
Athelstan Cl RH10 19 E6
Athelstan Rd BN13, BN14 182 A4
Athelstan Way RH13 58 E8
Athenaeum The 14 BN3 187 C6
Atkinson Ct RH6 2 B2
Atkinson Rd RH10 19 C4
Atlantic Ct 4 BN43 184 F6
Atlingworth St BN2 207 B4
Attlee Ho 5 RH11 18 B2
Attree Ct 6 BN2 188 C6
Attree Dr BN2 188 C6
Auchinleck Ct RH10 21 B7
Auckland Cl RH11 5 D1
Auckland Dr BN2 168 F1
Audrey Cl BN1 167 E5
Augusta Ct 5 PO19 153 A2
Augusta Ho 4 BN11 182 D1
Augusta Pl BN11 182 D1
Augustines Way RH16 85 F4
Aurum Cl RH6 2 B2
Austen Cl RH19 9 B1
Austens GU29 113 C8
Avalon Ct PO10 149 B2
Avalon Way BN13 181 D6
Avebury Cl Bracklesham PO20 202 C5
Horsham RH12 37 A7
Aveling Cl RH10 19 C4
Avenals The BN16 180 A5
Avenue App PO19 172 F7
Avenue Cl GU30 25 B4
Avenue Ct 19 BN3 187 C6
Avenue De Chartres PO19 172 F6
Avenue Gdns RH6 2 C2
Avenue The Bognor Regis PO21 195 B3
Brighton BN2 168 E1
Chichester PO19 153 A2
Dormansland RH19 10 B6
Funtington PO18 150 E7
Hambrook PO18 150 D1
Haslemere GU27 26 F7
Horley RH6 1 F2
Horsham RH13 57 D5
Liphook GU30 25 B4
Shoreham-by-Sea BN43 164 E1
Worthing BN12 181 C4
Avery Cl BN41 165 F4
Aviary Way RH10 8 C1
Avila Ho 3 BN11 182 C2
Avisford Park Rd BN18 156 F1
Avisford Terr PO21 194 D3
Avocet Quay PO10 169 C7
Avocet Trad Est RH15 106 F2
Avon Cl Bognor Regis PO22 196 D5
Lancing BN15 183 B6
Avon Ct BN15 183 B6
Avon Rd BN17 198 D5
Avon Wlk RH11 17 F5
Avondale Cl Horley RH6 2 A5
Worthing BN12 181 D3
Avondale Rd BN3 187 D7
Avonhurst RH15 107 B3
Awbrook Cl RH17 86 F3
Aylesbury BN3 187 E6
Aylwin Pl PO20 173 C1
Aymer Ho 4 BN3 187 A6
Aymer Rd BN3 187 A6
Aynsley Ct BN3 187 C8
Ayshe Court Dr RH13 36 E3
Azalea Dr GU27 26 F8
Azara Par PO20 202 B6

Babsham La PO21 194 F8
Back La
Balcombe Lane RH10, RH17 41 C7
Plaistow RH14 30 E2
Backwoods Cl RH16 86 B6
Backwoods La RH16 86 B6
Baden Dr RH6 1 E4
Baden Rd BN2 168 D1
Badger Cl BN41 166 B2
Badger Dr RH16 85 C5
Badger Way BN1 168 E6
Badgers Cl RH12 36 F6
Badgers Holt RH20 120 B1
Badgers Way
East Grinstead RH19 9 F2
Loxwood RH14 32 A4
Badgers Wlk Angmering BN16 179 F4
Burgess Hill RH15 107 D2
Badgers Wood RH20 119 D6
Baffin's La PO19 173 A6
Bailey Cl Horsham RH12 36 F7
Littlehampton BN16 179 A3
Bailing Hill RH12 35 D6
Baird Cl RH10 6 A1
Bakehouse Barn Cl RH12 36 E7
Bakehouse Rd RH6 2 A5
Baker Cl RH10 18 D4
Baker St BN1, BN2 207 A7
Baker's La RH13 79 B4
Bakerfield GU29 113 C8
Bakers Arms Hill BN18 158 B3
Bakers Cl RH13 57 F1
Bakers Ct BN13 181 E7
Bakers Mews RH13 60 A3
Bakery La PO21 195 C2
Bala Cres PO22 196 B6
Balchins Cl RH14 76 B8
Balcombe Ave BN14 182 C5
Balcombe CE (C) Prim Sch RH17 40 F2
Balcombe Ct Crawley RH10 19 D7
7 Worthing BN11 182 B1
Balcombe Gdns RH6 2 C2
Balcombe La Ardingly RH17 63 F8
Sharpthorne RH17, RH19 43 E2
Balcombe Rd
Balcombe Lane RH10, RH17 40 F8
Crawley RH10 19 D5
Haywards Heath RH16, RH17 85 D7
Horley RH6 2 B2
Tinsley Green RH10, RH6 6 D5
Balcombe Sta RH17 40 F1
Baldwin Cl Crawley RH10 19 C3
Middleton-on-Sea PO22 196 D6
Baldwins Hill Cty Prim Sch RH19 9 D3
Balfour Cty Inf Sch BN1 168 A3
Balfour Cty Jun Sch BN1 168 A3
Balfour Dr GU33 45 B4
Balfour Gdns RH18 23 E1
Balfour Rd BN1 168 A2
Ball Tree Croft 1 BN15 183 C7
Balliol Cl Bognor Regis PO21 194 E4
Crawley RH10 6 D1
Balmoral RH19 23 A8
Balmoral Cl Bognor Regis PO21 194 E2
Chichester PO19 173 D6
Balmoral Ct 6 Crawley RH11 18 B2
Hove BN3 167 A3
Worthing BN11 182 A2
Baltimore Ct 9 BN3 187 C7
Bamborough Cl RH13 58 A1
Bampfield St BN41 186 B8
Bancroft Rd RH10 19 D5
Banjo Rd BN17 198 E3
Bank La RH11 18 D6
Bank Pas BN44 143 D3
Bank Pass 9 BN11 182 D2
Banks Croft RH20 119 E2
Banks Rd Crawley RH10 19 C5
Scaynes Hill BN8 87 F1
Bankside Bolney RH17 83 C2
Brighton BN1 167 C5
Hassocks BN6 126 F5
Singleton PO18 133 E7
Bankview Cl 2 PO21 195 D4
Bannister Gdns RH20 119 E3
Bannister Way RH16 85 D6
Banstead Cl BN12 181 C1
Bar La RH13 80 B5
Baranscraig Ave BN1 168 A7
Barbary La BN12 200 E5
Barber Cl RH10 19 C2
Barclay Ho 2 BN2 188 C7
Barclays Ct 2 RH20 98 C2
Barcombe Pl BN1 168 F5
Barcombe Rd BN1 168 E4
Barfield Pk BN15 183 F6
Barford Rd PO19 173 A5
Barkdale RH15 107 D5
Barker Cl PO18 172 A7
Barkworth Way RH20 119 C7
Barlavington Way GU29 92 E5
Barley Cl RH10 18 D5
Barley Dr BN6 106 D4
Barleycroft
Albourne Green BN6 125 C6
Cowfold RH13 81 E1
Barleymead RH6 2 B4
Barlow Rd Chichester PO19 172 E8
Crawley RH11 17 E3
Barn Cl Albourne Green BN6 125 C6
Littlehampton BN17 178 E4
Pease Pottage RH11 39 B7
Worthing BN13 181 F7
Barn Cottage La RH16 86 A5
Barn Elm PO18 154 D3
Barn End BN5 123 F5
Barn Field PO22 195 F4
Barn Field Gdns 8 BN2 188 C6
Barn House La RH20 98 C2
Barn La PO22 175 D1
Barn Plat GU29 92 D8
Barn Rd PO20 201 F7
Barn Rise Barnham PO22 176 C5
Brighton BN1 167 D5
Barn Wlk PO20 201 F6
Barnard Gate RH16 85 E7
Barncroft Cl PO20 154 C1
Barnes Rd BN41 186 B8
Barnet Way Hove BN3 166 E3
Worthing BN13 181 D5
Barnett Cl PO20 175 E8
Barnett Rd BN1 168 B2
Barnett's Field PO20 175 D7
Barnfield Cl PO10 150 A1
Barnfield Cotts BN18 156 A2
Barnfield Dr PO19 173 C8
Barnfield Gdns BN6 127 E3
Barnfield Rd RH10, RH11 18 E7
Barnham Cty Prim Sch
Barnham PO22 176 C5
West Barnham PO22 176 B6
Barnham La BN18, PO22 176 C7
Barnham Rd PO20, PO22 176 A6
Barnhouse Cl 7 RH20 98 C2
Barnmead RH16 85 D7
Barns Farm La RH20 141 B7
Barnsfold La RH12, RH14 32 E6
Barnside PO18 171 D7
Barnside Ave RH15 107 D1
Barnside Way GU33 45 B3
Barnsite Cl BN16 199 B6
Barnsite Gdns BN16 199 B5
Barnsnap Cl RH12 36 D6
Barnum Sta PO22 176 B5
Barnwood Cl RH10 19 C7
Baron Cl PO20 175 D7
Barons Ct RH15 107 B2
Barons Mead PO21 205 A8
Barque Cl BN16 199 A6
Barrack La PO21 194 D2
Barrhill Ave BN1 167 F7
Barrington Cl
Haywards Heath RH16 85 F8
Worthing BN12 181 C2
Barrington Rd Crawley RH10 18 D3
Haywards Heath RH16 86 A8
Horsham RH13 36 E2
Worthing BN12 181 C2
Worthing BN12 181 E3
Barrington Wood RH16 85 F8
Barrow Cl BN1 168 C2
Barrow Hill Brighton BN1 168 C2
Henfield BN5 123 F3
Barrowfield RH17 84 F7
Barrowfield Cl BN3 167 C3
Barrowfield Dr BN3 167 D2
Barrowfield Lodge BN3 167 C2
Barry Cl RH10 18 E3
Barry Wlk BN2 188 C6
Bartholomew Cl GU27 27 D8
Bartholomew Sq BN1 207 A5
Bartholomew Way RH12 37 A7
Bartholomews BN1 207 A5
Barton Cl Bognor Regis PO21 194 A1
Worthing BN13 182 A5
Barton Cres RH19 23 A8
Barton Ct BN16 199 B5
Barton La GU28 95 F8
Barton Rd Bognor Regis PO22 195 A7
Chichester PO19 172 E7
Barton Way PO20 202 B6
Barton Wlk RH10 19 B4
Bartons Cty Inf Sch PO22 195 B6
Barttelot Rd RH12 36 D2
Barwell Gr PO10 149 A3
Bashford Way RH10 19 D8
Bashfords La BN14 182 D4
Bashurst Copse RH13 56 F8
Bashurst Hill RH13 56 E6
Basildon Way RH11 17 E2
Basin Rd PO19 173 A5
Basin Rd N BN41 186 B6
Basin Rd S BN3, BN41 186 B6
Basing Hill RH20, RH13 121 C7
Bassels La RH13 102 B5
Bassett Rd PO21 195 C3
Batchmere Est PO20 191 F1
Batchmere Rd PO20 192 A2
Batemans Cl BN13 181 B5
Batemans Ct RH10 19 A3
Bates Rd BN1 167 F2
Bath Ct BN3 187 A6
Bath Pl BN11 182 D1
Bath Rd Emsworth PO10 169 B8
Worthing BN11 182 B1
Bath St BN1 207 F7
Batts Dr BN5 123 D5
Batts La RH20 98 F1
Batworthpark Ho BN18 158 E1
Bavant Rd BN1 167 E2
Baxter Cl RH10 19 B4
Baxter St BN2 188 C7
Baxters La RH17 66 C6
Bay Cl RH6 1 E6
Bay Ct PO21 205 B8
Bay Tree Cl BN43 165 C1
Bay Tree Cotts BN18 156 D1
Bay Tree Gdn BN16 199 F5
Bay Trees Cl BN16 199 F5
Bay Wlk PO21 205 C8
Baycombe La BN18 156 D6
Bayfield Rd RH6 1 E4
Bayford Rd BN17 198 D4
Bayhams Field RH19 42 F6
Bayhorne La RH6 2 C1
Bayley Rd PO20 154 C1
Baylis Cres RH15 106 D4
Baylis Wlk RH11 18 B1
Baynards Rd RH12 12 A2
Bayton Ct PO19 173 B6
Baytree Cl PO19 152 F3
Beach Cl PO21 194 C1
Beach Ct 5 Rustington BN16 199 B4
10 Shoreham-by-Sea BN43 185 A6
Beach Gdns PO20 206 D5
Beach Gn BN43 184 E6
Beach Mews 3 BN17 198 F4
Beach Par BN11 182 F2
Beach Rd Bognor Regis PO21 205 A7
Emsworth PO10 169 A8
Littlehampton BN17 198 E4
Selsey PO20 206 F8
Shoreham-by-Sea BN43 184 E6
Beachcroft Pl BN15 183 F4
Beachside Cl BN12 181 E1
Beachy Rd RH11 18 A1
Beacon Cl BN1 168 A2
Beacon Ct RH13 37 A4

Beacon Hill Dormansland RH7 10 B8
Watersfield RH20 117 A4
Beacon Hurst BN6 127 B3
Beacon Rd BN6 127 D2
Beacon Sq PO10 169 A7
Beacon The RH19 42 E7
Beacon Way BN17 199 A6
Beaconsfield Cl PO22 196 E5
Beaconsfield Cotts RH17 86 F3
Beaconsfield Rd Brighton BN1 188 A8
Chelwood Gate RH17 66 D8
Littlehampton BN17 178 D3
Portslade-by-Sea BN41 186 B8
Beaconsfield Villas BN1 167 F1
Beaconsville Ct BN1 167 F1
Beagle Dr BN18 177 B2
Beal Cres BN1 168 B2
Beale Ct RH11 18 A3
Beale St RH15 106 F1
Bear Rd BN2 188 D8
Bearsden Way RH12 35 D3
Beatrice Ho PO22 195 E4
Beatty Ave BN1 168 D6
Beatty Rd PO21 195 C4
Beaufield Cl PO20 206 D5
Beaufield Gate GU27 27 D7
Beaufort Ct 4 BN16 199 A6
Beaufort Terr BN2 188 C6
Beaumont Cl RH11 17 E5
Beaumont Ct BN16 199 F6
Beaumont Pk BN16, BN17 199 A5
Beaumont Rd BN14 182 D5
Beaver Cl Fishbourne PO19 172 B6
Horsham RH12 36 F6
Beaver Ind Est GU30 25 C3
Beaver Units PO19 173 D5
Beccles Rd BN11 182 B2
Beckenham Terr PO10 149 D4
Becket Rd BN14 182 B3
Beckett La RH11 5 D1
Beckett Way 11 RH19 22 F8
Beckley Cl BN2 188 E5
Beckworth Cl
Haywards Heath RH16 86 A6
Worthing BN13 181 B5
Beckworth La RH16 86 A6
Bedale Cl RH11 18 C4
Bedales RH16 86 D4
Bedales Cnr RH16 86 D4
Bedales Hill RH16 86 D4
Bedelands Cl RH15 107 B5
Bedelands Farm
Local Nature Reserve RH15 107 B6
Bedenscroft PO21 195 A3
Bedford Ave PO21 195 A6
Bedford Pl BN1 187 E5
Bedford Rd RH13 36 D1
Bedford Row BN11 182 E2
Bedford Sq BN1 187 E5
Bedford St Bognor Regis PO21 195 D3
Brighton BN2 188 C4
Bedford Towers 13 BN1 187 E5
Bedham La RH20 97 B5
Beech Ave Bracklesham PO20 202 B6
Chichester PO19 172 E6
Beech Cl Findon BN14 161 E7
Portslade-by-Sea BN41 165 F3
Westergate PO20 175 D7
Beech Fields RH19 9 F3
Beech Gdns
Crawley Down RH10 21 A8
3 Worthing BN14 182 C4
Beech Gr Brighton BN2 168 E3
Midhurst GU29 92 E6
Storrington RH20 119 F3
Beech Hill RH16 86 B4
Beech Ho RH14 77 C8
Beech Holme RH10 21 B8
Beech Hurst Cl RH16 85 D4
Beech Rd Findon BN14 161 E7
Haslemere GU27 27 D8
Horsham RH12 37 B5
Beech Tree Cl RH11 18 D7
Beech View BN16 180 A6
Beech Wood BN5 144 F7
Beechcroft Cl GU30 24 D3
Beechers Rd BN41 165 F3
Beeches Ave BN14 182 D7
Beeches Cres RH10 18 E4
Beeches Head RH19 10 F5
Beeches La RH19 23 D6
Beeches The BN1, BN3 167 D3
Beechey Cl RH10 7 B3
Beechey Way RH10 7 B3
Beechfield Cotts GU28 72 B3
Beeching Way RH19 9 E1
Beechings BN5 123 D5
Beechlands Cl BN16 200 A5
Beechlands Ct BN16 200 A5
Beechside RH10 18 E5
Beechwood 9 Brighton BN1 167 E3
Southwater RH13 79 F8
Beechwood Ave Brighton BN1 167 F4
Worthing BN13 181 F7
Beechwood Cl BN1 167 F4
Beechwood Ct GU33 45 C6
Beechwood La GU28 115 B5
Beechwood Villas RH1 2 A7
Beechwoods RH15 107 A1
Beeding Ave BN3 166 F3
Beeding Cl Bognor Regis PO22 195 E7
Horsham RH12 37 A5
Lancing BN15 183 D8
Beeding Ct 4 BN43 185 B8
Beedingwood Dr RH12 37 F6
Beeechfield Pk PO20 175 C5
Beehive Cl BN12 200 F5
Beehive La BN12 200 F5
Beehive Ring Rd RH10, RH6 6 B4
Beggar's La BN45 146 D6
Beggarshouse La RH6 4 C8
Behenna Cl RH11 17 E5
Belbourne Ct 5 BN1 207 A6
Belfast St BN3 187 B7
Belgrave Cres PO19 172 F3
Belgrave Ct 3 RH20 98 C2
Belgrave Pl 11 BN2 188 D4
Belgrave St BN2 207 B6
Belgravia Ct RH6 2 B3
Belinus Dr RH14 77 C8
Bell Cl PO19 172 F8
Bell Ct PO21 194 C2
Bell Ctr RH10 5 F2
Bell Davies Rd BN17 198 F6
Bell Hammer RH19 22 E8
Bell Ho PO18 170 B7
Bell La Cocking GU29 112 C8
Mark Street TN22 66 F3
Somerley PO20 191 D2
Bell Mead 7 BN3 187 D7
Bell Rd Kingsley Green GU27 27 B3
Warnham RH12 36 A8
Bell Tower Ind Est 7 BN2 188 E4
Bell Vale La GU27 27 C4
Bellamy Rd RH10 19 C2
Belle Meade Cl PO20 175 D5
Belle Vue Ct BN2 188 D5
Bellevue Cotts BN2 188 F8
Bellevue Ct BN1 167 F1
Bellevue Gdns BN2 188 D4
Bellevue La PO10 149 B2
Bellingham Cres BN3 186 D8
Belloc Cl RH10 19 C7
Belloc Ct RH13 37 A3
Belloc Rd BN17 178 C3
Bellscroft Cl BN17 198 F6
Bellview Rd BN13 182 A5
Belmaine Ct 5 BN11 182 C1
Belmer Ct 6 BN11 182 A1
Belmont BN1, BN3 187 E7
Belmont Cl BN6 126 E5
Belmont La BN6 126 C5
Belmont St Bognor Regis PO21 195 D3
Brighton BN1 207 A6
Belmont Terr BN18 177 A2
Belmont Wlk BN13 181 D5
Belsize Cl BN11 182 B3
Belsize Rd BN11 182 B2
Belton Rd BN2 188 B8
Belvedere Ave BN15 183 D6
Belvedere Ct RH10 19 B7
Belyngham Cres BN17 198 D6
Bembridge St BN2 188 C8
Ben Turner Ind Est PO19 173 D6
Benbow Cl BN43 184 F6
Benchfield Cl RH19 10 B1
Benedict Cl BN11 183 B3
Benedict Dr BN11 183 A3
Benett Ave BN3 167 B2
Benett Dr BN3 167 B2
Benfield Cl BN41 166 C1
Benfield Cres BN41 166 C1
Benfield Ct BN41 186 C8
Benfield Cty Jun Sch BN41 186 C8
Benfield Valley Golf Course
BN3 166 C3
Benfield Way BN41 166 C1
Bengairn Ave BN1 168 A7
Benham Ct BN3 187 B5
Benhams Cl RH6 2 A5
Benhams Dr RH6 2 A5
Benizi Ct 11 PO21 195 D3
Benjamin Lodge RH15 107 D3
Benjamin Rd RH10 19 D4
Bennett Cl RH10 19 B2
Bennett Rd BN2 188 E4
Bennett's Terr 4 GU29 92 E7
Bennetts Cl PO20 201 F7
Bennetts Rd RH13 36 E1
Bens Acre RH13 37 A2
Benson Ct BN3 186 E7
Benson Rd BN5 123 F5
Benson's La RH12 16 C1
Bentham Rd BN2 188 C7
Bentons La RH13 101 E3
Bentswood Cres RH16 86 A5
Bentswood Rd RH16 85 F5
Bentworth PO22 176 B6
Bepton Cl GU29 92 D6
Bepton Rd GU29 92 B4
Berberis Ct BN43 165 B1
Beresford Ct 11 BN3 187 D7
Beresford Rd BN2 188 D5
Bereweeke Rd PO22 196 A4
Bergamot Cres BN43 165 C1
Berghestede Rd PO22 195 C6
Berkeley Cl RH11 17 E2
Berkeley Ct Bognor Regis PO21 195 D2
2 Hove BN3 187 E7
9 Littlehampton BN17 198 E4
Berkeley Sq BN11 182 A2
Berkshire Ct BN12 181 B3
Bermuda Ct 2 BN16 199 A6
Bernard Deegan Ho 2 PO21 195 C3
Bernard Pl BN2 188 C7
Bernard Rd Arundel BN18 157 F2
Brighton BN2 188 C7
Worthing BN11 181 F1
Berriedale Ave BN3 186 E6
Berriedale Cl BN15 183 C7
Berriedale Dr BN15 183 C7
Berriedale Ho BN3 186 E6
Berry Cl RH15 107 A5
Berry La Ardingly RH17 64 C7
Bognor Regis PO22 195 A7
Littlehampton BN17 198 F4
Berrybarn La PO20 201 B8
Berrylands GU33 45 C7
Berrylands Farm BN6 105 D1
Berrymeade Wlk RH11 17 E5
Berrymill Cl 6 PO21 195 D4
Berstead Wlk 1 RH11 17 F3
Bersted Green Ct PO22 195 C6
Bersted Mews PO22 195 D5
Bersted St
Bognor Regis PO21, PO22 195 C5
Bognor Regis PO22 195 D5
Bessborough Terr BN15 183 D4
Betchley Cl RH19 9 E3
Betchworth Works RH6 4 D6
Bethune Cl RH10 19 D5
Bethune Rd RH13 36 E1
Bethwines Cl PO18 172 A7
Betts Way RH11 5 D2
Bevan Ct RH11 18 B1
Bevendean Cres BN2 168 E2
Bevendean Prim Sch BN2 168 F1
Bevendean Rd BN2 168 D1
Beverley Cl PO20 206 F7
Beverley Ct 5 Pulborough RH20 98 C2
Southwick BN3 186 D7
3 Worthing BN11 182 B1
Beverley Gdns BN16 179 C3
Beverley Ho 5 BN15 183 E5
Bewbush Dr RH11 17 F3
Bewbush Fst Sch RH11 17 F3
Bewbush Manor RH11 17 E2
Bewbush Mid Sch RH11 17 F3
Bewley Rd BN16 179 F6
Bex La GU29 92 E2
Bickley Ct RH11 18 A3
Bickleys Ct 1 PO21 195 B2
Biggin Cl RH11 18 C4
Bignor Cl Horsham RH12 37 A7
Rustington BN16 199 D6
Bignor Park Rd RH20 116 E5
Bigwood Ave BN3 187 D8
Bilberry Cl RH11 18 B3
Bilbets RH12 36 C3
Billinghurst Rd RH20 120 F8
Billingshurst Inf Sch RH14 77 D8
Billingshurst Jun Sch RH14 77 D7
Billingshurst Rd RH12 35 D3
Billingshurst Sta RH14 77 D7
Billinton Dr RH10 19 B5
Bilsham Cnr BN18 196 F8
Bilsham Ct BN18 176 F2
Bilsham La BN18 176 E1
Bilsham Rd BN18 176 F1
Binderton La PO18 132 D2
Binney Ct RH10 6 E1
Binstead Ave PO22 196 A5
Binstead Cl RH11 18 B8
Binsted Cl BN16 199 B4
Binsted La BN18 177 B7
Birch Ave RH16 86 A3
Birch Cl Angmering BN16 179 F4
Arundel BN18 157 E1
Bognor Regis PO21 194 D3
Crawley Down RH10 21 C8
Haywards Heath RH16 86 B3
Lancing BN15 183 D4
Liss GU33 45 C4
Birch Ct BN42 166 A1
Birch Dr RH14 77 D7
Birch End RH20 119 D7
Birch Gr RH20 119 D5
Birch Grove Cres BN1 168 A5
Birch Lea RH10 6 A1
Birch Tree Cl PO10 149 B4
Birch Tree Ct BN11 182 E3
Birch Tree Dr PO10 149 B4
Birch Tree La RH20 119 E6
Birch Way
Haywards Heath RH16 86 A2
Heath Common RH20 120 B3
Birchen La RH16 85 F8
Birches Cl Selsey PO20 206 C7
Worthing BN13 181 C5
Birches Ind Est RH19 9 A3
Birches Rd RH12 37 B5
Birches The Crawley RH10 19 A7
Mannings Heath RH13 59 C7
West Chiltington Common RH20 119 C8
Birchgrove La RH17 44 A1
Birchgrove Rd RH17 65 E7
Bircholt Rd GU30 24 D4
Birchwood Cl Crawley RH10 19 C3
Horley RH6 2 B4
Birchwood Grove
Cty Prim Sch RH15 107 C1
Birchwood Grove Rd RH15 107 C1
Birdham CE (C) Prim Sch
PO20 191 E5
Birdham Cl Bognor Regis PO21 194 F5
Crawley RH11 18 B8
Birdham Pl BN2 168 E3
Birdham Rd
Apuldram PO19, PO20 172 D2
Brighton BN2 168 F3
South Hayling PO11 189 A2
Birkdale Cl BN13 181 D6
Birkdale Dr RH11 17 D5
Birkdale Rd BN13 181 D6
Birling Cl BN2 168 D1
Birthday Ho GU29 71 B2
Biscay Cl BN16 199 B6
Bishearne Gdns GU33 45 A5
Bishop Bell Mid Sch RH10 18 F3
Bishop Luffa CE Sch (A)
PO19 172 D7
Bishop Luffa Cl PO19 172 D7
Bishop Tufnell CE (A)
Inf Sch PO22 196 C5
Bishop Tufnell CE (A)
Jun Sch PO22 196 C5
Bishop's Cl BN6 126 A7
Bishopric RH12 36 B2
Bishopric Ct RH12 36 B2
Bishops Cl Bognor Regis PO21 205 A8
Fernhurst GU27 49 A6
Henfield BN5 123 E5
Worthing BN13 182 A4
Bishops Ctyd PO19 173 B6
Bishops Ho RH20 140 D8
Bishops Rd Hove BN3 167 C1
Tangmere PO20 154 D2
Bishopsgate Wlk PO19 173 B7
Bishopstone La BN6, RH17 106 A7
Bishopstone Wlk RH11 18 C1
Bitmead Cl RH11 17 E5
Bittern Cl RH11 17 D5
Black Dog Wlk RH10 18 E8
Black Gate La RH20 98 D7
Black Hill RH16 86 A7
Black Horse Way RH12 36 C2
Black Lion St BN1 207 A4
Black Swan Cl RH11 39 B7
Blackberry La Chichester PO19 173 C6
Felcourt RH7 9 E8
Blackberry Rd RH19, RH7 9 D8
Blackbird Cl BN6 106 D3
Blackboy La PO18 172 A7
Blackbridge Ct RH12 36 B2
Blackbridge La RH12 36 A1
Blackbrook La BN8 87 E2
Blackcap Cl Crawley RH11 18 C4
Red Hill PO9 128 C1
Blackdown Rd BN13 181 F7
Blackdown Rural Ind GU27 27 E4
Blackfold Rd RH10 19 A5
Blackgate La BN5 123 E4
Blackheath RH10 19 D8
Blackhouse La
Burgess Hill RH15 107 B4
Foxhill GU28 74 D5
Blackhouse Rd RH12, RH13 38 D5
Blacklands Cres RH18 23 F2
Blackman St BN1 207 A6
Blackman Way PO20 173 B1
Blackmill La PO18, PO20 155 C3
Blackpatch Gr 6 BN43 164 F1
Blacksmith's Cnr BN18 176 F8
Blacksmiths Cl RH20 121 A4
Blacksmiths Cres BN15 183 C8
Blackstone La Blackstone BN5 124 E6
Woodmancote BN5 124 D3
Blackstone Rise BN5 124 E5
Blackstone St BN5 124 E5
Blackstone Way RH15 107 A5
Blackthorn Cl Brighton BN1 167 D3
Crawley RH11 5 C1
Horsham RH13 37 A2
Portslade-by-Sea BN41 166 B2
Blackthorns
Haywards Heath RH16 86 A7
Hurstpierpoint BN6 125 F7
Blackthorns Cl RH16 86 A6
Blackthorns Cty Prim Sch
RH16 86 A6
Blackthorns The RH15 107 B5
Blackwater La RH10 19 D6
Blackwell Cty Prim Sch RH19 9 E3
Blackwell Farm Rd RH19 9 F3
Blackwell Hollow RH19 9 F2
Blackwell Rd RH19 9 F2
Blake Cl RH10 18 F2
Blake Cotts PO18 172 A6
Blake Ct 2 BN2 207 B6
Blakehurst La BN18 159 B3
Blakehurst Way BN17 198 D6
Blakemyle PO21 194 F2
Blaker St BN2 207 B5
Blakes Farm Rd RH13 58 A3
Blakes Rd PO22 196 A4
Blanches Rd RH13 103 A3
Blanches Wlk RH13 103 A3
Blanford Rd PO19 173 C8
Blatchen The BN17 198 F4
Blatchford Cl RH13 36 F3
Blatchford Rd RH13 36 F3
Blatchington Mill Sch BN3 166 F2
Blatchington Rd BN3 187 B7
Bleach's Yard Ind Est GU30 25 B2
Blendworth CE Inf Sch PO8 128 A8
Blendworth La PO8 128 A7
Blenheim Ave BN13 181 E5
Blenheim Cl Crawley RH10 6 D1
East Grinstead RH19 10 A3
Littlehampton BN16 179 B3
Blenheim Ct
Bognor Regis PO21 194 E4
1 Hove BN3 187 A6
Blenheim Dr BN16 179 B3
Blenheim Fields RH18 23 E3
Blenheim Gdns PO19 173 C6
Blenheim Pl 3 BN1 207 A6
Blenheim Rd Horsham RH12 36 D4
Lancing BN15 183 D4
Yapton BN18 176 F2
Bletchley Ct BN1 188 A8
Bligh Cl RH10 18 F4
Blindley Rd RH10 6 D1
Blomfield Dr PO19 153 A1
Blondell Dr PO21 194 D2
Bloomsbury Pl 17 BN2 188 C4
Bloomsbury St 16 BN2 188 C4
Bloor Cl RH12 36 D7
Blount Ave RH19 9 C1
Blue Cedars Cl BN16 179 E4
Bluebell Cl Crawley RH11 18 B3
East Grinstead RH19 9 B1
Haywards Heath RH16 85 F4
Horsham RH12 36 E5
Bluebell Rly RH17, RH19, TN22 43 A5
Bluebird Hill RH20 120 B1
Bluebird Ct 10 BN3 187 A6
Blundell Ave RH6 1 F4
Blunden Dr RH17 84 F8
Blunts Way RH12 36 C3
Blunts Wood Cres RH17 85 B6
Blunts Wood Rd RH17 85 C6
Blytons The RH19 9 B1
Booth Mus of Natural History
BN1 187 E8
Bob La RH17 104 E6
Boddingtons La BN6 127 D3
Bodiam Ave BN12 181 B2
Bodiam Cl Crawley RH10 19 C6
Southwater RH13 58 A2
Bodiam Ct 2 RH16 85 E5
Bodmin Cl BN13 181 D8
Bodmin Rd BN13 181 D8
Bognor Rd
Chichester PO19, PO20 173 C5
Warnham RH12, RH5 14 D4
Bognor Regis Com Coll
Bognor Regis PO21 194 F4
Bognor Regis PO22 195 A5
Bognor Regis Sta PO21 195 C3
Bohunt Com Sch GU30 25 B4
Bolding Way RH16 85 E2
Boleyn Dr PO21 194 B1
Bolney CE (C) Prim Sch RH17 83 C2
Bolney Chapel Rd RH17 105 B7
Bolney Crossways RH17 83 D1
Bolney Ct RH11 17 F3
Bolney Grange Ind Est RH17 105 F6
Bolney Lodge La RH17 83 B3
Bolney Rd BN2 168 F4
Bolney St RH17 83 C3
Bolnore RH16 85 B4
Bolnore Rd RH16 85 C4
Bolsover Rd Hove BN3 186 E8
Worthing BN13 181 E3
Bolters Rd RH6 2 A5
Bolters Rd S RH6 1 F6
Bolton Rd RH10 19 C2
Boltro Rd RH16 85 D5
Bonchurch Rd BN2 188 C7
Bond St Arundel BN18 158 A3
Brighton BN1 207 A5
Bonehurst Rd RH1, RH6 2 A7
Bonfire La RH17 65 D5
Bonnar Cl PO20 206 D6
Bonnar Rd PO20 206 D6
Bonnetts La RH11, RH6 5 A3
Bonny Wood Rd BN6 126 E3
Bookers La PO20 202 C8
Booth Rd RH11 17 E3
Borage Cl RH11 18 A3
Borde Hill Gdns RH17 63 C2
Bordehill La RH16, RH17 63 D3
Borden La GU30 69 A6
Border Chase RH10 7 A2
Border End GU27 26 D6
Border Rd GU27 26 D6
Borers Arms Rd RH10 7 C3
Borers Yard Ind Est RH10 7 C3
Borough Ho GU29 92 F8
Borough St BN1 187 E6
Borrow King Cl BN2 188 D8
Borrowdale Cl RH11 18 B4
Bosham Cty Prim Sch PO18 171 A5
Bosham La PO18 171 B5
Bosham Rd RH10 19 C3
Bosham Sta PO18 171 C7
Bosmere Gdns PO10 149 B1
Bosmere Rd PO11 189 A2
Bost Hill BN13, BN14 161 E3
Bostal Rd BN44 143 C1
Bostal The BN44 144 C1
Bostock Ave RH12 37 A5
Boston Ct RH16 86 A5
Boston Rd RH16 86 A5
Boston St BN1 207 A7
Boswell Rd RH10 19 C3
Botany Cl BN16 199 E4
Bough Beeches RH15 107 C1
Boulevard The
Crawley RH10, RH11 18 E6
Worthing BN12, BN13 181 E4
Boundary Cl Crawley RH10 18 E7
Worthing BN11 182 B1
Boundary Pas 6 BN3 187 E6
Boundary Rd Balcombe RH17 41 B4
Brighton BN2 188 F4
Crawley RH10 18 E7
Portslade-by-Sea BN3, BN41 186 C7
Shoreham-by-Sea BN15 184 B5
Worthing BN11 182 B1
Boundary Way BN16 200 B6
Boundstone Cl BN15 183 D7
Boundstone Com Coll BN15 183 D7
Boundstone La BN15 183 D6
Bourg-De-Peage Ave RH19 10 A1
Bourne Cl PO19 172 A7
Bourne Com Coll The PO10 149 F1
Bourne Ct Bracklesham PO20 202 A6
Brighton BN1 167 D4
Bourne The BN6 126 E5
Bourne View Cl PO10 149 F2
Bourne Way GU29 92 E6
Bourns Ct RH13 36 E3
Bowater Rd RH10 19 C3
Bowen Ct 4 BN3 187 C6
Bower La RH20 119 D6

Bower The RH16 85 D5
Bowerhill Cotts RH19 43 F6
Bowers Pl RH10 21 B8
Bowes Hill PO9 128 E3
Bowhill La PO18 151 D7
Bowley La PO20 193 E5
Bowling Green Cl PO21 194 B1
Bowling Green La RH12 36 D3
Bowman Ct RH11 18 D7
Bowmans Cl BN44 143 D4
Bowness Ave BN15 183 C5
Bowness Cl 7 RH11 17 D5
Bowring Way BN2 188 D4
Box Cl RH11 18 C1
Box La RH19 23 E6
Box Tree Ave BN16 199 B5
Box's La RH17 66 C6
Boxall Wlk RH13 36 D1
Boxes La RH17 65 C5
Boxgrove BN12 181 B4
Boxgrove CE Prim Sch PO18 154 D4
Boxgrove Cl BN15 183 F8
Boxgrove Gdns PO21 194 D2
Boxgrove Ho Boxgrove PO18 154 D3
Littlehampton BN17 178 B3
Boxham La PO20 192 D3
Boyce's St BN1 207 F5
Bracken Cl Copthorne RH10 7 B2
Crawley RH10 18 F8
Heath Common RH20 120 B2
Bracken Gr RH12 37 B5
Bracken La RH20 120 B2
Brackenbury Cl BN41 166 B2
Brackenside RH6 2 B4
Bracklesham Cl PO20 202 B6
Bracklesham Ct PO20 202 B6
Bracklesham La PO20 202 B7
Bracklesham Rd PO11 189 B2
Bracknell Wlk RH11 17 E3
Bradbury Rd RH10 19 C3
Brading Rd BN2 188 C7
Bradlond Cl PO21 195 A3
Bradshaw Rd PO19 173 C8
Braemar Ho 5 BN1 187 E6
Braemar Way PO21 194 F7
Braemore Ct BN3 186 E6
Braemore Rd BN3 186 E6
Braeside Ave BN1 168 A7
Braeside Cl GU27 26 F8
Brainsmead RH17 84 F7
Brainsmead Cl RH17 84 F7
Bramber Ave Hove BN3 166 F3
Storrington RH20 119 C2
Bramber Castle BN44 143 F2
Bramber Cl Bognor Regis PO21 195 A4
Crawley RH10 18 E8
Haywards Heath RH16 85 D4
Horsham RH12 37 B5
Lancing BN15 183 D8
Bramber Ct 8 Hove BN3 187 B7
2 Shoreham-by-Sea BN43 185 B8
2 Worthing BN11 181 F2
Bramber Cty Fst Sch BN14 182 F6
Bramber Rd Chichester PO19 173 B5
Steyning BN44 143 D2
Worthing BN14 182 E6
Bramber Sq BN16 199 C6
Bramber Way RH15 107 A4
Bramble Cl Copthorne RH10 7 B3
Worthing BN13 181 D7
Bramble Cres BN13 181 D8
Bramble Gdns RH15 106 D4
Bramble Hill RH17 40 F2
Bramble La BN13 181 D7
Bramble Mead RH17 40 F1
Bramble Rise BN1 167 C5
Bramble Twitten RH19 10 A1
Bramble Way BN1 168 C6
Brambledean Rd BN41 186 B7
Brambles BN6 126 F5
Brambles The RH17 85 A6
Brambletye Rd RH10 19 A5
Brambletye Sch RH19 23 C5
Brambletyne Cl BN16 180 A6
Brambling Cl RH13 37 A1
Brambling La GU29 70 C3
Brambling Rd Horsham RH13 37 A1
Red Hill PO9 128 D1
Bramblings The BN16 199 D5
Bramfield Rd PO22 196 C4
Bramlands La BN5 145 D8
Bramley Cl Crawley RH10 18 F6
Worthing BN14 182 D6
Bramley Gdns
Bognor Regis PO22 195 B7
Hermitage PO10 169 D8
Bramley Rd BN14 182 D6
Bramley Wlk RH6 2 C3
Brampton Cl PO20 206 D7
Brandy Hole La PO19 152 E2
Brangwyn Ave BN1 167 E5
Brangwyn Cres BN1 167 E6
Brangwyn Ct BN1 167 E5
Brangwyn Dr BN1 167 E5
Brangwyn Way BN1 167 E5
Brantridge La RH17 62 B6
Brantridge Rd RH10 18 F4
Brantridge Sch RH17 62 A8
Brasslands Dr BN41 165 F1
Braybon Ave BN1 167 F4
Braybon Bsns Pk RH15 106 E2
Braypool La BN1 167 D7
Brazwick Ave PO21 194 F7
Breach Ave PO10 150 A2
Breach Cl BN44 143 D4
Bread La BN17 197 F6
Bread St BN1 207 A6
Bream La PO20 206 B8
Brecon Cl BN13 181 F7
Brecon Ct 6 BN3 187 C7
Brede Cl BN2 188 F5
Breezehurst Dr RH11 17 F3
Bremner Ave RH6 1 F4
Brendon Rd BN13 181 E7
Brendon Way BN16 199 B6
Brent Ct PO10 169 A8
Brent Rd PO21 195 A4
Brentwood Cl BN1 168 B3
Brentwood Cres BN1 168 B3
Brentwood Rd BN1 168 B3
Brettingham Cl RH11 17 E3
Bretton RH15 106 E5
Brewells La GU33 46 A5
Brewer Rd RH10 18 E4
Brewer St BN2 207 B7
Brewers Yd RH20 119 D1
Brewery Hill BN18 158 B2
Brewhurst La RH14 32 A2
Breydon Wlk RH10 19 B4
Briar Ave PO20 190 F1
Briar Cl Angmering BN16 179 F4
Crawley RH11 5 C1
Oving PO20 174 C6
Yapton BN18 176 F3
Briar Wood GU33 45 C7
Briars Wood RH6 2 C4
Briarswood Cl RH10 19 D8
Brick Kiln Cl RH13 60 A3
Brickfield Cl PO21 195 B5
Bricklands RH10 21 B7
Brickyard La RH10 21 B8
Brideake Cl RH11 18 A3
Brideoake Cl PO19 172 E8
Bridge Cl Burgess Hill RH15 106 F4
Lancing BN15 183 E5
Worthing BN12 181 C4
Bridge Meadows GU33 45 B4
Bridge Rd Chichester PO19 173 C7
Emsworth PO10 149 B1
Haslemere GU27 27 C7
Haywards Heath RH16 85 F6
Littlehampton BN17 198 B6
Rudgwick RH12 33 D7
Worthing BN14 182 D3
Bridge Road Bsns Pk RH16 85 F7
Bridgefield Cl GU29 92 E6
Bridgefoot Path PO10 169 B8
Bridgelands RH10 7 A3
Bridgersmill RH16 85 D6
Bridges Ct RH12 37 A5
Bridgeway The PO20 206 D6
Bridgnorth Cl BN13 181 B5
Bridle Cl BN44 144 B2
Bridle Rd BN18 156 D4
Bridle Way RH10 19 D7
Bridle Way The PO20 206 D7
Bridorley Cl PO21 194 B2
Brierley Gdns BN15 183 F6
Brigden St BN1 207 F7
Brigham Pl PO22 196 D4
Brighton Coll BN2 188 C5
Brighton Coll of Tech
Brighton BN1 207 A6
Brighton BN2 207 B7
Brighton BN1 207 F8
Brighton Ctr The BN1 207 F5
Brighton General Hospl BN2 188 D7
Brighton & Hove
Golf Course BN41 166 D6
Brighton & Hove
High Sch for Girls BN3 187 E6
Brighton & Hove Stad BN3 167 B1
Brighton, Hove & Sussex
Sixth Form Coll BN3 187 E8
Brighton Marina BN2 188 F2
Brighton Marina Village BN2 188 F3
Brighton Mus & Art Gall BN1 207 A5
Brighton Pl BN1 207 A5
Brighton Race Course BN2 188 E7
Brighton Rd Crawley RH11 18 D4
Handcross RH17 61 C8
Hassocks BN6 126 D2
Horley RH6 1 F2
Hurstpierpoint BN6 125 F3
Lancing BN43 183 C3
Mannings Heath RH13 59 C6
Pease Pottage RH10, RH11 39 B4
Shoreham-by-Sea BN43 185 B7
Woodmancote BN5 124 A3
Worthing BN11, BN15, BN43 183 C3
Brighton Rd
(Pease Pottage Hill) RH11 39 C8
Brighton Road
Hornbrook Hill RH13 58 F8
Brighton Sea Life Ctr BN1 207 A4
Brighton Sq BN1 207 A5
Brighton Sta BN1 207 A6
Brills La BN1, BN2 207 A4
Brinfast La PO20 192 F4
Brinsbury Coll of Agriculture
& Horticulture RH20 76 F1
Brisbane Cl Crawley RH11 5 D1
Worthing BN13 181 C6
Brisbane Ho GU29 92 E6
Bristol Ave BN15 184 B5
Bristol Cl RH10 6 D1
Bristol Gate BN2 188 D4
Bristol Gdns Brighton BN2 188 E4
Chichester PO19 152 F2
Bristol Mews 3 BN2 188 E4
Bristol Pl BN2 188 E4
Bristol Rd BN2 188 C4
Bristol St BN2 188 E4
Britannia Ct PO18 171 A5
British Engineerium (Mus)
BN3 167 B2
Briton's Croft BN44 143 C3
Brittany Ct BN3 186 D7
Brittany Rd Hove BN3, BN41 186 D6
Worthing BN14 182 C4
Britten Cl RH11 17 F3
Britten's La BN18, PO18, PO20 155 E4
Broad Croft PO9 128 E3
Broad Green Ave RH15 107 C2
Broad Meadow PO18 170 D8
Broad Piece BN17 198 B6
Broad Rd PO18 150 D2
Broad Rig Ave BN3 166 D3
Broad St Brighton BN2 207 A4
Cuckfield RH17 85 A6
Broad Strand BN16 199 D3
Broad View PO20 206 F7
Broad Wlk Crawley RH10, RH11 18 D6
Heyshott PO18 113 D5
Broad Wlk The PO18 151 C6
Broadbridge Cotts RH20 121 A4
Broadbridge Ct PO18 171 C7
Broadbridge Dr PO18 171 C7
Broadbridge Heath Rd RH12 35 D4
Broadbridge La RH6 7 B8
Broadbridge Mill PO18 171 C7
Broadbridge Ret Pk RH12 35 E3
Broadfield RH19 42 E7
Broadfield Barton 4 RH11 18 B2
Broadfield Dr RH11 18 B3
Broadfield East Cty Fst Sch
RH11 18 C2
Broadfield East Cty Mid Sch
RH11 18 C2
Broadfield North Cty Fst &
Mid Sch RH11 18 B2
Broadfield Pl RH11 18 B2
Broadfields BN2 168 E3
Broadfields Rd BN2 168 E3
Broadford Bridge Rd RH20 99 E4
Broadlands Horley RH6 2 C4
Hurstpierpoint RH15 127 B8
Broadmark Ave BN16 199 C4
Broadmark Beach BN16 199 C3
Broadmark Ho 4 BN16 199 C5
Broadmark La BN16 199 C4
Broadmark Par 2 BN16 199 C5
Broadmark Way BN16 199 C4
Broadmead RH6 2 C4
Broadview Gdns BN13 181 E8
Broadwater Bvd BN14 182 D5
Broadwater CE (A) Prim Sch
BN14 182 C5
Broadwater Hall BN14 182 C4
Broadwater Ind Est BN14 182 F5
Broadwater La RH13 58 D2
Broadwater Manor Sch BN14 182 D5
Broadwater Rd BN11, BN14 182 D4
Broadwater St E BN14 182 D5
Broadwater St W BN14 182 C6
Broadwater Way BN14 182 D6
Broadway PO20 206 C8
Broadway Ct 11 BN43 185 C8
Broadway The Chichester PO19 153 A2
Crawley RH10 18 D6
Haywards Heath RH16 85 D4
Shoreham-by-Sea BN15 184 B5
Broadwood Cl RH12 37 A5
Broadwood Rise RH11 18 A2
Brock End RH17 84 E8
Brock Rd RH11 5 B1
Brockhurst BN2 188 F7
Brockhurst Cl RH12 35 F1
Brockhurst Farm RH20 117 B5
Brockley Cl BN14 182 C4
Bromley Cl BN6 127 A4
Bromley Rd BN2 207 B8
Brompton Cl BN1 167 E6
Brontes The RH19 9 D1
Bronze Cl PO22 195 C7
Brook Ave Bosham PO18 171 B5
Hassocks BN6 126 F3
Brook Barn Way BN12 181 E1
Brook Cl Bognor Regis PO21 194 F4
East Grinstead RH19 10 B1
Storrington RH20 119 F3
Worthing BN11 183 A4
Brook Cotts PO10 149 D3
Brook Gdns PO10 169 A8
Brook Gn RH17 62 E1
Brook Hill RH13 81 E3
Brook Ho 6 RH20 98 C2
Brook La Coldwaltham RH20 117 C5
Faygate RH12 37 C8
Ferring BN12 200 E6
Haywards Heath RH16 85 F8
Brook Rd RH12 36 E6
Brook St RH17 62 F2
Brook The RH13 58 A2
Brook Way BN15 183 F5
Brookdean Rd BN11 183 B3
Brookenbee Cl BN16 179 B3
Brooker Pl BN3 187 A7
Brooker St BN3 187 A7
Brooker's Rd RH14 77 D7
Brookfield La River GU28 72 D1
Upperton GU28 72 F2
Brookfield Way RH14 77 D6
Brookham Sch GU30 25 E2
Brookhill Cl RH10 7 A3
Brookhill Rd RH10 7 A3
Brookhouse Bottom RH17 66 D4
Brookland Way RH20 117 C5
Brooklands Bognor Regis PO21 194 A1
Shoreham-by-Sea BN15 184 C6
Brooklands Cotts PO18 130 E2
Brooklands
Pleasure Grounds The BN11 183 C4
Brooklands Rd RH11 18 C1
Brooklands Trad Est BN14 182 C3
Brooklands Way RH19 22 D8
Brooklyn Ave BN11 181 F2
Brooklyn Ct 4 BN11 181 F2
Brooks La Bognor Regis PO22 195 E4
Bognor Regis PO22 195 E5
Broadbridge PO18 171 D7
Brooks La W PO22 195 D5
Brooks The RH15 106 E5
Brooks Way RH20 98 C2
Brookside Ashington RH20 121 A4
Copthorne RH10 7 A3
Crawley RH10 18 F7
Runcton PO20 173 E1
Brookside Ave BN16 179 C3
Brookside Cl Ferring BN12 180 E3
Runcton PO20 173 E1
Brookside Ind Est BN16 179 F3
Brookside Rd BN12, BN16 200 D4
Brooksmead PO22 195 E4
Brookview Coldwaltham RH20 117 C5
Copthorne RH10 7 A3
Brookway Burgess Hill RH15 107 C3
Haywards Heath RH16 86 A8
Brookwood RH6 2 B4
Brookwood Ho RH6 2 B6
Broomcroft Rd PO22 196 C4
Broomdashers Rd RH10 18 F7
Broome Cl RH12 36 D5
Broomers Hill La RH20 98 E4
Broomers Hill Pk RH20 98 D5
Broomers La PO20 191 F6
Broomfield Ave BN13, BN14 182 B5
Broomfield Dr
Billingshurst RH14 77 E8
Portslade-by-Sea BN41 166 A3
Broomfield Gdns BN5 123 E5
Broomfield Rd Henfield BN5 123 E5
Selsey PO20 206 F8
Brou Cl BN16 200 B5
Brougham Ct 10 BN11 183 B3
Brougham Rd BN11 183 B3
Brougham Wlk 1 BN11 183 B3
Brow Cl RH20 119 B1
Brow The RH15 107 A2
Brown's La RH20 119 D1
Browning Cl RH10 19 C7
Browning Rd Lancing BN15 183 E8
Worthing BN11 182 B3
Browning's Hill RH13 81 C2
Brownings The 1 RH19 9 C1
Browns Wood RH19 9 E4
Broxmead La Bolney RH17 83 D4
Slough Green RH17 84 A5
Broyle Cl PO19 152 F1
Broyle Rd PO19 173 A8
Bruce Ave BN11 181 F3
Bruce Cl RH16 85 E3
Bruce Way BN11 181 F3
Brunel Ctr RH10 5 F2
Brunel Pl RH10 18 E5
Brunswick Cl
Bognor Regis PO22 196 A5
Crawley RH10 19 A4
Brunswick Ct RH10 19 A4
Brunswick Mews BN3 187 D5
Brunswick Pl BN3 187 D6
Brunswick Rd Hove BN3 187 D6
Shoreham-by-Sea BN43 184 F7
Worthing BN11 182 C1
Brunswick Row BN1 207 A7
Brunswick Sq BN3 187 D5
Brunswick St E BN3 187 D5
Brunswick St W BN3 187 D5
Brunswick Terr BN1, BN3 187 D5
Brushes La RH16 86 B8
Brushwood Rd RH12 37 B6
Bryce Cl RH12 37 A5
Buchans Lawn RH11 18 B2
Buci Cres BN43 165 C1
Buck Barn Bglws RH13 80 A2
Buckbarn Crossroads RH13 80 B2
Buckhurst Cl RH19 9 C3
Buckhurst Mead RH19 9 C4
Buckhurst Way RH19 9 C3
Buckingham Ave BN43 164 E1
Buckingham Cl
4 Brighton BN1 207 F7
Shoreham-by-Sea BN43 185 A8
Buckingham Ct Crawley RH11 18 B2
Worthing BN14 182 B7
Buckingham Cty Mid Sch
BN43 184 F8
Buckingham Dr
Chichester PO19 173 D6
East Grinstead RH19 23 A8
Buckingham Gate RH6 6 C7
Buckingham Lodge BN1 207 F7
Buckingham Mews 10 BN43 164 F1
Buckingham Pl BN1 207 F7
Buckingham Rd Brighton BN1 207 F6
Shoreham-by-Sea BN43 184 F8
Worthing BN11 182 D2
Buckingham St Brighton BN1 207 F6
Shoreham-by-Sea BN43 184 E7
Buckland Dr PO21 194 B2
Buckler St BN41 186 B8
Buckley Cl BN3 166 E4
Buckley Pl RH10 21 A8
Buckmans Rd RH11 18 D6
Bucknor Cl PO21 194 C2
Bucks Green Sch RH12 33 B7
Bucksham Ave PO21 194 F7
Buckshead Hill RH13 59 F7
Buckswood Dr RH11 18 A4
Buckwish La BN5 123 C4
Buddington La GU29 70 F3
Budgen Cl RH10 6 D1
Buffbeards La GU27 26 E6
Bugshill La GU29 91 D1
Bulbeck Cl RH15 106 E1
Bulkington Ave BN14 182 B4
Bull Hill GU33 46 A4
Bull's La RH13, RH17 82 D4
Bulldogs Bank RH19 42 F5
Buller Rd BN2 168 D1
Bullfinch Cl Horley RH6 1 E4
Horsham RH12 36 C7
Bunbury Cl RH20 120 B2
Bunch La GU27 27 B8
Bunch Way GU27 27 A6
Buncton Crossways BN44 142 C7
Buncton La RH17 83 E3
Bungalows The BN18 156 D1
Bunting Cl RH13 36 F3
Bunyan Cl RH11 17 E3
Burbeach Cl RH11 18 B3
Burch Gr BN18 156 D1
Burchell Ct BN15 183 F7
Burchens The BN14 182 C6
Burchett Wlk PO21 194 F5
Burchetts Cl RH16 85 E2
Burdett Cl RH10 19 D5
Burdock Cl RH11 18 A2
Burdocks Dr RH15 107 D1
Burford Cl BN13, BN14 182 A7
Burford Rd RH13 36 E2
Burgess Hill Sch RH15 107 B2
Burgess Hill Sta RH15 107 B2
Burgh Cl RH10 6 D1
Burgh Hill Rd GU30 25 A7
Burlands RH11 5 A1
Burleigh Cl RH10 21 B8
Burleigh Ct 4 BN11 182 C1
Burleigh Cty Inf Sch RH10 21 B8
Burleigh La RH10 21 C7
Burleigh Way RH10 21 B8
Burley Cl Lancing BN15 183 E6
Loxwood RH14 32 A4
Burley Rd PO22 196 D4
Burleys Rd RH10 19 C6
Burlington Ct BN11 181 F1
Burlington Gdns
Portslade-by-Sea BN41 166 C1
Selsey PO20 206 F6
Burlington Rd BN12 181 D3
Burlington St BN2 188 C4
Burlow Cl Birdham PO20 191 D4
Brighton BN2 188 E5
Burma Cl RH16 86 C4
Burmill Ct BN16 179 E3
Burndell Rd BN18 177 A2
Burners Cl RH15 107 D1
Burney Ct 5 RH11 18 A3
Burngreave Ct PO21 195 B3
Burnham Ave PO21 195 C3
Burnham Gdns PO21 195 C3
Burnham Pl RH13 36 D1
Burnham Rd BN13 181 E6
Burns Cl RH12 36 E7
Burns Gdns PO22 196 D6
Burns Rd RH10 19 C8
Burns Way Crawley RH12 17 C1
East Grinstead RH19 9 C1
Burnside Cres BN15 183 C5
Burnt House La RH12 17 A7
Burnthouse Bostall BN6 148 C8
Burnthouse La RH13 81 C4
Burrell Ave BN15 183 D5
Burrell Bldgs BN15 183 D5
Burrell Cl RH13 103 A3
Burrell Cotts RH17 84 E8
Burrell Ct RH11 17 F4
Burrell Gn RH17 84 F8
Burrell Rd RH16 85 D6
Burrells The BN43 185 B6
Bursledon Cl PO22 196 A5
Burstead Cl BN1 168 B3
Burston Gdns RH19 9 D4
Burstow Ho RH6 2 B6
Burstowhill La RH17 64 D6
Burton Cl RH6 2 A2
Burton Villas BN3 187 D8
Burtons Ct RH12 36 C2
Burwash Cl BN16 180 B3
Burwash Lodge 1 BN1 168 C1
Burwash Rd Crawley RH10 19 A5
Hove BN3 166 F3
Bury CE (A) Prim Sch RH20 137 F7
Bury Common Cotts RH20 116 F1
Bury Dr BN12 181 B2
Bury Hill BN18, RH20 137 F6
Bury Ho 3 BN14 182 D5
Bury Rd RH20 116 F3
Bush Farm Dr BN41 166 C3
Bushby Ave BN16 199 D5
Bushby Cl BN15 183 C5
Bushfield RH14 30 F2
Busticle La BN15 183 C7
Bute St BN2 188 D5
Butler's Green Ho RH16 85 B4
Butler's Green Rd RH16 85 C4
Butlers Rd RH13 37 B4
Butt La BN18 156 C6
Butterbox La BN8, RH17 87 D4
Buttercup Wlk BN1 168 B7
Butterfield RH19 9 B3
Buttermere Cl RH12 37 B6
Buttermere Way BN16 179 A3
Button Ct BN2 207 B7
Butts Cl RH11 18 B7
Butts Meadow RH14 54 B1
Butts Rd BN42 185 E7

Buxshalls Hill RH16 64 C2
Buxted Rise BN1 168 B5
Buxton Rd BN1 187 E7
By Sunte RH16 85 F8
Bycroft Way RH10 19 B8
Bye Way The PO21 205 C8
Byerley Cl PO10 149 D5
Byerley Way RH10 19 E7
Byeway The PO20 190 C1
Byfield Pl PO22 195 D6
Byfleets La RH12 35 D6
Bylands 3 BN2 188 F5
Bylanes Cl RH17 84 F7
Bylanes Cres RH17 84 F8
Byne Cl RH20 119 E1
Byrd Rd RH11 17 F3
Byron Cl Bognor Regis PO22 196 D6
Crawley RH10 19 B7
Horsham RH12 36 E6
Byron Ct 1 RH16 85 D5
Byron Gr 2 RH19 9 C1
Byron Rd Littlehampton BN16 199 A5
Worthing BN11 182 C1
Byron St BN3 187 A7
Bywater Way PO19, PO20 172 F4
Bywaves PO20 202 C4
Byway The Brighton BN1 168 E5
Middleton-on-Sea PO22 196 E5
Byways PO20 206 E5
Byworth Cl BN2 188 F6

Caburn Ct RH11 18 C4
Caburn Hts RH11 18 C4
Caburn Rd BN3 187 E7
Cackstones The RH10 19 D7
Caedwalla Dr PO20 154 C2
Caernarvon Rd PO19 173 D6
Caffins Cl RH10 18 E8
Cagefoot La BN5 123 E4
Caister's Cl BN3 187 C8
Caius Ct 16 BN43 185 C8
Cakeham Rd
East Wittering PO20 201 D8
East Wittering PO20 201 F7
Cakeham Way PO20 201 E7
Calbourne RH16 85 D5
Caldbeck Ho 7 RH11 17 F3
Calderdale Cl RH11 18 B4
Caledon Ave PO22 196 D5
Caledonian Ho RH11 18 D8
Caledonian Pl 1 BN11 182 D1
Caledonian Rd Brighton BN2 207 B8
Chichester PO19 173 B6
Caledonian Way RH6 6 B8
Callisto Cl RH11 17 E3
Calluna Dr RH10 7 A3
Calvecroft GU30 25 C4
Calvin Wlk RH11 17 E3
Camargue Ct 5 BN11 182 A3
Camber Cl Brighton BN2 188 F5
Crawley RH10 19 C6
Cambourne Ct 4 BN11 182 C2
Cambrai Ave PO19 173 B5
Cambria Cl PO18 171 C5
Cambridge Ave PO20 201 E8
Cambridge Dr PO21 194 F4
Cambridge Gr BN3 187 C7
Cambridge Rd Horsham RH13 36 D2
Hove BN3 187 D6
Worthing BN11 182 D3
Cambridge Wlk PO21 194 F4
Camden St BN41 186 C6
Camden Terr BN1 207 F6
Camelford St BN2 207 B4
Camelot Cl RH13 58 A2
Camelot Ct RH11 17 E6
Camelsdale Cty Fst Sch GU27 26 F5
Camelsdale Rd GU27 26 F5
Campbell Cres RH19 9 B1
Campbell Dr BN16 199 B6
Campbell Rd
Bognor Regis PO21 195 D3
Brighton BN1 207 F8
Crawley RH10 19 C5
Tangmere PO20 154 B1
Campion Rd RH12 36 E5
Canada Cnr GU31 89 B6
Canada Cotts GU29 71 A3
Canada Gr Bognor Regis PO21 195 C3
Easebourne GU29 71 A2
Canada Rd BN18 157 F3
Canal Rd BN18 176 F3
Canal Wharf PO19 172 F5
Canal Wharf Rd PO19 172 F5
Canberra Cl Crawley RH11 5 D1
Horsham RH12 36 F4
Canberra Pl Horsham RH12 36 F5
Tangmere PO20 154 D2
Canberra Rd
Thorney Island PO10 169 C3
Worthing BN13 181 C6
Candleford Gate GU30 25 C4
Canfield Cl BN2 168 D1
Canfield Rd BN2 168 D1
Canhouse La GU30, GU31, GU33 46 C3
Canning Rd PO22 195 F3
Canning St BN2 188 D5
Cannon Pl BN1 207 F5
Canon La PO19 172 F6
Canon's Cl PO21 194 D1
Canonbury Cotts RH12 16 F6
Canons Way BN44 143 E4
Cansiron La RH19 23 F6
Cantelupe Rd RH19 9 F1
Canter The RH10 19 E7
Canterbury Cl
Bognor Regis PO21 194 A1
Chichester PO19 172 F8
Canterbury Ct BN13 181 F3
Canterbury Dr 5 BN2 207 B7
Canterbury Rd Crawley RH10 18 E2
Rustington BN16 199 E6
Worthing BN13, BN14 182 A3
Canton 3 RH16 85 D6
Cants Cl RH15 107 C3
Cants La RH15 107 C3
Canute Rd PO18 171 B5
Canvey Cl RH11 18 C3
Cape Copse RH12 33 D7
Cape The BN16, BN17 199 A5
Capel La RH11 17 F5
Capel Rd RH12 16 A8
Capelia Ho BN11 182 A1
Capenors RH15 106 F1
Capricorn Cl RH11 17 E4
Capsey Rd RH11 17 E6
Capstan Dr BN16 179 A3
Caraway Cl RH11 18 B2
Card Hill RH18 23 F1
Carden Ave BN1 168 B6
Carden Cl BN1 168 A6
Carden Cres BN1 168 A6
Carden Cty Inf Sch BN1 168 B6
Carden Cty Jun Sch BN1 168 B6
Carden Hill BN1 168 B5
Cardew Rd GU33 45 C3
Cardinal Ct 4 BN11 182 A1
Cardinal Newman Sch BN3 187 D8
Cardinal's Dr PO21 194 B1
Carey Ho RH11 18 C6
Carfax RH12 36 C2
Cargo Forecourt Rd RH6 5 D7
Cargo Rd RH6 5 D7
Carisbrooke Cl BN15 183 E8
Carisbrooke Dr BN13 181 B5
Carisbrooke Rd BN2 188 D7
Carleton Rd PO19 172 E8
Carlingford Ct PO21 195 C4
Carlisle Gdns PO19 152 F1
Carlisle Rd BN3 186 F6
Carlton Ave PO21 194 C3
Carlton Ct Horley RH6 2 A5
Portslade-by-Sea BN3 186 C8
Carlton Hill BN2 207 B5
Carlton Hill Cty Prim Sch
BN2 207 B5
Carlton Ho 11 Brighton BN1 167 E2
Worthing BN13 182 A6
Carlton Mews BN11 182 A2
Carlton Pl 5 BN2 207 B5
Carlton Terr BN3 186 C8
Carlton Tye RH6 2 C3
Carlyle Ave BN2 168 D1
Carlyle St BN2 188 C7
Carman Wlk RH11 18 B1
Carnegie Cl BN14 182 C5
Carnegie Gdns BN14 182 D5
Carnegie Ho BN13 181 F6
Carnegie Rd BN14 182 C5
Carnforth Rd BN15 183 C5
Carol Cl BN1 167 F6
Caroline Ct RH11 18 D4
Carolyn Ho BN13 181 E5
Caron Cl BN15 183 E5
Carousel Ct PO21, PO22 195 B5
Carpenters RH14 77 D8
Carpenters Meadow RH20 98 C2
Carron La GU29 92 E7
Carter Rd RH10 19 D3
Carters Way RH14 76 B8
Cartersland GU30 47 B3
Carterslodge La RH17 60 E7
Cartersmead Cl RH6 2 B4
Carvel Way BN16, BN17 199 A6
Carylls Cotts RH12 16 F1
Casher Rd RH10 19 C3
Cashman Lodge BN1 168 A5
Caspian Ct 8 BN1 207 F7
Cassells Rd 2 PO19 153 A2
Cassidy Pl RH20 119 B1
Castle Cl Bramber BN44 143 E2
Worthing BN13 181 F4
Castle Ct BN13 181 F4
Castle Dr RH6 2 C2
Castle Gdns BN18 158 A3
Castle Goring Mews BN13 181 A8
Castle La Bramber BN44 143 E2
West Grinstead RH13 101 F7
Castle Rd
Broadridge Heath RH12 35 D3
Red Hill PO9 128 D1
Worthing BN13 181 F4
Castle Sq BN1 207 A5
Castle St BN1 187 E5
Castle The RH12 36 E7
Castle Way Bramber BN44 143 E3
Worthing BN13 181 F4
Castledean Sch BN2 168 C2
Castlegate RH20 119 B7
Castleman Rd PO19 173 C8
Castlereagh Gn PO22 196 A5
Castlewood Prim Sch RH13 58 A2
Castlewood Rd RH13 58 A2
Caterways RH12 36 A3
Cathedral of Our Lady &
St Philip Howard BN18 158 B3
Cathedral Way PO19 172 E5
Catherington Sch RH11 5 D2
Catkin Way RH16 86 A4
Catslands La BN5 145 C8
Causeway Ct BN18 158 C2
Causeway The Arundel BN18 158 C2
Bognor Regis PO21 205 A8
Causeway The Brighton BN2 188 D6
Horsham RH12 36 C1
Partridge Green RH13 103 A3
Selsey PO20 206 C8
Westlands PO20 191 F6
Worthing BN12 181 E3
Cavalier Cl GU29 92 E7
Cavalier Way RH19 22 F7
Cavell Rd RH10 19 C5
Cavendish Cl Horsham RH12 36 D7
Worthing BN12 181 D3
Cavendish Ho
Bognor Regis PO21 195 D2
12 Hove BN1 187 E5
Cavendish Pl BN1 187 E5
Cavendish Rd PO21 195 C3
Cavendish St 11 Brighton BN2 207 B5
Chichester PO19 172 F7
Cawley Rd PO19 173 A5
Caxton Cl RH10 18 E3
Caxton Ct 4 BN14 182 D4
Caxton Way 15 RH16 85 E4
Cecil Norris Ho 3 BN43 184 F7
Cecil Pashley Way BN43 184 D8
Cecil Rd BN15 183 E4
Cecilian Ave BN14 182 D4
Cedar Ave BN13 181 F6
Cedar Cl Bognor Regis PO21 194 D3
Burgess Hill RH15 107 B5
Crawley RH11 5 C1
Ferring BN12 200 E5
Horsham RH12 36 C3
Lancing BN15 183 D4
Worthing BN13 181 F6
Cedar Cl E PO21 194 D3
Cedar Ct Haslemere GU27 27 B6
Petworth GU28 95 E7
Cedar Dr Chichester PO19 172 E7
Southwater RH13 58 A1
Cedar Lodge RH11 18 D4
Cedar Way
Haywards Heath RH16 86 B4
Henfield BN5 123 F4
Cedars Farm Cl RH14 77 C8
Cedars Gdns BN1 167 E3
Cedars The 1 Brighton BN1 167 E3
1 Brighton BN2 207 B8
Haywards Heath RH16 85 D7
Rustington BN16 199 E6
Cedarwood 6 BN1 167 E3
Celandine Cl 1 RH11 18 B2
Cemetery La Tillington GU28 73 C1
Westbourne PO10 149 F3
Centenary Ho 9 BN1 167 E2
Centenary Ind Est 6 BN2 188 B8
Central Ave Bognor Regis PO21 195 A6
Littlehampton BN16 199 C4
Worthing BN14 161 F3
Central Bldgs 2 PO21 195 D3
Central CE (A) Jun Sch PO19 172 F7
Central Dr Bognor Regis PO21 195 A6
Middleton-on-Sea PO22 197 A5
Centrecourt Cl 5 BN14 182 C4
Centrecourt Rd BN14 182 C4
Centurion Rd BN1 207 F6
Ceres Pl PO22 196 D4
Chadborn Cl BN2 188 D5
Chadds Cotts RH17 39 C1
Chadwick Cl RH11 18 B1
Chaffer La PO20 191 D4
Chaffinch Cl Burgess Hill RH15 106 D4
Crawley RH11 18 D8
Horsham RH12 36 D7
Worthing BN13 181 C5
Chaffinch Way RH6 1 E4
Chailey Cl 2 RH11 18 A3
Chailey Ct 2 RH16 85 F3
Chailey Heritage Craft Sch &
Hospl New Heritage BN8 87 E1
Chailey Rd BN1 168 E4
Chainbridge La PO20 203 C1
Chalcraft Cl GU30 25 A4
Chalcraft La PO21, PO22 194 F5
Chalder La PO20 192 F3
Chaldon Rd RH11 18 C1
Chalet Cl BN12 200 E4
Chalet Gdns BN12 200 F4
Chalet Rd BN12 200 E4
Chalfont Cl PO22 196 E5
Chalfont Dr BN3 167 C3
Chalfont Way BN13 181 D6
Chalk La PO20 203 E7
Chalk Rd Goodwood Park PO18 134 A4
Ifold RH14 31 C3
Chalkdock La PO20 191 A5
Chalkers La BN6 126 B8
Chalkpit La PO18 153 B7
Chalky Rd BN41 166 A3
Challen Cl PO20 174 C6
Challen Ct RH12 36 B3
Challoners RH17 65 C4
Challow Cl BN6 126 E4
Chalmers Ct RH6 4 E6
Chaloner Cl RH16 86 B7
Chaloner Rd RH16 86 B7
Chalvington Cl BN1 168 E6
Champion's Gate RH13 81 A2
Chancellors Pk BN6 126 F4
Chancton Cl
Heath Common RH20 120 B3
Worthing BN11 181 F3
Chancton View Rd BN11 181 F3
Chanctonbury Cl RH20 141 E6
Chanctonbury Dr BN43 164 F1
Chanctonbury L Ctr RH20 119 C2
Chanctonbury Rd
Burgess Hill RH15 107 A1
Hove BN3 187 E7
Chanctonbury Rd
Littlehampton BN16 199 B4
Chanctonbury Ring Rd BN44 142 D6
Chanctonbury View BN5 123 D4
Chanctonbury Way RH11 18 C4
Chanctonbury Wlk RH20 119 D1
Chandler Cl RH10, RH11 18 D4
Chandler Rd PO19 172 E5
Chandlers Reach PO20 191 A7
Chandlers Way BN44 143 C2
Chandos Rd BN11 182 D2
Channel Ct BN15 183 E4
Channel Keep 11 BN17 198 E4
Channel View
Bognor Regis PO21 205 A8
13 Southwick BN42 185 E7
Chantlers Cl RH19 9 C2
Chantrey Rd RH10 18 E3
Chantry Cl Henfield BN5 123 E6
Horley RH6 1 F4
Storrington RH20 119 E1
Chantry Est The RH20 140 E8
Chantry La BN13, RH20 140 E6
Chantry Rd BN13 182 A6
Chantryfield Rd BN16 179 F6
Chapel Cl Burgess Hill RH15 106 F4
Littlehampton BN17 198 C6
Chapel La Ashurst Wood RH19 23 D6
Cootham RH20 119 A1
Copthorne RH10 7 F4
East Ashling PO18 152 A3
Forest Row RH18 23 F2
Horsted Keynes RH17 65 C5
West Wittering PO20 190 F2
Chapel Mews BN3 187 D5
Chapel Pl BN41 186 B7
Chapel Rd Barns Green RH13 56 F2
Charlwood RH6 4 F7
Southwick BN41 186 A7
Worthing BN11 182 D3
Chapel Row East Dean PO18 134 C6
West Hoathly RH19 42 E7
Chapel St Bognor Regis PO21 195 C2
Brighton BN2 207 B5
Chichester PO19 172 F6
Chapel Terr 2 BN2 188 D4
Chapel Wlk BN16 179 F5
Chapelfields RH17 84 F8
Chapman Ct BN13 181 F6
Chapman Rd RH10 19 C2
Chapman's La
East Grinstead RH19 9 B1
East Grinstead RH19 9 D1
Chappell Cl GU30 25 C4
Chappell Croft 2 BN11 182 B2
Charis Ct 18 BN3 187 C7
Charlecote Rd BN11 182 E2
Charles Ave Burgess Hill RH15 106 D2
Chichester PO19 173 D6
Charles Bennett Ct RH16 86 A4
Charles Cl BN3 167 A3
Charles Ct BN11 182 C3
Charles Ho BN12 181 D2
Charles St BN2 207 A4
Charlesfield Rd RH6 1 F4
Charleston Ct RH10 19 B3
Charlesworth Pk RH16 86 C4
Charlmead PO20 201 F6
Charlock Cl RH11 18 A2
Charlock Way RH13 58 A3
Charlotte Ct RH11 18 C6
Charlotte Ho PO22 195 E4
Charlotte St BN2 207 B4
Charlton Mill Way PO18 133 F6
Charlton Rd PO18 134 B6
Charlton St BN44 143 C3
Charltons The BN1 168 D6
Charlwood Cty Fst Sch RH6 4 F7
Charlwood Gdns RH15 107 C5
Charlwood La RH5 4 A5
Charlwood Rd
Burgess Hill RH15 107 D6
Charlwood RH11, RH6 4 E2
Crawley RH6 5 C4
Hookwood RH6 5 C8
Charlwood St PO21 195 B2
Charlwood Wlk RH11 5 B1
Charlwoods Bsns Ctr RH19 9 D2
Charlwoods Pl RH19 9 E3
Charlwoods Rd RH19 9 E3
Charm Cl RH6 1 E4
Charmandean La BN14 182 D8
Charmandean Rd BN14 182 D6
Charmans Cl RH12 37 B5
Charnwood Rd PO22 195 B6
Charrington Way RH12 35 C3
Chartfield BN3 167 A2
Chartfield Way BN3 167 B2
Chartwell Ct BN1 207 F5
Chartwell Rd BN15 183 D5
Chase Cl GU33 45 C4
Chase La GU27 27 E3
Chase Rd GU33 45 C4
Chase The Crawley RH10 19 A5
Nepcote BN14 161 E5
Chatelet Cl RH6 2 B4
Chates Farm Ct BN2 207 B6
Chatfield Rd Chichester PO19 173 C8
Cuckfield RH17 85 A6
Chatfield's Farm RH13 81 E6
Chatfields RH11 18 B4
Chatham Pl BN1 207 F7
Chatham Rd BN11 183 A3
Chatsmore Cath
High Sch (A) BN12 181 A3
Chatsmore Cres BN12 181 B3
Chatsmore Ho BN12 181 A2
Chatsworth Ave GU27 27 C8
Chatsworth Cl BN16 179 B3
Chatsworth Ct 5 BN43 184 F6
Chatsworth Dr BN16 179 B3
Chatsworth Rd Brighton BN1 187 E8
Chichester PO19 173 D6
Worthing BN11 182 D2
Chaucer Ave 3 RH19 9 C1
Chaucer Ct 2 RH16 85 D5
Chaucer Rd Crawley RH10 19 C8
Worthing BN11 182 B3
Chaucer Way PO22 196 D6
Chaucher Ave BN16 199 B5
Chawkmare Coppice PO21 194 F2
Chayle Gdns PO20 206 E6
Cheal Cl BN43 184 F6
Cheam Rd BN16 199 D4
Cheapside BN1 207 A6
Cheeleys RH17 65 C5
Cheesemans La PO18 150 E4
Chelsea Arc RH16 85 E4
Chelston Ave BN3 186 D7
Cheltenham Pl BN1 207 A6
Chelwood Ave BN12 181 C1
Chelwood Cl Brighton BN1 168 C6
Crawley RH10 18 F4
Chelwood Ct RH15 107 A4
Chelwood Gate Rd RH17 66 F7
Chennells Way RH12 36 E5
Chepstow Cl RH10 19 E6
Chepstow Ct BN1 168 F5
Chequer Grange RH18 23 E1
Chequer La PO18 171 D6
Chequer Rd RH19 9 F1
Chequers Cl RH6 2 A4
Chequers Ct RH13 36 E2
Chequers Dr RH6 2 A4
Chequers Quay PO10 169 C8
Cherington Cl BN6 126 B5
Chermont Ct BN16 199 F6
Cherrimans Orch GU27 26 F6
Cherry Ave BN18 177 A2
Cherry Cl Bognor Regis PO21 194 E2
Burgess Hill RH15 106 E3
Cherry Croft BN17 178 D3
Cherry Ct RH13 36 D1
Cherry Gdns Selsey PO20 206 D5
Worthing BN13 161 D1
Cherry La Birdham PO20 191 F5
Bolney RH17 83 C3
Brook Street RH17 62 F5
Crawley RH11 5 C1
Cherry Orchard Rd PO19 173 B5
Cherry Tree Ave GU27 26 F7
Cherry Tree Cl Billingshurst RH14 55 C1
Crawley RH10 19 D8
Worthing BN13 161 D1
Cherry Tree Dr PO20 175 F8
Cherry Tree Lodge 1 BN15 183 D6
Cherry Tree Wlk Horsham RH12 37 B6
Petworth GU28 95 E7
Cherry Trees RH17 84 E8
Cherry Wlk BN13 161 E1
Cherrytree Cotts PO22 176 C5
Cherrywood 5 BN1 167 E3
Cherwell Rd BN13 181 C8
Cherwell Wlk RH11 17 F5
Chesham Cl BN12 181 E2
Chesham Pl BN2 188 D4
Chesham Rd BN2 188 D4
Chesham St BN2 188 D4
Cheshire Cl PO21 195 D4
Cheshire Cres PO20 154 C1
Cheshire Way PO10 150 A2
Chesholt Cl GU27 49 B6
Chesley Cl BN13 181 C6
Chess Brook Gn BN5 123 F7
Chesswood Ave PO22 196 C6
Chesswood Cl BN11 182 F4
Chesswood Cty Mid Sch
BN14 182 E4
Chesswood Rd BN11 182 F4
Chester Ave Lancing BN15 183 E4
Worthing BN11 183 A3
Chester Ct 8 BN3 187 E7
Chester Lodge 1 BN11 182 A2
Chester Terr BN1 168 A1
Chesterfield Cl RH10 8 C4
Chesterfield Rd BN12 181 D3
Chesters RH6 1 E5
Chesterton Cl RH19 22 F7
Chesterton Ct RH13 37 A4
Chestnut Ave Chichester PO19 152 F3
Haslemere GU27 27 C7
Chestnut Cl Angmering BN16 179 F4
Burgess Hill RH15 107 B5
East Grinstead RH19 10 A1
Heath Common RH20 120 B3
Liphook GU30 25 D3
Midhurst GU29 92 E5
Chestnut Ct East Preston BN16 200 A5
Horsham RH13 36 E2
Chestnut End BN5 123 E5
Chestnut Gdns RH12 36 C5
Chestnut Gr Bognor Regis PO22 195 C6
Hurstpierpoint BN6 125 F7
Chestnut Rd Billingshurst RH14 77 D7
Horley RH6 2 B5
Chestnut Way BN5 123 E5
Chestnut Wlk Crawley RH11 5 C1
Felcourt RH19 9 C8
Pulborough RH20 98 B2
Tangmere PO20 154 C1
Worthing BN13 181 C5
Chestnuts Cl RH16 86 A7
Chestnuts The
Haywards Heath RH16 85 F7
Horley RH6 2 A5
Hunston PO20 193 A8

Chestnuts The
Sayers Common BN6 ..... 105 D1
Chesworth Cl RH13 ..... 58 C8
Chesworth Cres RH13 ..... 36 C1
Chesworth Gdns RH13 ..... 36 C1
Chesworth Jun Sch RH13 ..... 36 E3
Chesworth La RH12, RH13 ..... 36 C1
Chet Nole RH19 ..... 9 D2
Chetwood Rd RH11 ..... 17 D2
Cheveley Gdns PO21 ..... 194 E2
Chevening Cl RH11 ..... 18 C1
Cheviot Cl East Preston BN16 .. 200 A6
Worthing BN13 ..... 181 E8
Cheviot Rd BN13 ..... 181 E8
Cheviot Wlk RH11 ..... 18 B6
Cheyne Ct BN43 ..... 185 C7
Cheyne Wlk RH6 ..... 2 A1
Cheynell Wlk RH11 ..... 17 F4
Chichester By-Pass
Chichester PO20 ..... 173 D5
Stockbridge PO19 ..... 172 F4
Chichester Cath PO19 ..... 172 F6
Chichester Cl [15] Brighton BN2 188 D4
Crawley RH10 ..... 18 E2
Hove BN3 ..... 166 E4
Chichester Coll of Arts, Science & Tech PO19 ..... 172 E6
Chichester Ct
[8] Rustington BN16 ..... 199 C5
[1] Worthing BN11 ..... 182 A1
Chichester Dr PO20 ..... 154 D1
Chichester Festival Theatre PO19 ..... 173 A8
Chichester High Sch for Boys PO19 ..... 173 A5
Chichester High Sch for Girls PO19 ..... 172 F5
Chichester Inst of Higher Ed PO19 ..... 173 A6
Chichester Mus PO19 ..... 173 A6
Chichester Pl BN2 ..... 188 D4
Chichester Rd Arundel BN18 .. 157 E3
Bognor Regis PO21, PO22 ..... 195 B5
East Beach PO20 ..... 203 F1
Midhurst GU29 ..... 92 F3
Selsey PO20 ..... 206 E8
Street End PO20 ..... 192 E5
Chichester Sta PO19 ..... 172 F5
Chichester Terr
[19] Brighton BN2 ..... 188 D4
Horsham RH12 ..... 36 D2
Chichester Tutorial Unit PO20 ..... 173 C1
Chichester Way
Burgess Hill RH15 ..... 107 C5
Selsey PO20 ..... 206 G8
Chiddingley Cl BN2 ..... 188 F5
Chiddingly Cl RH10 ..... 19 B5
Chidham La PO18 ..... 170 E6
Chidholm Parochial (C) Prim Sch PO18 ..... 170 E4
Chilcomb RH15 ..... 107 C1
Chilcroft La GU27 ..... 27 B1
Chilcroft Rd GU27 ..... 26 F7
Chilcrofts Rd GU27 ..... 27 A1
Chilgrove Cl BN12 ..... 181 B3
Chilling St RH19 ..... 43 D3
Chillis Wood Rd RH16 ..... 85 C5
Chiltern Cl Crawley RH11 ..... 18 B6
East Preston BN16 ..... 200 A6
Haslemere GU27 ..... 27 B5
Shoreham-by-Sea BN43 ..... 185 C8
Chiltern Cres BN13 ..... 181 E7
Chiltington Cl Burgess Hill RH15 106 F5
West Chiltington Common RH20 119 C7
Chiltington Ct RH12 ..... 36 D4
Chiltlee Cl GU30 ..... 25 C4
Chiltlee Manor GU30 ..... 25 C3
Chiltley La GU30 ..... 25 D2
Chiltley Way GU30 ..... 25 C2
Chine The BN17 ..... 199 A4
Chipley Ct PO21 ..... 195 A4
Chippendale Rd RH11 ..... 18 B1
Chippers Cl BN13 ..... 181 F4
Chippers Rd BN13 ..... 181 F4
Chippers Wlk BN13 ..... 181 F4
Chithurst La
Chithurst GU29, GU30, GU31 .... 69 C4
Domewood RH6, RH7 ..... 7 F7
Chownes Mead La RH16, RH17 . 85 B4
Chrisdory Rd BN41 ..... 165 F3
Christ's Hospital Rd
Horsham RH13 ..... 57 E6
Itchingfield RH13 ..... 57 C6
Christ's Hospital (Sch) RH13 .. 57 D5
Christ's Hospital Sta (West Horsham) RH13 ..... 57 D7
Christchurch Cres PO21 ..... 194 E2
Christchurch Rd BN11 ..... 182 D3
Christie Pl PO22 ..... 195 D6
Christies RH19 ..... 22 D8
Christopher Rd RH19 ..... 9 E1
Christopher Way PO10 ..... 149 B2
Church App [1] BN17 ..... 198 E4
Church Ave RH16 ..... 85 E6
Church Cl Brighton BN1 ..... 167 F5
Burgess Hill RH15 ..... 107 A3
Clapham BN13 ..... 160 F1
Lancing BN15 ..... 183 E8
Lower Beeding RH13 ..... 60 A3
Pagham PO21 ..... 204 E7
Shipley RH13 ..... 101 D8
Upper Beeding BN44 ..... 144 A3
Church Cotts PO20 ..... 202 D6
Church Ct
[3] Haywards Heath RH16 ..... 85 E4
Hove BN3 ..... 166 F1
Church Farm Ct PO20 ..... 202 A8

Church Farm La PO20 ..... 202 A8
Church Farm Wlk BN44 ..... 144 A3
Church Gn BN43 ..... 185 C7
Church Gr RH20 ..... 99 D1
Church Hill Brighton BN1 ..... 167 E7
Midhurst GU29 ..... 92 F8
Pulborough RH20 ..... 98 B2
Pyecombe BN45 ..... 147 C6
Slindon BN18 ..... 156 C5
Church Ho BN17 ..... 198 D4
Church House Cl BN42 ..... 165 F1
Church La Albourne BN6 ..... 125 B5
Ardingly RH17 ..... 63 F8
Ashington RH20 ..... 121 A4
Ashurst BN44, RH13 ..... 122 D5
Barnham PO20 ..... 176 B4
Birdham PO20 ..... 191 E5
Bognor Regis PO22 ..... 195 C5
Boxgrove PO18 ..... 154 D3
Bramshott GU30 ..... 25 C6
Broadridge Heath RH12 ..... 35 D3
Burgess Hill RH16, RH17 ..... 107 F6
Burstow RH6 ..... 6 F7
Bury RH20 ..... 138 A7
Climping BN17, BN18 ..... 177 E1
Cocking GU29 ..... 112 D7
Coldwaltham RH20 ..... 117 C6
Copthorne RH10 ..... 7 B3
Danehill RH17 ..... 66 A3
Ditchling BN6 ..... 127 D3
East Grinstead RH19 ..... 9 F1
Eastergate PO20 ..... 175 E8
Ferring BN12 ..... 200 E6
Funtington PO18 ..... 151 A5
Haslemere GU27 ..... 27 D7
Henfield BN5 ..... 123 E5
Horsted Keynes RH17 ..... 65 C5
Hunston PO20 ..... 193 A8
Lancing BN15 ..... 183 A8
Lodsworth GU28 ..... 72 C2
Lower Beeding RH13 ..... 60 A5
Oving PO20 ..... 174 C7
Pagham PO21 ..... 204 E8
Partridge Green RH13 ..... 102 F3
Poynings BN45, BN6 ..... 146 E7
Pyecombe BN45 ..... 147 C6
Southwater RH13 ..... 57 E1
Southwick BN42, BN43 ..... 185 D7
Steyning BN44 ..... 143 D4
Street End PO20 ..... 192 E3
Tangmere PO20 ..... 154 C1
Upper Beeding BN44 ..... 144 A2
Yapton BN18 ..... 176 F4
Church Mead Keymer BN6 ..... 127 B3
Steyning BN44 ..... 143 E3
Church Meadow PO18 ..... 171 B5
Church Mews PO20 ..... 173 D1
Church Path [3] PO10 ..... 169 B8
Pulborough RH20 ..... 98 B2
Church Platt RH17 ..... 84 E5
Church Rd Aldingbourne PO20 .. 175 A8
Angmering BN16 ..... 179 F5
Bramshott GU30 ..... 25 C6
Broadridge Heath RH12 ..... 35 D3
Burgess Hill RH15 ..... 107 A3
Burstow RH6 ..... 7 A7
Chichester PO19 ..... 173 D7
Copthorne RH10 ..... 7 B3
Crawley RH6 ..... 5 E5
Crawley, Worth RH10 ..... 19 E6
East Wittering PO20 ..... 201 F8
Fernhurst GU27 ..... 49 B5
Haslemere GU27 ..... 27 C7
Haslemere, Shottermill GU27 .. 26 F1
Haywards Heath RH16 ..... 85 E4
Horley RH6 ..... 1 F2
Horley RH6 ..... 2 A3
Horsham RH12 ..... 37 B5
Hove BN3 ..... 187 B6
Littlehampton BN17 ..... 178 C6
Mannings Heath RH13 ..... 59 C5
North Mundham PO20 ..... 173 D1
Partridge Green RH13 ..... 102 F3
Portslade-by-Sea BN41 ..... 186 B7
Rustington BN16 ..... 199 C5
Scaynes Hill RH17 ..... 86 F3
Selsey PO20 ..... 206 E8
Southbourne PO10 ..... 169 F8
Turners Hill RH10 ..... 21 A3
West Hoathly RH19 ..... 42 F6
West Lavington GU29 ..... 93 A6
West Thorney PO20 ..... 169 F1
Westbourne PO10 ..... 149 D3
Worthing BN13 ..... 182 A4
Yapton BN18 ..... 176 F3
Church Road Ind Est RH6 ..... 5 E5
Church Road Trad Est RH6 ..... 5 E5
Church St Amberley BN18 ..... 138 D7
Brighton BN1 ..... 207 A5
Cox Green RH12 ..... 12 E1
Crawley RH11 ..... 18 C6
Cuckfield RH17 ..... 84 E6
Henfield BN5 ..... 123 E5
Liss GU33 ..... 45 A6
Littlehampton BN17 ..... 198 E5
Petworth GU28 ..... 95 F8
Portslade-by-Sea BN41 ..... 186 B7
Rudgwick RH12 ..... 33 E8
Shoreham-by-Sea BN43 ..... 184 F7
Steyning BN44 ..... 143 D3
Storrington RH20 ..... 119 D1
Warnham RH12 ..... 35 F8
West Chiltington RH20 ..... 99 E1
Church Terr Cowfold RH13 ..... 81 E2
Henfield BN5 ..... 123 E5
Church View PO10 ..... 149 D3
Church View Cl RH6 ..... 1 F2

Church Way Bognor Regis PO21 194 A1
[5] Brighton BN2 ..... 207 B6
Singleton PO18 ..... 133 D7
Worthing BN13 ..... 182 A5
Church Way Cl BN13 ..... 182 A5
Church Wlk Burgess Hill RH15 .. 107 A3
Horley RH6 ..... 1 F2
Worthing BN11 ..... 182 F2
Church Wood RH20 ..... 97 B4
Churcher Rd PO10 ..... 149 D4
Churchfarm La PO20 ..... 192 F2
Churchfield RH20 ..... 97 A3
Churchill Ave
Bognor Regis PO21 ..... 194 E4
Horsham RH12 ..... 36 B3
Churchill Ct Crawley RH10 ..... 6 A1
[3] Rustington BN16 ..... 199 C5
Churchill Dr PO10 ..... 149 B4
Churchill Ho Barnham PO22 .. 176 C5
Hove BN3 ..... 166 E4
Churchill Ind Est BN15 ..... 183 C4
Churchill Par RH15 ..... 199 C5
Churchill Sq BN1 ..... 207 F5
Churchill Way RH15 ..... 107 C2
Churchill Wlk PO21 ..... 205 A8
Churchmead Cl PO18 ..... 152 F6
Churchside PO19 ..... 173 A7
Churchwood Dr PO20 ..... 154 D1
Chute Ave BN13 ..... 161 E1
Chute Way BN13 ..... 181 E8
Cidermill La Cudworth RH12, RH5 . 3 F3
Newdigate RH5, RH12 ..... 3 F3
Cinder Hill RH19 ..... 43 B1
Circle The BN16 ..... 200 A4
Circus Par BN1 ..... 207 A7
Circus St BN2 ..... 207 A5
Cissbury Ave BN14 ..... 161 F2
Cissbury Cl RH12 ..... 37 A6
Cissbury Dr BN14 ..... 161 F3
Cissbury Gdns BN14 ..... 162 A2
Cissbury Hill RH11 ..... 18 C4
Cissbury Rd Burgess Hill RH15 .. 106 F1
Ferring BN12 ..... 180 E3
Hove BN3 ..... 187 E7
Worthing BN14 ..... 182 C6
Cissbury Way [5] BN43 ..... 164 F1
City Bsns Ctr Chichester PO19 .. 172 F5
Horsham RH13 ..... 36 D1
City Fields PO20 ..... 154 D2
City Fields Way PO20 ..... 154 D2
Civic Way RH15 ..... 107 A3
Claigmar Rd BN16 ..... 199 C5
Clair Ct [1] RH16 ..... 85 E5
Clair Rd RH16 ..... 85 E5
Clammer Hill GU27 ..... 27 F8
Clapham Cl BN13 ..... 160 F1
Clapham Comm BN13 ..... 180 E8
Clapham & Patching CE (C) Prim Sch BN13 ..... 160 E1
Clappers Gate RH10, RH11 ..... 18 D7
Clappers La Bracklesham PO20 .. 202 C6
Fulking BN5 ..... 145 F5
Clappers Meadow GU6 ..... 11 A3
Clare Cl RH10 ..... 6 C1
Clare Ct [5] BN17 ..... 198 E4
Clare Lodge [2] BN16 ..... 199 B5
Clare Wlk BN2 ..... 188 D5
Claremont Ct [15] PO21 ..... 195 D3
Claremont Way GU29 ..... 92 E7
Clarence Ave BN17 ..... 178 C3
Clarence Ct Horley RH6 ..... 2 D4
[3] Worthing BN11 ..... 182 F2
Clarence Dr
[2] East Grinstead RH19 ..... 22 F7
East Preston BN16 ..... 199 F6
Clarence Gate [10] PO21 ..... 195 D3
Clarence Rd Bognor Regis PO21 195 D3
Horsham RH13 ..... 36 E1
Clarence Sq BN1 ..... 207 F5
Clarendon Ho [2] BN2 ..... 188 B7
Clarendon Pl [15] Brighton BN2 . 188 C4
Portslade-by-Sea BN41 ..... 186 C6
Clarendon Rd Hove BN3 ..... 187 B7
Southwick BN42, BN43 ..... 185 D8
Worthing BN14 ..... 182 E6
Clarendon Terr [16] BN2 ..... 188 D4
Clarendon Villas BN3 ..... 187 B7
Clark Rd RH11 ..... 18 A1
Clarke Ave BN3 ..... 166 F3
Clarke Ct BN41 ..... 186 F6
Clarks Ind Est BN3 ..... 187 B8
Clay Hall La RH10 ..... 7 C4
Clay La Crossbush BN18 ..... 158 F1
Fishbourne PO18, PO19 ..... 172 B7
Storrington RH20 ..... 119 A1
West Ashling PO18 ..... 151 D1
Claypit La PO18 ..... 153 D2
Clays Cl RH19 ..... 22 E8
Clays Hill BN44 ..... 143 E2
Clayton Ave BN6 ..... 126 F3
Clayton Ct PO20 ..... 206 C6
Clayton Dr PO15 ..... 106 F1
Clayton Hill Crawley RH11 ..... 18 D7
Pyecombe BN45, BN6 ..... 147 D7
Clayton La PO20 ..... 202 B7
Clayton Pk BN6 ..... 126 E4
Clayton Rd Brighton BN2 ..... 188 D7
Ditchling BN6 ..... 127 C3
Selsey PO20 ..... 206 C6
Clayton Way BN3 ..... 166 D4
Clayton Wlk BN13 ..... 181 D5
Claytons Cnr PO20 ..... 191 E5
Clearwater La RH17 ..... 87 A3
Clearwaters La RH15 ..... 107 D8
Cleaver's La RH17 ..... 62 B2

Clement's Ct [1] BN43 ..... 184 F7
Clerks Acre BN6 ..... 127 A4
Clermont Ct [5] BN1 ..... 167 E2
Clermont Rd BN1 ..... 167 E2
Clermont Terr BN1 ..... 167 E2
Cleve Way RH14 ..... 77 D8
Cleveland Cl BN13 ..... 181 E8
Cleveland Gdns BN13 ..... 107 B2
Cleveland Rd Brighton BN1 ..... 168 A1
Chichester PO19 ..... 173 B5
Worthing BN13 ..... 181 F7
Clevelands Billingshurst RH14 .. 77 D8
Haywards Heath RH16 ..... 85 E6
Clevets The PO21 ..... 194 C1
Cliff App BN2 ..... 188 F4
Cliff Rd BN2 ..... 188 F4
Cliff The BN2 ..... 188 F4
Clifton Cl Chichester PO19 ..... 173 B5
[4] Worthing BN11 ..... 182 C3
Clifton Gdns BN11 ..... 182 C3
Clifton Hill BN1 ..... 207 F6
Clifton Mews BN1 ..... 207 F6
Clifton Pl BN1 ..... 187 E6
Clifton Rd Bognor Regis PO21 .. 195 C4
Brighton BN1 ..... 207 F6
Burgess Hill RH15 ..... 106 D5
Crawley RH10 ..... 19 C5
Littlehampton BN17 ..... 198 D4
Worthing BN11 ..... 182 C3
Clifton St BN1 ..... 207 F7
Clifton Terr BN1 ..... 207 F6
Cliftonville Ct [6] BN3 ..... 187 B7
Climping Cl RH16 ..... 85 D3
Climping Ct [2] BN16 ..... 199 B3
Climping Rd RH11 ..... 18 B8
Climping St BN17 ..... 197 E7
Clinton Hill RH7 ..... 10 A8
Clitherow Gdns RH10 ..... 18 E5
Clive Ave BN12 ..... 181 D2
Clive Way RH10 ..... 19 C6
Clivedale BN44 ..... 143 D3
Clivedale Gdns BN44 ..... 143 E3
Cliveden Ct BN1 ..... 167 E3
Clock Ho PO21 ..... 194 E1
Clock Pk PO22 ..... 195 E6
Clock Wlk PO22 ..... 195 D3
Close The Ardingly RH17 ..... 64 B7
Ashington RH20 ..... 121 A5
Bognor Regis PO21 ..... 194 C1
Boxgrove PO18 ..... 154 D3
Brighton BN1 ..... 167 E5
Burgess Hill RH15 ..... 107 C4
East Grinstead RH19 ..... 22 D8
Hassocks BN6 ..... 126 F4
Horley RH6 ..... 2 C1
Ifold RH14 ..... 31 D3
Lancing BN15 ..... 183 F4
Liphook GU30 ..... 25 C2
Littlehampton BN16 ..... 199 D4
Mid Lavant PO18 ..... 152 F5
Middleton-on-Sea PO22 ..... 197 A5
Selsey PO20 ..... 206 G8
Shoreham-by-Sea BN43 ..... 184 F8
Closewalks GU29 ..... 92 F7
Clothalls La RH13 ..... 102 B5
Clovelly Ave PO22 ..... 196 B5
Clovelly Rd Breach PO10 ..... 149 F1
Emsworth PO10 ..... 169 A8
Clover Ct [2] RH16 ..... 85 E4
Clover Field RH12 ..... 34 D4
Clover La BN12 ..... 200 E5
Clover Way BN41 ..... 166 B2
Cloverlands RH10 ..... 18 F8
Clovers Cotts RH12 ..... 16 F1
Clovers End Brighton BN1 ..... 168 B7
Horsham RH12 ..... 37 A5
Clovers Way RH12 ..... 37 D7
Club Wlk BN16 ..... 200 A4
Clun Rd BN17 ..... 198 C6
Clyde Cl BN13 ..... 181 C8
Clyde Rd Bognor Regis PO22 .. 195 F3
Brighton BN1 ..... 207 A8
Worthing BN13 ..... 181 C8
Clydesdale Ave PO19 ..... 173 B5
Clydesdale Gdns PO22 ..... 195 A7
Coach & Horses La RH17 ..... 66 C6
Coach House Cl PO20 ..... 206 E7
Coach House Mews BN11 ..... 182 C2
Coach La RH17 ..... 66 C6
Coach Rd Gatwick Airport, N Terminal RH6 ..... 5 F8
Gatwick Airport, S Terminal RH6 .... 6 B7
Shopwyke PO20 ..... 173 F7
Westhampnett PO18, PO20 ..... 153 E1
Coachmans Dr RH11 ..... 18 B2
Coastal Counties Ho [18] BN2 .. 207 B6
Coastal Rd BN16 ..... 200 C4
Coastguard Cotts BN16 ..... 200 A4
Coastguard La PO20 ..... 190 A1
Coastguard Par PO21 ..... 194 D1
Coastguard Rd BN17 ..... 198 D3
Coastguards Cotts PO20 ..... 190 A1
Coates Ct [11] BN42 ..... 185 E7
Coates La RH20 ..... 116 D8
Cob Cl RH10 ..... 21 C8
Cob La RH17 ..... 42 B1
Cob Wlk RH11 ..... 18 A6
Cobbett Cl RH10 ..... 19 C8
Cobbetts Mead RH16 ..... 86 B3
Cobblers RH12 ..... 34 C4
Cobbles Cres RH11 ..... 18 E7
Cobblewood PO10 ..... 149 B3
Cobden Ho GU29 ..... 92 E6
Cobden La GU27 ..... 27 D1
Cobden Rd Brighton BN2 ..... 188 C7
Midhurst GU29 ..... 92 E7
Worthing BN11 ..... 182 C1
Cobham Cl BN18 ..... 176 F2

Cobham Way RH10 ..... 6 B4
Cobnor Cl RH11 ..... 17 F4
Cobton Dr BN3 ..... 167 A3
Cockhaise Cotts RH16 ..... 87 B4
Cocking Hill GU29, PO18 ..... 112 C5
Cohen Cl RH11 ..... 175 D5
Cokeham Ct BN15 ..... 183 C7
Cokeham Gdns BN15 ..... 183 C6
Cokeham La BN15 ..... 183 C6
Cokeham Rd BN15 ..... 183 C6
Colbourne Ave BN2 ..... 168 D2
Colbourne Rd BN3 ..... 187 E7
Colchester Vale RH18 ..... 23 E2
Colchins RH15 ..... 106 F1
Coldean La BN1 ..... 168 D6
Coldean Cty Inf Sch BN1 ..... 168 D6
Coldean Cty Jun Sch BN1 ..... 168 D6
Coldean La BN1 ..... 168 D6
Coldharbour Farm Rd PO10 .. 149 B2
Coldharbour La BN13 ..... 160 D1
Coldwaltham La RH15 ..... 107 D2
Cole Cl RH11 ..... 18 B1
Colebrook Cl RH11 ..... 182 F3
Colebrook La RH20 ..... 117 B5
Colebrook Rd Brighton BN1 ..... 167 D4
Littlehampton BN17 ..... 178 C3
Southwick BN42 ..... 185 F7
Coleman Ave BN3 ..... 186 E7
Coleman St BN2 ..... 207 B7
Colemans Hatch Rd RH18 ..... 44 E5
Coleridge Cl Horsham RH12 ..... 36 E6
Worthing BN13 ..... 181 B3
Coleridge Cres BN12 ..... 181 A3
Coleridge Rd BN12 ..... 181 B3
Coleridge St BN3 ..... 187 A8
Colet Rd RH10 ..... 18 D3
Colgate Cl Brighton BN2 ..... 188 F6
Crawley RH11 ..... 18 B8
Colgate Cty Prim Sch RH13 .... 38 C6
Colhook Ind Pk GU28 ..... 51 D1
Colindale Rd BN12 ..... 200 E6
Colindale Rd N BN12 ..... 200 E6
Coll of St Barnabas RH7 ..... 9 F8
Coll of Tech
Three Bridges Outpost RH10 19 A7
Collard Way GU33 ..... 45 B4
Collards La GU27 ..... 27 D6
College Cl Bognor Regis PO21 .. 194 E4
East Grinstead RH19 ..... 9 F1
Portslade-by-Sea BN41 ..... 165 F3
Red Hill PO9 ..... 128 E1
College Ct PO22 ..... 195 E5
College Gdns Brighton BN2 ..... 188 C4
Worthing BN11 ..... 182 A2
College Hill Haslemere GU27 .... 27 C6
Steyning BN44 ..... 143 D2
College Hill Terr GU27 ..... 27 C6
College La Chichester PO19 .... 173 A8
East Grinstead RH19 ..... 9 F1
Hurst Wickham BN6 ..... 126 C6
College Pl Brighton BN2 ..... 188 C4
Hurst Wickham BN6 ..... 126 C6
College Rd Ardingly RH16, RH17 . 64 A5
Brighton BN2 ..... 188 C4
Crawley RH10 ..... 18 E6
Haywards Heath RH16 ..... 85 E7
Southwater RH13 ..... 57 E1
Upper Beeding BN44 ..... 144 C1
College St [11] BN2 ..... 188 C4
College Terr BN2 ..... 188 D5
Collendean La RH6 ..... 1 A5
Collier Row RH11 ..... 18 D4
Collingford La RH17 ..... 66 B4
Collingwood RH20 ..... 98 C3
Collingwood Cl
[4] East Grinstead RH19 ..... 22 F7
Horley RH6 ..... 2 B4
Horsham RH12 ..... 36 C4
Collingwood Ct [2] BN43 ..... 184 F6
Collingwood Rd Crawley RH10 .. 19 D5
Horsham RH12 ..... 36 B4
Worthing BN12 ..... 181 C4
Collins La GU31 ..... 89 C7
Collins Rd RH11 ..... 17 F4
Collins's La PO20 ..... 192 C4
Collyer Ave PO21 ..... 195 B5
Collyer's Sixth Form Coll RH12 ..... 36 D4
Collyers Cotts GU28 ..... 72 B7
Collyers Cres GU30 ..... 25 E4
Colmer Ct RH15 ..... 106 C3
Colmer Pl RH15 ..... 106 C3
Colne Cl BN13 ..... 181 C8
Colne Wlk RH11 ..... 17 F5
Colonades The RH20 ..... 98 B3
Colonsay Rd BN12 ..... 18 B3
Colt St PO20 ..... 206 D8
Colt's Bay PO21 ..... 194 C1
Coltash Rd RH10 ..... 19 A5
Coltsfoot Dr RH12 ..... 36 E5
Coltstaple La RH13 ..... 58 C4
Columbia Dr RH13 ..... 181 D6
Columbia Wlk BN13 ..... 181 C6
Colvill Ave RH15 ..... 85 F3
Colville Gdns RH16 ..... 85 F3
Colwell La
Haywards Heath RH16, RH17 .. 85 F1
Haywards Heath RH16, RH17 .. 86 B3
Colwell Rd RH16 ..... 85 F2
Colwood Hospl RH16 ..... 86 A3
Colwood La RH17 ..... 83 B6
Colwyn Cl RH11 ..... 17 F4
Combe Rd GU33 ..... 45 E1
Commerce Way BN15 ..... 183 C4
Commercial Rd RH15 ..... 106 F3

Commercial Sq RH16 85 E6
Common Hill RH20 119 D6
Common La BN6 127 D6
Common Rd PO10, PO18 150 D5
Common The RH20 119 C8
Common View GU29 69 F1
Commonside PO10 149 D5
Compass Cl BN17 199 A6
Compass Ct BN41 165 E3
Compassion Cl RH11 17 E5
Comper Cl RH11 17 E4
Compton Ave Brighton BN1 207 F7
Worthing BN12 181 B2
Compton Cl PO19 153 A3
Compton Ct BN16 199 C6
Compton Dr PO22 196 D6
Compton Rd Brighton BN1 167 D1
Haywards Heath RH16 86 B8
Compton & Up Marden CE (C) Prim Sch PO18 109 B2
Comptons Brow La RH13 37 A3
Comptons La RH12, RH13 36 F3
Conbar Ave BN16 199 C6
Concorde Cl RH20 119 F3
Condor Way RH15 106 E3
Conduit Mead PO19 173 C8
Coney Cl Crawley RH11 18 B8
East Wittering PO20 201 F6
Coney Croft RH12 37 B5
Coney Rd PO20 201 F6
Coney Six PO20 201 F6
Coneyhurst Rd RH14 77 F8
Congreve Rd BN14 182 E4
Conifer Dr PO18 150 E2
Conifers Cl RH12 37 B6
Conifers Sch GU29 71 A1
Conigar Rd PO10 149 B3
Coniston Cl Bognor Regis PO22 196 B6
Crawley RH11 17 D4
Horsham RH12 37 B6
Lancing BN15 183 C6
Coniston Ct 9 BN3 187 D7
Coniston Rd BN12 181 C4
Coniston Way BN16 179 A3
Connaught Ave BN43 184 E8
Connaught Ctr Brighton Coll of Tech & F Ed BN3 187 A6
Connaught Cty Jun Sch BN17 198 D5
Connaught Gdns RH11 18 D8
Connaught Ho 6 PO21 195 C2
Connaught Rd Hove BN3 187 A6
Littlehampton BN17 198 D5
Connaught Terr BN3 187 B7
Consort Way Burgess Hill RH15 106 E2
Horley RH6 2 A3
Consort Way E RH6 2 B2
Constable Dr PO20 206 F7
Constable Rd RH10 18 F2
Control Tower Rd RH6 5 D6
Convent Ct PO10 169 A8
Convent La PO10 169 B8
Conway Ct 1 BN3 187 B7
Conway Dr PO21 205 A8
Conway Pl BN3 187 A8
Conway St BN3 187 B8
Cook Rd Crawley RH10 18 F4
Horsham RH12 36 D6
Cook's Pond Rd GU30 69 A7
Cooks Hill RH12 33 A8
Cooks La Breach PO10, PO18 150 A1
Walderton PO18 130 D2
Cooks Mead RH12 16 D7
Cooks Meadow RH12 16 D7
Cooksbridge Rd BN2 188 E6
Coolham Ct RH11 17 F6
Coolham Dr BN2 188 E7
Coolham Rd RH13, RH20 100 C5
Coolhurst La RH13 37 A1
Coombe Cl Billingshurst RH14 55 D1
Crawley RH11 5 D1
Coombe Cres RH20 138 A7
Coombe Dr BN44 143 D2
Coombe Dro BN44 143 D2
Coombe Hall Sch RH19 22 D6
Coombe Hill RH14 55 D1
Coombe Hill Rd RH19 22 D6
Coombe La BN18 159 B7
Coombe Lea 22 BN3 187 C6
Coombe Rd Brighton BN2 168 D1
Steyning BN44 143 C2
Coombe Rise BN14 162 A2
Coombe Road Cty Prim Sch BN2 168 D1
Coombe Terr BN2 168 C1
Coombelands La RH20 98 A5
Coombers RH17 41 A1
Coombers La RH16 86 B5
Coombes Rd BN15 164 B4
Coomes Way BN17 178 D4
Cooper Row RH10 18 D3
Cooper St PO19 173 A6
Coopers Cl RH15 107 C5
Coopers The RH13 56 D4
Coopers Way BN5 123 F4
Coopers Wood RH17 39 C3
Coos La RH17 61 A6
Cootes Ave RH12 36 A3
Cootes Cotts RH20 116 B2
Cootes La PO22 196 F5
Cootham Gn RH20 119 B2
Copeland Rd PO22 196 A4
Copestake Dr RH15 107 D3
Copnall Way RH12 36 C2
Copper Cl BN6 106 C4
Copper Hall Cl 4 BN16 199 E6
Copperfield Pl RH12 36 B4
Copperfields RH13 59 B8
Copperfields Manor RH13 59 B8
Coppets Wood 7 BN16 199 B4
Coppice La PO20 206 D8
Coppice Rd RH12 37 A5
Coppice The Crawley Down RH10 21 B8
Scaynes Hill RH17 86 F3
Coppice Way RH16 85 D3
Coppice Wlk RH10 19 A7
Coppins Ct PO22 196 D5
Copsale Rd RH13 80 D6
Copse Cl Crawley Down RH10 21 B8
East Grinstead RH19 10 A3
East Liss GU33 45 C4
Horsham RH12 36 F6
Copse Cres RH11 18 C7
Copse Hill BN1 167 D5
Copse La Horley RH6 2 D4
Walberton BN18 156 D2
Copse Rd GU27 26 D5
Copse The Chichester PO19 153 B2
Haywards Heath RH16 86 B5
Southwater RH13 57 F2
Copse View BN16 199 F6
Copthorne Bank RH10, RH6 7 C4
Copthorne CE (C) Sch RH10 7 B3
Copthorne Cl BN13 182 A8
Copthorne Common Rd RH10 7 C3
Copthorne Ct 2 BN3 187 C6
Copthorne Hill BN13 181 F7
Copthorne Rd Copthorne RH10 6 F1
Felbridge RH10, RH19 8 D4
Copthorne Sch Trust Ltd RH10 7 E3
Copthorne Way
Bognor Regis PO21 194 D4
Copthorne RH10 6 F2
Copyhold Hill GU27 49 C8
Copyhold La Cuckfield RH17 85 A4
Haywards Heath RH16 63 E2
Copyhold Rd RH19 22 D8
Copythorne Ho RH16 85 E6
Corbishley Gn PO22 195 C6
Corbishley Rd PO22 195 C6
Corby Cl RH11 17 E3
Corbyn Cres BN43 185 A7
Corfe Cl Southwater RH13 58 A1
Worthing BN13 181 B5
Cormorant Way PO20 202 A6
Corn Ct 7 BN2 188 C6
Corner Garth BN12 200 F5
Cornfield Cl BN17 178 E3
Cornfield Sch BN17 178 E3
Cornford Cl RH15 106 E5
Cornwall Ct 2 BN3 187 C7
Cornwall Gdns Brighton BN1 167 E2
6 East Grinstead RH19 22 F8
Littlehampton BN17 198 D6
Cornwall Ho BN1 167 E2
Cornwall Rd BN17 198 D6
Coronation Bldgs BN11 183 A3
Coronation Homelets 9 BN11 183 B3
Coronation Rd
East Grinstead RH19 22 E7
South Hayling PO11 189 A1
Coronation St 7 BN2 188 C7
Coronet Cl RH10 19 E7
Coronet The RH6 2 C1
Corsletts Ave RH12 35 D3
Cortis Ave BN14 182 C5
Corunna Dr RH13 36 F2
Corvill Ct BN11 182 B2
Costells Edge RH17 86 F3
Cot La PO18 170 D6
Cote St BN13 161 C1
Cotland Rd PO20 206 F6
Cotsford RH11 39 B7
Cotswold Cl Crawley RH11 18 B6
Worthing BN13 181 E8
Cotswold Ct RH13 36 E2
Cotswold Pl 7 BN2 188 F5
Cotswold Rd BN13 181 E7
Cotswold Way BN16 200 A6
Cotswolds The BN42 185 E7
Cottage Bush Cl BN41 166 C2
Cottage Cl Bognor Regis PO21 194 C2
Horsham RH12 37 B6
Cottage Homes BN6 127 E6
Cottage Pl RH10 7 E3
Cottenham Rd BN11 182 F3
Cottesmore Golf Club RH11 38 E7
Cottesmore Sch RH11 39 A8
Cottesmore St Mary's RC Prim Sch BN3 187 D8
Cottingham Ave RH12 36 D7
Cotton Dr PO10 149 A3
Cotton Wlk RH11 18 A1
Cottrells The BN16 179 F5
Coulstock Rd BN6 106 C4
Council Cotts Charlwood RH6 4 C6
Clapham BN13 160 E1
Crosspost RH17 83 B1
High Cross BN6 125 A7
Loxwood RH14 32 A2
Plaistow RH14 30 D3
Sayers Common BN6 105 E3
Southwater RH13 79 F7
Sutton RH20 115 F3
Twineham Green RH17 105 B6
Warningcamp BN18 158 F2
Wepham BN18 159 A5
Countisbury Cl PO21 194 F3
Countryman La RH13 101 B7
County Mall RH10 18 E5
County Oak Ave BN1 168 B6
County Oak La RH11 5 D3
County Oak Ret Pk RH11 5 D2
County Oak Way RH11 5 D3
Courcels BN2 188 E3
Court Barn La PO20 191 E6
Court Cl Brighton BN1 167 E7
East Grinstead RH19 9 F1
Liphook GU30 25 B3
Court Cres RH19 9 F1
Court Est The 6 BN11 183 B3
Court Farm Rd BN3 167 A2
Court Lodge Cty Fst Sch RH6 1 F3
Court Lodge Rd RH6 1 F3
Court Meadow Sch RH17 85 A8
Court The PO21 194 A1
Courtfield Ho 4 PO21 195 B3
Courtfields BN15 183 D5
Courtlands 12 Brighton BN2 207 B6
Haywards Heath RH16 85 E3
Courtlands Cl BN12 181 E1
Courtlands Way
Bognor Regis PO22 196 C6
Worthing BN11, BN12 181 F1
Courtmead Rd RH17 84 F6
Courtney Gate BN3 187 B5
Courtney King Ct 8 BN2 188 C5
Courtney King Ho 1 BN2 188 D4
Courts Hill Rd GU27 27 B6
Courts Mount Rd GU27 27 B6
Courtup Hill RH13 80 E6
Courtwick La BN17 178 C4
Courtwick Rd BN17 178 C3
Courtyard The
Bognor Regis PO21 194 F2
Chichester PO19 172 F4
Crawley RH13 37 E4
East Grinstead RH19 10 B1
Haywards Heath RH16 64 C3
1 Horsham RH10 18 D5
Worthing BN13 182 A6
Worthing BN11 182 B3
Cousins Way RH20 98 C3
Cove Rd BN16 199 B4
Coventry Cl PO21 194 D4
Coventry St BN1 187 E8
Coverdale Ct RH19 9 C3
Covert Cl RH10 18 E7
Covert Mead RH17 61 B7
Covert The RH10 19 E8
Covington Rd PO10 149 D5
Cow La Sidlesham PO20 203 D7
South Harting GU31 89 C3
Cowdens Cl BN3 166 D4
Cowdown La PO18 108 F4
Cowdray GU29 93 A8
Cowdray Cl Crawley RH10 19 C5
Rustington BN16 179 B3
Worthing BN12 181 D1
Cowdray Ct 1 BN3 187 D7
Cowdray Dr Rustington BN16 179 B3
Worthing BN12 181 D1
Cowdray Park Golf Course GU29 71 D2
Cowdray Rd GU29 71 A2
Cowfold Cl RH11 17 F3
Cowfold Rd Brighton BN2 188 E5
Cowfold RH13 80 D2
Cowley Dr 1 BN15 183 F5
Cowper Rd BN11 182 B2
Cowper St BN3 187 A7
Cox Gr RH15 106 E5
Cox Green Rd RH12 12 C2
Cox Ho RH12 36 B2
Coxcomb Wlk RH11 18 A4
Coxes Rd PO20 206 D6
Coxham La BN44 143 C4
Crabbet Rd RH10 19 B7
Crabden La PO8 128 A8
Crablands PO20 206 D7
Crablands Cl PO20 206 C7
Crabtree Ave BN1 168 B5
Crabtree Gate RH13 81 F5
Crabtree La BN15 183 E6
Crabtree Lodge 2 BN15 183 D6
Crabtree Rd RH11 18 C7
Cradock Pl BN13 181 E8
Craggits La BN5 123 E5
Craigans RH11 18 A5
Craignair Ave BN1 167 F7
Craigwell La PO21 194 E2
Craigwell La PO21 194 E2
Craigwell Manor PO21 194 D1
Cranborne Wlk RH10 18 F4
Cranbourne Cl RH6 2 B5
Cranbourne St BN1 207 F5
Cranbrook 13 BN2 207 B6
Crane St PO19 173 A6
Cranford Gdns PO21 195 C4
Cranleigh Ct 6 BN11 182 C2
Cranleigh Rd BN14 182 C5
Cranley Ct BN3 186 D7
Cranmer Ave BN3 166 F1
Cranmer Rd BN13 182 A3
Cranmer Wlk RH10 19 C5
Cranston Rd RH19 9 F2
Cranworth Rd BN11 182 F3
Craven Rd Brighton BN2 188 D6
Crawley RH10 19 B5
Crawford Gdns RH13 36 E4
Crawfurd Way RH19 9 F3
Crawley Ave Crawley RH10 6 C1
Crawley RH10, RH11 18 A6
Crawley Coll of Tech RH10 18 E6
Crawley Coll (West Green Annexe) RH11 18 C7
Crawley Down CE (C) Prim Sch RH10 21 B8
Crawley Down Rd RH19 8 F4
Crawley Hospl (General) RH11 18 C6
Crawley La Balcombe RH17 40 E4
Crawley La Crawley RH10 19 C7
Crawley Rd Brighton BN1 168 D6
Crawley RH12 17 B1
Horsham RH12 37 B5
Crawley Sta RH10 18 E5
Crawters Cl RH10 18 F7
Cray La RH20 98 D5
Cray's La RH20 120 C8
Crayford Rd BN2 168 D1
Creasys Dr RH11 18 B1
Crede Cl PO18 171 C5
Crede La PO18 171 C5
Creek End Emsworth PO10 169 B7
Fishbourne PO19 172 B6
Crescent Cl RH15 107 B3
Crescent Mansions BN2 207 B8
Crescent Pl BN2 188 C4
Crescent Rd Bognor Regis PO21 195 C3
Brighton BN2 188 B8
Burgess Hill RH15 107 A3
East Grinstead RH19 9 D1
Worthing BN11 182 C2
Crescent Rise RH20 120 A3
Crescent The
Bognor Regis PO22 196 A4
Bognor Regis PO21 205 A8
Brighton BN2 168 E2
Cootham RH20 119 A2
East Wittering PO20 201 E7
Felcourt RH19 9 C8
Horley RH6 6 B8
Horsham RH12 36 A2
Keymer BN6 127 B3
Lancing BN15 183 E5
Littlehampton BN16 199 B5
Southbourne PO10 169 F8
Southwick BN42 185 F8
Steyning BN44 143 D2
West Kingston BN16 200 A4
Crescent Way
Burgess Hill RH15 107 A3
Horley RH6 2 A1
Crescenta Wlk PO21 195 A3
Crespin Way BN1 168 C2
Cressey Way PO19 153 A1
Crest Way BN41 166 B3
Crestway Par 1 BN1 168 C2
Crestway The BN1 168 C2
Crewdson Rd RH6 2 B3
Cricket Ct RH19 9 E3
Cricket Field Rd RH12 36 B1
Cricketers Par BN14 182 D6
Crimbourne La RH14 75 D3
Cripland Cl RH16 86 B6
Cripplecrutch Hill GU8 28 F5
Cripplegate La RH13 80 A8
Cripps Ho RH11 18 B2
Cripps La BN44 143 E3
Critchel's La PO20 192 C1
Critchfield Rd PO18 171 B5
Critchmere Dr PO20 175 F7
Critchmere Hill GU27 26 E7
Critchmere La GU27 26 E6
Critchmere Vale GU27 26 E6
Croat Ho PO20 206 D7
Crockford Rd PO10 149 D4
Crockham Cl RH11 18 C4
Crockhurst RH13 58 A2
Crockhurst Hill BN13, BN14 181 F8
Croft Ave BN42 185 F7
Croft Dr BN41 166 A3
Croft La BN5 123 E4
Croft Mead PO19 153 A2
Croft Rd Brighton BN1 167 D4
Selsey PO20 206 D7
Croft The Bognor Regis PO21 194 F5
Cocking GU29 112 D8
Crawley RH11 18 A6
East Preston BN16 200 A5
Hassocks BN6 126 F5
Lodsworth GU28 72 B3
Southwick BN42 185 E8
Yapton BN18 176 F4
Croft Villas BN5 123 E5
Croft Way Bognor Regis PO22 196 C6
Horsham RH12 36 A3
Selsey PO20 206 D7
Crofters Wood BN44 143 F2
Cromleigh Way BN42 165 E2
Crompton Fields RH10 5 E1
Crompton Way RH10 5 E1
Cromwell Ct 3 BN3 187 D7
Cromwell Pl 1 RH19 22 F7
Cromwell Rd Burgess Hill RH15 106 F3
Hove BN3 187 C7
Cromwell St BN2 188 C7
Crooked La PO20 191 E4
Crookthorn La BN17 197 E8
Crosbie Cl PO19 172 F3
Crosby Cl BN13 181 D6
Croshaw Cl BN15 183 D5
Cross Colwood La RH17 82 F5
Cross Gates BN18 139 A7
Cross Keys RH10, RH11 18 D6
Cross La Barns Green RH13 57 A1
Burstow RH6 7 C8
Findon BN14 161 E5
Cross Oak La RH1, RH6 2 C7
Cross Rd Rustington BN16 199 E5
Southwick BN42 185 D8
Cross St Brighton BN1 207 A7
Hove BN1, BN3 187 D5
Worthing BN11 182 C3
Crossbush La BN18 158 E1
Crossbush Rd
Bognor Regis PO22 196 C4
Brighton BN2 188 E6
Crossfield GU27 49 B5
Crossman Ct RH11 18 B1
Crosspath RH10 18 E7
Crosspost RH17 83 B1
Crosspost Ind Pk RH17 83 B1
Crossroad Cl BN42 185 D8
Crossway RH6 5 F8
Crossway The Brighton BN1 168 B2
Portslade-by-Sea BN41 166 A2
Crossways Crawley RH10 19 A7
Easebourne GU29 71 A2
East Preston BN16 180 B3
Middleton-on-Sea PO22 196 F5
Navant Hill GU28 50 E4
West Chiltington Common RH20 119 D7
Crossways Ave
East Grinstead RH19 9 C1
Worthing BN12 181 B4
Crossways Cl RH10 18 F7
Crossways Cotts
Alfold Crossways GU6 11 A3
Poynings BN45 146 C6
Tisman's Common RH12 32 F6
Crossways Ct GU27 49 B6
Crossways Pk RH20 119 D7
Crossways The Hassocks BN6 126 C4
Littlehampton BN17 178 C3
Crouch Cross La PO18 154 D3
Crouch Hill BN5 123 F7
Crouchlands Farm RH17 84 E8
Crowberry Cl RH11 18 A2
Crowborough Dr BN12 181 B2
Crowhurst Cl RH10 19 E6
Crowhurst Keep RH10 19 E6
Crowhurst Rd BN1 168 C7
Crown Bldgs BN15 183 C4
Crown Ct BN16 200 A4
Crown Gdns BN1 207 F5
Crown Hill 4 BN2 188 C6
Crown Point Ho BN6 126 F4
Crown Rd
Portslade-by-Sea BN41 186 A8
Shoreham-by-Sea BN43 185 B8
Crown St BN1 207 F5
Crowsbury Cl PO10 149 A3
Croxton La RH16 86 B6
Croy Cl PO19 172 E4
Crundens Cnr 5 BN16 199 E6
Crutchfield La RH6 1 B5
Crypt La GU29 112 C7
Cuckfield Cl RH11 17 F3
Cuckfield Cres BN13 181 F6
Cuckfield La RH17 61 B1
Cuckfield Rd
Burgess Hill RH15, RH17 106 E7
Goddards' Green BN6, RH17 106 A4
Slough Green RH17 62 A2
Cuckmere Cres RH11 17 F5
Cuckmere Way BN1 168 C5
Cudlow Ave BN16 199 C5
Cudlow Gdn Rustington BN16 199 C4
Rustington BN16 199 C5
Cudworth La RH5 3 E8
Cuffs Hill RH10 19 E2
Culimore Cl PO20 201 E7
Culimore Rd PO20 201 E7
Culpepper RH15 106 E4
Culpepper Cl BN2 168 D2
Culross Ave RH16 85 D5
Culver Ct BN15 183 E6
Culver Rd Bognor Regis PO22 196 A4
Lancing BN15 183 E6
Culvers GU31 89 D3
Cumberland Ave
New Brighton PO10 149 B4
Worthing BN12 181 D5
Cumberland Cres BN16 179 F5
Cumberland Dr BN1 167 E2
Cumberland Lodge 8 BN1 167 E2
Cumberland Rd
Angmering BN16 180 A6
Brighton BN1 167 E2
Cumbernauld Wlk RH11 17 E2
Cumbrian Cl BN13 181 E7
Cumnor House Sch RH17 66 B5
Cunliffe Cl PO20 190 C2
Cunningham Gdns PO22 196 C5
Curbey Cl RH20 99 D1
Curlescroft PO21 194 F2
Curlew Cl PO10 169 A7
Curlews The BN43 185 A8
Curteys Wlk RH11 18 A3
Curvins Way BN15 183 F7
Curwen Pl BN1 167 E3
Curzon Ave RH12 36 B3
Curzon Ct BN13 181 F6
Cutfield Cl PO19 172 F3
Cuthbert Rd BN2 188 C5
Cuttinglye La RH10 8 A1
Cuttinglye Rd RH10 8 C2
Cygnet Wlk PO22 195 B6
Cygnets The BN43 184 F8
Cylinders The GU27 49 B5
Cymens Ora PO20 203 D8
Cypress Ave BN12, BN13 181 C5
Cypress Cl 12 BN43 164 F1
Cypress Way PO21 194 D1
Cyprus Rd RH15 107 A3

D'Aubigny Rd BN2 188 B8
Dacre Gdns BN43 164 B7
Dagbrook La BN5 123 E3
Dagmar St BN11 182 E3
Dairy Farm BN12 181 A3
Dairy La Maudlin PO18, PO20 153 F1
Walberton BN18 156 D1
Dairyfields RH11 18 A5
Daisycroft The BN5 123 F4
Dakin Cl RH10 19 C2

Dakins The RH19 22 E8
Dale Ave Brighton BN1 167 F5
Keymer BN6 127 A3
Dale Cl RH12 36 F5
Dale Copse GU27 49 B6
Dale Cres BN1 167 F6
Dale Dr BN1 168 A6
Dale Hill BN45 147 A6
Dale Rd Forest Row RH18 23 F1
Worthing BN11 183 B4
Dale View Haslemere GU27 26 F5
Hove BN3 166 D2
Dale View Gdns BN3 166 D2
Dalewood Gdns
Burgess Hill RH15 107 C2
Crawley RH10 18 F8
Dallaway Gdns RH19 9 E1
Dallaway Rd PO19 173 B4
Dallington Rd BN3 186 F8
Dalloway Rd BN18 157 F1
Dalton Cl RH11 18 B1
Daltons Pl BN18 158 A2
Dame School Ct PO18 153 A5
Damer's Bridge GU28 95 F8
Damian Way BN6 127 B4
Dampier Wlk RH11 18 B1
Danbury Ct PO10 149 C2
Danefield Rd PO20 206 C6
Danehill CE Prim Sch RH17 66 B4
Danehill La RH17 65 E5
Danehill Rd BN2 188 F5
Danehurst 6 PO21 195 B3
Danehurst Cres RH13 36 F2
Daniel Cl BN15 183 F7
Dankton Gdns BN15 183 B7
Dankton La BN15 183 B7
Danley La GU27 26 A3
Danny Sheldon Ho 14 BN2 188 C4
Danworth La BN6 106 B3
Dapper's La BN16 180 A7
Darcey Dr BN1 168 A6
Darenth Way RH6 1 F6
Dark La PO21 194 F1
Darleydale RH11 18 C3
Dart Cl BN13 181 D8
Dart Ct RH19 10 A3
Dartmouth Cl BN2 168 F1
Dartmouth Cres BN2 168 F1
Darwin Cl RH12 36 F4
Daux Ave RH14 77 D6
Daux Hill RH12 36 B6
Daux Rd RH14 77 D7
Dauxwood Cl RH14 77 D6
Davenport Ct 3 BN11 181 F2
Davenport Rd PO22 196 B6
Davey Dr BN1 168 B1
Davids Cl PO21 194 F5
Davies Ct 11 BN11 182 A1
Davigdor Cty Inf Sch BN3 187 D6
Davigdor Rd BN3 187 E7
Davis Cl RH11 18 A1
Davison CE Girls' High Sch
BN11 182 F4
Davits Dr BN17 199 A6
Davys Ct PO18 151 A5
Dawes Ave BN11 182 F3
Dawes Cl BN11 182 F3
Dawlish Cl BN2 168 F1
Dawn Cl BN44 144 B1
Dawn Cres BN44 144 A1
Dawson Terr BN2 188 C6
Dawtrey Cl BN16 199 E6
Dawtrey Rd GU28 95 F7
Daynes Way RH15 106 E1
Days La PO18 155 F3
De Braose Way BN44 143 E2
De Courcel Rd BN2 188 E3
De La Warr Rd RH19 9 F1
De Montfort Rd BN2 188 C7
Deacon Trad Est BN14 182 F5
Deacon Way BN14 182 F5
Deacons Dr BN41 166 C2
Deacons Way BN44 144 B2
Deak's La RH17 84 B6
Dean Cl Littlehampton BN17 178 C3
Portslade-by-Sea BN41 166 C2
Dean Gdns BN41 166 C2
Dean La Finchdean PO8, PO9 128 F5
Upperton GU28 73 A1
Dean St BN1 187 E5
Dean Way RH20 119 C2
Deanland Rd RH17 41 A1
Deanway BN3 167 B3
Decoy Dr BN16 179 F7
Decoy Rd BN14 182 F5
Dedisham Cl RH10 19 A5
Dedisham Sch RH12 34 C6
Deep Dene GU27 26 E6
Deepdene Cl PO22 197 A5
Deepdene Sch BN3 186 D7
Deepfields RH6 1 F5
Deer Park La PO20 206 B8
Deer Pk BN5 123 E6
Deerswood Cl Crawley RH11 18 B7
Worthing BN13 181 B5
Deerswood Ct RH11 18 A7
Deerswood Lower Sch RH11 18 A8
Deerswood Rd RH11 18 B7
Deerswood Upper Sch RH11 18 A8
Deeside Ave PO19 172 B7
Deeside The BN1 168 A7
Defiance Pl PO22 196 C4
Delfryn BN41 165 F3
Dell Cl GU27 27 A7
Dell Dr BN16 179 F4
Dell La RH14 77 D8
Dell Quay Rd PO20 172 B2
Dell The Bognor Regis PO22 195 A6
Dell The East Grinstead RH19 10 B1
Haywards Heath RH16 85 C5
Horley RH6 2 B4
Wrays RH6 1 C5
Delling Cl PO18 171 B6
Delling La PO18 171 C6
Dellney Ave RH16 85 F3
Delta Bglws RH6 2 A1
Delta Dr RH6 2 A1
Delta Ho RH6 2 A1
Dempsey Rd 3 PO19 153 A2
Den Ave PO21 195 D3
Denbigh Rd GU27 27 D5
Denchers Plat RH11 5 D1
Dene Cl Haslemere GU27 27 C6
Horley RH6 1 E5
Dene The Hove BN3 166 D3
Southwater RH13 58 A2
Dene Tye RH10 19 D7
Dene Vale BN1 167 D5
Denecroft BN1 167 D5
Deneside BN1 167 D5
Deneway The Brighton BN1 167 D4
Lancing BN15 183 C6
Denham Cl PO22 196 E5
Denham Rd BN6, RH15 106 D3
Denison Ct 3 PO19 172 F7
Denman's Cl RH16 86 A8
Denman's La RH16 86 A7
Denmans RH10 19 D7
Denmans Gdns BN18, 155 F3
Denmans La BN18, PO20 155 E2
Denmark Rd BN41 186 C7
Denmark Terr BN1 187 E6
Denmark Villas BN3 187 B7
Denne Par RH12, RH13 36 C1
Denne Rd Crawley RH11 18 D5
Horsham RH12 36 C1
Dennis Ct RH20 98 C2
Dennis Hobden Cl BN2 168 E1
Dennis Way GU33 45 C3
Denny's Cl PO20 206 E7
Denshare Rd PO20 206 E8
Denshire Dr RH20 119 E2
Densihale PO21 195 A3
Denton Cl BN12 181 B3
Denton Dr BN1 168 A6
Departures Rd RH6 5 F8
Depot Rd Crawley RH11 5 D1
Horsham RH13 36 E2
Derby Ct 3 BN3 187 E7
Derby Pl 6 BN2 207 B5
Derby Rd GU27 27 B7
Derek Ave BN3, BN41 186 D6
Derek Ho BN3 186 F6
Derek Rd BN15 183 E8
Derwent Cl Crawley RH11 17 F5
Horsham RH12 37 B6
Lancing BN15 183 C5
Littlehampton BN16 179 A3
Tangmere PO20 154 D2
Derwent Ct BN1 207 F6
Derwent Dr BN12, BN13 181 D5
Derwent Gr PO22 196 B6
Desmond Anderson Cty Fst Sch
RH10 18 E2
Desmond Anderson Cty Mid Sch
RH10 18 E2
Desmond Way BN2 188 F6
Detling Rd RH11 18 C1
Devil's Dyke BN45 146 C3
Devil's Dyke Rd BN45 146 C1
Devils La GU30 25 E3
Devonian Ct BN2 207 B7
Devonport Pl BN11 183 A3
Devonport Rd BN11 183 A2
Devonshire Ct 1 BN3 187 C7
Devonshire Lodge 12 BN11 181 F2
Devonshire Pl
3 Bognor Regis PO21 195 C3
Brighton BN2 207 B5
Devonshire Rd
Bognor Regis PO21 195 C3
Horsham RH13 36 D2
Dewar Cl RH11 17 E5
Dewe Rd BN2 168 C1
Dexter Dr RH19 22 E8
Dial Cl PO22 176 C5
Diamond Cotts RH17 83 B1
Dickens Cl RH19 9 C1
Dickens Rd RH10 18 E3
Dickins Way RH13 58 F8
Dickinson Pl PO22 195 D6
Diggers The BN1 168 B3
Dinapore Ho 10 BN2 207 B6
Dingemans BN44 143 D5
Dingle The RH11 18 B6
Dingley Rd BN16 199 C5
Dinsdale Gdns BN16 199 C6
Dione Wlk RH11 17 E4
Dirty La RH19 23 E7
Discovery Pk RH10 6 A2
Ditcham Park Sch GU31 108 B8
Ditchfield Cl PO22 196 D6
Ditchling Beacon Nature Reserve
BN6 148 D7
Ditchling Bostall BN6 148 D7
Ditchling Cl BN12 181 B4
Ditchling Common Ctry Pk
BN6 107 F1
Ditchling Cres BN1 168 C5
Ditchling Ct 4 BN1 188 B8
Ditchling Gdns BN1 168 B1
Ditchling Hill RH11 18 C4
Ditchling Mus BN6 127 C3
Ditchling Rd Brighton BN1, BN2 168 B4
Westmeston BN1, BN6 148 D4
Ditchling Rise BN1 188 A8
Ditton Place Sch RH17 62 A8
Dobbins Pl RH11 17 E5
Dobson Rd RH11 5 D1
Dodsley Gr GU29 70 F2
Dodsley La GU29 71 A2
Dog Kennels GU28 115 B3
Dog La BN44 143 D3
Dolby Terr RH6 4 E6
Dollis Cl RH10 19 C5
Dolphin Cl Fishbourne PO19 172 B6
Haslemere GU27 26 E6
Dolphin Ct
4 Bognor Regis PO21 195 C2
5 Hove BN3 187 A6
Rustington BN16 199 D4
Dolphin Ind Est BN43 185 B7
Dolphin L Ctr The RH16 85 D6
Dolphin Lodge 12 BN11 182 A1
Dolphin Mews PO19 172 D6
Dolphin Rd
Haywards Heath RH16 85 D4
Shoreham-by-Sea BN43 185 B7
Dolphin Way
Littlehampton BN16 199 D4
Shoreham-by-Sea BN43 185 B7
Dominion Bldgs BN14 182 F4
Dominion Cl BN14 182 E5
Dominion Rd BN14 182 F5
Dominion Way
Rustington BN16 179 C3
Worthing BN14 182 F5
Dominion Way W BN14 182 F5
Donald Hall Rd BN2 188 D5
Doncaster Wlk RH10 19 A4
Donegal Rd PO19 152 F1
Donkey La RH6 6 D7
Donkey Mews BN3 187 D5
Donne Cl RH10 19 B8
Donnington Ct 2 RH11 17 F3
Donnington Pk PO20 172 D3
Donnington Pl 2 BN16 199 C6
Doomsday Gdn RH13 37 A1
Doone End BN12 200 F4
Dorchester Gdns BN11 182 A2
Dorking Rd RH12, RH5 15 B4
Dorman's Cl RH7 10 A8
Dormans RH11 18 A5
Dormans Gdns RH19 9 E6
Dormans High St RH7 10 A8
Dormans Park Rd
Dormans Park RH19 9 E6
East Grinstead RH19 9 D3
Dormans Sta RH7 9 F8
Dormans Station Rd RH7 9 F7
Dormansland Prim Sch RH7 10 A8
Dorothy Rd BN3 186 D8
Dorothy Stringer Sch BN1 167 F3
Dorset Ave RH19 9 C3
Dorset Cl BN17 198 E5
Dorset Ct BN41 186 F6
Dorset Gdns Brighton BN2 207 B5
East Grinstead RH19 9 C3
Dorset Ho RH14 78 E2
Dorset House Sch RH20 138 B7
Dorset Pl Brighton BN2 207 B5
4 Worthing BN13 182 A5
Dorset Rd PO21 195 C5
Dorset St BN2 207 A5
Dorsten Sq RH11 17 F3
Doubledays RH15 107 B2
Douglas Ave BN11 181 F2
Douglas Cl Burndell BN18 177 B2
Worthing BN11 181 F2
Douglas Martin Rd PO19 173 B7
Dove Cl RH11 18 D8
Dove Ct PO22 195 B5
Dovecote Mews BN15 183 C8
Dovedale Cres RH11 18 B4
Dover Cl RH13 57 F2
Dover Rd Brighton BN1 168 A2
Worthing BN11 182 A1
Dovercourt PO22 195 A6
Dower Wlk RH11 18 A5
Dowlands La RH10, RH6 7 D7
Down Cl GU29 113 C8
Down Cotts PO18 130 A8
Down St PO18 151 B3
Down Terr BN2 188 C6
Down The BN3 166 D4
Down View Rd BN11 182 A2
Downash Cl BN2 188 E6
Downe Cl RH6 1 E5
Downe Wlk BN13 181 D5
Downes Ct 9 BN43 185 C8
Downing Cl PO21 194 E4
Downland Ave BN42 165 E1
Downland Cl Findon BN14 161 E6
Southwick BN42 165 D1
Upper Beeding BN44 144 B2
Downland Cres BN3 166 F3
Downland Ct Chichester PO19 172 F8
Crawley RH11 18 C4
Portslade-by-Sea BN41 166 A2
Downland Dr Crawley RH11 18 C3
Hove BN3 166 F3
Downland Pl RH11 18 C4
Downland Rd BN44 144 B2
Downlands
Partridge Green RH13 102 F3
Pulborough RH20 98 D2
Worthing BN13 161 E2
Downlands Ave BN14 182 D6
Downlands Bsns Pk BN14 182 E8
Downlands Cl
Bognor Regis PO21 194 A2
Lancing BN15 183 C7
Downlands Gdns BN14 182 E7
Downlands La RH6 7 D7
Downlands Par BN14 182 E7
Downlands Ret Ctr BN14 182 E7
Downlands Sch BN6 126 F3
Downs Cl BN15 184 B6
Downs Cty Inf Sch BN1 207 B8
Downs Cty Jun Sch BN1 168 A1
Downs Mead BN15 183 C8
Downs Park Sch BN41 166 B2
Downs Rd Burgess Hill RH15 106 E4
West Stoke PO18 151 D6
Downs View Rd BN6 126 F3
Downs Way BN16 179 F3
Downsbrook Mid Sch BN14 182 E5
Downsbrook Trad Est BN14 182 E6
Downscroft Burgess Hill RH15 107 D6
Upper Beeding BN44 144 B1
Downside Brighton BN1 167 D5
Hove BN3 167 B3
Shoreham-by-Sea BN43 165 A1
Downside Ave BN14 161 F3
Downside Cl
Shoreham-by-Sea BN43 164 F1
Worthing BN14 161 F3
Downside Ct 6 BN16 199 B3
Downsman Ct RH10 18 D3
Downsview Hove BN3 166 D3
Hurstpierpoint BN6 126 A5
Small Dole BN5 144 F7
Downsview Ave RH20 119 E2
Downsview Cotts RH14 77 C8
Downsview Dr GU29 92 E5
Downsview Rd Horsham RH12 37 B6
Kingston Gorse BN16 200 D4
Portslade-by-Sea BN41 166 A2
Downsview Terr BN5 123 D5
Downsway
Shoreham-by-Sea BN43 164 F1
Southwick BN42 165 F1
Downview Ave BN12 180 E3
Downview Cl Burndell BN18 177 A3
East Wittering PO20 202 A6
Mid Lavant PO18 152 E6
Downview Ct 7 BN11 182 A1
Downview Cty Prim Sch PO22 195 F6
Downview Rd
Bognor Regis PO22 196 A5
Burndell BN18 177 A3
Ferring BN12 180 E3
Findon BN14 161 E7
Petworth GU28 95 E7
West Barnham PO22 176 A7
Downview Way BN18 177 A3
Dragons Green Council Cotts
RH13 79 C3
Dragons Green Rd RH13 79 C5
Dragons La Dragons Green RH13 79 C3
Little Parkminster RH13 103 E7
Drake Ave BN12 181 D4
Drake Cl RH12 36 E6
Drake Gr BN18 177 B2
Drake Pk PO22 196 C5
Drake Rd Crawley RH10 18 E3
Horley RH6 1 E3
Drakeleys Field GU30 47 B2
Drakes Cl BN15 184 B6
Draxmont Way BN1 167 F3
Draycliff Cl BN12 200 E5
Drayman's Mews PO19 173 B6
Drayton La PO20 174 A5
Drewitts Mews PO20 174 C7
Drift La Nutbourne PO18 170 E8
Selsey PO20 206 C7
Drift Rd Bognor Regis PO21 194 B2
Selsey PO20 206 G8
Drift The PO9 128 D1
Driftway The Rustington BN16 179 B3
Upper Beeding BN44 144 B3
Drive Lodge 10 BN3 187 C7
Drive The Bognor Regis PO21 194 D1
Bosham PO18 171 C4
Burgess Hill RH15 107 B4
Chichester PO19 153 A3
Copthorne RH10 7 C3
East Lavington GU28 114 E5
Horley RH6 2 B1
Hove BN3 187 C7
Ifold RH14 31 D2
Lancing BN15 183 D4
North Lancing BN15 164 B1
Shoreham-by-Sea BN43 164 F1
Southbourne PO10 169 F8
Southwick BN42 165 E1
West Kingston BN16 200 B4
Worthing BN11 181 F3
Driveway The BN43 164 F1
Droke La PO18 134 E6
Dropping Holms BN5 123 D4
Drove Cres BN41 166 A2
Drove La Earnley PO20 202 D5
Yapton BN18, PO22 176 D2
Drove Rd BN41 166 A1
Drove The BN1 167 D1
Drovers RH17 83 C3
Drovers Cl BN41 166 C2
Drovers Way RH15 107 C1
Droveway The
Haywards Heath RH16, RH17 85 C6
Hove BN3 167 B2
Hove BN3 167 C1
Drummond Cl RH16 85 D4
Drummond Ct RH16 85 D4
Drummond Rd Crawley RH11 17 E5
Worthing BN12 181 E1
Drungewick La RH14 32 D2
Drury Cl RH10 19 D4
Dryad Way PO22 196 D4
Dryad Wlk PO22 196 D4
Dryden Way GU30 25 A5
Drygrounds La PO22 195 F5
Duck La Midhurst GU29 92 F7
Selsey PO20 206 B8
Duckmead La GU33 45 D5
Dudeney Lodge BN1 168 B1
Dudley Rd BN1 168 B1
Dudley Terr GU33 45 C5
Duffield La PO10 150 A3
Duke Cl RH10 19 C2
Duke St Brighton BN1 207 F5
Littlehampton BN17 198 D5
Duke's Ct Chichester PO19 173 D5
2 Littlehampton BN17 198 D5
Duke's Dr RH5 3 D6
Duke's Hill RH20 120 A8
Duke's Mound BN2 188 D4
Duke's Rd BN18 155 F4
Dukes Barn Ct RH16 86 B7
Dukes Cl BN18 157 F2
Dukes La Brighton BN1 207 F5
Steyning BN44 143 D4
Dukes Meadow PO21 194 B3
Dukes Rd RH16 86 B8
Dukes Row RH20 119 A2
Dukes Yd BN44 143 D3
Dumbrells Court Rd BN6 127 D4
Dumbrells Ct BN6 127 D4
Dumbrills Cl RH15 107 A5
Dumpford La GU31 90 D8
Duncan Rd PO19 172 F8
Duncton CE (C) Prim Sch
GU28 115 B7
Duncton Cl Bognor Regis PO22 196 B4
Haywards Heath RH16 85 D4
Duncton High St GU28 115 B6
Duncton Ho BN6 126 E1
Duncton Rd BN16 199 C6
Dunes The PO21 205 C8
Dunford Hollow GU29 93 A3
Dunning's Rd RH19 22 E7
Dunnings Mill L Complex RH19 22 E6
Dunnock Cl PO9 128 D1
Dunsfold Cl RH11 18 A5
Dunsfold Rd GU8, RH14 30 D4
Dunstall Ave RH15 106 E4
Dunstall Farm Rd RH15 106 F4
Dunstan Cl PO19 153 A3
Dunster Cl BN1 168 B1
Durban Pk PO22 195 D5
Durban Rd PO22 195 D6
Durbans Rd RH14 54 C2
Durfold Rd RH12 36 D7
Durfold Wood RH14 30 D5
Durham Cl Bognor Regis PO21 205 A8
Crawley RH10 18 E2
Durham Ct BN3 187 B6
Durham Gdns PO19 152 F1
Durkins Rd RH19 9 D3
Durlston Dr PO22 195 B6
Durlston Par PO22 195 B6
Durnford Cl PO19 172 E7
Durrington Cty Fst Sch BN13 181 E7
Durrington Cty Mid Sch BN13 181 E7
Durrington Gdns BN12 181 D3
Durrington High Sch BN13 181 E5
Durrington Hill BN13 181 D7
Durrington La BN12, BN13 181 D6
Durrington-on-Sea Sta BN12 181 E3
Dutchells Copse RH12 36 E7
Duxhurst La RH6 1 B7
Dyall Cl RH15 106 E4
Dyers Almshouses RH10 18 D7
Dyers La BN18 156 C5
Dyke Cl Hove BN3 167 B4
Poynings BN45 146 C4
Dyke Golf Course BN1 146 D1
Dyke Rd BN1, BN3 187 E7
Dyke Road Ave BN1, BN3 167 C4
Dyke Road Dr BN1 187 F8
Dyke Road Pl BN1, BN3 167 C3
Dymock's The BN6 127 D3
Dymoke St PO10 149 A4
Dyson Wlk RH11 18 B1

Eady Cl RH13 36 F2
Eagle Est RH14 77 D7
Eagle Ho 10 PO21 195 B2
Eagles Chase BN17 178 D4
Earles Meadow RH12 37 B6
Earlswood Cl RH13 37 A4
Early Commons RH10 18 F7
Earnley Manor Cl PO20 202 D7
Earnley Rd Earnley PO20 202 D7
South Hayling PO11 189 B2
Eartham House
(Great Ballard Sch) PO18 155 D7
Earwig La RH17 82 E6
Easebourne La GU29 71 A1
Easebourne St GU28, GU29 71 D5
East Ave Middleton-on-Sea PO22 196 F6
Worthing BN12 181 F1
East Bank North End BN18 177 A5
Selsey PO20 206 F7
East Bank Wlk BN17 199 A4
East Beach Rd PO20 206 G8
East Bracklesham Dr PO20 202 B5
East Cl PO22 196 E5
East Court Way BN16 199 E6
East Dean PO22 195 D5
East Dr Angmering BN16 179 E3
Brighton BN2 188 C5
Middleton-on-Sea PO22 197 A5
East Field Cl PO10 150 A2
East Front Rd PO21 205 A7
East Gdns BN6 127 D3

East Grinstead Sta RH19 9 D1
East Gun Copse Rd RH13 57 D5
East Ham Rd BN17 198 D5
East Hampnett La PO20 154 F2
East Harting St GU31 89 F3
East Hill RH19 9 E6
East Hill Ct 1 BN11 182 D2
East Hill Dr GU33 45 C3
East Hill La RH10 7 D5
East Lake PO21 195 D4
East Lodge Lancing BN15 183 E4
Rogate GU31 68 B4
East Mascalls Rd RH16 86 E6
East Mead Bognor Regis PO21 205 A8
Ferring BN12 200 F5
East Meadway BN43 185 A6
East Onslow Cl BN12 200 E6
East Pallant PO19 173 A6
East Park La RH7 8 C8
East Pk RH10, RH11 18 D5
East Point 6 BN43 185 A6
East Preston Cty Inf Sch
BN16 200 A6
East Preston Cty Jun Sch
BN16 200 A6
East Row PO19 173 A6
East Row Mews 3 PO19 173 A6
East St Amberley BN18 138 E7
Billingshurst RH14 77 D8
Brighton BN1 207 A4
Chichester PO19 173 A6
Horsham RH12 36 C1
Lancing BN15 183 E4
Littlehampton BN17 198 E5
Petworth GU28 95 F8
Portslade-by-Sea BN41 186 C7
Rusper RH12 16 E7
Selsey PO20 206 E7
Shoreham-by-Sea BN43 184 F7
Turners Hill RH10, RH19 21 C4
West Chiltington RH20 99 E1
Westbourne PO10 149 D3
East Strand PO20 201 C8
East Tyne BN13 181 D6
East View Cl PO18 152 F7
East Walls PO19 173 A6
East Walls Cl 2 PO19 173 A6
East Way PO20 206 F7
East Wick RH16 86 C7
East Wittering Bsns Ctr PO20 202 A8
East Wittering Cty Prim Sch
PO20 201 F7
East Worthing Ind Est BN14 182 F5
East Worthing Sta BN11 182 F4
Eastbank BN42 165 F1
Eastbourne Rd Brighton BN2 168 D1
Felbridge RH7 8 E8
Eastbrook Rd BN41 186 B7
Eastbrook Way BN42 186 A7
Eastcourt Rd BN14 182 D4
Eastcroft Mews RH12 35 F1
Eastdale Rd RH15 107 D4
Eastdean Hill PO18 134 C5
Easteds La RH13 58 A2
Eastend La BN6 127 D3
Eastergate CE (C) Prim Sch
PO20 175 E7
Eastergate Cl BN12 180 F3
Eastergate Gn 6 BN16 199 C5
Eastergate La BN18, PO20 156 B1
Eastergate Rd BN2 168 F4
Eastern Ave BN43 185 A7
Eastern Cl East Preston BN16 200 B6
Shoreham-by-Sea BN43 185 A7
Eastern Cotts RH16 86 B7
Eastern Pl BN2 188 E4
Eastern Rd Brighton BN2 188 D4
Haywards Heath RH16 85 F3
Haywards Heath RH16 86 C7
Eastern Terr 10 BN2 188 D4
Eastern Terrace Mews 9
BN2 188 D4
Eastfield Cres BN1 168 A4
Eastfield La GU31 90 A4
Eastgate Ct PO19 173 B6
Eastgate Sq PO19 173 A6
Easthill Dr BN41 166 B2
Easthill Way BN41 166 B1
Easting Cl BN14 182 F5
Eastland Rd PO19 173 B5
Eastlands Cotts RH13 81 F1
Eastmead Ind Est PO18 152 E7
Eastoke Ave PO11 189 A2
Easton Cres RH14 77 E8
Easton La PO20 203 A6
Eastover Way PO22 195 F4
Eastshaw La GU29 70 C4
Eastway RH6 6 B7
Eastwick Cl BN1 168 B7
Eastwood RH10 18 F6
Eaton Ct 9 Hove BN3 187 B7
Worthing BN14 182 B6
Eaton Gardens Mansions 20
BN3 187 C7
Eaton Gate 17 BN3 187 C7
Eaton Gdns BN3 187 C7
Eaton Gr BN3 187 C7
Eaton Hall 19 BN3 187 C7
Eaton Manor 11 BN3 187 C7
Eaton Pl BN2 188 D4
Eaton Rd BN3 187 C7
Eaton Villas BN3 187 B7
Ecclesden 6 BN2 207 B6
Edburton Ave BN1 168 A1
Edburton Dro BN5 145 D6
Edburton Gdns BN43 164 F1
Eddington Hill RH11 18 B1
Eden Rd RH11 17 F4
Eden Vale RH19 9 E5
Edgar Cl RH10 19 E5
Edgehill Cl BN13 181 F7
Edgehill Way BN41 165 F2
Edgell Rd PO10 149 D4
Edgewood Ct GU33 45 D2
Edinburgh Cl
Bognor Regis PO21 194 E2
Southwater RH13 58 A1
Edinburgh Cotts 3 BN11 182 C1
Edinburgh Rd BN2 188 B8
Edinburgh Sq GU29 92 F7
Edinburgh Way RH19 22 F7
Edith Cotts PO18 151 A2
Edmonton Rd BN13 181 D6
Edrich Rd RH11 18 A1
Edward Ave BN3 167 A3
Edward Bryant Cty Prim Sch
PO21 195 D4
Edward Cl BN3 167 A3
Edward Ho BN3 186 F6
Edward Rd RH16 85 E2
Edward St BN2 207 B5
Edward Way RH15 106 D2
Edwards Ave PO20 154 C2
Edwards Way BN17 178 C4
Edwen Cl PO21 194 B3
Edwin Cl BN15 183 C6
Eels Cross PO20 206 B8
Effingham La RH10 7 E4
Effingham Rd RH10, RH6 7 D6
Egginton Rd BN2 168 F5
Egmont Ho GU29 71 A1
Egmont Rd Easebourne GU29 71 A1
Hove BN3 166 D1
Egremont Pl BN2 207 B5
Eighth Ave BN15 183 E7
Eirene Ave BN12 181 F1
Eirene Rd BN11, BN12 181 F1
Elanor Cl GU30 24 D8
Elbridge Cres PO21 194 C2
Elder Cl BN41 166 B2
Elder Pl BN1 207 A7
Elderfield Cl PO10 149 C3
Eldon Rd BN11 182 F3
Eldon Way BN17 198 B6
Eldred Ave BN1 167 D5
Eleanor Ct 1 BN11 181 F2
Eleanor Gdns PO22 196 D5
Elfin Gr PO21 195 B3
Elfn Mews 1 PO21 195 B3
Elger Way RH10 7 A4
Elgin Cl RH13 36 F3
Elgin Ct PO19 173 A5
Elgin Rd BN12 181 D2
Eliot Dr GU27 26 E6
Eliot Ho 4 RH16 85 E3
Elizabeth Ave
Bognor Regis PO21 194 D4
Hove BN3 167 A3
Elizabeth Cl Bognor Regis PO21 194 C3
Hove BN3 167 A3
Elizabeth Cres RH19 9 F3
Elizabeth Ct
5 Bognor Regis PO21 195 B2
Horley RH6 2 A3
7 Hove BN3 187 C7
7 Worthing BN11 181 F2
Elizabeth Ho
Bognor Regis PO22 195 E4
1 Worthing BN13 182 A5
Elizabeth Pl BN15 183 C5
Elizabeth Rd Chichester PO19 173 D7
Shoreham-by-Sea BN43 185 C8
Worthing BN11 182 C2
Elizabethan Way RH10 19 C5
Elkham Cnr GU28 52 C1
Ella Cl PO20 201 E7
Ellanore La PO20 190 B2
Ellasdale Rd PO21 195 B2
Ellen Ho 3 BN3 187 B7
Ellen St Hove BN3 187 B7
Portslade-by-Sea BN41 186 C7
Ellesmere Orch PO10 149 D5
Elliot Cl RH10 19 C4
Ellis Ave BN13 161 E1
Ellis Cl BN18 157 F2
Ellis Way PO21 205 A8
Ellman Rd RH11 17 F4
Ellson Cl RH10 19 C4
Elm Ave BN16 200 B6
Elm Cl Bognor Regis PO21 194 A1
Bracklesham PO20 202 B6
Hove BN3 167 C2
Shoreham-by-Sea BN43 164 F1
Elm Ct 1 Bognor Regis PO21 195 C2
Brighton BN1 187 E8
Southwick BN41 186 B8
Elm Dale PO22 176 A6
Elm Dr East Grinstead RH19 10 A1
Hove BN3 166 E1
Middleton-on-Sea PO22 197 B5
Elm Gr Bognor Regis PO21 195 A3
Brighton BN2 188 C7
Cowfold RH13 81 E2
Horsham RH13 36 E1
Lancing BN15 183 D5
Runcton PO20 173 E1
Selsey PO20 206 D7
West Barnham PO22 176 B7
Worthing BN11 181 F2
Elm Gr S PO22 176 A6
Elm Grove Cty Fst Sch BN11 181 F2
Elm Grove Cty Inf Sch BN17 198 E6
Elm Grove Cty Prim Sch BN2 188 C7
Elm Grove La BN44 143 D3
Elm Ho RH14 77 C8
Elm Pk Bosham PO18 171 C6
Ferring BN12 180 F3
Elm Pl BN16 199 D6
Elm Rd Portslade-by-Sea BN41 186 B8
Westergate PO20 175 E7
Worthing BN11 182 E2
Elm Rise BN14 161 E6
Elm Terr BN44 143 D3
Elm Tree Cl PO20 206 E8
Elmcroft Pl PO20 175 D6
Elmdene Ct PO20 202 B5
Elmeigh Ct GU29 92 E8
Elmer Cl PO22 197 B5
Elmer Ct PO22 197 C5
Elmer Rd PO22 196 F5
Elmgrove Rd BN17 198 F6
Elmhurst Cl BN16 180 A6
Elmhurst La RH13 56 C6
Elmleigh GU29 92 D8
Elmore Rd BN2 207 B6
Elms Dr BN15 183 D6
Elms La PO20 190 D1
Elms Lea Ave BN1 167 E3
Elms Ride PO20 190 C1
Elms Way PO20 190 C2
Elmsfield PO20 206 E7
Elmstead RH19 22 E8
Elmstead Gdns PO20 190 C2
Elmstead Park Rd PO20 190 C2
Elmstone Cl BN15 183 D6
Elmwood Ave PO22 195 D5
Elrington Rd BN3 167 C1
Elsaw Ct PO19 173 A5
Elsie Rd BN11 182 B1
Elsted Cl RH11 18 B8
Elsted Cres BN1 168 C6
Elsted Rd GU29 91 C7
Elverlands Cl BN12 200 F4
Elwood Cl RH15 106 F1
Ely Cl Crawley RH10 18 F2
East Wittering PO20 201 F8
Worthing BN13 181 F4
Ely Gdns PO21 194 D3
Ely Rd BN13 181 F4
Embassy Ct BN3 187 D5
Emberwood RH11 18 D8
Emerald Quay BN43 185 A6
Emlyn Rd RH6 1 E4
Emmabrook Ct BN16 199 A3
Emms La RH13 78 F7
Empire Villas RH1 2 B7
Emsbrook Dr PO10 149 B2
Emsworth Cl RH10 19 C3
Emsworth Common Rd
PO10, PO9 149 C6
Emsworth House Cl PO10 149 A1
Emsworth Prim Sch PO10 149 A1
Emsworth Rd PO10 169 D2
End Cotts BN18 138 E6
End La BN5 123 A5
Enfield Cl GU30 25 D3
Enfield Rd RH11 18 C2
Engalee RH19 9 C2
Englefield RH12 35 F2
English Cl BN3 186 E8
English Martyrs RC (A) Sch
BN12 181 D5
Ennerdale Cl RH11 18 B4
Ennerdale Dr BN15 183 B5
Ensign Way BN16 199 A6
Enterprise Ct BN12 181 C3
Enterprise Est BN1 168 C7
Epping Wlk RH10 18 F4
Epsom Gdns BN16 199 E6
Epsom Rd RH10 19 A4
Erica Way Copthorne RH10 7 A2
Horsham RH12 36 D5
Eridge Cl RH10 19 C6
Eridge Rd BN3 167 A2
Erin Way RH15 106 E3
Eriskay Ct BN13 181 B6
Eriswell Rd BN11 182 C1
Erles Rd GU30 25 C4
Ernest Cl PO10 149 B1
Erringham Rd BN43 164 E1
Erroll Rd BN3, BN41 186 C6
Erskine Cl RH11 17 E2
Esher Cl PO21 194 B2
Esher Dr BN17 198 F5
Eskbank Ave BN1 168 A7
Esmond Cl PO10 169 B8
Esmonde Cl BN17 198 F6
Esplanade The
Bognor Regis PO21 195 D2
Bognor Regis, Felpham PO22 195 F3
Worthing BN11 182 F2
Essex Ct BN11 182 A2
Essex Pl 3 BN2 188 C4
Essex Rd PO21 195 C5
Essex St BN2 188 C4
Estcots Cty Prim Sch RH19 10 A1
Estcots Dr RH19 10 A1
Estuary The BN17 198 F5
Ethel St BN3 187 B7
Ethelred Rd BN13, BN14 182 A4
Ethelwulf Rd BN13, BN14 182 A4
Eton Cl PO21 194 E4
Eton Dr PO20 201 F8
Eton Rd BN11 182 A3
Ettrick Cl PO19 173 B5
Ettrick Rd PO19 173 B5
Eurythmy Sch RH19 22 E6
Evans Cl RH10 19 D5
Evans Gdns 11 BN17 198 D5
Evans Pl PO22 195 D6
Evelyn Ave BN16 199 D4
Evelyn Ct BN41 186 A8
Evelyn Glennie Ct 7 BN2 188 C5
Evelyn Rd BN14 182 D4
Evelyn Terr BN2 188 C5
Everest Ho 2 BN3 186 F7
Eversfield RH13 58 B1
Eversfield Rd RH13 36 E1
Eversleigh Ct GU29 71 A2
Ewart St BN2 207 B6
Ewelands RH6 2 C4
Ewens Gdns PO22 176 A7
Ewhurst Cl RH11 18 C6
Ewhurst Rd Brighton BN2 168 C1
Crawley RH11 18 C7
Excalibur Cl RH11 17 E5
Excelsior The BN1 167 D4
Exchange Rd RH10 18 E6
Exeat Cl BN2 188 E6
Exeter Cl Bognor Regis PO21 194 F3
Crawley RH10 18 E2
New Brighton PO10 149 B2
Exeter Ct 2 BN11 182 A1
Exeter Rd PO19 152 E1
Exeter St BN1 187 E8
Exford Wlk BN13 181 D5
Exmoor Cl BN13 181 E7
Exmoor Cres BN13 181 E7
Exmoor Ct BN13 181 E7
Exmoor Dr BN13 181 E7
Exton Rd PO19 173 A4
Eyles Cl RH12 36 B4

Fabians Way BN5 123 D5
Fair View RH12 36 A3
Fairbanks RH16 85 E4
Fairbridge Way RH15 106 F5
Faircox La BN5 123 D5
Fairdene BN42 165 F1
Fairfield Ave RH6 2 A1
Fairfield Cl Ardingly RH17 64 A8
Bosham PO18 171 C5
Burgess Hill RH15 106 F4
New Brighton PO10 149 B2
Shoreham-by-Sea BN43 165 C1
Fairfield Cotts RH13 81 E2
Fairfield Cres BN6 126 A6
Fairfield Ct RH13 81 E2
Fairfield Gdns
Burgess Hill RH15 106 F4
Portslade-by-Sea BN41 166 B1
Fairfield Rd Ashington RH20 121 A4
Bosham PO18 171 B5
Burgess Hill RH15 106 F4
East Grinstead RH19 22 F8
Fairfield Rise GU28 95 F7
Fairfield Way Ashington RH20 121 A4
Haywards Heath RH16 85 D8
Fairfields 2 BN14 182 D4
Fairford Cl RH16 85 E5
Fairholme Dr BN18 177 A2
Fairlands Bognor Regis PO22 195 B6
East Preston BN16 200 A5
Fairlawn
1 Haywards Heath RH16 85 E4
Rustington BN16 199 C6
Fairlawn Cres RH19 9 B2
Fairlawn Dr East Grinstead RH19 9 B2
Worthing BN14 182 D4
Fairlawns Horley RH6 2 B2
8 Hove BN3 187 A6
Shoreham-by-Sea BN43 185 A8
Southwick BN41 186 F6
Fairlea Cl RH15 106 F4
Fairlea Rd PO10 149 B3
Fairlead BN17 198 F4
Fairlie Gdns BN1 167 E3
Fairlight Cty Prim Sch BN2 188 C8
Fairlight Pl 4 BN2 188 C8
Fairmead Cl RH20 97 A3
Fairmile Bottom BN18 157 B7
Fairmile Bottom Nature Trail
BN18 157 C8
Fairoak Ct 3 BN13 182 A5
Fairstone Ct RH6 2 B4
Fairview Ave BN12 181 C1
Fairview Cotts RH13 58 B3
Fairview Rd BN15 183 E8
Fairview Rise BN1 167 D5
Fairway Copthorne RH10 7 B2
Crawley RH11 17 D4
Littlehampton BN16, BN17 199 A4
Fairway Cl Copthorne RH10 7 A2
Liphook GU30 24 D3
Fairway Cres BN41 166 C2
Fairway Cty Inf Sch RH10 7 B3
Fairway The Bognor Regis PO21 205 B8
Midhurst GU29 92 E6
Rowland's Castle PO9 128 E2
Fairway Trad Est BN2 168 E4
Fairways BN1 187 E8
Faithfull Cres RH20 119 B2
Falcon Cl Crawley RH11 18 D8
Shoreham-by-Sea BN43 185 C6
Falcon Gdns BN17 178 C4
Falkland Ave BN17 198 F6
Falklands Cl PO22 195 D5
Falklands Dr RH13 37 B4
Fallow Deer Cl RH13 37 B4
Fallowfield Cl BN3 166 F2
Fallowfield Cres BN3 166 F2
Fallowfield Way RH6 2 B4
Falmer Ave BN12 181 B1
Falmer Cl Crawley RH11 18 D4
Worthing BN12 181 C1
Faraday Ave RH19 22 F6
Faraday Cl BN13 181 C5
Faraday Rd RH10 5 F2
Faresmead PO21 194 F2
Farhalls Cres RH12 36 F6
Farlington Ave RH16 85 F5
Farlington Cl RH16 85 F5
Farlington Sch RH12 35 B6
Farm Ave RH12 36 B3
Farm Cl Barns Green RH13 56 F2
Crawley RH10 19 A7
East Grinstead RH19 23 B8
Hassocks BN6 126 E4
Henfield BN5 123 E5
Loxwood RH14 32 A3
Middleton-on-Sea PO22 197 B5
Portslade-by-Sea BN41 166 A2
Warnham RH12 35 F7
Farm Cnr PO22 197 A5
Farm Cotts PO20 190 F6
Farm La Ditchling BN6 127 E3
Nutbourne PO18 170 B7
Farm Mews 8 BN3 187 D6
Farm Rd Bracklesham PO20 202 B5
Hove BN3 187 D6
Farm View PO10 149 B3
Farm Way Burgess Hill RH15 107 D1
Rustington BN16 199 B5
Southwick BN42 186 A7
Farmfield Dr RH6 5 B8
Farmfield Hospl RH6 1 B1
Farmleigh Cl RH10 19 C8
Farmway Cl BN3 166 D2
Farncombe Rd BN11 182 F2
Farndell Cl PO19 173 C7
Farne Cl PO20 191 E4
Farne La PO20 191 E4
Farney Close Sch
Bolney Court RH17 83 D2
Farnfold Rd BN44 143 D4
Farnham Ave BN6 127 A5
Farnham Cl RH11 39 C8
Farnham La GU27 27 A7
Farnham Rd GU33 45 A3
Farnhurst Rd PO22 176 B6
Farnlea RH15 107 D5
Faroes The BN17 199 A6
Farr Cl RH17 84 F8
Farriers Cl RH14 77 C7
Fastnet Way BN16, BN17 199 A6
Faulkners Way RH15 107 A5
Fay Rd RH12 36 C5
Faygate Bsns Ctr RH12 16 F1
Faygate Ct BN2 188 E6
Faygate La RH12 16 F4
Faygate Sta RH12 16 F1
Felbridge Ave RH10 19 D7
Felbridge Cl RH19 9 C3
Felbridge Ct RH19 9 A4
Felbridge Ctr The RH19 9 A3
Felbridge Cty Prim Sch RH19 8 F4
Felbridge Rd RH19 8 D3
Felcot Rd RH10 8 C4
Felcourt Cotts RH19 9 C8
Felcourt La RH19, RH7 9 C8
Felcourt Rd RH19, RH7 9 C7
Fellcott Way RH12 35 F1
Felpham Com Coll PO22 195 F5
Felpham Gdns PO22 196 B5
Felpham Ho BN17 178 B3
Felpham Rd PO22 195 F4
Felpham Way PO22 196 A5
Felride RH16 85 E3
Felwater Ct RH19 9 A3
Fenchurch Rd RH10 19 B4
Fender Ho RH12 36 B2
Fenhurst Cl RH12 35 F1
Fennel Cres RH11 18 B2
Fennel Wlk BN43 165 B1
Fereday Cl BN15 183 E6
Fermandy La RH10 8 A1
Fern Rd RH20 119 C1
Fern Way RH12 36 D5
Ferndale Rd Burgess Hill RH15 107 C2
Chichester PO19 153 A3
Hove BN3 187 D7
Ferndale Wlk BN16 180 A6
Fernden La GU27 27 C2
Fernden Sch GU27 27 B2
Ferndown Crawley RH10 6 D2
Horley RH6 2 A5
Ferndown Gdns PO22 196 A5
Fernhill Cl RH10 8 B1
Fernhill Rd RH6 6 D7
Fernhurst Cl Brighton BN1 168 B6
Crawley RH11 18 B8
Fernhurst Cres BN1 168 B5
Fernhurst Ct BN11 181 F1
Fernhurst Cty Prim Sch GU27 49 B6
Fernhurst Dr BN12 181 A2
Fernhurst Gdns PO21 194 D2
Fernhurst Gn GU27 49 B6
Fernwood Rise BN1 167 D5
Feroners Cl RH10 19 A4
Ferring CE (C) Prim Sch
BN12 200 F6
Ferring Cl Crawley RH11 18 B8
Ferring BN12 200 E4
Ferring Ct BN1 168 F5
Ferring Gdns PO22 196 A5
Ferring Grange Gdns BN12 200 E6
Ferring La BN12 180 F3
Ferring Marine BN12 200 F4
Ferring St BN12 200 E6
Ferringham La BN12 200 E5
Ferringham Way BN12 200 E4
Ferroners Ct RH10 19 A4
Ferry Rd Littlehampton BN17 198 B4
Shoreham-by-Sea BN43 184 F6
Festival Ct PO19 173 A7
Fetherston Rd BN15 183 E7
Feversham Cl BN43 185 B6

Fidlers Copse GU27 49 A6
Field Cl Burgess Hill RH15 106 E4
Lancing BN15 183 D6
Walberton BN18 156 D1
Field End RH20 119 E2
Field Ho Bognor Regis PO21 195 E3
East Preston BN16 199 F6
Field Pl Liphook GU30 25 C3
Littlehampton BN17 198 D5
Field Rd PO20 202 A7
Field Row 6 BN11 182 D2
Field Sch The BN3 186 D7
Fieldend RH12 37 B5
Fieldgate Cl RH13 59 C4
Fieldings Cotts RH14 55 F5
Fieldings The Horley RH6 2 C4
Southwater RH13 79 F7
Fields End Cl RH16 85 F4
Fieldview RH6 2 B4
Fieldway Ditchling BN6 127 D3
Haslemere GU27 27 C7
Haywards Heath RH16 85 F8
Fifth Ave Lancing BN15 183 E7
Worthing BN14 182 C8
Filbert Cres RH11 18 A6
Filey Cl RH11 17 F4
Filton Wlk BN13 181 D6
Finch Gdns PO22 195 B7
Fincham Cl BN16 199 F5
Fincham Ct BN16 199 F5
Finchdean Rd PO9 128 F3
Finches Cl Lancing BN15 183 D5
Littlehampton BN17 178 C4
Partridge Green RH13 103 A3
Finches Ct RH16 64 A1
Finches Gdns RH16 86 A8
Finches La Haywards Heath RH16 86 A8
West Chiltington Common RH20 119 C8
Finches Park Rd RH16 86 A8
Finches The BN43 185 A8
Findon By-Pass BN14 161 D6
Findon Cl BN3 166 F3
Findon Dr PO22 196 D6
Findon Rd Brighton BN2 188 F5
Crawley RH11 18 B8
Worthing BN14 161 F3
Findon Way RH12 35 D3
Finians Field RH13 56 F2
Finisterre Way BN17 199 A4
Finsbury Cl RH11 18 C2
Finsbury Lodge 1 BN2 188 C6
Finsbury Rd BN2 188 C6
Fir Tree Ave GU27 26 D6
Fir Tree Cl Crawley RH11 5 B1
Lower Beeding RH13 60 A3
West Chiltington Common RH20 119 D6
Fir Tree La RH20 119 D6
Fir Tree Way BN6 127 A4
Firbank Cotts RH6 7 C7
Fircroft Ave BN15 183 E8
Fircroft Cl Brighton BN1 167 E3
Worthing BN13 181 F6
Fircroft Cres BN16 179 D3
Firlands Haywards Heath RH16 85 F4
Horley RH6 2 B4
Firle Cl RH10 18 E8
Firle Rd Brighton BN2 188 D6
North Lancing BN15 163 E1
Firs Ave PO22 196 B5
Firs Ave W PO22 196 B5
Firsdown Cl BN13 161 E2
Firsdown Rd BN13 161 E2
Firsland Park Ind Est BN5 124 F8
First Ave Almodington PO20 191 F2
Bognor Regis PO22 196 B4
Bracklesham PO20 202 B5
Hove BN3 187 C6
Lancing BN15 183 E7
Middleton-on-Sea PO22 196 F6
Southbourne PO10 169 F8
Worthing BN14 182 C7
Firtoft Cl RH15 107 B3
Firview GU30 25 B3
Fish La Bognor Regis PO21 194 F2
Selsey PO20 206 B8
Fishbourne CE (C) Prim Sch PO19 172 B6
Fishbourne Rd W PO19, PO20 172 C6
Fishbourne Road E PO19 172 D6
Fishbourne Roman Palace PO19 172 B6
Fishbourne Sta PO19 172 B7
Fisher Cl RH10 18 E4
Fisher La Plaistow GU8 30 B7
South Mundham PO20 193 C7
Fisherman's Wlk
Bognor Regis PO21 194 D1
Selsey PO20 206 F7
Fishermans The PO10 169 C8
Fishermans Wlk
Shoreham-by-Sea BN43 184 D5
South Hayling PO11 189 A2
Fishers Cl BN16 199 A4
Fishers Ct RH12 36 C4
Fishersgate Cty Fst Sch BN41 186 A7
Fishersgate Sta BN41 186 C8
Fishersgate Terr BN41, BN42 186 A7
Fitch Dr BN2 168 F1
Fitchet Cl RH11 18 B8
Fittleworth CE (C) Fst Sch RH20 97 A3
Fittleworth Cl BN12 181 B4
Fittleworth Dr PO22 196 C7
Fittleworth Gdn 7 BN16 199 C5
Fittleworth Rd RH14 75 F5
Fitzalan Ct
3 Littlehampton BN17 198 E4
4 Rustington BN16 199 B3
Fitzalan Mews BN18 158 B2
Fitzalan Rd Arundel BN18 158 B2
Horsham RH12, RH13 37 A4
Littlehampton BN17 198 E4
Fitzherbert Dr BN2 188 D8
Fitzjohn Ct BN6 126 F3
Fitzleet Ho 9 PO21 195 C3
Fitzroy Ct BN17 198 E5
Fitzwilliam Cl PO21 194 F4
Five Acres Crawley RH10 18 E8
Funtington PO18 151 A5
Five Oaks Rd RH13, RH14 56 D7
Fixcroft Cotts BN5 104 D4
Flag Ct BN3 187 B5
Flag Sq BN43 184 F6
Flamsteed Hts RH11 18 B1
Flansham La PO22 196 C6
Flansham Pk PO22 196 D6
Flatt Rd PO18 170 D8
Flax Mean PO22 196 B5
Flax Mean Ho PO22 196 B5
Flaxman Ave PO19 172 D6
Fleet Cl BN17 199 A6
Fleet The RH20 97 B3
Fleming Ct PO21 194 A1
Fleming Way RH10, RH11 5 F2
Fletcher Cl Bognor Regis PO21 194 B2
Crawley RH10 18 E4
North Mundham PO20 173 D1
Fletcher Ho PO20 173 C1
Fletcher Pl PO20 173 C1
Fletcher Rd BN14 182 E5
Fletcher Way BN16 179 F6
Fletcher's Croft RH20 119 D2
Fletcher's La PO18 171 D1
Fletchers RH13 57 F3
Fletchers Cl RH13 36 E1
Fletchers Est PO20 192 D2
Fletchers Field GU30 25 C3
Fletchers Ho GU30 25 B3
Fletchers La PO20 192 D3
Fletching Cl BN2 188 F6
Flimwell Cl BN2 188 E5
Flint Cl Crawley RH10 19 B3
Portslade-by-Sea BN41 166 B2
Flint Cotts BN18 158 A3
Flint Ho 2 BN16 199 C4
Flora McDonald Cty Jun Sch BN17 198 C6
Floral Dean Ct BN14 162 A1
Florence Ave BN3 186 D8
Florence Cl PO20 191 D4
Florence Ct BN1 167 F2
Florence Pl BN1 168 B1
Florence Rd Brighton BN1 188 A8
Chichester PO19 173 C6
Florets The BN44 144 B1
Florida Cl BN12 200 F4
Florida Gdns BN12 200 F4
Florida Rd BN12 200 F4
Florlandia Cl BN15 183 B6
Flower Farm Cl BN5 123 D5
Foamcourt Waye BN12 200 E5
Fold Sch The BN3 186 D7
Folders Cl RH15 107 D1
Folders La BN6, RH15 107 D1
Follett Cl PO21 194 E2
Follis Gdns PO19 172 B8
Folly La GU28, RH20 115 E3
Fonthill Rd BN3 187 B8
Fontwell Ave BN18, PO20 155 F1
Fontwell Cl Fontwell BN18 156 A2
Littlehampton BN16 199 B4
Worthing BN14 182 A8
Fontwell Dr BN14 182 A8
Fontwell Park Race Course BN18 155 F2
Fontwell Rd Crawley RH10 19 A3
East Beach PO20 206 G8
Ford Airfield Ind Est BN18 177 C3
Ford La Ashurst BN44, RH13 122 D7
Ford BN18 177 C4
Ford Rd Arundel BN18 158 A2
Ford BN18 177 E3
Tortington BN18 177 F7
Fordingbridge Cl RH12 36 C1
Fordingbridge Ind Site PO22 176 A7
Fordwater Gdns BN18 177 B2
Fordwater La PO19 153 A2
Fordwater Rd
Chichester PO18, PO19 153 A3
East Lavant PO18 153 A5
Fordwater Sch PO19 153 A1
Foredown Cl BN41 166 B2
Foredown Dr BN41 166 C1
Foredown Rd
Portslade Village BN41 166 B4
Portslade-by-Sea BN41 166 B2
Forest Cl Crawley Down RH10 21 B8
Horsham RH12 37 B4
Mannings Heath RH13 59 C6
Forest Cnr GU33 45 C7
Forest Com Sch RH13 36 F1
Forest Lane Cl GU30 25 A4
Forest Lodge 2 RH19 22 F8
Forest Oaks RH13 37 B4
Forest Rd Brighton BN1 168 E6
Colgate RH12 38 D6
Liss Forest GU33 45 C7
Midhurst GU29 92 D6
Worthing BN14 182 D6
Forest Ridge RH19 43 A5
Forest Rise GU33 45 C6
Forest Row Bsns Pk RH18 23 F4
Forest Row CE Inf Sch RH18 23 F2
Forest View RH10 19 A3
Forest View Rd RH19 22 E6
Forester Rd RH10 18 E4
Forestfield Crawley RH10 19 B3
Horsham RH13 37 A3
Forge Cl Broadridge Heath RH12 35 D4
East Preston BN16 199 F6
Portslade-by-Sea BN41 166 B2
Stockbridge PO19 172 F3
Forge La Broadridge Heath RH12 35 D4
Crawley RH10 19 A7
Forge Rd RH10 19 A7
Forge The Handcross RH17 61 C8
Selsey PO20 206 D7
Southwater RH13 57 F1
Warnham RH12 35 E7
Forge Way Billingshurst RH14 77 C8
Burgess Hill RH15 107 A4
Forge Wood RH10 6 D3
Forge Wood Ind Est RH10 6 B3
Forrester Rd RH13 103 A3
Forsters Yd BN17 198 B5
Fort Haven BN43 185 C6
Fort Rd BN17 198 C6
Forty Acre La GU31 88 E3
Fosters Cl BN16 199 E4
Foundry Cl RH13 36 E4
Foundry Cotts GU29 93 C3
Foundry Ct RH15 107 B3
Foundry La Haslemere GU27 27 A6
Horsham RH12, RH13 36 E3
Foundry St BN1 207 A6
Fountains Cl Brighton BN1 168 C2
Crawley RH11 18 A4
Fourth Ave Bognor Regis PO22 196 C4
Hove BN3 187 B6
Lancing BN15 183 E7
Worthing BN14 182 D7
Fowey Cl BN43 185 B6
Fowler Cl RH10 19 C4
Fox Cl Burgess Hill RH15 106 F1
Crawley RH11 5 B1
Fox Ct RH20 119 B1
Fox Dell RH20 119 B1
Fox Hill RH16 85 E1
Fox Hill Cl RH16 85 F1
Fox Hill Village RH16 85 E1
Fox Lea BN14 161 E5
Fox Rd Easebourne GU29 71 A2
Haslemere GU27 26 E6
Fox Way BN41 166 B2
Foxbridge La RH14 31 C1
Foxbury La PO10 149 E4
Foxdale Dr BN16 179 F4
Foxes Cl RH13 79 F7
Foxes Croft PO22 176 C6
Foxfield Cotts RH13 79 F7
Foxfields RH20 119 C8
Foxglove Ave RH12 36 E6
Foxglove Wlk RH11 18 B3
Foxhill Ct 3 RH16 85 E3
Foxhole La RH17 83 B2
Foxholes RH12 33 D8
Foxhunters Rd BN41 165 F3
Foxleigh Chase RH12 36 F5
Foxley La BN13 181 F8
Foxwarren RH16 85 C5
Foxwarren Cl PO20 201 F7
Foxwells RH17 41 A1
Framfield 11 BN2 188 F5
Framfield Cl Brighton BN1 168 E6
Crawley RH11 18 A8
Frampton Ct BN12 181 C2
Framptons The BN16 200 B5
France La BN13 160 D1
Francis Edwards Way RH11 17 E2
Francis Rd RH16 86 B8
Francis St BN1, BN2 207 A7
Franciscan Way BN17 198 D5
Francislea RH16 85 E2
Francome Ho BN15 183 D3
Frandor Rd PO21 194 F5
Frankland Mead RH20 141 E6
Frankland Terr 2 PO10 169 C8
Franklands Cl
Burgess Hill RH15 107 B1
Worthing BN14 162 A1
Franklands Gdns RH15 127 A8
Franklands Way RH15 127 A8
Franklin Pl PO19 173 A7
Franklin Rd Brighton BN2 188 C7
Crawley RH10 19 C5
Portslade-by-Sea BN41 186 C7
Shoreham-by-Sea BN43 165 D1
Worthing BN13 181 E7
Franklin St BN2 188 C8
Franklynn Rd RH16 85 F3
Frankton Ave RH16 86 A3
Frant Rd BN3 167 A2
Fraydene PO10 169 F8
Fraser Cl PO20 206 F6
Fraser Ct 2 BN43 185 C8
Fraser Gdns PO10 150 A2
Fred Emery Ct 10 BN1 187 E5
Frederick Cotts RH16 86 B7
Frederick Gdns BN1 207 A6
Frederick Pl BN1 207 A6
Frederick Rd PO19 172 C7
Frederick St BN1 207 A6
Freehold St BN43 184 E7
Freehold Terr 1 BN2 188 C8
Freek's La RH15 107 A5
Freeman Cl BN18, PO20 156 B1
Freeman Rd RH12 35 F8
Freemans Cl RH14 77 C8
Freemans Rd BN41 186 A8
Freeways PO20 206 C8
French Gdns RH16 86 A6
Frenches RH20 119 D2
Frenches Mead RH14 77 C8
Freshbrook Cl BN15 183 E5
Freshbrook Ct 3 BN15 183 E5
Freshbrook Cty Fst Sch BN15 183 E6
Freshbrook Rd BN15 183 F5
Freshfield Bank RH18 23 E2
Freshfield Cl RH10 19 A5
Freshfield Halt RH17 87 B8
Freshfield La RH17 65 E2
Freshfield Pl BN2 188 C5
Freshfield Rd BN2 188 D6
Freshfield St BN2 188 C6
Freshfield Way BN2 188 C5
Freshfields Cl BN15 183 D6
Freshfields Dr BN15 183 D6
Friar Cl BN1 168 A4
Friar Cres BN1 168 A3
Friar Rd BN1 168 A3
Friar Wlk BN1 167 F4
Friars Cl BN6 126 E4
Friars Oak Rd BN6 126 E5
Friars Rookery RH10 18 F6
Friars Wlk BN13 181 F3
Friary Cl PO22 196 E5
Friary La PO19 173 A6
Friary Way RH10 18 E5
Friday St Faygate RH12 15 E6
Warnham RH12 35 E7
Friends Cl RH11 5 D1
Friston Cl BN2 168 F4
Friston Wlk RH11 18 A7
Frith Pk RH19 9 E3
Frith Rd Bognor Regis PO21 195 A4
Hove BN3 187 A8
Frobisher Cl BN12 181 D4
Frobisher Rd PO21 194 C2
Frobisher Way
Littlehampton BN16 199 E4
Worthing BN12 181 D4
Fry Cl RH11 18 B1
Fry Cres RH15 106 E5
Fryern Cl RH20 119 C2
Fryern Rd RH20 119 D3
Fryland La BN5, RH13 104 B4
Fuel Farm Rd RH6 5 E8
Fulfords Hill RH13 57 A7
Fulham Cl RH11 18 B2
Fullers Wlk BN17 178 D5
Fulmar Cl 1 Crawley RH11 17 D5
Hove BN3 167 D1
Fulmar Dr RH19 10 B3
Fulmar Way PO20 154 E1
Fulmer Ct 1 BN11 182 B1
Funtington Cty Prim Sch PO18 151 A3
Funtington Ho BN17 178 B3
Furlong Way RH6 5 F8
Furlonge Ho PO10 149 A1
Furlongs The BN44 143 D2
Furnace Dr RH10 18 F4
Furnace Farm Rd RH10 19 A4
Furnace Par RH10 19 A4
Furnace Pl RH10 19 A4
Furnace Rd RH10, RH19 8 C3
Furners La BN5 124 A5
Furners Mead BN5 123 F4
Furnston Gr PO10 150 A1
Furse Feld PO21 195 A2
Furze Cl BN13 161 D2
Furze Common Rd RH20 120 A6
Furze Croft BN3 187 D6
Furze Hill BN3 187 D6
Furze Hill Ct BN3 187 E6
Furze Hill Ho BN3 187 E6
Furze La RH19 9 B4
Furze Meadow GU31 90 A8
Furze Rd Rudgwick RH12 33 D8
Worthing BN13 161 E2
Furze View RH14 56 B6
Furzedene BN3 187 D6
Furzedown BN17 198 E4
Furzefield Crawley RH11 18 C7
East Wittering PO20 190 F1
Furzefield Chase RH19 9 E6
Furzefield Cl BN16 179 F7
Furzefield Rd
East Grinstead RH19 9 D4
Horsham RH12 37 B5
Furzeholme BN13 161 E2
Furzeland Way BN6 125 D8
Furzen La RH12, RH5 13 B4
Fyning La GU31 68 C5

Gables The Copthorne RH10 7 B3
Cowfold RH13 81 E1
Horsham RH12 36 D4
Southwater RH13 79 F8
Gableson Ave BN1 167 B4
Gabriel Rd RH10 19 C2
Gage Cl RH10 8 C1
Gage Ridge RH18 23 E2
Gaggle Wood RH13 59 C6
Gainsboro Rd PO21 195 C3
Gainsborough Ave BN14 182 E7
Gainsborough Dr PO20 206 F7
Gainsborough Ho 16 BN3 187 C7
Gainsborough Lodge 1 BN14 182 C4
Gainsborough Rd RH10 18 F3
Gaisford Cl BN14 182 C4
Gaisford Rd BN14 182 B4
Galahad Rd RH11 17 E6
Gales Dr RH10 18 F6
Gales Pl RH10 18 F6
Galliers Cl BN1 168 B6
Galsworthy Cl BN12 181 B3
Galsworthy Rd BN12 181 B3
Gamecock Terr PO20 154 D1
Gander Cl RH15 107 A5
Gander Gn RH16 85 F7
Gander Hill RH16 85 F7
Ganders Cl BN5 123 D5
Gandersgate La RH14 75 A7
Gannet Ho BN3 167 B1
Gannon Rd BN11 182 F3
Ganymede Ct RH11 17 E3
Garbitts La GU31 68 B4
Garcia Trad Est BN13 181 F3
Garden Ave PO20 202 B6
Garden Cl Angmering BN16 180 A7
East Grinstead RH19 22 F7
Lancing BN15 183 C6
Portslade-by-Sea BN41 186 C8
Shoreham-by-Sea BN43 165 B1
Storrington RH20 119 D2
Garden Cres PO22 176 C5
Garden Ct PO21 194 E2
Garden Head RH19 42 E6
Garden Ho PO19 152 F2
Garden Ho The BN1 207 F6
Garden House La RH19 22 F7
Garden Lodge PO21 194 A2
Garden Pl RH12 36 C4
Garden Wlk Crawley RH11 18 C6
Horsham RH12 36 C4
Garden Wood Cl RH20 119 D6
Garden Wood Rd RH19 22 C8
Gardener St BN41 186 B8
Gardeners Cl RH12 35 E8
Gardeners Ct RH13 36 D1
Gardeners Gn RH12 16 C6
Gardens The Fittleworth RH20 97 A3
Southwick BN42 185 F7
Gardner La RH10 21 A8
Gardner Rd BN41, BN42 186 A7
Gardner St BN1 207 A5
Garland Ave PO10 149 B3
Garland Cl PO19 173 B5
Garland Rd RH19 9 D2
Garland Sq PO20 154 D2
Garnet Ho 13 BN2 188 C4
Garrett Cl RH10 19 C4
Garrick Rd BN14 182 E4
Garrick Wlk RH10 18 E3
Garrones The RH10 19 E7
Garsons Rd PO10 169 F8
Garton Cl RH11 17 E5
Gaskyns Cl RH12 33 D7
Gasson Wood Rd RH11 17 E4
Gaston Way PO18 152 E7
Gatcombe Cl BN13 181 B5
Gateford Dr RH12 36 F6
Gatehouse La
Burgess Hill BN6, RH15 106 C4
Trotton GU31 69 A4
Gates Cl RH10 19 C2
Gatesmead RH16 85 F8
Gateway Lodge PO22 195 F4
Gatewick Terr BN44 143 D3
Gattons Cty Inf Sch The RH15 106 E3
Gattons The RH15 106 E3
Gatwick Airport Sta RH6 6 B7
Gatwick Airport-London RH6 5 F7
Gatwick Gate RH6 5 E5
Gatwick Metro Ctr RH6 2 B4
Gatwick Park Hospl RH6 1 E2
Gatwick Rd RH10, RH6 6 A3
Gatwick Way RH6 5 F8
Gatwick Zoo RH6 4 D6
Gaugemaster Way BN18 177 E5
Gay St RH20 99 C4
Gay Street La RH20 99 A6
Gaywood Wlk BN13 181 D5
Gemini Cl RH11 17 E4
Genistos The BN6 126 E4
Genoa Cl BN16 199 A6
George Denyer Cl GU27 27 C7
George IV Wlk PO22 196 A5
George Pinion Ct RH12 36 B3
George Pringle Sch BN12 181 D5
George St Brighton BN2 207 A5
Chichester PO19 173 A7
Hove BN3 187 B6
Portslade-by-Sea BN41 186 C7
Southwick BN41 186 A7
George V Ave
Shoreham-by-Sea BN15 184 B5
Worthing BN11, BN12 181 F2
Georges La RH20 120 C1
Georgia Ave BN14 182 D4
Georgian Cl RH10 19 D5
Georgian Gardens Cty Prim Sch BN16 199 E6
Georgian Gdns BN16 199 E6
Gerald Cl RH15 107 D3
Gerald Ct RH13 36 E2
Gerald Rd BN11 181 F1
Gerard St BN1 207 A8
Gerrard House Bsns Ctr BN16 199 F6
Ghyll Cres RH13 58 F8
Ghyll Ct RH13 57 F1
Ghyllside BN2 168 E1
Gibbons Cl RH10 19 C3
Giblets La RH12 36 F7
Giblets Way RH12 36 E7
Gibson Rd PO20 154 C2
Gibson Way PO21 195 D4
Giffards Cl RH19 9 F1
Gifford Rd PO18 171 C7
Gilbert Rd PO19 172 E8
Gilberts The BN16 199 B3
Giles Cl BN18 176 F2
Gilham La RH18 23 E2
Gillett Ct RH13 37 B4
Gillett Ho RH13 37 B4
Gillham's La GU27 26 A5

Gilligan Cl RH12 .... 36 B2
Gilligans The RH15 .... 106 F5
Gillmans Ind Est RH14 .... 77 D6
Gillway PO20 .... 206 G8
Gilmore Rd PO19 .... 173 C6
Gilpin Cl PO19 .... 172 B6
Gilwynes PO21 .... 194 F2
Gilwynes Ct PO21 .... 194 F2
Ginhams Rd RH11 .... 18 B6
Girton Ho BN41 .... 186 F6
Glade Cty Inf Sch The PO22 .. 195 A5
Glade The Bognor Regis PO21 .. 205 A8
  Crawley RH10 .... 19 A4
  Horsham RH13 .... 37 A3
Gladepoint 7 RH16 .... 85 E5
Glades The RH19 .... 10 B1
Gladonian Rd BN17 .... 178 D3
Gladstone Pl BN2 .... 188 C8
Gladstone Rd
  Burgess Hill RH15 .... 107 C4
  Horsham RH12 .... 36 D3
  Portslade-by-Sea BN41 .... 186 B7
  Yapton BN18 .... 176 F2
Gladstone Terr Brighton BN2 .. 207 B7
  Littlehampton BN17 .... 178 D3
Gladys Rd BN3 .... 186 D8
Glamis Ct PO21 .... 195 D3
Glamis St PO21 .... 195 D3
Glanville Wlk 7 RH11 .... 18 A3
Glaseby La PO20 .... 141 D4
Glasshouse La GU28, RH14 .... 74 F3
Glastonbury Rd BN3 .... 186 D6
Glatting La RH20 .... 115 E1
Glaziers La GU29 .... 71 B2
Gleave Cl RH19 .... 10 A2
Glebe Cl Crawley RH10 .... 18 E7
  Lancing BN15 .... 183 E7
  Norton PO22 .... 155 B1
  Southwick BN42 .... 185 F7
Glebe Cty Mid Sch BN42 .... 185 D7
Glebe Field Rd PO20 .... 191 A5
Glebe Rd Cuckfield RH17 .... 84 F6
  Fernhurst GU27 .... 49 B5
  Worthing BN13 .... 182 A5
Glebe The Copthorne RH10 ..... 7 B3
  Felbridge RH19 .... 9 A4
  Haywards Heath RH16 .... 86 A8
  Horley RH6 .... 1 F3
  Hurstpierpoint BN6 .... 126 A6
  Tangmere PO20 .... 154 C1
Glebe Twitten RH17 .... 84 F6
Glebe View RH17 .... 41 A1
Glebe Villas Hove BN3 ...... 186 D7
  Petworth GU28 .... 73 F1
Glebe Way Lancing BN15 .... 183 E7
  Wisborough Green RH14 .... 76 C8
Glebelands Crawley Down RH10 . 21 A7
  Loxwood RH14 .... 31 F4
  Pulborough RH20 .... 98 D2
Glebelands Cl BN43 .... 185 B8
Glebeside Ave BN14 .... 182 A5
Glebeside Cl BN14 .... 182 B5
Glen Cres PO20 .... 206 E7
Glen Dale PO9 .... 128 E1
Glen Gdns BN12 .... 200 F6
Glen Rise BN1 .... 167 B5
Glen Rise Cl BN1 .... 167 B5
Glen The Southwater RH13 .... 58 A2
  Worthing BN13 .... 182 A4
Glen Vue RH19 .... 9 E1
Glenbarrie Way BN12 .... 180 E3
Glencathara Rd PO21 .... 195 B3
Glendale Cl RH12 .... 37 A6
Glendale Rd Burgess Hill RH15 . 107 B2
  Hove BN3 .... 187 D7
Glendon Ho 9 RH11 .... 18 D5
Glendor Rd BN3 .... 186 E6
Glendyne Cl RH19 .... 23 A8
Glendyne Way RH19 .... 23 A8
Gleneagles Ct
  Crawley RH10, RH11 .... 18 D5
  13 Haywards Heath RH16 .... 85 E4
Glenelg Ct PO21 .... 194 F6
Glenfalls Ave BN1 .... 168 A7
Glenfield Cotts RH6 .... 4 D7
Glenham Ct RH19 .... 43 A5
Glenlea Hollow GU26, GU27 .... 26 E8
Glenmore Ct 13 BN17 .... 198 E4
Glenview Cl RH10 .... 18 F8
Glenville Rd BN16 .... 199 D4
Glenway PO22 .... 195 D4
Glenwood Ave PO22 .... 195 D4
Glenwood Rd PO10 .... 150 A1
Gleton Ave BN3 .... 166 D2
Globe Pl BN17 .... 178 D3
Gloster Dr PO21 .... 194 B2
Gloucester Cl RH19 .... 23 A8
Gloucester Ct BN12 .... 181 F1
Gloucester La BN17 .... 198 D5
Gloucester Pas 2 BN1 ..... 207 A6
Gloucester Pl
  Brighton BN1, BN2 .... 207 A6
  Littlehampton BN17 .... 198 D5
Gloucester Rd
  Bognor Regis PO21 .... 195 E3
  Brighton BN1 .... 207 A6
  Burgess Hill RH15 .... 106 F3
  Crawley RH10 .... 18 E2
  Littlehampton BN17 .... 198 C5
Gloucester St BN1, BN2 .... 207 A6
Gloucester Terr PO18 ...... 171 B4
Gloucester Way PO19 .... 152 F1
Glover's Rd RH6 .... 2 A3
Glovers Field GU27 .... 26 F6
Glynde Ave BN12 .... 181 A2

Glynde Cl BN12 .... 200 F6
Glynde Cres PO22 .... 196 A5
Glynde Ho BN3 .... 187 D6
Glynde Pl RH12 .... 36 C2
Glynde Rd BN2 .... 188 B6
Glyndebourne Ct 9 BN43 .... 184 F7
Glynleigh 17 BN2 .... 207 B6
Goda Rd BN17 .... 198 E5
Goddard Cl RH10 .... 19 B3
Goddards Green Hospl
(Cuckfield Hospl Annexe)
  BN6 .... 106 B5
Godman Cl PO21 .... 194 D2
Godmans Ct RH13 .... 81 E1
Godolphin Ct RH10, RH11 .... 18 D5
Godstalls La BN44 .... 143 C2
Godstrode La GU8 .... 29 A6
Godwin Cl PO10 .... 149 A3
Godwin Rd BN3 .... 166 D1
Godwin Way PO18 .... 172 A8
Goffs Cl RH11 .... 18 C5
Goffs La RH11 .... 18 B6
Goffs Park Rd RH11 .... 18 C4
Goldcrest Ave BN17 .... 178 C4
Goldcrest Cl RH6 .... 1 E4
Golden Acre
  Bognor Regis PO21 .... 205 A8
  West Kingston BN16 .... 200 B4
Golden Ave BN16 .... 200 B5
Golden Avenue Cl BN16 .... 200 B5
Golden Fields GU30 .... 25 D3
Golden Hill RH15 .... 107 D3
Golden La RH13 .... 122 E6
Golden Sq Henfield BN5 .... 123 E4
  Petworth GU28 .... 95 F8
Goldfinch Cl Crawley RH11 ... 18 D8
  Horsham RH12 .... 36 C7
Golding Barn Farm (Works)
  BN5 .... 144 E2
Golding La RH13 .... 59 D7
Goldsmid Rd BN1, BN3 ...... 187 E7
Goldsmith Rd BN14 .... 182 E4
Goldstone Cl BN3 .... 167 A2
Goldstone Cres BN3 .... 167 B2
Goldstone Ct BN3 .... 167 A3
Goldstone Cty Jun Sch BN3 . 166 E1
Goldstone Ho 4 BN3 .... 187 B7
Goldstone La BN3 .... 187 B8
Goldstone Rd BN3 .... 187 B7
Goldstone St BN3 .... 187 B7
Goldstone Villas BN3 ..... 187 B7
Goldstone Way BN3 .... 167 A2
Golf Club La RH20 .... 118 F7
Golf Dr BN1 .... 168 B3
Golf Links La PO20 .... 203 E1
Golf Links Rd PO22 .... 196 A6
Golfers La BN16 .... 179 D3
Goodacres PO22 .... 176 C5
Goodhew Ct BN18 .... 177 A3
Goodwin Cl RH11 .... 17 F3
Goodwins Ct RH19 .... 9 D3
Goodwood Ave PO22 .... 195 F5
Goodwood Cl Crawley RH10 .. 19 A3
  Midhurst GU29 .... 92 E5
  Rustington BN16 .... 199 E6
Goodwood Ct 2 Hove BN3 ... 187 D7
  Selsey PO20 .... 206 E8
  Southbourne PO10 .... 170 A8
Goodwood Ctry Pk PO18 .... 134 A4
Goodwood Gdns PO21 ...... 173 E1
Goodwood Ho PO18 .... 153 F6
Goodwood Rd BN13, BN14 ... 182 A7
Goodwood Way PO21 .... 168 F3
Goose Green Cl RH12 .... 36 D5
Goosegreen La RH20 .... 100 C2
Gooserye Ct GU30 .... 25 B3
Gorden Rd BN15 .... 183 D6
Gordon Ave
  1 Bognor Regis PO21 .... 195 D4
  Bognor Regis PO22 .... 195 D5
  Shoreham-by-Sea BN43 .... 185 A7
  Stockbridge PO19 .... 172 E3
Gordon Ave W PO22 .... 195 D5
Gordon Cl BN11 .... 85 E6
Gordon Ho
  8 Bognor Regis PO21 .... 195 C3
  Burgess Hill RH15 .... 107 C4
Gordon Rd Brighton BN1 .... 167 F2
  Burgess Hill RH15 .... 107 C4
  Haywards Heath RH16 ..... 85 E6
  Hermitage PO10 .... 169 D8
  Horsham RH12 .... 36 D4
  Portslade-by-Sea BN41 .... 186 C7
  Shoreham-by-Sea BN43 .... 185 A7
  Southwick BN41 .... 186 A7
  Worthing BN11 .... 182 D3
Gordon Terr PO18 .... 171 B6
Goreside La RH17 .... 84 F8
Goring Chase BN12 .... 181 A4
Goring Crossways BN12 .... 181 A4
Goring Ct BN1 .... 168 F5
Goring Hall Hospl (private)
  BN12 .... 181 B1
Goring Rd Steyning BN44 ... 143 C2
  Worthing BN11, BN12 ..... 181 D2
Goring St BN12 .... 181 A3
Goring Way
  Partridge Green RH13 .... 103 A3
  Worthing BN12 .... 181 A2
Goring's Mead RH13 .... 36 D1
Goring-by-Sea
  CE (A) Fst Sch BN12 .... 181 C2
Goring-by-Sea Sta BN12 ... 181 A3
Gorling Cl RH11 .... 17 E5
Gorringe Cl BN43 .... 185 D7
Gorringes Brook RH12 ...... 36 D6
Gorse Ave Bognor Regis PO22 . 196 B6
  Kingston Gorse BN12, BN16 . 200 D4

Gorse Ave Worthing BN14 .. 182 B6
Gorse Bank Cl RH10 .... 18 B1
Gorse Cl Copthorne RH10 .... 7 B2
  Crawley RH11 .... 18 B1
  Portslade-by-Sea BN41 .... 165 F4
Gorse Cotts GU27 .... 26 C8
Gorse End RH10 .... 18 B1
Gorse La BN13 .... 161 E2
Gorse Terr PO20 .... 192 D4
Gorselands RH14 .... 77 E8
Gosden Cl RH10 .... 19 A5
Gosden Rd BN17 .... 198 F6
Gospond Rd PO22 .... 176 B5
Gossamer La PO21 .... 194 D3
Gossops Dr RH11 .... 18 A5
Gossops Green Cty Fst Sch
  RH11 .... 18 A5
Gossops Green Cty Mid Sch
  RH11 .... 18 A5
Gossops Green La RH11 .... 18 A5
Gossops Par RH11 .... 17 F5
Goudhurst Cl RH10 .... 19 E6
Goudhurst Keep RH10 ...... 19 E6
Gower Rd Haywards Heath RH16 . 85 E3
  Horley RH6 .... 1 E3
Gowers Cl RH17 .... 64 B8
Grace Ct BN6 .... 126 E5
Grace Rd RH11 .... 18 A1
Graffham Cl Brighton BN2 .. 188 E6
  Chichester PO19 .... 153 A3
  Crawley RH11 .... 18 B8
Graffham Cty Prim Sch GU28 . 114 B6
Grafton Ave PO22 .... 196 C6
Grafton Cl BN16 .... 199 C6
Grafton Ct PO20 .... 206 E6
Grafton Dr BN15 .... 183 C6
Grafton Gdns BN15 .... 183 C6
Grafton Pl 5 BN11 .... 182 D2
Grafton Rd Selsey PO20 .... 206 E6
  Worthing BN11 .... 182 D2
Grafton St BN2 .... 207 B4
Graham Ave Brighton BN1 .. 167 F5
  Portslade-by-Sea BN41 .... 165 F4
Graham Cl BN41 .... 165 F4
Graham Cres BN41 .... 165 F4
Graham La BN17 .... 181 F1
Graham Rd Worthing BN11 .. 182 D2
  Yapton BN18 .... 176 F1
Graham's Cotts RH16 .... 64 B1
Grailands Cl GU27 .... 49 C6
Granary Cl RH6 .... 1 E3
Granary Way Horsham RH12 .. 36 A1
  Littlehampton BN17 ...... 178 D4
Grand Ave Hassocks BN6 ... 126 F4
  Hove BN3 .... 187 C6
  Lancing BN15 .... 183 E7
  Littlehampton BN17 ...... 178 C3
  Worthing BN11 .... 182 B1
Grand Avenue Mansions 23
  BN3 .... 187 C6
Grand Junction Rd BN1, BN2 . 207 A4
Grand Par Brighton BN2 .... 207 A5
  Crawley RH11 .... 18 D6
Grand Parade Mews BN2 .... 207 A5
Grange Cl Brighton BN1 .... 167 E1
  Burgess Hill RH15 .... 107 C5
  Crawley RH10 .... 19 A8
  Ferring BN12 .... 200 D5
Grange Cres RH10 .... 21 B7
Grange Ct Bognor Regis PO21 . 194 D2
  Middleton-on-Sea PO22 ... 196 F5
  9 Southwick BN42 .... 185 E7
Grange Field Way PO21 .... 194 D2
Grange Ind Est The BN42 ... 185 D7
Grange La PO20 .... 204 B2
Grange Park Rd BN12 ...... 200 E5
Grange Rd Crawley Down RH10 . 21 A7
  Hove BN3 .... 186 E8
  Midhurst GU29 .... 92 F7
  Southwick BN42 .... 185 E7
Grange The RH6 .... 2 A6
Grange Way RH13 .... 57 F2
Grangeway The BN16 ...... 199 C5
Grangeways BN1 .... 167 E5
Grangewood Dr PO21 ...... 194 D2
Granston Way RH10 .... 21 C8
Grant Cl PO20 .... 206 D7
Grant St BN2 .... 207 B7
Grantham Rd BN1 .... 168 A1
Grantsmead BN15 .... 183 E8
Granville Ct 10 BN3 ...... 187 B7
Granville Rd Hove BN3 .... 187 E7
  Littlehampton BN17 ...... 198 E4
Graperies The 3 BN2 ..... 188 C5
Grasmere Ave BN15 .... 183 B6
Grasmere Gdns RH12 ...... 37 B6
Grasmere Ho RH6 .... 2 C4
Grassmere Cl
  Bognor Regis PO22 ...... 195 F4
  Littlehampton BN17 ...... 179 A3
Grassmere Par PO22 ...... 195 F4
Gratten La
  Twineham BN5, RH17 ..... 105 A3
  Wineham BN5 .... 104 D3
Grattons Dr RH10 .... 6 C1
Grattons The RH13 .... 34 E3
Gratwicke Ct RH14 .... 77 D8
Gratwicke Rd BN11 .... 182 C2
Gravel La PO10 .... 173 C5
Gravelly Cres BN15 .... 183 F6
Gravelpit Cnr RH17 .... 39 C1
Gravelye Cl RH16 .... 86 B5
Gravelye La
  Haywards Heath RH16 ..... 86 A4
  Haywards Heath RH16 ..... 86 B6
Graveney Rd RH10 .... 18 C6
Gravett Ct RH15 .... 106 F2
Gravetye Cl RH10 .... 19 A4

Gravits La PO21 .... 195 B4
Graydon Ave PO19 .... 172 E4
Graylingwell Hospl PO19 .. 153 B1
Grays Cl GU27 .... 27 E8
Grays Wood RH6 .... 2 C3
Grayswood Ave PO20 .... 202 B6
Grayswood PO21 .... 27 E8
Grayswood Rd GU27 .... 27 D8
Great College St BN2 ..... 188 C4
Great Heathmead RH16 ..... 85 D6
Great House Ct 4 RH19 .... 22 F8
Great Walstead Sch RH16 ... 86 F6
Greatfield Way PO9 .... 128 D3
Greatham Ct BN1 .... 167 E6
Greatham Rd Crawley RH10 .. 19 C3
  Worthing BN14 .... 162 A1
Greatlake Ct RH6 .... 2 B4
Greatpin Croft RH20 ...... 97 A3
Grebe Cres RH11 .... 37 A1
Green Bushes Cl BN16 ..... 199 B4
Green Cl Southwater RH13 .. 57 F3
  4 Southwick BN42 .... 185 E7
Green Cross RH17 .... 84 C3
Green Ct East Wittering PO20 . 201 F7
  3 Southwick BN42 .... 185 E7
Green Field Cl BN42 ...... 185 E8
Green Hedges Ave RH19 ..... 9 D2
Green Hedges Cl RH19 ...... 9 D2
Green La Bosham PO18 .... 171 C6
  Broadbridge PO18 .... 171 A8
  Burstow RH6 .... 6 F6
  Chichester PO19 .... 173 B6
  Copthorne RH10 .... 7 F4
  Crawley RH10 .... 18 E8
  Crawley, Worth RH10 ..... 19 D6
  Faygate RH12 .... 15 F4
  Fernhurst GU27 .... 27 B4
  Merston PO20 .... 173 F4
  Newdigate RH5 .... 3 D8
  Runcton PO20 .... 173 F2
  Selsey PO20 .... 206 D6
  Sidlesham PO20 .... 203 C8
  Street End PO20 .... 192 E6
  West Grinstead RH13 .... 102 B8
Green Lane Cl BN18 ...... 157 F2
Green Meadows RH16 .... 86 B8
Green Pk BN1 .... 180 F3
Green Ridge BN1 .... 167 B5
Green The Bognor Regis PO21 . 205 A8
  Broadridge Heath RH12 ... 35 D4
  Copthorne RH10 .... 7 B3
  Crawley RH11 .... 18 C7
  East Lavington GU28 .... 114 E5
  Henfield BN5 .... 123 E4
  Hove BN3 .... 167 C2
  Liss GU33 .... 45 A5
  Pulborough RH20 .... 98 C4
  Southwick BN42 .... 185 E7
  Storrington RH20 .... 119 F2
Green View RH15 .... 106 E3
Green Way PO22 .... 196 F5
Green Way The BN12 ...... 181 B4
Green Wlk BN12 .... 181 B4
Greena Ct 7 BN11 .... 182 C2
Greenacre Ct RH20 .... 119 B1
Greenacres Ashington RH20 . 121 A6
  Brighton BN1 .... 167 F1
  Crawley RH10 .... 19 A5
  Horsham RH12 .... 36 C4
  Shoreham-by-Sea BN43 ... 184 B8
  Steyning BN44 .... 143 D2
  Westlands PO20 .... 191 D6
Greenacres Ring BN16 .... 180 A6
Greenbank PO22 .... 176 C5
Greencourt Dr PO21 ...... 195 A5
Greenfield RH20 .... 115 F2
Greenfield Cl Brighton BN1 . 168 A5
  Liphook GU30 .... 25 C5
Greenfield Cres RH11 ...... 37 A6
Greenfield Rd Chichester PO19 . 173 C7
  Slinfold RH13 .... 34 D3
Greenfield Way RH20 ..... 119 E2
Greenfields Liss GU33 .... 45 C4
  Littlehampton BN17 ..... 178 B3
  Nyewood GU31 .... 90 A7
Greenfields Cl Horley RH6 .. 1 E5
  Horsham RH12 .... 37 A6
  Nyewood GU31 .... 90 A8
Greenfields Rd Horley RH6 .. 1 F5
  Horsham RH12 .... 37 A5
Greenfields Sch RH18 ..... 23 C1
Greenfinch Way RH12 ...... 36 D7
Greengates GU28 .... 50 D2
Greenhill Pk RH16 .... 86 A2
Greenhill Way RH16 .... 86 A2
Greenhurst La RH20 ...... 119 E4
Greenland Rd BN13 .... 181 E7
Greenland Rd BN13 .... 181 E7
Greenland Wlk BN13 ...... 181 E7
Greenlands Cl RH15 ...... 127 B8
Greenlands Dr RH15 ...... 127 B8
Greenlea PO21 .... 194 B2
Greenleas BN3 .... 166 D2
Greenoaks BN15 .... 183 E8
Greenside BN17 .... 198 C6
Greenstede Ave RH19 .... 9 F2
Greentree La RH13 .... 103 C5
Greentrees Lancing BN15 .. 183 C6
  5 Worthing BN13 .... 182 B2
Greentrees Cl BN15 ...... 183 C6
Greentrees Cres BN15 .... 183 C6
Greenway RH12 .... 36 B3
Greenway Cty Prim Sch RH12 . 36 B3
Greenways Bognor Regis PO22 . 195 F4
  Haywards Heath RH16 ..... 85 F6
  Henfield BN5 .... 123 D5

Greenways
  Portslade-by-Sea BN41 .. 166 B1
  Southwick BN42 .... 165 F1
Greenways Cres Ferring BN12 . 200 F5
  Shoreham-by-Sea BN43 .... 165 A1
Greenways Wlk RH11 .... 18 C1
Greenwich Ct RH11 .... 18 C2
Greenwood Ave PO22 ...... 195 B6
Greenwood Cl PO22 .... 195 B6
Greenwood Ct 2 RH11 ..... 18 B1
Greenwood Dr BN16 .... 179 F4
Greet Rd BN15 .... 183 D7
Gregory Cl RH10 .... 19 C2
Gregsons RH12 .... 35 E8
Grendon Ct RH6 .... 1 F5
Grenfield Cl RH20 .... 149 B3
Grenville Ave BN12 ...... 181 D3
Grenville Cl Liphook GU30 .. 25 C4
  Worthing BN13 .... 181 D3
Grenville Gdns PO19 ..... 172 F4
Grenville St BN1 .... 207 F5
Gresham Wlk RH10 .... 18 E3
Grevatt's La BN17, BN18, PO22 . 197 B6
Grevatt's La W BN18, BN17 . 196 F8
Greville Gn PO10 .... 149 A3
Grey Alders RH16 .... 86 B6
Greyfriars BN3 .... 187 D6
Greyfriars Cl
  Bognor Regis PO21 ...... 194 F3
  Worthing BN13 .... 182 A6
Greyfriars La RH20 ...... 140 C8
Greyhound Slip RH10 ...... 19 D7
Greynville Ct PO21 ...... 194 C2
Greypoint Ho BN14 .... 161 E6
Greystoke Mews BN12 ..... 200 E6
Greystoke Rd BN12 .... 200 E6
Greystone Ave
  Bognor Regis PO21 ...... 194 F7
  Worthing BN13 .... 181 F5
Gribble La PO20 .... 174 B7
Grier Cl RH11 .... 17 E5
Griffin Cres BN17 .... 178 C4
Griffith's Ave RH15 ...... 183 B8
Grinstead Ave BN15 ...... 183 E6
Grinstead La Lancing BN15 . 183 E6
  Sharpthorne RH19 .... 43 C7
Grinstead Mount 4 BN2 ... 188 F5
Grisedale Cl RH11 .... 18 C4
Groombridge Way RH12 ..... 35 F1
Grooms The RH10 .... 19 D8
Groomsland Dr RH14 ...... 77 C6
Grosvenor Ct BN1 .... 167 E3
Grosvenor Gdns PO21 ..... 194 C3
Grosvenor Rd
  East Grinstead RH19 ...... 9 D1
  Stockbridge PO19 .... 172 F3
  3 Worthing BN11 .... 182 D2
Grosvenor St BN2 .... 207 B5
Grosvenor Way PO21 ...... 194 C3
Grouse Rd
  Barnsnap RH11, RH13 ..... 38 D3
  Mannings Heath RH13 .... 59 F7
Grove Bank 8 BN2 ...... 207 B6
Grove Cres BN17 .... 198 F6
Grove Ct 5 BN3 .... 187 C6
Grove Hill BN2 .... 207 B6
Grove La Petworth GU28 ... 96 A6
  West Chiltington Common RH20 . 119 E5
Grove Pk PO19 .... 172 E6
Grove Rd Burgess Hill RH15 . 107 B3
  Chichester PO19 .... 173 B5
  Horley RH6 .... 1 F4
  Selsey PO20 .... 206 E6
  Worthing BN14 .... 182 C6
Grove St Brighton BN2 .... 207 B6
  Petworth GU28 .... 95 F7
Grove The Bognor Regis PO22 . 196 A4
  Crawley RH11 .... 18 C6
  Ferring BN12 .... 200 E6
  Haywards Heath RH16 ..... 86 B3
  Horley RH6 .... 2 B2
  Liphook GU30 .... 25 A4
  Westbourne PO10 .... 149 D3
Grove Villa 3 BN1 .... 207 F7
Grovelands RH6 .... 2 B2
Grovelands Cl RH15 ...... 106 F1
Grovelands The BN15 ..... 183 E4
Grover Ave BN15 .... 183 D7
Guardian Ct BN13 .... 182 A6
Guernsey Cl RH11 .... 18 A2
Guernsey Farm La PO22 ... 196 D5
Guernsey Rd BN14 .... 200 F4
Guildbourne Ctr The BN11 . 182 E2
Guilden Rd PO19 .... 173 B6
Guildford Cl Breach PO10 . 150 A1
  Worthing BN14 .... 182 A3
Guildford Pl PO19 .... 152 F1
Guildford Rd Horsham RH12 . 36 A2
  Rowhook RH12 .... 34 C7
  Rudgwick RH12 .... 33 C5
  Rustington BN16 .... 199 E6
  Strood Green RH12 .... 35 B6
  Worthing BN14 .... 182 A3
Guildford St BN1 .... 207 F6
Guildhall St PO19 .... 173 A7
Guilford Rd RH11 .... 207 F6
Guillards Oak GU29 .... 92 E7
Guillemot Path 2 RH11 ... 17 D5
Guillods Cotts GU28 ..... 114 B7
Guinevere Rd RH11 .... 17 E6
Guinness Ct RH11 .... 18 A3
Gunning Cl RH11 .... 18 A3
Gunns Farm GU30 .... 25 C2
Gunwin Ct PO21 .... 194 D2
Guyhurst Spinney RH20 ... 120 A6
Gwydyr Mansions 4 BN3 ... 187 D6
Gwynne Gdns RH19 .... 9 C2

Habin Hill GU31 68 B3
Hackenden Cl RH19 9 E3
Hackenden La RH19 9 E3
Haddington Cl BN3 187 B6
Haddington St 11 BN3 187 B7
Hadley Ave BN14 182 D6
Hadley Cl PO22 196 E6
Hadlow Cl BN2 188 D6
Hadlow Way BN15 183 F6
Hadmans Cl RH12 36 C1
Hadrian Ave BN42 186 A8
Haglands Copse RH20 119 D7
Haglands La RH20 119 D7
Haig Ave BN1 168 D6
Haigh Cl BN15 184 B6
Hailsham Cl BN16 180 B3
Hailsham Rd BN11 181 F1
Hale Cl PO20 202 B6
Hales Field GU27 27 C6
Halewick Cl BN15 183 C8
Halewick La BN15 183 C8
Haleybridge Wlk PO20 154 D1
Half Moon Hill GU27 27 C6
Half Moon La BN13 181 F7
Halfrey Cl PO18 172 A7
Halfrey Rd PO18, PO19 172 B7
Halifax Cl RH10 6 E1
Halifax Dr BN13 181 C6
Hall Ave BN14 182 B7
Hall Cl BN14 182 A7
Halland Cl RH10 19 A7
Halland Rd BN2 168 F4
Halleighs RH17 84 E8
Hallett Rd BN2 188 D7
Halley Cl RH11 18 B1
Halley's Ct PO19 173 C6
Halliford Dr PO22 176 C6
Halliwick Gdns PO22 196 B4
Hallsland RH10 21 C8
Hallyburton Rd BN3 186 D8
Halnaker Barn La PO18 155 B4
Halnaker Gdns PO21 194 C2
Halnaker Wlk 8 RH11 17 F3
Halsbury Cl BN11 182 F3
Halsbury Rd BN11 182 F3
Halsford Croft RH19 9 B3
Halsford Gn RH19 9 B3
Halsford La RH19 9 C3
Halsford Park Cty Prim Sch RH19 9 C2
Halsford Park Rd RH19 9 C2
Halson Cl PO21 195 C4
Halton Shaws BN6 126 B5
Ham Bridge Trad Est BN14 183 A4
Ham Bsns Ctr BN43 185 A7
Ham Cl BN11, BN14 183 A4
Ham La Oving PO20 174 D7
Prinsted PO10 169 F7
Scaynes Hill RH17 86 E3
Ham Manor Cl BN16 179 E4
Ham Manor Farm Cotts BN16 179 D4
Ham Manor Way BN16 179 E4
Ham Rd Shoreham-by-Sea BN43 184 F7
Sidlesham PO20 203 C5
Worthing BN11, BN14 183 A3
Ham Way BN11 183 A4
Hamble Gdns BN13 181 C7
Hamble Rd BN15 183 B6
Hamble Way BN13 181 C7
Hambledon Pl PO21 195 B3
Hambleton Ct RH11 18 C4
Hambleton Hill RH11 18 C4
Hambrook RH15 107 C1
Hambrook Bsns Ctr PO18 150 D4
Hambrook Hill N PO18 150 D3
Hambrook Hill S PO18 150 D2
Hamilton Cl
Portslade-by-Sea BN41 166 A3
Stedham GU31 69 F1
Worthing BN14 182 E5
Hamilton Ct BN12 181 D4
Hamilton Gdns PO21 194 D2
Hamilton Lodge Sch BN2 188 D5
Hamilton Mansions BN3 187 B5
Hamilton Mews BN15 183 C6
Hamilton Rd Brighton BN1 207 F7
Horsham RH12 36 B3
Lancing BN15 183 D7
Hamlet The PO22 195 C6
Hamlin's Cnr BN6 106 A6
Hammer Hill Hammer GU27 26 C4
Staplefield RH17 62 A3
Hammer La Chithurst GU29, GU31 69 D4
Hammer GU27, GU30 26 B6
Hammer GU26 26 C5
Haslemere GU26 26 C8
Hammer Vale GU26 26 C6
Hammer Yd RH11 18 D5
Hammerpond Rd
Ashfold Crossways RH13, RH17 60 B6
Doomsday Green RH13 59 C8
Hammerwood Copse GU27 26 D5
Hammerwood Rd RH19 23 E6
Hammingden La RH17, RH19 42 E3
Hammond Dr BN13 181 E8
Hammond Pl 2 RH20 119 D1
Hammonds Ridge RH15 106 F1
Hammy Cl BN43 185 C8
Hammy La BN43 185 B8
Hammy Way BN43 185 B8
Hampden Cl Crawley RH10 6 E1
Middleton-on-Sea PO22 196 F5
Hampden Pl PO20 154 D2
Hampden Rd BN2 188 C7
Hamper's La RH13 37 A2
Hampers Common Ind Est GU28 73 F2
Hampers Ct RH13 36 D2
Hampers Gn GU28 73 E2
Hampers La RH20 120 B2
Hampshire Ave PO21 195 B5
Hampshire Ct BN2 207 B4
Hampshire Ho GU30 25 B7
Hampstead Rd BN1 167 D2
Hampton Cotts RH13 80 F6
Hampton Ct Bognor Regis PO21 194 F4
8 Littlehampton BN17 198 D5
Hampton Fields 4 BN17 198 D6
Hampton Lodge RH6 2 A2
Hampton Pl BN1 187 E5
Hampton St 14 BN1 187 E5
Hampton Way RH19 22 F7
Hamsey Cl BN2 188 F5
Hamsey Rd RH19 43 A6
Hamshire Hill RH17 60 F5
Hamsland RH17 65 C4
Hamstead Meadow PO18 170 E7
Hanbury La RH16 86 A5
Hanbury Park Sports Stad RH16 86 A5
Hanbury Rd RH11 17 E5
Handcross Cty Prim Sch RH17 39 C2
Handcross Park Sch RH17 39 C2
Handcross Rd Balcombe RH17 40 D3
Lower Beeding RH13, RH17 60 C5
Handford Way RH17 60 D6
Handsworth Ho 8 RH11 18 D5
Hangleton Cl BN3 166 D2
Hangleton Cty Inf & Jun Sch BN3 166 E2
Hangleton Gdns BN3 166 D1
Hangleton Grange BN12 180 E3
Hangleton La Hangleton BN12 180 D4
Hove BN3, BN41 166 C2
Portslade-by-Sea BN41 166 B2
Hangleton Manor Cl BN3 166 D2
Hangleton Rd BN3 166 E2
Hangleton Valley Dr BN3 166 D4
Hangleton Way BN3 166 D3
Hanlye La RH17 85 B8
Hannah Sq PO19 172 D7
Hannington Pl BN6 126 A7
Hanover Cl Bury RH20 138 A7
Crawley RH10 18 F3
Selsey PO20 206 F7
Hanover Cres BN2 207 B7
Hanover Ct Brighton BN2 207 B7
Haywards Heath RH16 85 D4
Horsham RH13 36 F3
Liphook GU30 25 B5
Worthing BN14 182 C6
Hanover Mews BN2 207 B7
Hanover St BN2 207 B7
Hanover Terr BN2 207 B7
Hanover Wlk RH20 119 D1
Harberton Cres PO19 153 A3
Harbolets Rd RH14, RH20 100 A5
Harborough Cl RH20 119 B8
Harborough Dr RH20 119 B8
Harborough Gorse RH20 119 B8
Harborough Hill RH20 119 B8
Harborough Meadow RH20 119 B8
Harbour Cotts PO18 171 A4
Harbour Ct Bosham PO18 171 C5
Southwick BN42 185 F7
Harbour Rd Bognor Regis PO21 204 F6
Bosham PO18 171 B4
Harbour View Rd PO21 205 A8
Harbour Way Bosham PO18 171 C4
Chidham PO18 170 F5
Emsworth PO10 169 C8
Shoreham-by-Sea BN43 185 B6
Harcourt Way PO20 206 F8
Hard The PO22 197 C5
Hard's Hill RH13 58 D5
Hardbarrow Woods RH20 120 A6
Hardham Cl Crawley RH11 18 A8
Rustington BN16 199 B4
Hardham Rd PO19 173 B5
Hardwick Rd BN3 166 E3
Hardwick Way BN3 166 E3
Hardy Cl Bognor Regis PO22 196 D5
Crawley RH10 19 C7
Horley RH6 1 E3
Horsham RH12 36 B4
Shoreham-by-Sea BN43 184 F6
Hare La Crawley RH11 18 B8
Selsey PO20 206 B8
Harebell Dr BN41 166 A3
Harefield Ave BN13 181 F4
Harefield Gdns PO22 196 F5
Harefield Rd PO22 196 F6
Hares La PO18 150 E6
Haresfield Terr PO20 154 D1
Haresfoot Cl PO18 150 F5
Harewood Cl RH10 6 A1
Harewood Ct 8 BN3 187 C6
Harfield Ct 6 PO21 195 D3
Harlands Cl RH16, RH17 85 C6
Harlands Cty Prim Sch RH16 85 D7
Harlands Rd RH16, RH17 85 D6
Harlech Cl BN13 181 B5
Harley Ct 6 BN11 182 B2
Harmans Dr RH19 10 B1
Harmans Mead RH19 10 B1
Harmony Cl RH11 17 E4
Harmony Dr PO20 202 B5
Harmsworth Cres BN3 166 E3
Harold Rd Crawley RH10 19 E5
Westbourne PO10 149 D4
Harold Terr PO10 149 B1
Haroldslea RH6 2 E2
Haroldslea Cl RH6 2 C1
Haroldslea Dr RH6 2 D1
Harper Dr RH10 19 C2
Harrier Ct RH10 6 D1
Harrington Ct 13 BN1 167 E2
Harrington Mansions 12 BN1 167 E2
Harrington Pl BN1 168 B2
Harrington Rd BN1 167 E2
Harrington Villas BN1 167 F2
Harriot's Hill RH13 81 A8
Harriots Cl RH13 59 A1
Harris Cl RH11 18 B3
Harris Ct GU30 25 B2
Harris La PO8 108 A5
Harrison Ct BN14 182 E5
Harrison Rd BN14 182 F5
Harrow Dr PO20 201 F7
Harrow Rd BN11 182 B3
Harrows The GU28 95 B8
Harrowsley Ct RH6 2 B4
Harsfold Cl BN16 199 B4
Harsfold Rd BN16 199 B4
Hartfield Ave BN1 168 A5
Hartfield Rd RH18 23 F2
Harting Cl BN12 181 B4
Harting Ct RH11 17 F3
Harting Rd BN17 178 D3
Hartings The PO22 196 D6
Hartington Pl BN2 188 C8
Hartington Rd BN2 188 C8
Hartington Terr BN2 188 C8
Hartington Villas BN3 187 B8
Hartland Ct PO10 149 F1
Harvest Cl RH16 86 B7
Harvest Hill Ansty RH17 84 D2
East Grinstead RH19 22 E8
Harvest Rd RH10 19 C4
Harvesters
Haywards Heath RH16 85 D2
Horsham RH12 36 D5
Harvestside RH6 2 C4
Harvey Cl Crawley RH11 18 A1
Sayers Common BN6 105 D1
Harvey Rd BN12 181 E1
Harvey Villas GU30 24 D8
Harwarden Cl RH10 21 C8
Harwood Ave BN12 181 D4
Harwood Pk RH1 2 A8
Harwood Rd
Horsham RH12, RH13 37 A3
Littlehampton BN17 198 C6
Harwood Road Ent Units BN17 198 C6
Harwoods Cl 3 RH19 22 F7
Harwoods La RH19 22 F7
Hascombe Ct RH11 18 A5
Hasle Dr GU27 27 B6
Haslemere & District Hospl GU27 27 D7
Haslemere Gdns PO11 189 B2
Haslemere Prep Sch GU27 27 D5
Haslemere Rd Breach PO10 149 F2
Fernhurst GU27 49 B7
Liphook GU27, GU30 25 D4
Haslemere Sta GU27 27 B6
Hasler's La PO18 132 E5
Haslett Ave E RH10 19 A6
Haslett Ave W RH10, RH11 18 D5
Haslingbourne La GU28 95 F5
Hassocks Ct 3 RH11 17 F3
Hassocks Cty Inf Sch BN6 126 F4
Hassocks Lodge BN6 126 F3
Hassocks Rd BN6 126 B5
Hassocks Sta BN6 126 E4
Haste Hill GU27 27 D5
Hastings Cl PO21 194 F4
Hastings Ct 9 BN11 182 A1
Hastings Rd Brighton BN2 188 C8
Crawley RH10 19 C6
Worthing BN11 182 A1
Hatch Cl GU6 11 A3
Hatch End RH18 23 F2
Hatch Hill GU27 27 B1
Hatch La East Liss GU33 45 E4
Kingsley Green GU27 27 B2
Hatchetts Dr GU27 26 D7
Hatchgate RH6 1 F2
Hatchgate Cl RH17 85 A6
Hatchgate La RH17 85 A6
Hatchlands RH17 84 F6
Hatfield Ct 16 BN3 187 C6
Hatfield Wlk Crawley RH11 17 E2
Worthing BN13 181 D5
Hatherleigh Cl PO21 195 A5
Hatherleigh Gdns PO21 195 A5
Hathersham La RH1, RH6 2 F6
Havant Rd PO10 169 A8
Havelock Cl PO22 195 F3
Havelock Rd
Bognor Regis PO21 195 C4
Brighton BN1 167 F1
Haven Cotts PO22 195 D5
Haven Ct PO20 201 F7
Haven Gdns RH10 8 B1
Haven Rd Rudgwick RH12, RH14 33 D3
South Hayling PO11 189 A1
Haven The Lancing BN15 183 F4
Rustington BN16 199 A5
Havengate RH12 36 F5
Havenside BN43 184 E6
Havenstoke Cl PO19 153 A1
Havenwood Cvn Pk BN18 157 B3
Haversham Cl RH10 18 F6
Haversham Ho RH6 2 B5
Hawke Cl BN16 199 E5
Hawkesbourne Rd RH12 36 F5
Hawkesmoor Rd RH11 17 E4
Hawkhurst Pl BN1 168 D6
Hawkhurst Rd BN1 168 D6
Hawkhurst Wlk RH10 19 B4
Hawkins Cl Bognor Regis PO21 194 B2
Hawkins Cl
Shoreham-by-Sea BN43 165 D1
Hawkins Cres BN43 165 D2
Hawkins Rd Crawley RH10 18 E4
Shoreham-by-Sea BN43 165 D1
Hawkley Rd GU33 45 A5
Hawkridge RH12 12 E1
Hawks Mead GU33 45 A5
Hawks Pl PO22 195 B6
Hawksfold La E GU27 49 A6
Hawksfold La W GU27 49 A6
Hawkshaw Cl GU30 25 D4
Hawley Rd BN16 199 B4
Hawmead RH10 21 C8
Hawth (Arts Ctr) The RH10 18 F5
Hawth Ave RH10 18 F4
Hawth Cl RH10 18 E4
Hawthorn Bank BN2 168 F4
Hawthorn Cl Burgess Hill RH15 107 D5
Chichester PO19 172 F7
Crawley RH11 5 C1
Horsham RH12 36 C4
Midhurst GU29 92 D6
6 Rustington BN16 199 C4
Hawthorn Cres BN14 182 D6
Hawthorn Gdns BN14 182 D6
Hawthorn Rd
Bognor Regis PO21, PO22 195 B4
Littlehampton BN17 178 D3
Worthing BN14 182 D6
Hawthorn Way
Portslade-by-Sea BN41 166 A3
Storrington RH20 119 D2
Hawthorne Cotts RH6 7 C7
Hawthorns Cty Fst Sch BN13 181 C5
Hawthorns The
Bognor Regis PO21 195 C4
Burgess Hill RH15 107 A5
West Chiltington Common RH20 119 E7
Hay Rd PO19 173 B4
Haybarn Dr RH12 36 E7
Haybourne Cl BN2 188 E7
Haybourne Rd BN2 188 E7
Haydon Cl PO21 194 C1
Hayes Cl Mid Lavant PO18 152 E7
Portslade-by-Sea BN41 186 C8
Hayes La RH13 34 D2
Hayes Wood Rd RH14 55 F5
Hayfields RH6 2 C4
Hayley Rd BN15 183 F7
Hayley's Gdns PO22 196 A4
Haylind Rd RH16 86 B5
Hayling Ct RH11 18 C3
Hayling Gdns BN13 161 E1
Hayling Rise BN13 161 E1
Haynes Rd BN13, BN14 182 B4
Haynes Way BN14 182 B4
Haystacks GU29 113 C8
Hayton Ct BN13 181 B5
Haywards RH10 6 D1
Haywards Cl PO22 196 B5
Haywards Heath Coll RH16 85 D6
Haywards Heath Golf Course RH16 63 F1
Haywards Heath Hospl RH16 85 C4
Haywards Heath Rd RH17 41 A1
Haywards Heath Sta RH16 85 E6
Haywards Rd Brighton BN1 168 A6
Haywards Heath RH16 85 E3
Hazel Bank 3 BN2 207 B7
Hazel Cl Crawley RH11 5 C1
Crawley Down RH10 21 C8
Portslade-by-Sea BN41 166 C3
Southwater RH13 58 A1
Hazel Gr Arundel BN18 157 E2
Bognor Regis PO21 194 D3
Burgess Hill RH15 107 B1
Hazel Rd PO22 195 B6
Hazel Way RH10 21 C8
Hazelbank Cl GU30 25 D4
Hazeldean Dr PO9 128 D1
Hazeldene Meads BN1 167 D2
Hazeldene Rd GU30 24 D4
Hazelgrove Gdns 8 RH16 85 E4
Hazelgrove Rd RH16 85 E4
Hazelhurst RH6 2 C4
Hazelhurst Cres Horsham RH12 35 F1
Worthing BN14 161 F3
Hazelhurst Dr RH10 19 E6
Hazelmead Dr BN16 200 A5
Hazelwick Ave RH10 19 B8
Hazelwick Mill La RH10 19 A8
Hazelwick Rd RH10 19 A7
Hazelwick Sch RH10 19 A8
Hazelwood Brighton BN1 167 D3
Crawley RH11 18 A5
Hazelwood Cl Crawley RH10 20 F8
Easebourne GU29 71 A3
Heath Common RH20 120 B2
Worthing BN14 182 F4
Hazelwood Cotts GU6 11 D4
Hazelwood Lodge 3 BN15 183 F5
Hazelwood Rd RH13 103 A3
Hazelwood Trad Est BN14 182 F5
Hazleden Cross RH19 22 B6
Headborough Ct BN15 183 E4
Headborough Gdns BN15 183 E4
Headlands Cotts RH17 39 C2
Headley Cl RH10 6 D1
Headley Rd GU30 25 B5
Hearn Cl PO20 154 C1
Hearnfield Rd BN17 178 D4
Heath Cl Broadridge Heath RH12 35 E3
9 Haywards Heath RH16 85 E4
Hunston PO20 193 A8
Mannings Heath RH13 59 D6
Sayers Common BN6 105 D1
Heath Ct Broadridge Heath RH12 35 E3
Heath Ct
6 Haywards Heath RH16 85 E5
Heath Hill Ave BN2 168 F1
Heath Pl PO22 195 D7
Heath Rd Hammer GU27 26 D5
Haywards Heath RH16 85 E5
Heath Sq RH16 85 D5
Heath Way RH12 36 D5
Heathcote Dr RH19 9 C2
Heathcourt BN17 198 F5
Heather Bank RH16 85 C5
Heather Cl Copthorne RH10 7 B2
Horsham RH12 36 D5
West Ashling PO18 151 C3
Heather Ct Chichester PO19 172 F5
9 Hove BN1 187 E6
Heather Ho BN15 183 F7
Heather La
West Chiltington Common RH20 119 C6
Worthing BN13 161 E2
Heather Way RH20 119 F1
Heather Wlk RH11 18 B3
Heatherlands Horley RH6 2 B4
Storrington RH20 119 F2
Heatherstone Rd BN11 183 B2
Heatherton Mews PO10 149 B3
Heatherway RH19, RH7 8 F7
Heatherwood GU29 92 E8
Heathfield RH10 19 D8
Heathfield Ave BN16 179 F3
Heathfield Cl 1 Midhurst GU29 92 E7
Worthing BN13 181 F5
Heathfield Copse RH20 119 C7
Heathfield Cres BN41 165 F3
Heathfield Dr BN41 165 F4
Heathfield Gate 2 GU29 92 E7
Heathfield Gdns GU29 92 E7
Heathfield Gn GU29 92 E7
Heathfield Pk GU29 92 E7
Heaven Farm Mus RH17 66 B1
Hebe Rd BN43 184 E7
Hechle Wood PO21 194 F2
Hedge End Rd PO22 176 C6
Hedgehog La GU27 27 B5
Hedgerow Gdns PO10 149 B3
Hedgers Hill BN18 156 F2
Hedgeside RH11 18 C1
Hedgeway PO22 196 D5
Hedingham Cl RH6 2 C4
Heene CE Fst (A) Prim Sch BN11 182 C3
Heene Pl BN11 182 C1
Heene Rd BN11 182 B2
Heene Terr BN11 182 B1
Heene Way BN11 182 B2
Heghbrok Way PO21 195 A2
Heights The Brighton BN1 167 B5
6 Haywards Heath RH16 85 E4
Worthing BN14 162 A1
Helen Ct 8 BN11 181 F2
Helena Cl BN41 166 C2
Helicon Ho RH11 18 C5
Hellingly Cl BN2 188 F5
Helston Dr PO10 149 B3
Helyer's Gn BN17 198 C6
Hemsby Wlk RH10 19 B4
Henbane Ct 2 RH11 18 B2
Henderson Rd RH11 18 B1
Henderson Way RH12 57 F8
Henderson Wlk BN44 143 D4
Hendon Ave BN16 199 A3
Hendon St BN2 188 D5
Henfield Bsns Pk BN5 124 A1
Henfield Cl Brighton BN2 188 F5
Worthing BN12 181 B4
Henfield Rd
Albourne Green BN6 125 B7
Upper Beeding BN44, BN5 144 D3
Henfield Way
Bognor Regis PO22 196 D6
Hove BN3 166 F3
Henge Way BN41 166 B2
Hengist Cl RH12 36 A1
Henley Ct BN2 188 F4
Henley Rd BN2 188 F4
Henry Ave BN16 199 B5
Henry Burt Way RH15 106 F1
Henry Cl PO19 173 D6
Henry St PO21 195 D4
Henshaw Cl RH11 17 F4
Henson Rd RH10 19 B7
Henty Cl Crawley RH11 17 E3
Walberton BN18 176 E8
4 Worthing BN14 182 C4
Henty Gdns PO19 172 F6
Henty Rd Ferring BN12 200 F4
Worthing BN14 182 C4
Heo Gn BN17 178 B3
Hepplewhite Cl RH11 18 B1
Herald Dr PO19 173 A5
Herbert Rd Brighton BN1 167 F2
North Lancing BN15 163 B1
Herbert Shiner Sch GU28 95 F7
Hercules Pl PO22 196 D5
Hereford Cl Chichester PO19 152 F1
Crawley RH10 18 E2
Hereford Ct 15 Brighton BN2 207 B5
15 Hove BN3 187 C7
Hereford St BN2 188 C5
Herington Rd BN18 157 F2
Heritage Lawn RH6 2 C4
Herm Cl RH11 18 A2
Herm Rd BN12 200 F4
Hermione Cl BN12 180 E3
Hermit Terr BN14 161 E6

Hermitage Cl PO20 173 D1
Hermitage La RH19 22 F8
Hermitage Rd RH19 9 D3
Hermitage The PO20 173 D1
Hermits Rd RH10 18 F7
Hermonger La RH12 12 F2
Hernbrook Dr RH13 58 E8
Herne Gdns BN16 199 D6
Herne La BN16 199 D6
Heron Cl Bognor Regis PO22 195 E1
Crawley RH11 18 C8
Mid Lavant PO18 152 E7
Selsey PO20 206 B8
Heron Ct PO19 173 D7
Heron Mead PO21 204 F7
Heron Pl RH19 22 F8
Heron Quay PO10 169 C7
Heron Way RH13 37 A1
Heron Way Cty Prim Sch RH13 37 A1
Heron's Ct Cl 3 BN16 199 C4
Heron's Rye 8 RH20 98 C2
Heron's Tye BN6 126 F3
Herondale GU27 26 E6
Herondean PO19 152 F2
Herons Cl Domewood RH10 8 B5
Kirdford RH14 53 B2
Herons Dale Sch BN43 165 C1
Herons Lea RH10 8 A4
Herons The BN43 185 A8
Herons Wood Ct RH6 2 B4
Herontye Dr RH19 23 A8
Herrick Cl RH10 19 C8
Herschel Wlk 9 RH11 18 B1
Hersee Way PO20 206 C7
Hertford Cl PO21 194 F3
Hertford Cty Inf Sch BN1 168 B2
Hertford Cty Jun Sch BN2 168 C2
Hertford Rd Brighton BN1 168 B2
Worthing BN11 182 D3
Heston Ave BN1 167 F7
Heston Gr PO21 194 C1
Hevers Ave RH6 2 A4
Hewart's La PO21 194 D4
Hewitts BN5 123 E4
Hewitts End BN5 123 E4
Hewshott Gr GU30 25 E5
Hewshott La GU30 25 E5
Hexham Cl RH10 19 E6
Heyshott Cl BN15 183 F8
Heyworth Cty Prim Sch RH16 85 F4
Hickling Wlk RH10 19 B4
Hickman's Cl RH16 86 B8
Hickman's La RH16 86 A8
Hickstead Int Arena RH17 105 D4
Hickstead La RH17 105 C5
Hickstead Pk BN6 105 D2
Hide Gdns BN16 199 B6
High Bank PO20 192 F8
High Bar La RH20 120 A6
High Beech La RH16 63 F1
High Beeches Cotts RH17 39 E2
High Beeches Gardens The RH17 39 F2
High Beeches La RH17 39 E2
High Cl BN41 166 A1
High La GU27 27 C8
High Meadow GU29 112 D8
High Oaks RH11 18 B4
High Park Ave BN3 166 E3
High Pines BN11 182 B2
High Point RH16 86 A3
High Ridge Cl BN18 157 F1
High Seat Gdns RH14 55 D1
High Spinney RH20 119 E5
High St Amberley BN18 138 E7
Angmering BN16 180 A5
Ardingly RH17 64 B8
Arundel BN18 158 B3
Balcombe RH17 40 C5
Billingshurst RH14 55 D1
Bognor Regis PO21 195 D3
Bosham PO18 171 A4
Brighton BN2 207 B5
Chichester PO19 172 F7
Crawley RH11 18 D6
Cuckfield RH17 84 E6
Ditchling BN6 127 D3
East Grinstead RH19 22 F8
Emsworth PO10 169 B8
Findon BN14 161 E6
Handcross RH17 61 C8
Haslemere GU27 27 D7
Haywards Heath RH16 86 B8
Henfield BN5 123 F4
Horley RH6 2 B3
Hurstpierpoint BN6 126 A5
Littlehampton BN17 198 D5
Oving PO20 174 C6
Partridge Green RH13 103 A3
Petworth GU28 95 F8
Portslade-by-Sea BN41 166 A1
Rusper RH12 16 D7
Selsey PO20 206 D7
Shoreham-by-Sea BN43 184 E7
Steyning BN44 143 D3
Storrington RH20 119 D1
Upper Beeding BN44 144 A2
Worthing BN11 182 E2
Worthing BN11 182 E3
Worthing, West Tarring BN13 182 A5
High Titten BN18 138 E5
High Trees Bognor Regis PO21 194 F2
Haywards Heath RH16 85 F5
Hunston PO20 173 A1
High Trees Ct RH6 1 A4
High View BN13 161 F1
Highams Hill RH11 17 F5
Highbank BN1 167 C5
Highbarn BN14 161 E7
Highbirch Cl RH12 37 B5
Highbrook Cl BN2 168 D3
Highbury Cotts RH17 61 B8
Highbury Gr GU27 27 C8
Highclere Way BN13 181 B5
Highcroft Ave PO22 195 D5
Highcroft Cl PO22 195 E5
Highcroft Cres PO22 195 E5
Highcroft Dr RH12 12 E1
Highcroft Lodge BN1 167 E1
Highcroft Rd RH19 43 A6
Highcroft Villas BN1, BN3 187 E8
Highden 2 BN2 188 C6
Highdown BN41, BN42 165 F1
Highdown Ave BN13 182 A5
Highdown Cl Ferring BN12 180 E3
Southwick BN41, BN42 165 F1
Highdown Ct Brighton BN1 167 E3
Crawley RH10 19 B3
Highdown Dr BN17 198 D6
Highdown Rd BN1, BN3 187 E7
Highdown Sch BN13 181 D5
Highdown Way Ferring BN12 180 E3
Horsham RH12 36 F6
Highercombe Rd GU27 27 E8
Highfield Horsted Keynes RH17 65 C4
Littlehampton BN17 178 B3
Highfield Cl Angmering BN16 180 A5
Easebourne GU29 71 A2
Highfield Cres BN1 168 A5
Highfield Ct 7 RH16 85 E4
Highfield Dr BN6 126 C5
Highfield Gdns
Bognor Regis PO22 195 D5
Liss GU33 45 D4
1 Rustington BN16 199 B5
Highfield La
Liphook GU27, GU30 25 E3
Oving PO20 174 C7
Highfield Rd
Bognor Regis PO22 195 D5
East Grinstead RH19 9 D3
Worthing BN13 182 A6
Highfield Sch GU30 25 E2
Highfields Brighton BN1 168 E5
Forest Row RH18 23 F2
Highgate Ct RH11 18 C2
Highgate Dr PO21 194 F6
Highgate Rd RH18 23 F1
Highground La PO22 176 B4
Highgrove Gdns BN11 182 B4
Highland Ave PO21 195 B4
Highland Cl PO10 169 A8
Highland Croft BN44 143 D3
Highland Ct RH16 85 E4
Highland Rd Chichester PO19 153 A2
Emsworth PO10 149 A1
Haywards Heath RH16 85 F3
Highlands Ave RH13 36 E2
Highlands Cl Keymer BN6 127 A3
Worthing BN13 161 E1
Highlands Cotts RH17 84 F8
Highlands Cres RH13 36 E2
Highlands Dr RH15 107 A4
Highlands Rd Horsham RH13 36 F2
Portslade-by-Sea BN41 166 B1
Highlands The RH17 84 F8
Highleigh 7 BN2 207 B6
Highleigh Rd PO20 192 C2
Highstanding La GU29 93 A6
Highstead La GU28 72 A8
Highview BN15 163 D1
Highview Ave N BN1 167 E6
Highview Ave S BN1 167 E6
Highview Rd Brighton BN1 167 E6
Eastergate PO20 175 F7
Highview Way BN1 167 E6
Highway Cl BN2 168 D2
Highway The BN2 168 D2
Highways BN41 166 B2
Hilary Lodge 2 BN2 188 C5
Hilary Rd PO19 172 E7
Hildon Cl BN13 181 D5
Hill Barn Golf Course BN14 182 B8
Hill Barn La BN14 182 C7
Hill Brow BN3 167 B3
Hill Brow Cl PO9 128 D1
Hill Brow Rd GU33 45 C3
Hill Cotts GU29 113 C8
Hill Crest RH19 9 E6
Hill Ct GU27 27 B6
Hill Dr BN3 167 B3
Hill Farm La RH20 98 B5
Hill Farm Way BN42, BN43 165 E2
Hill House Cl RH10 21 A5
Hill House Hill GU30 25 A6
Hill La Barnham PO22 176 C4
South Harting GU31 89 E2
Hill Manor RH12 36 A2
Hill Mead RH12 36 B3
Hill Pl RH11 18 C5
Hill Rd Haslemere GU27 27 C6
Littlehampton BN17 198 F6
Hill Top BN1 167 B5
Hill Top Cl BN41 165 F2
Hill View Elsted GU29 90 D4
Small Dole BN5 144 F7
Hillary Cl RH19 10 A3
Hillbank Cl BN41 165 F3
Hillbarn Ave BN15 163 D1
Hillbarn La GU29, PO18 112 D6
Hillbarn Par BN15 183 C8
Hillbrow Rd BN1 167 D4
Hillcrest BN1 167 C5
Hillcrest Cl Ashington RH20 121 A5
Crawley RH10 19 D6
Scaynes Hill RH17 86 F3
Hillcrest Ct BN1 167 C5
Hillcrest Dr RH20 121 A5
Hillcrest La RH17 86 F3
Hillcroft BN41 165 F2
Hillfield Rd PO20 206 D6
Hillhouse La RH12, RH14 11 F1
Hillingdale RH11 18 C1
Hillmead RH11 17 F6
Hillrise Ave BN15 183 D8
Hills Farm La RH12 35 F1
Hills Pl RH12 36 A2
Hills Rd BN44 143 C2
Hillsboro Rd PO21 195 C4
Hillside Brighton BN2 168 E2
Crawley Down RH10 21 B8
Forest Row RH18 23 E3
Horsham RH12 36 A2
Portslade-by-Sea BN41 166 C1
Southwick BN42 165 F1
Hillside Ave BN14 182 B7
Hillside Cl Crawley RH11 18 B4
East Grinstead RH19 9 E3
Hillside Cotts Clapham BN13 160 E1
East Marden PO18 110 B1
West Stoke PO18 152 A5
Hillside Cres BN16 180 A5
Hillside La BN5 144 E5
Hillside Rd Camelsdale GU27 26 F5
Heath Common RH20 120 A2
Sompting BN15 163 C1
Hillside Sch BN41 166 B2
Hillside Scout Camp BN5 144 E5
Hillside Terr BN44 143 D3
Hillside Way
Brighton, Moulsecoomb BN2 168 E2
Brighton, Westdene BN1 167 C4
Hillside Wlk
Haywards Heath RH17 85 C6
Heath Common RH20 120 A2
Hilltop Rd RH19 42 E6
Hillview Cres BN16 200 A6
Hillview Gdns RH11 39 C8
Hillview Rd BN14 161 F2
Hillview Rise BN14 161 F1
Hillybarn Rd RH11 4 C1
Hilton Ct RH6 2 C4
Hilton Pk PO20 202 A8
Hinde Rd PO22 196 C4
Hindhead Cl RH11 18 C4
Hindhead Rd GU26, GU27 26 E7
Hindle Cl RH20 119 D7
Hindleap Warren Activity Ctr RH18 44 D5
Hinton Cl BN1 168 C2
Hislop Wlk 12 PO21 195 D3
Hoad La RH16, RH17 64 D4
Hoathly Hill RH19 42 F5
Hobart Cl BN13 181 C7
Hobbs Ind Est RH7 8 D7
Hobbs Rd RH11 18 A2
Hobbs Way BN16 199 C5
Hobdens La RH17 64 B7
Hoblands RH16 86 B4
Hobs Acre BN44 144 B1
Hocken Mead RH10 19 D8
Hodshrove La BN2 168 E3
Hodshrove Pl BN2 168 E3
Hodshrove Rd BN2 168 E3
Hoe Ct North Lancing BN15 163 F1
Shoreham-by-Sea BN15 184 A8
Hoe La Bosham PO18 171 C1
Flansham PO22 196 B7
Walberton BN18 177 C7
Hoefield La PO18 112 C5
Hoewood BN5 144 F7
Hog La BN18 138 E7
Hogarth Rd Crawley RH10 18 F3
Hove BN3 186 F7
Hogspudding La RH5 3 C8
Hogwood Rd RH14 31 C3
Holbein Rd RH10 18 F3
Holbrook Cty Prim Sch RH12 36 E7
Holbrook School La RH12 36 E7
Holdens The PO18 171 A5
Holder Rd RH10 19 B3
Holders BN6 125 C6
Holdfast La GU27 27 F8
Hole St BN44, RH20 121 B2
Holford Gn PO20 206 F8
Holkham Cotts BN18 177 A3
Holland Cl PO21 194 F5
Holland Mews BN3 187 D5
Holland Rd Hove BN3 187 D6
Steyning BN44 143 E3
Holland St BN2 207 B6
Hollands La BN5 123 C4
Hollands Rd BN5 123 D5
Hollands The RH15 107 C4
Hollands Way
East Grinstead RH19 10 A4
Warnham RH12 35 F8
Hollies The PO21 194 F5
Hollin Ct RH10, RH11 5 E1
Hollingbourne Cres RH11 39 C8
Hollingbourne Ct 8 BN2 188 E4
Hollingbury Copse BN1 168 A4
Hollingbury Court Sch RH17 61 A1
Hollingbury Cres BN1 168 B2
Hollingbury Gdns BN14 162 A2
Hollingbury Ind Est BN1 168 C7
Hollingbury Park Ave BN1 168 A2
Hollingbury Park Golf Course BN1 168 B4
Hollingbury Pl BN1 168 B2
Hollingbury Rd BN1 168 B1
Hollingbury Rise BN1 168 B2
Hollingbury Rise W BN1 168 A3
Hollingbury Terr BN1 168 A2
Hollingdean La BN1, BN2 188 B8
Hollingdean Rd BN2 188 B8
Hollingdean St BN1 168 B1
Hollingdean Terr BN1 168 B2
Hollist La Easebourne GU29 70 E2
South Harting GU31 89 F4
Hollow La RH19, RH7 10 D6
Hollow The Bury RH20 138 A8
Crawley RH11 17 F5
Haywards Heath RH16 86 B5
Washington RH20 141 F8
West Chiltington RH20 99 D1
West Hoathly RH19 42 F6
Holly Bank 3 BN2 207 B8
Holly Cl Brighton BN1 167 E3
Crawley RH10 19 A8
Horsham RH12 37 B5
Storrington RH20 119 C1
West Chiltington RH20 99 D1
Worthing BN13 181 C5
Holly Ct Bognor Regis PO22 195 C6
Storrington RH20 119 C2
Holly Dr BN17 178 E4
Holly Rd RH16 86 A3
Hollybank La PO10 149 B4
Hollybush Rd RH10 18 E8
Hollycombe Cl GU30 25 C2
Hollycombe Cty Prim Sch GU30 47 D4
Hollycombe Steam Collection GU30 47 E7
Hollyridge GU27 27 B6
Hollywater Rd GU30, GU35 24 C8
Hollywood Ct 10 RH16 85 E5
Holman Cl RH11 39 B8
Holmans RH17 64 A8
Holmbury Cl RH11 18 C4
Holmbush Cl
Haywards Heath RH16 85 E2
Horsham RH12 36 D6
Shoreham-by-Sea BN43 165 D2
Holmbush Ct 8 BN43 185 C8
Holmbush Cty Fst Sch BN43 165 D1
Holmbush Ind Est GU29 92 E6
Holmbush La BN5 145 F8
Holmbush Way Midhurst GU29 92 E6
Southwick BN42, BN43 165 E1
Holmcroft RH10 18 E5
Holmcroft Gdns BN14 161 E6
Holmes Ave BN3 166 F1
Holmes Foundation BN18 158 B2
Holmes La BN16 199 B4
Holmesdale Rd RH15 107 A1
Holmfield Cl BN16 199 B6
Holmgarth BN5 123 F5
Holming End RH12 37 B5
Holmstead BN2 207 B7
Holmsted Hill RH17 62 A1
Holmwood Cl PO20 190 C1
Holmwood Ct BN6 126 F4
Holt Gdns PO9 128 D3
Holt Lodge 1 BN2 207 B7
Holt The Burgess Hill RH15 107 C2
Washington RH20 141 E6
Holtye Ave RH19 10 A3
Holtye Rd RH19 10 B3
Holtye Wlk RH10 19 A4
Holy Cross Hospl GU27 26 F7
Holy Trinity CE (A) Prim Sch RH17 84 F6
Holy Trinity CE (A) Sch The RH11 18 A4
Holy Trinity CE (C) Prim Sch RH13 60 A3
Holyrood RH19 23 A8
Holyrood Pl RH11 18 B2
Home Cl RH10 19 C8
Home Farm Bsns Ctr BN1 168 D3
Home Farm Ct RH17 65 C5
Home Farm Rd BN1 168 D3
Home Platt RH19 43 A6
Home Rd BN1 167 E1
Homecroft Ho 5 PO21 195 B3
Homedrive Ho BN3 187 C8
Homefield Ave PO22 196 C6
Homefield Cl RH6 2 B4
Homefield Cotts GU33 45 A5
Homefield Cres BN18 156 D1
Homefield Rd
Westbourne PO10 149 D4
Worthing BN11 182 E3
Homegreen Ho GU27 27 A6
Homehaven Ct 2 BN43 184 E7
Homelands Ave BN16 200 A4
Homelands Copse GU27 49 D4
Homeleigh BN1 167 E5
Homepier Ho 7 BN11 182 B2
Homesearle Ho BN12 181 C2
Homestall Rd RH19 23 E8
Homestead The BN16 200 A5
Homesteyne Ho 3 BN14 182 D4
Homewood BN14 161 E7
Homing Gdns PO22 195 B7
Honer La PO20 193 D3
Honey Croft BN3 166 D4
Honey La BN16 180 A5
Honeybridge La
Ashurst BN44, RH13, RH20 122 A6
Dial Post RH13 101 E1
Honeysuckle Cl Horley RH6 2 C4
North Lancing BN15 163 D1
Honeysuckle La Crawley RH11 5 C1
Worthing BN13 161 C3
Honeysuckle Wlk RH12 37 A5
Honeywood La RH5 13 F5
Honeywood Rd RH13 37 A4
Hooe Farm Ind Est BN18 156 D2
Hooe The BN17 199 A5
Hook La
Bognor Regis PO21, PO22 195 E4
Bognor Regis, Rose Green PO21 194 B3
Bosham PO18 171 F2
West Hoathly RH17, RH19 42 D4
Woodgate PO20 175 C6
Hooklands La RH13, RH20 101 B3
Hooks The BN5 123 E4
Hop Garden La PO20 193 D8
Hop Garden The GU31 89 D3
Hope Cotts BN42 185 E8
Hope Ct RH11 18 B1
Hopedene Ct 5 BN11 182 C2
Hopgarton The PO21 194 E3
Hophurst Cl RH10 21 B8
Hophurst Dr RH10 21 B8
Hophurst Hill RH10, RH19 8 D2
Hophurst La RH10 8 B1
Hopkins Ct RH11 18 B1
Hordens The RH13 56 F2
Hordern Ho RH12 36 A1
Horley Cty Fst Sch RH6 2 A3
Horley Lodge La RH1 2 A8
Horley Pl BN2 188 E6
Horley Rd RH6 5 B7
Horley Row RH6 2 A4
Horley Sta RH6 2 B2
Hormare Cres RH20 119 C2
Horn La BN5 124 B1
Hornbeam Cl
Bognor Regis PO21 194 F1
Horsham RH13 36 F1
Hornbeam Way GU29 92 D5
Hornbrook Copse RH13 58 F8
Hornby Rd BN2 168 F1
Horndean Cl RH10 6 D2
Horndean Rd PO10 149 A3
Hornet Ent Ctr PO19 173 B6
Hornet Rd PO10 169 C3
Hornet The PO19 173 B6
Horns La PO21 193 F1
Hornshill La RH12 32 F7
Horse Hill RH6 1 B4
Horse Shoe The PO20 206 D7
Horsebridge Hill RH14 75 E2
Horsed Keynes Sta RH17 65 A7
Horsefield Rd PO20 206 D8
Horsemere Green La BN17 177 D1
Horseshoe Cl RH10 19 D7
Horsgate Ho RH17 85 A8
Horsgate La RH17 85 A6
Horsham Bsns Pk RH12 15 C4
Horsham Cl BN2 188 F6
Horsham Com Hospl RH12 36 C3
Horsham Golf Course RH13 58 A6
Horsham Rd
Alfold Crossways GU6, RH14 11 C1
Ashurst BN44 143 C7
Cranleigh RH12 12 B8
Crawley RH11 18 B4
Findon BN14 161 D8
Five Oaks RH14 56 A6
Handcross RH17 61 B7
Kingsfold RH5 15 C8
Littlehampton BN17 198 F6
Pease Pottage RH11 39 B6
Petworth GU28 74 B2
Rowhook RH5, RH12 13 D5
Rusper RH12 16 B5
Steyning BN44 143 C4
Wallis Wood RH5 13 D8
Horsham Rd W BN17 198 F6
Horsham Sta RH13 36 D2
Horsted Ho 1 RH16 85 F3
Horsted Keynes Ind Est RH17 65 B7
Horsted Keynes Sta RH17 65 A7
Horsted La Danehill RH17 66 A4
Sharpthorne RH19 43 B3
Horton Rd BN1 168 B1
Hoskins Pl RH19 10 A4
Hospital Villas 5 RH16 85 F3
Hotham Gdns PO22 195 E4
Hotham Way PO21, PO22 195 D4
Houghton Bridge BN18 138 D4
Houghton Ho BN17 178 B3
Houghton La BN18, RH20 138 A6
Houghton Rd RH10 19 C3
Hova Villas BN3 187 B6
Hove Bsns Ctr BN3 187 B8
Hove Ent Ctr BN41 186 C6
Hove General Hospl BN3 187 A7
Hove Manor 7 BN3 187 A6
Hove Mus & Art Gall BN3 187 A6
Hove Park Gdns Hove BN3 167 B1
Hove BN3 187 B8
Hove Park Rd BN1, BN3 167 C1
Hove Park Sch (Lower) BN3 166 D2
Hove Park Sch (Upper) BN3 167 A1
Hove Park Villas BN3 187 B8
Hove Park Way BN3 167 C1
Hove Pl BN3 187 B5
Hove St BN3 187 A6
Hove Sta BN3 187 B8
Hovedene BN3 187 A6
Howard Ave Burgess Hill RH15 106 E4
East Wittering PO20 201 D7
Howard Ct BN3 167 A2
Howard Ho PO21 195 A4
Howard Pl Brighton BN1 207 F7
5 Littlehampton BN17 198 D5
Howard Rd Arundel BN18 158 A2
Brighton BN2 188 C7
Crawley RH11 17 D2
Horsham RH13 37 A4
Littlehampton BN17 198 C5

Howard Rd Sompting BN15 .... 163 C1
Howard St BN11 .... 182 C3
Howard Terr BN1 .... 207 F7
Howards Way BN16 .... 199 B3
Hoylake Cl RH11 .... 17 D5
Hoyle La GU29 .... 93 D2
Huddlestones BN16 .... 179 F6
Hudson Cl BN13 .... 181 D6
Hudson Dr BN16 .... 199 E4
Hudson Rd RH10 .... 18 E4
Huffwood Trad Est
Billingshurst RH14 .... 77 D7
Partridge Green RH13 .... 103 A3
Hughes Cl PO21 .... 194 F4
Hughes Rd BN2 .... 188 B8
Hugo Platt GU31 .... 68 A4
Humber Ave BN13 .... 181 C7
Humber Cl Littlehampton BN17 . 198 F4
Worthing BN13 .... 181 C7
Humphrey Lodge RH15 .... 107 D3
Humphrey's Gap BN43 .... 185 A7
Humphrys Rd 4 BN11 .... 182 D2
Hundredsteddle La PO20 .... 191 D2
Hungers La GU28 .... 95 D6
Hunstanton Cl RH11 .... 17 D5
Hunt's Gate BN8 .... 87 E3
Hunter Ho RH10 .... 18 D3
Hunter Rd Crawley RH10, RH11 ... 18 D4
Thorney Island PO10 .... 169 C3
Hunter's Mead BN6 .... 125 C6
Hunters Chase GU30 .... 25 B5
Hunters Cl PO21 .... 194 C1
Hunters Mead RH13 .... 103 A3
Hunters Race PO19 .... 152 E3
Hunters Way PO19 .... 152 F3
Hunterscroft Gdns RH13 .... 81 E1
Huntingdon Way RH15 .... 107 D5
Huntsbottom La GU33 .... 45 D3
Hurley Rd BN13 .... 181 E6
Hurst Ave Horsham RH12 .... 36 D3
Worthing BN11 .... 181 F2
Hurst Cl Amberley BN18 .... 138 E7
Crawley RH11 .... 17 F4
Liphook GU30 .... 25 A5
Hurst Cotts BN18 .... 138 E7
Hurst Cres BN41 .... 186 B8
Hurst Ct RH12 .... 36 D3
Hurst Farm Rd RH19 .... 22 D7
Hurst Gdns BN6 .... 125 F7
Hurst Hill BN1 .... 168 C5
Hurst Rd Hassocks BN6 .... 126 D4
Horley RH6 .... 1 E4
Horsham RH12 .... 36 D3
Rustington BN16 .... 199 E6
Hurst Wickham Cl BN6 .... 126 C5
Hurstfield BN15 .... 183 D5
Hurstfield Cl RH16 .... 86 A2
Hurstlands RH14 .... 77 C7
Hurston Cl BN14 .... 182 A8
Hurston Gr RH20 .... 119 B3
Hurston La RH20 .... 119 B3
Hurstpierpoint Coll BN6 .... 126 B8
Hurstwood 6 BN2 .... 188 F5
Hurstwood Ave PO10 .... 150 A1
Hurstwood Ct GU29 .... 92 E5
Hurstwood La
Haywards Heath RH16 .... 86 A2
Sharpthorne RH17, RH19 .... 43 D1
Hutchins Way RH6 .... 1 F5
Hutton Rd BN1 .... 168 B3
Huxley's Experience Bird of Prey Ctr RH13 .... 58 F8
Hyde Dr RH11 .... 17 E5
Hyde Heath Ct RH10 .... 19 D8
Hyde La BN44 .... 144 B2
Hyde Sq BN44 .... 144 B2
Hyde St BN44 .... 144 B1
Hyde The BN2 .... 188 F8
Hylands Cl RH10 .... 19 A5
Hylters's La PO18 .... 132 B7
Hyperion Ct RH11 .... 17 E4
Hyperion Wlk RH6 .... 2 B1
Hythe Cl BN11 .... 182 A1
Hythe Rd Brighton BN1 .... 168 A2
Worthing BN11 .... 182 A1

Icarus Way PO22 .... 196 C5
Icklesham Ho 9 RH11 .... 17 F3
Iden Cl BN2 .... 188 E5
Iden Hurst BN6 .... 126 A7
Idsworth Cl PO8 .... 128 A6
Ifield Ave RH11 .... 18 C7
Ifield Com Sch RH11 .... 18 A7
Ifield Cty Jun Sch RH11 .... 18 A6
Ifield Cty Mid Sch RH11 .... 18 A6
Ifield Fst Sch RH11 .... 18 A8
Ifield Gn RH11 .... 5 A1
Ifield Rd Charlwood RH6 .... 4 E5
Crawley RH11 .... 18 C6
Ifield St RH11 .... 17 F8
Ifield Sta RH11 .... 18 A6
Ifield Wood RH11 .... 4 E1
Ifold Bridge La RH14 .... 31 D4
Ifoldhurst RH14 .... 31 C2
Ilex Cl BN16 .... 199 C4
Ilex Ct Portslade-by-Sea BN42 .. 166 A1
Worthing BN12 .... 181 B2
Ilex Ho 1 BN16 .... 199 C4
Ilex Way
Middleton-on-Sea PO22 .... 196 E6
Worthing BN12 .... 181 B2
Image Cross Flats RH19 .... 43 A5
Imberhorne La RH19 .... 9 B2
Imberhorne Lower Sch RH19 ..... 9 D3
Imberhorne Sch RH19 .... 9 B3
Imberhorne Way RH19 .... 9 B3
Imperial Arc BN1 .... 207 F5
Independent Bsns Pk The RH19 9 A3
Infirmary Dr RH13 .... 57 E6
Infirmary Terr PO19 .... 172 F8
Ingfield Manor Sch RH14 .... 55 E6
Ingham Dr BN1 .... 168 D6
Ingle Green Cl BN12 .... 200 E4
Inglecroft Ct 4 BN15 .... 183 C7
Inglenook RH13 .... 79 F7
Ingleside Cres BN15 .... 183 F5
Ingleside Rd BN15 .... 183 E5
Inglewood Cl PO21 .... 194 C1
Inglewood Dr PO21 .... 194 B1
Ingram Cl Horsham RH12 .... 36 A2
Rustington BN16 .... 199 B5
Steyning BN44 .... 143 D2
Ingram Cres E BN3 .... 186 E8
Ingram Cres W BN3 .... 186 E8
Ingram Ct BN3 .... 186 E7
Ingram Rd BN44 .... 143 D2
Ingram's Green La GU29 .... 91 C4
Inholmes Cl RH15 .... 107 C3
Inholmes Cotts RH17 .... 84 E8
Inholmes Park Rd RH15 .... 107 B3
Ink Pen La RH18 .... 23 E1
Inlands Rd PO18 .... 170 B8
Innerwyke Cl PO22 .... 196 B5
Innes Rd RH12 .... 36 F4
Inval Hill GU27 .... 27 C8
Inverness Rd BN2 .... 188 C8
Inwood Cres BN1 .... 167 E1
Inwood Rd GU33 .... 45 C3
Iona Cl RH11 .... 18 B3
Iona Way 12 RH16 .... 85 E4
Iping La GU29 .... 69 E4
Irene Ave BN15 .... 183 D7
Irons Bottom Rd RH6 .... 1 A6
Irvine Rd BN17 .... 198 E4
Irving Wlk RH10 .... 18 E3
Irwin Dr RH12 .... 36 A2
Isaac's La Burgess Hill RH15 .... 106 F6
Haywards Heath RH16, RH15 .... 85 A2
Isabel Cres BN3 .... 186 E8
Isfield Rd BN1 .... 168 C2
Island La PO20 .... 206 B8
Island Loop PO20 .... 206 B8
Isle of Thorns (Univ of Sussex) RH17 .... 44 D1
Islingword Pl BN2 .... 188 C6
Islingword Rd BN2 .... 188 C7
Islingword St BN2 .... 207 B6
Itchenor Rd
Shipton Green PO20 .... 191 A4
South Hayling PO11 .... 189 B2
Itchingfield Cty Prim Sch
Barns Green RH13 .... 56 F3
Itchingfield RH13 .... 57 A6
Ithaca Terr PO22 .... 195 F3
Ivanhoe Cl RH11 .... 5 D1
Ivanhoe Pl PO22 .... 196 C5
Iveagh Cl RH11 .... 18 C1
Ivory Pl BN2 .... 207 B6
Ivory Wlk RH11 .... 17 E3
Ivy Arch Cl BN14 .... 161 F6
Ivy Arch Rd BN14 .... 182 D3
Ivy Cl Ashington RH20 .... 121 A5
Southwater RH13 .... 57 F1
Westergate PO20 .... 175 D7
Ivy Cotts RH17 .... 84 E8
Ivy Cres PO22 .... 195 D5
Ivy Dene La RH19 .... 23 D6
Ivy La Bognor Regis PO22 .... 195 D5
Westergate PO20 .... 175 E7
Ivy Pl Hove BN1, BN3 .... 187 D5
Worthing BN11 .... 182 B1
Ivydale Rd PO21 .... 195 A4
Ivydene Cres PO18 .... 170 D7
Ivydore Ave BN13 .... 181 D8
Ivydore Cl BN13 .... 181 D7

Jackdaw Cl RH11 .... 18 C8
Jackdaw La RH12 .... 36 E6
Jacket's Hill RH20 .... 120 A5
Jackrells La RH13 .... 58 B2
Jackson Rd RH11 .... 39 B8
Jackson St BN2 .... 207 B7
Jacobean Cl RH10 .... 19 C5
Jacqueline Du Pre Ct 6 BN2 188 C5
James Cl BN13 .... 181 F6
James St PO20 .... 206 E6
James Watt Way RH10 .... 6 A4
Jane Murray Way
Burgess Hill BN6, RH15 .... 106 D5
Burgess Hill RH15 .... 106 E1
Jane's La RH15 .... 107 E4
Janes Cl RH15 .... 107 C5
Janes La Burgess Hill RH15 ...... 107 D4
River GU28 .... 72 E3
Janeston Ct 4 BN3 .... 187 C7
Japonica Cl BN43 .... 165 B1
Jarvis Cl RH11 .... 39 B8
Jarvis Cotts BN44 .... 143 D3
Jarvis La BN44 .... 143 D3
Jarvis Rd BN18 .... 157 F2
Jasmine Ct Brighton BN1 .... 167 F5
Horsham RH12 .... 36 C2
Javelin Ct RH10 .... 6 D1
Javelin Rd PO10 .... 169 C3
Jay Cl RH13 .... 58 A2
Jay's La GU27 .... 28 C3
Jays Cl BN17 .... 198 D6
Jays The RH15 .... 106 E4
Jeans Ct 10 RH11 .... 18 B1
Jefferies RH17 .... 65 C4
Jefferies La BN12 .... 181 C1
Jeffreys Ave PO19 .... 153 A1
Jengers Mead RH14 .... 55 D1
Jenner Rd RH10 .... 5 F3
Jeremy's La RH17 .... 83 C6
Jerrard Rd PO20 .... 154 D2
Jersey Rd Crawley RH11 .... 18 A2
Ferring BN12 .... 200 F4
Jersey St BN2 .... 207 B6
Jervis Ave BN16 .... 199 D5
Jesmond Cl BN3 .... 186 E7
Jesmond Rd BN3 .... 186 E7
Jessie Younghusband Cty Prim Sch PO19 .... 172 F8
Jesters RH15 .... 107 C7
Jetty The PO22 .... 197 A5
Jevington Cl BN13 .... 181 B5
Jevington Ct
Shoreham-by-Sea BN43 .... 185 D6
Worthing BN13 .... 181 B5
Jevington Dr BN2 .... 168 D1
Jew St BN1 .... 207 A5
Jib Cl BN16 .... 179 A3
Jireh Ct 4 RH16 .... 85 E5
Joan Nightingale Ho RH16 .... 85 C4
Job's Cnr RH17 .... 105 E5
Job's La BN6, RH17 .... 105 F5
Jobes RH17 .... 40 F1
Jobson's La GU27 .... 28 D2
Jockey Mead RH12 .... 36 A1
John Arundel Rd PO19 .... 172 E7
John Horniman Sch BN11 .... 182 E2
John King Shipyard PO10 .... 169 C8
John Pounds Ho RH11 .... 18 D4
John Selden Cty Fst Sch BN12 .... 181 D4
John Selden Mid Sch BN12 ...... 181 D4
John St Bognor Regis PO21 ...... 195 D3
Brighton BN2 .... 207 B6
Shoreham-by-Sea BN43 .... 184 E7
John Whittle Lodge 4 BN2 ...... 168 C1
Johnson Bank 4 BN2 .... 188 C7
Johnson Dr RH15 .... 107 D3
Johnson Way BN18 .... 177 B2
Johnson Wlk RH10 .... 18 E3
Jolesfield Crawley RH11 .... 17 F3
Partridge Green RH13 .... 102 F4
Jolesfield CE (C) Prim Sch RH13 .... 103 A4
Jolliffe Rd PO20 .... 201 D7
Jordan Ct BN3 .... 186 E8
Jordans Cl RH11 .... 18 D8
Jordans Cres RH11 .... 5 D1
Jordans The RH19 .... 22 E8
Joy Wlk 6 PO19 .... 173 A6
Joyce Cl BN17 .... 178 C3
Joys Croft PO19 .... 173 B7
Joys Croft Ct PO19 .... 173 B7
Jubilee Ave BN16 .... 199 C6
Jubilee Cl RH16 .... 86 A4
Jubilee Ct BN2 .... 168 E2
Jubilee Ho Crockerhill PO18 .... 155 B3
Emsworth PO10 .... 149 A1
Jubilee Rd Burgess Hill RH15 .... 106 E2
Chichester PO19 .... 173 A7
Portslade-by-Sea BN41 .... 186 A8
Rudgwick RH12 .... 33 D8
Jubilee St BN1 .... 207 A6
Jubilee Terr Chichester PO19 .... 173 A7
Westbourne PO10 .... 149 D3
Jubilee Way RH20 .... 119 F3
Jubilee Wlk RH10 .... 19 A6
Judge's Terr RH19 .... 22 E8
Juggs La RH20 .... 99 E1
Juggs The RH20 .... 99 E1
Julian Ct 5 BN43 .... 185 C8
Julian Rd BN3 .... 187 E7
Junction Cl Burgess Hill RH15 ... 107 C4
Burndell BN18 .... 177 B2
Junction Pl GU27 .... 26 F6
Junction Rd Brighton BN1 .... 207 F6
Burgess Hill RH15 .... 107 B3
June Cl PO21 .... 204 F8
June La GU29 .... 92 E8
June Meadows GU29 .... 92 D8
June Rise GU29 .... 92 E8
Juniper Cl
Middleton-on-Sea PO22 .... 196 E6
Portslade-by-Sea BN41 .... 166 B3
Worthing BN13 .... 181 C5
Juniper Rd RH11 .... 5 C1
Juniper Wlk BN43 .... 165 C1
Jupp's La BN12 .... 181 C3
Jura Cl RH11 .... 18 B3
Jury La PO20 .... 192 D5
Juxon Cl Chichester PO19 .... 173 A5
Crawley RH11 .... 17 F4

Kaithwood Ho RH12 .... 37 B5
Karenza Ct BN1 .... 188 A8
Kearsley Dr BN14 .... 162 A1
Keats Cl RH12 .... 36 F7
Keats Pl RH19 .... 9 D1
Keats Wlk PO21 .... 195 B3
Kebbell Lodge 12 BN2 .... 207 B5
Keble Cl Bognor Regis PO21 ..... 194 F3
Crawley RH10 .... 6 D1
Keelson Way BN16 .... 199 A6
Keepers Wood PO19 .... 152 F3
Keir Hardie Ho 7 RH11 .... 18 B1
Kelly Rd BN3 .... 167 D1
Kelsey Ave PO10 .... 150 A1
Kelsey Cl East Liss GU33 .... 45 C5
Horley RH6 .... 1 F3
Kelsey Ct RH15 .... 107 D3
Kelso Cl Crawley RH10 .... 19 E7
Lancing BN15 .... 183 B7
Worthing BN13 .... 181 E4
Kelvin Bsns Ctr RH10 .... 5 F2
Kelvin La RH10 .... 5 F2
Kelvin Way RH10 .... 5 F2
Kemnal Pk GU27 .... 27 D7
Kemp Ct BN2 .... 188 E4
Kemp St BN1 .... 207 A6
Kemp Town Pl 18 BN2 .... 188 D4
Kemps BN6 .... 125 F7
Kempshott Rd RH12 .... 36 B4
Kemptown Mews 11 BN2 .... 188 E4
Kendal Cl BN16, BN17 .... 179 A3
Kendal Rd Hove BN3 .... 186 F8
Lancing BN15 .... 183 C6
Kenhurst BN16 .... 200 A5
Kenilworth Cl RH11 .... 18 B2
Kenilworth Rd PO21 .... 195 B4
Kenlegh PO21 .... 194 F2
Kenmara Cl RH10 .... 6 A1
Kenmara Ct RH10 .... 6 A2
Kenmure Ave BN1 .... 168 A7
Kennard Ct RH18 .... 23 E3
Kennedy Ave RH19 .... 9 D3
Kennedy Rd RH13 .... 36 D1
Kennel Hill PO18 .... 133 E1
Kennel La Hookwood RH6 .... 1 D2
Maplehurst RH13 .... 80 E2
Kennet Cl Crawley RH11 .... 17 F5
Worthing BN13 .... 181 D7
Kensett's Cnr RH20 .... 121 A3
Kensington Cl RH20 .... 119 C7
Kensington Gdns BN1 .... 207 A6
Kensington Pl BN1 .... 207 A6
Kensington Rd
Chichester PO19 .... 173 D6
Crawley RH11 .... 18 C2
Kensington St BN1 .... 207 A6
Kent Cl BN43 .... 185 C7
Kent Rd Chichester PO19 .... 173 B7
Littlehampton BN17 .... 198 D6
Kent St RH13, RH17 .... 104 C6
Kenton Rd BN3 .... 186 D7
Kents Rd RH16 .... 85 F3
Kentstreet La RH13 .... 82 C1
Kentwyns Dr RH13 .... 58 E8
Kenwards BN1 .... 168 D7
Kenya Ct Horley RH6 .... 1 F4
3 Hove BN1 .... 187 E6
Kerdale Cl RH10 .... 19 C2
Kerrison Mews BN3 .... 187 D5
Kerves La RH13 .... 58 D6
Kestrel Cl Bracklesham PO20 .... 202 A6
Crawley RH11 .... 18 C8
Horsham RH12 .... 36 E5
Hove BN3 .... 187 D8
Kestrel Ct Bognor Regis PO21 .... 204 F7
Chichester PO19 .... 173 D7
Kestrel Way BN17 .... 178 C4
Kestrels The BN43 .... 185 A8
Keswick Cl Crawley RH11 .... 17 D4
Worthing BN12 .... 181 D5
Ketch Rd BN16, BN17 .... 199 A4
Ketche's La RH17 .... 87 E7
Kew Gdns PO21 .... 194 F5
Kew St BN1 .... 207 F6
Kewell's Cnr PO20 .... 191 E5
Keymer Cres BN12 .... 181 D1
Keymer Ct RH15 .... 107 B2
Keymer Gdns RH15 .... 107 B1
Keymer Par RH15 .... 107 B2
Keymer Pk BN6 .... 127 B3
Keymer Rd Brighton BN1 .... 168 B6
Burgess Hill RH15 .... 107 B1
Crawley RH11 .... 18 D4
Keymer BN6 .... 127 B3
Keymer Way BN12 .... 181 C1
Keynor La PO20 .... 203 E8
Keysford La RH16, RH17 .... 64 E3
Kidborough Rd RH11 .... 17 F4
Kidbrook RH16 .... 86 B6
Kidbrooke Park (Michael Hall Sch) RH18 .... 23 D1
Kidbrooke Rise RH18 .... 23 E2
Kidders La BN5 .... 123 D8
Kidmans Cl RH12 .... 36 F5
Kidworth Cl RH6 .... 1 F5
Kilbarn Ct RH16 .... 85 D2
Kilbarn Way RH16 .... 85 D2
Killingthurst La GU8 .... 28 D8
Kilmore Cl BN14 .... 161 E6
Kiln Field GU33 .... 45 A5
Kiln Fields GU27 .... 27 C8
Kiln La Haywards Heath RH16 .... 86 B5
Horley RH6 .... 2 A5
Kiln Rd RH10 .... 21 B7
Kiln The RH15 .... 107 C3
Kilnfield Rd RH12 .... 33 D8
Kilnmead RH10, RH11 .... 18 E7
Kilnmead Cl RH10 .... 18 E7
Kilnwood Cl PO20 .... 206 F7
Kilnwood La RH12 .... 17 B3
Kilwich Cl PO22 .... 196 D6
Kimber Cl BN15 .... 183 D5
Kimberley Cl RH6 .... 1 E3
Kimberley Rd Brighton BN2 ..... 168 D1
Crawley RH10 .... 19 B7
Kimbridge Pk PO20 .... 202 A6
Kimbridge Rd PO20 .... 202 A6
Kindersley Cl RH19 .... 10 B3
Kinfauns Dr BN13 .... 161 D2
King Alfred Cl BN44 .... 143 D3
King Alfred (Swimming Pool & Sports Ctr) BN3 .... 187 A5
King Bsns Ctr BN6 .... 105 C1
King Charles Pl 8 BN43 .... 185 A6
King Edward Ave BN14 .... 182 E4
King Edward Cl Horsham RH13 .. 57 D6
Worthing BN14 .... 182 E4
King Edward Rd RH13 .... 57 D6
King Edward VII Hospl GU29 .... 70 E6
King George Ave RH19 .... 9 C3
King George Ct PO21 .... 195 B4
King George Rd BN43 .... 185 D8
King George VI Ave BN1, BN3 . 167 A3
King George VI Dr BN3 .... 167 A4
King George VI Mansions BN3 .... 166 F2
King James La BN5 .... 123 E4
King John Ct 4 BN43 .... 185 A6
King Pl BN1 .... 207 F5
King St Arundel BN18 .... 158 A3
Brighton BN1 .... 207 A5
East Grinstead RH19 .... 9 E1
Emsworth PO10 .... 169 C8
Westbourne PO10 .... 149 D3
Worthing BN14 .... 182 D4
King's Arms Hill BN18 .... 158 B3
King's Ave PO19 .... 172 F4
King's Barn La BN44 .... 143 F4
King's Barn Villas BN44 .... 143 E3
King's Ct PO21 .... 195 E3
King's Dr GU29 .... 70 F7
King's Espl BN3 .... 187 A5
King's Gdns BN3 .... 187 B5
King's La RH13 .... 104 B8
King's Manor Sch BN43 .... 185 D8
King's Par PO21 .... 195 A2
King's Rd Brighton BN1, BN3 ..... 187 E5
Emsworth PO10 .... 169 A8
Haslemere GU27 .... 27 A6
Haywards Heath RH16 .... 85 F3
Horsham RH12, RH13 .... 36 E3
King's Stone Ave BN44 .... 143 F3
King's Terr 6 PO10 .... 169 B8
Kingfisher Cl Crawley RH10 ...... 6 A1
Rowland's Castle PO9 .... 128 D1
Worthing BN13 .... 181 C5
Kingfisher Ct PO22 .... 196 F5
Kingfisher Par PO20 .... 201 F7
Kingfisher Rise RH19 .... 22 F8
Kingfisher Way RH12 .... 36 C5
Kingley Vale Nature Reserve PO18 .... 131 E2
Kingmere 10 BN17 .... 198 E4
Kings Barn End BN44 .... 143 F3
Kings Cl Burndell BN18 .... 177 A3
Lancing BN15 .... 183 F5
Red Hill PO9 .... 128 C1
Kings Copse 9 RH19 .... 22 F8
Kings Cres BN43 .... 184 D5
Kings Ct Horsham RH13 .... 36 E3
Lancing BN15 .... 183 F4
Selsey PO20 .... 206 E8
Shoreham-by-Sea BN43 .... 184 D5
Kings Dr Bognor Regis PO21 ..... 205 B8
Hassocks BN6 .... 126 F4
Shoreham-by-Sea BN43 .... 184 D5
Kings Gap BN43 .... 184 D5
Kings Gate BN3 .... 187 C8
Kings La Coldwaltham RH20 ...... 117 C6
Marehill RH20 .... 98 F1
Southwater Street RH13 .... 58 A4
Kings Mews BN3 .... 187 B6
Kings Par BN1 .... 168 A2
Kings Platt RH13 .... 101 D8
Kings Rd Horley RH6 .... 2 A3
Lancing BN15 .... 183 F5
Southwick BN42 .... 165 E1
Kings Ride RH15 .... 107 D1
Kings Way Burgess Hill RH15 .... 107 D2
Red Hill PO9 .... 128 C1
Kings Wlk BN43 .... 184 D5
Kingsbridge Mews BN13 .... 181 D7
Kingsbury Rd BN1 .... 207 A7
Kingsbury St BN1, BN2 .... 207 A7
Kingscliffe Sch BN2 .... 188 C5
Kingscote Hill RH11 .... 18 B4
Kingscote Lodge BN1 .... 168 F5
Kingscote Sta RH19 .... 21 F4
Kingsdene BN11 .... 182 B2
Kingsey Ave PO10 .... 169 A8
Kingsfield Henfield BN5 .... 123 E5
Storrington RH20 .... 119 E2
Kingsfield Cl BN42 .... 185 E8
Kingsfold 2 BN2 .... 188 F5
Kingsfold Cl RH14 .... 77 D6
Kingsfold Ct RH12 .... 15 B5
Kingsham Ave PO19 .... 173 B5
Kingsham Cty Prim Sch PO19 173 B4
Kingsham Rd PO19 .... 173 A5
Kingsland RH5 .... 3 A8
Kingsland Cl
Shoreham-by-Sea BN43 .... 185 B7
Storrington RH20 .... 119 E2
Kingsland Cotts BN6 .... 105 C1
Kingsland Rd BN14 .... 182 D6
Kingslea RH13 .... 36 E3
Kingsley Cl Horley RH6 .... 1 F5
Worthing BN14 .... 182 F4
Kingsley Ct 11 BN1 .... 187 E5
Kingsley Rd Brighton BN1 .... 167 D1
Crawley RH11 .... 18 A3
Horley RH6 .... 1 F5
Kingsmead Bognor Regis PO22 . 195 F3
Littlehampton BN17 .... 178 C5
Kingsmead Cl Horsham RH12 .... 37 B6
Steyning BN44 .... 143 D1
Kingsmead Gdns PO22 .... 197 A6
Kingsmead Pl RH12 .... 35 C3
Kingsmead Rd Ancton PO22 ..... 197 A5
Broadridge Heath RH12 .... 35 D3
Kingsmere BN1 .... 167 E2
Kingsmill Rd PO22 .... 176 C6
Kingspit La GU28 .... 96 D8
Kingsthorpe Rd BN3 .... 186 F8
Kingston Bay Rd BN43 .... 185 C6
Kingston Broadway BN42, BN43 .... 165 D1
Kingston Buci Cty Fst Sch BN43 .... 185 B8

Kingston Cl Brighton BN1 168 E6
Hove BN3 166 E2
Shoreham-by-Sea BN43 185 C8
Kingston Ct 17 BN43 185 C8
Kingston La East Preston BN16 200 B5
Southwick BN41, BN42, BN43 185 D7
Kingston Way BN42, BN43 165 D1
Kingsway Bognor Regis PO21 194 D1
Hove BN3 187 B5
Selsey PO20 206 F6
Worthing BN12 181 F2
Kingsway Ct BN3 187 C5
Kingsway Sch The BN18 176 F3
Kingswood RH20 119 C7
Kingswood Cl RH11 39 C8
Kingswood Flats BN2 207 B5
Kingswood St BN2 207 A5
Kinnell Cl PO10 169 B8
Kinrara Ho 10 PO21 195 C3
Kinsale Ct 5 BN3 187 D7
Kipling Ave BN12 181 B3
Kipling Cl RH10 19 C8
Kipling Ct
3 Haywards Heath RH16 85 D5
Horsham RH13 37 A4
Kipling Way RH19 9 C1
Kippens La RH13 80 B2
Kirdford Cl Burgess Hill RH15 107 C1
Crawley RH11 18 A8
3 Littlehampton BN16 199 B4
Kirdford Cty Jun Sch RH14 53 B2
Kirdford Rd BN18 158 A2
Kirkby Cl PO18 154 D3
Kirkland Cl BN16 199 B5
Kites Cl RH11 18 C6
Kithurst Cl Crawley RH11 18 D4
Littlehampton BN16 199 F4
Worthing BN12 181 B4
Kithurst Cres BN12 181 B4
Kithurst Farm Rd RH20 140 B8
Kithurst La RH20 119 C1
Kithurst Pk RH20 119 B1
Kitilear Ct 5 BN3 187 D6
Kitsmead RH10 7 A2
Kittiwake Cl RH11 17 D4
Knap La PO20 206 D7
Knepp Cl Brighton BN2 168 F2
Crawley RH10 19 C6
Knight's Hill PO18 133 E5
Knighton Cl RH10 6 D2
Knights Cotts PO18 151 B3
Knightscroft Ave BN16 199 C4
Knightscroft Cl 4 BN16 199 B4
Knob Hill RH12 15 A1
Knockhundred Row GU29 92 F8
Knole Cl RH10 19 D7
Knole Gr RH19 9 C3
Knoll Bsns Ctr The BN3 186 D8
Knoll Cl BN3 166 D1
Knoll Cty Inf Sch BN3 166 D1
Knowle Cl RH10 7 C3
Knowle Dr RH10 7 B3
Knowle La GU6, RH12 11 D4
Knowle The RH17 84 E7
Knowles Cl BN5 123 E5
Knowles Meadow GU33 45 D1
Knoyle Rd BN1 167 E2
Knyveton Ct RH15 107 B3
Kymer Gdns BN6 127 A3
Kynon Gdns PO22 196 D6
Kyoto Ct PO21 195 B3

Laburnum Ave BN3 166 E1
Laburnum Cl Ferring BN12 200 F5
Lancing BN15 183 D4
Laburnum Gr
Bognor Regis PO22 195 C6
Brighton BN1 168 B3
Chichester PO19 173 A5
Laburnum Grove Cty Jun Sch The PO22 195 C6
Laburnum Way RH16 86 B4
Laburnum Wlk BN16 199 C6
Lacey Ho PO19 172 F5
Lackenhurst La RH13 79 A6
Ladbroke Rd RH6 2 B5
Ladies Mile BN1 168 B7
Ladies Mile Cl BN1 167 F6
Ladies' Mile Ct BN1 167 E6
Ladies' Mile Rd BN1 167 F6
Lady Bee Ind Est BN42 185 E6
Lady Margaret Rd RH11 18 A7
Lady Margaret Wlk RH11 18 A7
Ladydell Rd BN11 182 F3
Ladymead RH15 107 C5
Ladymead Cl RH10 19 C3
Ladysmith Rd BN2 188 D8
Lagoon Rd PO21 204 F7
Lagwood Cl BN6 126 F3
Laine Cl BN1 167 E3
Laines Rd BN44 143 C2
Lake Cotts PO22 176 D6
Lake La Barnham BN18, PO22 176 D6
Horley RH1, RH6 2 C6
Lake Rd PO19 173 C6
Lake View Bognor Regis PO21 194 A1
1 Brighton BN2 188 C5
Lake View Rd
Dormans Park RH19 9 F5
Furnace Wood RH10 8 C4
Lakers Lea RH14 31 F1
Lakers Meadow RH14 77 D8
Lakeside Horsham RH12 36 C5
Midhurst GU29 92 E6
Shoreham-by-Sea BN15 184 B5
Lamberhurst Wlk RH10 19 A5
Lambert's La GU29 92 F8
Lambeth Cl RH11 18 B2
Lambleys La BN14 182 F8
Lambourn Cl RH19 9 E3
Lambourne Cl Brighton BN1 168 C2
Crawley RH10 18 F4
Lambourne La GU29, GU30 47 E2
Lambourne Rd BN1 168 C2
Lambs Cres RH12 36 F5
Lambs Farm Cl RH12 37 A5
Lambs Farm Rd RH12 37 A6
Lambs Green Rd RH12 16 F6
Lambs Lease GU33 45 D3
Lambyn Croft RH6 2 C4
Lammas Cl BN17 178 E3
Lamorna Gdns Ferring BN12 200 F4
Westergate PO20 175 D6
Lamorna Gr BN14 182 C6
Lanark Cl RH13 36 E2
Lancaster Cl RH10 6 D1
Lancaster Ct 11 BN3 187 A6
Lancaster Dr RH19 10 A3
Lancaster Pl PO22 195 C6
Lancaster Rd Brighton BN1 207 F7
Worthing BN12 181 E2
Lancasterian Grange PO19 172 F6
Lancastrian Cty Inf Sch PO19 172 F7
Lancelot Cl RH11 17 E6
Lancing Cl Crawley RH11 18 A8
Lancing BN15 183 D6
Lancing Coll BN15 164 A2
Lancing Ct 5 Brighton BN2 188 F5
Horsham RH12 37 A4
Lancing Manor L Ctr BN15 183 F8
Lancing Pk BN15 183 D4
Lancing Sta BN15 183 E5
Landen Pk RH6 1 E5
Landseer Dr PO20 206 F7
Landseer Rd BN3 187 A8
Lane End Dr PO10 169 B8
Lane End Rd PO22 197 A5
Lane Ho RH13 36 D2
Lane The Chichester PO19 153 A2
Ifold RH14 31 C4
Lanercost Rd RH11 18 C5
Lanfranc Rd BN14 182 B4
Langbury Cl BN12 180 D3
Langbury La BN12 180 E3
Langdale Ave PO19, PO20 173 C4
Langdale Cl BN15 183 C5
Langdale Ct BN41 186 F6
Langdale Gdns BN3 186 F6
Langdale Rd Crawley RH11 17 D4
Hove BN3 186 F6
Langham Ct 4 BN11 182 A2
Langham Gdns BN11 182 A2
Langhurst Cl RH12 15 E4
Langhurst La RH12 17 A8
Langhurstwood Rd RH12 15 D3
Langley Dr RH11 18 D8
Langley Gr PO21 194 C1
Langley Green Cty Fst Sch RH11 5 D1
Langley Green Cty Mid Sch RH11 18 C8
Langley La RH11 18 A8
Langley Par RH11 5 C1
Langley Pl RH11 5 C1
Langley Wlk RH11 5 B1
Langmead Cl BN17 197 E8
Langridge Dr
East Grinstead RH19 22 E8
Portslade-by-Sea BN41 166 B3
Langridge Ho RH12 36 B2
Langridge La RH16 86 A5
Langridge Way RH15 106 E5
Langshott RH6 2 D4
Langshott La RH6 2 C4
Langshott Sch RH6 2 C3
Langstone Cl RH10 19 C3
Langton Cl PO20 206 D6
Langton La BN6 125 E7
Langton Pl 4 RH20 119 D1
Langton Rd Chichester PO19 172 E7
Worthing BN14 182 D4
Lanka Ct PO20 201 E7
Lansbury Rd RH11 18 B1
Lansdown Cl RH12 37 B6
Lansdown Terr PO10 149 D5
Lansdowne Cl Angmering BN16 179 F6
Worthing BN11 182 A2
Lansdowne Ct BN11 182 A2
Lansdowne Mews 9 BN3 187 D6
Lansdowne Pl BN3 187 D6
Lansdowne Rd
Angmering BN16 179 F6
Hove BN1, BN3 187 D6
Littlehampton BN17 178 D3
Worthing BN11 182 A2
Lansdowne Sq BN3 187 D5
Lansdowne St BN3 187 D6
Lansdowne Way BN16 179 F6
Lanyards BN16 179 A3
Lanyon Cl RH12 37 A6
Lanyon Mews RH12 37 A6
Lapwing Cl RH13 36 F3
Larch Cl Bognor Regis PO22 195 C7
Chichester PO19 152 F2
Liphook GU30 25 B3
Rustington BN16 199 D5
Larch End Horsham RH12 36 B4
West Chiltington Common RH20 119 D7
Larch Way RH16 86 B4
Larches The RH12 37 C6
Larches Way RH10 21 C8
Larchfield Cl PO21 194 D1
Large Acres PO20 206 D7
Lark Hill BN3 166 E3
Lark Rise Crawley RH11 18 C8
Liphook GU30 25 A5
Larke Cl BN43 185 C7
Larkfield Cl BN15 183 F5
Larkfield Way BN1 168 A4
Larkins Rd RH6 5 D7
Larkspur Way RH13 58 A3
Lashmar Rd BN16 200 A6
Lashmere RH10 7 D3
Laski Ct RH11 18 B1
Latham Rd PO20 206 D6
Latimer Cl RH11 5 D1
Latimer Rd BN11 181 F1
Laud Dr RH10 19 D5
Lauder Cl PO10 149 F2
Laughton Rd RH12 36 F5
Laundry La RH17 44 D1
Laurel 2 RH16 85 D6
Laurel Cl Burgess Hill RH15 107 D5
Crawley RH10 19 A3
Worthing BN13 181 C5
Laurel Dene RH19 9 F1
Laurel Gr PO22 195 C6
Laurel Mount RH20 98 C2
Laurel Wlk RH13 36 F1
Laurels Cty Fst Sch The BN13 181 B6
Laurels The 4 Brighton BN2 207 B8
Crawley RH10 6 A1
Henfield BN5 123 E5
Southwater RH13 57 F2
Laurence Gn PO10 149 B4
Lauriston Rd BN1 167 E2
Lavant CE (C) Prim Sch PO18 152 E6
Lavant Cl Crawley RH11 17 F5
Worthing BN12 181 A4
Lavant Down Rd PO18 152 E7
Lavant Ho (Rosemead Sch) PO18 152 E5
Lavant Rd PO18, PO19 152 F3
Lavender Hill BN43 165 B1
Lavender Ho BN2 207 B4
Lavender St BN2 207 B4
Lavington Cl RH11 18 A7
Lavington Rd BN14 182 B6
Lavinia Ct Bognor Regis PO21 194 F4
Worthing BN12 181 C3
Lavinia Way BN16 200 A5
Lawn The PO21 194 E2
Lawns Rd RH12 12 A3
Lawns The Lancing BN15 183 C8
West Kingston BN16 200 A4
Lawrence Ave BN16 199 D6
Lawrence Rd BN3 186 F7
Lawrie La RH16 86 B5
Laws Cl RH11 17 E5
Lawson-Hunt Ind Pk RH12 35 C4
Lawyer's La BN5 123 C4
Laylands Ct BN41 186 A7
Laylands Rd BN41 186 A7
Layne The PO22 197 A5
Lazy Acre PO10 169 F8
Le May Cl RH6 2 A4
Lea Cl RH11 17 F5
Lea Farm La RH20 97 C2
Lea Ho PO22 195 A6
Leach Ct BN2 188 C5
Leahurst Court Rd BN1 167 E3
Leahurst Ct 4 BN1 167 E3
Leamon Cl PO22 196 F5
Leander Rd PO18 171 C5
Leas Ct PO22 195 C5
Leas The Angmering BN16 179 E3
Burgess Hill RH15 106 F4
Leatherbottle La PO19 173 C6
Lechford Rd RH6 2 A1
Leconfield Rd BN15 183 C5
Ledbury Way PO21 194 B2
Ledgers Meadow RH17 84 F6
Ledra Dr PO21 205 B8
Lee St RH6 1 E4
Leechpond Hill RH13 59 F2
Leechpool La RH12, RH13 37 A4
Leechpool Lane Cty Prim Sch RH13 37 A4
Leechwood & Owlbeech Wood Nature Reserve RH13 37 B3
Leecroft PO21 194 E2
Leeds Cl Southwater RH13 58 A2
Worthing BN13 181 B5
Leemark Ho 4 BN17 198 E4
Lees Cnr BN16 199 B5
Leeward Cl BN13 181 F5
Leeward Rd
Littlehampton BN16, BN17 199 A5
Worthing BN13 181 F5
Legion Way PO20 202 A6
Legsheath La RH18, RH19 43 F8
Leicester St BN2 207 B5
Leicester Villas BN3 186 D7
Leigh Ct PO20 202 C4
Leigh Rd Chichester PO19 172 F5
Worthing BN14 182 D6
Leighlands RH10 19 C8
Leighton Ave BN14 182 E6
Leighton Rd
Horsted Keynes RH17 65 C5
Hove BN3 187 A8
Leighton Villas RH17 65 C5
Leinster Gdns PO22 196 D4
Leith View Rd RH12 37 A5
Lemmington Way RH12 37 A7
Lenhurst Way BN13 181 F4
Lennox Rd Chichester PO19 173 B7
Hove BN3 186 F8
Shoreham-by-Sea BN43 185 B8
Worthing BN11 182 D3
Lennox St Bognor Regis PO21 195 D2
Lennox St Brighton BN2 207 B5
Leonardslee Ct RH10 19 B3
Leonardslee Gardens RH13 82 A8
Leonora Dr PO21 194 B2
Leopold Cl PO22 196 A5
Leopold Rd Brighton BN1 207 F6
Crawley RH11 18 C6
Lesser Foxholes BN43 164 D1
Letchworth Cl BN12 200 E5
Letchworth Ct RH11 17 E3
Level Mare La PO20 155 E2
Leveret La RH11 18 B8
Leverton Ave PO22 196 D4
Levine Ct 4 PO21 195 D4
Lewes Cl Bognor Regis PO21 194 F4
Crawley RH10 19 C6
Lewes Cres BN2 188 E4
Lewes Rd Ashurst Wood RH19 23 C6
Brighton BN1, BN2 168 E3
Chelwood Gate RH17, RH18 44 C1
Danehill RH17 66 B3
Ditchling BN6 127 F2
Forest Row RH18 23 E2
Haywards Heath RH16 86 B7
Horsted Keynes RH17 65 C5
Scaynes Hill RH16, RH17 86 D4
Lewes St BN2 207 B6
Lewin Cl BN15 183 F7
Lewis Ct 2 Brighton BN2 188 C8
Worthing BN13 181 B5
Lewis La BN18 177 B2
Lewis Rd Chichester PO19 173 B7
Lancing BN15 183 D8
New Brighton PO10 149 C3
Selsey PO20 206 E7
Lewisham Cl RH11 18 C2
Ley Rd PO22 196 B4
Leybourne Cl RH11 18 C1
Leyfield BN6 125 D5
Leylands Pk RH15 107 B5
Leylands Rd RH15 107 B4
Leys The Fernhurst GU27 49 A5
Singleton PO18 133 D7
Leythorne Cotts PO20 173 E3
Leyton Lea RH17 84 E6
Library Pl BN11 182 E1
Lichfield Ct 10 Brighton BN2 188 F5
3 Worthing BN11 182 A1
Lichfield Gdns PO21 194 E3
Lidsey Rd PO20, PO22 175 D4
Lifeboat Way PO20 206 E5
Lilac Cl Middleton-on-Sea PO22 196 E6
Worthing BN13 181 B5
Lillywhite Cl RH15 106 F5
Limbourne La RH20 97 B3
Limbrick Cl BN12 181 C3
Limbrick La BN12 181 C4
Limbrick Way BN12 181 C4
Lime Ave RH12 37 A4
Lime Chase RH20 119 D2
Lime Cl Chichester PO19 173 B7
Copthorne RH10 7 B3
Crawley RH11 5 C1
Lime Gr BN16 179 F4
Lime Kiln Rd RH13 59 D6
Lime Rd BN14 161 E6
Lime Tree Ave BN14 161 F2
Lime Tree Cl BN16 199 F6
Lime Tree Gr RH16 86 C7
Limes Ave RH6 2 B1
Limes Cl Bramshott GU30 25 C7
Liss GU33 45 B4
Limes The East Grinstead RH19 9 A5
Yapton BN18 177 A3
Limmard Way PO22 196 C4
Limmer La PO22 196 B4
Limney Rd BN2 188 E7
Linacre Dr GU6, RH12 12 C4
Lincett Ave BN13 181 F4
Lincett Ct BN13 181 F4
Lincett Dr BN13 181 F3
Linch Rd GU29, GU27 70 B7
Linchmere BN2 188 F7
Linchmere Pl RH11 18 A7
Linchmere Rd Hammer GU27 26 D5
Linchmere GU27 26 C4
Lincoln Ave PO21 194 C4
Lincoln Cl Crawley RH10 18 E3
Horley RH6 2 A2
Lincoln Cotts BN2 207 B6
Lincoln Ct Hove BN3 187 C8
Liphook GU30 25 C4
Lincoln Gn PO19 152 F1
Lincoln Rd
Portslade-by-Sea BN41 186 B7
Worthing BN13 181 F4
Lincoln St BN2 207 B7
Lincoln Wood RH16, RH17 85 C5
Lindale Pl 5 RH20 119 D1
Linden Ave RH19 9 C2
Linden Cl Crawley RH10 19 A3
Horsham RH12 36 E4
Linden Ct
1 Bognor Regis PO21 195 C3
Petworth GU28 95 E7
Linden Dr GU33 45 B4
Linden Gr RH16 86 B7
Linden Pk BN17 198 C5
Linden Rd Bognor Regis PO21 195 C4
Littlehampton BN17 198 C5
Lindens Cl PO10 149 B2
Lindens The 4 Brighton BN2 207 B7
Copthorne RH10 7 B3
Lindfield BN41 166 A1
Lindfield Ct 2 BN1 168 C2
Lindfield Cty Inf Sch RH16 86 A7
Lindfield Cty Jun Sch RH16 86 B7
Lindfield Ent Pk RH16 86 C6
Lindfield Rd RH17 64 C6
Lindgren Wlk RH11 18 B1
Lindsey Ct PO22 196 A6
Lindum Rd BN13 181 F5
Lindum Way BN13 181 F5
Lineside Ind Est BN17 198 B6
Lineside Way BN17 198 B6
Linfield Copse RH20 119 F6
Lingfield Cl BN13 181 F6
Lingfield Dr RH10 19 E7
Lingfield Rd RH19 9 D3
Lingfield Way PO20 206 F7
Link Hill RH20 119 B1
Link La RH20 98 C2
Link The RH11 18 D6
Link Way PO21 194 A1
Links Ave PO22 195 F4
Links Cl Portslade-by-Sea BN41 186 C8
Red Hill PO9 128 D1
Links La PO9 128 D2
Links Rd Lancing BN15 183 F6
Portslade-by-Sea BN41 186 C8
Worthing BN14 182 A8
Linkway RH6 6 C7
Linkway The Brighton BN1 168 B1
Worthing BN11 182 C3
Linton Ho GU28 73 C1
Linton Rd BN3 186 F8
Lintott Gdns RH13 36 E3
Lion Cl GU27 26 F7
Lion Ct PO21 194 B2
Lion Gn GU27 26 F6
Lion La Haslemere GU27 26 F7
Turners Hill RH10 21 A4
Lion Mead GU27 26 F6
Lion Mews 4 BN3 186 F7
Lion Rd PO21 194 A2
Lion St PO19 173 A6
Lionel Ave PO22 196 C6
Lions Ct BN2 188 E5
Lions Dene BN1 167 D4
Lions Gdns BN1 167 D2
Liphook CE (C) Jun Sch GU30 25 B4
Liphook Cl BN1 168 C1
Liphook Cty Inf Sch GU30 25 B4
Liphook Golf Course GU30 47 A7
Liphook Rd Haslemere GU27 26 F6
Hollywater GU35 24 A8
Linchmere GU27 26 B4
Liphook Sta GU30 25 C2
Lisher Rd BN15 183 F7
Lisle Way PO10 149 A3
Lismore Cres RH11 18 B3
Liss Inf Sch GU33 45 C3
Liss Jun Sch GU33 45 C3
Lister Ave RH19 22 F6
Listers RH17 60 F1
Litten Terr PO19 173 A7
Little Ashfield GU29 92 E8
Little Babbsham PO21 194 E2
Little Barn Pl GU33 45 D4
Little Bentswood RH16 85 F5
Little Bentswood Cl RH16 85 F5
Little Black Hill RH16 86 B7
Little Boultons PO20 193 A8
Little Breach PO19 172 F8
Little Bridges Cl RH13 57 F1
Little Cl RH13 79 F7
Little Comptons RH13 36 F2
Little Copse Rd BN6 126 E4
Little Court Rd GU29 92 D8
Little Crabtree RH11 18 C7
Little Dipper's RH20 98 C2
Little Dr BN12 200 E5
Little Dro BN44 143 D2
Little East St Billingshurst RH14 55 D1
Brighton BN2 207 A4
Little Finches RH13 103 A3
Little Gables BN13 181 F6
Little George St BN2 207 A4
Little Grebe RH12 36 C5
Little Haven La RH12 36 F5
Little Hayes Cotts RH14 55 F5
Little High St
Shoreham-by-Sea BN43 184 E7
Worthing BN11 182 D3
Little Hill RH20 119 C8
Little King St RH19 9 E1
Little London PO19 173 A6
Little London Mews 5 PO19 173 A6
Little Oak RH13 103 A3
Little Paddocks BN12 200 E5
Little Paddocks Way BN12 200 F5
Little Park Enterprises RH6 4 E3
Little Pembrokes BN11 182 A3
Little Preston St BN1 187 E5
Little Western St 1 BN1 187 E5
Littlecote GU28 95 F7
Littledrove Cotts PO18 133 D7
Littlefield Cl PO20 206 E7
Littlefield Rd PO19 173 B5
Littlefield Sch GU30 25 D2
Littlegreen Sch PO18 109 A4
Littlehampton Com Sch The BN17 198 E6
Littlehampton Hospl BN17 198 E5
Littlehampton Marina BN17 198 B5
Littlehampton Rd
Ferring BN12, BN16 180 D3
Worthing BN12, BN13 181 D5
Littlehampton Sta BN17 198 D5
Littlehaven Sch RH12 36 F5
Littleheath Rd BN18 155 E4
Littlemead Gram Sch PO20 174 A7
Littlestone Rd BN13 181 E6
Littleworth La RH13 103 A6
Liverpool Bldgs 7 BN11 182 D2
Liverpool Gdns BN11 182 D2

Liverpool Rd BN11 182 D2
Liverpool Terr BN11 182 D2
Livesay Cres BN14 182 D4
Livingstone Ho 5 BN3 187 B7
Livingstone Rd
Burgess Hill RH15 106 F3
Crawley RH10 18 E4
Horsham RH13 36 D1
Hove BN3 187 B7
Livingstone St BN2 188 D5
Lizard Head BN17 199 A6
Lloyd Cl BN3 187 C8
Lloyd Goring Cl BN16 179 F6
Lloyd Rd BN3 187 C8
Lloyds Ct RH10 5 E1
Loats La PO21, PO22 194 F7
Lobs Wood La RH20 119 D2
Lobster La PO20 206 B8
Lock La PO20 191 F6
Locke Rd GU30 25 D4
Lockgate Rd PO20 192 C4
Locks Cres BN41 166 B1
Locks Ct 10 BN42 185 E7
Locks Hill BN41 166 B1
Locksash Cl PO20 190 C2
Locksash La PO18 130 C7
Lockwood Cl RH12 37 A5
Lockwood Ct RH10 18 F8
Loddon Cl BN13 181 C8
Loder Gdns BN14 182 C5
Loder Pl BN1 167 F2
Loder Rd BN1 167 F2
Loders RH17 64 B8
Lodge Cl Crawley RH11 18 C6
East Grinstead RH19 9 D1
Middleton-on-Sea PO22 197 A5
Portslade-by-Sea BN41 165 F2
Lodge Ct Bognor Regis PO21 194 E2
Shoreham-by-Sea BN43 164 E1
Lodge Hill La BN6 127 C4
Lodge La Forestside PO9 129 F6
Horley RH6 1 E8
Keymer BN6 127 B2
Lodge The BN2 207 B8
Lodgebury Cl PO10 170 A8
Lodgelands RH17 64 B6
Lodsworth Cl BN2 188 F7
Lodsworth Rd PO21 194 B3
Lombard St GU28 95 F8
Lomond Ave BN1 168 B7
Londerry Ind Est The PO20 206 D8
London Fields Ho RH11 18 C2
London La RH17 84 F6
London Meed Cty Prim Sch RH15 107 A1
London Rd Arundel BN18 157 E6
Arundel BN18 158 A3
Ashington RH20 121 A4
Balcombe RH17 40 F2
Bognor Regis PO21 195 D3
Brighton BN1 207 A7
Brighton, Withdene BN1 167 D4
Burgess Hill RH15 106 F5
Clayton BN1, BN45 147 C4
Coldwaltham RH20 117 D6
Crawley RH11 5 E3
Cuckfield RH17 84 F7
Danehill RH17 66 A4
East Grinstead RH19 9 C3
Fontwell BN18 156 A3
Forest Row RH18 23 E4
Hassocks BN6, RH15 126 E6
Heath Common RH20 120 E2
Henfield BN5 123 F6
Hill Brow GU31, GU33 67 B8
Horsham RH12 36 C2
Hurstpierpoint BN6 125 E2
Liphook GU30 25 C5
Pyecombe BN45, BN6 146 F7
London Road Cotts BN18 158 A4
London Road Sta BN1 188 A8
London St BN11 182 C3
London Terr BN1 207 A7
Lonesome La RH6 1 D8
Loney Ct 1 BN43 185 C8
Long Acre RH10 21 A8
Long Cl RH10 19 D6
Long Copse Ct PO10 149 B4
Long Copse La PO10 149 C4
Long Furlong BN13, BN14 161 B5
Long Hill RH13 81 F8
Long La Arundel BN18 157 D4
East Marden PO18 110 A3
Long Mead BN18 156 D1
Long Meadow BN14 162 A3
Long Park Cnr BN6 127 D2
Long Wlk RH16 86 B4
Longacre Liss GU33 45 C4
Selsey PO20 206 D6
Longacre Cres RH17 84 F8
Longacre La PO20 206 E6
Longacre Pk BN18 176 F5
Longbridge Gate RH6 5 E8
Longbridge Rd Crawley RH6 5 F8
Horley RH6 1 F1
Longbridge Rdbt RH6 1 E2
Longbridge Wlk RH6 1 F1
Longbrook PO22 195 F3
Longchamp Cl RH6 2 C3
Longcroft 4 BN43 184 E7
Longdene Rd GU27 27 B6
Longfellow Cl RH12 36 E7
Longfellow Rd BN11 182 B3
Longfield Rd
New Brighton PO10 149 B3
Tower Hill RH12 58 A8
Longford Rd PO21 195 C4
Longfurlong La BN13 160 E4
Longhurst 9 Brighton BN2 188 E4
Burgess Hill RH15 107 D2
Longhurst Rd RH11 18 A1
Longland Ave RH20 119 C2
Longlands BN14 182 D8
Longlands Glade BN14 182 D8
Longlands Rd
East Wittering PO20 201 F6
Southbourne PO10 169 F8
Longlands Spinney BN14 182 D8
Longmead GU33 45 B4
Longmeadow Gdns PO20 191 E4
Longmere Rd RH11 18 D8
Longmoor Dr GU30 24 D4
Longmoor Rd GU30 24 E4
Longport Rd PO22 196 B4
Longships BN16 199 A6
Longwood View RH10 19 A3
Longyard Ho RH6 2 B5
Loop The PO22 196 C4
Loose La BN15 183 B6
Loppets Rd RH10 18 F3
Lordings La RH20 119 D7
Lordings Rd RH14 77 A6
Loriners RH10 18 D3
Loriners Ct BN3 186 D8
Lorna Rd BN3 187 D7
Lorne Rd BN1 207 A8
Lorraine Ct 7 BN3 187 E7
Lotts La BN15 183 C6
Loudoun Rd BN17 198 C5
Lourier Ct 1 BN14 182 D4
Love La RH20 119 D2
Lovegrove Ct BN3 186 E8
Loveletts RH11 18 A5
Lovells Cl PO21 194 B2
Lover's Wlk BN1 187 F8
Lovett Ct BN12 181 C4
Loveys Rd BN18 176 F2
Lowdells Cl RH19 9 C4
Lowdells Dr RH19 9 D4
Lowdells La RH19 9 C3
Lowe Cl RH11 39 B8
Lower Barn Cl RH12 36 F5
Lower Beach Rd BN43 184 F6
Lower Bevendean Ave BN2 168 E1
Lower Bognor Rd PO20, PO21 194 D5
Lower Chalvington Pl BN2 188 E5
Lower Church Rd RH15 106 F3
Lower Dene RH19 10 A1
Lower Dr BN42 165 E1
Lower Faircox BN5 123 D5
Lower Forecourt RH6 6 B7
Lower Hanger GU27 26 D6
Lower Hone La PO18 171 A2
Lower Market St BN3 187 D5
Lower Mere RH19 22 F8
Lower Rd East Lavant PO18 153 A5
Forest Row RH18 23 F3
Lower Rock Gdns BN2 207 B4
Lower Sq RH18 23 E3
Lower St Fittleworth RH20 97 A2
Haslemere GU27 27 C6
Pulborough RH20 98 C2
Lower Station Rd
Billingshurst RH14 77 D6
Henfield BN5 123 D4
Lower Tanbridge Way RH12 36 B2
Lowestoft Wlk RH10 19 B4
Lowfield Heath Rd RH6 4 F5
Lowfield Rd
Haywards Heath RH16 85 F3
Slinfold RH13 34 D3
Lowfield Way RH6 5 E5
Lowlands Rd RH15 107 B5
Lowther Rd Brighton BN1 168 A2
Worthing BN13 181 F7
Loxdale (The Swedish Folk High Sch) BN41 166 B1
Loxley Gdns 2 BN14 182 C4
Loxwood BN16 180 B3
Loxwood Ave BN14 182 B5
Loxwood Cty Prim Sch RH14 32 A4
Loxwood Rd
Alfold Crossways GU6 11 A3
Bucks Green RH12 33 A6
Ifold RH14 31 A2
Loxwood RH12, RH14 32 D4
Loxwood Wlk RH11 18 A8
Lucas RH17 65 D5
Lucas Cl RH19 10 A1
Lucas Field GU27 26 E6
Lucas Grange RH16 85 D5
Lucas Rd RH12 35 F8
Lucas Way RH16 85 C5
Lucastes Ave RH16, RH17 85 D6
Lucastes La RH16, RH17 85 C6
Lucastes Rd RH16 85 C5
Lucerne Cl BN41 166 B1
Lucerne Ct PO21 194 E2
Lucerne Dr RH10 19 D4
Lucerne Rd BN1 168 A1
Lucking La PO22 196 F5
Lucraft Rd BN2 168 F5
Ludlow Cl PO21 194 E2
Luffs Meadow GU28 51 A7
Lullington Ave BN3 186 F8
Lumley Ct RH6 2 A4
Lumley Gdns PO10 169 C8
Lumley Rd Horley RH6 2 A3
Lumley PO10 149 C1
Lumley Terr PO10 149 C1
Lunce's Hill RH16, RH17 107 F8
Lundy Cl Crawley RH11 18 C3
Littlehampton BN16 199 A4
Lurgashall RH15 107 C1
Lutener Rd GU29 71 A1
Luth The Wisborough Green RH14 54 B1
Luth The
Wisborough Green RH14 76 A8
Luther St BN2 188 C7
Lutman St PO10 149 A4
Lutyens Cl RH11 17 E4
Luxford Cl RH12 36 F5
Luxford Rd RH16 86 B7
Luxford's La RH19 23 B6
Lychgates The BN18 176 F4
Lydon Ho RH11 5 D1
Lye La East Ashling PO18 151 F4
West Stoke PO18 151 F5
Lyminster Ave BN1 168 A5
Lyminster Cty Inf Sch BN17 178 D3
Lyminster Gate BN17 178 D4
Lyminster Rd Crossbush BN18 158 D1
Littlehampton BN17, BN18 178 D6
Lyn Rd BN13 181 C6
Lynch Down PO18 151 A6
Lynchborough Rd GU30 24 D8
Lynchet Cl BN1 168 C3
Lynchet Down BN1 168 C2
Lynchet Wlk BN1 168 C2
Lynchets Cres BN3 166 D3
Lynchette The BN43 164 F1
Lynchmere Ave BN15 183 D8
Lynchpole Wlk BN12 181 B3
Lynden Ct 6 BN1 167 E2
Lyndhurst Cl RH11 18 D5
Lyndhurst Ct BN3 187 D7
Lyndhurst Cty Fst Sch BN11 182 F3
Lyndhurst Farm Cl RH19 8 D4
Lyndhurst Rd Chichester PO19 173 B5
Hove BN3 187 D7
Worthing BN11 182 F3
Lynton Cl East Grinstead RH19 10 A2
Hurstpierpoint BN6 126 B5
Lynton Park Ave RH19 10 A2
Lynton St BN2 188 C7
Lynwick St RH12 33 C8
Lynwood Ct RH12 36 C3
Lyon Cl Crawley RH10 19 C2
Hove BN3 187 D7
Lyon Ct 1 Bognor Regis PO21 195 D3
Horsham RH13 36 E2
Lyon St PO21 195 D3
Lyon St W PO21 195 D3
Lyons Cl RH13 34 D3
Lyons Farm Ret Pk BN14 182 E8
Lyons Rd RH13 34 E3
Lyons Way BN14 182 E7
Lyoth La RH16 86 C4
Lyoth Villas RH16 86 C4
Lyric Cl RH10 19 D4
Lysander Ho RH20 119 E1
Lysander Way PO20 154 D1
Lytton Dr RH10 19 D7

M'tongue Ave PO18 171 C7
Mackerel La PO20 206 B8
Mackie Ave Brighton BN1 168 A7
Keymer BN6 127 A5
Mackley's Ind Est BN5 144 F6
Macklin Rd PO22 195 E4
Macleod Rd RH13 36 F1
Madehurst Cl Brighton BN2 188 D5
Littlehampton BN16 199 F4
Madehurst Ct Crawley RH11 17 F3
6 Littlehampton BN17 198 D5
Madehurst Way BN17 198 D6
Madeira Ave
Bognor Regis PO22 195 E5
Horsham RH12 36 C2
Worthing BN11 182 E2
Madeira Dr BN2 188 C4
Madeira Par PO22 195 E5
Madeira Pl BN2 207 B4
Madgwick La PO18 153 D1
Mafeking Rd BN2 168 D1
Magdalene Cl RH10 6 C1
Magellan Terr RH10 6 A2
Magnolia Cl BN13 181 B5
Magnolia Ct RH6 2 A3
Magpie Cotts PO9 128 E4
Magpie La Horsham RH13 58 F6
Selsey PO20 203 C1
Magpie Rd PO8 128 E5
Magpie Wlk RH10 18 F8
Maiden La RH11 18 C8
Maidenbower Cty Fst Sch RH10 19 C4
Maidenbower Dr RH10 19 D4
Maidenbower La RH10 19 C4
Maidenbower Pl RH10 19 C4
Maidenbower Sq RH10 19 C4
Maidment Cl BN5 123 F6
Main Dr PO22 196 F5
Main Rd Birdham PO20 191 E4
Broadbridge PO18, PO19 171 D7
East Dean PO18 134 C6
Nutbourne PO10, PO18 170 B7
Yapton BN18 176 F3
Maines Farm Rd BN44 144 C1
Mainstone Rd 1 BN3 186 F7
Maizecroft RH6 2 C4
Major Cl BN1 168 B1
Major's Hill RH10 20 C5
Malcolm Cl BN12 200 E5
Malcolm Gdns RH6 1 D1
Malcolm Rd Tangmere PO20 154 C1
Tangmere PO20 154 C2
Malden Pl 3 RH20 119 D1
Malden Way PO20 206 D7
Maldon Rd BN1 167 D2
Malham Cl RH10 19 C3
Malin Rd BN16 199 A5
Malla Way BN5 123 E6
Mallard Cl Haslemere GU27 26 E6
Mallard Cl Horley RH6 2 A5
Horsham RH12 36 C5
Mallard Cres PO21 204 F7
Mallard Pl RH19 22 F8
Mallard Rd PO9 128 D1
Mallion's La RH17 61 E2
Mallon Dene BN16 199 D4
Mallory Rd BN3 167 C2
Mallow Cl RH12 36 E6
Malmayne Ct PO21 194 E3
Malt House Trad Est BN43 185 B7
Malthouse Cl Arundel BN18 158 A2
Lancing BN15 183 B7
Malthouse Cotts Cocking GU29 112 D7
West Ashling PO18 151 B3
West Wittering PO20 190 D3
Worthing BN12 181 C1
Malthouse Ct 14 BN2 207 B5
Malthouse La
Burgess Hill BN6, RH15 106 C2
West Ashling PO18 151 B3
Malthouse Meadows GU30 25 C4
Malthouse Pas 3 BN17 198 D6
Malthouse Rd
Crawley RH10, RH11 18 D4
Selsey PO20 206 E7
Malthouse Trad Est BN43 185 B7
Maltings Gn BN44 143 D2
Maltings The Burgess Hill BN6 106 D4
Chichester PO19 172 F6
Liphook GU30 25 D4
Maltravers Ct 2 BN17 198 E4
Maltravers Dr BN17 198 E4
Maltravers Rd BN17 198 E4
Maltravers St BN18 158 B3
Malvern Cl BN11 183 B3
Malvern Mews PO10 149 B1
Malvern Rd Crawley RH11 18 C5
Hill Brow GU33 45 D2
Malvern St 12 BN3 187 B7
Malvern Way PO21 194 B1
Manaton Cl RH16 85 F4
Manchester St BN2 207 A4
Manchester Terr PO10 149 D4
Mandalay Ct BN1 167 D4
Manet Sq PO22 195 B6
Manhattan Ct BN1 167 D4
Manhood Com Coll The PO20 206 D8
Manhood Cotts PO20 202 F7
Manhood La PO20 203 F8
Manitoba Way BN13 181 C6
Manley's Hill RH20 119 E1
Manning Cl RH19 9 D2
Manning Rd Chichester PO19 173 C7
Littlehampton BN17 198 C6
Mannings 8 BN43 184 F7
Mannings Cl RH10 6 D1
Mannings Heath Golf Course RH13 59 F6
Mannock Rd PO20 154 B1
Manor Ave BN6 127 A5
Manor Cl Bognor Regis PO22 196 A4
Brighton BN2 188 E5
Burgess Hill RH15 107 D4
East Preston BN16 199 F5
Haslemere GU27 26 E6
Henfield BN5 123 F5
Horley RH6 1 F3
Lancing BN15 183 F7
Shoreham-by-Sea BN15 184 B6
Southwick BN42 186 A8
Stockbridge PO19 172 F3
Storrington RH20 119 D1
Worthing BN11 182 B2
Manor Cotts BN6 125 F5
Manor Cres Brighton BN2 188 E5
Haslemere GU27 26 E6
Manor Ct Elmer PO22 197 B5
Horsham RH12 37 A5
North Lancing BN15 183 D8
Rustington BN16 199 B6
Southwick BN42 186 A7
Worthing BN11 182 B1
Manor Dr Cuckfield RH17 84 E7
Horley RH6 1 F3
Manor Farm Cl PO20 206 E8
Manor Farm Ct PO20 206 E8
Manor Field Ct BN14 182 D5
Manor Fields
Horsham RH12, RH13 37 A4
Liphook GU30 25 D4
Manor Gdns Breach PO10 149 F1
Brighton BN2 188 E5
Hurstpierpoint BN6 125 F6
Rustington BN16 199 B5
Manor Gn BN2 188 E5
Manor Hall Cty Fst Sch BN42 185 F7
Manor Hall Cty Mid Sch BN42 185 F8
Manor Hall Rd BN42 185 F8
Manor Hill BN2 188 E6
Manor Ho BN11 182 B2
Manor House Pl BN15 183 F8
Manor La East Beach PO20 206 F8
South Mundham PO20 193 D6
Manor Lea Haslemere GU27 26 E6
Worthing BN11 182 B1
Manor Lodge Rd PO9 128 C1
Manor Paddock BN2 188 E4
Manor Par BN13 181 D7
Manor Pk PO21 194 A1
Manor Pl Bognor Regis PO21 195 C2
Brighton BN2 188 E4
Manor Rd Breach PO10 149 F1
Brighton BN2 188 E5
Burgess Hill RH15 107 D4
East Grinstead RH19 9 C2
Horsham RH12 37 A5
Hurstpierpoint BN6 125 F6
Manor Rd Lancing BN15 183 E8
Portslade-by-Sea BN41 166 B1
Rustington BN16 199 B6
Selsey PO20 206 E7
Upper Beeding BN44 144 B2
West Kingston BN16 200 A4
Worthing BN11 182 B2
Manor Royal RH10, RH11 5 E1
Manor The 3 BN11 182 B2
Manor View Ct BN14 182 D5
Manor Villas PO18 171 C5
Manor Way Bognor Regis PO21 194 C1
Breach PO10 149 F1
Brighton BN2 188 E5
Henfield BN5 123 F6
Lancing BN15 183 F7
Middleton-on-Sea PO22 197 B5
Manorfields RH11 17 D2
Mansell Ct RH15 107 B3
Mansell Rd BN43 185 B8
Manser Rd BN18 156 F1
Mansfield Cl BN11 183 A4
Mansfield Cotts PO18 170 D7
Mansfield Rd
Bognor Regis PO21, PO22 195 B6
Hove BN3 186 E7
Worthing BN11 183 A4
Mansion Cl RH15 107 D3
Mant Cl RH20 119 D1
Mant Rd GU28 95 F7
Mantell Ho 2 BN2 207 B5
Mantling Rd BN17 198 D5
Manton Rd BN2 168 E1
Mants Farm Ct PO21 194 C3
Maple Cl Billingshurst RH14 55 D1
Burgess Hill RH15 107 B5
Crawley RH11 5 C1
Haywards Heath RH16 86 B3
Horsham RH12 37 A5
Middleton-on-Sea PO22 196 E6
New Brighton PO10 149 B2
Worthing BN13 161 E1
Maple Ct 6 BN11 181 F2
Maple Dr Burgess Hill RH15 107 A5
East Grinstead RH19 10 A1
Maple Gdns Bognor Regis PO22 195 C7
Hove BN3 166 F1
Maple Ho BN12 181 A4
Maple Leaf RH20 117 D6
Maple Par BN18 176 E8
Maple Rd Billingshurst RH14 77 D7
Walberton BN18 176 E8
Maple Wlk Lancing BN15 183 B7
Rustington BN16 199 C6
Mapledown Cl RH13 57 F2
Maplehurst Rd Chichester PO19 153 B2
Maplehurst RH13 81 A3
Portslade-by-Sea BN41 166 A1
Maples The
3 Bognor Regis PO21 195 B3
Ferring BN12 200 F4
Maplewood 7 BN1 167 E3
Mapsons La PO20 192 B3
Marama Gdns BN16 199 B3
March CE Prim Sch The PO18 153 E1
Marchants Cl BN6 126 A6
Marchants Rd BN6 126 A6
Marchants Way RH15 106 F5
Marches Rd RH12 14 E4
Marchwell Ind Unit PO19 153 B1
Marchwood PO19 153 A3
Marcuse Fields PO18 171 B6
Mardale Rd BN13 181 F6
Marden Ave PO19 172 E3
Marden Ho Barnham PO22 176 C6
Littlehampton BN17 178 B3
Mardens The RH11 18 B7
Mardyke BN43 184 D6
Mare Hill Rd RH20 98 E1
Maresfield Rd BN2 188 E5
Margaret Cl PO21 194 E3
Margaret Cotts RH13 81 E2
Margaret Ho PO22 195 E4
Margaret St BN2 207 B4
Margery Rd BN3 186 D8
Marian Way PO21 195 E3
Marigolds Lodge 2 BN16 199 B4
Marina Cl PO10 169 C7
Marina Way BN2 188 F3
Marine Ave BN3 186 E6
Marine Cl East Wittering PO20 201 E6
Worthing BN11 182 A1
Marine Cres BN12 181 D1
Marine Ct BN43 184 D5
Marine Dr Brighton BN2 188 F3
East Wittering PO20 201 E7
Selsey PO20 206 F7
Worthing BN12 181 B1
Marine Dr W
Bognor Regis PO21 195 A2
East Wittering PO20 201 D7
Marine Gdns Brighton BN2 207 B4
Selsey PO20 206 D5
Marine Par Bognor Regis PO21 195 B2
Brighton BN2 188 C4
Worthing BN11 182 D1
Marine Pk 3 PO21 195 B2
Marine Pl BN11 182 D1
Marine Point 13 BN11 182 A1
Marine Sq BN2 188 C4
Marine Terrace Mews 7 BN2 188 C4
Marine View 3 BN2 207 B5
Mariners Cl BN43 184 D5
Mariners Quay BN2 188 F3

Mariners Terr PO18 ...... 171 B4
Mariners The BN15 ...... 183 D3
Mariners Wlk BN16 ...... 199 D4
Marineside PO20 ...... 202 B5
Marion Rd RH10 ...... 19 B3
Marisfield Pl PO20 ...... 206 F8
Marjoram Pl BN43 ...... 165 B1
Market Cl PO22 ...... 176 B6
Market Field BN44 ...... 143 E3
Market Pl Burgess Hill RH15 ...... 107 A2
 Haywards Heath RH16 ...... 85 E6
Market Rd PO19 ...... 173 A6
Market Sq Horsham RH12 ...... 36 C1
 Midhurst GU29 ...... 92 F7
 Petworth GU28 ...... 95 F8
Market St Bognor Regis PO21 ...... 195 C2
 Brighton BN1 ...... 207 A5
 10 Worthing BN11 ...... 182 D2
Markfield PO22 ...... 195 B6
Markwick Mews BN11 ...... 182 E3
Marlborough Bsns Ctr BN15 ...183 C4
Marlborough Cl
 Chichester PO19 ...... 173 D6
 Crawley RH11 ...... 18 C2
 Horsham RH12 ...... 36 D5
Marlborough Ct
 Bognor Regis PO21 ...... 194 F5
 Burgess Hill RH15 ...... 106 E3
 1 Hove BN3 ...... 187 C6
Marlborough Dr RH15 ...... 107 C2
Marlborough Mews BN1 ...... 207 F5
Marlborough Pl BN1, BN2 ...... 207 A6
Marlborough Rd Lancing BN15 183 D4
 Worthing BN12 ...... 181 D2
Marlborough St BN1 ...... 207 F5
Marlborough Way BN12 ...... 181 D2
Marle Ave RH15 ...... 107 A4
Marles La RH14 ...... 55 C8
Marley Combe Rd GU27 ...... 26 F4
Marley Hanger GU27 ...... 27 A3
Marley La GU27 ...... 26 E4
Marley Lodge BN2 ...... 207 B7
Marley Way RH20 ...... 119 E2
Marlinspike The BN43 ...... 185 A6
Marlow Ct Brighton BN2 ...... 207 B7
 Crawley RH10, RH11 ...... 18 D7
Marlow Dr RH16 ...... 86 C4
Marlow Rd BN2 ...... 188 F4
Marlowe Cl PO22 ...... 196 D6
Marlowe Rd BN14 ...... 182 E5
Marlpit Cl RH19 ...... 9 E4
Marlpit La Oving PO20 ...... 174 B7
 Woodmancote PO10 ...... 150 C4
Marlpit Rd RH19 ...... 43 A6
Marlpost Rd RH13 ...... 57 C1
Marmion Rd BN3 ...... 186 F7
Marquis Way PO21 ...... 194 E1
Marringdean Rd RH14 ...... 77 E4
Marsh Barns PO20 ...... 173 F2
Marsh Ct RH11 ...... 18 B1
Marsh Ho 3 BN43 ...... 185 D7
Marsh La Chidham PO18 ...... 170 C4
 Crockerhill PO20 ...... 155 A2
 Merston PO20 ...... 174 A2
 Mid Lavant PO18 ...... 152 F6
Marshall Ave
 Bognor Regis PO21 ...... 195 B4
 Worthing BN11 ...... 161 F3
Marshall Cl PO22 ...... 176 B5
Marshall Rd RH10 ...... 19 C4
Marshalls Row BN1 ...... 207 A7
Marston Ct 6 BN3 ...... 187 E7
Marston Rd BN14 ...... 182 E4
Martello Ent Ctr BN17 ...... 178 C4
Martha Gunn Cl BN2 ...... 168 E1
Martin Cl RH11 ...... 18 D8
Martin Rd BN3 ...... 166 D1
Martins La PO20 ...... 191 F5
Martins The RH10 ...... 21 C8
Martlet Cl PO19 ...... 173 A5
Martlet Ho BN1 ...... 188 A8
Martlet Rd GU28 ...... 95 E7
Martlet The BN3 ...... 167 D1
Martlet Way PO21 ...... 204 F7
Martlets RH20 ...... 119 D8
Martlets Cl RH12 ...... 36 C5
Martlets Ct BN18 ...... 158 B2
Martlets The Burgess Hill RH15 107 A3
 Crawley RH10 ...... 18 E6
 Lancing BN15 ...... 183 C6
 Littlehampton BN16 ...... 199 A4
 Shoreham-by-Sea BN43 ...... 184 F8
Martlets Trad Est BN12 ...... 181 C3
Martlets Way BN12 ...... 181 C3
Marts The RH12 ...... 33 D7
Martyn Cl BN5 ...... 123 E5
Martyns Pl RH19 ...... 23 A8
Martyrs Ave RH11 ...... 5 D1
Marvell Cl RH10 ...... 19 C8
Marylands RH16 ...... 85 F5
Marylands Cres PO22 ...... 195 E5
Masefield Rd RH11 ...... 17 E3
Mash Barn La BN15 ...... 184 A1
Mason Cl RH10 ...... 9 E2
Mason Rd RH10 ...... 18 E4
Masons Field RH13 ...... 59 C6
Masons Way RH20 ...... 98 D5
Massetts Rd RH6 ...... 2 A2
Matlock Rd BN1, BN3 ...... 167 D2
Matthews Dr RH19 ...... 19 C3
Matthey Pl RH10 ...... 6 D1
Maudlin La BN44 ...... 143 E1
Maudlyn Cl BN44 ...... 143 E1

Maudlyn Parkway BN44 ...... 143 D1
Maudlyn Pk BN44 ...... 143 D1
Mauldmare Cl PO21 ...... 194 F2
Maunsell Pk RH10 ...... 19 B6
Maxton Wlk RH11 ...... 18 B2
Maxwell Rd Arundel BN18 ...... 157 F1
 Littlehampton BN17 ...... 198 C5
Maxwell Way RH10 ...... 6 A1
May Cl Bognor Regis PO22 ...... 195 D5
 Sidlesham PO20 ...... 203 F8
 Worthing BN12 ...... 181 C4
May Rd BN2 ...... 188 D7
May Tree Ave BN14 ...... 161 F3
Maybridge Cres BN12 ...... 181 C3
Maybridge Sq BN12 ...... 181 C4
Maybush Dr PO18 ...... 170 D7
Maydwell Ave RH13 ...... 34 C2
Mayes Cl RH10 ...... 19 C5
Mayes La RH12 ...... 14 F3
Mayfair Ct PO19 ...... 172 F7
Mayfield Crawley RH10 ...... 19 D6
 East Preston BN16 ...... 180 B3
Mayfield Cl Bognor Regis PO21 ... 194 B3
 Brighton BN1 ...... 168 A5
 Worthing BN14 ...... 162 A1
Mayfield Cres BN1 ...... 167 F5
Mayfield Ct RH15 ...... 107 B3
Mayfield Rd PO21 ...... 195 A4
Mayflower Cl RH10 ...... 19 D5
Mayflower Ct
 Haywards Heath RH16 ...... 85 F4
 9 Shoreham-by-Sea BN43 ...... 185 A6
Mayflower Rd RH15 ...... 85 F4
Mayflower Sq BN1 ...... 207 A7
Mayflower Way BN16 ...... 180 A3
Mayhouse Rd RH15 ...... 106 F1
Mayo Cl 5 BN2 ...... 188 B8
Mayo Rd BN2 ...... 188 B8
Maypole La BN18 ...... 176 F5
Maypole Pk BN18 ...... 176 F5
Maypole Rd Ashurst Wood RH19 23 E6
 East Grinstead RH19 ...... 9 D2
Mayridge PO20 ...... 206 B8
Maytree Cl Angmering BN16 ...... 179 F4
 Lancing BN15 ...... 183 B6
Maytree Wlk BN15 ...... 166 L1
McKerchar Cl BN3 ...... 183 F7
McIndoe Rd RH19 ...... 9 D3
McIver Cl RH19 ...... 8 F4
McRae Ct PO20 ...... 206 D7
Mead La
 Bognor Regis PO21, PO22 ...... 195 A4
 Storrington RH20 ...... 119 E2
Mead Rd RH10 ...... 18 F7
Mead Sway BN18 ...... 156 D4
Mead The Liphook GU30 ...... 25 B5
 Liss GU33 ...... 45 B4
Mead Way GU29 ...... 92 E6
Meadow Brook Ind Ctr RH10 ... 6 A1
Meadow Cl Balcombe RH17 ...... 41 A1
 Copthorne RH10 ...... 7 A3
 Horsham RH12 ...... 37 A5
 Hunston PO20 ...... 193 A8
 Liphook GU30 ...... 25 C4
 Portslade-by-Sea BN41 ...... 166 B2
 Southwick BN42 ...... 186 A8
 Worthing BN11 ...... 183 B3
Meadow Court Est 2 BN11 ... 183 B3
Meadow Cres BN11 ...... 183 A3
Meadow Croft RH6 ...... 6 C8
Meadow Ct 4 Emsworth PO10 .169 B8
 Middleton-on-Sea PO22 ...... 196 D6
Meadow Dr RH10 ...... 86 B6
Meadow End GU30 ...... 25 C5
Meadow Farm La RH12 ...... 37 A5
Meadow La Burgess Hill RH15 .. 106 F1
 Haywards Heath RH16 ...... 86 B6
 Lancing BN15 ...... 183 E5
 West Wittering PO20 ...... 190 D2
Meadow Rd BN11 ...... 183 B3
Meadow Road Ind Est BN11 .. 183 B4
Meadow Sweet Cl BN13 ...... 181 A5
Meadow The RH10 ...... 7 A3
Meadow Vale GU27 ...... 27 A6
Meadow Way
 Bognor Regis PO21 ...... 194 B1
 Bognor Regis PO22 ...... 195 A6
 Ferring BN12 ...... 200 E6
 Liphook GU30 ...... 25 C5
 Littlehampton BN17 ...... 198 F5
 Petworth GU28 ...... 95 E7
 Tangmere PO20 ...... 154 D2
 Westergate PO20 ...... 175 D6
Meadow Wlk Liss GU33 ...... 45 B4
 Middleton-on-Sea PO22 ...... 197 A5
Meadowbank RH14 ...... 76 B8
Meadowcroft Cl Crawley RH11 .. 17 F5
 East Grinstead RH19 ...... 9 C2
Meadowfield Dr PO19 ...... 173 B7
Meadowland PO20 ...... 206 D6
Meadowlands Crawley RH11 ... 18 C6
 Rowland's Castle PO9 ...... 128 E3
Meadows BN6 ...... 126 F5
Meadows Rd PO20 ...... 202 A7
Meadows The
 East Preston BN16 ...... 200 A5
 Hove BN3 ...... 166 C3
 Walberton BN18 ...... 176 E8
Meadowside Angmering BN16 .. 180 A6
 Horley RH6 ...... 2 B4
 Storrington RH20 ...... 119 D1
Meadowside Ct BN12 ...... 181 A2
Meadowview BN2 ...... 168 E1
Meadowview Rd BN15 ...... 183 D8
Meads Ave BN3 ...... 166 C3
Meads Cl BN3 ...... 166 C3

Meads Cty Prim Sch The
 RH19 ...... 22 E7
Meads The Brighton BN1 ...... 168 D5
 East Grinstead RH19 ...... 22 E7
 Fulking BN5 ...... 145 F4
 Haslemere GU27 ...... 26 F6
 South Harting GU31 ...... 89 D4
Meadvale RH12 ...... 35 F2
Meadway Haslemere GU27 ...... 26 F6
 Rustington BN16 ...... 199 D5
Meadway Cres BN3 ...... 166 F2
Meadway Ct
 Southwick BN42, BN43 ...... 185 D8
 Worthing BN13 ...... 181 E4
Meadway The Brighton BN2 ... 188 F5
 Horley RH6 ...... 2 C3
 Portslade-by-Sea BN41 ...... 186 B6
 Shoreham-by-Sea BN43 ...... 184 F7
Measham Cl RH11 ...... 200 F5
Meath Green Ave RH6 ...... 1 F5
Meath Green Cty Fst Sch RH6 .. 1 F5
Meath Green Cty Jun Sch RH6 .. 1 F5
Meath Green La RH1, RH6 ...... 1 E6
Medina Pl BN3 ...... 187 B6
Medina Terr BN3 ...... 187 B5
Medina Villas BN3 ...... 187 B6
Medlar Cl RH11 ...... 5 C1
Medmerry Cty Prim Sch The
 PO20 ...... 206 D7
Medmerry Hill BN2 ...... 168 E2
Medmerry RH10 ...... 21 A5
Medway Cl BN13 ...... 181 D7
Medway Cotts BN18 ...... 176 F2
Medway Ct RH12 ...... 37 B5
Medway Dr East Grinstead RH19 . 22 D6
 Forest Row RH18 ...... 23 F2
Medway Rd RH11 ...... 17 F5
Medwyn Wlk RH12 ...... 36 C2
Meeds Rd RH15 ...... 107 A2
Meeting House La BN1 ...... 207 A5
Melanie's Gdns 10 PO21 ...... 195 D4
Melbourne Ave BN11 ...... 181 C2
Melbourne Rd Chichester PO19 173 B7
 Worthing BN12 ...... 181 D2
Melbourne St BN2 ...... 188 C8
Melbourne Way Horsham RH12 . 36 F5
 Worthing BN12 ...... 181 C2
Melksham Cl RH13 ...... 36 E1
Melrose Ave
 Portslade-by-Sea BN41 ...... 166 A1
 Worthing BN13 ...... 181 E4
Melrose Cl Brighton BN1 ...... 168 C2
 Worthing BN13 ...... 181 E4
Melrose Pl RH20 ...... 120 C3
Melton Ave RH20 ...... 119 D3
Melton Cl RH20 ...... 119 E3
Melton Dr RH20 ...... 119 E3
Melville Rd BN3 ...... 187 E7
Melville Way RH10 ...... 181 C4
Mendip Cl BN16 ...... 200 A6
Mendip Cres BN13 ...... 181 E7
Mendip Cl 1 BN16 ...... 199 C6
Mendip Rd BN13 ...... 181 E7
Mendip Wlk RH11 ...... 18 B6
Mercer Cl RH10 ...... 19 C3
Mercer Rd RH12 ...... 36 C8
Mercers Mead RH13 ...... 81 E1
Merchant St PO21 ...... 195 C3
Mercury Cl RH11 ...... 17 E3
Meredith Rd BN14 ...... 182 F4
Mereworth Dr RH10 ...... 19 D8
Meridian Gr RH6 ...... 2 C4
Meridian Way RH19 ...... 9 F3
Merle Way GU27 ...... 49 A6
Merlin Cl Crawley RH11 ...... 17 E6
 Hove BN3 ...... 187 D8
Merlin Ct BN13 ...... 181 F6
Merlin Ctr RH11 ...... 5 D2
Merlin Way East Grinstead RH19 . 10 A3
 Middleton-on-Sea PO22 ...... 196 D6
Merrion Ave PO21, PO22 ...... 195 B5
Merrivale Ct PO10 ...... 149 F1
Merry End PO22 ...... 196 D5
Merryfield Cres BN16 ...... 180 A6
Merryfield Dr Horsham RH12 .... 36 A3
 Selsey PO20 ...... 206 F7
Merryfield Rd RH20 ...... 119 D2
Merryfield Way RH20 ...... 119 D2
Merryhills La RH14 ...... 32 A5
Merryweather Rd PO18 ...... 171 B5
Merrywood Ho RH20 ...... 120 B3
Merrywood La RH20 ...... 120 B4
Mersey Cl BN13 ...... 181 C7
Mersey Rd BN13 ...... 181 C7
Mersham Gdns BN12 ...... 181 C2
Merton Ave BN16 ...... 199 D4
Merton Cl PO21 ...... 194 E4
Merton Dr 1 BN17 ...... 198 D6
Metcalf Way RH11 ...... 5 D2
Meteor Rd PO19 ...... 169 C3
Metropole Ct 19 BN1 ...... 187 E5
Mews Ct RH19 ...... 22 F6
Mews The
 14 Bognor Regis PO21 ...... 195 C3
 Bognor Regis PO22 ...... 195 E4
 Brighton BN1 ...... 167 E2
 Broadridge Heath RH12 ...... 35 D4
 Pulborough RH20 ...... 98 D2
Meyers Wood RH13 ...... 103 A2
Meyners Cl BN3 ...... 166 C3
Michael Ayres
 Cty Jun Sch The PO22 ...... 195 A5
Michael Cres RH6 ...... 2 A1
Michael Fields RH18 ...... 24 B3
Michel Gr BN16 ...... 199 F5
Michelbourne Cl RH15 ...... 106 E1

Michelgrove Cotts BN13 ...... 160 C5
Michell Cl RH12 ...... 36 A2
Micklam Cl PO21 ...... 194 C2
Middle Mead
 Littlehampton BN17 ...... 199 A5
 Steyning BN44 ...... 143 D4
Middle Meadow GU33 ...... 45 C4
Middle Onslow Cl BN12 ...... 180 E3
Middle Rd Brighton BN1 ...... 167 E1
 Lancing BN15 ...... 183 D5
 Partridge Green RH13 ...... 103 A3
 Shoreham-by-Sea BN43 ...... 185 B7
Middle Row 1 RH19 ...... 22 F8
Middle St Brighton BN1 ...... 207 F5
 Horsham RH12 ...... 36 C2
 Petworth GU28 ...... 95 F8
 Portslade-by-Sea BN41 ...... 186 B6
 Shoreham-by-Sea BN43 ...... 184 F7
Middle Street Cty Prim Sch
 BN1 ...... 207 F5
Middle Tyne BN13 ...... 181 D5
Middle Way Burgess Hill RH15 .. 107 B3
 Kingston Gorse BN16 ...... 200 D4
Middlefield Horley RH6 ...... 2 C4
 West Wittering PO20 ...... 190 C1
Middlefield La PO18 ...... 153 C7
Middleton Ave BN3 ...... 186 D6
Middleton Bsns Pk PO22 ...... 196 E6
Middleton Cl PO20 ...... 202 B6
Middleton Gdns PO20 ...... 154 D2
Middleton Rd Horsham RH12 .... 36 A2
 Middleton-on-Sea PO22 ...... 196 D5
Middleton Rise BN1 ...... 168 E5
Middleton Way RH11 ...... 17 E5
Midfields RH15 ...... 107 B3
Midfields Dr RH15 ...... 107 B3
Midfields Wlk RH15 ...... 107 B4
Midgley Rd RH10 ...... 18 F8
Midholme BN16 ...... 199 F5
Midhurst CE (C) Prim Sch
 GU29 ...... 92 E7
Midhurst Cl Crawley RH11 ...... 18 A7
 Ferring BN12 ...... 200 C1
Midhurst Cottage Hospl GU29 . 70 F1
Midhurst Dr BN12 ...... 181 A2
Midhurst Gram Sch GU29 ...... 70 F1
Midhurst Gram Sch (C) GU29 .. 92 F8
Midhurst Rd Fernhurst GU27 .... 49 A4
 Haslemere GU27 ...... 27 B5
 Liphook GU30 ...... 25 C2
 Petworth GU28 ...... 95 E7
Midhurst Rise BN1 ...... 168 B6
Midhurst Wlk BN3 ...... 166 F3
Midway The PO22 ...... 196 A4
Mighell St BN2 ...... 207 B5
Milborne Rd RH10 ...... 19 C2
Milbury Cl PO21 ...... 200 F4
Milcote Ave BN3 ...... 186 F8
Mile End Cotts BN1 ...... 167 E6
Mile End La PO20 ...... 172 C2
Mile Oak Cres BN42 ...... 165 F1
Mile Oak Cty Prim Sch BN41 . 165 F3
Mile Oak Gdns BN41 ...... 166 A1
Mile Oak Rd
 Portslade-by-Sea BN41, BN42 ... 165 F3
 Southwick BN41, BN42 ...... 165 F1
Miles Cl BN18 ...... 177 B2
Miles Cotts PO18 ...... 171 A5
Milford Ct BN15 ...... 183 D3
Mill Ave BN43 ...... 164 F1
Mill Bay La RH12 ...... 36 B1
Mill Cl Crabtree RH13 ...... 82 A7
 East Grinstead RH19 ...... 22 E7
 Fishbourne PO19, PO20 ...... 172 B6
 Haslemere GU27 ...... 26 E6
 Horley RH6 ...... 1 E4
 Portslade-by-Sea BN41 ...... 166 C1
 Poynings BN45 ...... 146 C5
 Rustington BN16 ...... 199 D6
Mill Copse Rd GU27 ...... 27 B4
Mill Cotts East Grinstead RH19 .... 22 E7
 Rudgwick RH12 ...... 33 D5
Mill Ct BN45 ...... 146 C5
Mill Dr Henfield BN5 ...... 123 F4
 Hove BN3 ...... 167 A3
Mill End Hermitage PO10 ...... 169 B8
 West Chiltington Common RH20 119 C8
Mill Farm Rd RH13 ...... 37 A4
Mill Gdns PO20 ...... 201 F7
Mill Green Rd RH16 ...... 85 E6
Mill Hill BN43 ...... 164 E3
Mill Hill Cl Haywards Heath RH16 85 E7
 Shoreham-by-Sea BN43 ...... 164 E1
Mill Hill Dr BN43 ...... 164 E1
Mill Hill Gdns BN43 ...... 164 E1
Mill Ho 4 BN11 ...... 183 B3
Mill House Gdns BN11 ...... 182 A2
Mill La Amberley BN18 ...... 138 E6
 Arundel BN18 ...... 158 B3
 Ashington RH20 ...... 120 F4
 Balcombe RH17 ...... 41 C1
 Clayton BN45, BN6 ...... 147 E7
 Cocking GU29 ...... 112 C8
 Coolham RH13 ...... 78 D3
 Copthorne RH10 ...... 7 E3
 Crabtree RH13 ...... 82 B7
 Crawley RH11 ...... 18 A8
 Dumpford GU31 ...... 69 A1
 Dumpford GU33 ...... 90 F8
 Felbridge RH19 ...... 8 E5
 Felcourt RH7 ...... 9 E8
 Fernhurst GU27 ...... 27 C3
 Fishbourne PO19 ...... 172 B6
 Goddards' Green BN6 ...... 106 A3
 Heyshott Green GU29 ...... 93 A2
 Hookwood RH6 ...... 1 C3
 Littlehampton BN17 ...... 178 D5
 Littleworth RH13 ...... 102 F5

Mill La Portslade-by-Sea BN41 .. 166 B6
 Poynings BN45 ...... 146 C5
 Runcton PO20 ...... 173 E1
 Rustington BN16 ...... 179 D3
 Sayers Common BN6, RH17 ...... 105 C2
 Selsey PO20 ...... 206 C7
 Shoreham-by-Sea BN43 ...... 184 F8
 Sidlesham PO20 ...... 203 F7
 Slindon BN18 ...... 156 C6
 South Harting GU31 ...... 89 D4
 Stedham GU29 ...... 70 A2
 Storrington RH20 ...... 119 D2
 Walberton BN18 ...... 156 D1
 West Chiltington Common RH20 119 C8
 Westbourne PO10 ...... 149 D3
 Worthing BN13 ...... 161 F1
Mill Lodge PO21 ...... 194 A2
Mill Mead RH20 ...... 121 A4
Mill Park Rd PO21 ...... 194 B2
Mill Pk RH15 ...... 107 B3
Mill Quay PO21 ...... 169 C7
Mill Race BN6 ...... 126 E8
Mill Rd Angmering BN16 ...... 179 F5
 Arundel BN18 ...... 158 C3
 Brighton BN1 ...... 167 C6
 Burgess Hill RH15 ...... 107 B3
 Crawley RH10 ...... 19 B3
 Lancing BN15 ...... 183 E8
 Liss GU33 ...... 45 C4
 Southwick BN41 ...... 186 B7
 Steyning BN44 ...... 143 C3
 Walberton BN18 ...... 156 D3
 West Ashling PO18 ...... 151 A3
 West Chiltington Common RH20 119 C8
 Westbourne PO10 ...... 149 D4
 Worthing BN11 ...... 182 A2
Mill Rd Ind Est BN41 ...... 186 B7
Mill Rise BN1 ...... 167 C5
Mill Road Ave BN16 ...... 179 F5
Mill Straight BN5 ...... 79 F8
Mill Stream Meadow RH16 ...... 85 D7
Mill Vale Meadows GU30 ...... 47 B3
Mill View Rd BN18 ...... 176 F2
Mill Way Billingshurst RH14 ...... 55 C1
 Billingshurst RH14 ...... 55 D1
 East Grinstead RH19 ...... 22 E7
Mill Wood RH15 ...... 107 B3
Millais RH13 ...... 37 A3
Millais Cl RH11 ...... 17 F2
Millais Ct RH13 ...... 37 A4
Millais Sch RH28 ...... 36 F2
Millais Sch Lower Sch RH13 ... 36 F2
Milland Cl GU30 ...... 47 A5
Milland Rd GU30, GU29 ...... 47 C2
Millars Ct PO21 ...... 194 B1
Millbank RH15 ...... 107 B4
Millbank The RH11 ...... 17 F6
Millbrook Cl GU33 ...... 45 C4
Millcroft BN1 ...... 167 C5
Millcroft Ave BN42 ...... 165 E1
Millcroft Gdns BN42 ...... 165 E1
Millcross Rd BN41 ...... 166 B1
Miller's Rd BN1 ...... 167 E1
Millers Cl BN16 ...... 199 D6
Millers Gate RH12 ...... 36 D6
Millers The BN18 ...... 176 F2
Millers Way RH15 ...... 107 B4
Millfield Lancing BN15 ...... 183 C4
 Southwater RH13 ...... 80 A7
Millfield Cl Chichester PO19 .... 173 C8
 Littlehampton BN16 ...... 199 B5
Millfield Cotts 8 BN2 ...... 188 D4
Millpond La RH12 ...... 151 B3
Millstream The GU27 ...... 26 E5
Millthorpe Rd RH12 ...... 36 F4
Millwood RH19 ...... 21 E5
Milne Cl RH11 ...... 17 E3
Milner Flats BN2 ...... 207 B5
Milner Rd BN2 ...... 168 D1
Milnthorpe Rd BN3 ...... 186 F6
Milnwood Rd RH12 ...... 36 C3
Milton Ave BN16 ...... 199 B5
Milton Cl Lancing BN15 ...... 183 F5
 Rustington BN16 ...... 199 B5
Milton Cres RH19 ...... 22 C3
Milton Ct
 6 Haywards Heath RH16 ...... 85 D5
 2 Worthing BN11 ...... 182 C1
Milton Dr BN42 ...... 185 E8
Milton Mount Ave RH10 ...... 6 D1
Milton Mount Ave RH10 ...... 19 D8
Milton Mount Fst & Mid Sch
 RH10 ...... 19 C8
Milton Rd Brighton BN2 ...... 207 B4
 Crawley RH10 ...... 19 C7
 Haywards Heath RH16 ...... 85 D5
 Horsham RH12 ...... 36 C3
 Worthing BN11 ...... 182 C1
Milton St BN11 ...... 182 C1
Milward Ct 3 BN43 ...... 185 C8
Milwood Cl PO20 ...... 172 F7
Mimmack Cl BN44 ...... 143 D4
Mimosa Cl BN1 ...... 168 B3
Mindleheim Ave RH19 ...... 10 B2
Minnels The BN6 ...... 127 A3
Minsted Rd GU29 ...... 91 F7
Minster Cl BN17 ...... 178 C4
Mint Rd GU33 ...... 45 D6
Minton Rd PO20 ...... 196 B4
Miranda Wlk RH11 ...... 17 E4
Mitchamer Cotts PO18 ...... 130 F2
Mitchell Gdns RH13 ...... 34 E3
Mitchells Rd RH10 ...... 18 F6
Mitford Wlk 10 BN1 ...... 18 A3
Mitre Ho 15 BN1 ...... 187 E5
Moat La RH20 ...... 98 B2
Moat Rd RH19 ...... 9 E2
Moat The RH20 ...... 98 C2

Moat Way BN12 ... 181 E1
Moat Wlk RH10 ... 19 C7
Moatfield La RH13 ... 104 A8
Mocatta Way RH15 ... 106 D5
Model Buildings Cotts RH13 ... 80 B2
Modena Rd BN3 ... 186 F7
Mole Cl RH11 ... 18 B8
Mole The BN17 ... 199 A5
Molecomb Broadwalk PO18 ... 134 A2
Molesworth St BN3 ... 186 F8
Molins Ct 4 RH11 ... 18 A3
Monarch Cl RH11 ... 18 A3
Monastery La RH20 ... 119 C1
Monk Cl BN1 ... 168 E6
Monk's Hill PO10 ... 149 C5
Monkmead Copse RH20 ... 119 C6
Monkmead La RH20 ... 119 B6
Monks Ave BN15 ... 183 F6
Monks Cl BN15 ... 183 F6
Monks Ct BN15 ... 183 E6
Monks La RH5 ... 13 F5
Monks Wlk BN44 ... 144 B2
Monksfield RH10 ... 18 F7
Monmouth St 13 BN3 ... 187 B7
Mons Ave PO21 ... 195 B5
Montagu Rd PO19 ... 172 E8
Montague Cl BN43 ... 185 D7
Montague Ct 6 Brighton BN2 ... 188 C4
Lancing BN15 ... 183 B7
2 Shoreham-by-Sea BN43 ... 185 D7
Montague Ctr 8 BN11 ... 182 D2
Montague Pl Brighton BN2 ... 188 C4
Worthing BN11 ... 182 D1
Montague Rd GU29 ... 71 A2
Montague St 4 Brighton BN2 ... 188 C4
Worthing BN11 ... 182 C1
Montalan Cres PO20 ... 206 B8
Montefiore Rd BN3 ... 187 E7
Monterey Ct BN1 ... 167 E3
Montes Hill RH16 ... 86 F8
Monteswood La RH16, RH17 ... 87 B8
Montford Cl BN43 ... 185 D8
Montfort Rise RH6 ... 1 F8
Montgomery Dr PO22 ... 196 D6
Montgomery St BN3 ... 187 A7
Montpelier Cotts RH20 ... 141 E8
Montpelier Cres BN1 ... 187 E6
Montpelier Gdns RH20 ... 141 E8
Montpelier Lodge 8 BN1 ... 187 E6
Montpelier Pl 7 BN1 ... 187 E6
Montpelier Rd Brighton BN1 ... 187 E5
East Preston BN16 ... 200 A5
Montpelier St BN1 ... 187 E6
Montpelier Terr 10 BN1 ... 187 E6
Montpelier Villas BN1 ... 187 E6
Montreal Rd BN2 ... 207 B6
Montreal Way BN13 ... 181 C6
Montreux Ct RH11 ... 18 B6
Montrose Cl BN12 ... 181 C2
Monument La PO18 ... 150 B7
Monument View BN2 ... 188 D6
Moon's La RH19, RH7, TN8 ... 10 E8
Moons La RH13 ... 36 E1
Moor Park Cres RH11 ... 17 D5
Moor Pl RH19 ... 9 D2
Moor Rd GU27 ... 26 C5
Moorcroft Cl RH11 ... 18 B7
Moore Ct RH12 ... 36 A1
Moorfield GU27 ... 26 F5
Moorfoot Rd BN13 ... 181 F7
Moorhead Rd RH12 ... 37 B5
Moorhen Way PO22 ... 195 B6
Moorhouse La GU29 ... 69 D6
Moorings The
East Grinstead RH19 ... 9 A3
Lancing BN15 ... 183 F8
5 Littlehampton BN16 ... 199 A6
Shoreham-by-Sea BN43 ... 185 C6
Moorland Cl RH10 ... 19 C3
Moraunt Dr PO22 ... 196 E6
Morecambe Cl RH11 ... 17 F4
Morecambe Rd BN1 ... 168 A6
Moreton Rd PO18 ... 171 B5
Morland Ave BN14 ... 182 E7
Morley St BN2 ... 207 B6
Morleys RH20 ... 121 A4
Mornington Cres
Bognor Regis PO22 ... 196 A5
Hove BN3 ... 186 D7
Mornington Mansions BN3 ... 186 D7
Morrell Ave RH12 ... 36 F6
Morris Way RH20 ... 119 C7
Morrison Ct 5 RH11 ... 18 B1
Mortimer Rd BN3 ... 187 A8
Morton Cl RH11 ... 39 B8
Morton Rd RH19 ... 22 E7
Mosdell Rd PO10 ... 170 A8
Mosford Cl RH6 ... 1 F5
Moss Cl GU33 ... 45 C4
Mosse Gdns PO19 ... 172 B7
Moulsecoomb Cty Inf Sch BN2 ... 168 E3
Moulsecoomb Cty Jun Sch BN2 ... 168 E3
Moulsecoomb Sta BN2 ... 168 D2
Moulsecoomb Way BN2 ... 168 F4
Mount Cl RH10 ... 19 D7
Mount Ct PO20 ... 206 E7
Mount La Chichester PO19 ... 172 F6
Turners Hill RH10 ... 21 A4
Mount Noddy RH17 ... 84 C3
Mount Pk BN44 ... 143 D1
Mount Pleasant Arundel BN18 ... 158 A3
Brighton BN2 ... 207 B5
Mount The Lambs Green RH12 ... 17 B8
Rusper RH11, RH12 ... 4 B1
Mount Way BN15 ... 163 E1
Mount Zion Pl BN1 ... 207 F6
Mountbatten Cl RH11 ... 18 C2
Mountbatten Ct
Bognor Regis PO21 ... 195 D2
Hove BN3 ... 186 E8
7 Littlehampton BN16 ... 199 A6
Mountfields BN1 ... 168 C2
Mountview Rd BN15 ... 163 C1
Mountwood Rd Breach PO10 ... 149 F1
Selsey PO20 ... 206 F8
Mouse La BN44 ... 142 E6
Mouthey's La PO18 ... 151 E2
Mowbray Dr RH11 ... 17 F4
Mowden Sch BN1 ... 167 D1
Moyne Cl BN3 ... 166 E1
Moyne Rd RH11 ... 18 C2
Mudberry La PO18 ... 171 A8
Muggeridge's Hill RH5, RH12 ... 15 E8
Muirfield Cl Crawley RH11 ... 17 D5
Worthing BN13 ... 181 E6
Muirfield Ct 16 RH16 ... 85 E4
Muirfield Rd BN13 ... 181 E6
Mulberry Cl Brighton BN1 ... 167 F3
Ferring BN12 ... 200 E6
Horsham RH12 ... 36 C5
Lancing BN15 ... 183 E6
Shoreham-by-Sea BN43 ... 165 D1
Worthing BN12 ... 181 C3
Mulberry Ct Bognor Regis PO21 ... 205 A7
Petworth GU28 ... 95 E7
Worthing BN12 ... 181 C2
Mulberry Gdns BN12 ... 181 C2
Mulberry La Ditchling BN6 ... 127 D3
Worthing BN12 ... 181 C2
Mulberry Rd RH11 ... 5 B1
Mullein Wlk RH11 ... 18 A2
Mumford Pl PO19 ... 173 B4
Munmere Way 3 BN16 ... 199 E6
Munnion Rd RH17 ... 64 B7
Munns Dr RH15 ... 107 B4
Muntham Dr RH13 ... 56 F3
Muntham House Sch RH13 ... 56 E4
Murina Ave PO21 ... 195 C5
Murray Ct Crawley RH11 ... 18 A1
Horsham RH13 ... 37 B4
Murray Rd PO20 ... 206 D6
Museum Hill GU27 ... 27 D6
Musgrave Ave RH19 ... 22 E8
Mustang Cl BN18 ... 177 B2
Muster Ct RH16 ... 85 D4
Muster Gn N RH16 ... 85 D4
Muster Gn S RH16 ... 85 D4
Mutton Hill RH7 ... 10 B7
Mutton's La RH20 ... 120 D3
Myrtle Cres BN15 ... 183 D5
Myrtle Gr BN16 ... 199 F5
Myrtle La RH14 ... 77 D7
Myrtle Rd BN15 ... 183 D5
Mytchett Ho 1 PO19 ... 153 A2
Mytten Bank RH17 ... 84 F6
Mytten Cl RH17 ... 84 F6
Nab Tower La PO20 ... 206 B8
Nab Wlk PO20 ... 201 F6
Nagels Cl PO20 ... 202 A6
Naiad Gdns PO22 ... 196 D5
Naldrett Cl RH12 ... 36 F4
Naldretts La RH12 ... 33 D5
Namrik Mews BN3 ... 187 A6
Nanson Rd BN1 ... 168 D6
Napier Ho 3 BN2 ... 188 C7
Napier Way RH10 ... 6 A1
Nappers Wood GU27 ... 49 A6
Nash La RH17 ... 87 B4
Nash Rd RH10 ... 18 E3
Nash Way BN18 ... 156 D1
Natal Rd BN2 ... 168 D1
Natts La RH14 ... 77 D6
Naunton Rd PO19 ... 153 B1
Navarino Rd BN11 ... 183 A2
Neale Cl RH19 ... 9 B3
Need's Hill RH13 ... 102 F6
Needlemakers PO19 ... 173 B6
Needles Cl RH12 ... 36 B1
Nell Ball RH14 ... 30 E2
Nelson Cl Crawley RH10 ... 19 C5
Lancing BN15 ... 183 D8
Tangmere PO20 ... 154 D2
Nelson Ct BN43 ... 184 D5
Nelson Pl 16 BN2 ... 207 B6
Nelson Rd Bognor Regis PO21 ... 195 A3
Horsham RH12 ... 36 C3
Worthing BN12 ... 181 D4
Nelson Row Brighton BN2 ... 207 B5
Ford BN18 ... 177 E3
Nep Cl BN5 ... 123 E4
Nep Town Rd BN5 ... 123 E4
Nepcote La BN14 ... 161 F5
Nepcote Par BN14 ... 161 E6
Nepfield Cl BN14 ... 161 F5
Neptune Cl RH11 ... 17 E4
Neptune Ct PO22 ... 196 D4
Neptune Way BN16 ... 199 A4
Nesbit Ct RH11 ... 17 E3
Nesbitt Rd BN2 ... 168 D1
Nestor Ct BN1 ... 167 E1
Netherton Cl Selsey PO20 ... 206 E7
Southwater RH13 ... 57 F4
Netherwood RH11 ... 18 B4
Netherwoods Rd RH13 ... 79 B6
Netley Cl RH11 ... 39 C8
Nettleton Ave PO20 ... 154 C2
Nettleton Ct BN1 ... 168 B1
Nevile Cl RH11 ... 18 A3
Nevill Ave BN3 ... 166 F1
Nevill Cl BN3 ... 167 A2
Nevill Cotts BN6 ... 127 D2
Nevill Ct BN3 ... 167 A1
Nevill Gdns BN3 ... 167 A2
Nevill Pl BN3 ... 167 A2
Nevill Rd BN3 ... 167 A2
Nevill Way BN3 ... 167 A2
Neville Gdns PO10 ... 149 A3
Neville Rd Bognor Regis PO22 ... 195 D4
Chichester PO19 ... 172 D7
New Barn Cl
Portslade-by-Sea BN41 ... 166 B2
Shoreham-by-Sea BN43 ... 165 B1
New Barn Hill PO18 ... 154 B7
New Barn La RH20 ... 119 B8
New Barn Rd Amberley BN18 ... 138 D5
Shoreham-by-Sea BN43 ... 165 B1
New Brighton Rd PO10 ... 149 B2
New Broadway BN14 ... 182 A3
New Church Rd BN3, BN41 ... 186 E7
New Cotts Scaynes Hill RH17 ... 86 F1
Turners Hill RH10 ... 21 A4
Washington RH20 ... 141 E6
New Courtwick La BN17 ... 178 C4
New Cut BN18 ... 158 B3
New Dorset St BN1 ... 207 F6
New England Coll BN18 ... 177 E7
New England Ho BN1 ... 207 A7
New England Rd Brighton BN1 ... 207 F7
Haywards Heath RH16 ... 85 F4
New England Rise BN41 ... 166 A4
New England St BN1 ... 207 A7
New Farthingdale RH7 ... 10 B8
New Hall La BN5 ... 144 E7
New House La RH1 ... 2 E8
New La GU31 ... 89 D2
New Life Sch RH19 ... 9 D2
New Moorhead Dr RH12 ... 37 C6
New Par East Wittering PO20 ... 201 E7
Worthing BN11 ... 182 F2
New Park Rd PO19 ... 173 A7
New Place Rd RH20 ... 98 C3
New Rd Billingshurst RH14 ... 56 B2
Brighton BN1 ... 207 A5
Camelsdale GU27 ... 26 F5
East Dean PO18 ... 134 D8
Keymer BN6 ... 127 B2
Littlehampton BN17 ... 198 D4
Midhurst GU29 ... 92 E6
Rustington BN16 ... 179 E3
Shoreham-by-Sea BN43 ... 184 F7
South Ambersham GU29 ... 93 E4
Southbourne PO10 ... 170 A8
Southwater RH13 ... 57 F4
Upper Beeding BN44 ... 144 B1
Upperton GU28 ... 73 A2
Westbourne PO10 ... 149 D3
Westerton PO18 ... 153 D4
Worthing BN13 ... 181 C7
New Row BN44 ... 143 C3
New Salts Farm Rd BN43 ... 184 C6
New St Crawley RH10 ... 19 A7
Horsham RH13 ... 36 D2
Petworth GU28 ... 95 F8
2 Worthing BN11 ... 182 D1
New Steine BN2 ... 207 B4
New Steine Mews BN2 ... 207 B5
New Sussex Hospl BN3 ... 187 E6
New Town 10 Chichester PO19 ... 173 A6
Copthorne RH10 ... 7 B3
New Town Rd RH20 ... 119 B1
New Way La BN6 ... 126 B2
Newark Pl BN2 ... 207 B6
Newark Rd RH10 ... 18 F8
Newbarn La
Bognor Regis, Felpham PO22 ... 196 B6
Bognor Regis, N Bersted PO21 ... 194 F6
Henfield BN5 ... 123 F2
Walderton PO18 ... 150 B8
Newbridge Cl RH12 ... 35 C3
Newbridge Rd RH14 ... 77 B8
Newbury La RH17 ... 84 E5
Newdigate Rd RH12 ... 16 C8
Newells La Broadbridge PO18 ... 171 A7
Monk's Gate RH13 ... 59 D2
West Ashling PO18 ... 150 F1
Newfield Rd Liss Forest GU33 ... 45 C6
Selsey PO20 ... 206 G8
Newhall Cl PO21 ... 194 F3
Newham Cl BN44 ... 143 C3
Newham La BN44 ... 143 C2
Newhaven St BN2 ... 207 B6
Newhouse La East Dean PO18 ... 134 D8
Heath Common RH20 ... 120 C3
Newick House Sch RH15 ... 107 C1
Newick Rd BN1 ... 168 E4
Newland Rd
Upper Beeding BN44 ... 144 B2
Worthing BN11 ... 182 D3
Newland St BN11 ... 182 D3
Newlands RH17 ... 40 F1
Newlands Cl Horley RH6 ... 1 F5
Keymer BN6 ... 127 B3
Newlands Cres RH19 ... 9 D2
Newlands La PO19 ... 172 D8
Newlands Pk RH10 ... 7 E3
Newlands Pl RH18 ... 23 F3
Newlands Rd Crawley RH11 ... 18 C5
Horsham RH12 ... 36 C4
Newling Way BN13 ... 161 E1
Newman Cl RH10 ... 19 C4
Newman's Gdns BN15 ... 183 B7
Newmarket Rd Brighton BN2 ... 188 C8
Crawley RH10 ... 19 A4
Newmarket Terr 8 BN2 ... 188 C8
Newport Dr PO18, PO19 ... 172 B7
Newport Mews BN11 ... 183 B3
Newport Rd RH15 ... 106 F3
Newport St BN2 ... 207 B7
Newpound RH14 ... 54 E3
Newpound La RH14 ... 54 D1
Newstead 5 BN1 ... 207 F7
Newtimber Ave BN12 ... 181 B3
Newtimber Dr BN41 ... 166 A1
Newtimber Gdns BN43 ... 164 F1
Newton Ave RH19 ... 22 F6
Newton Cl RH16 ... 86 B7
Newton Ct 3 RH16 ... 85 E5
Newton Rd Crawley RH10 ... 5 F2
Haywards Heath RH16 ... 86 C7
Newtown Ave PO21, PO22 ... 195 A6
Newtown Ct RH13 ... 36 E1
Newtown Rd Hove BN3 ... 187 B8
Liphook GU30 ... 25 C3
Nicholsfield RH14 ... 31 F4
Nicolson Dr BN43 ... 184 F8
Nightingale Cl Crawley RH11 ... 18 C8
East Grinstead RH19 ... 22 D7
Red Hill PO9 ... 128 C1
Storrington RH20 ... 119 E1
Nightingale Ct PO22 ... 196 F5
Nightingale La
Burgess Hill RH15 ... 126 F8
Hambrook PO18 ... 150 D3
Storrington RH20 ... 119 E1
Nightingale Pk RH20 ... 119 E1
Nightingale Rd RH12 ... 36 D3
Nightingale Wlk RH14 ... 77 E8
Nightingales Findon BN14 ... 161 E7
West Chiltington Common RH20 ... 119 D7
Nightingales Bsns Pk RH20 ... 98 C5
Nile St Brighton BN1 ... 207 A5
Emsworth PO10 ... 169 B8
Nimbus Cl BN17 ... 199 A6
Nimrod Ct RH10 ... 6 D1
Nine Acres GU29 ... 92 D8
Ninfield Ct RH11 ... 17 F2
Ninfield Pl BN2 ... 188 E7
Niven Cl RH10 ... 19 D5
Nizells Ave BN3 ... 187 E7
Noah's Ct RH10 ... 21 A4
Noah's Farm Yard Nature Trail GU28 ... 94 E8
Noahs Ark La RH16 ... 86 C7
Noel Gn RH15 ... 107 B4
Noel Rise RH15 ... 107 B4
Nonnington La GU28 ... 94 B1
Nookery The BN16 ... 200 A5
Nor'bren Ave PO21 ... 195 A5
Norbury Cl BN15 ... 183 F8
Norbury Dr BN15 ... 183 F8
Nordseter Lodge 1 BN16 ... 199 B4
Nore Down Way PO18 ... 130 A8
Norfolk Bldgs 2 BN1 ... 187 E5
Norfolk Cl
5 Bognor Regis PO21 ... 195 C2
Crawley RH11 ... 17 E2
Horley RH6 ... 2 A2
Norfolk Cotts Bury RH20 ... 138 A7
Steyning BN44 ... 143 D3
Norfolk Ct Horsham RH12 ... 37 B5
8 Rustington BN16 ... 199 B4
1 Worthing BN11 ... 182 C3
Norfolk Gdns BN17 ... 198 F4
Norfolk Ho PO22 ... 195 F4
Norfolk Mews 3 Hove BN1 ... 187 E5
Littlehampton BN17 ... 198 F4
Norfolk Pl BN17 ... 198 F4
Norfolk Rd Horsham RH12, RH13 ... 36 D2
Hove BN1 ... 187 E6
4 Littlehampton BN17 ... 198 F4
Norfolk Sq Bognor Regis PO21 ... 195 C2
Hove BN1 ... 187 E5
Norfolk St Bognor Regis PO21 ... 195 C2
4 Hove BN1 ... 187 E5
Worthing BN11 ... 182 C3
Norfolk Terr
Horsham RH12, RH13 ... 36 D2
Hove BN1 ... 187 E6
Norfolk Way PO22 ... 197 B5
Norman Cl BN17 ... 198 F5
Norman Cres 9 BN43 ... 164 F1
Norman Rd Burgess Hill RH15 ... 107 A3
Hove BN3 ... 186 E6
Norman Way BN44 ... 143 D4
Norman's Dr PO22 ... 196 B6
Normandy RH12 ... 36 C1
Normandy Cl Crawley RH10 ... 19 C4
7 East Grinstead RH19 ... 22 F8
Normandy Ct 5 BN11 ... 182 B1
Normandy Dr BN16 ... 200 A4
Normandy Gdns RH12 ... 36 C1
Normandy Ho 3 BN3 ... 187 C6
Normandy La BN16 ... 200 A4
Normandy Rd BN14 ... 182 C4
Normanhurst 9 Brighton BN2 ... 207 B6
4 Shoreham-by-Sea BN43 ... 184 F7
Normanhurst Cl Crawley RH10 ... 18 F6
Rustington BN16 ... 199 C4
Normanscourt 8 BN43 ... 164 F1
Normanton Ave PO21 ... 195 B3
Normanton St 8 BN2 ... 188 C7
Norris The BN16 ... 200 B5
North Ash RH12 ... 36 C4
North Ave
Middleton-on-Sea PO22 ... 196 F5
Worthing BN12 ... 181 E1
North Ave E PO22 ... 197 A5
North Ave S PO22 ... 197 A5
North Bank BN6 ... 126 E4
North Bay PO10 ... 169 C3
North Bersted St PO22 ... 195 A7
North Cl Chichester PO19 ... 173 A7
Crawley RH10 ... 18 F7
Portslade-by-Sea BN41 ... 166 A2
North Ct BN6 ... 126 E4
North Dr Angmering BN16 ... 179 F4
Brighton BN2 ... 188 C6
North End BN6 ... 127 D4
North End Cl GU28 ... 73 F1
North End Cotts BN14 ... 161 E8
North End Rd BN18 ... 176 F4
North Farm Cotts BN14 ... 141 D2
North Farm Ct BN15 ... 183 E6
North Farm Rd BN15 ... 183 F6
North Gdns BN1 ... 207 F6
North Ham Rd BN17 ... 198 D6
North Heath Cl RH12 ... 36 D5
North Heath Cty Prim Sch RH12 ... 36 D5
North Heath Est RH12 ... 36 D6
North Heath La RH12 ... 36 E6
North Holmes Cl RH12 ... 37 B5
North La Buriton GU31 ... 88 A5
Charlton PO18 ... 134 A7
East Preston BN16 ... 200 B6
Littlehampton BN16 ... 199 B6
Portslade-by-Sea BN41 ... 166 A3
South Harting GU31 ... 89 D4
West Hoathly RH19 ... 42 E6
Wiston BN44 ... 121 C2
North Lancing Cty Fst & Mid Sch BN15 ... 183 E8
North Lodge PO21 ... 194 A2
North Mead RH10 ... 18 E8
North Mundham Cty Prim Sch PO20 ... 173 D1
North Pallant PO19 ... 173 A6
North Par RH12 ... 36 C3
North Pl Brighton BN1 ... 207 A5
14 Littlehampton BN17 ... 198 E4
North Point 1 BN43 ... 185 A6
North Pound BN18 ... 156 D1
North Rd Brighton BN1 ... 207 A6
Brighton, Preston BN1 ... 167 E1
Broadbridge PO18 ... 171 C7
Crawley RH10 ... 19 A7
Haywards Heath RH16 ... 86 A4
Lancing BN15 ... 183 E6
Portslade-by-Sea BN41 ... 166 A2
Selsey PO20 ... 206 E7
North St Brighton BN1 ... 207 A5
Chichester PO19 ... 173 A7
Emsworth PO10 ... 149 B1
Horsham RH12, RH13 ... 36 D3
Littlehampton BN17 ... 178 D3
Midhurst GU29 ... 92 F8
Petworth GU28 ... 73 F1
Portslade-by-Sea BN41 ... 186 C7
Shoreham-by-Sea BN43 ... 184 E7
Storrington RH20 ... 119 D1
Turners Hill RH10 ... 21 A4
Westbourne PO10 ... 149 D4
Worthing BN11 ... 182 D3
North Terminal App RH6 ... 5 F8
North View BN5 ... 124 E5
North Walls Chichester PO19 ... 172 F6
Chichester PO19 ... 172 F7
North Way Bognor Regis PO22 ... 195 F4
Petworth GU28 ... 95 E7
Northbourne Cl BN43 ... 184 F8
Northbrook Cl BN14 ... 182 E6
Northbrook Coll
Worthing, Goring-by-Sea BN13 ... 181 B4
Worthing,West Worthing BN11 ... 182 D2
Northbrook Coll Design & Tech BN14 ... 182 D5
Northbrook Coll of Design & Tech RH12 ... 36 C4
Northbrook Rd BN14 ... 182 E6
Northbrook Trad Est BN14 ... 182 E6
Northchapel Cty Prim Sch GU28 ... 51 A7
Northcliffe Rd PO22 ... 195 E4
Northcote Rd PO21 ... 195 A4
Northcourt Cl BN16 ... 199 E6
Northcourt Rd BN14 ... 182 C4
Northcroft BN5 ... 123 E5
Northdown Cl RH12 ... 36 F4
Northdown Terr RH19 ... 9 D3
Northease Cl BN3 ... 166 D2
Northease Dr BN3 ... 166 E3
Northease Gdns BN3 ... 166 E3
Northend La BN6 ... 105 F3
Northerlea BN41 ... 166 A1
Northern Breach RH17 ... 84 E6
Northern Cres PO20 ... 201 F7
Northfield PO20 ... 206 F7
Northfield Rd BN13 ... 182 A6
Northfield Rise BN3 ... 166 D4
Northfield Way BN1 ... 168 A4
Northfields La PO20 ... 155 D1
Northgate PO19 ... 173 A7
Northgate Ave RH10 ... 18 F7
Northgate Cl BN15 ... 183 C6
Northgate Cty Fst Sch RH10 ... 18 E7
Northgate Cty Mid Sch RH10 ... 18 E7
Northgate Pl RH10 ... 18 E7
Northgate Rd
Crawley RH10, RH11 ... 18 D6
Gatwick Airport RH6 ... 5 F8
Northlands PO19 ... 152 B1
Northlands Ave RH16 ... 86 B4
Northlands La RH20 ... 119 E4
Northlands Rd RH12 ... 14 D2
Northlands Wood Cty Prim Sch RH16 ... 86 B4
Northmead GU28 ... 73 F1
Northside PO18 ... 152 E7
Northview Terr BN14 ... 161 E6
Northway Burgess Hill RH15 ... 107 C4
Gatwick Airport RH6 ... 5 F8
Northway Rd BN17 ... 178 D4
Northwood Pk RH10 ... 6 A2
Northwyke Cl PO22 ... 196 C5

Northwyke Rd PO22 .... 196 C5
Norton Cl BN3 .... 187 B6
Norton La PO20 .... 155 B1
Norton Rd Hove BN3 .... 187 B6
Lancing BN15 .... 183 D5
Norway La BN17 .... 178 F3
Norway St BN41 .... 186 C7
Norwich Cres BN2 .... 168 F2
Norwich Dr BN2 .... 168 F2
Norwich Rd Chichester PO19 ... 152 F1
Crawley RH10 .... 19 B5
Norwood BN1 .... 168 A4
Norwood La N GU28 .... 114 E6
Norwood La S GU28 .... 114 E5
Norwoodhill Rd RH6 .... 4 E8
Notre Dame Int Sch RH10 .... 19 D6
Nowhurst La RH12 .... 35 A5
Nuffield Cl PO21 .... 194 E3
Nursery Cl
Haywards Heath RH16 .... 85 D5
Hurstpierpoint BN6 .... 125 F7
Lancing BN15 .... 183 D7
New Brighton PO10 .... 149 B3
Portslade-by-Sea BN41 .... 165 E4
Shoreham-by-Sea BN43 .... 185 B8
West Barnham PO22 .... 176 B6
West Kingston BN16 .... 200 A4
Nursery Field GU33 .... 45 A3
Nursery Gdns BN17 .... 178 D3
Nursery La
Fishbourne PO18, PO19 .... 172 B7
Hookwood RH6 .... 1 D2
Worthing BN11 .... 182 C1
Nursery The RH15 .... 107 C4
Nurserylands RH11 .... 18 A6
Nutbourne Halt PO18 .... 170 D8
Nutbourne La PO20 .... 99 A4
Nutbourne Manor Vineyard
RH20 .... 99 B2
Nutbourne Rd
Nutbourne Common RH20 .... 99 A1
South Hayling PO11 .... 189 A1
Worthing BN14 .... 182 B4
Nutcombe La GU26, GU27 .... 26 E8
Nutcroft PO20 .... 98 C3
Nutham La RH13 .... 58 A1
Nuthatch Cl PO9 .... 128 D1
Nuthatch Way RH12 .... 36 D7
Nuthurst Cl Brighton BN2 .... 188 F6
Crawley RH11 .... 18 A7
Nuthurst Pl BN2 .... 188 F5
Nuthurst Rd Maplehurst RH13 .. 80 F6
Monk's Gate RH13 .... 59 B3
Nuthurst St RH13 .... 59 A2
Nutley Ave BN12 .... 181 C1
Nutley Cl Hove BN3 .... 166 F3
Worthing BN12 .... 181 C1
Nutley Cres BN12 .... 181 C1
Nutley Dr BN12 .... 181 C1
Nye La Ditchling BN6 .... 127 D1
Westmeston BN6 .... 148 D8
Nye Rd RH15 .... 107 C3
Nyes Cl BN5 .... 123 F5
Nyes La RH13 .... 57 F3
Nyetimber Cl
Bognor Regis PO21 .... 194 B2
West Chiltington Common RH20 119 C6
Nyetimber Copse RH20 .... 119 C7
Nyetimber Cres PO21 .... 194 B2
Nyetimber Hill BN2 .... 168 E2
Nyetimber La
Bognor Regis PO21 .... 194 B2
West Chiltington Common RH20 119 C7
Nyetimber Mill PO21 .... 194 A2
Nyetimbers The PO21 .... 194 A2
Nyewood CE Inf (A) Sch
PO21 .... 195 A4
Nyewood CE Jun (A) Sch
PO21 .... 195 A3
Nyewood Gdns ② PO21 .... 195 B3
Nyewood Pl PO21 .... 195 B3
Nyewood Pl PO21 .... 195 B2
Nymans Cl RH12 .... 37 A7
Nymans Cotts RH17 .... 61 C7
Nymans Ct RH10 .... 19 B3
Nymans (NT) RH17 .... 61 D7
Nyton Rd PO20 .... 175 C8

Oak Ave Chichester PO19 .... 172 E7
Heath Common RH20 .... 120 B3
Oak Bank RH16 .... 85 F7
Oak Cl Bognor Regis PO22 ...... 195 C6
Brighton BN1 .... 167 E3
Chichester PO19 .... 172 E7
Copthorne RH10 .... 7 A3
Southwater RH13 .... 79 F7
Storrington RH20 .... 119 F2
Worthing BN13 .... 161 E1
Oak Cotts GU27 .... 26 E6
Oak Croft RH19 .... 23 A8
Oak Dell RH10 .... 19 C7
Oak End Arundel BN18 .... 157 E2
West Chiltington Common RH20 119 D8
Oak Gr Bognor Regis PO22 ..... 195 C6
Loxwood RH14 .... 32 A4
Oak Hall Pk RH15 .... 107 B1
Oak Ho RH14 .... 55 C1
Oak La RH12 .... 35 E3
Oak Meadow PO20 .... 191 E6
Oak Rd Crawley RH11 .... 18 C5
Southwater RH13 .... 57 E1
Oak Tree Cotts
Burgess Hill RH15 .... 107 B3
Danehill RH17 .... 66 A4
Oak Tree Ct GU29 .... 92 E6

Oak Tree Dr Liss GU33 .... 45 C4
New Brighton PO10 .... 149 B4
Oak Tree Farm PO18 .... 150 D1
Oak Tree La Haslemere GU27 ... 26 D6
Woodgate PO20 .... 175 D5
Oak Tree Way RH13 .... 36 F4
Oak View PO20 .... 192 F7
Oak Way RH10 .... 18 E8
Oak Wlk RH12 .... 36 E1
Oakapple Cl Cowfold RH13 ...... 81 E1
Crawley RH11 .... 18 B1
Oakapple Rd BN42 .... 165 E1
Oakcroft Gdns BN17 .... 178 F3
Oakdale 6 RH16 .... 85 F3
Oakdene Brighton BN2 .... 168 F4
7 Haywards Heath RH16 .... 85 D5
Oakdene Ave BN41 .... 165 E3
Oakdene Cl BN41 .... 165 E3
Oakdene Cres BN41 .... 165 E3
Oakdene Gdns BN41 .... 165 E3
Oakdene Rise BN41 .... 165 E4
Oakdene Way BN41 .... 165 E4
Oakendene RH13 .... 82 B1
Oakenfield RH15 .... 107 A5
Oakfield Lodsworth GU28 .... 72 B3
Plaistow RH14 .... 30 E2
Oakfield Ave PO20 .... 201 F7
Oakfield Cl RH16 .... 86 A7
Oakfield Rd Cowfold RH13 ...... 81 F1
East Wittering PO20 .... 201 F7
Oakfield Way RH19 .... 9 F3
Wallis Wood RH5 .... 13 D8
Oakfields Crawley RH10 .... 19 D7
Wallis Wood RH5 .... 13 D8
Oakhaven RH10, RH11 .... 18 D4
Oakhill Cotts RH13 .... 81 E1
Oakhill Rd RH13 .... 36 E2
Oakhurst Haywards Heath RH16 .. 85 D8
Henfield BN5 .... 123 F6
Midhurst GU29 .... 92 D7
Sayers Common BN6 .... 105 D2
Oakhurst Gdns
East Grinstead RH19 .... 9 C2
Rustington BN16 .... 199 E6
Oakhurst La
Haywards Heath RH16 .... 85 D8
Loxwood RH14 .... 31 F1
Oakhurst Mews RH13 .... 36 E2
Oakland Ct Bognor Regis PO22 .. 196 A4
Bognor Regis, Nyetimber PO21 .. 194 A1
7 Littlehampton BN17 .... 198 E4
5 Shoreham-by-Sea BN43 .... 184 F7
Worthing, Goring-by-Sea BN12 .. 181 A1
2 Worthing, W Worthing BN11 182 C2
Oaklands Ardingly RH17 .... 64 B8
Billingshurst RH14 .... 77 D7
Haslemere GU27 .... 27 C7
Horley RH6 .... 2 C3
Horsham RH13 .... 36 E2
2 Lancing BN15 .... 183 F5
Oaklands Bsns Ctr BN11 .... 181 F3
Oaklands Ct PO19 .... 172 F8
Oaklands La GU29 .... 92 F5
Oaklands Rd RH16 .... 85 D5
Oaklands Way PO19 .... 173 A7
Oakleigh Annexe
(Queen Victoria Hospl) RH19 23 C7
Oakleigh Cl BN11 .... 183 A4
Oakleigh Ct
2 Bognor Regis PO21 .... 195 B2
Southwater RH13 .... 80 A7
Worthing BN14 .... 183 A4
Oakleigh Rd Horsham RH12 ..... 36 F4
Worthing BN11, BN14 .... 183 A4
Oakley Cl RH19 .... 23 B7
Oakley Cotts Ashurst Wood RH19 23 C7
Handcross RH17 .... 61 C8
Oakley Gdns BN16 .... 200 A5
Oakmead Rd RH15 .... 106 F1
Oakmeadow Cl PO10 .... 149 C3
Oakmeeds Com Sch RH15 ..... 107 A2
Oakroyd Cl RH15 .... 107 D5
Oaks Cl Horsham RH12 .... 37 B6
Westergate PO20 .... 175 D6
Oaks The Burgess Hill BN6 ..... 106 C4
East Grinstead RH19 .... 23 B8
Haywards Heath RH16 .... 86 A4
Haywards Heath RH16 .... 86 C4
Rustington BN16 .... 199 E5
Small Dole BN5 .... 144 E6
Southwater RH13 .... 57 F2
Oakside Cl RH6 .... 2 C4
Oakside La RH6 .... 2 C4
Oaktree Cotts BN18 .... 176 C8
Oakway RH13 .... 59 C6
Oakwood Haywards Heath RH16 . 85 D4
Partridge Green RH13 .... 103 A3
Oakwood Cl Burgess Hill RH15 107 B2
Midhurst GU29 .... 92 E7
Tangmere PO20 .... 154 D2
Oakwood Ct GU28 .... 95 E7
Oakwood Gdns PO21 .... 195 C4
Oakwood Ind Pk RH10 .... 6 A2
Oakwood Pk RH18 .... 22 E2
Oakwood Rd Burgess Hill RH15 107 B2
Haywards Heath RH16 .... 85 D4
Horley RH6 .... 2 B4
Oakwood Sch
East Ashling PO18 .... 151 F2
Horley RH6 .... 2 C3
Oates Wlk RH10 .... 18 F3
Oathall Ave RH16 .... 85 F6
Oathall Com Coll RH16 .... 85 F6
Oathall Rd RH16 .... 85 E5
Oatlands Crawley RH11 .... 18 A5
Horley RH6 .... 2 C4
Oberon Way RH11 .... 17 E3
Ocean Cl BN12 .... 200 E4

Ocean Dr BN12 .... 200 E4
Ocean Par BN12 .... 200 E4
Ockenden La RH17 .... 84 E6
Ockenden Way BN6 .... 126 E3
Ockley Ct PO21 .... 195 C3
Ockley Hill BN6, RH15 .... 127 B6
Ockley La Burgess Hill RH15 ... 127 B7
Keymer BN6 .... 127 B4
Ockley Rd PO21 .... 195 C3
Ockley Way BN6 .... 127 A5
Octagon The BN2 .... 188 F3
Offington Ave BN13, BN14 ..... 182 B6
Offington Cnr BN13 .... 182 A8
Offington Ct BN14 .... 182 C6
Offington Dr BN14 .... 182 B7
Offington Gdns BN14 .... 182 A6
Offington La BN13, BN14 .... 182 A7
Okehurst La RH14 .... 55 D4
Okehurst Rd RH14 .... 55 A6
Old Barn Cl RH16 .... 85 D2
Old Barn Way BN42 .... 186 A7
Old Boat Cnr BN1 .... 168 C7
Old Boat Wlk BN1 .... 168 B7
Old Bridge Rd PO18 .... 171 C7
Old Bridge St PO18 .... 171 C7
Old Brighton Rd N RH11 .... 39 C7
Old Brighton Rd S
Crawley RH11, RH6 .... 5 E5
Pease Pottage RH11 .... 39 B6
Old Broyle Rd PO19 .... 152 D2
Old Buddington La GU29 .... 70 E3
Old Church Ho The PO21 .... 195 A6
Old Coastguard Cotts PO20 ... 206 C7
Old Coastguards PO22 .... 195 F3
Old Control Rd RH6 .... 5 D6
Old Convent The RH19 .... 9 E2
Old Cottage Cl PO20 .... 154 C1
Old Cotts BN14 .... 161 E7
Old Court Cl BN1 .... 167 F4
Old Crawley Rd RH12 .... 37 C7
Old Denne Gdns RH12 .... 36 C1
Old Farm Cl PO21 .... 194 D2
Old Farm Ct BN15 .... 184 C6
Old Farm La PO10 .... 149 E3
Old Farm Rd BN1 .... 167 F5
Old Fort Rd BN43 .... 185 B6
Old Glebe GU27 .... 49 B6
Old Granary The PO18 .... 154 D4
Old Guildford Rd RH12 .... 35 E4
Old Haslemere Rd GU27 .... 27 C5
Old Holbrook RH12 Faygate RH12 ... 15 F2
Horsham RH12 .... 36 E7
Old Horsham Rd RH11 .... 18 B4
Old London Rd Brighton BN1 .. 167 E6
Coldwaltham RH20 .... 117 D6
Washington RH20 .... 141 E8
Old Manor Cl RH11 .... 18 A8
Old Manor House Gdns PO22 .. 196 B5
Old Manor Rd BN16 .... 199 B6
Old Market Ave 9 PO19 .... 173 A6
Old Martyrs RH11 .... 5 D1
Old Mead Rd BN17 .... 178 C5
Old Mill Cl Brighton BN1 .... 167 E5
Southwick BN41 .... 186 A7
Old Mill Dr RH20 .... 119 D1
Old Mill Pl RH20 .... 98 D1
Old Mill Sq RH20 .... 119 D1
Old Mill The PO19 .... 173 A7
Old Millmeads RH12 .... 36 C5
Old Museum Ct GU27 .... 27 D6
Old Orchards RH10 .... 19 E6
Old Park Cl RH17 .... 85 A6
Old Park La PO18 .... 171 E5
Old Patcham Mews BN1 .... 167 E6
Old Pl PO21 .... 194 E3
Old Point PO22 .... 196 E4
Old Quarry The GU27 .... 26 F4
Old Rd RH9 .... 9 F1
Old Rectory Cl PO10 .... 149 D3
Old Rectory Dr PO20 .... 175 E7
Old Rectory Flats PO22 .... 196 A4
Old Rectory Gdns
Bognor Regis PO22 .... 196 A4
Southwick BN43 .... 185 D8
Old Rectory The PO22 .... 196 A4
Old Salts Farm Rd BN15 .... 184 A5
Old School Cl PO20 .... 191 E4
Old School Mews PO20 .... 196 A5
Old School Pl RH15 .... 106 F2
Old School Rd GU33 .... 45 B4
Old School The RH20 .... 97 A2
Old Shoreham Rd
North Lancing BN15 .... 184 A8
Portslade-by-Sea
BN1, BN3, BN41, BN42 .... 186 C8
Shoreham-by-Sea BN43 .... 184 E8
Old Stables The PO22 .... 195 F4
Old Station Cl RH10 .... 21 B7
Old Steine BN1, BN2 .... 207 A5
Old Thorns Golf Course GU30 . 24 D3
Old Viaduct Ct 6 BN2 .... 188 C8
Old Wickham La RH16 .... 85 E7
Old Wickhurst La RH12 .... 35 D2
Old Worthing Rd BN16 .... 180 B3
Older Way BN16 .... 179 F6
Oldfield Cres BN42 .... 185 E8
Oldfield Rd RH6 .... 1 F1
Oldhouse La Balls Green RH14 .. 78 B3
Broadford Bridge RH14, RH20 ... 100 A4
Sidlesham PO20 .... 203 C7
West Marden PO18, PO9 .... 130 A6
Oldlands Ave Balcombe RH17 ... 41 A1
Keymer BN6 .... 127 A4
Oldlands Way PO22 .... 195 E7
Oldwick Meadows PO18 .... 152 F5
Olive Rd BN3 .... 186 D8
Oliver Cl BN2 .... 188 C5

Oliver Ho BN3 .... 187 B5
Oliver Rd RH12 .... 36 A1
Oliver Whitby Rd PO19 .... 172 E7
Olivers Meadow PO20 .... 175 D7
Olivier Ct PO21 .... 195 A6
Olivier Rd RH10 .... 19 D5
Onslow Ct 7 BN11 .... 183 B3
Onslow Dr BN12 .... 200 E6
Ontario Cl BN13 .... 181 C6
Ontario Gdns BN13 .... 181 C6
Open Mkt The BN1 .... 207 A7
Ophir Rd BN11 .... 183 A3
Orange Row Brighton BN1 ..... 207 A5
Emsworth PO10 .... 169 B8
Orchard Ave Chichester PO19 .. 172 F7
Hove BN3 .... 167 A1
Lancing BN15 .... 183 E7
Selsey PO20 .... 206 E6
Worthing BN14 .... 182 B5
Orchard Bsns Ctr The RH1 .... 2 A8
Orchard Cl Bognor Regis PO21 .. 195 B3
East Harting GU31 .... 90 A4
Elsted GU29 .... 90 D4
Ferring BN12 .... 180 E3
Haywards Heath RH16 .... 85 D8
Horley RH6 .... 1 F4
Petworth GU28 .... 95 F7
Scaynes Hill RH17 .... 86 F3
Shoreham-by-Sea BN43 .... 184 E8
Small Dole BN5 .... 144 F6
Southwick BN42 .... 185 F8
Worthing BN14 .... 182 B5
Orchard Cott RH16 .... 86 B5
Orchard Cott RH17 .... 84 F6
Orchard Cotts Charlwood RH6 ... 4 F7
Fishbourne PO18 .... 172 A8
Woodgate PO20 .... 175 D5
Orchard Cres BN18 .... 156 A3
Orchard Dell RH20 .... 99 E2
Orchard Gdns Chichester PO19 172 F7
Hove BN3 .... 167 B1
Rustington BN16 .... 199 D6
Woodgate PO20 .... 175 D5
Orchard Hill RH12 .... 33 C7
Orchard Ho BN15 .... 183 E6
Orchard La Ditchling BN6 .... 127 D4
Hassocks BN6 .... 126 F4
Hermitage PO10 .... 169 D8
Orchard Par PO20 .... 206 F8
Orchard Pl BN18 .... 156 A3
Orchard Rd Burgess Hill RH15 .. 106 E3
East Preston BN16 .... 200 A6
Horsham RH13 .... 36 E2
Hove BN3 .... 167 B1
West Itchenor PO20 .... 191 A7
Orchard Side PO20 .... 193 A8
Orchard St Chichester PO19 ... 172 F7
Crawley RH10 .... 18 D6
Orchard The
Bognor Regis PO20 .... 194 C1
Haslemere GU27 .... 26 F5
Hassocks BN6 .... 126 F3
Bolney RH17 .... 83 D8
Burgess Hill RH15 .... 106 E3
East Grinstead RH19 .... 9 E1
Fontwell BN18 .... 156 A3
Haywards Heath RH16 .... 85 D8
Hurstpierpoint BN6 .... 125 F6
Lancing BN15 .... 183 E7
Midhurst GU29 .... 92 F8
Pulborough RH20 .... 98 C3
Orchards The Brighton BN2 ... 168 E3
4 Crawley RH11 .... 17 D5
11 Haywards Heath RH16 ...... 85 E4
Horsham RH12 .... 36 F5
Orchid Dr RH13 .... 36 A3
Orchid Pk RH16 .... 86 C4
Orchid View BN1 .... 168 C6
Orde Cl RH10 .... 6 D1
Oriel Cl Crawley RH10 .... 6 C1
West Barnham PO22 .... 176 B6
Orient Rd BN15 .... 184 C5
Oriental Pl BN1 .... 187 E5
Orion Ct RH11 .... 17 D4
Orion Par BN6 .... 126 F3
Orkney Ct BN13 .... 181 B5
Orltons La RH12 .... 3 F2
Orme Cotts BN16 .... 179 F6
Orme Rd BN11 .... 182 C3
Ormerod Ct 5 RH16 .... 85 E5
Ormesby Cres PO22 .... 196 A6
Ormesby Wlk RH10 .... 19 B4
Ormonde Ave PO20 .... 173 B6
Ormonde Way BN43 .... 184 D6
Orpen Pl PO20 .... 206 F7
Orpen Rd BN3 .... 167 D1
Osborn Cres PO19 .... 153 A1
Osborne Cl BN15 .... 183 C6
Osborne Cres PO19 .... 173 D6
Osborne Ct Crawley RH11 .... 18 B2
7 Shoreham-by-Sea BN43 .... 185 D6
Osborne Dr BN15 .... 183 C6
Osborne Rd BN1 .... 168 A2
Osborne Villas BN3 .... 187 B6
Osmond Rd BN3 .... 187 B7
Osmonde Cl BN14 .... 182 C4
Osmund Cl RH10 .... 19 E6
Osmunda Bank RH19 .... 9 E6
Osney Ct RH11 .... 18 C5
Osprey Cl BN17 .... 178 D4
Osprey Gdns PO22 .... 195 C7
Osprey Ho 8 BN1 .... 187 E5
Osprey Quay PO10 .... 169 C7
Ostlers View BN14 .... 77 C7
Otard Cl PO20 .... 206 E7
Otford Cl RH11 .... 39 C8

Ottafield Ct RH16 .... 85 F6
Otter Cl PO19 .... 172 E8
Otway Cl RH11 .... 17 F4
Otway Rd PO19 .... 153 A2
Oulton Wlk RH10 .... 19 B4
Our Lady of Sion RC Jun Sch
BN11 .... 182 D2
Our Lady of Sion Sch BN11 .... 182 C2
Our Lady Queen of Heaven
RC (A) Prim Sch RH11 .... 18 B8
Outerwyke Ave PO22 .... 196 A6
Outerwyke Gdns PO22 .... 196 B6
Outerwyke Rd PO22 .... 196 A6
Outram Ho PO22 .... 195 F3
Outram Rd PO22 .... 195 F3
Oval Cl PO20 .... 206 E5
Oval The Findon BN14 .... 161 E2
Liss GU33 .... 45 B4
Worthing BN13 .... 182 A5
Oval Waye BN12 .... 200 A4
Over St BN1 .... 207 A6
Overdene Dr RH11 .... 18 A6
Overdown Rd PO22 .... 196 B5
Overdown Rise BN41 .... 165 E4
Overhill BN42 .... 165 E1
Overhill Dr BN1 .... 167 E5
Overhill Gdns BN1 .... 167 E5
Overhill Way BN1 .... 167 E6
Overmead BN43 .... 184 E8
Overstrand Ave BN16 .... 199 C4
Overton Ct PO19 .... 173 C6
Overton Shaw RH19 .... 9 E4
Oving Ct PO19 .... 173 C6
Oving Rd Chichester PO19 ..... 173 C6
Oving PO20 .... 174 B7
Oving Terr PO19 .... 173 C6
Owen Cl RH15 .... 106 F1
Owers Way PO20 .... 201 E7
Owlbeech Ct RH13 .... 37 B4
Owlbeech Pl RH13 .... 37 B4
Owlbeech Way RH13 .... 37 B4
Owletts RH10 .... 19 D7
Owlscastle Cl RH12 .... 36 D5
Oxen Ave BN43 .... 184 F8
Oxen Ct BN43 .... 184 F8
Oxford Cl PO20 .... 201 F7
Oxford Ct Brighton BN1 .... 207 A7
5 Midhurst GU29 .... 92 E7
Oxford Dr PO21 .... 194 F3
Oxford Mews BN3 .... 187 C7
Oxford Pl BN1 .... 207 A7
Oxford Rd Crawley RH10 .... 18 F2
Horsham RH13 .... 36 E2
Worthing BN11 .... 182 C3
Oxford St Bognor Regis PO21 .. 195 B2
Brighton BN1, BN2 .... 207 A7
Oxford Terr BN44 .... 143 D2

Pacific Ct 3 BN43 .... 184 F6
Packer Ct RH11 .... 10 A3
Packham Way RH15 .... 106 F4
Paddock Cl GU27 .... 49 B5
Paddock Ct BN41 .... 165 F3
Paddock Gdns RH19 .... 22 E7
Paddock Gn BN16 .... 199 E6
Paddock La PO20 .... 206 D8
Paddock The
Bognor Regis PO22 .... 195 C6
Crawley RH10 .... 19 D7
Haslemere GU27 .... 27 A8
Hove BN3 .... 167 C6
Littlehampton BN17 .... 178 C6
Shoreham-by-Sea BN43 .... 164 D1
Paddock Way Findon BN14 .... 161 E6
Liphook GU30 .... 25 C5
Paddockhall Rd RH16 .... 85 D5
Paddockhurst La RH17 .... 41 D3
Paddockhurst Rd Crawley RH11 18 A5
Turners Hill RH10 .... 20 C2
Paddocks PO22 .... 176 B6
Paddocks The Lancing BN15 ... 183 F5
Upper Beeding BN44 .... 144 B3
Padstow Wlk RH11 .... 17 F4
Padwick Rd RH13 .... 37 A2
Page Ct RH13 .... 36 D1
Pages Cnr BN11 .... 183 A3
Pages La BN11 .... 183 A4
Paget Cl RH13 .... 58 E8
Pagham Cl PO10 .... 169 C8
Pagham Gdns PO11 .... 189 B2
Pagham Harbour Nature Reserve
PO20, PO21 .... 204 C6
Pagham Ho BN17 .... 178 B3
Pagham Rd
Bognor Regis PO20, PO21 ..... 194 A3
Runcton PO20 .... 173 C1
Pain's Flat RH15, RH17 .... 106 D8
Palace Pl BN1, Bn 207 A5
Palace Yd PO19 .... 172 E6
Palatine Rd BN12, BN13 .... 181 D4
Palings Way GU27 .... 49 A5
Pallant The BN12 .... 181 B4
Pallingham Dr RH10 .... 19 C3
Pallingham La RH14 .... 75 F2
Palm Court Cotts BN16 .... 200 A4
Palm Ct BN13 .... 181 E7
Palmeira Ave BN3 .... 187 D6
Palmeira Ct 20 BN3 .... 187 C6
Palmeira Ho 6 BN3 .... 187 D7
Palmeira Mansions 18 BN3 .... 187 C6
Palmeira Pl BN3 .... 187 D7
Palmeira Sq BN3 .... 187 C6
Palmer Cl Horley RH6 .... 1 F5
Storrington RH20 .... 119 F2
Palmer Pl PO20 .... 173 C1
Palmer Rd Angmering BN16 ... 179 F7
Crawley RH10 .... 19 C3
Palmer's Rd PO10 .... 149 B1

Palmers Way BN13 161 D1
Palmerston Ave BN12 181 C2
Pangdean La BN6 106 C4
Pangdene Cl RH15 106 F1
Pankhurst Ave BN2 188 D6
Pankhurst Ct 11 RH11 18 B1
Pannell Cl RH19 9 D1
Pannett RH15 106 E4
Pantiles The BN12 200 E5
Panton Cl PO10 149 A3
Parade Mansions BN16 200 A4
Parade The Bognor Regis PO21 205 A7
East Wittering PO20 201 F7
Hove BN3 166 E2
West Kingston BN16 200 A4
Paradise La PO10 149 D4
Parchment St PO19 172 F7
Parham Cl Brighton BN2 188 D5
Littlehampton, Rustington BN16 199 B4
Littlehampton, Wick BN17 198 D6
Worthing BN14 161 F1
Parham Ct 3 BN11 182 A2
Parham House RH20 118 D1
Parham Rd Crawley RH11 17 F7
Worthing BN14 161 F1
Parish Ho 6 RH11 18 D5
Parish La RH10 39 E6
Park Ave Hove BN3 186 E7
Keymer BN6 127 A2
Selsey PO20 206 F7
Shoreham-by-Sea BN43 185 A8
Worthing BN11 182 E3
Park Cl Brighton BN1 168 E5
Burgess Hill RH15 106 F4
Hove BN3 166 E3
Hurstpierpoint BN6 126 A6
Portslade-by-Sea BN41 166 B1
Worthing BN14 182 A7
Park Copse PO20 204 C1
Park Cotts BN6 125 F6
Park Cres Brighton BN2 207 B7
Emsworth PO10 149 A1
Midhurst GU29 92 E8
Portslade-by-Sea BN41 186 A8
Selsey PO20 206 G8
Worthing BN11 182 C2
Park Crescent Pl BN2 207 B7
Park Crescent Rd BN2 207 B7
Park Crescent Terr BN2 207 B7
Park Ct Brighton, Patcham BN1 167 E6
Brighton, Preston BN1 167 F1
Burgess Hill RH15 107 A3
4 Haywards Heath RH16 85 E4
Park Dr Bognor Regis PO22 196 D5
Burndell BN18 177 A2
Ferring BN12 200 F6
Rustington BN16 199 D6
Park Farm Cl RH12 36 D7
Park Farm Rd RH12 36 D7
Park Gate BN3 187 D6
Park Hill BN2 207 B5
Park Ho 3 BN11 183 B3
Park La Aldingbourne PO20 175 B7
Aldsworth PO10, PO18 149 E8
Ashurst Wood RH19 23 D6
Bosham PO18 171 D2
East Beach PO20 204 A1
Fernhurst GU27 49 B6
Halnaker PO18 154 D5
Haywards Heath RH16 64 D2
Maplehurst RH13 81 B6
Slindon BN18 156 C4
Southwick BN42, BN43 185 D7
Warminghurst RH20 120 D5
West Grinstead RH13 102 D8
Park Lodge BN3 187 D8
Park Manor BN1 167 D4
Park Pl Arundel BN18 158 A3
Horsham RH12 36 C1
Park Rd Barnham PO22 176 D6
Breach PO10 149 F1
Brighton BN1 168 E5
Burgess Hill RH15 107 A3
Burndell BN18 177 A2
Dormans Park RH19 9 F6
East Grinstead RH19 9 D1
Faygate RH12 16 F1
Forest Row RH18 23 F2
Goodwood Park PO18 153 F8
Handcross RH17 61 B6
Haslemere GU27 27 C5
Haywards Heath RH16 85 E4
Henfield BN5 123 E4
Petworth GU28 95 F8
Selsey PO20 206 G8
Shoreham-by-Sea BN43 185 A8
Slinfold RH13 34 D3
Worthing BN11 182 E3
Park Rise Horsham RH12 36 B4
Hove BN3 166 E3
Petworth GU28 95 E7
Park Road Terr 4 BN2 207 B5
Park Royal BN1 187 E6
Park St Brighton BN2 207 B5
Horsham RH12 36 D2
Park Street RH13 34 C3
Park Terr Bognor Regis PO21 195 B2
Tillington GU28 73 C1
Park Terr E RH13 36 D1
Park Terr W RH13 36 D1
Park View Brighton BN1 187 E8
Brighton BN2 188 C6
Haywards Heath RH16 85 E6
Horley RH6 2 A3
Park View Ct BN16 199 C6
Park View Rd BN3 167 B1
Park View Terr BN1 187 E8
Park Way Crawley RH10 19 C7
Park Way Easebourne GU29 71 B2
Horsham RH12 36 C2
Southwick BN42 185 F8
Park Way Cl BN42 185 F8
Parker Cl RH10 19 D5
Parker Ct BN41 166 B2
Parker's Cotts PO18 153 A6
Parkers RH13 56 F3
Parkfield RH12 36 C3
Parkfield Ave PO21 194 D3
Parkfield Cl RH11 17 F6
Parkfield Ct BN13 182 A4
Parkfield Rd BN13 182 A4
Parkhurst Gr RH6 1 F4
Parkhurst Rd RH6 1 E4
Parklands BN43 185 C8
Parklands Ave
Bognor Regis PO21 195 B4
Worthing BN12 181 D1
Parklands Ct BN12 181 D2
Parklands Cty Prim Sch PO19 172 E7
Parklands Rd Chichester PO19 172 F7
Hassocks BN6 126 F3
Parklawn Ave RH6 1 F5
Parkmead BN2 207 B7
Parkmore Terr BN1 207 F8
Parkside 8 Bognor Regis PO21 195 D4
Burgess Hill RH15 106 F3
Crawley RH10 18 E6
East Grinstead RH19 9 C1
Keymer BN6 127 A4
Shoreham-by-Sea BN43 165 A1
Worthing BN11 182 E3
Parkside Ave BN17 198 F5
Parkside Ct BN17 198 F5
Parkside Mews RH12 36 D2
Parkview BN6 126 A5
Parkway Bognor Regis PO21 195 A3
Horley RH6 2 A3
Parkway The BN16 199 D5
Parnell Cl RH10 19 D4
Parry Dr BN16 199 B5
Parson's Hill BN18 158 B3
Parsonage Bsns Pk RH12 36 E4
Parsonage Est GU31 68 B4
Parsonage Rd Henfield BN5 123 E6
Horsham RH12, RH13 36 E4
Parsonage Way RH12 36 E4
Parsons Cl Haslemere GU27 27 C8
Horley RH6 1 E4
Parsons Gn GU27 27 C8
Parsons Wlk Horsham RH12 57 F8
Walberton BN18 176 E8
Parthings La RH12, RH13 57 F8
Pascoe Ct 2 PO19 172 F7
Pashley Ct 10 BN43 184 F7
Passfield Ent Ctr GU30 24 D8
Passfield Rd GU30 24 E8
Paston Pl BN2 188 D4
Pasture Hill Rd RH16 85 D6
Pasture The RH10 19 C6
Patcham By-Pass BN1 167 E6
Patcham Cty Inf Sch BN1 167 E6
Patcham Cty Jun Sch BN1 167 F6
Patcham High Sch BN1 167 F6
Patcham House Sch BN1 167 E6
Patchdean BN1 167 F5
Patching Cl Crawley RH11 17 F7
Worthing BN12 181 B4
Patching Lodge 5 BN2 188 C5
Patchings RH13 36 F3
Paterson Wilson Rd BN17 198 E6
Path Link RH10 18 E7
Pathfield Cl RH12 33 D7
Pathfield Rd RH12 33 D7
Pathfields Cl GU27 27 D7
Patnore PO18 152 E7
Patricia Ave BN12 181 D1
Patricia Cl BN12 181 D1
Patrick's Cl GU33 45 C4
Patrick's Copse Rd GU33 45 C4
Patrington Cl RH11 18 A3
Patterdale Cl RH11 18 C4
Paulus Ct 1 PO19 172 F7
Pavilion Bldgs BN1 207 A5
Pavilion Cl BN6 126 E5
Pavilion Ct 11 BN1 187 E7
Pavilion Par BN2 207 A5
Pavilion Rd BN14 182 B3
Pavilion Ret Pk BN2 168 C1
Pavilion St BN2 207 A5
Pavilion Way RH19 22 E8
Pax Cl RH11 17 E4
Paxhill Park Golf Course RH16 86 E8
Paxmead Cres BN14 182 F6
Payne Ave BN3 186 F8
Payne Cl Bognor Regis PO21 205 A8
Crawley RH10 19 D8
Payne Terr BN1 168 B1
Paynesfield RH17 83 C3
Paythorne Cl BN42 165 D1
Paythorne Dro BN5 145 D4
Payton Dr RH15 106 E2
Payton Ho RH15 107 D3
Peace Cl BN1 168 C1
Peacemaker Cl RH11 17 E4
Peacheries The PO19 173 C5
Peachey Rd PO20 206 D6
Peacock Ind Est BN3 187 D7
Peacock La BN1 167 E4
Peacock Wlk 8 RH11 18 A3
Peacock's Hill RH13 81 D6
Peacocks La RH20 100 C1
Peak La BN16 200 C4
Peak The PO9 128 E2
Pear Tree Hill RH1 2 A8
Pearson Rd Arundel BN18 157 F2
Crawley RH10 19 C6
Pearsons Retreat BN11 183 B3
Peartree Cl RH15 106 E3
Peartree Cnr RH13 81 C2
Peary Cl RH12 36 D6
Pease Croft GU31 89 D3
Pease Pottage Service Area
RH10 39 C7
Pebble Ct PO22 195 E5
Pebble Wlk BN16 179 A3
Peckhams Copse La PO20 173 D3
Peeks Brook La Fernhill RH6 6 E7
Horley RH6 2 F2
Peel Cl BN17 198 C6
Peel Ctr The PO22 195 D7
Peel Rd BN2 188 F4
Peerley Cl PO20 202 A6
Peerley Rd PO20 202 A6
Pegasus Cl GU27 26 D5
Pegasus Ct RH11 17 E4
Pegasus Way RH19 10 B3
Pegwell Cl RH11 17 F4
Pelham Ct Crawley RH11 18 B2
Horsham RH12 36 B2
2 Worthing BN13 182 A5
Pelham Dr RH11 18 A2
Pelham Pl RH11 18 B2
Pelham Place Cotts RH16 86 A7
Pelham Rd
Haywards Heath RH16 86 A6
Worthing BN13 182 A5
Pelham Sq BN1 207 A6
Pelham St BN1 207 A6
Pelham Terr Brighton BN2 168 C1
Lumley PO10 169 C8
Pelleys La PO19 172 F1
Pemberton Cl BN15 183 E7
Pembley Gn RH10 7 E3
Pembroke Ave Hove BN3 187 A7
Worthing BN11 181 F2
Pembroke Cres BN3 187 A7
Pembroke Ct 2 BN3 187 A6
Pembroke Gdns BN3 187 A6
Pembroke Rd RH10 6 C1
Pembroke Way PO21 194 E4
Pembury Cl
Haywards Heath RH16 86 B3
Worthing BN14 182 D4
Pembury Rd BN14 182 D4
Pempeys Terr BN44 143 C4
Penarth Gdns BN17 178 D5
Pende Cl BN15 183 D8
Pendean RH15 107 C1
Pendine Ave BN11 183 A3
Pendragon Ct BN3 187 A8
Penfold La BN16 179 C3
Penfold Rd Crawley RH10 19 B2
Worthing BN14 182 E5
Penfold Way BN44 143 D2
Penfolds Pl BN18 158 A2
Penhill Rd BN15 183 E5
Penhurst Ct Worthing BN13 181 B5
Worthing, Broadwater BN14 182 C6
Penhurst Pl BN2 188 F6
Penland Cl RH16 85 D7
Penland Ct BN44 143 D2
Penland Rd RH16, RH17 85 D7
Penland's Cl BN44 143 D2
Penlands Rise BN44 143 C2
Penlands Vale BN44 143 C2
Penlands Way BN44 143 D2
Penleigh Cl BN15 183 F5
Penn Cl Crawley RH11 5 D1
Middleton-on-Sea PO22 196 E5
Penn Cres RH16 86 A5
Penn Gdns RH20 120 E5
Pennels Cl GU30 47 B2
Pennine Cl RH11 18 B6
Pennington Ho RH16 86 A3
Penns Ct BN44 143 C4
Penny La PO10 169 D8
Pennycress Ave BN12, BN13 181 A5
Pennyfields PO22 196 C5
Penrith Ct BN14 182 D5
Pensfold La RH12, RH13 33 E5
Penshurst Cl RH10 19 D7
Penstone Cl BN15 183 D6
Penstone Ct 4 BN43 185 C8
Penstone Pk BN15 183 E6
Penthorpe Sch RH12 33 C7
Pentland Rd BN13 181 E8
Penwarden Way PO18 171 C7
Penwith Dr GU27 26 E5
Peperham Ho GU27 27 C7
Peperham Rd GU27 27 C8
Pepper Ct BN17 198 C5
Pepper Dr RH15 106 F1
Pepper's La BN44 122 C5
Peppering La BN18 159 A7
Pepperscoombe La BN44 144 B2
Perche Ct GU29 92 D6
Perching Dro BN5 145 E4
Percival Terr 14 BN2 188 D4
Percy Rd RH12 36 B3
Percy Row GU28 95 F8
Peregrine Rd BN17 198 F6
Perimeter Rd E RH6 6 B6
Perimeter Rd N RH6 5 D7
Perimeter Rd S RH6 5 E5
Perkstead Ct 6 RH11 18 A3
Perrots La BN44 143 C2
Perry Ave RH19 9 E3
Perryfield Ho 7 RH11 18 D5
Perryfield La RH13 82 C6
Perryfield Rd RH11 18 D5
Perryfields RH15 106 E4
Perrylands RH6 4 F7
Perrylands La RH6 2 F2
Perryman's La RH17 66 D3
Perrymount Rd RH16 85 E5
Perth Cl RH11 5 D1
Perth Ho GU29 92 E6
Perth Way RH12 36 F4
Pescott's Cl PO20 191 E5
Peskett Cl RH13 56 F3
Peter Gladwin Cty Prim Sch
BN41 166 B2
Peter Rd BN15 183 C4
Peter Weston Pl PO19 173 B6
Peter's La PO20 206 A8
Peter's Pl PO20 206 A8
Peterborough Rd RH10 18 E2
Peterhouse Cl PO21 194 F4
Peterhouse Par RH10 6 C1
Peterlee Wlk RH11 17 E2
Petersfield Rd GU29 92 E8
Petlands Gdns 4 RH16 85 F3
Petlands Rd RH16 85 E3
Pett Cl BN2 188 F6
Petworth Ave BN12 181 C1
Petworth CE (C) Prim Sch
GU28 95 F7
Petworth Ct Crawley RH11 17 F3
Haslemere GU27 27 D6
5 Rustington BN16 199 B3
Petworth Dr Burgess Hill RH15 107 A4
Horsham RH12 36 F7
Petworth Pk GU28 73 D2
Petworth Rd
Ansteadbrook GU27, GU8 28 B6
Brighton BN1 168 B6
Pevensey Cl RH10 19 C5
Pevensey Gdn BN11 182 A1
Pevensey Rd
Bognor Regis PO21 195 A4
3 Brighton BN2 188 C8
Southwater RH13 58 A2
Worthing BN11 182 A1
Peverel Rd Crawley RH11 17 E5
Worthing BN13 182 A4
Peveril Cl BN15 183 A6
Peveril Dr BN15 183 B6
Pharos Quay BN17 198 C5
Pheasant Cotts PO18 132 F6
Philip Ct 8 BN3 187 C7
Phillips Bsns Ctr PO19 172 E5
Philliswood La PO18 110 D3
Philpots Manor Sch RH19 42 C5
Phoenix Brewery Halls BN2 207 B7
Phoenix Cl PO19 173 A5
Phoenix Cres BN42 185 D8
Phoenix La RH19 23 E6
Phoenix Pl BN2 207 B6
Phoenix Way BN42 185 D8
Phrosso Rd BN11 181 F1
Pickers Gn RH16 86 A8
Picketts La RH1 2 C8
Pickhurst La RH20 98 B6
Pickwell La RH17 85 A1
Picton St BN2 188 C7
Picts Hill RH13 58 A7
Picts La RH13 82 A4
Pier Rd BN17 198 D4
Pierpoint Cl BN6 125 F6
Pigbush La RH14 32 A7
Pigeonhouse La BN16 199 E4
Piggery Hall La PO20 190 F1
Piggott Ct RH13 36 E1
Piggott's Bsns Pk 5 BN11 182 C3
Pike The RH20 141 E7
Pilgrim Ct RH16 86 A5
Pilgrims Cl 1 BN14 182 B3
Pilgrims Terr BN13 182 A3
Pilgrims Way PO21 194 B1
Pilgrims Wlk BN13 182 A3
Pilot Ho 1 BN2 207 B5
Piltdown Rd BN2 188 F6
Pine Cl Billingshurst RH14 55 C1
Crawley RH11 5 C1
Heath Common RH20 120 B3
Midhurst GU29 92 F5
Pine Cotts GU33 45 C7
Pine Ct PO10 149 B4
Pine Gdns RH6 2 A2
Pine Gr Chichester PO19 152 C1
East Grinstead RH19 9 B3
Pine Shaw RH10 19 D7
Pine Tree Cl BN6 126 B5
Pine Trees Cl BN16 179 F7
Pine Trees Ct BN6 126 D4
Pine View Cl GU27 27 C8
Pine Way Cl RH19 22 E7
Pine Wlk Bognor Regis PO21 194 D4
Liss Forest GU33 45 C6
Pineham Copse RH16 85 F4
Pinehurst Burgess Hill RH15 107 A1
Horsham RH12 36 C4
Pinehurst Pk PO21 194 D4
Pines Ave BN14 182 D7
Pines Rd GU30 24 E4
Pines The Angmering BN16 179 F4
2 Brighton BN2 207 B7
Haywards Heath RH16 86 B4
Horsham RH12 37 C5
Hove BN3 187 E6
Yapton BN18 176 F3
Pinetrees Cl RH10 7 B3
Pinewood 8 BN1 167 E3
Pinewood Cl
Broadridge Heath RH12 35 D3
East Preston BN16 200 A6
Pinewood Ct
Haywards Heath RH16 85 D2
West Lavington GU29 93 A6
Pinewood Gdns PO21 195 A3
Pinewood Way
Haywards Heath RH16 85 D2
Pinewood Way Midhurst GU29 92 E5
Pinfold 4 RH16 85 D6
Pinkhurst La RH13 35 A2
Pinks La PO20 191 D3
Pinland Rd RH13 102 F1
Pipers Cl Hove BN3 166 C3
Southwater RH13 57 F1
Pipers End RH13 34 E3
Pipers La Ebernoe GU28 52 A4
Northchapel GU28 51 A7
Pirles Pl RH12 36 C2
Pit Rd BN6 126 A5
Pitcroft La GU31 88 B5
Pitcroft The PO19 173 C8
Pitfold Ave GU27 26 D6
Pitfold Cl GU27 26 E6
Pitsham La GU29 92 D5
Pitsham Wood GU29 92 D6
Plainfields Ave BN1 168 A7
Plainwood Cl PO19 152 F2
Plaistow Cl BN2 188 F6
Plaistow Cty Inf Sch RH14 30 F3
Plaistow Rd Ifold RH14 31 D1
Kirdford RH14 53 B5
Plantain Cres RH11 18 A2
Plantation Cl BN13 181 F7
Plantation Rd GU33 45 D2
Plantation Rise BN13 182 A7
Plantation The
East Preston BN16 200 A5
Storrington RH20 119 B1
Worthing BN13, BN14 182 A7
Plantation Way
Storrington RH20 119 C1
Worthing BN13 181 F7
Plat The RH12 36 A3
Platt The Dormansland RH7 10 A8
Handcross RH17 61 C8
Haywards Heath RH16 86 B5
Plaw Hatch La RH18, RH19 43 E5
Playden Cl 1 BN2 188 E4
Playden Ct 3 RH11 18 A3
Pleasant La PO10 169 F1
Plough Cl RH11 17 F8
Plough La RH12 36 E5
Plover Cl Bognor Regis PO22 195 C7
Bracklesham PO20 202 A6
Crawley RH11 18 C8
Plovers Rd RH13 36 F3
Plovers The BN15 184 A5
Plumb Pudding Cnr RH20 96 D6
Plummerden La RH16 64 F2
Plumpton Rd BN2 188 D6
Plumtree Cross RH13 57 A5
Plumtree Cross La RH13 57 A5
Plymouth Ave BN2 168 F1
Polecat La RH13 80 C8
Poles La RH11, RH6 5 C3
Polestub La RH17 84 F7
Poling Cl BN12 181 B4
Poling St BN18 179 B7
Pollard Ct BN11 182 A2
Pollard's Hill RH13 80 A6
Pollards RH11 18 A5
Pollards Dr RH13 36 F2
Polperro Cl BN12 200 E5
Pomper La BN6 106 A2
Pond Cl RH14 31 F4
Pond Copse La RH14 31 F5
Pond Farm Cl RH13 57 F4
Pond La BN13 181 D7
Pond Mews BN13 181 D7
Pond Rd Bracklesham PO20 202 B6
Shoreham-by-Sea BN43 184 F7
Pond Rise RH20 99 E1
Pond Way RH19 10 B1
Pond Wood Rd RH10 19 A8
Pondcroft Rd RH16 86 B7
Pondfield Rd RH12 33 D8
Pondtail Cl RH12 36 D6
Pondtail Dr RH12 36 D7
Pondtail Rd RH12 36 D6
Pony Farm BN14 161 F6
Pook La PO18 153 A5
Pookbourne La BN6, RH17 105 E4
Pool Valley BN2 207 A4
Popes Mead GU27 27 C7
Poplar Ave BN3 166 E3
Poplar Cl Brighton BN1 167 F2
Crawley RH11 5 C1
Hove BN3 166 E3
Poplar Ct RH20 98 A2
Poplar Rd BN13 181 C5
Poplar Way GU29 92 E5
Poplars The Burndell BN18 177 A3
Ferring BN12 200 E4
Horsham RH13 36 E3
Keymer BN6 127 A3
Poppy Cl RH13 58 A3
Porchester Cl RH13 58 A2
Port Hall Ave BN1 187 E8
Port Hall Mews BN1 187 E8
Port Hall Pl BN1 187 E8
Port Hall Rd BN1 187 E8
Port Hall St BN1 187 E8
Portfield Ave BN1 168 A6
Portfield Ret Pk PO19 173 D7
Portfield Way PO19, PO20 173 D8
Portland Ave BN3 186 E7
Portland Cl BN16 199 A6
Portland Gate BN3 186 E7
Portland Ho 5 RH19 22 F8
Portland Pl 18 BN2 188 C4
Portland Rd Burgess Hill RH15 106 F3
East Grinstead RH19 22 F8

Portland Rd Hove BN3 186 E7
Worthing BN11 182 D2
Portland Road Trad Est BN3 186 D8
Portland Sq GU33 45 B4
Portland St BN1 207 F5
Portland Villas BN3 186 D7
Portside BN2 188 F3
Portslade Com Coll (Lower) BN41 166 A3
Portslade Com Coll (Sixth Form) BN41 166 A1
Portslade Cty Inf Sch BN41 186 B8
Portslade Sta BN3 186 C8
Portsmouth La RH16 85 F8
Portsmouth Rd Bramshott GU30 25 E6
Liphook GU30 25 B2
Portsmouth Wood RH16 85 F8
Portsmouth Wood Cl RH16 85 F8
Portway BN44 143 C2
Post Office La PO20 173 D1
Post View RH20 140 E8
Potters Croft RH13 36 E2
Potters Field GU33 45 C4
Potters Gn RH13 81 E2
Potters La RH15 106 F1
Potters Mead BN17 178 C3
Pottersfield RH10 18 D7
Pottery La PO18 170 D8
Poulner Cl PO22 196 A5
Poulter's Cnr BN13 182 A6
Poulter's La BN13, BN14 182 B6
Pound Cl Loxwood RH14 31 F5
Petworth GU28 95 F7
Pound Cnr RH13 101 D7
Pound Farm Rd PO19 173 C6
Pound Gate BN6 126 D3
Pound Hill Cty Fst & Mid Schs RH10 19 C7
Pound Hill Par RH10 19 C7
Pound Hill Pl RH10 19 C6
Pound La
Little Parkminster RH13 103 D8
Mannings Heath RH13 59 C6
Shipley RH13 79 D2
Upper Beeding BN44 144 B2
Pound Rd Walberton BN18 156 D1
West Wittering PO20 190 B2
Pound St GU28 95 F8
Pound The Bognor Regis PO21 194 E2
Burgess Hill RH15 106 F4
Poundfield La RH14 31 B3
Povey Cross Rd RH6 1 E1
Poveys Cl RH15 106 D3
Powell Cl RH6 1 E4
Powis Gr BN1 207 F6
Powis Rd BN1 187 E6
Powis Sq BN1 187 E6
Powis Villas BN1 207 F6
Poynes Rd RH6 1 E5
Poynings Crossways BN45 125 B1
Poynings Dr BN3 166 F3
Poynings Rd RH11 17 E5
Poynter Rd BN3 187 A8
Poyntz Cl PO19 172 F3
Pratton Ave BN15 183 D7
Prawn Cl PO20 206 C8
Prebendal Sch The PO19 172 F6
Precinct The PO21 194 F4
Prescott Gdns RH15 107 A3
Preston Ave BN16 199 D5
Preston Cir BN1 207 A7
Preston Dro BN1 167 F2
Preston Grange BN1 167 E1
Preston Manor (Mus) BN1 167 E1
Preston Paddock BN16 199 E5
Preston Park Ave BN1 167 F1
Preston Park Sta BN1 167 D2
Preston Rd BN1 187 F8
Preston St BN1 187 E5
Prestonville Ct 1 BN1 207 F7
Prestonville Rd BN1, BN3 207 F7
Prestwick Cl RH11 17 D5
Prestwood Cl RH11 5 B1
Prestwood La RH11, RH12, RH6 4 C3
Pretoria Ave GU29 92 E7
Pretoria Rd GU29 92 E7
Price Way RH17 64 B7
Priceholm RH17 64 B7
Priest Croft Cl RH11 18 A6
Priestley Way Crawley RH10 6 A3
Middleton-on-Sea PO22 196 D5
Prime Cl BN18 176 E8
Primrose Ave RH6 2 B1
Primrose Cl RH11 18 B3
Primrose Copse RH12 36 E7
Primrose La GU33 45 F4
Prince Albert St BN1 207 A5
Prince Ave BN15 184 B5
Prince Charles Cl BN41, BN42 166 A1
Prince Of Wales Ct BN41 186 F6
Prince Regent's Cl BN2 188 E4
Prince Regent's Ct 2 BN2 188 E4
Prince William Cl BN14 182 A8
Prince William Ct 4 PO21 195 D3
Prince's Cres BN2 207 B8
Prince's Dr PO18 133 E1
Prince's Pl BN1 207 A5
Prince's Rd BN1, BN2 188 B8
Prince's St BN2 207 A5
Prince's Terr BN2 188 E4
Princes Ave BN3 187 A6
Princes Cres BN3 187 A6
Princes Croft PO21 194 A1
Princes Ct 6 BN3 187 A6
Princes Gate BN11 181 F2
Princes Sq BN3 187 A6
Princess Anne Rd RH12 33 D6
Princess Ave
Bognor Regis PO21 195 A2
Worthing BN13 181 F4
Princess Ct BN13 181 F3
Princess Margaret Rd RH12 33 D7
Princess Rd RH11 18 C6
Princess Royal Hospl The RH16 85 F2
Prings La RH13 81 C8
Prinsep Rd BN3 187 A8
Prinsted La PO10 169 F7
Priors Acre PO18 154 D3
Priors Cl Breach PO10 150 A1
Upper Beeding BN44 144 A2
Priors Leaze La PO18 150 C1
Priors Waye PO21 194 A2
Priors Wlk RH10 18 F6
Priors Wood GU27 26 F6
Priory Cl Bognor Regis PO21 205 B8
Boxgrove PO18 154 D3
Horley RH6 1 F4
Lancing BN15 183 B7
Worthing BN13 182 A4
Priory Ct 14 Bognor Regis PO21 195 D3
Brighton BN1 187 F8
Priory Field BN44 144 A2
Priory Gate BN15 183 E6
Priory Lanes PO19 173 A7
Priory Rd Arundel BN18 157 F2
Burgess Hill RH15 107 A1
Chichester PO19 173 A7
Forest Row RH18 23 D2
Hassocks BN6 126 E5
Rustington BN16 199 B6
Priory The Brighton BN1 167 D5
Hove BN3 187 B5
Priory Way RH16 85 F4
Proctor Cl RH10 19 C4
Promenade The
Emsworth PO10 169 B7
Littlehampton BN17 198 E3
Pronger's Cnr RH13 59 E3
Prospect Pl Crawley RH11 18 C6
3 Worthing BN11 182 D1
Providence Pl Brighton BN1 207 A7
6 Chichester PO19 172 F7
Providence Terr BN11 182 E2
Providence The 5 PO19 172 F7
Pruetts La GU31, GU33 45 B1
Pryors Gn PO21 194 C2
Pryors La PO21 194 C1
Puckshott Way GU27 27 D8
Pudding La RH6 4 E7
Puffin Rd RH11 17 D5
Pulborough Cl BN2 188 F7
Pulborough Rd RH20 119 B2
Pulborough Sta RH20 98 A2
Pulborough Way PO22 196 D6
Pump Ho The BN3 186 D8
Punch Copse Rd RH10 18 F7
Punches La PO20 193 D5
Punnetts Ct RH11 17 F2
Purbeck Pl BN17 198 C5
Purcell Rd RH11 17 F3
Purton Rd RH12 36 B4
Putmans La GU31 89 B7
Puttock Cl GU27 26 D5
Pyecombe Ct 4 RH11 17 F3
Pyecombe Golf Course BN45 147 E6
Pyecombe St BN45 147 A6
Pyrford Cl PO21 194 B2

Quadrangle The BN14 161 E4
Quadrant BN1 207 F5
Quadrant The Keymer BN6 127 A4
Worthing BN12 181 C3
Quail Cl RH12 36 D7
Quakers La RH16 86 A5
Quantock Cl Crawley RH11 18 B6
Worthing BN13 181 F8
Quantock Rd BN13 181 F7
Quantocks 2 BN17 198 D6
Quarries The RH13 59 D6
Quarry Bank Rd BN1 168 B2
Quarry Cl Burgess Hill RH15 107 D3
Horsham RH12 36 F6
Quarry Hill RH17 85 C6
Quarry La PO19 173 C5
Quarry Lane Ind Est PO19 173 C5
Quarry Rise RH19 10 A3
Quarry Way RH13 57 F2
Quarterbrass Farm Rd RH12 36 D7
Quashetts The Worthing BN14 182 D4
Worthing BN14 182 D5
Quay Ct BN43 185 B6
Quay The 5 BN43 185 A6
Quayside BN17 198 B5
Quebec St BN2 207 B6
Queen Alexandra Ave BN3 167 A3
Queen Caroline Cl BN3 167 A3
Queen Elizabeth Ave RH15 107 A2
Queen Elizabeth II Jubilee Sch The RH13 36 F1
Queen Elizabeth Rd RH12 33 D7
Queen Mary Ave BN3 167 A3
Queen Sq BN1 207 F5
Queen St Arundel BN18 158 B2
Emsworth PO10 169 C8
Horsham RH13 36 D1
Littlehampton BN17 198 D5
Worthing BN14 182 C4
Queen Victoria Ave BN3 167 A3
Queen Victoria Hospl The RH19 9 F3
Queen's Ave PO19 172 F4
Queen's Ct RH16 85 F6
Queen's Gdns Brighton BN1 207 A6
Queen's Gdns Hove BN3 187 C5
Stockbridge PO19 172 F4
Queen's Par BN3 166 E2
Queen's Park Cty Prim Sch BN2 188 C5
Queen's Park Rd BN2 188 C6
Queen's Park Rise BN2 188 C6
Queen's Park Terr BN2 188 C6
Queen's Pl Brighton BN1 207 A7
Hove BN3 187 C6
Shoreham-by-Sea BN43 184 F7
Queen's Rd Brighton BN1 207 F6
East Grinstead RH19 9 E1
Horley RH6 2 A3
Worthing BN11 182 C1
Queen's Sq PO21 195 D3
Queens Cres RH15 107 A2
Queens Dr BN6 126 F4
Queens Fields E PO21 194 F4
Queens Fields W PO21 194 F4
Queens Fields Wlk PO21 194 F4
Queens Gate RH6 6 A8
Queens La BN18 158 B2
Queens Rd
Haywards Heath RH16 85 E6
Lancing BN15 183 F5
Liphook GU30 24 C3
Southwick BN42 165 E1
Queens Sq RH10 18 D6
Queens St GU29 70 A2
Queensborough Ct 6 BN11 182 A3
Queensbury Mews BN1 187 E5
Queensdown Sch BN1 168 C3
Queensdown School Rd BN1, BN2 168 D2
Queensmead PO21 204 F8
Queensway Bognor Regis PO21 195 C3
Bognor Regis, Aldwick PO21 194 E1
Brighton BN2 188 D6
Crawley RH10 18 E6
East Grinstead RH19 9 E1
Horsham RH13 36 C1
Lancing BN15 183 E6
Queensway Ho 7 PO21 195 C3
Quell Farm Ind Est RH20 117 E4
Querneby Cl BN43 185 D7
Quest Cl PO19 173 B6

Racecourse Rd RH6 5 F8
Racecourse Way RH6 5 F8
Rackfield GU27 26 D7
Rackham Cl Crawley RH11 18 D4
Worthing BN13 181 F5
Rackham Rd Amberley BN18 138 F7
3 Littlehampton BN16 199 B3
Worthing BN13 181 F5
Rackham St Amberley BN18 139 A8
Rackham BN18, RH20 139 C8
Racton Rd PO10 149 C3
Radford Rd
Bognor Regis PO21, PO22 195 B5
Tinsley Green RH10, RH6 6 C4
Radinden Dr BN3 167 D1
Radinden Manor Rd BN3 187 D8
Radnor Cl BN13 181 F4
Radnor Rd BN13 181 F4
Raglan Ave BN13 181 E5
Raglan Ct Brighton BN1 207 F5
2 Worthing BN11 182 A2
Raglan Terr PO10 149 C1
Railey Rd RH10 18 E7
Railway App East Grinstead RH19 9 E1
Worthing BN11 182 D3
Railway Cotts Cinder Hill RH19 65 A8
Maplehurst RH13 80 E2
Railway St BN1 207 F6
Railway Terr GU29 92 D7
Rainbow Way RH20 119 F3
Rake Bsns Pk GU33 46 B4
Rake CE (C) Prim Sch GU33 46 B5
Rake Rd Liss GU33 45 D4
Milland GU30 47 A2
Rakers Ridge RH12 36 D5
Raleigh Cl BN43 184 F6
Raleigh Cres BN12 181 D3
Raleigh Ct RH10 6 A3
Raleigh Rd PO21 194 C3
Raleigh Way BN12 181 C3
Raleigh Wlk RH10 18 E4
Rambledown La RH20 119 C6
Ramblers Way RH11 39 B8
Ramillies Gdns PO22 196 C5
Ramsey Cl Horley RH6 1 F3
Horsham RH12 36 D5
Ramsey Ct 17 RH11 18 B1
Randall Schofield Ct RH10 19 A7
Randiddles Cl BN6 126 B4
Ranelagh Villas BN3 187 B8
Ranmore Cl RH11 39 C8
Ransome Cl RH11 17 E3
Ranville Cl GU28 95 E7
Ranworth Cl PO22 195 F5
Rapeland Hill RH12 15 F2
Raphael Rd BN3 186 F7
Rapley Ave RH20 119 B2
Rascals Cl RH13 79 F7
Rastrick Cl RH15 106 F1
Ratham La Broadbridge PO18 171 C8
West Ashling PO18 151 C1
Rathbone Ho RH11 18 B1
Rathlin Rd RH11 18 B3
Raughmere Ct PO18 152 F4
Raughmere Dr PO18, PO19 152 F4
Raven Cl RH12 36 E6
Raven La RH11 18 C8
Raven's Rd BN43 184 F7
Ravendene Ct 3 RH11 18 D5
Ravens Croft 7 BN16 199 C4
Ravens Way PO22 195 B6
Ravensbourne Ave BN43 164 F1
Ravensbourne Cl 11 BN43 164 F1
Ravenscroft RH20 140 D8
Ravenscroft Ct RH12 36 C3
Ravenswood BN6 126 E4
Ravenswood Ct BN13 182 A4
Ravenswood Rd RH15 107 B3
Ravenwood Ct PO21 194 E2
Raworth Cl RH10 19 C4
Rawson Villas BN16 199 C6
Raycroft Cl PO21 194 F2
Rayden Cl BN17 198 E5
Raymer Wlk RH6 2 C4
Rayner Ct BN5 123 E4
Reading Rd BN2 188 F4
Reapers Cl RH12 36 D5
Record Rd PO10 149 A1
Rectory Cl Ashington RH20 121 A5
Hove BN3 186 D7
Pulborough RH20 98 C2
Southwick BN43 185 D7
Storrington RH20 119 D1
Rectory Ct 15 BN43 185 C8
Rectory Farm Rd BN15 183 B7
Rectory Gdns BN14 182 C5
Rectory La Angmering BN16 179 F5
Bramshott GU30 25 D7
Charlwood RH6 4 D7
Church Norton PO20 204 B3
Crawley RH11 17 F8
Pulborough RH20 98 C2
Warminghurst RH20 120 E6
Rectory Rd Southwick BN43 185 D7
Storrington RH20 119 D1
Worthing BN13, BN14 182 A5
Rectory Wlk Lancing BN15 183 C7
Storrington RH20 119 D1
Red Admiral St RH12 36 E5
Red Deer Cl RH13 37 B4
Red House Ct GU31 68 B4
Red La RH13 79 D1
Red Lion St GU29 92 F7
Red Oak Ct GU29 71 A2
Red Ridges PO21 195 A2
Red River Ct RH12 36 B5
Redcotts 1 BN11 182 B2
Redditch Cl RH11 17 E2
Redehall Rd RH6 7 C8
Redford Ave RH12 36 B4
Redgarth Ct RH19 9 B3
Redgrave Dr RH10 19 D5
Redhill Cl BN1 167 C5
Redhill Distribution Ctr RH1 2 A8
Redhill Dr BN1 167 C5
Redhill Rd PO9 128 D1
Redhouse Mews GU30 25 C2
Redkiln Cl RH13 36 F4
Redkiln Way RH12, RH13 36 F3
Redlands La New Brighton PO10 149 B4
New Brighton PO10 149 C4
Shipton Green PO20 190 F3
Redmoor PO20 191 E4
Redshank Ct 5 RH11 17 D5
Redvers Rd BN2 168 D1
Redwing Cl Horsham RH13 36 F3
Littlehampton BN17 178 C4
Redwood Cl Crawley RH10 18 E8
Worthing BN13 181 C5
Redwood Ct BN17 198 F5
Redwood Dr RH16 85 D3
Redwood Manor GU27 27 C7
Redwood Pl PO21 194 E2
Reed Cl RH20 119 C1
Reed Pond Wlk RH16 86 A4
Reed's La BN6 125 B8
Reedings RH11 17 D4
Reeds La Liss Forest GU33 45 F6
Southwater Street RH13 58 B3
Reef Cl BN17 198 F4
Reeves Hill BN1 168 D5
Regal Dr 10 RH19 22 F8
Regency Ct BN13 182 A6
Regency Mews 16 BN1 187 E5
Regency Rd BN1 207 F5
Regency Sq BN1 187 E5
Regent Arc BN1 207 A5
Regent Bsns Pk RH15 106 E2
Regent Cl BN15 184 B6
Regent Hill BN1 207 F5
Regent Row BN1 207 F5
Regent St BN1 207 A5
Regents Cl RH11 18 C2
Regents Way PO21 194 F4
Regis Ave PO21 205 B8
Regis Ct Bognor Regis PO21 195 D3
Worthing BN11 182 A1
Reigate Cl RH10 6 D1
Reigate Ct BN11 181 F2
Reigate Rd Brighton BN1 167 D1
Hookwood RH6 1 C4
Worthing BN11 181 F3
Renoir Ct PO22 195 A6
Renoir Mews PO22 195 A6
Renton Cl RH14 77 D8
Rew La PO19 152 F3
Reynard Cl RH12 37 B5
Reynolds La BN18 156 D4
Reynolds Pl RH11 18 C7
Reynolds Rd Crawley RH11 18 C7
Hove BN3 186 F7
Rhodes Way RH10 18 F3
Ribbetts Ho BN6 126 A5
Ribbetts The BN6 126 A5
Rices Hill RH19 9 E1
Richard Allen Ct 2 BN2 168 C1
Richardson Ct 10 Crawley RH11 18 B1
5 Hove BN3 186 F7
Richardson Rd BN3 186 F7
Richmond Ave
Bognor Regis PO21 195 B2
Chichester PO19 153 A1
Richmond Ave W PO21 195 A3
Richmond Cl 1 BN16 199 E6
Richmond Ct 5 Hove BN3 187 E7
3 Rustington BN16 199 B5
Worthing BN11 182 C2
Richmond Hts 11 BN2 207 B6
Richmond Ho 11 PO21 195 C3
Richmond Par BN2 207 B6
Richmond Pl BN2 207 A6
Richmond Rd
16 Bognor Regis PO21 195 C3
Brighton BN2 188 B8
Horsham RH12 36 D4
Westerton PO18 153 F3
Worthing BN11 182 D2
Richmond Rd N 5 PO21 195 D4
Richmond Sq RH19 9 D2
Richmond St BN2 207 B6
Richmond Terr BN2 207 B7
Richmond Villas PO22 195 F3
Richmond Way RH19 22 F8
Rickfield RH11 18 A5
Rickman's La RH14 31 B2
Rickwood RH6 2 B4
Riddens The RH12 33 A6
Ride The Brighton BN1 167 F1
Ifold RH14 31 C2
Ridge Cl BN41 166 A4
Ridge View BN1 168 E5
Ridge Way RH16 86 B2
Ridgedale RH10 21 B8
Ridgehurst Dr RH12 35 F1
Ridgeside RH10 18 F6
Ridgeside Ave BN1 167 E5
Ridgeway East Grinstead RH19 22 E7
Shoreham-by-Sea BN41, BN42 165 F1
Ridgeway Cl BN42 165 F1
Ridgeway The
Burgess Hill RH15 107 B4
Chichester PO19 172 E7
Fernhurst GU27 49 B6
Horley RH6 2 A1
Horsham RH12 36 B4
Ridgway The PO22 196 B4
Ridings The Bognor Regis PO21 194 C1
Burgess Hill RH15 107 C2
Crawley RH10 19 D7
Liss GU33 45 D4
Littlehampton BN16 199 F4
Steyning BN44 143 D1
Ridleys RH19 42 E6
Rife La PO20 206 B8
Rife Way Bognor Regis PO22 195 F4
Ferring BN12 200 E6
Rifeside Gdns BN12 180 E3
Rigden Rd BN3 167 C1
Rikkyo Sch in England RH14 32 D8
Riley Rd BN2 168 C1
Rill Wlk RH19 10 B1
Rillside RH10 19 A3
Rimmer Cl RH11 39 B8
Ring Rd BN15 163 F1
Ring Rd N RH6 6 C8
Ring Rd S RH6 6 C7
Ringley Ave RH6 2 A2
Ringley Oak RH12 36 F4
Ringley Rd RH12 36 E4
Ringmer Cl BN1 168 E4
Ringmer Rd Brighton BN1 168 E4
Brighton BN1 168 F4
Worthing BN13 181 E5
Ringwood Cl RH10 18 E4
Ripley Rd BN11 181 F3
Ripon Gdns PO21 194 E3
Rise The Crawley RH10 19 D6
East Grinstead RH19 22 F8
Haywards Heath RH16 86 B5
Partridge Green RH13 103 A4
Portslade-by-Sea BN41 165 F2
Rissom Ct BN1 167 E2
River Cl BN43 184 E6
River La River GU28 72 E3
Watersfield RH20 117 B4
River Mead Crawley RH11 5 A1
Horsham RH12 36 B1
River Rd Arundel BN18 158 B2
Littlehampton BN17 198 C5
River St PO10 149 D4
River's Rd RH16 63 D3
Riverhill La GU28, RH20 96 E7
Rivermead RH20 98 D1
Rivermead Ct PO10 149 C3
Riverside Chichester PO19 173 B7
Forest Row RH18 23 E3
Horley RH6 2 A1
Horsham RH12 36 A2
Littlehampton BN17 198 C4
Shoreham-by-Sea BN43 184 F6
Southwick BN42 185 E7
Storrington RH20 119 D2
Upper Beeding BN44 144 A2
Riverside Bsns Ctr 11 BN43 184 F7
Riverside Cl GU33 45 B4
Riverside Ct RH20 98 A1
Riverside Ind Est BN17 198 B5
Riverside Rd BN43 184 F6
Rixons Cl RH17 65 C5
Rixons Orch RH17 65 C5
Robell Way RH20 119 F3
Robert Lodge BN2 188 F4
Robert May Cty Fst Sch The RH10 18 F4
Robert St BN1 207 A6
Robert Way RH12 36 F7

Roberts Cl RH13 .... 57 F4
Roberts Rd BN15 .... 183 E4
Robertson Rd BN1 .... 167 D1
Robin Cl Crawley RH11 .... 18 C8
  East Grinstead RH19 .... 9 F2
  Littlehampton BN17 .... 178 C4
  Southwater RH13 .... 58 A2
Robin Davis Cl BN2 .... 168 E1
Robin Dene BN2 .... 188 E4
Robin Hood La RH12 .... 35 F5
Robin Rd BN6 .... 106 D2
Robin's Cl PO20 .... 206 E8
Robinia Lodge 1 BN1 .... 167 E2
Robins Dr PO21 .... 194 D3
Robins La GU29 .... 69 D7
Robins Row RN41 .... 166 A1
Robinson Cl BN15 .... 183 E6
Robinson Rd RH11 .... 18 D5
Robinswood Ct RH12 .... 36 F4
Robson Rd BN11, BN12 .... 181 E2
Rochester Cl Chichester PO19 .. 152 F1
  2 Hove BN3 .... 187 D6
  Worthing BN13 .... 181 B5
Rochester Ct 8 BN3 .... 187 D6
Rochester Gdns BN3 .... 187 D6
Rochester St BN2 .... 188 D5
Rochester Way PO21 .... 194 E3
Rock Cl BN42 .... 185 E7
Rock Gdns PO21 .... 195 C2
Rock Gr BN2 .... 188 E4
Rock La RH20 .... 120 E1
Rock Pl BN2 .... 207 B4
Rock Rd RH20 .... 120 C2
Rock St BN2 .... 188 E4
Rockall Cl BN16 .... 179 A3
Rockingham Cl BN13 .... 181 E6
Rockpit Cotts GU33 .... 45 D4
Rocks La RH17 .... 40 F1
Rocks The RH19 .... 23 D6
Rocky La RH16, RH15 .... 85 D1
Rodgate La GU8 .... 28 E5
Rodmell Pl BN1 .... 168 A6
Rodmell Rd BN13 .... 181 E5
Rodney Cl PO21 .... 194 C3
Rodney Cres BN18 .... 177 D4
Roebuck Cl RH13 .... 37 B4
Roedale Rd BN1 .... 168 B1
Roedean Ct BN2 .... 188 F4
Roedean Rd Brighton BN2 .... 188 F4
  Worthing BN13 .... 181 E6
Roedeer Copse GU27 .... 26 E6
Roffey Cl RH6 .... 1 F3
Roffey Cnr RH12 .... 37 B4
Roffey Ct RH13 .... 37 A4
Roffey's Cl RH10 .... 7 A4
Rogate CE (C) Prim Sch GU31 .. 68 D4
Rogate Cl Lancing BN15 .... 183 B7
  Worthing BN13 .... 182 A6
Rogate Rd BN13 .... 182 A6
Roger's La RN14 .... 161 E4
Rolfe Dr RH15 .... 107 D3
Rollaston Pk BN18 .... 177 C2
Romaine Cl RH15 .... 107 D5
Roman Acre BN17 .... 198 C6
Roman Cres BN42 .... 185 E8
Roman Landing PO20 .... 190 B2
Roman Rd Bramber BN44 .... 143 E3
  Hove BN3 .... 186 D6
  Southwick BN42 .... 185 E8
Roman Way Billingshurst RH14 ... 55 D1
  Fishbourne PO19 .... 172 B6
  Southwick BN42 .... 185 E8
Roman Wlk BN15 .... 183 B7
Romany Cl RN41 .... 186 B8
Romany Rd BN13 .... 181 B5
Romney Broadwalk PO22 .... 195 B6
Romney Ct RH11 .... 181 F1
Romney Garth PO20 .... 206 F7
Romney Rd BN11 .... 181 F1
Romsey Cl BN1 .... 168 C2
Rona Cl RH11 .... 18 B3
Rook Way RH12 .... 36 F6
Rookcross La RH13 .... 102 A4
Rookery La PO20 .... 203 F8
Rookery The Lumley PO10 .... 149 C1
  Selsey PO20 .... 206 F8
Rookery Way RH16 .... 85 E1
Rookwood La PO20 .... 190 D4
Rookwood Pk RH12 .... 35 F3
Rookwood Rd PO20 .... 190 C2
Rope Wlk Littlehampton BN17 .. 198 C4
  Shoreham-by-Sea BN43 .... 184 E7
Ropeland Way RH12 .... 36 E7
Ropes La GU27 .... 49 C5
Ropetackle BN43 .... 184 E7
Rosamund Rd RH10 .... 19 B3
Rosary Ct RH15 .... 107 B2
Rose Ave PO22 .... 196 F5
Rose Cottage La RH17 .... 62 A3
Rose Cotts RH14 .... 66 A4
Rose Ct Bognor Regis PO21 .... 194 D3
  Chichester PO19 .... 173 A7
  Hassocks BN6 .... 126 E4
  7 Littlehampton BN17 .... 198 D5
Rose Green Cty Inf Sch PO21 194 C2
Rose Green Cty Jun Sch
  PO21 .... 194 C3
Rose Green Rd PO21 .... 194 C3
Rose Hill BN2 .... 207 B7
Rose Hill Cl BN1, BN2 .... 207 A7
Rose Hill Ct BN1 .... 207 A7
Rose Hill Terr BN1 .... 207 A7
Rose Wlk BN11, BN12 .... 181 E1
Rosebarn Cl RH15 .... 107 C1
Rosebery Ave BN12 .... 181 E2
Rosecroft Cl BN15 .... 183 E5
Rosedale Ct RH11 .... 18 A4
Rosehill RH14 .... 55 D1

Roseleigh Gdns RH17 .... 86 F3
Rosemary Ave RN44 .... 143 E3
Rosemary Cl Bramber BN44 .... 143 E3
  Haywards Heath RH17 .... 85 B6
  Petworth GU28 .... 95 F8
  Storrington RH20 .... 119 D1
Rosemary Ct Haslemere GU27 ... 27 C7
  Horley RH6 .... 1 E4
Rosemary Cl BN16 .... 165 C1
Rosemary La Charlwood RH6 .... 4 E7
  Horley RH6 .... 2 B3
  Petworth GU28 .... 95 F8
Rosewood RH10 .... 21 A8
Rosier Commercial Ctr RH14 .. 77 F7
Rosier Way RH14 .... 77 E6
Roslan Ct RH6 .... 2 B2
Ross Cl Bognor Regis PO21 .... 194 B2
  Crawley RH10 .... 18 F3
Rossalyn Cl PO21 .... 194 B3
Rossiter Rd BN15 .... 183 E8
Rosslyn Ave BN43 .... 185 A7
Rosslyn Cl BN43 .... 184 F7
Rosslyn Rd BN43 .... 184 F7
Rossmore Ct RH10 .... 6 D2
Rostock Cl PO20 .... 202 B6
Rotary Ho BN15 .... 183 E4
Rotary Lodge BN16 .... 168 E6
Rotary Point BN41 .... 166 B1
Rothbury Rd BN3 .... 186 D7
Rother Cl RH20 .... 119 F3
Rother Cres RH11 .... 17 F5
Rother Ho GU33 .... 45 B3
Rother La GU33 .... 69 A1
Rotherbank Farm La GU33 .. 45 C6
Rotherbridge La GU28 .... 95 E5
Rotherfield Cl RH11 .... 168 B6
Rotherfield Cres BN1 .... 168 B5
Rothermead GU28 .... 95 E7
Rothervale RH6 .... 1 F5
Rothesay Cl BN13 .... 181 E4
Rothley Chase RH16 .... 85 F4
Rotten Row PO20 .... 192 E3
Rough Field RH19 .... 9 D4
Rough Way RH12 .... 36 F5
Round Hill Rd 2 BN1, BN2 .... 188 B8
Round Hill St 3 BN2 .... 188 B8
Round Piece PO20 .... 206 C8
Round Piece La PO20 .... 206 B8
Roundabout Copse RH20 .. 119 D5
Roundabout Cotts 33 C5
Roundabout La RH20 .... 119 D6
Roundhill Cres BN2 .... 188 B8
Roundhouse Meadow PO10 .. 169 C7
Roundle Ave PO22 .... 196 C6
Roundle Rd PO22 .... 196 C5
Roundle Sq PO22 .... 196 B5
Roundle Square Rd PO22 196 B5
Roundstone By-Pass Rd
  BN16 .... 180 A3
Roundstone Cres BN16 .... 200 A6
Roundstone Dr BN16 .... 200 A6
Roundstone La BN16 .... 180 A4
Roundstone Way PO20 .... 206 F8
Roundway BN1 .... 168 E5
Roundway Ct RH11 .... 18 D8
Roundway The BN16 .... 199 D4
Roundwood La RH16 .... 85 F8
Row Hill La RH17 .... 62 E7
Rowan Ave BN3 .... 166 E1
Rowan Cl Crawley RH10 .... 18 F6
  Haywards Heath RH16 .... 86 B4
  Horsham RH12 .... 37 B5
  Portslade-by-Sea BN41 .... 166 A1
  Storrington RH20 .... 119 F2
Rowan Ct RH14 .... 55 D1
Rowan Dr RH14 .... 55 C1
Rowan Ho BN12 .... 181 A4
Rowan Tree Cl GU33 .... 45 C4
Rowan Way Bognor Regis PO22 195 C2
  Horsham RH12 .... 37 C5
Rowena Ho RH11 .... 5 D7
Rowens The BN11 .... 182 A2
Rowfant Bsns Ctr RH10 .... 20 E6
Rowhook Hill RH12 .... 34 F8
Rowhook Rd Rowhook RH12 .... 13 E1
  Slinfold RH12 .... 35 A8
Rowland Cl RH10 .... 7 E5
Rowlands Castle Rd PO8 .. 128 B6
Rowlands Castle Sta PO9 .. 128 C2
Rowlands Rd Horsham RH12 .. 37 A6
  Worthing BN11 .... 182 B1
Rowner Rd RH14 .... 55 A2
Rowplatt La RH19 .... 8 E4
Roxburgh Cl BN13 .... 181 F7
Royal Alexandra Hospl for
  Sick Children The BN1 207 F6
Royal Ashdown Forest
  Golf Course RH18 .... 44 F8
Royal Bldgs BN15 .... 183 C4
Royal Cl PO19 .... 173 C6
Royal Cres BN2 .... 188 C4
Royal Crescent Mansions 10
  BN2 .... 188 C4
Royal Crescent Mews 8 BN2 188 C4
Royal Gdns PO9 .... 128 C5
Royal George Par BN43 .... 165 C4
Royal George Rd RH15 .... 106 E3
Royal Oak Cotts BN45 .... 146 C5
Royal Oak Ho RH10 .... 21 B7
Royal Par PO21 .... 195 A6
Royal Pavilion BN1 .... 207 A5
Royal Sussex Cty Hospl
  (General) BN2 .... 188 D4
Royal West Sussex Hospl
  PO19 .... 172 F8
Royce Cl PO20 .... 190 C1
Royce Rd PO20 .... 6 A3
Royce Way PO20 .... 190 C1

Royston Cl RH10 .... 6 A2
Roystons The BN16 .... 199 F4
Ruckmans La RH5 .... 14 B7
Rucrofts Cl PO21 .... 194 F3
Rudford Ind Est BN18 .... 177 D2
Rudgwick Ave BN12 .... 181 A2
Rudgwick Cl BN16 .... 199 B4
Rudgwick Cty Prim Sch RH12 .. 33 D7
Rudgwick Rd RH11 .... 17 F7
Rudwick Way PO22 .... 196 C4
Rudwick's Cl PO22 .... 196 C4
Rufwood RH10 .... 21 A8
Rugby Ct 5 Brighton BN2 .... 188 E4
  3 Worthing BN11 .... 182 A3
Rugby Pl BN2 .... 188 E4
Rugby Rd Brighton BN1 .... 168 A1
  Worthing BN11 .... 182 A3
Ruislip Gdns PO21 .... 194 C2
Rumbolds Cl PO19 .... 173 C5
Rumbolds Hill GU29 .... 92 F7
Rumbolds La RH11 .... 5 B1
Rumboldswyke CE (C)
  Prim Sch PO19 .... 173 C5
Runcorn Cl RH11 .... 17 E2
Runcton La PO20 .... 193 E7
Runnymede Ct PO21 .... 194 F5
Runshooke Ct 9 RH11 .... 18 A3
Rusbridge Cl PO21 .... 194 D4
Rushams Rd RH12 .... 36 B3
Rushes The RH16 .... 86 C4
Rushetts Pl RH11 .... 5 C1
Rushetts Rd RH11 .... 5 B1
Rushfield Rd GU33 .... 45 B3
Rushlake Cl BN1 .... 168 E5
Rushlake Rd BN1 .... 168 E5
Rushwood Cl RH16 .... 86 B4
Ruskin Cl Crawley RH10 .... 6 C1
  Selsey PO20 .... 206 F7
Ruskin Rd Hove BN3 .... 186 F8
  Worthing BN14 .... 182 F4
Rusper Cty Prim Sch RH12 ... 16 C7
Rusper Rd Brighton BN1 .... 168 D6
  Crawley RH11, RH12 .... 17 D7
  Crawley RH11 .... 17 E6
  Faygate RH12 .... 16 A1
  Horsham RH12 .... 36 F6
  Newdigate RH12, RH5 .... 3 C4
  Rusper RH5 .... 15 E8
  Worthing BN13 .... 181 E5
Rusper Rd S BN13 .... 181 F5
Ruspers RH15 .... 107 D2
Ruspers Keep RH11 .... 17 F7
Russ Hill RH5, RH6 .... 4 C5
Russell Cl BN14 .... 182 E5
Russell Cres BN1, BN3, BN2 207 F7
Russell Ct 4 BN15 .... 183 E5
Russell Mews 17 BN1 .... 187 E5
Russell Pl
  7 Bognor Regis PO21 .. 195 D3
  Brighton BN1 .... 207 F5
Russell Rd Brighton BN1 .... 207 F5
  East Wittering PO20 .... 201 E7
Russell Sq BN1 .... 207 F5
Russell St PO19 .... 173 C6
Russell Way RH10 .... 19 A5
Russell's Cl BN16 .... 200 B6
Russells Cres RH6 .... 2 A2
Russells Dr BN15 .... 183 E5
Russet Cl RH6 .... 2 C3
Russet Ct GU27 .... 49 B5
Rustington Cty Prim Sch
  BN16 .... 199 B6
Rustington Rd BN1 .... 168 A5
Rustington Trad Est BN16 .... 199 F7
Rustlings Ct RH16 .... 86 B5
Ruston Ave BN16 .... 199 D5
Ruston Cl RH10 .... 19 C3
Ruston Pk BN16 .... 199 E5
Rutherford Way RH10 .... 6 A3
Rutherwick Cl RH6 .... 1 F3
Rutland Cl BN3 .... 186 F6
Rutland Gdns BN3 .... 186 F7
Rutland Rd BN3 .... 187 A7
Rutland Way PO18, PO20 .. 173 D8
Rycroft Cl BN12 .... 181 C1
Rydal Cl Crawley RH11 .... 17 D4
  Littlehampton BN16 .... 179 A3
Ryde Ct BN3 .... 166 D1
Ryde Rd BN2 .... 188 D7
Ryders Way RH12 .... 36 F7
Rydon Com Sch The RH20 .. 120 A2
Rye Ash RH10 .... 19 A7
Rye Cl BN11 .... 182 A1
Rye Farm La RH13 .... 57 A2
Ryecroft 5 Brighton BN2 .... 188 F5
  Haywards Heath RH16 .... 85 E3
Ryecroft Dr RH12 .... 36 A3
Ryecroft Gdns BN12 .... 181 C2
Ryecroft La RH20 .... 119 D1
Ryecroft Meadow RH13 .... 59 C3
Ryecroft Rd RH17 .... 83 C3
Ryelands Crawley RH11 .... 18 A5
  Horley RH6 .... 2 C4
Ryelands Dr BN2 .... 168 D3

Sabre Rd PO10 .... 169 C3
Sack La PO22 .... 175 E2
Sackville Rd RH19 .... 9 C3
Sackville Coll RH19 .... 9 F1
Sackville Cres BN14 .... 182 E5
Sackville Ct 3 RH19 .... 22 F8
Sackville Gdns
  East Grinstead RH19 .... 9 C3
  Hove BN3 .... 186 F6
Sackville La RH19 .... 9 C3
Sackville Rd Hove BN3 .... 187 A7
  Worthing BN14 .... 182 A4
Sackville Sch RH19 .... 10 A1

Sackville Trad Est BN3 .... 187 B8
Sackville Way BN14 .... 182 E4
Saddle La PO20 .... 206 D8
Saddler Row RH10 .... 18 D3
Saddler's Row GU28 .... 95 F8
Saddlers Cl RH15 .... 107 D1
Sadler St PO21 .... 195 C2
Sadler Way BN2 .... 188 F6
Sadlers Wlk
  4 Chichester PO19 .... 173 A6
  Lumley PO10 .... 169 C8
Saffron Cl Crawley RH11 .... 18 A3
  Shoreham-by-Sea BN43 .... 165 C1
Saffron Ct BN3 .... 182 A3
Saffrons The RH15 .... 106 F5
Saint Hill Rd RH19 .... 22 C5
St Agnes Rd RH19 .... 9 E2
St Andrew's CE (A) Prim Sch
  BN3 .... 187 B6
St Andrew's CE Boys High Sch
  BN14 .... 182 E4
St Andrew's CE (C) Prim Sch
  BN44 .... 143 D4
St Andrew's CE Fst & Mid Sch
  RH10 .... 19 A4
St Andrew's Cl Ferring BN12 .. 200 E6
  Oving PO20 .... 174 C6
St Andrew's Gdns BN13 .... 182 A4
St Andrew's Prim Sch (CE)
  RH13 .... 59 A1
St Andrew's Rd Brighton BN1 .. 168 A1
  Portslade-by-Sea BN41 .... 186 C7
  Worthing BN13 .... 181 F4
St Andrews Rd
  Burgess Hill RH15 .... 107 D3
  Crawley RH11 .... 17 D5
St Ann's Ct 12 BN3 .... 187 D7
St Ann's Hill GU29 .... 92 F7
St Anne's Ct 3 Brighton BN2 .. 188 C4
  6 Brighton BN1 .... 207 F7
  East Wittering PO20 .... 201 F7
St Anne's Gdns BN6 .... 127 A3
St Anne's Ho 7 BN1 .... 207 F7
St Anne's Rd RH10 .... 6 C2
St Annes Well Ho 7 BN3 .. 187 D6
St Anselm's Rd BN14 .... 182 B4
St Anthony's Sch PO19 .... 172 F8
St Anthony's Cl 1 BN16 .... 199 D6
St Anthony's Wlk PO21 .... 194 D3
St Aubin Cl RH11 .... 17 F2
St Aubins Cl BN12 .... 200 F4
St Aubins Rd BN12 .... 200 F4
St Aubyn's Cres BN41 .... 186 B7
St Aubyn's Rd
  Portslade-by-Sea BN41 .... 186 C7
  Southwick BN41 .... 186 A7
St Aubyns BN3 .... 187 B6
St Aubyns S BN3 .... 187 A5
St Augustine Cl RH17 .... 86 F3
St Augustine Rd 12 BN17 .. 198 E4
St Barnabas Ct RH10 .... 19 C7
St Bartholomew CE Prim Sch
  GU27 .... 27 C7
St Bartholomew's CE Prim Sch
  BN1 .... 207 A7
St Bartholomews Cl PO19 ...... 172 E4
St Bernadette's RC Prim Sch
  BN1 .... 167 E2
St Bernards Ct BN15 .... 183 E5
St Blaises Rd PO18 .... 154 C4
St Botolph's Rd BN11 .... 182 B3
St Botolphs Ct 2 BN11 .... 182 B3
St Brelades Rd RH11 .... 17 F2
St Catherine's RC (A) Prim Sch
  BN17 .... 198 D6
St Catherine's Ct BN17 .... 198 D4
St Catherines Ct BN17 .... 198 D4
St Catherines Rd RH10 .... 6 D1
St Christopher's Cl
  Fishbourne PO19 .... 172 C6
  Haslemere GU27 .... 27 A6
St Christopher's Gn GU27 .. 27 A6
St Christopher's Rd
  Haslemere GU27 .... 27 A6
  Hurstpierpoint BN6 .... 126 A6
St Christopher's Sch BN3 .. 187 A6
St Christophers RH12 .... 36 D4
St Christophers Day Hospl
  RH12 .... 36 D3
St Clement Rd RH11 .... 17 F2
St Cuthman's Rd BN44 .... 143 D4
St Cuthman's Sch GU29 .... 70 A6
St Cuthmans Ct BN2 .... 188 F6
St Cyriacs PO19 .... 173 A7
St David's Gate 4 BN15 .... 183 D6
St Dunstan's Rd BN13, BN14 .. 182 A3
St Edmund Cl RH11 .... 5 D1
St Edmund's Rd RH16 .... 85 F3
St Edward's Cl RH19 .... 9 C1
St Elmo Rd BN14 .... 182 B4
St Flora's Rd BN17 .... 198 F5
St Francis Cl RH16 .... 85 F2
St Francis of Assisi RC (A)
  Prim Sch RH10 .... 18 E4
St Francis Wlk RH11 .... 17 E4
St Gabriels Rd BN14 .... 77 E8
St George's Cl PO20 .... 206 E8
St George's Dr PO19 .... 172 C5
St George's Gdns
  Horsham RH13 .... 36 C4
  2 Worthing BN11 .... 182 F2
St George's La BN6 .... 126 D5
St George's Mews BN1 .... 207 A6
St George's Pl Brighton BN1 .. 207 A6
  Hurstpierpoint BN6 .... 126 D5
St George's Rd Brighton BN2 .. 188 D4
  Worthing BN11 .... 182 F2
St George's Terr 5 BN2 .... 188 C4

St Georges Cl RH6 .... 2 B3
St Georges Ct Crawley RH11 .. 18 D8
  East Grinstead RH19 .... 9 C3
St Georges Rd RH13 .... 103 A3
St Georges Wlk PO20 .... 175 F7
St Giles CE Prim Sch RH17 ...... 65 C6
St Giles BN43 .... 185 B8
St Helen's Cres BN3 .... 166 D3
St Helen's Dr BN3 .... 166 D3
St Helen's Rd BN2 .... 188 D7
St Helier Cl RH11 .... 18 A2
St Helier Ct BN12 .... 200 F4
St Helier Rd BN2 .... 200 F4
St Heliers Ave BN3 .... 186 E7
St Hilda's Cl Crawley RH10 .... 6 C1
  Horley RH6 .... 2 B3
  Selsey PO20 .... 206 E6
St Hugh's Cl RH10 .... 6 C1
St Itha Cl PO20 .... 206 E7
St Itha Rd PO20 .... 206 E6
St Ives RH10 .... 19 C7
St Ives Sch GU27 .... 27 E8
St James Ave BN15 .... 183 E8
St James CE Prim Sch PO10 .. 149 B2
St James Ct PO19 .... 173 B7
St James Wlk RH11 .... 18 C2
St James' CE (C) Prim Sch
  RH20 .... 117 C6
St James' Cty Prim Sch PO19 173 C7
St James' Ho 13 BN2 .... 207 B5
St James' Ind Est PO19 .... 173 C7
St James' Rd Chichester PO19 .. 173 C7
  Emsworth PO10 .... 149 B1
St James's Ave BN2 .... 207 B5
St James's Cl PO20 .... 191 E5
St James's Rd RH19 .... 9 D1
St James's Sq PO19 .... 173 C7
St James's St BN2 .... 207 B5
St James's Street Mews BN2 . 207 B5
St Joan Cl RH11 .... 5 D1
St John Baptist (A) Prim Sch
  BN14 .... 161 E6
St John Cl RH13 .... 36 E1
St John the Baptist RC (A)
  Prim Sch BN2 .... 188 D5
St John's Ave
  Burgess Hill RH15 .... 106 F4
  Worthing BN11 .... 181 D1
St John's Cl Bognor Regis PO21 194 E4
  East Grinstead RH19 .... 9 E2
  Midhurst GU29 .... 92 E7
  Worthing BN11 .... 181 D1
St John's Cres RH12 .... 35 E3
St John's Ct BN15 .... 183 D6
St John's Mews Cotts 7
  BN43 .... 184 E7
St John's Mount 8 BN2 .... 207 B5
St John's Pl Brighton BN2 .... 207 B5
  10 Hove BN3 .... 187 C6
St John's RC Prim Sch RH12 .. 36 A1
St John's Rd Breach PO10 .... 149 F1
  Crawley RH11 .... 18 C6
  East Grinstead RH19 .... 9 E2
  Haywards Heath RH16 .... 85 E2
  Hove BN3 .... 187 C5
St John's Sch BN2 .... 188 D5
St Johns Cl PO20 .... 175 D5
St Johns Ct RH15 .... 107 A3
St Johns Rd RH15 .... 107 A3
St Joseph's Cl BN2 .... 187 A8
St Joseph's Dominican Sch
  RH20 .... 140 C8
St Joseph's RC (A) Cty Prim Sch
  BN2 .... 168 C1
St Joseph's RC (A) Prim Sch
  RH16 .... 85 E4
St Josephs Trad Est BN3 .... 187 B8
St Josephs Way RH16 .... 85 E4
St Julian's La BN43 .... 185 D7
St Julians Cl BN43 .... 185 C7
St Keyna Ave BN3, BN41 .... 186 D6
St Lawrence Ave BN14 .... 182 B4
St Lawrence CE (A) Prim Sch
  BN6 .... 126 A6
St Lawrence Way BN6 .... 126 A7
St Leodegar's Way RH13 .... 173 A1
St Leonard's Ave BN3, BN41 .. 186 C7
St Leonard's Gdns BN3, BN41 186 D7
St Leonard's Rd
  5 Brighton BN2 .... 188 C8
  Hove BN3, BN41 .... 186 C7
St Leonards Cty Inf Sch RH13 .. 36 E2
St Leonards Dr RH10 .... 19 A4
St Leonards Pk RH19 .... 9 E1
St Leonards Rd RH13 .... 37 A1
St Louie Cl BN42 .... 186 A8
St Luke's Cl BN11 .... 183 B4
St Luke's Cty Inf Sch BN2 .... 188 C6
St Luke's Cty Jun Sch BN2 .. 188 C6
St Luke's Rd BN2 .... 188 C6
St Luke's Terr BN2 .... 188 C6
St Lukes Ct RH15 .... 107 A3
St Mald Ct BN12 .... 200 F4
St Malo Cl BN12 .... 200 F4
St Margaret CE Prim Sch
  BN6 .... 127 D3
St Margaret's Ave RH19 .... 9 F6
St Margaret's CE (A) Prim Sch
  Angmering BN16 .... 179 F7
  Crawley RH11 .... 18 B7
St Margaret's Cotts GU27 .... 49 B6
St Margaret's Pl BN1 .... 207 F5
St Margaret's Rd RH19 .... 9 F3

St Margaret's Sch GU29 .... 92 E8
St Margarets Ct RH12 .... 35 F7
St Mark's CE (C) Prim Sch
RH17 .... 61 F5
St Mark's CE Prim Sch BN2 .. 188 C5
St Mark's Cres BN11 .... 183 B4
St Mark's La RH12 .... 36 E6
St Mark's St BN1 .... 188 E4
St Martin's Flats **6** BN2 ...... 188 C7
St Martin's La **3** BN17 .... 198 D5
St Martin's Pl BN2 .... 188 C7
St Martin's Sq PO19 .... 173 A7
St Martin's St Brighton BN2 .... 207 B8
Chichester PO19 .... 173 A6
St Martins CE Prim Sch BN2 .. 188 C8
St Martins Rd BN17 .... 198 D5
St Mary Magdalen RC
Prim Sch BN1 .... 187 E5
St Mary Magdalene St BN2 .. 207 B8
St Mary & St Paul CE (C)
Fst Sch GU31 .... 89 D3
St Mary's CE (A) Prim Sch
Climping RH17 .... 197 E8
East Grinstead RH19 .... 9 D2
Pulborough RH20 .... 98 C3
St Mary's CE Fst Sch BN12 .. 181 C2
St Mary's CE Prim Sch RH20 . 141 D6
St Mary's Cl Billingshurst RH14 .. 77 D8
Littlehampton BN17 .... 198 E5
Mid Lavant PO18 .... 152 E7
Pulborough RH20 .... 98 C2
Shoreham-by-Sea BN43 .... 184 F7
St Mary's Ct Bramber BN44 .. 143 F2
Worthing BN13 .... 181 D6
St Mary's Dr Crawley RH10 .... 19 B8
Rustington RH16 .... 199 F5
St Mary's Gdns Horsham RH12 .. 36 C1
1 Littlehampton BN17 .... 198 E5
St Mary's Ho RH12 .... 36 C1
St Mary's House BN44 .... 143 F2
St Mary's Lodge **1** PO19 .... 173 A6
St Mary's Pl BN2 .... 207 B5
St Mary's RC (A) Prim Sch
PO21 .... 195 D3
St Mary's RC Prim Sch
Portslade-by-Sea BN41 .... 186 B7
Worthing BN11 .... 182 C2
St Mary's Rd Boxgrove PO18 .. 154 C4
Burgess Hill RH15 .... 106 F4
Liss GU33 .... 45 B4
Shoreham-by-Sea BN43 .... 184 F7
St Mary's Rd W RH15 .... 106 E4
St Mary's Sch RH12 .... 36 C1
St Mary's Sq **17** BN2 .... 188 D4
St Mary's Terr **6** BN43 .... 184 E7
St Mary's Way BN17 .... 198 E5
St Marys Cl Bognor Regis PO22 . 195 D5
Lancing BN15 .... 183 B7
St Marys Meadow BN18 .... 176 F4
St Marys Pl **3** BN43 .... 185 A6
St Matthew's Rd BN11 .... 182 C3
St Matthews Ct BN2 .... 188 C5
St Maur's Rd BN12 .... 200 E6
St Michael's St BN11 .... 182 B2
St Michael's Pl BN1 .... 187 E6
St Michael's Rd
Portslade-by-Sea BN41 .... 186 B7
Worthing BN11 .... 182 B2
St Michaels Cl GU28 .... 51 A7
St Michaels Rd RH19 .... 9 E2
St Michaels Way RH13 .... 103 A3
St Nicholas' CE Jun Sch
BN41 .... 186 B8
St Nicholas Ct Crawley RH10 .. 19 C7
Haywards Heath RH16 .... 86 A6
Middleton-on-Sea PO22 .... 196 E5
St Nicholas' Ct **3** BN15 .... 183 D6
St Nicholas' La PO22 .... 196 F5
St Nicholas Lodge BN1 .... 207 F5
St Nicholas Pl **2** BN43 ...... 185 A6
St Nicholas Rd Brighton BN1 . 207 F6
Mid Lavant PO18 .... 152 E6
Portslade-by-Sea BN41 .... 186 B7
St Nicolas Ct BN43 .... 184 D8
St Nicolas La BN43 .... 184 D8
St Nicolas & St Mary CE (A)
Prim Sch BN43 .... 185 A8
St Osmund Rd BN12 .... 200 E6
St Pancras PO19 .... 173 B7
St Pancras St PO19 .... 173 B6
St Patrick's La GU33 .... 45 F5
St Patrick's Rd BN3 .... 187 A7
St Paul's Ave BN11, BN15 ..... 183 B4
St Paul's CE Prim Sch BN1 ... 207 F6
St Paul's Cl RH16 .... 85 F5
St Paul's Gdns PO19 .... 172 F7
St Paul's RC (A) Sec Sch RH16 . 85 F5
St Paul's Rd PO19 .... 172 F8
St Paul's St BN2 .... 207 B8
St Peter's PO19 .... 173 A7
St Peter's CE (A) Prim Sch
Cowfold RH13 .... 81 E2
Henfield BN5 .... 123 D5
St Peter's CE (C) Prim Sch
RH17 .... 64 A8
St Peter's Cl Cowfold RH13 .... 81 E1
Hove BN3 .... 166 F2
St Peter's Cres PO20 .... 206 E8
St Peter's Cty Inf Sch BN41 .. 186 B7
St Peter's Gn BN44 .... 144 A2
St Peter's Pl Brighton BN1, BN2 .. 207 B8
Lancing BN15 .... 183 C4
St Peter's RC (A) Prim Sch
East Grinstead RH19 .... 9 C1
Shoreham-by-Sea BN43 .... 185 A8

St Peter's Rd Crawley RH11 ...... 18 C6
Portslade-by-Sea BN41 .... 186 B7
St Peter's Sch RH15 .... 107 A4
St Peter's Sq **7** PO10 .... 169 B8
St Peter's St BN1 .... 207 A7
St Peters Cl PO21 .... 194 E4
St Peters Ct **1** PO10 .... 169 C8
St Peters Rd RH15 .... 107 A4
St Peters View BN5 .... 123 E6
St Philip Howard
High Sch The PO22 .... 176 A6
St. Philip's RC (A) Prim Sch
BN18 .... 158 A3
St Philips Mews **3** BN3 .... 186 F7
St Raphael's Rd BN11 .... 181 F2
St Richard's Cotts GU31 .... 90 A4
St Richard's Ct BN3 .... 166 D1
St Richard's Dr PO21 .... 194 D3
St Richard's Flats BN41 .... 186 B7
St Richard's Hospl PO19 ...... 173 B8
St Richard's Mews PO19 .... 18 F6
St Richard's RC Prim Sch
PO19 .... 173 A5
St Richard's Rd BN41 .... 186 B7
St Richard's Wlk PO19 .... 194 D3
St Richards GU29 .... 92 D8
St Richards Cotts
Codmore Hill RH20 .... 98 D6
Lower Fittleworth RH20 .... 97 A2
St Richards Rd PO20 .... 175 E7
St Robert Southwell RC
Prim Sch BN1 .... 37 A6
St Robert's Lodge **1** BN15 . 183 E5
St Roche's Cl PO18 .... 152 F7
St Sampson Rd RH11 .... 17 F2
St Saviours Ct BN1 .... 188 B8
St Stephen's Cl GU27 .... 26 F6
St Stephens Cl GU27 .... 27 C7
St Swithun's Ct RH19 .... 9 F1
St Thomas Ct PO21 .... 205 A8
St Thomas Dr PO21 .... 204 F8
St Thomas's Rd BN14 .... 182 B4
St Valerie Rd BN1 .... 182 A1
St Vincent Cl RH10 .... 19 D5
St Wilfred's Ct **5** RH16 ..... 85 E4
St Wilfred's Rd BN14 .... 182 A4
St Wilfreds Cl PO20 .... 206 G8
St Wilfreds Rd RH15 .... 107 B4
St Wilfrid Rd PO19 .... 172 D7
St Wilfrid's CE (A) Prim Sch
RH16 .... 85 E4
St Wilfrid's RC (A) Prim Sch
Angmering BN16 .... 179 F6
Crawley RH11 .... 18 B5
St Wilfrid's Way RH16 .... 85 E4
St Wilfrids RC (A) Prim Sch
RH15 .... 106 F2
St Wilfrids View PO20 .... 206 C6
St Winefride's Rd BN17 .... 198 E4
St Winifred's Cl PO21 .... 195 B2
Sake Ride La BN5 .... 104 C1
Salbrook Rd RH1 .... 2 A8
Salehurst Rd RH10 .... 19 E6
Salisbury Rd Crawley RH10 .... 18 F2
Hove BN3 .... 187 C6
Tower Hill RH12, RH13 .... 58 A8
Worthing BN11 .... 182 D2
Salisbury Way PO19 .... 152 F1
Salt Box Cl RH13 .... 56 F2
Saltdean Cl RH10, RH11 .... 18 D3
Salterns Rd RH10 .... 19 C3
Saltham La PO20 .... 173 E1
Salthill La PO19 .... 172 C8
Salthill Rd PO19 .... 172 B7
Saltings The Birdham PO20 ... 191 E4
Lancing BN15 .... 183 F5
Littlehampton BN16 .... 199 A6
Shoreham-by-Sea BN43 .... 184 D6
Saltings Way BN44 .... 144 A2
Salvington Ct BN13 .... 181 D7
Salvington Ct BN13 .... 161 F2
Salvington Gdns BN13 .... 181 F6
Salvington Hill BN13 .... 161 E1
Salvington Rd Crawley RH11 .. 17 F3
Worthing BN13 .... 181 E7
Samaritan Cl RH11 .... 17 E4
Samphire Cl RH11 .... 18 A3
Samphire Dr BN13 .... 181 A5
Sampsons Dr PO20 .... 174 C7
San Feliu Ct RH19 .... 10 B2
Sanctuary La RH20 .... 120 C1
Sandbrook BN6 .... 126 F3
Sandcroft PO20 .... 175 D7
Sandeman Way RH13 .... 58 F8
Sanders Ho BN3 .... 186 E8
Sanderstead **1** BN2 .... 188 F5
Sandfield Ave BN17 .... 178 D4
Sandgate La RH20 .... 120 A2
Sandgate Rd BN1 .... 168 A2
Sandhawes Hill RH19 .... 10 A4
Sandhill La Crawley Down RH10 .. 21 B7
Washington RH20 .... 141 E7
Sandhills Rd RH13 .... 56 F3
Sandhurst Sch BN11 .... 182 F2
Sandown Ave BN12 .... 181 C1
Sandown Cl BN12 .... 181 C1
Sandown Ct Hove BN3 .... 166 D1
1 Worthing BN11 .... 182 C1
Sandown Rd Brighton BN2 ... 188 D7
Southwick BN42 .... 185 E8
Sandpiper Cl RH11 .... 17 D4
Sandpiper Rd PO20 .... 202 A6
Sandridge La RH10 .... 63 F1
Sandringham Cl
Bracklesham PO20 .... 202 B5
East Grinstead RH19 .... 23 A8
Hove BN3 .... 167 A3

Sandringham Dr BN3 .... 167 A3
Sandringham Lodge **13** BN3 . 187 C6
Sandringham Mews
Worthing BN13 .... 181 D7
Worthing BN14 .... 182 D6
Sandringham Rd
Chichester PO19 .... 173 C6
Crawley RH11 .... 18 B2
Sandringham Way PO21 .... 195 B4
Sandrock Haslemere GU27 .... 27 C6
Midhurst GU29 .... 92 D8
Sandrock Cotts GU28 .... 51 A7
Sandrocks Way RH16 .... 85 E2
Sands La BN5 .... 144 F6
Sands The RH20 .... 121 A5
Sandwich Rd BN11 .... 181 F1
Sandy Beach Est PO11 .... 189 B1
Sandy La Crawley Down RH10 .. 21 A8
East Ashling PO18 .... 151 D4
East Grinstead RH19 .... 9 F1
Fittleworth RH20 .... 97 A2
Haslemere GU26, GU27 .... 26 C7
Heath Common RH20 .... 118 B2
Henfield BN5 .... 123 D4
Midhurst GU29 .... 92 D8
Rake GU33 .... 46 A4
Watersfield RH20 .... 117 A5
West Hoathly RH19 .... 42 E6
Sandy Point La PO20 .... 206 B8
Sandy Point Rd PO11 .... 189 A1
Sandy Rd PO21 .... 205 A7
Sandy Vale RH16 .... 85 E2
Sandygate La RH13 .... 59 F3
Sandymount Ave PO22 .... 195 B6
Sandymount Cl PO22 .... 195 C6
Sangers Cty Jun Sch RH6 ...... 1 F3
Sangers Dr RH6 .... 1 F3
Sanyhils Ave BN1 .... 167 F7
Sarel Way RH10 .... 2 B5
Sargent Cl RH10 .... 18 F2
Sarisbury Cl PO22 .... 196 A5
Sark Cl RH11 .... 18 A2
Sark Gdns BN12 .... 200 F4
Satellite Bsns Village The RH10 . 5 E2
Satinwood Cl PO22 .... 196 E6
Saturn Cl RH11 .... 17 E4
Saucelands Rd RH13 .... 100 E7
Saunders Cl RH10 .... 19 B7
Saunders Hill BN1 .... 168 D7
Saunders Park Rise **3** BN2 . 168 C1
Saunders Park View BN2 ...... 168 C1
Savernake Wlk RH10 .... 18 F3
Savill Rd RH10 .... 86 A8
Saville Ct RH14 .... 77 D7
Saville Gdns RH14 .... 77 D7
Sawyers Cl RH15 .... 107 D1
Saxby Rd RH15 .... 106 D4
Saxifrage Way BN12, BN13 ... 181 A5
Saxley RH6 .... 2 C4
Saxon Cl Bognor Regis PO21 . 204 F8
East Preston BN16 .... 180 B3
Saxon Cres RH12 .... 36 B4
Saxon Ct BN3 .... 186 D6
Saxon Meadow PO20 .... 154 C1
Saxon Rd Bramber BN44 ...... 143 F3
Crawley RH10 .... 19 E5
Hove BN3 .... 186 D6
Saxonbury **15** BN2 .... 207 B6
Saxons BN43 .... 164 F1
Saxony Rd BN14 .... 182 C4
Sayers The **5** RH19 .... 9 C1
Scallows Cl RH10 .... 19 A7
Scallows Rd RH10 .... 19 A7
Scamps Hill RH16 .... 86 C6
Scant Rd E PO18 .... 150 F2
Scant Rd W PO18 .... 150 E2
Scarborough Rd BN1 .... 167 D1
Scaynes Hill CE (C) Prim Sch
RH17 .... 86 F3
Sceptre **2** BN1 .... 167 E2
Scholars Ct RH10 .... 21 A8
School Cl Burgess Hill RH15 . 106 F2
Fittleworth RH20 .... 97 A3
Horsham RH12 .... 37 A6
1 Southwick BN42 .... 185 E7
School Dell PO18 .... 151 A4
School Hill Findon BN14 .... 161 E6
Slindon BN18 .... 156 C5
Storrington RH20 .... 119 E1
Warnham RH12 .... 35 F8
School La Arundel BN18 .... 158 A2
Ashurst BN44 .... 122 D5
Ashurst Wood RH19 .... 23 E6
Bosham PO20 .... 171 C5
Compton PO18 .... 109 B2
Danehill RH17 .... 66 B5
Eastergate PO20 .... 175 F7
Emsworth PO10 .... 169 B8
Fittleworth RH20 .... 97 A3
Liss GU33 .... 45 B4
Lodsworth GU28 .... 72 B4
North Mundham PO20 .... 173 D2
Nutbourne PO18 .... 170 B7
Pyecombe BN45 .... 147 C6
Selsey PO20 .... 206 B8
Shipley RH13 .... 79 C1
Stedham GU29 .... 69 F1
Steyning BN44 .... 143 D3
Storrington RH20 .... 119 C1
Sutton RH20 .... 115 F4
Washington RH20 .... 141 E7
Westbourne PO10 .... 149 D5
School Rd Amberley BN18 ..... 138 E7
Camelsdale GU27 .... 26 F6
Hove BN3 .... 186 F8
Upper Beeding BN44 .... 144 B2
School Rise BN2 .... 188 E6
Schooner Ct **3** BN16 .... 199 A6

Scolliers Crossways RH13 ..... 79 B3
Scory Cl RH11 .... 18 A3
Scotland La GU27 .... 27 C5
Scotland St BN2 .... 207 B6
Scotlands Cl GU27 .... 27 B5
Scotlands Dr GU27 .... 27 C5
Scotney Cl RH13 .... 181 B5
Scott Cl PO21 .... 195 C2
Scott Rd Crawley RH10 .... 18 F3
Hove BN3 .... 186 F7
Scott St PO21 .... 195 C2
Scrace Hill Terr RH16 .... 107 F8
Scrase Lodge RH15 .... 107 D3
Scratchings La GU28 .... 52 C6
Sea Ave BN16 .... 199 D5
Sea Cl Middleton-on-Sea PO22 . 196 E5
Worthing BN12 .... 181 E2
Sea Dr Bognor Regis PO22 ... 196 D4
Ferring BN12 .... 200 F4
Sea Ho **14** BN42 .... 185 E7
Sea La Bognor Regis PO21 ... 204 F7
Ferring BN12 .... 200 F5
Kingston Gorse BN16 .... 200 D4
East Preston BN16 .... 199 F4
Rustington BN16 .... 199 B4
Middleton-on-Sea PO22 .... 196 E5
Worthing BN12 .... 181 C1
Sea Lane Cl East Preston BN16 . 199 F5
Ferring BN12 .... 200 F6
Sea Lane Gdns BN12 .... 200 F5
Sea Pl BN12 .... 181 E1
Sea Rd Bognor Regis PO22 ... 195 F3
Littlehampton BN16, BN17 .... 199 A3
West Kingston BN16 .... 200 A5
Sea View Cotts PO10 .... 169 B8
Sea View Rd BN11 .... 182 B1
Sea Way Bognor Regis PO22 . 204 F8
Elmer PO22 .... 197 B5
Middleton-on-Sea PO22 .... 196 E4
Seabright **8** BN11 .... 182 B1
Seabrook Ct BN15 .... 183 E4
Seacourt Cl PO21 .... 194 D2
Seafarers Wlk PO11 .... 189 B1
Seafield Ave BN12 .... 181 D1
Seafield Cl East Wittering PO20 . 202 A6
Littlehampton BN16 .... 199 C4
Seafield Rd Hove BN3 .... 187 B6
Littlehampton BN16 .... 199 C4
West Kingston BN16 .... 200 A4
Seafield Terr **4** PO21 .... 195 B2
Seafield Way PO20 .... 202 A6
Seafields Bracklesham PO20 . 202 C5
Emsworth PO10 .... 169 B8
Shoreham-by-Sea BN43 .... 184 F8
Seaford Coll GU28 .... 114 E5
Seaford Rd Crawley RH11 ..... 18 A2
Hove BN3, BN41 .... 186 C6
Seagate Ct PO20 .... 201 E6
Seagate Wlk BN17 .... 199 A4
Seagull Cl PO20 .... 203 C1
Seagull Rd PO10 .... 149 B1
Seahaven Gdns BN43 .... 184 D5
Seal Cl PO20 .... 206 D7
Seal Rd PO20 .... 206 D5
Seal Cty Prim Sch PO20 ...... 206 E7
Seal Rd PO20 .... 206 D5
Seal Sq PO20 .... 206 D5
Seamill Ct **5** BN11 .... 183 B3
Seamill Park Ave BN11 .... 183 B3
Seamill Park Cres BN11 .... 183 B3
Seamill Way BN11 .... 183 B3
Searle's View RH12 .... 36 E5
Seasaw Way BN2 .... 188 F7
Seaside Ave BN15 .... 183 F5
Seaside Cl BN15 .... 183 F5
Seaside Rd BN15 .... 183 F5
Seaton Cl BN17 .... 178 D4
Seaton La BN17 .... 178 D4
Seaton Park Cotts BN17 ...... 178 D4
Seaton Pk BN17 .... 178 D4
Seaton Rd BN17 .... 178 D4
Seaview Ave
Kingston Gorse BN16 .... 200 D4
West Kingston BN16 .... 200 A4
Seaview Ct
2 Bognor Regis PO21 ..... 195 C2
Lancing BN15 .... 183 D4
Selsey PO20 .... 206 D6
4 Worthing BN11 .... 182 B1
Seaview Est BN42 .... 185 F7
Seaview Gdns **5** BN16 ..... 199 C4
Seaview Rd BN16 .... 200 A4
Seaward Ct **6** PO21 .... 195 C3
Seaward Dr PO20 .... 190 C1
Seawaves Cl BN16 .... 200 A5
Seawood Ho PO20 .... 201 F7
Second Ave Almodington PO20 . 191 F1
Bognor Regis PO22 .... 196 B4
Hove BN3 .... 187 C6
Lancing BN15 .... 183 E7
Southbourne PO10 .... 169 F8
Worthing BN14 .... 182 D7
Sedbury Rd BN15 .... 183 C8
Seddon Ct RH11 .... 18 B1
Sedgefield Cl RH10 .... 19 E7
Sedgewick Cl RH10 .... 19 C6
Sedgwick La RH13 .... 58 E4
Sefter Rd PO20 .... 194 B3
Sefton Ave PO21 .... 194 D3
Sefton Cl BN13 .... 181 D6
Sefton Rd BN41 .... 165 F3
Selba Dr BN2 .... 168 A3
Selborne Pl BN3 .... 187 C7
Selborne Rd Hove BN3 .... 187 C6
Littlehampton BN17 .... 198 E4
Worthing BN11 .... 182 F3
Selborne Way BN16 .... 199 D4
Selbourne Cl RH10 .... 6 D2
Selby Ct RH16 .... 85 E3

Selden La Hammerpot BN13 . 160 B1
Worthing BN13 .... 182 F2
Selden Rd BN11 .... 182 F2
Selden's Mews BN13 .... 181 F6
Selden's Way BN13 .... 181 F7
Sele Gdns BN44 .... 144 B2
Selham CI Brighton BN1 .... 168 D6
Chichester PO19 .... 153 A3
Crawley RH11 .... 18 A7
Selham Dr BN1 .... 168 D6
Selham Pl BN1 .... 168 D6
Selham Rd GU29 .... 93 C6
Selhurst Cl BN16 .... 199 F5
Selhurstpark Rd PO18 .... 135 B4
Selkirk Cl BN13 .... 181 E4
Selmeston Pl BN2 .... 188 F6
Selmestone Rd BN2 .... 188 F5
Selsey Ave PO21 .... 195 A2
Selsey Cl Brighton BN1 .... 168 E6
South Hayling PO11 .... 189 B2
Worthing BN13 .... 181 F5
Selsey Ct **3** Crawley RH11 . 18 B2
6 Rustington BN16 .... 199 B4
Selsey PO20 .... 206 D6
Selsey Rd Crawley RH11 .... 18 A2
Sidlesham PO20 .... 203 F7
Stockbridge PO19 .... 172 E3
Street End PO20, PO19 .... 192 D7
Selsfield Dr BN2 .... 168 D3
Selsfield Rd
Little London RH17, RH19 ..... 42 A4
West Hoathly RH19 .... 42 C7
Selway La BN17 .... 198 F6
Selwyn Ave BN17 .... 178 F3
Selwyn Cl Bognor Regis PO21 . 194 F4
Crawley RH10 .... 6 C1
Semley Rd Brighton BN1 ...... 168 A1
Hassocks BN6 .... 126 E4
Senator Gdns PO19 .... 172 A7
Sequoia Pk RH11 .... 18 D4
Sergison Cl RH16 .... 85 D5
Sergison Rd RH16 .... 85 D5
Serrin Way RH12 .... 36 E5
Service Rd
Gatwick Airport, N Terminal RH6 . 5 F8
Gatwick Airport, S Terminal RH6 . 6 B7
Servite Cl PO21 .... 195 B4
Servite Ho PO21 .... 195 B4
Sevelands Cl BN2 .... 188 F7
Seven Dials BN1 .... 207 F2
Sevenfields BN6 .... 106 D4
Seventh Ave BN15 .... 183 E8
Severals Rd GU29 .... 92 C7
Severn Rd RH10 .... 19 C5
Seville St BN2 .... 188 C7
Sewill Cl RH6 .... 4 F7
Sextant Ct **6** BN16 .... 199 A4
Seymore Pl **2** PO21 .... 195 C3
Seymour Ho **5** BN2 .... 188 D4
Seymour Rd RH11 .... 18 B2
Seymour Sq **3** BN2 .... 188 D4
Seymour St **4** BN2 .... 188 D4
Shackleton Rd RH10 .... 18 F3
Shadwells Cl BN15 .... 183 F7
Shadwells Ct BN15 .... 183 F7
Shadwells Rd BN15 .... 183 F7
Shaftesbury Ave
BN11, BN12, BN13 .... 181 E3
Shaftesbury Ct **4** BN16 .... 199 C4
Shaftesbury Pl BN1 .... 188 A8
Shaftesbury Rd Brighton BN1 . 207 A8
Crawley RH10 .... 19 D4
Littlehampton BN16 .... 199 C4
Shakespeare Rd BN11 .... 182 C3
Shakespeare St BN3 .... 187 A8
Shalbourne Cres PO20 .... 202 C5
Shalesbrook La RH18 .... 23 F1
Shamrock Ct Bosham PO18 . 171 C5
Chichester PO19 .... 173 B8
Shandon Gdns BN14 .... 182 D6
Shandon Rd BN14 .... 182 D6
Shandon Way BN14 .... 182 D6
Shands BN6 .... 126 F3
Shandys Ct RH12 .... 36 A1
Shanklin Ct **7** Brighton BN2 . 188 C8
Hove BN3 .... 166 D1
Shanklin Rd BN2 .... 188 C8
Shannon Cl RH11 .... 199 A4
Shardeloes Rd BN16 .... 179 F6
Sharon Cl RH10 .... 19 A4
Sharpthorne Cl RH11 .... 17 F6
Sharpthorne Cres BN41 .... 166 C1
Sharrow Cl **9** RH16 .... 85 E5
Shaves Wood La BN6 .... 125 A2
Shaw Cl PO22 .... 196 F5
Shaw's La RH13 .... 57 D1
Shawcross Ho **10** BN1 ...... 167 E2
Shaws Rd RH12 .... 36 E5
Shearwater Ct **6** RH11 ...... 17 D5
Shearwater Dr PO22 .... 195 C6
Sheddingdean Bsns Ctr RH15 . 106 F3
Sheddingdean Cl RH15 .... 107 A4
Sheddingdean Ct RH15 .... 106 F4
Sheddingdean Cty Inf Sch
RH15 .... 107 A5
Sheddingdean Cty Prim Sch
RH15 .... 107 A5
Sheep Fold Ave BN16 .... 199 E6
Sheep La GU29 .... 92 F8
Sheep Pen La BN44 .... 143 D3
Sheepbell Cl BN41 .... 166 B3
Sheepdown Cl GU28 .... 96 A7
Sheepdown Dr GU28 .... 96 A7
Sheepwash La
East Lavant PO18 .... 152 F5
Shipton Green PO20 .... 190 E4
Sheffield Cl RH10 .... 19 B4
Shelby Rd BN13 .... 181 C6

Sheldon Cl RH10 19 D5
Sheldon Ct BN11 182 B1
Shell La RH17 41 C1
Shellbridge Rd BN18 156 E3
Shelldale Ave BN41 186 B7
Shelldale Cres BN41 186 B7
Shelldale Rd BN41 186 B8
Shelley Cl RH10 19 C8
Shelley Ct 4 RH16 85 D5
Shelley Dr RH12 35 C3
Shelley Rd Bognor Regis PO21 195 B3
East Grinstead RH19 9 D1
Horsham RH12 36 B3
Hove BN3 186 F7
Worthing BN11 182 C2
Shelley Wood BN6 106 D4
Shelly Cty Prim Sch RH12 35 E3
Shellys Ct RH13 37 A3
Shenfield Way BN1 168 B3
Shenstone RH16 86 B8
Shepherd Cl RH10 18 E3
Shepherd's Hill GU27 27 C6
Shepherd's Hill Bglws GU27 27 C6
Shepherds Croft Brighton BN1 167 C4
Findon BN14 161 E6
Shepherds La GU28 72 B3
Shepherds Mead
Burgess Hill RH15 106 F4
Worthing BN14 162 A2
Shepherds Way Horsham RH12 37 A5
Liphook GU30 25 D3
Shepherds Wlk BN6 126 F5
Shepherdsgrove La RH19 10 F5
Sheppard Way BN41 166 A3
Sheppey Cl RH11 18 C3
Sheppeys RH16 85 D2
Sheraton Wlk 12 RH11 18 B1
Sherborne Rd PO19 172 E7
Sherbourne Cl BN3 166 D3
Sherbourne La PO20 206 B8
Sherbourne Rd BN3 166 D3
Sherbourne Way BN3 166 D3
Sherbrooke Cl BN13 181 D6
Sherburne Hospl The PO19 152 F1
Sheridan Cl RH19 9 C1
Sheridan Mansions BN3 187 A8
Sheridan Rd BN14 182 E5
Sheridan Terr BN3 187 A8
Sherlock Ave PO19 172 E7
Shermanbury Ct
Horsham RH12 36 D4
Lancing BN15 183 C5
Shermanbury Dr RH20 119 C2
Shermanbury Rd BN14 182 B4
Sherston Cl RH20 119 E2
Sherwood Cl
Bognor Regis PO22 195 B6
Liss Forest GU33 45 C7
Sherwood Dr RH16 85 C5
Sherwood Rd PO21, PO22 195 B6
Sherwood Wlk RH10 18 F3
Shetland Cl RH10 19 E7
Shetland Ct BN13 181 B5
Shillinglee Park Golf Course GU8 29 D6
Shilpey CE (C) Prim Sch RH13 79 B1
Shingle Rd BN43 185 A6
Shingle Wlk PO20 201 F6
Shinwell Wlk 3 RH11 18 B1
Ship St Brighton BN1 207 F5
East Grinstead RH19 22 E8
Shoreham-by-Sea BN43 184 E7
Ship Street Gdns BN1 207 F5
Shipfield PO21 194 F2
Shipley Bridge La RH10 7 A3
Shipley Ct GU30 25 C3
Shipley Rd Crawley RH11 18 A6
Southwater RH13 79 E5
Shipleybridge La RH10, RH6 6 F4
Shipton Green La PO20 191 B4
Shire Par RH10 19 D7
Shirlands Ct 2 BN16 199 D6
Shirley Ave BN3 167 B2
Shirley Cl Bognor Regis PO21 205 A8
Crawley RH11 17 E2
Littlehampton BN16 199 D4
Southwick BN43 185 D8
Worthing BN14 182 B7
Shirley Dr Bognor Regis PO22 196 A6
Hove BN3 167 C2
Worthing BN14 182 B6
Shirley Rd BN3 187 C8
Shirley St BN3 187 B7
Shirleys BN6 127 E2
Shirleys Gdn PO22 196 B5
Shooting Field BN44 143 D4
Shop La PO18 153 A5
Shopfield Cl BN16 199 C6
Shopping Ctr The PO20 206 D7
Shopsdam Rd BN15 183 F4
Shopwhyke Ind Ctr PO20 173 D7
Shopwhyke Rd PO19, PO20 173 E7
Shore Rd Bosham PO18 171 B3
Bosham PO18 171 B4
East Wittering PO20 201 E7
Shorecroft PO21 194 F1
Shoreham Airport BN15, BN43 184 C8
Shoreham Beach Cty Fst Sch BN43 185 A6
Shoreham By-Pass
BN41, BN42, BN43, BN15 165 D2
Shoreham Coll BN43 185 D7
Shoreham Cty Fst Sch BN43 184 E8
Shoreham Rd Crawley RH10 19 C3
Small Dole BN5 144 F8
Upper Beeding BN43, BN44 164 B7
Shoreham-by-Sea Sta BN43 184 F7
Shoreside Wlk PO20 201 F7
Short Cl RH11 18 D8
Short Furlong BN17 198 F5
Short Gallop RH10 19 D7
Shortgate Rd BN2 168 F4
Shortsfield Cl RH12 36 C5
Shotford PO20 203 F8
Shotterfield Terr GU33 45 B4
Shottermill RH12 37 A7
Shottermill Cty Fst Sch GU27 26 F7
Shottermill Cty Jun Sch GU27 26 F7
Shottermill Rd GU27 26 E5
Shotters RH15 106 E1
Shovelstrode La RH19 23 D8
Shripney La PO22 175 C1
Shripney Rd Bognor Regis PO22 195 D5
Bognor Regis PO22 195 E7
Shrubbs Dr PO22 196 E5
Sickle Rd GU27 27 A5
Sidehill Dr BN41 165 F2
Sidings The RH12 33 D7
Sidlesham Cl PO11 189 B2
Sidlesham Cty Prim Sch PO20 203 D8
Sidlesham La PO20 192 A4
Silchester Dr RH11 18 B4
Silkin Wlk 8 RH11 18 B1
Sillwood Ct 7 BN1 187 E5
Sillwood Hall 6 BN1 187 E5
Sillwood Pl 9 BN1 187 E5
Sillwood Rd BN1 187 E5
Sillwood St BN1 187 E5
Silver Birch Cl GU33 45 C4
Silver Birch Dr
Middleton-on-Sea PO22 196 E6
Worthing BN13 181 C5
Silver Birches
Haywards Heath RH16 86 A4
Small Dole BN5 144 F7
Silver Glade RH20 119 E6
Silver La RH14 77 D8
Silver Way PO20 202 C4
Silver Wood RH20 119 B7
Silver Wood Copse RH20 119 B7
Silverdale Coldwaltham RH20 117 C5
Keymer BN6 127 B3
Silverdale Ave BN3 187 D7
Silverdale Cl PO21 205 A8
Silverdale Dr BN15 183 C5
Silverdale Ind Est BN11 183 B3
Silverdale Rd Burgess Hill RH15 107 C2
Hove BN3 187 D7
Silverlea Gdns RH6 2 C2
Silverlock Pl PO10 149 D5
Silverston Ave PO21 195 A2
Silvertrees PO10 149 B2
Simon Ct 13 PO21 195 C3
Sinclair Cl RH10 19 C4
Sincox La RH13 100 D6
Singing Hills Golf Course BN6 125 B4
Singleton CE (C) Prim Sch PO18 133 D7
Singleton Cl PO21 194 C1
Singleton Cres BN12 200 F6
Singleton Cres W BN12 180 F3
Singleton Ho BN17 178 B3
Singleton Rd Brighton BN1 168 A6
Broadridge Heath RH12 35 D3
Singleton Way RH15 107 C1
Sinnocks RH20 99 E1
Sir George's Pl BN44 143 C3
Sir Robert Peel Ct 11 PO21 195 D4
Siskin Cl RH12 36 E5
Sissinghurst Cl RH10 19 D7
Six Acres Cl RH13 56 F2
Skelmersdale Wlk RH11 17 E2
Skeyne Dr 4 RH20 98 C2
Skiff La RH14 53 F5
Skipton Way RH6 2 B5
Skye Cluan Cl PO22 176 B6
Skylark View RH12 36 D7
Slade La GU31 67 F5
Slattsfield Cl PO20 206 F7
Slaugham Ct RH11 17 F3
Slaugham La RH17 61 A2
Sleets Rd RH12 35 E3
Slider's La Ferners Green TN22 87 F6
Furner's Green RH17 66 B1
Slimbridge Rd RH15 106 F3
Slindon Bottom Rd BN18 156 A4
Slindon CE (C) Prim Sch BN18 156 D4
Slindon Cl BN14 182 D6
Slindon Coll BN18 156 B5
Slindon Rd BN14 182 D6
Slinfold CE (C) Sch RH12 34 D4
Slinfold Park (Golf & Ctry Pk) RH12 34 A2
Slinfold Wlk RH11 18 A6
Slinford Cl BN2 188 D5
Slipper Rd PO10 169 C8
Sloane Ct 4 BN2 188 C5
Slonk Hill Rd BN43 165 A1
Sloughbrook Cl RH12 36 F6
Sloughgreen La RH17 61 E1
Slugwash La RH16, RH17 86 D2
Small's La RH11 18 C6
Smallcroft Cl BN17 198 C5
Smallcuts Ave PO10 149 F1
Smallfield Rd RH6 2 D3
Smallmead RH6 2 B3
Smalls Mead RH11 18 C6
Smith Cl RH10 18 D3
Smith La PO10 169 F1
Smith's Cross RH13 82 C3
Smithbarn RH13 37 A2
Smithbarn Cl RH6 2 B4
Smithers Cotts RH12 33 F7
Smithers Hill La RH13 79 B2
Smithy The RH13 81 E1
Smock Alley RH20 119 E7
Smokejack Hill RH5 13 D7
Smokyhouse La GU28 94 B5
Smolletts RH19 22 C8
Smuggler's La PO18 171 B1
Smugglers' La
Barns Green RH13 56 D3
Barns Green RH13 56 F3
Paynes Green RH12, RH5 14 E7
Smugglers Way RH13 56 F2
Smugglers Wlk BN12 181 E1
Snapes Rd RH20 119 F3
Snell Hatch RH11 18 B6
Snipe La GU27 27 A1
Snow Hill RH10 8 A4
Snow Hill Bsns Ctr RH10 8 A4
Snowdrop Cl RH11 18 A2
Snowdrop La RH16 86 C4
Snowflakes La RH16 86 D6
Snowhill La RH10 7 F5
Soames Ct RH15 106 F4
Soane Cl RH11 17 E4
Solent Cl BN16 179 A3
Solent Rd PO20 201 F6
Solent Way PO20 206 E5
Solway Ave BN1 167 F7
Solway Cl BN17 199 A5
Somergate RH12 35 F2
Somerhill Ave BN3 187 D7
Somerhill Ct 10 BN3 187 D7
Somerhill Cty Jun Sch BN3 187 D6
Somerhill Lodge 6 BN3 187 D6
Somerhill Rd BN3 187 D6
Somerley La PO20 191 E1
Somersbury La GU6, RH12 12 F7
Somerset Cl BN13 182 A5
Somerset Ct 3 BN3 187 C7
Somerset Gdns PO21, PO22 195 C5
Somerset Hospl GU28 95 F8
Somerset Point 1 BN2 188 C4
Somerset Rd
East Preston BN16 200 B6
Ferring BN12 200 F4
Somerset St BN2 188 C5
Somerstown PO19 172 F8
Somerton Gn PO22 195 F5
Somerville Dr RH10 6 C1
Somping Rd BN14 182 E7
Sompting Abbotts Sch BN15 183 A8
Sompting Ave BN14 182 D5
Sompting By-Pass BN14 182 E7
Sompting Cl BN2 188 F7
Sompting Ct 3 BN43 185 B8
Sompting Rd Lancing BN15 183 D5
Worthing BN14 182 E6
Sopers La BN44 163 C7
Sorrel Cl RH11 18 A2
Sorrel Rd RH12 36 E5
South Acre GU31 89 D3
South Ash BN44 143 D4
South Ave Bognor Regis PO21 194 F3
Brighton BN2 188 C5
Hurstpierpoint BN6 126 A5
Worthing BN12 181 E1
South Bank Hassocks BN6 126 E3
Stockbridge PO19 172 F4
South Bank Ct BN15 184 A4
South Bay PO10 169 C3
South Beach 6 BN15 184 F6
South Bersted CE (C) Prim Sch PO22 195 D5
South Bersted Ind Est PO22 195 D6
South Cl Burgess Hill RH15 106 E3
Crawley RH10 18 F7
South Dr Angmering BN16 179 E3
Bognor Regis PO22 196 C5
Burgess Hill RH15 106 E3
Ferring BN12 200 E4
South Farm Inds BN14 182 C5
South Farm Rd BN11, BN14 182 C5
South Gr Horsham RH13 36 D1
Petworth GU28 95 F7
South Holmes Rd RH13 37 B4
South La Breach PO10 150 A2
Houghton BN18 138 B3
Tillington GU28 94 F7
Woodmancote PO10 150 A3
South Lodge
Bognor Regis PO21 194 A2
9 Brighton BN2 188 F5
3 Lancing BN15 183 C7
South Lodge Cl RH15 106 F4
South Pallant PO19 173 A6
South Par RH6 1 F4
South Pas BN17 198 F4
South Pier Rd RH6 6 B7
South Point 7 BN43 185 A6
South Rd Bognor Regis PO22 195 F5
Brighton BN1 167 E1
Haywards Heath RH16 85 E4
Liphook GU30 25 D1
South St Brighton BN1 207 F5
Chichester PO19 173 A6
Cuckfield RH17 84 E6
Ditchling BN6 127 D3
Emsworth PO10 169 B8
Horsham RH12 36 C2
Lancing BN15 183 E4
Midhurst GU29 92 F7
Partridge Green RH13 103 A3
Portslade-by-Sea BN41 166 A1
Worthing BN11 182 D1
Worthing, West Tarring BN11, BN13, BN14 182 A4
South Strand BN16 200 A4
South Strand Par BN16 200 A4
South Terr Bognor Regis PO22 195 D5
Littlehampton BN17 198 E4
South View Copthorne RH10 7 E3
Ditchling BN6 127 E5
West Kingston BN16 200 B4
South View Terr BN5 123 E4
South Way PO21 195 A5
South Wlk PO22 196 E5
South Woodlands BN1 167 E5
Southall Ave BN2 168 D2
Southampton St BN2 207 B6
Southan View BN15 183 C3
Southbourne Ave PO10 169 D8
Southbourne Cty Inf Sch PO10 170 A8
Southbourne Cty Jun Sch PO10 170 A8
Southbourne Halt PO10 170 A8
Southbrook RH11 18 C1
Southbrook Rd
West Ashling PO18 151 B2
West Ashling PO18 151 C3
Southcote Ave PO20 201 E7
Southcourt Cl BN16 199 E6
Southcourt Rd BN14 182 C3
Southdean Cl PO22 196 F5
Southdean Dr PO22 196 F5
Southdown Ave Brighton BN1 168 A1
Portslade-by-Sea BN41 186 C8
Southdown Cl
Haywards Heath RH16 85 D2
Horsham RH12 37 A5
Midhurst GU29 92 D6
Southdown Ct PO20 202 A7
Southdown Ho BN12 181 D2
Southdown Pl BN1 168 A1
Southdown Rd
Bognor Regis PO21 195 C3
Brighton BN1 168 A1
Portslade-by-Sea BN41 166 A2
Shoreham-by-Sea BN43 184 F7
Southwick BN42 185 E7
Southdown Sch BN44 143 D3
Southdown Terr BN44 143 E3
Southdown View Cl BN14 182 F5
Southdown View Rd BN14 182 F5
Southdown View Way BN14 182 E6
Southdown Way RH20 119 F3
Southern Cross Ind Est PO22 195 E7
Southern L Ctr PO20 173 D3
Southern Rd PO20 206 E6
Southey Rd BN11 182 C1
Southfield Ind Pk PO18 171 B6
Southfield Rd BN14 182 D5
Southfields Cl PO19 172 F3
Southfields Rd BN17, BN16 198 F5
Southgate PO19 172 F5
Southgate Ave RH10, RH11 18 E4
Southgate Cty Fst & Mid Sch RH10 18 D4
Southgate Cty West Fst & Mid Sch RH11 18 C4
Southgate Dr RH10, RH11 18 E4
Southgate Par RH10 18 D4
Southgate Rd RH10, RH11 18 D4
Southlands East Grinstead RH19 22 E7
Horley RH6 1 F3
Southlands Ave RH6 2 A4
Southlands Ct 1 BN43 185 B8
Southlands General Hospl BN43 185 B8
Southlands La RH20 119 E8
Southlands Pk GU29 92 E5
Southleigh Rd PO10, PO9 149 B3
Southleys GU27 49 A5
Southmount BN1 168 B1
Southon Cl BN41 165 F3
Southover Pl BN2 207 B7
Southover Rd PO21 195 C3
Southover St BN2 207 B6
Southover Way PO20 173 A1
Southsea Ave BN12 181 E1
Southside RH20 98 D2
Southview Scaynes Hill RH17 86 F3
Small Dole BN5 144 F6
Southview Cl BN42 165 E1
Southview Dr BN11 182 A2
Southview Gdns BN11 182 A2
Southview Rd
Bognor Regis PO22 196 B4
Findon BN14 161 E6
Southwick BN42 185 E8
Southwark Cl RH11 18 B2
Southwark Wlk PO21 194 E4
Southwater Bsns Pk RH13 57 F1
Southwater Cl Brighton BN2 188 D6
Worthing BN12 181 B3
Southwater Cty Inf Sch RH13 57 F2
Southwater Cty Jun Sch RH13 57 F2
Southwater St RH13 58 A4
Southway Burgess Hill RH15 106 D3
Littlehampton BN17 198 F4
Southway Cty Jun Sch RH15 106 D3
Southways Ave BN14 182 E6
Southways Pk RH11 5 D3
Southwick Cl RH19 9 D2
Southwick Ho RH19 9 D2
Southwick Sq BN42 185 E7
Southwick St BN42 185 E8
Southwick Sta BN42 185 E7
Southwold Cl BN13 161 E1
Southwood Rd PO11 189 A1
Sovereign Ct 16 PO21 195 D3
Spa Ct BN3 187 B5
Spanish Ct RH15 107 B4
Spark's La RH17 62 E2
Sparks Ct BN17 198 D5
Sparrow Way BN6 106 D3
Sparshott Rd PO20 206 E5
Spartan Cl PO10 169 C3
Spatham La BN6 127 F4
Spear Hill RH20 121 A7
Speedwell Cl BN13 181 A5
Speedwell Way RH12 36 E5
Spencer Ave BN3 166 D3
Spencer Rd Lancing BN15 183 D5
New Brighton PO10 149 A4
Spencer St PO21 195 D4
Spencer's Rd RH12 36 B3
Spencers La RH6 1 A2
Spencers Pl RH12 36 B4
Spencers Rd RH11 18 D5
Spey Cl BN13 181 C8
Spicers Cl RH15 106 F5
Spierbridge Rd RH20 119 C2
Spiers Way RH6 2 B1
Spindle Way RH10 18 F5
Spinnaker Cl BN16, BN17 199 A5
Spinnals Gr BN42 185 D7
Spinney Cl Crawley Down RH10 21 C8
Horsham RH12 37 B6
Hurstpierpoint BN6 126 C5
Spinney La
West Chiltington Common RH20 119 D5
West Itchenor PO20 191 A6
Spinney North RH20 98 D2
Spinney The Bognor Regis PO21 194 E3
Burgess Hill RH15 107 B5
Crawley RH11 18 B4
Haslemere GU27 27 C8
Hassocks BN6 126 F5
Haywards Heath RH16, RH17 85 D8
Horley RH6 2 A5
Hove BN3 167 C3
Pulborough RH20 98 D2
West Itchenor PO20 191 A5
West Kingston BN16 200 A4
Spinney Wlk PO22 176 B6
Spitalfield La PO19 173 B7
Spitfire Ct PO20 154 D2
Spithandle La BN44 122 B3
Spooners Rd RH12 37 A4
Spring Copse Copthorne RH10 7 C3
East Grinstead RH19 9 D3
Spring Gdns Brighton BN1 207 A5
Copthorne RH10 7 C3
Emsworth PO10 169 C8
Heath Common RH20 120 E2
6 Southwick BN42 185 E7
Spring Hill Wildfowl Pk RH18 23 A1
Spring La Clayton BN6 147 E8
Haywards Heath RH16 64 B1
Slinfold RH13 34 C3
Spring Meadow RH18 23 F1
Spring Meadows GU29 92 E6
Spring Plat RH10 19 C6
Spring Plat Ct RH10 19 C6
Spring St BN1 187 E5
Spring Way RH19 10 A4
Springate Rd BN42 185 F8
Springbank PO19 152 F1
Springfarm Rd GU27 26 E5
Springfield Bognor Regis PO21 194 A2
East Grinstead RH19 9 D4
Liss GU33 45 B4
Springfield Cl Birdham PO20 191 F5
Bolney RH17 83 C4
Mid Lavant PO18 152 F7
Rustington BN16 199 E5
Springfield Cotts RH17 83 C4
Springfield Cres RH12 36 B2
Springfield Ct RH12 36 C2
Springfield Fst Sch BN14 182 E4
Springfield Gdns BN13 182 A7
Springfield La RH12, RH13 38 B5
Springfield Park Rd RH12 36 B2
Springfield Rd Brighton BN1 188 A8
Crawley RH11 18 D5
Horsham RH12 36 C2
Springfields Farm Ind Est RH17 107 F5
Springhead Farm Cotts BN18 139 E7
Springhills BN5 123 E4
Spronkett's La RH17 82 E3
Sproule Cl BN18 177 B2
Sproutes La RH13 100 D8
Spur Rd PO19 173 D5
Spurgeon Cl RH11 18 C7
Spy La RH14 32 A4
Square Dr Fernhurst GU27 49 B7
Marley Heights GU27 27 B1
Square The Brighton BN1 167 E6
Crawley RH11 18 D6
Findon BN14 161 E6
Prinsted PO10 169 F7
South Harting GU31 89 D4
Storrington RH20 119 D1
Washington BN14 141 C3
West Barnham PO22 176 B5
Westbourne PO10 149 D3
Squire Way BN5 123 E4
Squires Cl RH10 21 A8
Squires Cotts RH20 138 A7
Squirrel Cl RH11 5 B1
Squirrels Copse RH20 120 C3
Stable Cotts Crawley RH11 39 A8
Shopwyke PO20 173 F7
Stable Field PO22 197 B5
Stable Flats RH11 39 A8
Stable La BN14 161 E6
Stace Way RH10 19 E8
Stackfield Rd RH11 17 E5

Stafford House F Ed Ctr BN6 127 A3
Stafford Rd Brighton BN1 187 E8
Crawley RH11 5 B1
Stafford Way BN6 127 A3
Staffords Cl BN16 199 B6
Staffords Pl RH6 2 B2
Stag Cl BN5 123 E6
Stagelands RH11 18 C8
Stagelands Ct RH11 18 C8
Stairbridge La RH17 105 E7
Stakers La RH13 80 A8
Stalham Way PO22 196 A6
Stall House La RH20 99 A8
Stamford 6 RH16 85 D6
Stamford Lodge 7 BN1 167 E2
Stammerham Bsns Ctr RH5 15 E7
Stammers Hill BN5 145 F3
Stan Hill RH6 4 D8
Stanbridge Cl RH11 17 E6
Stanbridge Way RH17 64 B7
Stanbrok Cl PO21 194 E3
Stanbury Cl PO18 171 C7
Standean Cl BN1 168 D6
Standen Cl RH19 9 A4
Standen Ct BN44 144 B2
Standen (NT) RH19 22 D4
Standen Pl RH12 37 A7
Standgrove Pl RH17 64 A6
Standinghall La RH10 20 A3
Stane St Billingshurst RH14, RH20 77 B4
Codmore Hill RH20 98 D6
Five Oaks RH14, RH13 55 E4
Park Street RH12, RH13 34 C4
Strettington PO18 154 B3
Stane Street Cl RH20 98 C4
Stanford Ave Brighton BN1 168 A1
Hassocks BN6 126 E4
Stanford Cl Bognor Regis PO22 195 E5
Hassocks BN6 126 E4
Hove BN3 167 C1
Stanford Ct BN1 187 F8
Stanford Cty Inf Sch BN1 187 E8
Stanford Cty Jun Sch BN1 187 F8
Stanford Orch RH12 35 F8
Stanford Rd BN1 187 F8
Stanford (Scout Camp Site) RH11 39 B8
Stanford Sq BN11 182 E2
Stanford Terr BN6 126 E4
Stanford Way RH12 35 D3
Stanhope Rd
Littlehampton BN17 198 E5
Worthing BN11 182 D3
Stanier Cl RH10 19 B5
Stanley Ave BN41 165 F3
Stanley Cl Bognor Regis PO21 195 D4
Crawley RH10 18 E4
Stanley Ctr RH10 5 F2
Stanley Deason L Ctr BN2 188 F5
Stanley Deason Sch BN2 188 F5
Stanley Rd Brighton BN1 207 A7
Emsworth PO10 169 C8
Littlehampton BN17 178 D3
Portslade-by-Sea BN41 186 A8
Worthing BN11 182 D3
Stanley St BN2 207 B6
Stanley Wlk RH13 36 D2
Stanmer BN1 168 F8
Stanmer Park Rd BN1 168 B2
Stanmer St BN1 168 B2
Stanmer Villas BN1 168 B2
Stanmore Gdns PO21 194 E2
Stanover La PO22 196 B7
Stansfield Ct BN16 199 D6
Stanstead Cl PO9 128 E2
Stansted House PO9 129 E1
Stanton Dr PO19 153 A3
Stanwater La GU29 69 F3
Staple La PO18 152 F8
Staplecross Ct 1 RH11 18 A3
Staplefield Dr BN2 168 F3
Staplefield Place Sch RH17 61 E5
Staplefield Rd Cuckfield RH17 84 C8
Stapleford RH17 61 E4
Staples Barn BN5 123 D5
Staples Barn La BN5 123 D5
Staples Hill RH13 102 F4
Stapleton Ct PO21 194 D2
Stapley Ct BN3 186 D8
Stapley Rd BN3 166 D1
Star Rd RH13 103 A2
Starboard Ct BN2 188 F3
Starboard Wlk 9 BN17 198 F4
Starborough Cotts RH7 9 F7
Station App Haslemere GU27 27 B6
Hassocks BN6 126 F4
Horley RH6 2 B2
Horsted Keynes RH17 65 A7
Hove BN3 187 B8
Station Approach Rd RH6 6 B7
Station Cl RH13 36 D2
Station Cotts Hassocks BN6 126 E4
Horsham RH13 57 D7
Station Hill RH10 19 B7
Station Par 2 Lancing BN15 183 E5
6 Rustington BN16 199 E6
1 Worthing BN11 182 A3
Station Rd Angmering BN16 179 F4
Billingshurst RH14 77 D7
15 Bognor Regis PO21 195 C3
Brighton BN1 167 D3
Broadbridge PO18 171 C7
Burgess Hill RH15 107 B2
Cowfold RH13 81 B2
Cranleigh RH12 12 C3
Station Rd Crawley RH10, RH11 18 D5
Crawley Down RH10 21 B8
Crossbush BN18 158 D1
East Grinstead RH19 9 D1
Ford BN18 177 E4
Forest Row RH18 23 F3
Henfield BN5 123 D5
Horley RH6 2 B3
Horsham RH13 36 D2
Horsted Keynes RH17 65 C5
Liphook GU30 25 C2
Liss GU33 45 B4
Littlehampton BN16 199 E5
Loxwood RH14 32 A3
Midhurst GU29 92 D7
Petworth GU28 95 E5
Portslade-by-Sea BN3, BN41 186 C7
Pulborough RH20 98 A2
Rudgwick RH12 33 D7
Sharpthorne RH19 43 A6
Southwater RH13 57 F1
7 Southwick BN42 185 E7
Steyning BN44 143 E3
Tower Hill RH13 57 D7
Warnham RH12 36 B8
Worthing BN11 182 E3
Station St BN1 207 A6
Station Way RH10, RH11 18 D5
Staunton Ctry Pk PO9 128 A2
Stavely Gdns PO19 152 F3
Stean Furlong BN17 178 C3
Stedham Cty Prim Sch GU29 69 F1
Stedham La GU29 70 A3
Steeds Cnr RH13 80 D6
Steele Cl RH20 99 E1
Steels La PO18 170 E5
Steep Cl BN14 161 E5
Steep La BN14 161 E5
Steepdown Rd BN15 183 C8
Steeple View BN13 182 A5
Steeres Hill RH12 16 C6
Steers La RH10 6 C4
Stein Rd PO10 149 F2
Steine Gdns BN2 207 A5
Steine La BN1, BN2 207 A5
Steine St BN2 207 A4
Stemp Dr RH14 77 C8
Stempswood Way PO22 176 C6
Stephen Cl RH11 5 D1
Stephens Rd BN1 168 B2
Stephenson Dr RH19 22 F7
Stephenson Pl RH10 19 B6
Stephenson Way RH10 19 B6
Stepney Cl RH10 19 C4
Sterling Bldgs RH12 36 C2
Sterling Par 1 BN16 199 C5
Sternway BN17 199 A5
Stevenage Rd RH11 17 E3
Stevens Ct BN3 186 E7
Stevenson Rd BN2 188 C5
Stewards Rise BN18 157 F1
Steyne Gdns BN11 182 E2
Steyne St PO21 195 C3
Steyne The Bognor Regis PO21 195 C2
Worthing BN11 182 E2
Steyning Ave BN3 166 F3
Steyning By-Pass BN44 143 E3
Steyning Cl Crawley RH10 18 E8
Lancing BN15 183 D8
Worthing BN12 181 B3
Steyning Cres RH20 119 C2
Steyning Ct 7 BN3 187 B7
Steyning Gram Sch
Steyning BN44 143 D3
Steyning BN44 143 D4
Steyning Ho 1 BN14 182 D5
Steyning Mus BN44 143 D4
Steyning Rd
Shoreham-by-Sea BN43 164 C4
Shoreham-by-Sea, Mill Hill BN43 164 D1
West Grinstead RH13 102 C7
Steyning Way PO22 195 E7
Stile Gdns GU27 26 F6
Stipenhoks BN5 123 F4
Stirling Cl Burgess Hill RH15 107 C4
Crawley RH10 19 C5
Stirling Court Rd RH15 107 C4
Stirling Ct 5 BN3 187 C7
Stirling Pl BN3 187 A6
Stirling Rd PO19 173 A5
Stirling Way Bognor Regis PO21 194 E2
East Grinstead RH19 10 B3
Horsham RH13 36 E3
Stirrup Way RH10 19 D7
Stoatley Hollow GU27 27 A8
Stoatley Rise GU27 27 A8
Stock Ho BN15 183 A7
Stockbridge Gdns PO19 172 E4
Stockbridge Pl PO19 172 F4
Stockbridge Rd PO19 172 F4
Stockcroft Rd RH17 41 A1
Stocker Rd PO21 195 B2
Stockfield RH6 2 B4
Stocklands Cl RH17 84 F8
Stocks Cl RH6 2 B2
Stocks Field BN44 121 D1
Stocks La Bracklesham PO20 202 A6
Chichester PO18 153 C3
Stocks Mead RH20 141 E6
Stockwell Ct Burgess Hill RH15 106 F3
1 Haywards Heath RH16 85 E3
Stockwell Rd RH19 22 E6
Stockwell Works RH10 19 A6
Stodham La Hill Side GU33 45 C2
Prince's Marsh GU33, GU31 45 B1
Stoke Abbott Ct 2 BN11 182 D2
Stoke Abbott Rd BN11 182 D2
Stoke Brunswick Sch RH19 23 E7
Stoke Rd BN18 138 D3
Stokes Cl RH10 19 C3
Stone Cl BN13 181 F6
Stone Cross RH16 64 D3
Stone Ct GU29 92 D8
Stone Hatch GU6 11 A3
Stone La BN13 181 F6
Stone Quarry Rd RH17 66 D7
Stone St BN1 187 E5
Stoneage Cl PO22 195 C7
Stonebridge Ct Crawley RH11 18 C2
Horsham RH12 36 A2
Stonecourt Cl RH6 2 C3
Stonecourt Cotts RH17 62 A5
Stonecroft BN44 143 D3
Stonecroft Cl BN3 166 E4
Stonecrop Cl RH11 18 B3
Stonecross La RH16 64 E3
Stonecross Rd BN2 168 F4
Stonefield Cl RH10, RH11 18 D5
Stonefield Way RH15 106 F5
Stonefields BN16 199 D5
Stonehall La RH17 63 C6
Stoneham Rd BN3 186 F7
Stonehill Cres PO21 194 B3
Stonehouse La RH13 81 B1
Stonehouse Rd GU30 25 D4
Stonehurst Ct BN2 188 C6
Stonehurst Rd BN13 182 A5
Stoneleigh Ave BN1 167 F6
Stoneleigh Cl Brighton BN1 167 F6
East Grinstead RH19 9 F1
Stonepit La BN5 123 C5
Stonepound Crossroads BN6 126 D4
Stonepound Rd BN6 126 E4
Stoners Cl RH6 5 E7
Stonery Cl BN41 166 A2
Stonery Rd BN41 166 A2
Stoney La Balcombe Lane RH17 41 B5
Bracklesham PO20 202 D4
Shoreham-by-Sea BN43 185 C8
Stoney Stile Cl PO21 194 C2
Stoney Stile La PO21 194 C1
Stoneybrook RH12 35 F1
Stoneycroft Wlk 3 RH11 17 D5
Stoneyfield Cotts PO20 156 B1
Stoneywish Ctry Pk BN6 127 E3
Stopham Cl BN14 182 A5
Stopham Rd Crawley RH10 19 C3
Stopham RH20 97 E1
Stor Meadow RH20 119 D2
Storrington Cl
Fishbourne PO18, PO19 172 B7
Hove BN3 166 E2
Storrington Cty Prim Sch RH20 119 C2
Storrington Rd
Heath Common RH20 120 A5
Washington RH20 141 C8
Storrington Rise BN14 161 F4
Story Rd PO19 173 C7
Stour Cl BN13 181 C8
Stour Rd BN13 181 C8
Strachey Ct 1 RH11 18 B1
Strand Cl RH10 19 D4
Strand Par BN12 181 E3
Strand The Brighton BN2 188 F3
Ferring BN12 200 E4
Worthing BN12 181 C3
Strand Way PO22 196 B4
Strange Gdn PO21 194 E1
Strathfield Cl RH16 85 F4
Strathmoor Gdns GU29 70 F1
Strathmore Cl BN13 181 E4
Strathmore Rd Crawley RH11 5 A1
Worthing BN12, BN13 181 E4
Stratton Ct PO22 195 E5
Strawberry La RH20 120 B5
Stream Cl PO18 171 B5
Stream La RH20 99 B1
Stream Pk RH19 9 A3
Streathleigh Ct PO21 195 A2
Streel's La GU28 51 F5
Street End La PO20 192 E3
Street End Rd PO20 192 E3
Street Hill RH10 19 E5
Street La RH17 64 A8
Street The Albourne Green BN6 125 C6
Boxgrove PO18, PO20 154 D4
Bramber BN44 143 F2
Bury RH20 138 A7
Charlwood RH6 4 E7
Clapham BN13 160 E1
East Preston BN16 199 F6
Lancing BN15 183 F8
Nutbourne RH20 99 A2
Patching BN13 160 D2
Plaistow RH14 30 E2
Rustington BN16 199 C5
Shoreham-by-Sea BN43 164 E1
Slinfold RH13 34 D4
Stedham GU29 70 A1
Thakeham RH20 120 B7
Walberton BN18 156 D1
Walberton BN18 176 E8
Warninglid RH17 82 F8
Washington RH20 141 D6
West Itchenor PO20 190 F7
Westmeston BN6 148 F8
Streete Ct 7 PO21 195 B2
Streetfield Rd RH13 34 E3
Stretch Hill RH20 97 A5
Strettington La PO18 154 A3
Strettons Copse GU30 47 B2
Strickland Cl RH11 17 E5
Stringer Way BN1 167 F3
Strone Ct BN11 181 F1
Strood La RH12 35 C7
Stroud Green Dr PO21 194 F5
Stroudley Cl RH10 19 B5
Stroudley Ct BN16 199 E6
Strouds La PO21 194 F5
Strudgate Cl RH10 19 B4
Stuart Cl Crawley RH10 19 D5
Worthing BN11 182 F4
Stuart Way RH19 22 F7
Stuarts Meadow GU28 114 C8
Stubbermere PO9 149 B8
Stubcroft La PO20 202 B7
Stubfield RH12 36 A3
Stubpond La RH19, RH7 8 D7
Stumblemead RH17 41 A1
Stumblets RH10 19 C7
Stumps End PO18 171 C4
Stumps La PO18 171 C4
Sturges Rd PO21 195 C3
Sturt Ave GU27 26 F5
Sturt Rd GU27 26 F5
Sudbury Cl PO21 194 C1
Sudeley Pl BN2 188 D4
Sudeley St BN2 188 D4
Sudeley Terr 6 BN2 188 D4
Sudley Gdns PO21 195 D3
Sudley Rd PO21 195 D3
Suffolk Cl RH6 2 A2
Suffolk St BN3 186 F8
Sugar La RH17 65 C4
Sugden Rd BN11 182 F3
Sugworth Cl RH16 85 D7
Sullington Cl BN2 168 F4
Sullington Copse RH20 119 F2
Sullington Gdns BN14 161 F3
Sullington Hill RH11 18 D4
Sullington La RH20 140 F7
Sullington Mead RH12 35 E3
Sullington Way BN43 185 A8
Sullivan Dr RH11 17 E3
Sultan Rd PO10 149 B1
Summer Cl BN41 186 A7
Summer La PO21 193 F1
Summerdale Rd BN3 166 D2
Summerdown Cl BN13 181 B5
Summerdown Ct BN13 181 B5
Summerfield Rd PO20 190 C2
Summerfields BN14 161 E6
Summerfold House Sch RH15 107 A4
Summerhill Cl
Bognor Regis PO22 196 D6
Haywards Heath RH16 85 F7
Summerhill Dr
Bognor Regis PO22 196 C6
Haywards Heath RH16 86 A7
Summerhill Grange RH16 85 F7
Summerhill La RH16 85 F7
Summerlea Gdns 5 BN17 198 E5
Summerley La PO22 196 B5
Summers Ho GU29 92 D6
Summersdale Ct PO19 152 F3
Summersdale Rd PO19 153 A1
Summersdeane BN42 165 F1
Summersfield GU33 45 B4
Summersvere Cl RH10 6 A1
Sumners RH17 64 B7
Sun Brow GU27 27 A5
Sun Ct Chichester PO19 173 A5
10 Worthing BN11 182 A1
Sun Park Cl PO21 195 A6
Sundale La PO22 196 E5
Sunderland Cl PO20 154 D2
Sundew Cl RH11 18 A2
Sunneymead Cl PO20 206 E6
Sunningdale Ct Crawley RH11 18 D4
Worthing BN12 181 C3
Sunningdale Gdns
Bognor Regis PO22 195 B7
East Wittering PO20 201 D7
Sunningdale Rd BN13 181 E6
Sunninghill Ave BN3 166 F2
Sunninghill Cl BN3 166 E2
Sunny Ave RH10 21 A8
Sunny Cl BN12 181 E1
Sunny Way PO18 171 B5
Sunnybox La BN18 156 E4
Sunnycroft Cl RH17 86 E2
Sunnydale Ave BN1 168 A6
Sunnydale Cl BN1 168 A6
Sunnydown Ct BN16 199 A3
Sunnyhill Cl RH10 21 A8
Sunnymead Crawley RH11 18 D6
Crawley Down RH10 21 B8
Sunnymead Cl PO22 197 A6
Sunnymead Dr PO20 206 E6
Sunnywood Dr RH16 85 D3
Sunset La RH20 119 C5
Sunte Ave RH16 85 F7
Sunte Cl RH16 85 E7
Sunvale Ave GU27 26 D6
Sunvale Cl GU27 26 D6
Surrenden Cl BN1 167 F4
Surrenden Cres BN1 167 E4
Surrenden Holt BN1 167 F3
Surrenden Lodge BN1 167 F2
Surrenden Pk BN1 168 A4
Surrenden Rd BN1 167 F3
Surrenden Rise RH11 39 C8
Surrey Cott 5 BN17 198 F4
Surrey Ho 12 BN2 188 D4
Surrey St Arundel BN18 158 A2
Brighton BN1 207 F6
Littlehampton BN17 198 D5
Worthing BN11 182 C1
Surrey Wharf BN18 158 B2
Surry St BN43 184 F7
Sussex Bsns Village The PO22 176 E6
Sussex Ct Elmer PO22 197 B5
2 Haywards Heath RH16 85 E3
Horsham RH13 36 E1
13 Hove BN3 187 C6
Sussex Cty Cricket Gd BN3 187 C7
Sussex Dr PO21 194 A1
Sussex Eye Hospl BN2 188 D4
Sussex Gdns
Haywards Heath RH16 86 B3
Rustington BN16 199 C6
Sussex Hts 18 BN1 187 E5
Sussex House Ind Est BN3 186 F8
Sussex Lodge RH12 36 C4
Sussex Manor Bsns Pk RH10 6 A2
Sussex Mews 4 BN2 188 E4
Sussex Nuffield Hospl BN3 186 F7
Sussex Pl BN2 207 B6
Sussex Rd Haywards Heath RH16 85 E3
Hove BN3 187 B5
Nursted GU31 88 D7
Worthing BN11 182 D3
Sussex Sq Brighton BN2 188 E4
17 Haywards Heath RH16 85 E4
Sussex St Bognor Regis PO21 195 D3
Brighton BN2 207 B5
Littlehampton BN17 198 D6
Sussex Terr BN2 207 B6
Sussex Toy & Model Mus BN1 207 A6
Sussex Village PO22 197 B5
Sussex Way RH15 106 E5
Sutherland Cl
Bognor Regis PO21 195 C3
Rustington BN16 199 B5
Sutherland Ct 4 PO21 195 C3
Sutherland Rd BN2 188 C5
Sutton Ave BN16 199 C4
Sutton Cl PO22 195 F6
Swainsthorpe Cl RH16 85 F3
Swaledale Cl RH11 18 C3
Swallow Rd RH11 18 C8
Swallowfield Cl RH13 59 C5
Swallows Cl 3 BN15 184 C5
Swallows Green Dr BN13 181 C5
Swallows La RH13 101 F6
Swallows The BN17 198 D4
Swallowtail Rd RH12 36 E6
Swan Barn Rd GU27 27 D6
Swan Cl Emsworth PO10 169 C8
Southwater RH13 58 A2
Storrington RH20 119 C2
Swan Ct RH20 98 B2
Swan Dene PO21 204 F7
Swan La RH6 4 F7
Swan Sq RH12 36 C2
Swan View RH20 98 C1
Swan Wlk RH12 36 C2
Swanborough Ct 7 BN43 184 F7
Swanborough Dr BN2 188 F7
Swanborough Pl BN2 188 F7
Swanbourne Cl BN15 183 F8
Swanbourne Rd BN17 178 D3
Swandean Hospl BN13 181 D8
Swanfield Dr PO19 173 C8
Swann Cl RH15 107 D3
Swann Way RH12 35 E3
Swans Ghyll RH18 23 E3
Swansea Gdns PO21 195 B2
Sweda Ct 13 BN2 188 D4
Sweetlands BN6 127 B5
Swift La RH11 18 C8
Swift Rd PO10 169 C3
Swift Way BN17 178 C4
Swillage La BN16 180 A8
Swindon Rd RH12 36 B4
Swiss Gdns BN43 184 E7
Swissland Hill RH19, RH7 9 E7
Sycamore Ave RH12 37 C6
Sycamore Cl Angmering BN16 179 F4
Crawley RH11 5 C1
Portslade-by-Sea BN41 166 C3
Sycamore Dr RH19 10 A1
Sycamore Rd PO22 195 C7
Sycamores The
Chichester PO19 173 A7
Sayers Common BN6 105 D1
Sydenham Terr PO10 149 D5
Sydney Rd RH16 85 E6
Sydney St BN1 207 A6
Sydney Tidy Ho 5 BN2 188 C6
Syers Rd GU33 45 B4
Sylvan Cl RH16 86 B4
Sylvan Rd Crawley RH10 19 A4
Lancing BN15 183 B6
Sylvan Way PO21 195 B3
Sylvester Way BN3 166 C3
Sylvia Cl PO21 194 A1
Symbister Rd BN41 186 C7
Syresham Gdns RH16 85 F4

Tabard Gate PO21 194 B1
Tack Lee Rd BN18 176 F3
Talbot Cres BN1 168 D6
Talbot La RH12 36 C1
Talbot Rd BN17 198 C5
Tallis Cl RH11 17 F3
Talman Cl RH11 17 E5
Tamar Ave BN13 181 C7
Tamar Cl Crawley RH10 19 C5
Worthing BN13 181 C7
Tamar Way PO20 154 D2
Tamarisk Cl PO22 195 C6
Tamarisk Way Ferring BN12 200 F5
Littlehampton BN16 199 F4
Tamarisk Wlk PO20 201 F6
Tamworth Rd BN3 186 F7
Tanbridge House Sch RH12 35 F2
Tanbridge Pk RH12 36 B1

Tanbridge Pl RH12 36 B1
Tandridge Rd BN3 186 E6
Tanfield Ct RH12 36 B2
Tangle Oak RH19 8 E4
Tangmere Cty Prim Sch PO20 154 D2
Tangmere Gdns PO21 194 D2
Tangmere Military Aviation Mus PO20 154 D1
Tangmere Rd Brighton BN1 168 A6
Crawley RH11 17 F6
Oving PO20 174 B8
Tankerdale La GU33 45 A1
Tanners La GU27 27 C7
Tanners Mead RH17 61 E5
Tannery Cl RH13 34 D3
Tansy Mead RH20 119 B2
Tanyard Ave RH19 23 A8
Tanyard Cl Crawley RH10 19 C3
Horsham RH13 36 E1
Tanyard Cotts BN44 143 C3
Tanyard La Danehill RH17 66 C4
Steyning BN44 143 D3
Tanyard Way RH6 2 B4
Tarham Cl RH6 1 E5
Tarmount La BN43 184 F7
Tarner Rd BN2 207 B6
Tarragon Way BN43 165 C1
Tarrant St BN18 158 B3
Tarrant Wharf BN18 158 B2
Tarring Gate BN13 182 A4
Tarring Rd BN11 182 B3
Tasman Cl BN16 199 D4
Tasman Way BN13 181 C6
Tatchells GU29 92 D6
Tate Cres RH15 106 F5
Tate's Way RH12 33 D7
Tatham Ct RH11 18 B1
Taunton Cl RH10 19 D6
Taunton Rd BN2 168 F1
Taverner Pl PO19 173 B5
Tavistock Down BN1 168 C2
Tavistock & Summerhill Sch RH16 85 F7
Tavy Cl BN13 181 C6
Tavy Rd BN13 181 C6
Taw Cl BN13 181 D7
Taylor Wlk RH11 18 C6
Taylor's La PO18 171 C4
Taylors Field GU29 92 E6
Taylors Rise GU29 92 E6
Teal Cl RH12 36 C5
Teal La PO20 206 C8
Teasel Cl RH11 18 B3
Teesdale RH11 18 C3
Teg Cl BN41 166 C2
Teign Wlk BN13 181 C8
Teknol Ho RH15 106 E2
Telegraph La GU31 90 A3
Telegraph St 12 BN2 188 C4
Telford Pl RH10 18 E5
Telgarth Rd BN12 200 F4
Telham Ct 5 RH11 17 F3
Templars Cl PO22 196 D6
Templars Cty Fst Sch BN15 183 B6
Templars The BN14 182 E7
Temple Cl RH10 19 D5
Temple Ct 2 BN17 198 E5
Temple Gdns BN1, BN3 187 E6
Temple Gr RH15 106 D4
Temple La RH12 3 A4
Temple Rd GU33 45 C6
Temple St BN1 187 E6
Templesheen Rd PO22 197 B5
Ten Acres BN11 183 A3
Tenacre Cl PO19 173 C8
Tenantry Down Rd BN2 188 E8
Tenantry Rd BN2 188 D8
Tennis Rd BN3 186 E6
Tennyson Ave BN16 199 B5
Tennyson Cl Crawley RH10 19 B8
Horsham RH12 36 E6
Tennyson Ct 5 RH16 85 D5
Tennyson Rd
Bognor Regis PO21 195 B3
Worthing BN11 182 C2
Tennyson Rise RH19 22 C8
Tennyson's La GU27 27 E4
Tennysons GU27 27 E4
Terminus Mill PO19 172 F5
Terminus Pl 9 Brighton BN1 207 F7
Littlehampton BN17 198 D5
Terminus Rd Brighton BN1 207 F7
Chichester PO19 172 E5
Littlehampton BN17 198 C5
Terminus Road Ind Est PO19 172 E5
Terminus St BN1 207 F6
Tern Rd RH11 17 D5
Terrace The Crossbush BN18 158 E1
Lancing BN15 183 E4
Sidlesham PO20 203 F7
Worthing BN12 181 C2
Terringes Ave BN13 181 F5
Terry Rd RH11 18 B1
Terry's Cross BN5 124 C2
Terwick La GU31 91 A8
Terwick Rise GU31 68 D6
Test Rd BN15 183 B6
Testers Cl RH13 80 A7
Teville Gate BN14 182 D3
Teville Inds BN14 182 F5
Teville Pl BN11 182 C3
Teville Rd BN11 182 D3
Thackeray Rd BN14 182 F4
Thakeham Cl
East Preston BN16 180 B3
Worthing BN12 181 A2
Thakeham Copse RH20 120 B3
Thakeham Cty Prim Sch RH20 120 B7
Thakeham Dr BN12 181 A2
Thakeham Rd RH20 119 F2
Thalassa Rd BN11 183 B3
Thames Cl Brighton BN2 207 B5
Littlehampton BN16, BN17 199 A4
Thames Way BN13 181 D7
Thatch Cott BN15 183 F8
Thatcher Cl RH10 18 D3
Thatchers Cl Burgess Hill RH15 107 D1
Horley RH6 2 B5
Horsham RH12 36 E4
Thatchway Cl BN17 198 D6
Thatchway The
Angmering BN16 179 E5
Littlehampton BN16 199 D4
Theatre La PO19 173 A6
Theatre Pl 8 PO19 173 A6
Thelton Ave RH12 35 D3
Theobalds Rd RH15 107 D6
Theobold Ho 1 BN1 207 A6
Thesiger Cl BN11 183 A4
Thesiger Rd BN11 183 A4
Theydon Cl RH10 19 A4
Thicket La PO18 155 B5
Third Ave Almodington PO20 202 E8
Bognor Regis PO22 196 B4
Bracklesham PO20 202 B5
Hove BN3 187 B6
Lancing BN15 183 E7
Worthing BN14 182 D7
Thirlmere Cres BN14, BN15 183 B5
Thirlmere Rd RH11 17 D4
Thirlmere Way PO22 196 B6
Thistledowne Gdns PO10 169 D8
Thomas a'Becket Cty Fst Sch BN13 182 A5
Thomas a'Becket Cty Mid Sch BN14 182 A5
Thomas Bennett Com Coll RH10 18 D3
Thomas Bennett Com Sch RH10 18 E2
Thompson Ct 15 RH11 18 B1
Thompson Rd BN1 168 C1
Thompson's Hospital GU28 73 F1
Thorgate Rd BN17 178 B3
Thorn Rd BN11 182 C1
Thornberry Cty Middle Sch BN15 183 F5
Thornbush Cres BN41 166 B3
Thorncroft Rd BN17 198 F6
Thorndean Rd BN2 168 D3
Thornden RH13 81 E2
Thorndene Ave PO21 195 B4
Thorndyke Cl RH10 19 D5
Thorney Dr PO20 206 C7
Thorney Island Cty Prim Sch PO10 169 C3
Thorney Old Pk PO10 169 F1
Thorney Rd PO10 169 D6
Thornham La PO10 169 D6
Thornham Marina PO10 169 E6
Thornhill Ave BN1 168 A7
Thornhill Cl BN3 166 E2
Thornhill Rise BN41 166 A4
Thornhill Way BN41 166 A3
Thornscroft BN44 143 D4
Thornsdale 4 BN2 207 B6
Thornton Cl RH6 1 E3
Thornton Ct 2 BN16 199 E6
Thornton Meadow RH14 76 B8
Thornton Pl RH6 1 F3
Threal's La RH20 119 E6
Threals Copse RH20 119 E5
Three Acres RH12 36 A1
Three Bridges Cty Fst Sch RH10 19 A7
Three Bridges Cty Mid Sch RH10 18 F6
Three Bridges Rd RH10 19 A6
Three Bridges Sta RH10 19 B6
Three Gates La GU27 27 E8
Threestile Rd RH12 14 F1
Thrusloes PO21 194 F3
Thurlow Rd BN11 182 F3
Thurne Way RH12 33 D7
Thyme Cl BN43 165 C1
Ticehurst Cl RH10 19 E6
Ticehurst Rd BN2 188 F5
Tichborne Cotts RH16 86 C6
Tichborne St BN1 207 A5
Tideway BN16, BN17 199 A4
Tidy St BN1 207 A6
Tilbury Pl BN2 207 B5
Tilbury Way BN2 207 B6
Tile Barn Est PO20 191 C1
Tile Barn La PO20 191 C1
Tilers Cl RH15 107 D3
Tilgate Cl BN2 188 D6
Tilgate Dr RH10, RH11 18 E2
Tilgate Forest Bsns Ctr RH11 18 D1
Tilgate Forest Golf Course RH10 19 A2
Tilgate Forest Recn Ctr RH10 18 D1
Tilgate Forest Row RH11 39 C5
Tilgate Par RH10 18 E3
Tilgate Pl RH10 18 E3
Tilgate Way RH10 18 E3
Tilletts La RH12 35 E8
Tillinghurst La RH17 42 A2
Tillington BN2 188 F7
Tillington Cotts BN18 176 F3
Tillotson Cl RH10 19 D5
Tillstone Cl BN2 168 D2
Tillstone St BN2 207 B5
Tiltwood Dr RH10 21 C8
Timber Cl BN13 181 C5
Timber Ct RH12 36 C3
Timber Mill RH13 57 F2
Timberham Farm Rd RH6 5 D8
Timberham Link RH6 5 E8
Timberham Way RH6 5 E8
Timberlaine Ind Est PO19 173 C5
Timberlaine Trad Est BN14 182 F5
Timberlands 13 Crawley RH11 18 B1
Storrington RH20 119 E2
Timberlea Cl RH20 121 A5
Timberleys 1 BN17 199 A6
Timbermill Ct GU27 26 F6
Timbers The RH13 59 C6
Tindal Cl RH15 107 D3
Tinghall PO21 194 E3
Tinsley Gn RH10 6 B4
Tinsley La RH10 6 A1
Tinsley La N RH10 6 B3
Tinsley La S RH10 19 A8
Tintagel Ct Horsham RH13 36 D1
6 Shoreham-by-Sea BN43 184 F7
Tintern Cl BN1 168 B1
Tintern Rd RH11 18 A4
Tinwood La PO18 154 E5
Tipper La GU31 89 D3
Tiree Path RH11 18 B3
Tisbury Rd BN3 187 C6
Titch Hill BN15 163 A3
Titchfield Cl RH15 107 D1
Tithe Barn BN15 183 E8
Tithe Barn Chalets PO20 206 B8
Tithe Barn Cl PO21 194 C1
Tithe Barn Ct PO21 205 B8
Tithe Barn Way PO21 194 B1
Tithe Gn BN16 199 B5
Tithe Orch RH19 8 E4
Titian Rd BN3 186 F7
Titmus Dr RH10 18 F2
Titnore La BN12, BN13 181 A6
Titnore Way BN12, BN13 181 A6
Tivoli 3 BN1 167 E2
Tivoli Cres BN1 167 D1
Tivoli Cres N BN1 167 D2
Tivoli Pl BN1 167 D2
Tivoli Rd BN1 167 D2
Toat Hill RH13 56 E8
Toat La RH20 98 A8
Tobias Sch of Art RH19 22 E6
Toddington La BN17 178 E4
Toddington Pk BN17 178 E3
Todds Cl RH6 1 E5
Toftwood Cl RH10 19 C5
Tollbridge Ho BN43 184 D8
Tollgate RH16 86 B8
Tollgate Hill RH11 18 C1
Tollgate La RH17 84 E8
Tollhouse Cl PO19 172 F6
Tompset's Bank RH18 23 F1
Tongdean Ave BN3 167 C2
Tongdean Ct BN1 167 D4
Tongdean La
Brighton BN1, BN3 167 C4
Brighton BN1 167 D4
Tongdean Rd BN3 167 C3
Tongdean Rise BN1 167 C4
Toomey Rd BN44 143 D5
Top Rd Sharpthorne RH19 43 B5
Slindon BN18 156 C5
Top St RH17 83 C4
Torcross Cl BN2 168 E1
Toronto Cl BN13 181 D6
Toronto Terr BN2 188 C6
Torrance Cl BN3 166 F1
Torridge Cl BN13 181 C7
Torton Hill Rd BN18 157 F2
Tote La GU29 70 A5
Totland Rd BN2 188 D7
Tott Hill BN6 126 B5
Tottington Dr BN5 144 F6
Tottington Way BN43 165 B1
Tower Cl Chichester PO19 172 F7
East Grinstead RH19 9 E2
Horley RH6 1 F3
Liphook GU30 25 B4
Tower Hill RH12 58 A8
Tower Ct RH19 9 E2
Tower Hill RH12, RH13 58 A8
Tower Ho 4 Brighton BN1 167 E2
Burgess Hill RH15 107 B2
Tower House Cl RH17 84 E7
Tower Pl PO20 201 F7
Tower Rd Brighton BN2 188 C6
Colgate RH12 38 A7
Lancing BN15 183 D5
Liphook GU30 25 B4
Worthing BN11 182 E3
Tower St Chichester PO19 172 F6
Emsworth PO10 169 C8
Towergate BN1 167 E2
Towers Convent Sch The BN44 144 B1
Towers Rd BN44 144 B2
Town Barn Rd RH11 18 C7
Town Cross Ave PO21 195 C4
Town La PO18 133 C4
Town Mead RH11 18 D7
Town Place Farm Cotts RH17 87 C7
Townfield RH14 53 B2
Townsend Cres BN17 198 F6
Tozer Ct BN41 186 B7
Tozer Way PO19 173 B6
Trafalgar Ct
8 Bognor Regis PO21 195 B2
Brighton BN1 207 A6
Trafalgar Cty Inf Prim Sch RH12 36 B4
Trafalgar Gate BN2 188 F3
Trafalgar La BN1 207 A6
Trafalgar Pl BN1 207 A6
Trafalgar Rd Horsham RH12 36 C4
Portslade-by-Sea BN41 186 B8
Trafalgar St BN1 207 A6
Trafalgar Terr BN1 207 A6
Tramway Cl PO20 192 F8
Treadcroft Dr RH12 36 E5
Treadwheel Rd PO8 128 D6
Tredcroft Rd BN3 167 C2
Tree Ave GU27 26 F8
Treemans Rd RH17 65 B2
Treetops RH13 79 F7
Treeview RH11 18 C1
Trefoil Cl RH12 36 E5
Trefoil Cres RH11 18 A2
Tregarth Rd PO19 153 A2
Tregenna Ho GU30 25 B5
Treharne Cl BN13 181 D7
Treloar Rd PO11 189 B1
Trendle Gn PO21 194 F2
Trenear Cl RH13 36 E2
Trent Cl Crawley RH11 17 F4
Lancing BN15 183 C6
Trent Rd BN11, BN12 181 E2
Tretawn Gdns PO20 206 F6
Trevanne Plat RH10 19 D7
Treveor Cl BN11 182 C2
Treyford Cl RH11 17 F6
Triangle Rd RH16 85 E3
Triangle The BN15 183 C4
Trinity Cl RH10 19 C8
Trinity Rd BN6 126 A6
Trinity St BN2 207 B7
Trinity Way Bognor Regis PO21 194 F4
Littlehampton BN17 198 F4
Tripp Hill RH20 116 F7
Tristram Cl BN15 183 B7
Triton Pl PO22 196 C5
Troon Cl RH11 17 D5
Trotton Cl RH10 19 C3
Trotton Rd GU29, GU31 91 A7
Trotyn Croft PO21 194 F2
Trout La RH13 79 A7
Trout Rd GU27 26 E6
Troymede RH17 41 A1
True Blue Prec BN17 178 D3
Truggers RH17 61 C8
Truleigh Cl BN44 144 B2
Truleigh Dr BN41 166 A4
Truleigh Rd BN44 144 B2
Truleigh Way BN43 165 A1
Trumpers La GU28 95 F8
Trundle Cl PO18 152 E6
Trundle Mead RH12 36 C5
Trundle View Cl PO22 176 B6
Truro Cl PO19 152 F1
Truro Cres PO21 194 E3
Trusler's Hill BN6 124 F6
Tryndel Way PO22 196 B4
Tudor Ave PO10 149 A4
Tudor Cl Chichester PO19 152 F2
Crawley RH10 19 D5
East Grinstead RH19 22 F8
Findon BN14 161 E6
Hove BN3 166 F2
Marehill RH20 98 F1
Middleton-on-Sea PO22 196 D5
Tudor Ct 9 PO22 195 D4
Tudor Dr Upper Beeding BN44 144 A3
Westergate PO20 175 D8
Tudor Gdns RH15 106 F4
Tudor Ho RH13 36 F3
Tudor View BN17 198 C4
Tudor Village RH20 120 C3
Tuff's Hard PO18 191 C7
Tufts Field GU29 92 D6
Tufts Meadow GU29 92 E6
Tuggles Plat RH12 35 E7
Tulip Ct RH12 36 C4
Tullett Rd RH10 19 B2
Tunbridge Cres GU30 25 B5
Tunbridge La GU30 25 B6
Tunnmeade RH11 17 E5
Tungsate BN44 143 D3
Tuppenny La PO10 169 E8
Turkey La RH15 107 B3
Turnberry Ct 14 RH16 85 E4
Turnbull Rd PO19 173 B7
Turner Ct RH19 10 A3
Turner Rd BN14 182 E6
Turner Way PO20 206 F7
Turner's Hill Rd RH19 22 B6
Turners Hill CE (C) Sch RH10 21 A3
Turners Hill Rd RH10 21 A7
Turners Mead RH20 119 B2
Turners Mill Cl RH16 85 D7
Turners Mill Rd RH16 85 D6
Turners Way RH15 106 F4
Turnpike Cl PO19 172 F3
Turnpike Pl RH11 18 D8
Turnpike Rd BN18 138 F6
Turret Ct RH19 9 C3
Turton Cl BN2 188 D5
Tuscan Ave PO22 196 F5
Tuscany Gdns RH10 18 E8
Tushmore Ave RH10, RH11 5 E1
Tushmore La RH10, RH11 18 E8
Tushmore Rdbt RH11 18 D8
Tussock Cl RH11 18 A4
Tuxford Cl RH10 19 C4
Tweed La RH11 4 F1
Twineham CE (C) Prim Sch RH17 105 A4
Twineham Cl BN2 188 F7
Twineham La BN6, RH17 105 A3
Twitten Cl 2 BN42 185 E7
Twitten La RH19 8 E4
Twitten The
Albourne Green BN6 125 C6
Burgess Hill RH15 107 B4
Ditchling BN6 127 D3
Southwick BN42 185 E7
Twitten Way BN13, BN14 182 A4
Two Barns La PO18 152 D6
Two Mile Ash Rd RH12, RH13 57 D3
Two Ways RH14 32 A4
Twyford Cl BN13 181 E6
Twyford Gdns BN13 181 E6
Twyford Rd Brighton BN1 168 E6
Worthing BN13 181 E6
Twyhurst Ct RH19 9 D3
Twyne Cl RH11 17 F4
Twyner Cl RH6 2 D4
Tye La BN18 156 E1
Tylden Way RH12 36 F6
Tyler Rd RH10 18 D3
Tyler's Gn RH16, RH17 85 B4
Tylston Meadow GU30 25 B5
Tymperley Ct RH13 36 E3
Tyne Cl Crawley RH10 19 C5
Worthing BN13 181 C7
Tyne Way PO21 194 D4
Tynings The BN15 183 E5
Tyson Pl 9 BN2 207 B5
Tythe Barn RH17 83 C3
Tythe Barn Rd PO20 206 E6

Uckfield Cl BN2 188 F6
Ullswater Dr BN16 179 A3
Ullswater Gr PO22 196 B6
Ullswater Rd BN15 183 B5
Underdown Rd BN42 185 E8
Underhill La Clayton BN45, BN6 147 E8
Westmeston BN6 148 C8
Undermill Rd BN44 144 B2
Underwood Cl RH10 21 B8
Underwood Rd GU27 26 F7
Unifax BN12 181 C3
Union Pl BN11 182 D2
Union Rd BN2 207 B7
Union St BN1 207 A5
Univ of Brighton BN1 207 A5
Univ of Brighton (Belgrave St Annexe) BN2 207 B6
Univ of Brighton (Cockcroft/ Watts Annexes) BN2 168 D2
Univ of Brighton (Finsbury Rd Annexe) BN2 207 B6
Univ of Brighton (St Peter's Ho) BN2 207 A6
Upfield RH6 2 A1
Upfield Cl RH6 2 A1
Upfield Villas RH14 54 C2
Uphill Way PO20 193 A8
Uplands Ave BN13 181 F8
Uplands Cl GU27 27 D8
Uplands Rd Brighton BN1 168 C2
Rowland's Castle PO9 128 E2
Uplands Sch BN2 168 C2
Uppark GU31 109 B8
Uppark Gdns RH12 36 F6
Uppark Way PO22 196 D7
Upper Abbey Rd BN2 188 D4
Upper Bedford St BN2 188 C4
Upper Beeding Cty Prim Sch BN44 144 A2
Upper Bevendean Ave BN2 168 E1
Upper Bognor Rd 3
Bognor Regis PO21, PO22 195 D4
Bognor Regis PO21 195 E4
Upper Boundstone La
Lancing BN15 183 D7
Lancing BN15 183 D8
Upper Brighton Rd
Lancing BN15 183 C8
Worthing BN14 182 D7
Upper Chalvington Pl BN2 188 E5
Upper Cl RH18 23 F2
Upper Dr BN16 200 B4
Upper Dr The BN3 187 D8
Upper Forecourt RH6 6 B7
Upper Gardner St BN1 207 A6
Upper Gloucester Rd BN1 207 F6
Upper Hamilton Rd BN1 207 F8
Upper High St BN11 182 E3
Upper Hollingdean Rd BN1, BN2 168 B1
Upper Kingston La BN42, BN43 165 D1
Upper Lewes Rd BN2 207 B7
Upper Lodges BN1 168 D8
Upper Market St BN3 187 D5
Upper Mount GU33 45 A3
Upper North St BN1 207 F5
Upper Park Pl 7 BN2 207 B5
Upper Rock Gdns BN2 207 B5
Upper Roedale Cotts BN1 168 B4
Upper Shoreham Rd BN43 185 A8
Upper Sq RH18 23 E3
Upper St RH20 97 A3
Upper St James's St BN2 207 B4
Upper St Johns Rd RH15 107 A4
Upper Station Rd BN5 123 D5
Upper Sudeley St 7 BN2 188 D4
Upper Wellington Rd 5 BN2 188 C7
Upper West Dr BN12 200 E5
Upper West La BN15 183 E8
Upper Winfield Ave BN1 167 F6
Upperfield GU29 70 F2
Upperton Rd GU28 73 C1
Upton Ave BN42 165 E1
Upton Ct BN13 181 F3

Upton Gdns BN13 181 F4
Upton Rd Stockbridge PO19 172 F4
Worthing BN13 181 F4
Upways Cl PO20 203 F1
Ursula Ave PO20 206 D6
Ursula Ave N PO20 206 D6
Ursula Sq PO20 206 D5

Vachery La GU6 11 E7
Vale Ave Brighton BN1 167 E7
Worthing BN14 161 F2
Vale Ct BN41 186 B7
Vale Cty Fst & Mid Sch BN14 161 F2
Vale Dr Horsham RH12 36 B3
Worthing BN14 161 F2
Vale Gdns BN41 186 B7
Vale Rd Haywards Heath RH16 85 E2
Portslade-by-Sea BN3, BN41 186 C7
Vale Wlk BN14 161 F1
Valebridge Cl RH15 107 C6
Valebridge Dr RH15 107 C5
Valebridge Rd RH15 107 C6
Valencia Rd BN11 182 A3
Valentine Cl BN14 182 B7
Valentine Ct 14 BN3 187 C7
Valentine Dr RH15 106 E4
Valentines Gdns PO21 194 C2
Valentines Lea GU28 51 A8
Valerie Cl BN41 166 C2
Valetta Pk PO10 169 A8
Valetta Rd PO10 169 F1
Valewood Cl RH14 56 D1
Valewood La RH13, RH14 56 D1
Valewood Rd GU27 27 C4
Valiant Rd PO10 169 F1
Vallance Cl RH15 106 E4
Vallance Gdns BN3 187 A6
Vallance Rd BN3 187 A6
Vallensdean Cotts BN41 166 C2
Valley Cl BN1 167 C4
Valley Dr BN1 167 C4
Valley Rd Lancing BN15 183 C8
Portslade-by-Sea BN41 166 A2
Valley Side GU30 25 B5
Valverde Ho 13 BN3 187 C7
Van Dyck Pl PO22 195 A6
Van Gogh Pl PO22 195 B6
Vanbrugh Cl RH11 17 E3
Vanbrugh Ct 21 BN3 187 C7
Vancouver Cl BN13 181 D6
Vancouver Dr RH11 5 D1
Vancouver Rd BN13 181 D6
Vann Bridge Cl GU27 49 A6
Vann Rd GU27 49 A6
Vanners RH10 18 E7
Vanzell Rd GU29 71 A1
Varndean Cl BN1 167 E3
Varndean Coll BN1 167 F3
Varndean Dr BN1 167 E3
Varndean Gdns BN1 167 E3
Varndean Holt BN1 167 F3
Varndean Rd BN1 167 E3
Varndean Sch BN1 168 A3
Varsity Rd PO10 169 F1
Velyn Ave PO19 173 B6
Ventnor Villas BN3 187 B6
Venus La PO21 204 E7
Veras Wlk RH20 120 C1
Verbania Way RH19 10 B1
Vere Rd BN1, BN2 207 A8
Veric 12 BN3 187 C7
Verica Ct PO19 172 A7
Vermont Dr BN16 200 A5
Vermont Way BN16 200 A5
Vernon Cl Horsham RH12 37 A4
Rustington BN16 199 C5
Vernon Ct 4 BN1 187 E6
Vernon Terr BN1 187 E7
Veronica Cl BN16 200 A4
Veronica Way BN2 207 B4
Viaduct Rd BN1, BN2 207 A7
Vicarage Fields BN13 181 D7
Vicarage La Bognor Regis PO22 196 A4
East Preston BN16 199 F5
Haslemere GU27 26 F6
Horley RH6 1 F4
Lodsworth GU28 72 B2
Scaynes Hill RH17 86 F3
Steyning BN44 143 D3
Vicarage Rd RH10 21 A8
Vicars Cl 7 PO19 173 A6
Viceroy Ct BN12 200 E5
Viceroy Lodge 9 BN3 187 A6
Victor Ct RH10 6 D1
Victor Rd PO10 169 F1
Victoria Ave Burgess Hill RH15 106 E3
Easebourne GU29 71 A1
Victoria Cl Burgess Hill RH15 106 E3
Burgess Hill RH15 106 F2
Horley RH6 2 A3
3 Midhurst GU29 92 E7
Victoria Cottage Hospl PO10 169 B8
Victoria Ct
6 Bognor Regis PO21 195 B2
Horsham RH13 36 D2
21 Hove BN3 187 C6
Portslade-by-Sea BN41 186 C8
3 Shoreham-by-Sea BN43 184 E7
3 Worthing BN11 182 C3
Victoria Dr PO21 195 B3
Victoria Gdns
Burgess Hill RH15 106 F2
Westergate PO20 175 D7
Victoria Gr 9 BN3 187 C6
Victoria Ind Est RH15 106 E2
Victoria Park Gdns 2 BN11 182 C3
Victoria Pl 11 Hove BN1 187 E6
Liphook GU30 47 E8
Victoria Rd Balcombe RH17 41 A1
Bognor Regis PO21 195 B2
Brighton BN1 187 E6
Burgess Hill RH15 106 E2
Chichester PO19 173 C7
Crawley RH11 18 C6
Emsworth PO10 149 A1
Haywards Heath RH16 86 A3
Horley RH6 2 B2
Portslade-by-Sea BN3, BN41 186 C8
Shoreham-by-Sea BN43 184 E7
Southwick BN41, BN42 185 D7
Worthing BN11 182 C3
Victoria Rd S PO21 195 B2
Victoria St Horsham RH13 36 D2
Hove BN1 187 E6
Victoria Terr
Bognor Regis PO22 195 F3
Lumley PO10 149 C1
Westbourne PO10 149 D3
Victoria Villas BN18 177 A3
Victoria Way Burgess Hill RH15 106 F2
East Grinstead RH19 22 F7
Victory Ct 9 PO21 195 B2
Victory Rd RH12 36 B3
View Terr RH7 10 A8
View The PO21 205 A8
Views Path RH16 86 B4
Villa Plage PO22 197 A5
Village Barn The BN1 167 E7
Villiers Ct BN1 207 A6
Vinall Gdns RH12 35 D4
Vincent Cl Horsham RH13 36 F2
Lancing BN15 183 D6
Vincent Rd PO20 206 C6
Vine Pl BN1 207 F6
Vine St BN1 207 A6
Vineries Cl BN13 182 A6
Vineries The Burgess Hill RH15 107 D3
1 Hove BN3 187 B6
Vinery Ct BN13 182 A6
Vines Cross Rd BN2 188 F7
Vinnetrow Rd PO20 173 E3
Vinols Cross RH19 42 F6
Vinson Rd GU33 45 C4
Viscount Dr PO21 205 B8
Vivienne Cl RH11 5 D1
Volks Electric Rly BN1, BN2 188 C4
Vowels La RH19 21 E2
Vulcan Cl RH11 18 C2
Vulcan Rd PO10 169 F1

Wad The PO20 190 B1
Waddington Cl RH11 18 A3
Wade End PO20 206 C8
Wadeway The PO20 206 C8
Wadeys The RH14 77 C8
Wadham Cl RH10 6 C1
Wadhurst Cl PO21 195 B4
Wadhurst Ct 4 BN13 182 A3
Wadhurst Dr BN12 181 B2
Wadhurst Rise BN2 188 F5
Wadlands Brook Rd RH19 9 D5
Wagg Cl RH19 10 A1
Wagtail Cl RH12 36 D7
Wain End RH12 36 D5
Wainwrights RH11 18 D3
Wakefield Rd BN2 207 B8
Wakefield Way PO21 194 E4
Wakehams Green Dr RH10 6 D1
Wakehurst Dr RH10, RH11 18 D3
Wakehurst La RH17 64 A8
Wakehurst Mews RH12 35 F1
Wakehurst Pl BN16 199 C6
Wakehurst Place
(Royal Bot Gdn) RH17 41 F3
Wakenhurst Ct BN11 182 F3
Wakestone La RH20 75 A2
Walberton & Binstead CE (C)
Prim Sch BN18 156 E1
Walberton Cl PO22 196 B5
Walberton Ct BN11 181 F1
Walberton Pk BN18 176 E8
Waldby Ct RH11 18 A3
Waldegrave Rd BN1 168 A1
Walders Rd BN16 199 B6
Waldron Ave BN1 168 D6
Waldron Pl BN1 168 D6
Walesbeech RH10 19 A5
Walker Rd RH10 19 C4
Wall Hill Rd RH18, RH19 23 E5
Wallace Ave BN11 181 F1
Wallace Ct 11 BN11 181 F2
Wallace Par 5 BN11 181 F2
Wallace Rd BN16 179 C3
Wallage La RH10 20 D6
Walled Gdn The RH14 31 F7
Wallfield PO21 194 F2
Wallis Ct RH10 5 D2
Wallis Ho RH19 9 E1
Wallis Way Burgess Hill RH15 106 E4
Horsham RH13 37 A4
Wallner Cres PO22 196 C5
Wallrock Wlk PO10 149 B4
Walmer Cl RH13 58 A2
Walmsleys Way PO20 202 C5
Walnut Ave Chichester PO19 172 F8
Rustington BN16 199 B5
Walnut Cl BN1 167 E3
Walnut Ct RH13 36 E1
Walnut La RH11 5 B1
Walnut Lodge BN14 182 C4
Walnut Pk RH16 86 B4
Walnut Tree Cotts RH14 77 A3
Walnut Tree Dr PO10 150 A3
Walnut Tree Way BN13 181 B5
Walpole Ave BN12 181 D2
Walpole Rd BN2 188 D5
Walpole Terr BN2 188 D5
Walsham Cl PO22 195 F6
Walsingham Rd BN3 186 F6
Walstead Ho 2 RH10 18 D5
Walter May Ho 13 BN2 188 F5
Waltham Park Rd RH20 117 B6
Walton Ave PO21 195 E3
Walton Bank BN1 168 E5
Walton Cl BN13 181 F6
Walton Heath RH10 19 D8
Walton La PO18 171 C5
Walton Lodge BN13 181 F6
Walton Rd PO21 195 E3
Wandle Cl RH10 19 C5
Wandleys Cl PO20 155 F1
Wandleys Dr PO20 155 F1
Wandleys La BN18, PO20 156 A2
Wandleys Lane Cvn Site PO20 155 F1
Wansford Way PO22 196 C4
Wantage Cl RH10 19 C3
Wantley Hill Est BN5 123 F6
Wantley La RH20 119 E2
Wantley Rd BN14 162 A1
War Memorial Hospl PO22 195 C5
Warble Heath Cl PO18 152 F6
Warblers Way PO22 195 B7
Warbleton Cl BN2 188 E5
Warbleton Ho 6 RH11 17 F3
Warblington Rd PO10 169 A8
Warburton Cl RH19 23 A8
Ward Cres PO10 149 C3
Warden Ct RH17 85 A6
Warden Park Sch RH17 85 A5
Wardley Cotts GU30 47 D4
Ware Ct RH15 107 D3
Warelands RH15 106 F1
Waremere Ct BN18 177 A3
Warenne Rd BN3 166 C4
Warleigh Rd BN1, BN2 207 A8
Warltersville Way RH6 2 C1
Warmdene Ave BN1 167 F6
Warmdene Cl BN1 167 F5
Warmdene Rd BN1 167 F6
Warmdene Way BN1 167 F6
Warner Ct RH15 107 A3
Warner Rd Selsey PO20 206 C6
Worthing BN14 182 F4
Warner's La PO20 206 C8
Warnham CE (C) Prim Sch
RH12 35 F8
Warnham Court Sch RH12 35 F7
Warnham Ct BN3 187 C5
Warnham Nature Reserve
RH12 36 B6
Warnham Rd
Broadridge Heath RH12 35 D4
Crawley RH10 19 B4
Horsham RH12 36 B5
Worthing BN12 181 D2
Warnham Rise BN1 168 A5
Warnham Sta RH12 36 C8
Warninglid Cty Prim Sch RH17 61 A2
Warninglid La RH13, RH17 60 D2
Warren Cl RH19 8 E3
Warren Cotts Handcross RH17 61 B8
West Dean PO18 132 F6
Warren Cres BN16 200 A6
Warren Croft RH20 119 B1
Warren Ct Lancing BN15 183 D5
Worthing BN14 182 B7
Warren Dr Crawley RH11 18 A8
Southwater Street RH13 58 A3
Warren Farm La PO19 152 F2
Warren Gdns BN14 182 B7
Warren Rd Brighton BN2 188 E8
Liss Forest GU33 45 E7
Worthing BN14 182 B7
Warren Side GU31 89 D3
Warren The Burgess Hill RH15 107 C1
Ferring BN12 200 F4
Handcross RH17 60 E6
Warren Way PO22 176 B6
Warrington Cl RH11 17 E2
Warrior Cl BN41 166 B2
Warrs Hill La BN8 87 E1
Warwick Cl PO21 194 B2
Warwick Ct Arundel BN18 158 A2
5 Emsworth PO10 169 B8
4 Hove BN3 187 E7
Warwick Gdns BN11 182 E2
Warwick La BN11 182 E2
Warwick Mount 2 BN2 188 C4
Warwick Pl Bognor Regis PO22 196 D5
Worthing BN11 182 E2
Warwick Rd BN11 182 E2
Warwick St BN11 182 E2
Warwick Wlk 3 BN43 164 F1
Washbrooks Farm BN6 125 F5
Washington Bostal RH20 141 D5
Washington Cotts RH20 141 D8
Washington Rd
Buncton BN44, RH20 142 E8
Crawley RH11 17 E3
Emsworth PO10 149 B1
Haywards Heath RH16 86 A5
Storrington RH20 119 E1
Washington RH20 141 A8
Washington St Brighton BN2 207 B7
Chichester PO19 172 F7
Wassand Cl RH10 19 A6
Water La Angmering BN16 179 F5
Buncton BN44 142 C8
Littlehampton BN17 198 D6
Selden BN13, BN16 180 C7
Storrington RH20 119 F2
Water Lane Ind Est RH20 119 E3
Water Lea RH10 19 A5
Water Tower Bldgs 3 PO21 195 D3
Water View RH6 2 C3
Waterbury Hill RH17 65 B5
Waterdyke Ave BN42 185 E7
Waterfield Cl RH13 36 E3
Waterfield Cty Fst Sch RH11 17 E4
Waterfield Gdns RH11 17 E4
Waterhall Golf Course BN1 167 A7
Waterhall Rd BN1 167 C6
Waterlands La RH12 13 E1
Waterloo Pl 1 BN1 207 B6
Waterloo Rd PO22 196 A4
Waterloo Sq PO21 195 C2
Waterloo St BN3 187 D5
Waterplat The PO19 173 C8
Waters Edge PO21 194 E1
Waters Edge Gdns PO10 169 B8
Watersfield Rd BN14 182 B5
Waterside East Grinstead RH19 10 B1
Horley RH6 2 A5
Waterside Cl RH11 17 E4
Waterside Dr PO19, PO20 172 F4
Waterstone Cl PO20 191 A7
Watery La Chichester PO20 173 A4
Funtington PO18 151 A4
Watling Cl 5 BN42 185 E7
Watling Ct 8 BN42 185 E7
Watling Rd BN42 185 E7
Watney Cotts RH17 42 E1
Watson Cl RH10 19 C4
Watts Lodge RH15 107 D3
Waveney Wlk RH10 19 B4
Waverley Cres BN1 168 C1
Waverley Ct RH12 36 B2
Waverley Rd
Bognor Regis PO21 195 A4
Rustington BN16 199 D5
Wavertree Rd BN12 181 D3
Way The BN16 200 A4
Wayfield Ave BN3 166 F1
Wayland Ave BN1 167 C3
Wayside Brighton BN1 167 D6
Crawley RH11 17 E4
Lancing BN15 183 C5
Wayside Ave BN13 181 D7
Weald Ave BN3 186 F8
Weald Cl Horsham RH13 58 E8
Hurstpierpoint BN6 125 F6
Weald Ct RH14 77 D7
Weald Day Hospl The RH11 18 C6
Weald Dr RH10 19 A4
Weald Dyke BN43 184 F6
Weald Rd RH15 106 E3
Weald Rise RH16 85 E1
Weald Sch The RH14 77 D7
Weald The RH19 9 F4
Wealden Way RH16 85 D4
Wealdon Cl RH13 79 F7
Wear Cl BN13 181 C7
Wear Rd BN13 181 C7
Weare St RH5 14 D7
Weatherhill Cl RH6 2 F3
Weatherhill Rd RH6 2 F3
Weaver Cl RH11 17 E5
Weavers Cl Burgess Hill RH15 107 D1
Easebourne GU29 70 F2
Weavers Hill BN16 180 A5
Weavers La BN5 123 E4
Weavers Ring BN16 180 A5
Webb Cl Bognor Regis PO21 205 A7
Crawley RH11 18 B1
Weddell Rd RH10 18 F3
Wedges The RH13 56 D5
Wedgwood Rd PO22 196 A4
Weir Wood Resr
(Nature Reserve) RH19 22 D1
Weirbrook RH10 19 A3
Welbeck Ave BN3 186 E6
Welbeck Cl RH15 107 D4
Welbeck Dr RH15 107 D4
Welkin The RH16 86 B8
Well La GU27 27 D6
Well Lodge PO21 194 A2
Well Rd PO21 204 F7
Welland Cl BN13 181 D8
Welland Rd BN13 181 D8
Wellcroft Cotts BN6 125 C5
Weller Cl RH10 19 D5
Wellesey Ct BN11 181 F1
Wellesley Ave BN12 181 D2
Wellesley Ct 8 BN17 198 E4
Wellfield RH19 23 C7
Wellfield Cotts GU31 89 D3
Wellhouse La RH15 127 C7
Wellingham La BN13 161 E1
Wellington Cl RH10 6 E1
Wellington Gdns PO20 206 E8
Wellington Rd
Bognor Regis PO21 195 B3
Brighton BN2 207 B7
Chichester PO19 153 A1
Horsham RH12, RH13 36 D2
Portslade-by-Sea BN41 186 B6
Wellington St BN2 188 C7
Wellington Town Rd RH19 9 D2
Wellington Way RH6 1 F5
Wellingtonia Cl 11 BN1 167 E3
Wells Cl RH12 35 F2
Wells Cres Bognor Regis PO21 194 E4
Chichester PO19 152 F1
Wells Ho GU29 92 E6
Wells Lea RH19 9 D3
Wells Meadow RH19 9 D3
Wells Rd RH10 18 E2
Wells The GU27 27 C6
Wellsbourne 8 BN2 188 F5
Wellsfield PO20 190 C1
Wellswood Gdns PO9 128 E3
Wellsworth La PO9 128 E3
Wellwood Cl RH13 37 B4
Welwyn Cl RH11 17 E2
Wembley Ave BN15 183 D6
Wembley Gdns BN15 183 D6
Wembury Pk RH7 8 E8
Wenban Rd BN11 182 D3
Wenceling Cotts 4 BN15 184 C5
Wendover Grange 3 BN3 187 A6
Wendy Ridge BN16 199 B6
Wenlock Cl RH11 18 A4
Wensley Gdns PO10 149 B3
Wensleydale RH11 18 C3
Wentworth Cl
West Barnham PO22 176 B7
Worthing BN13 181 F8
Wentworth Ct BN16 200 A4
Wentworth Dr RH10 19 D7
Wentworth St BN2 207 B4
Weppons 2 BN43 184 F7
Wesley Cl Crawley RH11 17 E3
Horley RH6 2 A5
Wessex Ave Bognor Regis PO21 195 B2
East Wittering PO20 202 A7
Wessex Ct 1 BN11 182 C2
Wessex Wlk 1 BN43 164 F1
West Ashling Rd
Hambrook PO18 150 D3
Hambrook PO18 150 E3
West Ave Bognor Regis PO21 194 F3
Crawley RH10 19 A8
Middleton-on-Sea PO22 196 F6
Shoreham-by-Sea BN15 184 A5
Worthing BN11 182 A2
West Bank BN18 177 A5
West Beach Rd BN43 184 D5
West Blatchington Inf Sch
BN3 166 E4
West Blatchington Jun Sch
BN3 166 E4
West Bldgs BN11 182 D1
West Bracklesham Dr PO20 202 A6
West Brook Cl PO18 171 A5
West Broyle Dr PO19 152 C2
West Burton La RH20 137 E8
West Burton Rd RH20 137 D8
West Chiltington Cty
Prim Sch RH20 99 E1
West Chiltington La
Balls Green RH14 77 F2
Coneyhurst RH14, RH13 78 C6
West Chiltington Rd
West Chiltington RH20 100 A2
West Chiltington Common RH20 119 D5
West Cl Bognor Regis PO22 196 B4
Fernhurst GU27 49 B6
Middleton-on-Sea PO22 196 D5
West Comm RH16 85 F6
West Common Dr RH16 86 A7
West Dean CE (C) Prim Sch
PO18 132 F5
West Dean Coll PO18 133 A6
West Dr Angmering BN16 179 D4
Bognor Regis PO21 194 B1
Brighton BN2 188 C6
Ferring BN12 200 E4
Middleton-on-Sea PO22 197 A5
West End La Ansteadbrook GU8 28 D8
Henfield BN5 123 B5
West End Way BN15 183 D3
West Front Rd PO21 204 F7
West Furlong Ct BN6 126 A5
West Furlong La BN6 126 A5
West Green Cty Fst Sch RH11 18 C7
West Green Dr RH11 18 C6
West Gun Copse Rd RH13 57 D5
West Head BN17 198 F4
West Hill Ardingly RH17 63 E8
Dormans Park RH19 9 E6
East Grinstead RH19 22 D8
Worthing BN13 161 E2
West Hill Cl BN13 161 E2
West Hill Pl BN1 207 F6
West Hill Rd BN1 207 F6
West Hill St BN1 207 F7
West Hoathly CE (C) Prim Sch
RH19 42 E6
West Hoathly Rd RH19 22 D4
West Hove Cty Inf Sch BN3 186 F7
West Hove Cty Jun Sch BN3 186 F6
West Hove Golf Course BN3 166 C5
West La East Grinstead RH19 22 D8
Lancing BN15 183 E7
West Lavington CE (A)
Prim Sch GU29 93 A6
West Leigh RH19 22 E7
West Mallion RH16 85 F3
West Mare La RH20 98 F1
West Mead BN16 199 E4
West Mead Dr PO21 194 F4
West Meade GU30 47 B2
West Onslow Cl BN12 180 E3
West Pallant PO19 173 A6
West Par Horsham RH12 36 C4
Worthing BN11 182 A1
West Park CE (C) Fst &
Mid Sch BN12 181 D2
West Park Cres RH15 106 D4
West Park Rd Domewood RH10 7 F5
Domewood RH7, RH10 8 B7
Handcross RH17 61 B7
West Preston Manor BN16 199 E5
West Preston Mews BN16 199 E5
West Rd Emsworth PO10 169 A8
Pyecombe BN45 146 E7
Southwick BN41 186 A7

West Ridings BN16 199 F4
West Sands Cvn Pk PO20 206 B8
West Sands La PO20 206 B7
West Side GU28 95 B8
West St Billingshurst RH14 77 C8
Bognor Regis PO21 195 C2
Brighton BN1 207 F5
Burgess Hill RH15 106 E4
Chichester PO19 172 F6
Crawley RH11 18 D5
Ditchling BN6 127 D3
East Grinstead RH19 22 E8
Emsworth PO10 169 B8
Haslemere GU27 27 C6
Horsham RH12 36 C2
Lancing BN15, BN14 183 B7
Midhurst GU29 92 F7
Portslade-by-Sea BN41 186 C7
Selsey PO20 206 C7
Shoreham-by-Sea BN43 184 E7
Storrington RH20 119 D1
Worthing BN11 182 C1
West Stoke Rd PO19 152 C3
West Strand PO20 201 B8
West Tyne BN13 181 D5
West View Fishbourne PO19 172 B6
Haywards Heath RH16 86 B6
Hove BN3 187 C8
West View Cotts Breach PO10 150 A2
Haywards Heath RH16 86 B6
West View Dr BN18 176 F2
West View Gdns RH19 22 E8
West Walberton La BN18 156 C2
West Way Chichester PO19 152 C2
Crawley RH10 19 A7
Hove BN3 166 D2
Littlehampton BN17 178 C3
Shoreham-by-Sea BN15 184 B5
Slinfold RH13 34 D3
Worthing BN13 161 D1
West Wittering Parochial (C) Prim Sch PO20 190 B2
West Worthing Sta BN13 182 A3
Westbourne Ave
New Brighton PO10 149 C2
Worthing BN14 182 D4
Westbourne Cl PO10 149 C2
Westbourne Cty Prim Sch PO10 149 D4
Westbourne Gdns BN3 187 A7
Westbourne Gr BN3 187 A7
Westbourne House Sch PO20 173 F7
Westbourne Pl BN3 187 A6
Westbourne Rd PO10 149 C3
Westbourne St BN3 187 A7
Westbourne Villas BN3 186 F6
Westbrook RH18 23 E3
Westbrook Field PO18 171 A5
Westbrook Way BN42 185 F7
Westbrooke BN11 182 D2
Westbury Ct 4 BN11 182 B2
Westcombe 1 BN1 187 E7
Westcott Cl RH11 39 C8
Westcourt Pl BN14 182 C3
Westcourt Rd BN14 182 C4
Westdean Rd BN14 182 B5
Westdene Cty Prim Sch BN1 167 C5
Westdene Dr BN1 167 C5
Westdown Ct 2 BN11 182 A3
Westergate Cl BN12 200 F6
Westergate Com Coll
Westergate PO20 175 D6
Westergate PO20 175 E7
Westergate Mews PO20 175 D8
Westergate Rd BN2 168 E4
Westergate St PO20 175 D6
Westerley Gdns PO20 202 B6
Western Apron Rd RH6 5 F8
Western Ave PO10 169 A8
Western Cl BN15 183 C4
Western Espl BN3, BN41 186 D6
Western Lodge 2 BN15 183 C7
Western Par PO10 169 A7
Western Pl BN11 182 C1
Western Rd Burgess Hill RH15 106 E3
Haywards Heath RH16 85 F4
Hove BN1, BN3 187 E5
Hurstpierpoint BN6 125 F6
Lancing BN15 183 C4
Liss GU33 45 B4
Littlehampton BN17 198 F4
Selsey PO20 206 E6
Shoreham-by-Sea BN43 184 F7
Western Rd N BN15 183 C6
Western Row BN11 182 C1
Western St BN1 187 D5
Western Terr 5 BN1 187 E5
Westfield PO22 195 B7
Westfield Ave BN16 200 A4
Westfield Cl BN1 168 A4
Westfield Cres BN1 168 A5
Westfield Ct 1 BN17 198 F4
Westfield Rd RH11 18 B6
Westgate PO19 172 E6
Westgate L Ctr PO19 172 F5
Westgrove Gdns 8 PO10 169 B8
Westhampnett Rd
Chichester PO19 173 C7
Westhampnett PO18 153 E1
Westhill Dr RH15 106 E3
Westingway PO21 195 A3
Westlake Cl BN13 181 E5
Westlake Gdns BN13 181 F5
Westland Ave BN14 182 A4
Westland Ct BN41 186 A7
Westland's Copse La GU28 73 A4
Westlands Ferring BN12 200 E5
Horsham RH13 36 E3
Westlands Littlehampton BN16 199 A6
Westlands La PO20 191 D5
Westlands Rd
Haywards Heath RH16 86 B5
Hunston PO20 193 A8
Westleas RH6 1 E5
Westloats Gdns PO21 195 A5
Westloats La PO21 195 B5
Westmead Gdns BN11 181 F2
Westmead Rd PO19 172 C6
Westminster Ct 1 BN11 182 F2
Westminster Dr PO21 194 E3
Westminster Rd RH10 19 C5
Westmorland Ct 12 BN1 187 E7
Westmorland Dr PO22 196 B6
Westmorland Wlk 2 BN43 164 F1
Westmount 3 BN2 188 C6
Westmount Cl BN42, BN43 185 D8
Weston La PO18 150 F5
Westons Cl RH12 36 D7
Westons Hill RH13 57 B6
Westpark La BN11, BN12 181 E2
Westup Rd RH17 40 E2
Westview Terr BN14 161 E6
Westward Cl PO18 171 C5
Westward Ho PO19 172 C6
Westward La RH20 119 C6
Westway Bognor Regis PO22 195 D5
Copthorne RH10 7 A3
Gatwick Airport RH6 6 B7
Westway Cl BN41 165 E4
Westway Gdns BN41 165 E4
Westwood Cl PO10 149 C3
Wey Hill GU27 27 A6
Wey Lodge Cl GU30 25 D4
Weycombe Rd GU27 27 C8
Weydown Ct GU27 27 B7
Weydown Ind Est GU27 27 B8
Weydown Rd GU27 27 B7
Weyland Cl GU30 25 C5
Weysprings GU27 27 A6
Whapple The 7 BN17 198 F4
Wharf Rd Hove BN3 186 D6
Littlehampton BN17 198 C5
Wharf The GU29 92 F7
Wheatcroft BN17 178 C3
Wheatfield Rd PO20 206 F8
Wheatfield Way Brighton BN2 168 F3
Horley RH6 2 C4
Wheatlands Ave PO11 189 A1
Wheatlands Cres PO11 189 A1
Wheatsheaf Cl
Burgess Hill RH15 106 E5
Horsham RH12 36 E5
Wheatsheaf La RH17 85 A6
Wheatstone Cl RH10 6 B3
Wheelbarrow Castle GU29 71 A2
Wheeler Rd RH10 19 B4
Wheelers Way RH19 8 E3
Wheelwright La RH15 107 D1
Wheelwrights RH20 99 E1
Whichelo Pl BN2 188 C6
Whippingham Rd BN2 188 C7
Whippingham St BN2 188 C8
Whistler Ave PO19 153 A1
Whistler Cl RH10 18 F3
Whistler Ct BN1 167 F1
Whitaker Pl PO20 174 B7
White Acre BN17 178 C3
White City GU29 92 E7
White Hart Ct RH12 36 C4
White Horse Cnr PO20 175 A8
White Horse Ct 1 RH20 119 D1
White Horse Sq BN44 143 D3
White Horses Way BN16 199 A5
White Lion Ct 6 BN43 184 E7
White Lodge Hove BN3 187 C8
4 Littlehampton BN17 198 E5
White St BN2 207 B5
White Styles C ty Mid Sch BN15 183 B6
White Styles Rd BN15 183 B7
White Styles Terr BN15 183 B7
White's Cl BN6 126 A7
Whitebeam Rd BN13 181 C5
Whitebeam Way
Middleton-on-Sea PO22 196 E6
Tangmere PO20 154 D1
Whitechimney Row PO10 149 D3
Whitecroft 5 BN16 199 C5
Whitecross St BN1 207 A6
Whitehall Dr RH11 17 E6
Whitehawk Cl BN2 188 E5
Whitehawk Cres BN2 188 E5
Whitehawk Cty Inf Sch BN2 188 E6
Whitehawk Hill Rd BN2 188 D5
Whitehawk Jun Sch BN2 188 E6
Whitehawk Rd Brighton BN2 188 E6
Brighton BN2 188 F5
Whitehawk Way BN2 188 F6
Whitehorse Rd RH12 37 B6
Whitelands PO22 196 A6
Whitelea Rd BN17 198 D6
Whitelot Cl BN42 165 E2
Whitelot Way BN42 165 E2
Whitely Hill RH10 19 F1
Whiteman's Cl RH17 84 E8
Whitemans Gn RH17 84 E8
Whiterock Pl BN42 185 E7
Whites La GU27 48 E3
Whiteside Cl PO19 173 B7
Whitethorn Dr BN1 167 B4
Whitethroat La RH17 62 D6
Whiteways PO22 195 A6
Whiteways Cl
Bognor Regis PO22 195 A6
Littlehampton BN17 198 D6
Whitfield Cl PO22 195 E5
Whitfield Rd GU27 27 C8
Whitgift Wlk RH10 18 D3
Whitley Cl PO10 149 D5
Whitmore Way RH6 1 E3
Whittingehame Gdns BN1 167 F3
Whittington Coll RH19 9 A4
Whittington Ct 1 PO10 169 B8
Whittington Rd RH10 18 E3
Whittle Way RH10 6 A3
Whitworth Rd RH11 5 D2
Whyke Cl PO19 173 B4
Whyke Ct PO19 173 B4
Whyke La PO19 173 B5
Whyke Rd PO19, PO20 173 B5
Whylands Ave BN13 181 D8
Whylands Cl BN13 181 D8
Whylands Cres BN13 181 D8
Whytemead Cty Fst Sch BN14 182 E5
Whytings RH13 59 C6
Wick Cl PO22 196 B5
Wick Farm Rd BN17 198 C6
Wick Hall BN3 187 D6
Wick La Bognor Regis PO22 196 B5
Easebourne GU29 71 B4
Wick Par BN17 178 D3
Wick St BN17 178 D3
Wickbourne Cty Inf Sch BN17 198 C6
Wickbourne Ho BN17 198 C6
Wickets The RH15 106 F5
Wickham Cl
Haywards Heath RH16 85 E7
Horley RH6 1 F4
Wickham Dr BN6 126 C5
Wickham Hill BN6 126 C4
Wickham Way RH16 85 E7
Wickhurst Cl BN41 165 F2
Wickhurst Gdns RH12 35 E3
Wickhurst La RH12 35 E3
Wickhurst Rd BN41 166 A2
Wickhurst Rise BN41 165 F3
Wickland Ct RH10 18 D3
Wickor Cl PO10 149 C2
Wickor Way PO10 149 C2
Wicks Cotts BN18 177 C4
Wicks Rd RH14 77 C8
Widdicombe Way BN2 168 E2
Widewater Cl 1 BN15 184 C5
Widewater Ct 7 BN15 184 C5
Widgeon Cl PO20 206 B8
Widgeon Way RH12 36 C5
Widworthy Mews 7 PO21 195 B3
Wigmore Cl BN1 168 B1
Wigmore Rd BN14 182 D6
Wigmore Trad Est BN14 182 F5
Wilberforce Cl RH11 39 C8
Wilbury Ave BN3 187 C8
Wilbury Cres BN3 187 D7
Wilbury Gdns BN3 187 C8
Wilbury Gr BN3 187 C6
Wilbury Grange 7 BN3 187 C6
Wilbury Lodge 11 BN3 187 C6
Wilbury Rd BN3 187 C6
Wilbury Villas BN3 187 C7
Wilby Ave BN42 165 E1
Wild Orchid Way RH13 58 A3
Wild Park Cl BN2 168 E3
Wildacre Cl RH14 31 D3
Wilderness Rd BN6 126 A6
Wilderness Rise RH19 10 A6
Wilderness The RH16 86 B8
Wilderwick Rd RH19, RH7 10 A5
Wildgoose Dr RH12 35 F3
Wildwood Golf Course GU6 11 B3
Wildwood La GU6 11 C5
Wilfrid Rd BN3 166 D1
Wilkinson Ct 4 RH11 18 B1
Willett Cl GU28 115 B7
William Allen La RH16 86 B6
William Morris Way RH11 39 C8
William Penn (C) Prim Sch RH13 78 E2
William Rd PO19 173 D6
William St Bognor Regis PO21 195 D3
Brighton BN2 207 A5
Southwick BN41 186 B7
William Sutton Ho BN1 207 A5
Williams Rd Broadbridge PO18 171 C7
Shoreham-by-Sea BN43 185 C8
Williams Way RH10 19 B5
Willingdon Rd BN2 168 E1
Willington Ct 2 BN11 182 B1
Willow Ave BN16 199 E5
Willow Brean RH6 1 E5
Willow Brook BN17 178 C3
Willow Cl Crawley RH10 18 E8
East Grinstead RH19 9 D3
Liphook GU30 25 D3
2 Shoreham-by-Sea BN15 184 C5
Steyning BN44 143 D4
West Chiltington Common RH20 119 E6
Willow Cnr RH6 4 F7
Willow Cres BN13 181 C5
Willow Ct Chichester PO19 172 D6
Horley RH6 2 B6
4 Hove BN3 187 D7
Worthing BN11 182 A3
Willow Dr RH14 77 D8
Willow Gdns
Hurstpierpoint BN6 126 A7
Liphook GU30 25 D3
Westbourne PO10 149 D4
Willow Ho Hassocks BN6 126 E5
Worthing BN12 181 A4
Willow Mead 8 RH19 22 F8
Willow Pk RH16 86 B4
Willow Rd Horsham RH12 37 B5
Liss GU33 45 B4
Willow Ridge RH10 21 A3
Willow Way Ashington RH20 121 A4
Bognor Regis PO21 194 B1
Hurstpierpoint BN6 125 F8
Willow Wlk GU28 95 E7
Willowbed Ave PO19 173 C4
Willowbed Dr PO19 173 C4
Willowbrook Pk BN15 184 A5
Willowbrook Rd BN14 183 A4
Willowbrook Way BN6 127 A3
Willowfield 4 RH11 18 D5
Willowhale Ave PO21 194 D2
Willowhale Gn PO21 194 C2
Willowhayne Ave BN16 200 A4
Willowhayne Cl BN16 200 A4
Willowhayne Cres BN16 200 A4
Willowhayne Ct BN16 200 A4
Willows Cty Fst Sch The BN15 183 E7
Willows The
Bognor Regis PO21 195 C4
2 Brighton BN2 207 B8
Burgess Hill RH15 107 C5
Findon BN14 161 E6
Ford BN18 177 E5
Hassocks BN6 126 E4
Horsham RH12 36 D5
Lancing BN15 183 E5
Pulborough RH20 98 A1
Rustington BN16 199 D6
Selsey PO20 206 E8
Wills Cl BN18 177 B2
Wilman Gdns PO21 194 D2
Wilmington Cl Brighton BN1 168 A5
Crawley RH11 18 C1
Hassocks BN6 126 F4
Wilmington Par BN1 167 F5
Wilmington Way Brighton BN1 168 A5
Haywards Heath RH16 86 A5
Wilmot Ct 6 BN43 185 C8
Wilmot Rd BN43 185 C8
Wilson Ave BN2 188 F6
Wilson Cl Chichester PO19 172 D7
Crawley RH10 19 D3
Wilson Ct BN18 177 B2
Wilton 1 RH16 85 D6
Wilton Cl Bracklesham PO20 202 C5
Partridge Green RH13 103 A3
Wilton Villas RH17 41 A1
Wiltshire Ho 16 BN2 207 B5
Wimblehurst Ct RH12 36 C4
Wimblehurst Rd RH12 36 C4
Wimborne Ct BN11 181 F2
Wimland Hill RH12 16 D2
Wimland Rd Faygate RH12 16 D1
Rusper RH12 16 C4
Wimlands La RH12 16 E3
Winchelsea Ct 8 BN11 182 A1
Winchelsea Gdns BN11 182 A1
Winchester Dr PO19 172 F8
Winchester Rd Crawley RH10 18 E2
Rustington BN16 199 E6
Worthing BN11 182 C2
Winchester St BN1 207 A8
Wincombe Rd BN1, BN3 167 D1
Winden Ave PO19 173 B6
Windermere Cres BN12 181 D5
Windermere Ct 9 BN2 188 C6
Windermere Rd RH16 85 F4
Windlesham Ave BN1, BN3 187 E6
Windlesham Cl BN41 166 A1
Windlesham Ct 10 Hove BN1 187 E7
Littlehampton BN17 178 D3
5 Worthing BN11 182 A1
Windlesham Gdns
East Preston BN16 200 A6
Hove BN1, BN3 187 E7
Shoreham-by-Sea BN43 184 F8
Windlesham House Sch BN14 141 D3
Windlesham Rd Hove BN1 187 E6
Shoreham-by-Sea BN43 184 F8
Windlesham Sch BN1 187 E8
Windmill Ave BN6 126 F3
Windmill Cl Ashington RH20 121 A5
Bognor Regis PO21 194 B1
Horley RH6 2 B3
Horsham RH13 37 A4
Hove BN3 166 F2
Upper Beeding BN44 144 B2
Windmill Copse RH20 119 E2
Windmill Ct Crawley RH11 18 D8
East Wittering PO20 201 F7
Tangmere PO20 154 D1
Windmill Dr Brighton BN1 167 D6
Burgess Hill RH15 107 A4
Rustington BN16 199 D6
Windmill Field PO18 171 A5
Windmill La Ashurst Wood RH19 23 C7
East Grinstead RH19 9 D3
Nep Town BN5 123 E4
Windmill Par BN42 165 E1
Windmill Platt RH17 61 C8
Windmill Rd
Littlehampton BN17 198 D4
Southwick BN42 165 E1
Windmill St BN2 207 B6
Windmill Terr 19 BN2 207 B6
Windmill View BN1 168 B7
Windmills Cty Jun Sch BN6 127 A3
Windrum Cl RH12 57 F8
Windrush Cl Crawley RH11 17 F4
Worthing BN13 181 C8
Windsor Cl Bognor Regis PO21 194 E4
Crawley RH11 18 C2
Hove BN3 167 A3
Southwater RH13 58 A1
Windsor Ct Brighton BN1 207 F5
Brighton, Withdene BN1 167 D4
Horsham RH13 36 F3
Windsor Ct Worthing BN11 183 A2
Windsor Dr
East Wittering PO20 201 F7
Rustington BN16 179 B3
Windsor Lodge BN3 187 B6
Windsor Pl RH19 23 A8
Windsor Rd Chichester PO19 173 D6
Selsey PO20 206 E6
Worthing BN11 182 F3
Windsor St BN1 207 F5
Windsor Way BN15 184 B6
Windward Cl BN16, BN17 199 A5
Windyridge RH11 18 A5
Wineham La BN5, RH13, RH17 104 D5
Winfield Ave BN1 167 F6
Winfield Cl Brighton BN1 167 F5
Portslade-by-Sea BN41 166 A3
Winfield Gr RH5 3 A8
Winfield Way PO10 149 B4
Wingle Tye Rd RH15 127 A8
Winkfield Ct RH16 85 D5
Winkhurst Way RH15 107 D1
Winnals Pk RH16 85 D5
Winner Way RH6 5 D6
Winnet Way RH13 58 A2
Winston Bsns Ctr BN15 183 C5
Winston Cl PO21 194 F6
Winston Cres PO21 194 F6
Winston Rd BN15 183 D4
Winter Knoll The BN17 198 F5
Winterbourne Horsham RH12 36 F7
Horsham RH12 37 A7
Winterbourne Cl BN13 181 B5
Winterbourne Ct BN13 181 B5
Winterbourne Rd PO19 153 A2
Winterbourne Way BN13 181 B5
Winterfold RH10 19 A3
Winterpit Cl RH13 59 D6
Winterpit La RH13 59 E6
Winters Cotts 6 GU29 92 E7
Winters La GU29 71 A4
Winterton Ct RH13 36 D2
Winterton Lodge BN17 198 E5
Winterton Way BN43 185 B6
Winton Pl BN11 182 D3
Wire Mill La RH7 8 F8
Wireless Mus RH16 86 B7
Wisborough Ct Crawley RH11 17 F3
Worthing BN13 181 F6
Wisborough Gdns RH14 76 D8
Wisborough Green Cty Prim Sch RH14 54 C1
Wisborough La RH20 119 E1
Wisden Ave RH15 106 E5
Wish Ct BN3 186 E8
Wish Rd BN3 186 E6
Wiston Ave Stockbridge PO19 172 E4
Worthing BN13, BN14 182 B5
Wiston Cl BN14 182 B5
Wiston Ct Crawley RH11 17 F3
12 Shoreham-by-Sea BN43 185 C8
Wiston Rd BN2 188 F6
Wiston Way BN2 188 F7
Withdean Ave Brighton BN1 167 D2
Worthing BN12 181 B1
Withdean Cl BN1 167 D3
Withdean Court Ave BN1 167 D3
Withdean Cres BN1 167 E3
Withdean Ct 10 BN1 167 E3
Withdean Hall 3 BN1 167 E3
Withdean Rd BN1 167 D3
Withdean Rise BN1 167 E3
Wither Dale RH6 1 E4
Withey Brook RH6 1 D1
Withey Meadows RH6 1 D1
Withy Bush RH15 106 E5
Withypitts RH10 21 A3
Withypitts E RH10 21 A3
Wittering Rd PO11 189 B2
Wivelsfield Cty Prim Sch RH16 107 F6
Wivelsfield Rd RH16 85 E2
Wivelsfield Sta RH15 107 C4
Woburn Pl BN1 168 F5
Woburn Rd RH11 18 A4
Woelfs Cl RH20 121 A5
Wold Cl RH11 17 F4
Woldhurstlea Cl RH11 18 A4
Wolseley Rd Brighton BN1 168 D6
Portslade-by-Sea BN41 186 A8
Wolsey Cl PO21 194 B1
Wolstead Lodge 3 RH16 85 F3
Wolstenbury Rd BN16 179 C3
Wolstonbury Cl Crawley RH11 18 C4
Hurstpierpoint BN6 126 B4
Wolstonbury Ct RH15 107 B2
Wolstonbury Rd BN3 187 E7
Wolstonbury Way RH15 107 B2
Wolstonbury Wlk 7 BN43 164 F1
Wolverstone Dr BN1 168 C2
Wolverton Cl RH6 1 F1
Wolverton Gdns RH6 1 F2
Wood Cl RH1 2 A8
Wood End RH12 37 C5
Wood La BN5 144 F7
Wood Ride RH16 85 D3
Wood St Bognor Regis PO21 195 B2
East Grinstead RH19 9 D1
Wood View BN18 158 A2
Wood's Mill Countryside Ctr BN5 144 F8
Woodard Rd BN15 183 F7
Woodards View BN43 184 D5
Woodberry La
Rowland's Castle PO9 128 F1

Woodberry La
Stubbermere PO10, PO9 149 B7
Woodbine Ct 7 PO21 195 D4
Woodbourne Ave BN1 168 A4
Woodbourne Cl GU33 45 C4
Woodbridge Ct RH12 37 A5
Woodbridge Pk BN16 200 A5
Woodbury Ave RH19 10 B1
Woodbury Cl RH19 23 B8
Woodcock Hill RH19, RH7 8 F6
Woodcote Graffham GU28 114 A8
Horley RH6 2 C4
Woodcote La
Harwoods Green RH20 97 D5
Littlehampton BN17 178 D5
Woodcote Rd RH18 23 F2
Woodcourt RH11 18 C1
Woodcrest Rd RH15 106 F1
Woodcroft RH15 106 F5
Woodcroft Rd RH11 17 D4
Woodcutters RH17 86 F3
Wooddale La RH14 56 A2
Woodend Bognor Regis PO21 195 A4
West Ashling PO18 151 C5
Woodend Cl RH10 19 A8
Woodfield RH13 57 F1
Woodfield Cl
Bognor Regis PO21 205 A7
Crawley RH10 18 E7
Tangmere PO20 154 D1
Woodfield Park Rd PO10 169 D8
Woodfield Rd Crawley RH10 18 F7
Rudgwick RH12 33 D7
Woodfield Terr RH13 81 E1
Woodgate Cl PO20 175 D5
Woodgate Pk PO20 175 D6
Woodgate Rd PO20 175 D5
Woodgates Cl RH13 36 F3
Woodhall Cl RH17 84 F7
Woodhatch RH13 57 F2
Woodhayes RH6 2 B4
Woodhorn Cotts PO20 174 E6
Woodhorn La PO20 174 D6
Woodhouse Cl BN3 186 E7
Woodhouse La
Blendworth PO8 128 C6
Rowland's Castle PO8, PO9 128 E4
Woodhouse Rd BN3 186 E7
Wooding Gr 14 RH11 18 B1
Woodland Ave
Burgess Hill RH15 107 C4
Hove BN3 167 B3
Worthing BN13 161 F1
Woodland Cl
Burgess Hill RH15 107 C4
Five Oaks RH14 55 E6
Woodland Cl Horsham RH13 37 B4
Woodland Cl Hove BN3 167 B2
Woodland Cotts RH20 120 A7
Woodland Cres RH15 107 C4
Woodland Ct BN3 167 B4
Woodland Dr
Crawley Down RH10 21 B8
Hove BN3 167 B3
Woodland La RH13 38 C3
Woodland Par BN3 167 B3
Woodland Pl PO19 153 A3
Woodland Rd PO20 206 D6
Woodland Villas PO20 155 F1
Woodland Way Brighton BN1 167 F4
Horsham RH13 37 B4
Woodlands Crawley RH10 19 D8
Horley RH6 2 C4
Hove BN3 167 C2
Woodlands Ave
New Brighton PO10 149 B3
Rustington BN16 199 C6
Woodlands Cl
Angmering BN16 180 A7
Clapham BN13 160 F1
Crawley Down RH10 21 B7
Rustington BN16 199 C6
Woodlands Cotts BN16 199 C6
Woodlands La
Chichester PO19 172 F8
Haslemere GU27 26 F7
Heath Common RH20 120 C3
Hill Side GU33 45 D3
Walderton PO18 130 B2
Woodlands Pk BN18 176 F3
Woodlands Rd
Bognor Regis PO22 195 B6
East Grinstead RH19 10 A4
Haywards Heath RH16 85 F4
Littlehampton BN17 198 E4
Woodlands The BN1 167 E5
Woodlands Way
Billingshurst RH14 77 E6
Southwater RH13 79 E8
Woodlands Wlk RH13 59 C5
Woodlea Rd BN13 182 A4
Woodleigh Rd RH15 107 C4
Woodmancote Ct RH12 36 D5
Woodmancote La
PO10, PO18 150 B4
Woodmancote Rd BN14 182 B4
Woodmans Hill RH11 18 C2
Woodpecker Cres BN6 106 D3
Woodpecker La RH20 119 E1
Woodpecker Rd GU28 95 E7
Woodpecker Way BN13 181 C5
Woodridge Cl RH16 86 A3
Woodroffe Wlk PO10 149 B4
Woodroyd Ave RH6 1 F2
Woodroyd Gdns RH6 1 F1
Woodruff Ave BN3 167 C2
Woodruff Bsns Ctr The
PO19 172 E5
Woods Hill Cl RH19 23 D6
Woods Hill La RH19 23 D6
Woods Ho BN3 187 A8
Woods Mill Cl BN5 144 E6
Woods Way BN12 181 C3
Woodside Horsham RH13 37 B4
West Barnham PO22 176 B6
Woodside Ave BN1 167 D2
Woodside Cl
Cornerhouse RH13 103 D4
Storrington RH20 119 E2
Woodside Ct 6 BN17 198 E4
Woodside Lodge BN1 167 D2
Woodside Rd Crawley RH10 18 F8
Worthing BN14 182 B4
Woodsland Cross RH16 64 E3
Woodslands Cl BN6 126 F4
Woodslands Rd BN6 126 F4
Woodstock RH19 9 C2
Woodstock Cl RH12 36 D5
Woodstock Gdns PO21 194 F2
Woodview BN43 164 F1
Woodview Cl BN1 168 D6
Woodwards RH11 18 C1
Woodwards Cl RH15 107 B1
Wool La GU29 92 F7
Woolbeding La GU29 70 B4
Woolborough Cl RH10 18 E7
Woolborough La Crawley RH10 5 F1
Crawley RH10 19 A8
Horley RH1 2 F8
Woolborough Rd RH10 18 E7
Woolmer Hill Rd GU26, GU27 26 D7
Woolmer Hill Sch GU27 26 D7
Woolmer St PO10 149 A4
Woolstaplers The PO19 172 F6
Woolven Cl RH15 106 E1
Woolven Row BN5 123 F5
Wophams La PO20 192 D7
Worcester Cl PO21 194 E3
Worcester Ct 2 BN3 187 E6
Worcester Rd Chichester PO19 152 F2
Crawley RH10 18 E2
Worcester Villas BN3 186 C7
Wordsworth Cl RH10 19 B8
Wordsworth Gdns PO22 196 D6
Wordsworth Pl RH12 36 E7
Wordsworth Rd BN11 182 C1
Wordsworth Rise 6 RH19 9 C1
Wordsworth St BN3 187 A7
Worms La PO22 196 E7
Worsted La RH19 23 B8
Worth Abbey & Sch RH10 20 B1
Worth Park Ave RH10 19 C7
Worth Rd RH10 19 C6
Worth Way RH10 19 E5
Worthing Golf Course BN14 162 B1
Worthing High Sch BN14 182 C4
Worthing Hospl BN11 182 E3
Worthing Rd Dial Post RH13 101 E3
East Preston BN16 199 F6
Littlehampton BN17 178 E3
Rustington BN16, BN17 179 B3
Southwater RH13 57 F2
Tower Hill RH12, RH13 58 A7
West Grinstead RH13 102 A6
Worthing Sixth Form Coll
BN13 181 E3
Worthing Sta BN11 182 C3
Wray Cl RH19 23 D6
Wraysbury Park Dr PO10 149 B4
Wren Cl Horsham RH12 36 D7
Pulborough RH20 98 B2
Wren Cres PO22 195 B6
Wren Ct RH10 18 E3
Wrenfield Pl 3 PO21 195 C2
Wrentham Ho RH15 107 B3
Wroxham Way PO22 195 F6
Wroxham Wlk RH10 19 B4
Wyatt Cl RH14 54 B1
Wyatt Ct PO20 201 F7
Wyatts La RH17 65 D5
Wyberlye Rd RH15 107 A4
Wychcroft 4 BN17 198 D5
Wychperry Rd RH16 85 D5
Wychwood Cl PO21 194 E1
Wychwood Gdns BN11 183 B3
Wychwood Wlk PO21 194 E1
Wyck Ct BN41 186 A7
Wycliffe Ct RH11 17 E3
Wyde Feld PO21 194 F2
Wye Cl RH11 39 C8
Wye Ho BN11 182 B2
Wyke Ave BN11 182 E2
Wyke La N PO22 196 C6
Wykeham Cl BN44 143 D3
Wykeham Ct BN11 182 C2
Wykeham Rd BN11 182 C2
Wykeham Terr BN1 207 F5
Wykeham Way RH15 107 C2
Wykwood GU30 25 D4
Wylde Green La GU33 45 D5
Wyncombe Cl RH20 97 B3
Wyndham Lea RH20 119 D6
Wyndham Pk GU29 92 D7
Wyndham Rd GU28 95 F7
Wyndham St BN2 207 B4
Wynlea Cl RH10 21 A8
Wynnes Mews BN3 187 A7
Wynnstay RH15 107 B2
Wysemead RH6 2 C4
Wyshe The BN45 147 C6
Wythering Cl PO21 204 F7
Wythwood RH16 85 E1
Wyvern Cl PO20 154 E1
Wyvern Ct 6 BN11 182 C1

Yachtsmens Cotts PO18 171 A5
Yapton CE (C) Prim Sch BN18 176 F4
Yapton La BN18 176 F7
Yapton Rd
Barnham BN18, PO22 176 D4
Horsemere Green BN17, BN18 177 C1
Middleton-on-Sea BN18, PO22 196 E7
Yarbrook PO18 152 E7
Yardlea Cl PO9 128 D1
Yardley St BN1 207 A8
Yarmouth Cl RH10 19 A4
Yarrow Cl RH12 36 E5
Yattendon Rd RH6 2 B3
Yattendon Sch RH6 2 A4
Yeoman Rd BN12, BN13 181 B5
Yeoman Way BN13 181 B4
Yeomans Acre PO21 194 F3
Yeomans Field PO18 150 D1
Yeomans La GU30 25 A4
Yew La RH19 9 B3
Yew Tree Cl
Bognor Regis PO22 195 B6
Horley RH6 2 A4
Lancing BN15 183 E5
Yew Tree Cotts RH15 107 B3
Yew Tree Ct RH17 84 F6
Yew Tree Pl GU33 45 C4
Yew Tree Rd RH6 4 E7
Yewlands Wlk RH11 17 D4
Yewtree Cl RH13 81 E2
York Ave East Grinstead RH19 23 A8
Hove BN3 187 E6
York Chase PO19 152 F1
York Cl Horsham RH13 36 F3
Southwater RH13 58 A1
York Ct 9 BN3 187 E7
York Gdns BN17 198 D5
York Gr BN1 207 F7
York Hill BN1 207 A7
York Ho BN41 186 B8
York Pl BN1, BN2 207 A6
York Rd Bognor Regis PO21 195 D3
Burgess Hill BN6, RH15 106 D2
Chichester PO19 173 C5
Crawley RH10 18 E2
Hove BN1, BN3 187 E6
Littlehampton BN17 198 D5
Selsey PO20 206 E5
Worthing BN11 182 E2
York Villas BN1 207 F7
Yorkhurst Hill PO18 112 F1
Yorkwood GU33 45 B4
Young St 4 PO19 153 A2
Youngsmere Cl BN1 168 C6

Zachary Merton Com Hospl
BN16 199 D4

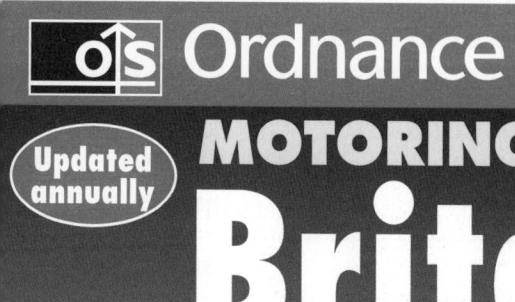

Ordnance Survey
MOTORING ATLAS
Updated annually

Britain

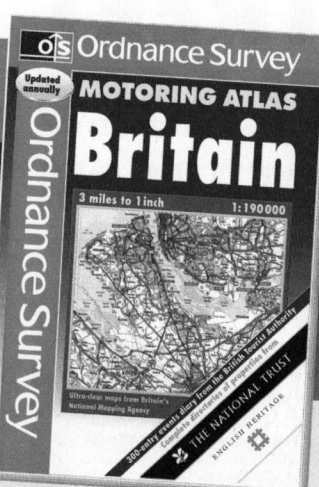

The best-selling *OS Motoring Atlas Britain* uses unrivalled and up-to-date mapping from the Ordnance Survey digital database. The exceptionally clear mapping is at a large scale of 3 miles to 1 inch (Orkney/Shetland Islands at 5 miles to 1 inch).

A special feature of the atlas is its wealth of tourist and leisure information. It contains comprehensive directories, including descriptions and location details, of the properties of the National Trust in England and Wales, the National Trust for Scotland, English Heritage and Historic Scotland. There is also a useful diary of British Tourist Authority Events listing more than 300 days out around Britain during the year.

Available from all good bookshops or direct from the publisher:
Tel: 01933 443863

The atlas includes:
- ◆ 112 pages of fully updated mapping
- ◆ 45 city and town plans
- ◆ 8 extra-detailed city approach maps
- ◆ route-planning maps
- ◆ restricted motorway junctions
- ◆ local radio information
- ◆ distances chart
- ◆ county boundaries map
- ◆ multi-language legend

STREET ATLASES
ORDER FORM

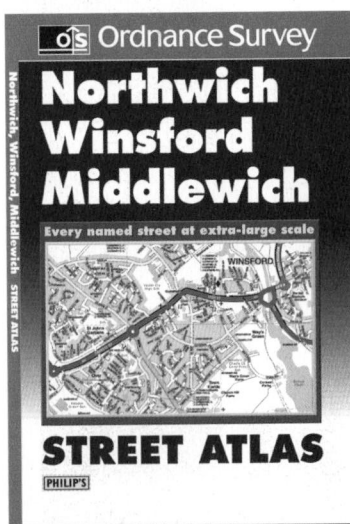

PHILIP'S

The Street Atlases are available from all good bookshops or by mail order direct from the publisher. Orders can be made in the following ways. **By phone** Ring our special Credit Card Hotline on **01933 443863** during office hours (9am to 5pm) or leave a message on the answering machine, quoting your full credit card number plus expiry date and your full name and address. **By post or fax** Fill out the order form below (you may photocopy it) and post it to: **Philip's Direct, 27 Sanders Road, Wellingborough, Northants NN8 4NL** or fax it to: **01933 443849**. Before placing an order by post, by fax or on the answering machine, please telephone to check availability and prices.

COLOUR LOCAL ATLASES

	PAPERBACK	
	Quantity @ £3.50 each	£ Total
CANNOCK, LICHFIELD, RUGELEY	☐ 0 540 07625 2	➤ ☐
DERBY AND BELPER	☐ 0 540 07608 2	➤ ☐
NORTHWICH, WINSFORD, MIDDLEWICH	☐ 0 540 07589 2	➤ ☐
PEAK DISTRICT TOWNS	☐ 0 540 07609 0	➤ ☐
STAFFORD, STONE, UTTOXETER	☐ 0 540 07626 0	➤ ☐
WARRINGTON, WIDNES, RUNCORN	☐ 0 540 07588 4	➤ ☐

COLOUR REGIONAL ATLASES

	HARDBACK	SPIRAL	POCKET	
	Quantity @ £10.99 each	Quantity @ £8.99 each	Quantity @ £5.99 each	£ Total
BERKSHIRE	☐ 0 540 06170 0	☐ 0 540 06172 7	☐ 0 540 06173 5	➤ ☐
	Quantity @ £10.99 each	Quantity @ £8.99 each	Quantity @ £4.99 each	£ Total
MERSEYSIDE	☐ 0 540 06480 7	☐ 0 540 06481 5	☐ 0 540 06482 3	➤ ☐
	Quantity @ £12.99 each	Quantity @ £9.99 each	Quantity @ £4.99 each	£ Total
DURHAM	☐ 0 540 06365 7	☐ 0 540 06366 5	☐ 0 540 06367 3	➤ ☐
HERTFORDSHIRE	☐ 0 540 06174 3	☐ 0 540 06175 1	☐ 0 540 06176 X	➤ ☐
EAST KENT	☐ 0 540 07483 7	☐ 0 540 07276 1	☐ 0 540 07287 7	➤ ☐
WEST KENT	☐ 0 540 07366 0	☐ 0 540 07367 9	☐ 0 540 07369 5	➤ ☐
EAST SUSSEX	☐ 0 540 07306 7	☐ 0 540 07307 5	☐ 0 540 07312 1	➤ ☐
WEST SUSSEX	☐ 0 540 07319 9	☐ 0 540 07323 7	☐ 0 540 07327 X	➤ ☐
SOUTH YORKSHIRE	☐ 0 540 06330 4	☐ 0 540 06331 2	☐ 0 540 06332 0	➤ ☐
SURREY	☐ 0 540 06435 1	☐ 0 540 06436 X	☐ 0 540 06438 6	➤ ☐
	Quantity @ £12.99 each	Quantity @ £9.99 each	Quantity @ £5.50 each	£ Total
GREATER MANCHESTER	☐ 0 540 06485 8	☐ 0 540 06486 6	☐ 0 540 06487 4	➤ ☐
TYNE AND WEAR	☐ 0 540 06370 3	☐ 0 540 06371 1	☐ 0 540 06372 X	➤ ☐
	Quantity @ £12.99 each	Quantity @ £9.99 each	Quantity @ £5.99 each	£ Total
BIRMINGHAM & WEST MIDLANDS	☐ 0 540 07603 1	☐ 0 540 07604 X	☐ 0 540 07605 8	➤ ☐
BUCKINGHAMSHIRE	☐ 0 540 07466 7	☐ 0 540 07467 5	☐ 0 540 07468 3	➤ ☐

STREET ATLASES ORDER FORM

COLOUR REGIONAL ATLASES

	HARDBACK	SPIRAL	POCKET	£ Total
	Quantity @ £12.99 each	Quantity @ £9.99 each	Quantity @ £5.99 each	
CHESHIRE	☐ 0 540 07507 8	☐ 0 540 07508 6	☐ 0 540 07509 4	➤ ☐
DERBYSHIRE	☐ 0 540 07531 0	☐ 0 540 07532 9	☐ 0 540 07533 7	➤ ☐
SOUTH HAMPSHIRE	☐ 0 540 07476 4	☐ 0 540 07477 2	☐ 0 540 07478 0	➤ ☐
NORTH HAMPSHIRE	☐ 0 540 07471 3	☐ 0 540 07472 1	☐ 0 540 07473 X	➤ ☐
OXFORDSHIRE	☐ 0 540 07512 4	☐ 0 540 07513 2	☐ 0 540 07514 0	➤ ☐
WARWICKSHIRE	☐ 0 540 07560 4	☐ 0 540 07561 2	☐ 0 540 07562 0	➤ ☐
WEST YORKSHIRE	☐ 0 540 06329 0	☐ 0 540 06327 4	☐ 0 540 06328 2	➤ ☐
	Quantity @ £14.99 each	Quantity @ £9.99 each	Quantity @ £5.99 each	£ Total
LANCASHIRE	☐ 0 540 06440 8	☐ 0 540 06441 6	☐ 0 540 06443 2	➤ ☐
NOTTINGHAMSHIRE	☐ 0 540 07541 8	☐ 0 540 075426 6	☐ 0 540 07543 4	➤ ☐
STAFFORDSHIRE	☐ 0 540 07549 3	☐ 0 540 07550 7	☐ 0 540 07551 5	➤ ☐

BLACK AND WHITE REGIONAL ATLASES

	HARDBACK	SOFTBACK	POCKET	£ Total
	Quantity @ £11.99 each	Quantity @ £8.99 each	Quantity @ £3.99 each	
BRISTOL AND AVON	☐ 0 540 06140 9	☐ 0 540 06141 7	☐ 0 540 06142 5	➤ ☐
	Quantity @ £12.99 each	Quantity @ £9.99 each	Quantity @ £4.99 each	£ Total
CARDIFF, SWANSEA & GLAMORGAN	☐ 0 540 06186 7	☐ 0 540 06187 5	☐ 0 540 06207 3	➤ ☐
EDINBURGH & East Central Scotland	—	☐ 0 540 06181 6	☐ 0 540 06182 4	➤ ☐
EAST ESSEX	☐ 0 540 05848 3	☐ 0 540 05866 1	☐ 0 540 05850 5	➤ ☐
WEST ESSEX	☐ 0 540 05849 1	☐ 0 540 05867 X	☐ 0 540 05851 3	➤ ☐
	Quantity @ £12.99 each	Quantity @ £9.99 each	Quantity @ £5.99 each	£ Total
GLASGOW & West Central Scotland	☐ 0 540 06183 2	☐ 0 540 06184 0	☐ 0 540 06185 9	➤ ☐

Post to: Philip's Direct, 27 Sanders Road, Wellingborough, Northants NN8 4NL

◆ Free postage and packing

◆ All available titles will normally be dispatched within 5 working days of receipt of order but please allow up to 28 days for delivery

☐ Please tick this box if you do not wish your name to be used by other carefully selected organisations that may wish to send you information about other products and services

Registered Office: Michelin House, 81 Fulham Road, London SW3 6RB

Registered in England number: 3597451

I enclose a cheque / postal order, for a **total** of ☐
made payable to *Octopus Publishing Group Ltd*, or please debit my

☐ Access   ☐ American Express   ☐ Visa   ☐ Diners

account by ☐

Account no ☐☐☐☐ ☐☐☐☐ ☐☐☐☐ ☐☐☐☐

Expiry date ☐☐ ☐☐

Signature...

Name..

Address..

....

....

....POSTCODE

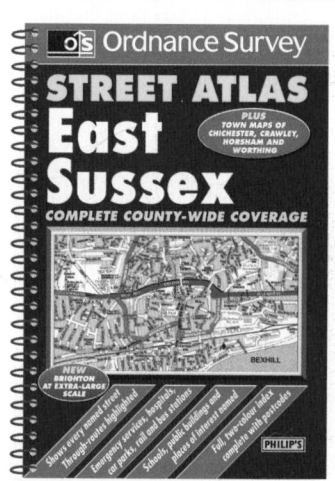

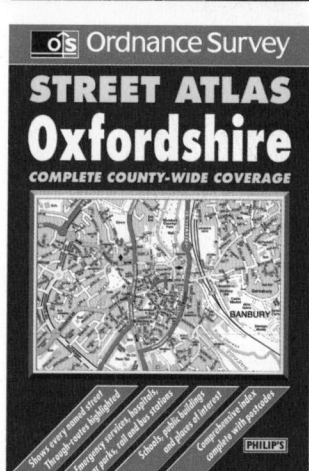

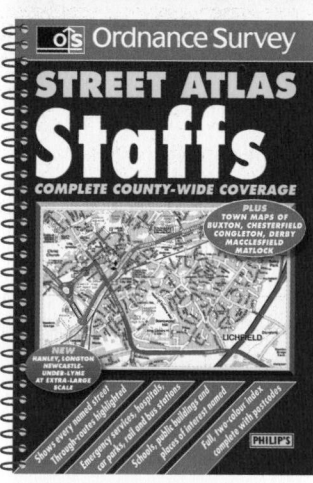